PREVENTING PALESTINE

Preventing Palestine

A POLITICAL HISTORY
FROM CAMP DAVID TO OSLO

Seth Anziska

PRINCETON UNIVERSITY PRESS
PRINCETON & OXFORD

Published by Princeton University Press
41 William Street, Princeton, New Jersey 08540
6 Oxford Street, Woodstock, Oxfordshire OX20 1TR

press.princeton.edu

LCCN: 2018934034
ISBN 978-0-691-17739-7

British Library Cataloging-in-Publication Data is available

Editorial: Fred Appel and Thalia Leaf
Production Editorial: Nathan Carr
Jacket/Cover Design: Leslie Flis
Jacket image: Camp David Accords, 1978. Courtesy of the Jimmy Carter Presidential Library.
Production: Erin Suydam
Publicity: Tayler Lord

This book has been composed in Miller

Printed on acid-free paper. ∞

Printed in the United States of America

10 9 8 7 6 5 4 3 2 1

CONTENTS

ILLUSTRATIONS

The Road from Gush Etzion

ON SEPTEMBER 27, 2017, the Israeli government celebrated a half century of territorial expansion in the West Bank. The occasion was marked with an official state commemoration in a field outside the Gush Etzion settlement of Alon Shvut. Thousands of guests gathered for "50 Years of Settlement in Judea and Samaria," referring to the biblical term the government had adopted for the territory in 1967. Featuring music, dancers, and fireworks, the ceremony echoed across the hilltops between Jerusalem and Hebron. "Settlement is important to you my friends," Prime Minister Benjamin Netanyahu told the assembled crowd. "It is no less important to me and therefore, I tell you clearly and before anything: There will be no further uprooting of settlements in the land of Israel!"[1]

The location of the ceremony was historically significant. Gush Etzion, or the Etzion Bloc, is a cluster of settlements that consists of many heavily populated towns and includes Kfar Etzion, the first religious kibbutz established in the West Bank after the 1967 War. Before the emergence of Israel in 1948, the area was the site of pre-state Jewish agricultural communities founded between the 1920s and 1940s. After the November 1947 UN vote to partition Palestine, the area was designated as part of a Palestinian state. During the 1948 War, Gush Etzion's children were evacuated from the area, but women and men remained behind to defend the settlement.

On May 13, armed villagers and the Arab Legion broke into Kfar Etzion, killing over a hundred Jewish residents. The neighboring kibbutzim surrendered the following day to the Arab Legion, as the State of Israel was declared in Tel Aviv.[2] Gush Etzion then came under Jordanian control for the next nineteen years, until Israel's conquest of the West Bank in the June 1967 War. That war, referred to as the "Six Day War" in Israel, and the Naksa, or "setback" in the Arab world, led to a lightning-fast Israeli victory over combined Arab forces yielding the capture of the Sinai Peninsula and Gaza Strip from Egypt, the Golan Heights from Syria, and East Jerusalem and the West Bank from Jordan.

Having kept the memory of the kibbutz alive while growing up in Israel, the children of Kfar Etzion's former residents immediately sought to return. The Israeli cabinet granted them permission to do so in September 1967, despite advice by the legal counsel of the Foreign Ministry at the time, Theodor Meron. A civilian settlement would contravene the Fourth Geneva Conventions, Meron argued, as the territory was deemed "occupied" by Israel after the war. To circumvent these legal strictures, Kfar Etzion was established as a military outpost, even though it was in effect a civilian settlement.[3]

The reestablishment of Kfar Etzion, which followed similar initiatives in the Golan Heights, was the basis for a much broader effort by successive Labor and Likud governments to settle Jews beyond the 1949 Armistice line (known as the "Green Line") in the newly occupied territories. Five decades later, their number reached over six hundred thousand people, including residents of East Jerusalem.[4] For Israeli government officials in 2017, Gush Etzion was therefore a fitting place to mark the anniversary of the war and the birth of the settlement project. In their planning announcement of the ceremony, Naftali Bennett, Israel's education minister, and Miri Regev, Israel's culture minister, remarked that "Israel's glorious victory in the Six Day War and the liberation of Judea and Samaria, the Golan Heights and the Jordan Valley" should be celebrated with "the respect it deserves."[5]

Government opposition members decried the choice of location, which flaunted the ongoing occupation of Palestinians living in the same territories. "Israel has controlled millions of people for 50 years, treads on them every day anew and denies them rights and sovereignty," the left-wing Meretz party chairwoman Zehava Galon told the *Haaretz* newspaper. "Bennett and Regev want us to continue living with this reality alongside us without considering the heavy price it extracts from us," she concluded.[6] The ceremony and the surrounding debate embodied the dissonant feelings that 1967 still arouses in Israel, of conquest and military victory alongside unanswered questions about the war's consequences and Israeli state control over local Palestinian life and territory ever since.

I know Gush Etzion well. In August 2001, when I was eighteen years old, I arrived in the settlement of Alon Shvut for a year of intensive study at Yeshivat Har Etzion, a preparatory academy of religious learning focused on immersion in the Torah, Talmud, and Jewish thought. The yeshiva, commonly known as the "Gush," was originally established in Kfar Etzion in 1968, before it expanded to bigger quarters nearby. It has programs for both Israeli students, who integrate their religious learning with active service in the Israeli army, and overseas Jewish students from across the United States, Canada, the United Kingdom, and South Africa. My time at the Gush was in line with the expectations of the Modern Orthodox American Jewish community in which I grew up, where it was common practice to spend a gap year before college living in Israel. Most young men and women study at a religious seminary, an experience that is meant to strengthen traditional observance and one's connection to the land of Israel.

I had been raised with a strong attachment to Zionism, traveling across Israel as part of a summer camp teen tour and participating in a wide array of activities to support the Jewish state. Although I was not particularly eager to pore over pages of Talmud, the social and familial expectations to spend a year abroad were strong, as was the encouragement of my school rabbis. The Gush seemed less restrictive than some of the other yeshiva options. It had a reputation for deep and critical inquiry, where students and teachers drew on ancient and modern Jewish thought to explore the texts of a religious tradition with analytical rigor and robust debate. This particular theological outlook was also coupled with openness to the wider world. With some trepidation, but also a degree of excitement, I found myself arriving in the West Bank for a year of study between high school and university in New York City.

My arrival at the Gush coincided with the height of the second Palestinian Intifada, or uprising. It was a year of extreme violence throughout Israel and the occupied territories, with a stream of suicide bombings and military operations that unleashed havoc on civilian life. The events of that year led to a gradual and painful personal and political awakening about the circumstances that had led me there. I was often close to the violence, making regular trips out of the settlement for weekend breaks. The dark green Egged company buses that I rode to and from Gush Etzion were bulletproof. There were frequent shooting attacks on the cars and buses driving on the settler-only roads in the West Bank, especially near the tunnels that passed under Palestinian villages above. I had macabre thoughts on those trips, wondering where it was best to sit in the event of a suicide bombing and whether a bullet round could make it through the gaps under the double-plated windows. On the announcement board in the yeshiva's study hall, or Beit Midrash, small notices regularly went up with the Hebrew names of the injured, asking students to pray for those who had been victims of a terror attack.

One Saturday night, headed back to yeshiva after the Jewish Sabbath, I missed a particularly gruesome triple suicide bombing on West Jerusalem's Ben Yehuda Street by just a few minutes. I remember visiting a student from my high school who had been injured in the bombing and can still distinctly recall the ball bearings that had been removed from his body sitting in a small plastic cup nearby. It was hard to focus on tractates of Talmud in this surreal environment. I often retreated to my dorm room, where I read local newspapers and tried to make sense of events unfolding around me. In the spring of 2002, I could feel my room shake as the Israeli army launched Operation "Defensive Shield," occupying nearby Bethlehem, as well as Jenin, Nablus, and other major Palestinian cities. The operation was launched following a string of attacks that culminated in a Passover suicide bombing by a Hamas bomber at the Park Hotel in the seaside town of Netanya. It was the largest military operation in the West Bank since the 1967 War.

Amid all this upheaval, I recall very little discussion with our yeshiva's rabbis about the drivers of Palestinian violence or the relationship of the yeshiva and the Gush Etzion settlement bloc to the wider context of the occupation. For many Jewish religious leaders in the settlements or elsewhere this would not be surprising, given their deep-seated belief in the divine right to the land and intimate knowledge of biblical scripture invoked to support continued Jewish presence there, generally to the exclusion of others. But the founder of the institution, an inspiring educator named Rabbi Yehuda Amital, was a figure who possessed a unique worldview. Born in what was then Transylvania, he had survived the Nazi invasion of Hungary and arrived in Palestine in 1944. His entire family had perished in the Holocaust. Rabbi Amital would often tell students the famous story of a rabbinic scholar studying Torah in a room next to his grandson and hearing a baby cry in a third room beyond. The elder rabbi got up to calm the baby, walking past his grandson, who was too involved in the religious text to notice. Returning to his own room, the grandfather criticized his grandson: "If someone is studying Torah and fails to hear a baby's cry, there is something very wrong with his learning." This was the founding philosophy of the Gush: to be immersed in the realm of the spiritual but attuned to the everyday concerns of the physical world beyond.

After the yeshiva was founded, Rabbi Amital shifted from a messianic view of Zionism toward the idea of territorial compromise with the Palestinians. He had been shaken by the loss of students at the yeshiva who had fought and died in Israel's 1973 Yom Kippur War and 1982 Lebanon War.[7] He founded the left-leaning Meimad (Jewish State, Democratic State) movement in 1988, and served as a Minister without Portfolio in the Labor government of Shimon Peres in 1995–96. Soon after the November 1995 assassination of Prime Minister Yitzhak Rabin by the religious extremist Yigal Amir, Rabbi Amital castigated the religious Zionist community for their role in fostering an environment in which such violence was condoned.[8] On a day-to-day basis, however, I often wondered how he and the other rabbis really felt about living in a settlement and the ethical implications of their actions for the daily lives of Palestinians. In youthful deference to their stature and the environment of the yeshiva I never asked, even as I increasingly wondered what I was doing in the middle of it all myself.

Leaving the settlement for Jerusalem or travels farther afield, the Egged bus would often make its way through the nearby settlement of Efrat, a sprawling suburb founded in part by American Jews from New York City's Upper West Side.[9] On Fridays, the main grocery store would be bustling with mothers doing family shopping for their Shabbat meals. Once the route linked up with the main highway, we would pass through a large checkpoint on the outskirts of Beit Jala, a Palestinian town adjacent to Bethlehem. There would always be a long line of Palestinians sitting in their cars or standing nearby, waiting to pass. As our bus bypassed the line and zipped through the checkpoint, I would peer at them from the bulletproof window.

Something did not sit right with me on those frequent journeys. The growing knowledge that my ease of access to travel around the West Bank and Israel as an American Jew came at the expense of local Palestinian inhabitants made me uncomfortable. Their conditions seemed bleak, and the contrast with the Jewish population living or traveling through the West Bank was stark. We lived in verdant hilltop settlements with manicured lawns, and from the little I could discern, their towns seemed a jumble of unfinished buildings on the horizon that had to be avoided. The entire road system that we traveled on had been designed to bypass Palestinian areas, but we could still see them from a distance. It was strange to inhabit space so close together and yet have no real interaction with these neighbors.

While the disparity of movement and restrictions that separated Palestinians from Jews now seems so obvious, it was a slow realization at the time. In the Jewish community of my youth, I had no direct contact with Arabs, let alone much interaction with non-Jews. Ironically, the biblical "Land of Israel" was far more present in my life, a storied place of great religious significance that evoked the long sweep of Jewish history and whose modern "redemption" verged on the miraculous. As kids, we sang songs of the Jewish return to the holy city of Hebron and the Tomb of the Patriarchs, and felt strongly that this faraway land belonged to us, the Jewish people. Each year, our school marched proudly down New York City's Fifth Avenue in the annual "Salute to Israel Day Parade," blending notions of religious return with the modern miracle of statehood. In our insular context, we did not comprehend or even recognize the presence or rights of another people.

This image of biblical Israel cultivated at a distance was shattered on those bus rides, which inadvertently exposed the reality of the West Bank. With the overwhelming obsession over the land of Israel, no one seemed to take much notice of the non-Jewish inhabitants living there. How could we not have seen them? Here were Palestinian mothers and their children waiting at the Beit Jala checkpoint on a Friday morning, not far from their Jewish counterparts in the bustling Efrat kosher supermarket. The cognitive dissonance was astounding. What could possibly explain this disparity? Why were Palestinians unable to move freely, in the very same space where I, a U.S. citizen, could come and go as I pleased? It seemed to me that the only difference was based on religion or ethnicity, one system for Jews and another for Arabs. Friends in yeshiva talked about the need for security, but I felt uncomfortable drawing distinctions along these lines.

Over the course of that year in yeshiva, deeply troubled by these questions, I took a much greater interest in the political nature of the conflict between Israel and the Palestinians. My limited but growing awareness of the underlying dynamics was often out of step with the views of many friends and family who did not grasp things the same way I did. For those who did notice something amiss, the disparity was easily justified. Among some friends in Israel or my community back home in the United States, the explanation was that Palestinians brought misery upon themselves. "Look at all the violence they perpetrate!" they would say. "They are not interested in peace," or "This is our land, God gave it to us," others would tell me. One particularly savvy educator responded to my piercing questions with the following response: "You know, Seth, as bad as things have gotten, it's important to remember that we need to care about our own first, before we address the needs of the other side."

The justifications offered to me did not mitigate the daily reality I was witnessing. I had grown up saturated with conversations about the Israeli-Palestinian conflict, yet crucial pieces of the story were missing. Living in the West Bank provided an immediacy that had been lacking in my American context. I had arrived from the United States with a very strong image of the land and a belief in who it belonged to, and yet the visceral encounter with Israel, the occupied territories, and the mechanics of the occupation chipped away at faraway projections. Through conversations with numerous other American Jews over the years, similar moments of disenchantment have often been described to me, the feeling of incongruence and even self-deception that lies at the heart of discovering certain uncomfortable truths about the relationship between Israel and the Palestinians.

Moreover, as an American citizen who grew up viewing U.S. diplomacy as a force for good in the Middle East, there was something particularly curious about my own country's role in this disturbing reality. As a child in the 1990s, I remember my family saving a copy of the newspaper with the cover of President Bill Clinton presiding over the signing of the Oslo Accords with the sense that a new reality was beginning. This was encapsulated in the photo of the handshake between Israeli prime minister Yitzhak Rabin and Palestinian leader Yasser Arafat on the White House lawn. Close to a decade later, why was I sitting in bulletproof buses, full of fear that a fellow passenger might be a suicide bomber? And how could those suicide bombers be willing to blow up random civilians on Ben Yehuda Street? These were heavy questions for an eighteen-year-old and led to many tense discussions with my parents back home in the United States about why I was in the West Bank.

A desire to find answers to these and other questions drove me to study the history, languages, and politics of the region following the formative experience in Gush Etzion and eventually led to this book. I became interested in understanding how and why the Palestinians still lived under Israeli control without equal rights, lacking a state of their own. What explained Oslo's unraveling? How had the American government mediated the conflict for so long without an end to the Israeli occupation that began in 1967? I also wanted to understand how the expansion of Israeli territory beyond the Green Line had affected daily reality, and why the very "peace process" that was presumably intended to address the fate of the West Bank and Gaza Strip had not in fact facilitated the independence of the territories. Rather, the diplomatic process seemed to solidify their absorption into Israel, blurring borders and making it very easy for me to get on a public bus in West Jerusalem and less than an hour later end up in Gush Etzion without noticing a demarcated crossing.

In different guises, the search to answer these questions took me back to the West Bank, this time to Bethlehem and Hebron and Jenin and Nablus and Ramallah, but also to Syria and Lebanon and Jordan and Egypt, to state archives in Jerusalem, London, and Washington, private collections and U.S. presidential libraries, interviews with diplomats and legal advisors, thousands of documents, and unsurprisingly, countless more questions. My inquiry ultimately stretched back to the 1970s, particularly to the emergence of the Camp David Accords in September 1978. This was the first moment since the establishment of Israel in 1948—what Palestinians refer to as the Nakba, or "catastrophe"—that Palestinian self-determination was the subject of international diplomatic negotiations. While much of the focus on issues at the heart of the Israeli-Palestinian conflict like settlements, territory, and political sovereignty dwells on diplomacy in the 1990s, the foundations of that era were actually laid fifteen years earlier.

A great deal of this early history has been ignored or glossed over in broader accounts of the Israeli-Palestinian conflict. The complex legacy of Camp David, particularly concerning the political fate of the Palestinians, is often eclipsed by the beaming image of U.S. president Jimmy Carter, hands intertwined with Egyptian president Anwar al-Sadat and Israeli prime minister Menachem Begin. Egypt's accord with Israel is an event that demands broader reexamination, especially given the availability of new historical sources.

I arrived at the Israel State Archives early on in my research just as the records from this period were released to the public under the thirty-year rule of declassification. While in the archives, I was also among the first to gain access to newly available records about the 1982 Israeli war in Lebanon, which followed on the heels of the political discussions at Camp David and focused on a military solution to the problem of Palestinian nationalism. Taken together—and alongside newly available sources that I examined in the United States, Europe, and the Middle East—a clearer picture emerged of a formative moment in the international history of the Arab-Israeli conflict and the battle over Palestinian self-determination.

The forty-year anniversary of the triple handshake between Carter, Begin, and Sadat after Camp David coincides in September 2018 with twenty-five years marking the Arafat-Rabin handshake of the Oslo Accords. Rather than engendering regional peace or statehood for the Palestinians, this fateful twin constellation is marked by an entrenched stalemate. Israel has successfully maintained and expanded its presence in the West Bank and East Jerusalem, even with a withdrawal from settlements in the Gaza Strip, which remains subject to an Israeli blockade. Palestinian geographic and political fragmentation has grown ever more acute, and the lack of meaningful sovereignty remains a formative element of the contemporary Palestinian condition. The celebration of fifty years of the settlement project in Gush Etzion merely underscores the failure of the peace process, highlighting how it has also facilitated Israel's territorial expansion. At the ceremony, Prime Minister Netanyahu spoke to the assembled guests from a stage adorned with a large banner that read in Hebrew: "We have returned to Judea and Samaria."[10] For stateless Palestinians living nearby, the echo of the music and fireworks must have been particularly lacerating.

Only in retrospect do I recognize that the dissonance engendered by a year living in Gush Etzion launched a much longer quest for historical understanding about Israel's establishment and its control of the occupied territories, the fate of the Palestinians, and the absence of Palestine. This book is an attempt to provide an answer to some of my questions. I am well aware that it lands in a field saturated with fierce debate and a depth of emotion, raising questions of political allegiance, ideology, objectivity, and competing claims of responsibility. But I am also certain that confronting an ongoing tragedy and advancing a conversation about where things might be headed begins with greater consciousness about how we got here in the first place.

PREVENTING PALESTINE

Introduction

"I FEAR FOR THE SPIRIT OF CAMP DAVID," wrote its chief architect, former U.S. president Jimmy Carter, in a 2016 plea to outgoing
president Barack Obama. Before leaving office, Carter told Obama,
his administration should "grant American diplomatic recognition
to the state of Palestine." The thirty-ninth president invoked his
own efforts to reach a peace agreement between Israel and Egypt
in 1978, based on United Nations Security Council Resolution 242,
passed in the aftermath of the 1967 War. This resolution, Carter
underscored, formed the basis of U.S. policy toward the region and
should guide a renewed commitment to ensure the viability of a
"two-state solution" to the Israeli-Palestinian conflict. By recognizing a Palestinian state, Carter argued, Obama would clear the way
for other countries and the UN Security Council to take action,
"countering the one-state reality that Israel is imposing on itself
and the Palestinian people."[1]

"The primary foreign policy goal of my life has been to help bring
peace to Israel and its neighbors," Carter concluded. He recalled
with pride his speech to a joint session of Congress in September
1978 after Israeli prime minister Menachem Begin and Egyptian
president Anwar al-Sadat had reached their agreement at Camp
David. "Blessed are the peacemakers, for they shall be called the
children of God," the president had said to loud applause and a
standing ovation, looking at the two leaders in the balcony above.
It was a moment broadcast live on television and the radio, etched
into public consciousness as the high point of Carter's time in office.

Forty years since negotiations were convened in the isolated Catoctin Mountain Park presidential retreat, Camp David still endures as a moment of rare triumph for a U.S. administration beset by domestic challenges and struggles abroad. Under Carter's guidance, the United States acted as an effective broker to secure a peace agreement between Egypt and Israel that has persisted as the cornerstone of regional politics in the Middle East. For many observers, Camp David's success underscores the importance of skilled American mediation and burnishes the image of judicious U.S. engagement abroad. But could such a positive interpretation be a misreading of history? Is the invocation of Camp David as a model for peacemaking to help solve the Israeli-Palestinian conflict truly appropriate? Might Carter's great diplomatic success have helped ensure the prevention of a Palestinian state?

There is in fact a competing view of Camp David that focuses on its more troubling legacy for the Middle East. From the vantage point of Palestinian nationalists in Beirut and in the streets of other Arab capitals at the time, the 1978 summit was a formative moment of disenfranchisement. Palestinians, whose struggle for self-determination had been moving definitively from armed resistance to diplomatic engagement in the years prior to this deal, had high hopes for a shift in the American approach to their political fate in the late 1970s. Yet at the very moment when their demands for self-determination were under serious consideration for the first time, they found themselves shut out of an incipient peace process and consigned to the sidelines. In exchange for peace with Egypt and the return of the Sinai Peninsula negotiated at Camp David, Israel was able to exercise continued control of the West Bank and Gaza Strip.

The bilateral peace agreement that Carter brokered between Begin and Sadat was therefore castigated as an abandonment of the Palestinian cause. Sidestepping the question of Palestinian self-determination in East Jerusalem, the West Bank, and Gaza Strip, the accords ultimately shifted negotiations to the question of possible local autonomy for Arab residents living in the occupied territories. The emergence of these subsequent "autonomy talks," which were held between representatives of Egypt, Israel, and the United States from 1979 to 1982, were premised on a non-sovereign resolution to Palestinian national aspirations. Although often ignored or dismissed as insignificant in accounts of this period, the autonomy discussions became the basis of limited self-rule and, eventually, the emergence of the Palestinian National Authority after the Oslo Accords were signed in 1993.

Four decades since the signing of the Camp David Accords, the Palestinian quest for self-determination remains unfulfilled. Without an independent state in the West Bank, Gaza Strip, and East Jerusalem, Palestinians continue to live as non-citizens under Israeli occupation, deprived of basic rights like the freedom of movement. They are stateless subjects under Israeli military control, suspended between limited autonomy within enclaves of self-rule and the continuing encroachment of Israeli settlements.[2] This result did not appear out of the blue, nor was it inevitable. A non-statist outcome emerged directly from the diplomatic negotiations meant to resolve their political fate, in line with what Israeli officials intended.

Camp David's narrow outcome was not at all what President Carter had envisioned when entering office in January 1977. Unlike his predecessors, Carter sought to include the Palestinians as part of a comprehensive regional peace settlement to resolve the unanswered questions of the 1967 War once and for all. He was the first U.S. president to speak openly of a Palestinian "homeland," using the controversial term at a news conference a few months after he took office.[3] But through a series of protracted diplomatic negotiations following on the heels of the Camp David Accords, which began while Carter was in the White House and continued after the administration of Ronald Reagan took over, the expansive vision that had guided the thirty-ninth president yielded a far more troubling legacy.

This book traces the fate of the "Palestinian question"—the diplomatic negotiations over Palestinian self-determination—from its emergence as a central feature of a Middle East settlement under Carter in the late 1970s to the onset of the Madrid and Oslo peace process that finally brought Palestinian leaders to the negotiating table in the early 1990s. It is the first study based on primary sources of how Palestinian self-determination was conceptualized and debated by American, Israeli, Egyptian, Palestinian, and transnational actors in this crucial period, predating the years traditionally demarcated as formative for the negotiations of a Palestinian political future.

A tendency to canonize Camp David—even by President Carter himself—has obscured the structural deficiencies enshrined by these early negotiations. While an Egyptian-Israeli settlement was indeed a significant achievement, it was reached at great and recurring expense. For Israel, the primary outcome of the peace treaty was the end of the traditional military rivalry with a neighboring Arab state. Concurrently, however, it also helped secure legitimacy for the extension of Israeli state sovereignty beyond the 1967 borders. For the Palestinians, Camp David was a crucial moment of state prevention. It marked the first instance of post-1948 discussion of their plight on a global scale, yet excluded them from the negotiations that would decide their political fate. By reassessing the negotiations that led to the summit and its consequences, this account complicates the dominant interpretation of Camp David as "heroic diplomacy."[4]

The diplomacy around Camp David actually served more troubling ends. Alongside the linkage to autonomy provisions and settlement expansion plans, it connected directly to Israel's military invasion of Lebanon in 1982, which in turn shaped the outbreak of the first Palestinian Intifada in 1987. Taken together, these successive developments reshaped Israel's relations with the Palestinians as well as broader regional politics in the Middle East during the late twentieth century. Given its transnational dimension, Camp David also affected crucial domestic currents in the United States, from the resurgence of Cold War conservatism to the shifting political allegiance of American Jewry. Yet beyond essential accounts of the summit itself, the linkage between Camp David and the wider transformations of this period remain unexamined.[5]

In order to understand why the Palestinian question remains among the most vexing problems of international diplomacy, we must revisit the years in which the very terms of political engagement were first substantively debated by American, Israeli, British, and Arab officials. In recounting this history, *Preventing Palestine* demonstrates how a confluence of global and regional politics, as well as shifting local developments on the ground, has produced an outcome of indefinite occupation, statelessness, and deep fragmentation for Palestinians. After surveying Israel's territorial conquest and the resurgence of Palestinian national politics after 1967, as well as the American approach to resolving regional conflict in the wake of the war, chapters 1 and 2 turn to the rise of new leadership in the United States and Israel in the 1970s. The clash between President Jimmy Carter's expansive vision of Palestinian political aspirations and Prime Minister Menachem Begin's more sobering approach explains how two competing worldviews led to a more limited Egyptian-Israeli peace at Camp David. Chapters 3 and 4 explain how Egyptian and American acquiescence in the face of Israeli statecraft led in turn to the triumph of "autonomy" as a rubric for addressing the Palestinians, while facilitating the extension of Israeli sovereignty inside the occupied territories.

Troubling dynamics unleashed in the 1970s were exacerbated in the 1980s. Rising neoconservative influence and the election of Ronald Reagan, as chapter 5 examines, positioned the Palestinians as a proxy of the Soviet Union in a revived Cold War and offered legal legitimacy to the settlement project. While bolstering Israel's restrictive notion of autonomy, the Reagan administration facilitated a turn from political suppression to military intervention as the Camp David process gave way to the 1982 Israeli invasion of Lebanon. Chapter 6 explores the central role of the Israeli-American relationship in the lead-up to the war and during the fighting itself, which targeted Palestinian nationalists in their Lebanese stronghold. The unforeseen consequences of the war, from the Sabra and Shatila massacre to Iranian-backed proxy attacks on U.S. Marines, underscored the limits of American support for Israeli actions and undercut U.S. influence in the Middle East. It also highlighted the futility of thwarting Palestinian nationalism, which rebounded in the wake of the expulsion of the Palestine Liberation Organization (PLO) from Beirut. Continued attempts to sideline the movement—which included economic initiatives and Jordanian circumvention, as chapter 7 demonstrates—were ultimately unsuccessful. The 1987 outbreak of the first Intifada led to U.S. recognition of the PLO in 1988, one of Reagan's final acts in office.

The end of the Cold War reordered U.S. relations with the Middle East, reviving a political track on the Palestinian front. Chapter 8 explores the onset of formal peace negotiations in the 1990s and the continuing influence of diplomatic models first introduced through the Camp David Accords. While the Madrid Conference crucially brought the Palestinians to the negotiating table in 1991, and the secret Oslo Accord of 1993 secured the return of the exiled Palestinian leadership to the West Bank and Gaza Strip, meaningful sovereignty and the possibility of statehood remained elusive. Rooted in the autonomy model enshrined by Menachem Begin, the negotiations ensured an ongoing Israeli presence in the occupied territories. Twenty-five years after the signing of the Oslo Accord and the subsequent establishment of the Palestinian National Authority, the Palestinians are no closer to self-determination. Many would argue that a separate state of Palestine is even farther away from reality and that Palestinians are alternatively no closer to securing equal rights within an expanded one-state entity between the Mediterranean Sea and the Jordan River. The book's conclusion examines the persistence of statelessness and its long-term consequences against this historical backdrop.

At the heart of this story is a struggle between two competing political projects: the first of an Israeli government emboldened by the conquests of 1967 and seeking to extend control into the newly occupied territories while preventing Palestinian self-determination from taking hold. The second is of a Palestinian national movement finding its political voice in the wake of the same war and seeking sovereignty on a portion of their ancestral homeland.[6] The race between these two projects was ultimately won by Israel, in part as a result of U.S. and Egyptian acquiescence in the wake of Camp David, as well as through Israel's military victory in Lebanon. But Israel's success also bred its own version of failure, as the crushing military and political defeat of the PLO brought the Palestinian plight to world attention. This development opened a space for global agitation on their behalf, as the visibility was solidified by the outbreak of the first Intifada. Inversely, the Palestinian achievement in gaining international recognition and opening a dialogue with the United States ultimately yielded a diplomatic agreement that did not resolve the core issues of contention. Diplomacy in the 1990s, like the autonomy talks in the 1970s, helped assure Israel's expansion of settlements in the occupied territories, now extant for more than fifty years. When those territories first came under Israeli control, neither the conquerors nor the inhabitants could have imagined what would follow.

In the Wake of 1967

For many Israelis and their supporters abroad, the capture of the West Bank, Gaza Strip, Golan Heights, Sinai Peninsula, and the old city of Jerusalem in June 1967 was greeted with ecstatic revelry. It seemed to fulfill the redemptive hopes of messianic Zionism, or else a secular variant of nationalist fervor.[7] The swift but surprising war had first been a source of existential dread, ultimately giving way to celebration.[8] At the same time, the expansion of Israel's territory raised profound political and demographic questions for Israeli leaders. During the earliest security cabinet discussions about the future of the newly occupied territories, the specter of how to manage the Palestinian population took on central importance. While the assembled Israeli ministers broadly agreed that the newly acquired Golan Heights and Sinai Peninsula would be bargaining chips for possible peace treaties with Syria and Egypt, the status of Jerusalem, the West Bank, and the Gaza Strip remained a matter of extensive debate.[9]

The conquest of territory greatly expanded the young state's borders, but it now left Israel in control of more than one million inhabitants living on the land that it had occupied. Officials argued over the fate of the Palestinians in the West Bank who had previously been under Jordanian rule. What would become of these residents? Would they acquire rights and an ability to vote in Israel? What of their citizenship? A consensus emerged against either annexation or granting rights to the Arab residents, with the cabinet of Israeli prime minister Levi Eshkol making a "decision not to decide" on the status of the newly occupied territories. The land would be utilized for Jewish settlements, and the Palestinians living there would de facto be deprived of sovereign control or the right to self-determination.[10]

The cabinet's "decision not to decide" evolved into a permanent condition of military occupation, and it enabled the building of settlements under the Labor-led government in the decade after the war.[11] Legal and historical arguments about the state's right to the conquered territories expanded with the rise of the messianic Gush Emunim movement, or "Bloc of the Faithful." Founded in 1974 by Orthodox followers of Rabbi Tzvi Yehuda Kook, the group's ideological support base had grown in the wake of the 1967 War. The movement called for the reclamation of land in the territories— labeled by their biblical name, Yehuda v' Shomron (Judea and Samaria)—to establish Jewish settlements.[12] While nationalists and the religious right were advocating for settlements, secularists from the dominant Labor party had in fact long been ushering a wave of expansion on the ground in the territories. A project that began under the Labor government of Eshkol expanded dramatically under the Likud-led governments that followed. In combination, Israeli control over the territory yielded one of the longest—if not *the* longest—military occupations of the modern era.[13]

Beyond the decisions inside the Israeli cabinet room in 1967, a struggle for self-determination was taking shape among Palestinians themselves. A reinvigorated national movement helped revive global attention to the Palestinian plight, which had been sidelined as a humanitarian problem after the creation of Israel in 1948. In the course of the war, over seven hundred thousand Palestinians were expelled or fled from territories that had become the Israeli state.[14] Against the backdrop of dispersion and infiltration that followed, as well as inter-Arab rivalry and internal divisions in the 1950s and 1960s, the quest for self-determination strengthened in the wake of the 1967 War.[15] Disillusioned with the failure of Arab nationalism, Palestinian leaders seized the struggle for their future away from discredited regional power brokers.[16] The PLO, founded in 1964, was given new life in the aftermath of Israel's victory.[17] In their quest for political recognition, the Palestinians found allies across Europe and the Global South, seizing on other examples of decolonization, from the struggles of Algerian independence to the Vietnam War.[18]

The 1967 War was therefore a watershed moment for the United States in the Middle East and for the reemergence of the Palestinian question. Israel's rapid defeat of the Arab states was a decisive blow to the prestige of the Soviet military who backed them. U.S. support for Israel during the war placed Washington at the center of postwar diplomatic efforts to resolve the Arab-Israeli conflict. President Lyndon Johnson did not want to return to the status quo that had prevailed before 1967 and supported Prime Minister Eshkol's bid to retain the territories until the Arab states recognized Israel and made peace.[19] This stance was codified in November 1967 via United Nations Security Council Resolution 242, which was understood internationally as a guideline for pursuing an exchange of "land for peace," meaning the return of territories for Israel's full recognition by the Arab world. At the same time, UN resolution 242 did not refer to the Palestinians directly, calling for a "just settlement to the refugee problem," without mentioning the fate of the West Bank and Gaza Strip. According to some opinions, it did not call for full Israeli withdrawal from all the captured territories.[20]

Nevertheless, by the mid-1970s, the PLO had gained international prominence through a combination of diplomatic overtures and violent acts of political terrorism on the global stage.[21] After first pursuing "total liberation" over the entirety of historic Palestine via armed struggle, the organization gradually shifted toward territorial partition and separate statehood alongside Israel. Moderating influences within the Palestinian national movement also gained ground after the 1973 War, generating measured support for a negotiated settlement.[22] At the Arab League Summit in 1974, the PLO was officially recognized as the representative voice of Palestinian concerns in the Arab world. But how, exactly, were Palestinians going to be able to get any territory for a state? Beyond armed struggle, the PLO needed international backing for its diplomatic track, particularly from the United States. It was an effort riven with difficulty, given internal Palestinian debates over military tactics and the parameters for diplomatic engagement, as well as long-standing U.S. policy toward Israel and the Middle East.[23]

A crucial regional development followed the September 1970 death of the champion of pan-Arab nationalism, Egyptian president Gamal Abdel Nasser. The new president, Anwar al-Sadat, pivoted his country westward, seeking to align Egypt with the United States rather than the Soviet Union.[24] Sadat was also determined to break the hold of Israel's dominant territorial position in the region, seeking to reclaim the Sinai Peninsula. He tried to negotiate a territorial exchange with Israel and signaled his determination to align with

Western powers. Israeli officials were not responsive to his overtures, and President Richard Nixon's powerful National Security Advisor, Henry Kissinger, was determined to maintain the strategic balance of détente. Joining forces with Syrian president Hafez al-Assad, Sadat launched the 1973 October War against Israel as a way to break this regional stalemate and create a "crisis of détente."[25]

The surprise attack broke out on Yom Kippur, the holiest day of the Jewish calendar. Israeli reservists were not at their bases, as the leadership of the country had not heeded the warnings of intelligence channels on the eve of the fighting.[26] The ensuing battle shattered Israel's cloak of invincibility that had been dominant in the wake of 1967. Although Israel defeated the Egyptian and Syrian forces, Israeli leaders had to seek U.S. military aid to turn the tide of the fighting. A massive American airlift of tanks, airplanes, and ammunition reversed the Egyptian and Syrian advances. With Nixon distracted by the Watergate scandal, Kissinger negotiated the terms of agreement to end the war. These terms were passed as UN Security Council Resolution 338, which called for a "just and durable peace in the Middle East" along the lines of UN Security Council Resolution 242 after the 1967 War.[27] Kissinger, as Nixon's envoy and later as secretary of state to President Gerald Ford, pursued a step-by-step approach to achieve a diplomatic solution between Israel and its neighbors.

Within Israel, the 1973 War brought the downfall of Prime Minister Golda Meir's government. A committee of inquiry, known as the Agranat Commission, found deep lapses of judgment among the leadership of the Israel Defense Forces (IDF) and held several military leaders to account for Israeli losses.[28] Meir's replacement was Yitzhak Rabin, a Labor party leader and decorated commander of the Israeli army who had served for five years as Israel's ambassador to Washington. Primarily concerned with rebuilding Israeli military deterrence after the war, Rabin entertained U.S. efforts to maintain postwar calm with interim arrangements. Alongside Sadat, who had been seeking out U.S. patronage and aid since assuming the Egyptian presidency, the two leaders helped ensure the success of Kissinger's diplomacy.[29]

In December 1973, a few months after the end of the Yom Kippur War, the United States and the Soviet Union convened a short-lived Geneva Conference that included representatives from Egypt, Jordan, and Israel. Although largely in a ceremonial role, it was to be the last time the United States accepted the Soviet Union as an equal partner in the Middle East, leading to a period of American diplomatic dominance in the region. The PLO leadership, which thought that Palestinians would be included in these discussions, began to rethink its diplomatic options.[30] While the Geneva Conference did not achieve a comprehensive solution to the Arab-Israeli conflict, it fostered Kissinger's "shuttle missions" to Egypt, Syria, and Israel between 1973 and 1975. These missions led to disengagement agreements between the three countries, as well as the Sinai Interim Agreement (Sinai II), which signaled a willingness to resolve conflict between Israel and Egypt "by peaceful means."[31]

While strengthening bilateral relations with Israel and Egypt, the American approach also prolonged broader regional conflict indefinitely.[32] Sinai II included further Israeli withdrawals from the Sinai Peninsula and the establishment of a UN buffer zone in the area. In pulling Cairo out of the Arab-Israeli conflict, the United States hoped to reduce the likelihood of another dangerous armed conflict, which threatened to destabilize great power relations in the Middle East. Kissinger's approach was a means of conflict management: by removing Egypt as a strategic and diplomatic threat, Israel's position would be secured and American dominance in the region would be preserved.

Palestinian national aspirations, which remained a central point of contention between Israel and the Arab states during this period, were ignored by Kissinger's diplomatic initiatives. In focusing on limited cease-fires between warring states, Kissinger's effort favored a piecemeal approach that separated the Palestinian issue from broader regional concerns.[33] This served Kissinger's agenda of conflict management, and also assuaged the anxieties of the Rabin government. Israel was deeply opposed to the possibility of Palestinian self-determination, and in 1975 Kissinger formally promised that the United States would not engage with the PLO unless it acknowledged Israel's right to exist and accepted UN Security Council Resolutions 242 and 338. This ban on dealing with the PLO was formative in shaping U.S. relations with the

Palestinians, forestalling meaningful engagement just as the PLO was moving purposefully toward diplomacy.[34]

During the 1976 presidential campaign, a new U.S. approach to the Middle East began taking shape. Gerald Ford's Democratic opponent, Georgia governor Jimmy Carter, had grander plans for U.S. foreign policy in the Global South.[35] Carter was viewed in the United States as a political outsider and foreign policy neophyte, but he also ran for office at a time when Cold War détente was under assault and human rights were emerging as an alternative basis on which to formulate the trajectory of U.S. international- ism.[36] The governor was developing a regional, rather than strictly Cold War, approach to foreign policy, marked by a concern with localized political dynamics.[37]

In his campaign speeches on the Middle East, Carter stressed a shift away from Kissinger's gradualist approach to regional peace- making. "A limited settlement," Carter argued, "leaves unresolved the underlying threat to Israel. A general settlement is needed— one which will end the conflict between Israel and its neighbors once and for all."[38] This comprehensive tone, which sought a resolution with countries like Jordan, Lebanon, Syria, and Saudi Arabia, marked a more expansive agenda while privileging U.S. relations with Israel. Carter also placed the Palestinian question at the heart of a comprehensive solution. In a break with long- standing policy, Carter spoke of a Palestinian "homeland," offer- ing the possibility of a radically new American policy toward self- determination.[39] For the first time since 1948, U.S. officials had come to recognize the centrality of Palestinian political—rather than humanitarian—rights.

The eventual outcome of the Carter administration's extensive diplomatic efforts in 1977 and 1978 was the Camp David Accords, which secured the bilateral peace agreement between Egypt and Israel. In effect, the accords were the triumph of Kissinger's dip- lomatic architecture. They left the Palestinian issue subject to fur- ther negotiations over autonomy after the ratification of the 1979 Egyptian-Israeli peace treaty. These autonomy talks sidestepped the PLO and served to prevent a territorial resolution of Palestinian national aspirations, solidifying a condition of statelessness and de- liberately undermining sovereignty claims. While the peace treaty with Egypt was being implemented, Israel's Likud government introduced new plans for the territories, expanding settlements that had first started under the Labor governments in the decade after the 1967 victory.

Despite their significance, the autonomy talks have largely been absent from historical accounts of the Israeli-Palestinian conflict. Among the leading studies, Israeli historian Benny Morris dismisses autonomy as a "nonstarter," while other scholars downplay or ignore the negotiations in the wake of Camp David.[40] Dominant narratives of the peace process instead trace the beginning of a serious engagement with the Palestinian question to the Madrid and Oslo negotiations of the 1990s, often ignoring the diplomatic mechanisms that constrained Palestinian self-determination in the 1970s and 1980s.[41] Those who do examine this earlier period, like one recent study of the Carter administration's approach, paint a more sympathetic portrait of American attempts to create a process leading to "genuine Palestinian self-determination" by challenging the Begin government on settlement expansion and territorial withdrawal.[42] But the U.S. role in the autonomy talks—and the very substance of the negotiations themselves—actively undermined the prospects of a solution to the Palestinian question.

Israeli prime minister Menachem Begin's autonomy scheme was in fact a formidable and sophisticated piece of statecraft. While it was designed to frustrate Palestinian nationalism, its ingenuity was to sustain the fiction of serious movement on the Palestinian front. Far from representing a diplomatic dead end, the talks were an integral, dynamic, and highly consequential component of Israel's diplomatic strategy. The recent revival of interest in the autonomy plan among right-wing politicians in Israel attests to the deep imprint it continues to have on Israel's approach to the Palestinians.[43]

While Begin was indefatigable as a negotiator and relentless in advocating for his ideas, he received a great deal of help from his new ally, Egypt. The country's formal withdrawal from the Arab-Israeli conflict as a consequence of Camp David relieved Israel of military pressure from the southwest and enabled the intensification of the occupation of Palestinian land. However, Cairo was also a willing partner in the political project that Begin had conceived for the Palestinians. Despite Sadat's loud exhortations as the chief defender of Palestinian rights, Egypt explicitly countenanced the Israeli notion that autonomy would preclude, rather than facilitate, the achievement of Palestinian statehood. Verbatim records of successive rounds of negotiations between delegations from these two countries reveal how an initial Egyptian insistence on a meaningful outcome for the Palestinians gave way to functional autonomy and the preservation of a bilateral peace alone.[44] Egypt's permissive role underscores a causal link between the "breakthrough" of Camp David and the subsequent thwarting of Palestinian statehood.

Global constraints also played a large part in the limits of Carter's achievements in the Middle East. After Camp David, events in 1979 fueled a shift in Carter's attention, notably with the overthrow of the Shah of Iran and the Soviet invasion of Afghanistan.[45] As a result of the Iranian Revolution and the hostage crisis in Tehran, the latter part of Carter's time in office was not devoted to the intricacies of the Arab-Israeli conflict as it had been in the early years. Heightened tensions in the Cold War, which have often been ascribed to Reagan's election and the revival of global conflict in the 1980s, actually emerged in part as a reaction to Carter's actions.[46] By his 1980 State of the Union address, the articulation of a "Carter Doctrine" signaled a more muscular American posture toward the international arena. This would only increase during the early years of the Reagan administration.[47]

There are many ways to narrate the Palestinian struggle for self-determination in the late twentieth century and a multiplicity of perspectives to account for. I have focused here on the interactions between the United States, Israel, Egypt, and the Palestinians themselves, although the latter were often excluded from the discussions over their political fate. Grassroots activists and various movement-based organizations were also pivotal in framing (and opposing) this struggle, and I have incorporated the constraining voices of domestic groups like the American Jewish community and Cold War conservatives. While examining local developments, this is not an internal history of the Israeli Likud or the PLO's military and diplomatic strategy, although those dynamics are discussed. Nor does this book seek to cover all the developments within inter-Arab politics or international and nongovernmental organizations, even as organizations like the United Nations and the Arab League, as well as European governments, played a crucial role and appear as well. Rather I explain how and why a host of influential state and non-state actors engaged with the question of Palestinian self-determination in political terms and reflect on the broader outcome of those discussions at a pivotal moment in the international history of the Middle East.[48]

The persistence of Palestinian statelessness since the years under examination in this book remains intimately tied to the triumph of a political vision for limited self-rule first articulated by Israeli leaders in the 1970s, as well as the very real consequences of settlement expansion in the occupied territories. These processes are linked together. But while visible evidence of Israel's fifty-year-old occupation is well-documented, the evolution of its intellectual, legal, and political architecture is only recently coming under sustained scrutiny.[49] By examining the genesis of diplomatic negotiations prior to Camp David and the repercussions in the decade that followed, I am therefore suggesting we rethink the conventional periodization of the peace process to more directly account for the 1970s and 1980s. This deeper history is often obscured by the immediate concerns of the present, but the architecture of this process extends much farther back than has been acknowledged.

My argument by no means implies that independent statehood was necessarily the preferred outcome for Palestinians, or even considered a viable option as far back as the 1970s. Other ideas were always circulating in diplomatic corridors, from confederation with Jordan to limited self-rule by local elites and other non-state alternatives. Rather than presume statist outcomes, it is important to remember that the articulation of self-determination in the 1970s and 1980s looked rather different than it might in the early twenty-first century.[50] The central claim of *Preventing Palestine* is also not to say that Palestine, as a real or imagined place, was irrevocably foreclosed in the period under examination. At multiple junctures, horizons had opened for possible Palestinian self-determination, and may very well still exist.

But in writing a history of contingent and unfolding events during the formative period between Camp David and Oslo, it is clear that certain avenues for sovereignty were closed down in the process, and the effect—if not the intent—has been the elision of a political solution for the Palestinians. In tracing a history of failure—the genealogy of a non-event, as it were—the historian must be mindful of clashing dynamics at play, haphazard intentionality, and a predetermined reading of the recent past. As this book makes clear, a series of diplomatic decisions and military interventions, shifting legal ideas about settlements, and conceptual debates over the meaning of autonomy and self-determination all contributed to the prevention of Palestine at the very moment when demands for sovereignty were first being heard.

CHAPTER ONE

Jimmy Carter's Vision

WITH A LARGE BLUE VELVET KIPPAH covering his head, former Georgia governor Jimmy Carter rose to speak to an overflowing crowd of more than two thousand congregants at the Jewish Educational Center in Elizabeth, New Jersey. It was June 1976, the summer before the national election that would bring Carter to the White House. "The land of Israel has always meant a great deal to me," Carter told his audience. "As a boy I read of the prophets and martyrs in the Bible—the same Bible we all study together."[1]

A devout Southern Baptist, navy veteran, and successful agriculturalist, Carter was largely unfamiliar to American Jews in the Northeast. Many were skeptical of his southern roots and were wary of supporting an untested politician with no experience in the Middle East.[2] The hostility ran deep. One Jewish campaign advisor recalled the views of his coreligionists. "You mean you are supporting that guy? I thought he was anti-Semitic."[3]

To counter these anxieties, the Democratic Party's nominee for president chose a large Orthodox congregation to deliver one of his most important campaign speeches. "As an American," Carter told the audience, "I have admired the State of Israel and how she, like the United States, opened her doors to the homeless and the oppressed."[4] This affirmation of a deep commitment to Israel in part reflected personal experience, as well as the steady growth of cultural and intellectual bonds between political Zionism and American liberalism since the 1940s.[5]

Carter's speech at the synagogue came against the backdrop of tense Israeli relations with the wider Arab world. Attempts at regional peacemaking after the 1973 War had left unresolved core issues of political contention, as well as the fate of the Palestinian question. "All people of good will can agree it is time—it is far past time—for permanent peace in the Middle East," Carter told the congregants in Elizabeth that day. This peace "must be based on absolute assurance of Israel's survival and security," he assured the assembled crowd. "As President, I would never yield on that point. The survival of Israel is not just a political issue, it is a moral imperative."[6]

The rising political star argued that only a "change of attitudes" would lead to "Arab recognition of the right of Israel to live as a Jewish State." When speaking of the Palestinians, he stuck with more humanitarian themes. "Too many human beings, denied a sense of hope for the future, are living in makeshift and crowded camps where demagogues and terrorists can feed on their despair," Carter remarked.[7] This language was deliberate and designed to assuage the concerns of his audience. "Our constant and unwavering goal must be the survival of Israel as a Jewish State and the achievement of a just and lasting peace."[8]

Conspicuously absent from Carter's synagogue address was a direct discussion of the Palestinians in national terms. The omission was in line with dominant U.S. policy at the time, given strong domestic American Jewish opposition to the PLO in the United States and the unwelcome claims of self-determination the organization had been making globally in the 1970s. The specter of armed Palestinian resistance had not dissipated, despite the PLO's growing commitment to diplomacy in place of military action. Carter had a national race to win, and in the view of a campaign liaison to the American Jewish community, the Elizabeth speech helped clinch the election by preventing a big loss in the New Jersey primary.[9]

The Georgia governor's support for Israel extended well beyond political expedience. In his memoir, *Keeping Faith*, Carter later reflected on his 1973 visit to the country, which underscored religious attachments as well. "In my affinity for Israel, I shared the sentiment of most other Southern Baptists that the holy places we revered should be preserved and made available for visits by

Christians . . . I considered this homeland for the Jews to be compatible with the teachings of the Bible, hence ordained by God." It was a perspective that had direct bearing on his approach to political solutions in the Middle East, as Carter felt strongly that regional stability depended on continued U.S. alignment with Israel. In his view, "moral and religious beliefs made my commitment to the security of Israel unshakable."[10]

What of Carter's early attitude toward the Arab world and Palestinians? Initially, religious blinders and limited experience in the Middle East precluded a more substantial engagement with divergent perspectives.[11] As the president himself declared in his memoirs, "I had no strong feelings about the Arab countries. I had never visited one and knew no Arab leaders."[12] At the same time, Carter took issue with Palestinian political disenfranchisement, growing out of his domestic orientation toward greater civil rights and equality. This was a function of his childhood in the segregated South, where racial inequality was a direct feature of his daily life.[13] He highlighted the linkage in very forthright terms years later, writing in his memoir about "the continued deprivation of Palestinian rights" and the need for American involvement in securing these rights. "It was imperative that the United States work to obtain for these people the right to vote, the right to assemble and to debate issues that affected their lives, the right to own property without fear of its being confiscated, and the right to be free of military rule," Carter reflected. "To deny these rights was an indefensible position for a free and democratic society."[14]

Throughout his presidential campaign, however, Carter consistently used language that avoided the endorsement of Palestinian statehood, and he continued to avoid it during his time in office. Such a position fit well in mainstream American political discourse, which did not countenance the idea of a state or sovereignty for Palestinians.[15] After the election, closer attention to the region and the complexities of the conflict yielded startlingly original ideas that pushed the boundaries of what might be possible diplomatically, including arrangements for territory administered by Palestinians themselves. While Carter's initial framing of this issue had largely been in the context of human rights and humanitarian concerns, his evolving rhetoric signaled a willingness to engage more directly with the question of Palestinian aspirations in political terms.[16] Over the course of Carter's first few months in office, the evolution of his thinking about the meaning of self-determination and the floating of specific ideas drew fierce opposition from both the Israeli government and domestic constituencies in the United States.

Carter's Turn

On November 2, 1976, Carter and his running mate, Minnesota senator Walter Mondale, defeated the incumbent president Gerald Ford and his running mate, Kansas senator Bob Dole. Carter's foreign policy advisors had been busy outlining priorities for the first six months of the administration even before he had won the election. Like many untested transition teams, they were ambitious and envisioned a "protracted architectural process to reform and reshape the existing international system."[17] In the realm of the Middle East, they stressed the need to pursue a comprehensive settlement to the Arab-Israeli conflict instead of Kissinger's interim agreements negotiated under Nixon and Ford. Underscoring that a new approach to the Arab-Israeli conflict was under development, Carter's advisors emphasized that this would mean "a settlement in which the Arab countries trade full normalization of relations with Israel for return of territories occupied in 1967, with such changes as may be mutually agreed, and some form of self-determination for Palestinians on the West Bank."[18] Rather than put forward detailed American proposals or "impose" a solution from the outside, the United States would encourage negotiations by working as an external broker.

The newly appointed National Security Advisor, Zbigniew Brzezinski, worked closely with the president to craft this comprehensive approach. Brzezinski was a member of the political science faculty at Columbia University when he first met Carter. He also served as the executive director of the North American branch of the Trilateral Commission, a forum for government, business, and academic representatives from the United States, Europe, and Japan to discuss issues of the developed and developing world. After a 1975 speech in Japan, at which Carter had argued for utilizing a balanced approach to achieve peace in the Middle East,

Brzezinski decided to become more actively involved in the campaign and quickly emerged as a top foreign policy tutor to the governor. He saw Carter as realistic and determined, sensing that he was "able to combine principle with power, the only prescription for a successful American foreign policy."[19]

Brzezinski was a Soviet specialist, a clear indication that the Carter administration was still working in the context of a U.S.-Soviet power struggle.[20] But the waning influence of détente, which had shaped U.S. foreign policy around the globe in the early 1970s, provided space for a new sort of American internationalism. Carter's aim was to articulate a stance abroad that was rooted in the rhetoric of human rights and that was responsive to decolonization in the developing world. This stance would often be applied unevenly, and its impact would be more rhetorical than substantive. Nevertheless, Carter's intention was to break with dominant Cold War constraints of the decade.[21]

Even with this new emphasis, the great power rivalry of the Cold War continued to cast a shadow during the presidential transition. Not long before entering the White House, Carter met with the outgoing secretary of state, Henry Kissinger. Kissinger had jointly convened a meeting in December 1973 with the Soviet Union under the auspices of the United Nations intended to negotiate a solution to the Arab-Israeli conflict in the wake of the 1973 War. Carter was attuned to this geopolitical rivalry, and off the record he assured Kissinger that he would try to avoid a revival of the Geneva Conference "out of concern for the role the Soviets might play there."[22]

Two major influences shaped the development of Brzezinski's views of the Middle East. The first, as had been the case for Carter, was a trip to the region in the summer of 1976, right before the presidential election. This visit convinced Brzezinski that security for Israel would depend on formalized borders, close to the 1967 Green Line. Such a conclusion came into conflict with Israeli settlement expansion, which Brzezinski understood as extending Israeli sovereignty beyond internationally recognized borders.[23] Brzezinski's second formative exposure to Arab-Israeli issues was his participation in a 1975 Middle East Study Group hosted by Washington's Brookings Institution. This was a think-tank gathering of leading experts who sought to articulate an alternative for the region through a collaborative effort between "pro-Israel," "pro-Arab," and non-aligned parties.[24] According to one member of the study group, the Brookings report grew out of the realization that Kissinger's step-by-step approach to Middle East diplomacy, first articulated in the 1973 Geneva Conference, was not working.[25]

The Brookings report called for an integrated settlement that would include security for Israel and a territorial withdrawal to the 1967 Green Line. Explicitly, it also argued for some form of Palestinian self-determination. "This might take the form either of an independent Palestinian state accepting the obligations and commitments of the peace agreements or of a Palestinian entity voluntarily federated with Jordan but exercising extensive political autonomy," the authors explained.[26] Rather than a simple matter of human rights, the assembled experts drew a line between the need for permanent Israeli borders and the importance of framing the Palestinian question in national terms. Rita Hauser, a prominent lawyer and former fund-raiser for Richard Nixon, emphasized the importance of the Brookings study to Carter's foreign policy: "[Carter] took this report and he read it, and he campaigned on it, and he made it his Bible."[27] In the view of another study group participant, the report stated openly "what those in government could not say about the need for a comprehensive solution that would involve the Palestinians."[28]

Brzezinski had coauthored a 1975 article in the journal *Foreign Policy* that called for an independent Palestinian state in the West Bank and Gaza Strip.[29] In his first official meeting with Israeli officials, the National Security Advisor got a sense of how far apart the administration's views were from leading voices in Israel. General Moshe Dayan, a prominent Israeli Labor politician and military hero who had been defense minister during the 1967 War, met with Brzezinski on January 31, 1977, to discuss the contours of a peace settlement. While Dayan spoke about interim avenues with Syria and Jordan, he felt peace with the Arab world was "far off," even if an "end to the state of war" might be possible.[30] Dayan took the Arabs seriously in their readiness to sign peace treaties but also told Brzezinski that "Israel is not willing to pay the price." The general acknowledged this left Israel in an "awkward position" with regard to U.S. and world opinion.[31] When it came to territorial division, Dayan was clear that the West Bank, unlike the Golan Heights and the Sinai Peninsula, posed non-security-related challenges. "Israel has every right to be there," Dayan remarked. "Any division of the area is unacceptable. . . . A West Bank-Gaza state is not a solution."[32] Dayan would soon be appointed foreign minister in the Likud government of Menachem Begin, where he would help negotiate the Camp David Accords. In January 1977, however, he made it clear that "if Israel were offered peace tied to full withdrawal, he [Dayan] would oppose peace."[33]

Like Brzezinski, Carter's newly appointed secretary of state, Cyrus Vance, was convinced of the need to address the question of Palestinian self-determination. Vance was a graduate of Yale University and a veteran of the U.S. Navy who joined the New York law firm of Simpson Thacher & Bartlett after completing his military service. He later transitioned into the government as general counsel of the Department of Defense and secretary of the army in the administration of John F. Kennedy, followed by a stint as the deputy secretary of defense under President Lyndon B. Johnson.[34] In his memoir, Vance wrote explicitly of the Palestinian plight. He described how they were "ejected from their homes, embittered, radicalized, living in squalor and desperation," and argued that the Palestinian question remained the "central, unresolved human rights issue of the Middle East." Reflecting on his approach to diplomacy in the region, Vance wrote that he and Carter were convinced a lasting solution to conflict in the Middle East required "a just answer" to the Palestinian question, "one almost certainly leading to a Palestinian homeland and some form of self-determination."[35] Vance was also mindful of the constraints inhibiting a change in U.S. policy after 1967. He pointed out that UN Security Council Resolution 242 only dealt with the Palestinians as a refugee problem, not a political group seeking self-determination. The international community was not initially focused on statehood. "It was only in 1969 and 1970 that serious attention began to focus on the Palestinian people and their aspiration for a homeland in the West Bank and Gaza."[36]

A Palestinian Evolution

Part of the reason for the delayed engagement with the political dimensions of Palestinian self-determination was a result of

an evolution within Palestinian nationalism itself. The 1967 War
had revitalized the national movement, which was easily eclipsed
by inter-Arab political rivalries before Israel's victory. There was
a split between the PLO, created by the Arab League in 1964 as
a means to defuse nationalist agitation among Palestinians, and
the Fatah movement, an independent liberation movement whose
founders included Yasser Arafat.[37] Arafat was born in Cairo to parents from Gaza and Jerusalem, and he engaged in politics early
on, demonstrating against British colonial rule in Egypt and then
fighting in the 1948 War. While completing his engineering studies
at Cairo University he became the head of the Palestinian Studies
Union, drawing the attention of the secret police. He left Egypt for
Kuwait in 1957, where he headed a successful construction company but remained involved in political activity through the creation of Fatah in 1959.[38]

In 1965, Fatah began launching guerilla attacks into Israel from
Jordan, Syria, and Lebanon to "liberate" Palestine and keep the national struggle alive. The movement gained a great deal of attention
and prestige after 1967, seen as the only legitimate resistance movement against Israel. Fatah soon joined the PLO and became the
dominant force of the umbrella organization, with Arafat taking
over the leadership in 1969.[39] There were several constituent factions within the organization, including the Popular Front for the
Liberation of Palestine (PFLP), headed by George Habash, and the
Democratic Front for the Liberation of Palestine (DFLP), headed
by Nayaf Hawatmeh. Smaller groups included the Syrian-backed
Al-Saiqa force and the Iraqi-backed Arab Liberation Front. All of
these groups utilized armed violence and some engaged in highly
visible global attacks like plane hijackings to advance their struggle,
while also balancing the use of force with a need to maintain relations with Arab states from where they operated. Arafat was at
the helm of the PLO throughout this formative period, balancing
various factional interests through challenges like the Jordanian
civil war. He was an indomitable force, although he ruled by factional consensus and was therefore heavily constrained by other
resistance actors within the organization. There is a risk of reading
Palestinian national history exclusively though his actions given the
wider balance of power between clashing factions.[40]

FIGURE 1.1. *Leader of the PLO* Yasser Arafat by John Austin Hanna. 1982.
Courtesy of Liberation Graphics and the Palestine Poster Project Archives.

Between 1969 and 1973, the PLO's primary objective was the re-
covery of a Palestinian homeland and the establishment of a "secular democratic state," without leaving Israel in place. Tactically, this
included armed struggle as well as diplomatic means.[41] The 1973
War launched a new phase in the PLO's struggle, oriented toward

partition and the acknowledgment of Israel's presence. In the aftermath of the October War, the PLO sought a place within the comprehensive diplomatic negotiations, which required political compromise and the eventual embrace of a state on far less territory than historic Palestine.[42] This was not a simple position to take, nor did it elicit uniform support, with early stirrings for a political solution leading to a violent backlash by more extreme factions. In June 1974, the Palestine National Council (the PLO "parliament in exile") passed a ten-point program that denoted a more targeted struggle for "every part of Palestinian land that is liberated," implying an acceptance of a political solution on a limited piece of territory.[43]

By the time that Carter took office in 1977, advocates for a separate state on a part of Palestinian territory had gained ground within the PLO, and the national movement's political demands were increasingly visible on the global stage.[44] The United Nations General Assembly had granted the PLO observer status in 1974, and Arafat had spoken in the chamber, a signal that the national movement was increasingly acceptable as a political interlocutor. The U.S. government, however, continued to officially oppose diplomatic engagement with the PLO, codified by the 1975 ban on discussions with the organization. *Palestine*, the PLO's Information Bulletin published in Beirut, noted the movement's growing international prominence and the attendant constraints of American policy. Describing hard-won victories in forums like the United Nations, the magazine's editors asserted the centrality of the Palestinian cause to regional stability even as mounting violence in Lebanon's civil war was generating new complications.[45]

The views articulated by Carter's advisors were discussed widely in the American media and think tanks, strengthening Palestinian hopes that the incoming administration might be open to the notion of Palestinian statehood. For the PLO, this new U.S. attitude denoted a break from the previous administration. Yasser Arafat had singled out Henry Kissinger, the architect of the 1975 ban, for his intransigent approach. "If the imperialist forces are unable to liquidate the Revolution, then they are not averse to taming it or trimming its wings, turning it into a disarmed, restricted entity, void of the active militant spirit which disturbs the dreams of the imperialists and Zionists."[46] Skeptical of American attitudes, Palestinian nationalists had looked elsewhere for diplomatic backing.

Over the course of the mid-1970s, the PLO was making quiet inroads with Western diplomats in Europe. British Embassy officials across European capitals, the United States, and the Middle East had regular "discreet and informal contact with the PLO," including monthly lunches between the Middle East desk officer in London and Said Hammami, the PLO representative in the city.[47] UK officials were mindful of Israeli opposition to these contacts but stressed the importance of hearing the PLO's ideas and "feed[ing] ideas directly to them."[48] In France and Belgium, the PLO had attained some official recognition, and the organization was gaining ground with the German government as well. Among Europeans, there was a growing consensus to support the organization, increasingly seen as the legitimate vehicle for achieving Palestinian self-determination.[49]

Israeli leaders, long opposed to Palestinian national rights and deeply shaken by the violence of armed groups during the 1970s, sought to quash any effort to engage with Palestinians as a national entity. This position was bolstered by Kissinger's promise to the Israelis not to speak with the PLO as long as it refused to accept UN Security Council Resolutions 242 and 338.[50] By contrast, Carter's incoming administration included critics who had opposed the PLO ban and were more attuned to the broader sweep of decolonization across the Global South. They found themselves in a position to craft Washington's new Middle East policy in a way that accounted for Palestinian aspirations as well.

"Possible Elements of a Middle East Settlement"

Since 1967, America had played the leading role in conflict mediation between Israel and the Arab states, working to shape diplomatic efforts as part of what had become known as the "peace process."[51] While not always perceived as a balanced mediator, Washington was the driving force for a regional settlement.[52] With Carter assuming office, several key State Department experts collectively began formulating a comprehensive approach to solving the Arab-Israeli conflict, including the Palestinian issue.[53] They suggested Carter embrace U.S. mediation as the lead driver for talks in the region as he sought to break from Kissinger's shuttle diplomacy. Carter's European allies voiced private skepticism of his administration's ambitions. "Israel is enormously dependent on the United States," British ambassador John Mason wrote from Tel Aviv, "but the scope for the new U.S. Administration to use this dependence to force the Israeli government to concede points which they judge vital to their security is subject to severe constraints."[54]

Aware of these difficulties, Carter's National Security Council settled on the idea of arranging a new version of the brief 1973 Geneva Conference, which had been premised on a comprehensive solution before yielding Kissinger's narrow shuttle diplomacy. They hoped to convene such a gathering in the fall of 1977, with the goal of negotiating the large and seemingly intractable policy questions prior to that date. Kissinger's unwillingness to confront the Israelis directly on a permanent settlement had undermined the effectiveness of his shuttle diplomacy, and Brzezinski believed that a breakthrough would only occur if the American government took a harder line against Israel by demanding the establishment of permanent borders.[55] Such a confrontation could not be sustained indefinitely in light of Israeli dependence on their American allies. "Most Israelis would instinctively shrink back from overt defiance of the United States," Brzezinski remarked, "*provided* they were convinced the United States meant business."[56] With the model of a Geneva-like conference that included U.S. and Soviet cochairmanship as well as UN endorsement in mind, State Department experts prepared detailed proposals focused on content.

In a closely held secret proposal circulated to the president, Brzezinski, and Vance, a striking vision emerged of a possible comprehensive settlement that included an entity akin to a Palestinian state.[57] The details of the plan covered Israel's relations with Egypt, Syria, and the Palestinians and examined the fate of Jerusalem while providing maps of possible permanent borders. Egypt was viewed as a key component in this settlement, but a separate peace between Egypt and Israel was "not in the cards."[58] An agreement that included the Palestinians was intended to proceed along with the participation of other Arab states, particularly Syria, in direct contrast to Kissinger's bilateral approach. The State Department was hopeful that Syrian president Hafez al-Assad could endorse a settlement and provide "explicit acknowledgement of Israel's right to exist," which had been out of reach since the emergence of the Israeli state in 1948.[59] This would include support for a solution to the Palestinian refugee question and "recognition of a final, sovereign border between Israel and a Palestinian entity."[60] In return, Syria would regain control over the Golan Heights, captured by Israel in 1967, and full diplomatic relations would be established between the two countries.

In the West Bank and Gaza, the details of a possible agreement focused on a viable resolution that would balance Palestinian national aspirations with Israeli concerns. Several political configurations were offered, but two "extreme outcomes" were eliminated. The first was a "reconstitution of the Hashemite Kingdom of Jordan on a pre-1967 basis," which would fail to address Palestinian self-determination. The second was "a radical Soviet-armed PLO-dominated state on the West Bank and Gaza," which would be "unacceptable to Israel and could be a destabilizing force in the region." Instead, the study suggested that the areas from which Israel would withdraw "would be administered by the Palestinians and would have a recognized Palestinian political identity."[61]

State Department analysts envisioned a Palestinian homeland linked to Jordan in loose confederation, with an elected administration supervising the police, courts, a capital, flags, taxation, and passports. The Palestinians would be allowed "internal security forces" without heavy military equipment crossing the Jordan River. Jordan would be responsible for foreign policy and defense, and could intervene for internal security matters. Any arrangement would rely on political and economic relationships between the Palestinian entity and Jordan, with Palestinian representatives participating in negotiations and approval being secured by local referendum. In essence, an interim Palestinian administration would work with Jordan to set up this confederation, cooperating with the United Nations prior to internal elections.

Carter wondered whether a Palestinian commitment to the terms of a peace agreement—including "Israel's right to exist as a sovereign state"—would require the PLO's participation at a Geneva Conference, a matter of some debate in the ensuing weeks.[62] But the initial plan called for an agreement on the West Bank and Gaza signed between Israel, Jordan, and "Palestinians accepted by these Arab governments and the PLO as representative of the Palestinian people." Syria, Egypt, and Saudi Arabia would also associate themselves in the pursuit of this political entity "constituting a homeland for the Palestinians."[63]

The recommendations outlined the borders of such a homeland. Aside from the Israeli government's unilateral annexation of East Jerusalem in June 1967, the rest of the territory captured during the war had not been formally annexed and boundaries remained indeterminate. The administration sought a first-stage Israeli withdrawal to the 1967 lines, excluding a fifteen-kilometer strip along Jordan and the Dead Sea with West Bank access via Jericho. Furthermore, it envisioned that this strip would be extended to embrace Israeli settlements in Hebron and around the Latrun area near Jerusalem. A further ten-kilometer strip would remain under Israeli control along the western boundary of the West Bank north of Latrun, the Gush Etzion settlement bloc, and a two-kilometer strip either side of the Jerusalem corridor. After a second stage of withdrawal, Israel would still retain Hebron and half the area north of Latrun.[64] Demilitarized security zones would follow in the West Bank, Gaza, and a portion of the Jordanian side of the border, with Israeli surveillance stations on high points over the Jordan valley and UN observer posts at the border crossing. This peace would require mutual recognition, "free access" for Israelis and Palestinian entity residents in each other's territory, and eventual diplomatic recognition. If Israel would not withdraw from most of the territories without mutual security offers from the United States, the proposal recommended a separate treaty to come to Israel's defense in the event of aggression.

The status of Jerusalem was to be adjudicated with particular criteria in mind. These included the requirement that the city would be "undivided physically," with the Jewish population remaining part of Israel. Israelis would control Jewish areas in what was described as their capital, although the plan stipulated that "no authority has sovereignty over [the] entire city." Later, the report expanded, "It is important, but probably not such an imperative, that the local Arab entity, whatever it may be, has its capital in

Jerusalem as well."[65] The proposal for Jerusalem included a Jewish mayor and Arab deputy, Jewish and Arab community councils, respective courts and schools, unhindered access, and an international commission under the United Nations to oversee free operation and use of religious institutions.[66] As for the Israeli settlements that housed 40,000–50,000 Jewish inhabitants in the East Jerusalem neighborhoods of French Hill and Neve Yaacov, what the report euphemistically called "Jewish housing projects in Arab Jerusalem," options included representation on Jewish or Arab councils or the abandonment of these settlements and the movement of people and institutions to Jewish areas in the west.[67]

Among the most charged issues addressed was the long-standing dilemma of the Palestinian refugee problem. According to Carter's Middle East advisors, it "would be resolved primarily through compensation and resettlement in the West Bank-Jordan area, with only token repatriation to Israel."[68] In detail, the principles of a settlement included the acknowledgment of injustice, the stipulation that "refugees have right [*sic*] to homes but developments since 1948 affect practicality," and offering compensation as a replacement where necessary. Carter, who had closely commented on this plan, scribbled on the side, "Most will not want to live there—this is my guess."[69] Furthermore, the memo stated that Jews who left Arab countries have claims, "but not against Palestinians." A special Israeli-Palestinian/Jordanian Commission under UN auspices, intended to organize refugee choices, screen returns, and calculate compensation, would facilitate the practicalities. The actual movement of the refugees would be done under direct UN auspices, via a Refugee Resettlement and Development Commission that would initiate development for resettlement and eventually subsume the operations of the long established United Nations Relief and Works Agency for Palestine (UNRWA).

As a statement of the opening U.S. position for peace in the Middle East in early 1977, the State Department proposal was a bold document. Its contents, many of which have since returned as the central components of any negotiated settlement, outlined the beginnings of what at the time was an equitable solution to Israel's conflict with the Palestinians and the wider Arab world. Arguably, it was the first detailed American outline of a grand regional settlement, placing territorial division at the core. It can also be read as an early iteration of what would eventually emerge as the "two-state solution." Although the Palestinian component was limited to a homeland linked with Jordan rather than an independent state, it contained the seed of plausible sovereignty to address Palestinian aspirations for self-determination. In dealing with the most contentious aspects of the conflict, including refugees and the right of return, the status of Jerusalem, and the demarcation of a permanent border, this February 1977 plan was the first comprehensive U.S. idea for resolving the unanswered questions of the 1967 War.

Carter himself was well aware that the State Department proposal went beyond the existing ceiling of negotiations, which had been limited to bilateral truces in the Nixon and Ford administrations. On the cover note of the entire memo, which had been distributed on National Security Council stationery to only eight people "aware of its existence," the president wrote that it "probably asks too much of Israel." He suggested his advisors limit themselves to specific items, which he listed in his handwriting as "a) '67 borders & minor adjustments; b) real peace; c) Palestine homeland; refugee problem resolved; d) no specifics re Jerusalem; no PLO contact absent UN 242 endorsement, etc. J.C."[70] The new president was certainly thinking beyond the existing script of Middle East diplomacy but remained attuned to the limits of what might be possible.

Vance to the Middle East

To initiate movement on this new approach, Secretary of State Vance made plans for an extensive trip to the Middle East. A series of meetings were arranged in Washington at President Carter's behest throughout the spring of 1977, including with Israeli prime minister Yitzhak Rabin in March, Egypt's president Sadat and King Hussein of Jordan in April, and Saudi Arabia's Crown Prince Fahd in May. Optimism abounded among regional experts. The U.S. Consul General in Jerusalem, Michael H. Newlin, wrote to Vance of the "real possibility" of peace given Arab willingness to recognize Israel's legitimacy in exchange for territorial withdrawal along the lines of UN resolution 242. "The complicated and interrelated problems of peace, withdrawals, security, a Palestinian entity, and the future of the PLO, while truly formidable, do not appear inherently insoluble."[71] Newlin was, however, aware of the irony that inhabitants of the Palestinian territories themselves would be excluded from the negotiations.[72]

Gaps between the initial American position and the views of regional leaders did not take long to appear. Vance's first stop was in Jerusalem, where he had an official lunch with Prime Minister Yitzhak Rabin, Defense Minister Shimon Peres, Foreign Minister Yigal Allon, and several leading diplomats from both countries in Rabin's private office. Rabin had taken over from Golda Meir in June 1974 at the age of fifty-two, the first native-born Israeli leader. He had transitioned from a soldier to a diplomat and finally to a Labor party politician, an evolution that his biographer explains was "neither smooth nor easy."[73] In his meeting with Vance, Rabin spoke of Israel's readiness for territorial compromise to advance peace, but he said it would "not be a total withdrawal to the 1967 borders." The prime minister suggested that changes to sovereignty and questions about the control over territory would be subject to negotiation.[74]

In an evening telegram to the State Department in Washington, Vance recounted Rabin's views about normalization with Arab states and the establishment of "defensible borders" rather than full withdrawal to the 1967 Green Line.[75] The prime minister's stance was a clear sign that the expansion of settlements would still be encouraged by the Israeli Labor government, despite American fears that these settlements would undercut Palestinian claims for territorial control. Vance's telegram contained a great deal of eye-opening reportage. Defense Minister Peres, who would later be celebrated as a leading Israeli dove, had defended the situation in the occupied territories.[76] Peres had spoken of an "Open Bridge" policy facilitating population movement between the West Bank and Jordan, and praised the rise of employment and improved living conditions among local residents. He also complimented Jordan's shadow role in the West Bank, where it was paying local salaries of public officials and supporting municipalities. With regard to the Gaza Strip, Peres spoke proudly of Israeli housing schemes and employment opportunities for Palestinians: "It is the most tranquil part of the area under Israeli administration . . . Israel feels that whatever happens, it must behave as a responsible government and permit a normal life for the Gazans." This nod to a policy of pacification drew on a longer tradition of colonial control over native territories, a stance that was common within the Labor government since the 1967 War.[77] As Peres told Vance, "Israel hopes to maintain a humane presence in the territories."[78]

Arriving in Cairo for meetings on February 17, Vance joined Deputy Egyptian Prime Minister Ismail Fahmy and his advisors to discuss the state of U.S.-Egyptian relations and the peace process. Fahmy was a close confidant of Sadat, who had appointed him as the foreign minister after the 1973 War, a position that had exposed Fahmy to Kissinger's negotiations of the Sinai Disengagement Agreements. Vance stressed that the United States hoped to be "a facilitator of peace" but that it also "has no plan" and he had "come to learn."[79] This sentiment underscored the American approach of gathering information and gauging positions rather than suggesting parameters for diplomatic negotiations, even as it had developed ideas privately.

Fahmy stressed the importance of engaging with the PLO directly on matters related to the Palestinians. Despite Kissinger's earlier promise to the Israelis on non-engagement, there was already formal American communication with PLO leaders in the context of security procedures around the Lebanese civil war that had broken out in 1975 and a modus vivendi had emerged between U.S. officials and Yasser Arafat's organization. This had expanded into more general discussions over the organization and its role in the region.[80] The Egyptian minister had met with PLO leader Yasser Arafat the same morning that he saw Vance and was pushing the Palestinians toward a more moderate stance that might yield American recognition. But Fahmy stressed to Vance that he "could not and would not wish to negotiate for others, including the Palestinians."[81] Fahmy elaborated on the willingness of the Egyptians to reach a comprehensive settlement with Israel, including full recognition in exchange for complete withdrawal and "secure boundaries."

That evening, Vance met with Egyptian president Anwar al-Sadat and Vice President Hosni Mubarak. He was assured that for the first time in over twenty-five years, Arabs and Israelis "both now have full confidence in the U.S. and in President Carter" to act as a mediator.[82] Sadat was born to a poor Nubian family in the Egyptian Nile Delta, one of thirteen siblings, later graduating from the Royal Military Academy in Cairo. He met Gamal Abdel Nasser in the army, where several junior officers formed the secret Free Officers Movement, which sought to free Egypt and Sudan from British rule. In the Egyptian Revolution of 1952, the group overthrew the corrupt King Farouk, and Sadat went on to serve under Nasser's government as vice president. The curtailed influence of Egypt's secret police and the empowering of Egypt's Islamist movement, which Nasser had suppressed, bolstered his political rise.[83]

Sadat spoke of his own efforts to reach out to the United States from the time he came to office in 1970, recalling his statements of support for a peace agreement with Israel and his proposals to complete such an agreement swiftly.[84] He also recalled his decision to order Soviet troops out of Egypt and his work with Kissinger on the disengagement agreements. The Egyptian president was caustic about the Soviet Union, saying they had "nothing to offer except their ability to undermine and create chaos so that the Arabs will have to ask for Soviet assistance."[85] As for the Palestinians, Sadat believed they should have a state on the West Bank and Gaza Strip connected by a corridor running through Israel.

Vance reflected on the dissonance of his meetings with Israelis one day and Egyptians the next in a telegram to Carter that evening: "The suspicion and distrust of each other's intentions are profound and are matched by an almost total inability on each side to understand the other's political realities."[86] The Israelis sought a peace process at a "measured pace," stressing their need to retain some Arab territory for security purposes and opposing a separate Palestinian state or dealings with the PLO. The Egyptians viewed PLO participation and the establishment of a Palestinian state as "the crux of the problem" and were willing to find creative ways to ensure their participation in Geneva.[87] Sadat privately assured Vance that he was deeply committed to a peace deal, and "he said he could bring the other Arabs along by virtue of his substantial influence."[88]

Before returning to Washington, Vance shuttled to Amman, Beirut, and finally Damascus, where he met with President Hafez al-Assad on February 20.[89] Assad, like King Hussein of Jordan and President Elias Sarkis of Lebanon, agreed that a comprehensive solution to the Middle East conflict was a necessity. He was adamant that a withdrawal from the territories occupied during the 1967 War signified the areas in their entirety. "Even if a state of war continued for hundreds of years with clashes every other year, Syria would not give up one inch of its territory under any pretext or condition," Assad stressed.[90] Privately, Vance spoke with Assad about the Arab states finding common ground on the Palestinian issue.[91] Back in his room at Damascus's Hotel Meridien that evening, Vance scribbled out the areas of agreement and division that had emerged during his visit to Arab capitals. All the parties, Vance wrote, were willing to go to a Geneva Conference in the second half of 1977, and they were prepared to have substantive discussions on the "core elements of a final settlement: peace, withdrawal, resolution of the Palestinian question."[92] The disagreements that Vance described centered on the method of resolving these issues and the question of PLO participation.

Vance reported back on his trip to President Carter, Vice President Mondale, Brzezinski, and several other senior officials at the National Security Council (NSC). He reiterated the common agreement on going to Geneva for an overall settlement and the "essential" U.S. role in facilitating these discussions. The question of Israeli withdrawal divided the Arabs who were demanding full pull back from the 1967 lines and the Israelis, who held onto the notion of secure recognized borders. As Vance relayed, there was "little consensus" on the Palestinian question, "even among the Arabs."[93] America's role, the NSC meeting participants agreed, was to help the parties articulate their positions and to outline general principles governing a settlement. Brzezinski stressed the need to deal with substance ahead of Geneva, like separating out the discussion of security and sovereignty and a "sharper definition" of the Palestinian issue.[94]

In their discussion of Israel's position on negotiations, Carter wondered about the impact of an impending Israeli election on foreign policy and the willingness of any Israeli government—left wing or right wing—to recognize the PLO. The organization remained a pariah group in the view of leading Israeli politicians.

Vance suggested more U.S. willingness to grant visa applications to PLO spokespeople wanting to travel to the United States, "a limited sign we are prepared to move off dead center." Carter entertained the idea but also raised his concern about U.S. conformity with the Helsinki Agreement, which necessitated the preservation of civil and human rights: "Can we keep people like this out of our country? This is not so much a question just of the PLO, but we have to be clean on the human rights issue."[95]

Following up with Carter after the meeting, Brzezinski argued that permitting the PLO to come to the United States would be a "major concession" requiring something in return. The National Security Advisor warned that Carter should only "add to the PLO's prestige" when the timing was right for broader American efforts in the Middle East. "The moderate Arabs are making an effort to get the PLO under control," Brzezinski suggested, and this would "diminish their stature." Such action was in the U.S. interest, Brzezinski concluded, "and we should not undercut them by suddenly giving the PLO a big public shot in the arm."[96] On the margin of the memo, Carter noted his agreement. The president's position underscored the dissonance between his invocation of human rights as a replacement for Cold War détente and the reality of subjecting regional politics to a strategic advantage.

Brzezinski worked to develop a strategic view of the American approach to peacemaking. He advised Carter that Israel had to understand that a Geneva Conference was not a "substitute for stalemate." Rather than simply attend and let the conference stumble, Brzezinski argued that in Carter's upcoming talks with Rabin, the president should emphasize real movement, and the administration should not be shy to contribute substantive thoughts of its own. Carter underlined "not shy" on the memo, writing that "we should play a *strong* & discreet role, but first we must decide what we want—ultimately & step-by-step."[97]

Rabin to the White House

Rabin's March visit presented an opportunity for the two leaders to discuss the substance of a possible settlement to the Arab-Israeli conflict. In his first meeting with Carter, the Israeli prime minister

FIGURE 1.2. "Jimmy Carter with Yitzhak Rabin, Prime Minister of Israel." March 7, 1977. White House Staff Photographers Collection at the Jimmy Carter Library.

emphasized an approach to territorial compromise that did not denote full withdrawal, especially in the West Bank. At the same time, he stressed that the territories were not being annexed: "Under international law, these are administered territories under Israeli control, but they are not part of our sovereign territory. We believe that their future is still to be decided in negotiations."[98] But when Rabin was pushed by Vance to clarify whether Israel required or claimed sovereignty in occupied territories like the Golan Heights, the Israeli prime minister was noncommittal: "We may claim it, but we have not annexed any other territory. We have left it open."[99] The echo of the Eshkol government's 1967 "decision not to decide" was unmistakable.

The talks between Carter and Rabin also highlighted the difficulty of the U.S. convincing Israel to yield on the Palestinian question. In Rabin's view, there should be two states, "Israel, as a Jewish state," and a "Jordanian-Palestinian state," *not* an independent Palestinian entity between the Jordan River and the Mediterranean. According to Rabin, this Jordanian-Palestinian state would be the only address for the Palestinians. "How the Palestinian identity is worked out within that state is not our business. It is up to them. But we want two states. It can consist of two entities, but there can only be one state."[100] Carter pushed Rabin, asking about a possible U.S. model of two states within a federation, where Jordan would control defense and foreign policy and the West Bank state would be demilitarized. Rabin reiterated that "there can be no third state."[101] In his view, negotiations should only proceed between governments, underscoring the limits of Israeli willingness to accommodate any Palestinian national entity with attributes of sovereignty outside of a Jordanian context. Later that evening, Brzezinski noted the Israeli prime minister's firm positions and encouraged Carter to "make clear to Rabin that we want greater specificity . . . we are prepared to support Israel in a genuine search for peace, but that he should have no illusion about the United States indefinitely supporting a stalemate."[102]

Rabin had also made it clear that forging any agreement with the PLO at a possible Geneva Conference was out of the question, as the organization refused to recognize Israel or accept UN resolution 242.[103] These procedural difficulties would complicate preparations for a possible conference, given the Arab demands for Palestinian participation. In an earlier meeting with Israeli foreign minister Yigal Allon during his February trip to the region, Secretary of State Vance broached the possibility that the PLO could amend its charter to accept Israel and adopt UN resolution 242, to which Allon responded, "A PLO that accepts 242 would no longer be the PLO."[104] As Vance's visit to the Middle East had signaled, the administration was already pursuing the possibility of PLO reform and discussing modes of engagement with the organization in successive talks with Arab leaders.

During the second extended session between Rabin, Carter, and senior advisors from both countries, Carter more firmly articulated the American position on territory and the Palestinian question. "Your settlements in the occupied territories are illegal," Carter told Rabin. "Your control over territory in the occupied regions will have to be modified substantially in my view."[105] As for the PLO, Carter invoked global comparisons to soften Rabin's opposition to engagement: "We, of course, deplore terrorism, but even we sometimes have had to swallow our pride. We talked to the North Koreans and the French talked to the FLN [Front de Libération Nationale] . . . we don't know of any Palestinian leaders other than the PLO." He called for greater Israeli flexibility on moving toward Geneva with Palestinian representation, and Rabin's response evinced frustration with such an activist U.S. stance: "I hope that you, Mr. President, will not take clear substantive positions before negotiations."[106]

For Rabin, a broader Israeli position on the Palestinian issue could be separated from the question of PLO representation, which he opposed. But Carter and Vance made it clear that the issues were intertwined, and the U.S. government would not shy away from either. As Carter concluded, "My only goal is to bring about a permanent peace in the Middle East," and this would require movement from all parties. "We will be just as insistent in dealing with the Arabs," Carter added. "We will insist that they recognize you, that they open their borders, and that they end belligerency. But I do not intend to tell them where the borders should be." The president did not share the same skepticism toward the Arab states as Rabin. "We want a partnership with you in peace, and I understand how difficult it will be for you to accept the proposition that the Arabs really do now want peace."[107]

Personal accounts of the visit underscore the deep divide that was emerging between the United States and Israel.[108] Rabin recalled his meeting with some disdain in his memoirs: "It seemed to me that Carter was set on the Brookings report and intended to 'sell' it to me piecemeal."[109] In Rabin's opinion, "the Brookings plan had absolutely nothing in common with Israel's views about final borders."[110] The Israeli prime minister was especially frustrated with Carter's insistence on frank talk and clear objectives, growing "increasingly concerned about the effect his 'new style' would have on our region." "If he publicized his views on the Middle East," Rabin noted, "he would bring comfort to the Arabs and weaken Israel's negotiating position."[111]

Carter also felt uneasy about his meetings with Rabin. Ten days later, aboard Air Force One, he told a domestic affairs advisor "he liked Rabin but didn't think Rabin liked him." In private talks in the White House residence, Carter had asked Rabin about a possible peace and promised that "he could raise with Sadat any point on behalf of Israel that Rabin wanted." But Carter had been "disappointed" by Rabin's "lack of response."[112] In the context of American ambitions to solve the Arab-Israeli conflict, Rabin's circumspect reaction was disheartening.

Tensions generated by the visit also worried leaders of the American Jewish community. On the evening of Rabin's departure, a delegation from the Conference of Presidents of Major Jewish Organizations gathered in the State Department with Secretary Vance.[113] The conference had been founded in 1954 during the administration of Dwight D. Eisenhower, in response to an Israeli military massacre of Palestinians in the West Bank village of Qibya. American Jewish leaders had mobilized during this crisis in U.S.-Israeli relations and sought to facilitate a central address for engaging the growing and often fractious communal organizations.[114] Rabbi Alexander Schindler, the chairman of the organization and the leader of the Union of American Hebrew Congregations (the congregational arm of Reform Judaism in North America), expressed concern over Carter's meeting with Rabin. Vance assured the assembled Jewish representatives that the special relationship between the United States and Israel was as strong as ever. His assurance would not last very long.

A Palestinian "Homeland"

The breaking point between the Carter administration and American Jewish supporters of Israel came just ten days after the talks with Rabin. At a town hall meeting in Clinton, Massachusetts, Carter responded to a question on the Middle East saying "there has to be a homeland provided for the Palestinian refugees who have suffered for many, many years."[115] The frank language and insistence that accommodating Palestinians was central to any movement on Arab-Israeli policy fit with Carter's decisive break from his predecessors. In particular, Carter's choice of the word "homeland"—which was actually invoked with similar language in both the Brookings report and the State Department secret memo—elicited a great deal of public criticism from Israeli and American Jewish leaders.[116]

Almost 70 percent of American Jews had cast a vote for Carter in the 1976 election, but deep suspicion lingered with regard to the administration's policy toward Israel. The remarks at the Clinton town hall bolstered these anxieties. *Time* magazine printed scathing reactions to the "homeland" comment from communal leaders, with sources commenting that "Carter's pronouncement seems both premature and imprecise."[117] The President's chief of staff, Hamilton Jordan, recognized this mounting concern and worked to rectify it, along with other members of the administration including Stuart Eizenstat, the leading domestic policy advisor, and Mark Siegel, the administration's designated Jewish communal liaison. Their reactions to the Clinton remarks and the subsequent discussions about Carter's approach to Israel indicate that the domestic pressures on the administration's approach to the Middle East were real and ongoing from the very first months of 1977.[118]

The brunt of the internal effort to soothe relations with American Jewry fell under the remit of the office of the chief of staff. As Hamilton Jordan's young deputy in charge of Jewish outreach, Siegel was an active advisor who guided the early response of the White House to criticism of Carter's policies on Israel. Siegel had been appointed executive director of the Democratic National Committee (DNC) in 1974, leading to his position within the administration.[119] In the wake of the Clinton town hall, Siegel co-authored a breathtaking White House memo titled "Jewish Identity, Zionism and Israel." The internal document demonstrated increased executive branch awareness of the need to be cognizant of domestic Jewish concerns in the articulation of foreign policy. Siegel later recalled scrambling to finish the memo for Jordan, who feared that domestic support was "slipping away." In the memo, Siegel referred specifically to Carter's "homeland" statement, writing that "the Jewish community here is in almost morbid fear of a separate, politically independent Palestinian entity on the West Bank of the Jordan River."[120]

Siegel captured the zeitgeist among American Jews in his memo, describing how "the fear and disgust of the PLO reaches almost Nazi-hating quality of emotion." This disgust is what animated domestic criticism to the town hall statement. "The American Jewish community," Siegel explained, was "terribly concerned by the President's reference to a Palestinian homeland." The liaison also made several recommendations for Carter to reach out to American Jews, who were convinced "that the State and Defense Departments are populated with anti-Semitic Arabists." As Siegel suggested, "a token of 'objectivity' must be introduced into the departments, even if it is the placement of one obviously sympathetic, non-career person, in each. At the very least, this will give the lobby someone to bitch to that they feel will at least listen." A similar suggestion was made regarding the National Security Council and the White House, in line with the belief that a better explanation of administration policies would have long-lasting strategic benefits. As Siegel concluded, "above all, they [American Jews] must come to feel that their voices have been heard and that they have been part of the process. Only then could they be called on to help sell the result to their people and the Hill."[121]

As a constituency long engaged in political activism, the American Jewish community had been working tirelessly to tighten its support among Congress and among sympathetic allies in the White House, building a powerful lobby to steer its agenda. This increasing focus on Israel was a pronounced shift in the activity of organizations like the American Jewish Committee (AJC) and the Anti-Defamation League (ADL), older advocacy groups traditionally focused on domestic matters of concern like civil rights and immigration.[122] The effort to shape American policy through domestic lobbying grew exponentially during the 1970s, with the American Israel Public Affairs Committee (AIPAC) making significant inroads alongside other American Jewish organizations.[123] This domestic mobilization was partially rooted in the psychologically damaging effects of Israel's military losses in the surprise attack of the 1973 War, which still hung over Jewish organizational life.

The negative reaction among American Jewish leaders was largely the result of a mounting perception that Carter was taking sides in the Middle East debate, to the detriment of Israel's national interest. Brzezinski admitted in his memoir that without any Arab concessions, the town hall remark "helped to create the impression that the new administration was tilting away from Israel."[124] It was coupled with decisions around the same time not to sell cluster bombs to Israel or allow the sale of Israeli-made Kfir bombers to

Latin American countries. As a result, the Carter administration was viewed in some quarters of the American Jewish community as having distanced itself from its alliance with Israel. By June 1977, the perception among domestic supporters of Israel that the country was being unfairly targeted by the administration led members of AIPAC to compile a list of twenty-one grievances, demanding the dismissal of Carter's Middle East experts. The White House was inundated with letters attacking Carter's "pro-Arab" policies.[125]

Carter attempted to counter this public outcry, saying "he never called for an independent Palestinian country" and expressing support for the idea that "if there is a Palestinian entity established in the West Bank . . . it ought to be associated with Jordan."[126] Brzezinski, too, reassured Israeli officials that the term was far more innocuous than they imagined, calling Ambassador Simcha Dinitz to clarify that the word change was not monumental.[127] One administration official, however, portrayed Carter's statement as deliberate, arguing that the president wanted to move the negotiating process forward in his first year.[128] The concept of a "homeland" implied certain inalienable rights for Palestinians, addressing the refugee issue and acknowledging Israel's role in fomenting the dispossession of 1948. That may have been too much for some allies to countenance. In the late 1970s and 1980s, many supporters of Israel took issue with the view that Palestinians were an actual nation, a position that persisted well beyond Carter's time in office.[129]

Outside of the United States, the American call for a "homeland" was a welcome development. Carter's remarks were considered a sign of the administration's seriousness in advancing toward Geneva and resolving the Palestinian question. The British Foreign Office emphasized their agreement. "We consider that the Palestinians should have a land of their own," one official wrote. "How this should be realized is one of the matters for negotiations between the parties."[130] The PLO leadership in Beirut also praised Carter's declaration as a "step forward in U.S. Middle Eastern policy, and an encouragement for the Palestinian people in their resistance to Zionist expansion and settler colonialism."[131] PLO officials still sought out a more specific reference to the location of this possible homeland, insisting on an independent state rather than a confederal arrangement with Jordan.[132] While mindful of declarations that had not altered the situation on the ground, the Palestinian reaction reflected a wider embrace of a diplomatic solution in the 1970s and a grudging willingness to live side by side with Israel.[133] The president's broader appeal for human rights elicited particular praise, with the hope that he would "relieve the sufferings of all oppressed peoples of the world, including the Palestinians."[134]

This linkage of the administration's Middle East stance with an emerging human rights agenda was touted as a successful departure from the approach of earlier decades domestically as well. As Zbigniew Brzezinski wrote to the president, "the public clearly understands that the Carter foreign policy is derived from an affirmative commitment to certain basic human values. Moreover, you have defined these values as 'human rights,' which is both broader and more flexible than such words as 'liberty' or 'freedom.' This gives our foreign policy a wider appeal, more in tune with the emerging political consciousness of mankind—which is concerned both with liberty and equity."[135] Brzezinski suggested that the vision offered by the president contained the kernel of an entirely new way of conceiving of the U.S.-dominated Arab-Israeli peace process, one based on greater flexibility in dealing with intractable issues. He believed the parties would see that the United States was serious about its peacemaking efforts, which could lead to more substantive negotiations. "This is a significant step forward from almost anything that the United States has said on the subject for at least ten to fifteen years," the NSC advisor concluded.[136]

Arab Dissonance

What did other Arab parties think of this new American approach to the region? Continuing the series of meetings that Vance had initiated on the Middle East, Carter hosted Egyptian president Sadat at the White House for his first face-to-face conversation with an Arab leader. At their discussion in the Cabinet Room on April 4, the connection between the two men was immediate. Sadat spoke of the common principles shared by the two villagers, both from religious backgrounds. "You have to be optimistic if you are a farmer," Carter replied. "You have to always believe that things will be better next year."[137] Their discussions about the Palestinian issue, representation at Geneva, and Egypt's willingness to pursue a permanent peace with Israel were frank and far-reaching. Sadat was eager to establish his unique role for Carter: "I am the only leader in the Arab world who can take real steps toward peace. . . . No other Arab leader, even in Jordan, will go as far as I will."[138] Underlying Sadat's optimism about peacemaking was an acute concern about the state of Egypt's economy and the need for greater Western investment to bolster the country's domestic and regional security.[139]

King Hussein of Jordan visited the White House after Sadat, and Carter pushed him on the specifics of Jordanian-Palestinian relations in the West Bank.[140] Hussein, the long-standing monarch of the Jordanian Kingdom since 1952, had a storied secret relationship with successive Israeli leaders.[141] It remained unclear how sovereignty for Palestinians in the West Bank would affect Palestinians in Jordan, and how to achieve an independent entity given the dominance of the PLO. As King Hussein argued, "The PLO prefers its own state before discussing the future, and they realize the need for close links with us. The PLO is the creation of Arab summits, not the choice of the Palestinian people."[142] Hussein had been pressured to agree to the 1974 Rabat Summit declaration, in which the Arab League members recognized the PLO as the sole representative of the Palestinian people, with inducements of annual subsidies from oil-producing states. His antipathy toward organized Palestinian nationalism was a legacy from the 1970 civil war in Jordan and the Hashemite Kingdom's long history of control over the West Bank. Jordan's direct annexation of the West Bank in 1950 had a formative impact on the Palestinian national movement, and it lasted until King Hussein formally relinquished claims on the territory west of the Jordan River in 1988. In the interim, it was difficult for Palestinians to represent their own interests on a global stage, as demands were made that they participate in diplomatic discussions jointly with Jordan. This was a core structural impediment to the possibility of direct contacts with the PLO, which officials in the Carter White House sought to address.[143]

The paramount concern within the administration during these consultations was not PLO representation but the composition of a defined territorial entity for Palestinians and how to account for refugees from the 1948 War. Carter raised these matters directly during his first meeting with Syria's president Hafez al-Assad, which took place in Geneva's Intercontinental Hotel on May 9. "How do you see a practical solution?" he asked Assad. "I don't believe that Israel can agree to take all of the Palestinians into their territory. What does Arafat have in mind that is practical?" Assad searched for an answer. He felt that any Palestinian state in the West Bank and Gaza would be too small to accommodate the refugees, and Israel would have to accept some. Carter asked him how many there were. Assad was taken aback, whispering to his foreign minister about the numbers of Palestinians in each Arab country. "I am anxious to provide you with a reply, but I don't want to mislead you," he told Carter. The conversation turned to the possible formation of a Palestinian homeland, and Assad admitted that there was internal dissonance between King Hussein and the Palestinians. Carter sensed the Arab states "do not favor a fully independent Palestinian nation. It could become radicalized with a Qadhafi-like leader. The Soviets might gain influence there." Assad explained the divergent schools of thought, one that saw Jordanian hegemony over the West Bank and Gaza preventing the emergence of a Palestinian state, and the other saw a demilitarized entity for Palestinians as part of a Jordanian state. "These propositions would divest the Palestinians of anything allowing themselves to demonstrate their own personality," Assad concluded.[144]

Inter-Arab disagreements about the nature of Palestinian self-determination persisted throughout Carter's bilateral discussions with the Egyptian, Jordanian, and Syrian leadership. The problem for the Carter administration was not merely a question of internal Arab confusion about how to manage the fate of the Palestinians. It extended into questions of representation, the nature of political sovereignty, and the extent to which the United States might recognize the possibility of self-determination for Palestinians.[145] This was particularly vexing in light of shifting PLO views about how best to exercise national aspirations after the Rabat Summit. Arab recognition had spurred Arafat's diplomatic gains at the United Nations, while also raising "the expectation of a showdown with the more extreme guerilla organizations" skeptical of the diplomatic track.[146] If a "homeland" was a dangerous prospect for Carter to float in the United States, Palestinians themselves were still debating the nature of a political outcome that would be premised on independent statehood alongside Israel.

The Carter administration's planning for a comprehensive peace was upended by a sea change in Israeli politics in the spring of 1977. In a startling development, Prime Minister Yitzhak Rabin announced his resignation from office on April 8. The decision was a consequence of a bank account scandal involving his wife while he was ambassador to the United States. Coming on the heels of several corruption and nepotism investigations, the "Dollar Account Affair" set in motion a political upheaval in Israel.[147] The electoral success of Menachem Begin in May and the arrival of a Likud government to power would further challenge the possibility of Palestinian national sovereignty inside the West Bank or Gaza Strip. Carter's early efforts to reorient American involvement in the region, away from Kissinger's limited cease-fires and toward a comprehensive solution involving the Palestinians, now faced new hurdles in Jerusalem.

CHAPTER TWO

Menachem Begin's Reality

IN HIS MEMOIR, President Carter recalled watching an interview when Menachem Begin was running for prime minister, in which the candidate stated "that the entire West Bank had been 'liberated' during the Six Day War, and that a Jewish majority and an Arab minority would be established there." At the time Carter exclaimed, "I could not believe what I was hearing."[1] But Begin's views were not at all surprising to anyone paying attention to his long career in politics. Begin was a leader of the revisionist faction of the Zionist movement and a disciple of its founder, Ze'ev Jabotinsky. His early years had been marked by the upheaval of war in Europe and the tragedy of losing his parents and brother in the Holocaust. After arriving in Palestine and commanding the underground Irgun militia, Begin headed the opposition in the Israeli Knesset as the head of the Herut and then Likud party, a position from which he passionately articulated his views on a host of fractious issues, including the territories.[2]

Begin saw the West Bank as central to Israeli identity, always referring to it using the biblical name of "Judea and Samaria."[3] When the territories were first conquered by Israel in 1967, Begin was deeply opposed to granting Arab inhabitants political rights or any form of territorial control that could lead to Palestinian statehood.[4] Running counter to this exclusivist approach was Begin's more inclusive conception of nationalism, based in part on the model of European thinkers who had elevated a progressive version of the nation-state that should provide individual rights to minorities.[5] Together, the influence of Jabotinsky's ideas about Jewish territorial dominance and the discourse of liberal nationalist thinkers fed Begin's emerging conception of Palestinian Arabs as a minority that could be granted rights under Israeli rule rather than a self-determining political entity deserving of sovereignty.

This inherent tension engendered an evolution in Begin's thinking as he campaigned for the 1977 elections a decade later.[6] In the lead-up to the May election in Israel, Begin stressed the impossibility of a Palestinian state or some form of national self-determination for Arabs in the West Bank or Gaza Strip. The Labor party that had been ruling Israel since 1948 was no less opposed to such a development but remained wary of the political limbo that confronted the young country after the territorial conquests of the 1967 War. Leading Labor politicians like Levi Eshkol, Golda Meir, and Yitzhak Rabin therefore had spoken publicly of offers to exchange territory for peace between 1967 and 1977.[7] At the same time, they had facilitated the installation of military outposts and civilian settlements in the territory itself.[8] The grounds for this encroachment were always articulated in terms of security, although common cause was made with the religious right and secularists involved in the "Greater Land of Israel" movement, which sought the expansion of Israel's borders.

Unlike Labor politicians, Begin was less circumspect about Israel's choices regarding the territories and did not try to hide his views. "To whom are we going to give it back?" Begin responded to one interviewer. "[In 1948] King Abdullah invaded this country from Jordan, he killed our people, destroyed our synagogues and he occupied part of it. Then in the early '50s he annexed it. Nobody recognized that annexation but Britain and Pakistan. The U.S. never recognized it. So give what back? It doesn't belong to them."[9] In the style of liberal nationalists in interwar Europe, Begin viewed the "Arabs of Judea and Samaria" as a minority that should be treated with a degree of fairness but without collective rights for self-determination. The Likud election platform had provisions for dealing with the Palestinians in Israel as well as the West Bank and Gaza Strip. It delineated their choice to adopt Israeli citizenship, which would provide full rights and include voting for the Knesset. Alternatively, if Arabs in the territories chose not to take up Israeli citizenship, they would retain full rights without voting. In either circumstance, the electoral platform stated that the "Arab nationality in Eretz Israel will enjoy cultural autonomy," a term that was distinct from political sovereignty and would emerge as a central tenant of Begin's approach to the Palestinians while in power.[10]

The Likud Revolution

In an unexpected political earthquake, Begin's Likud party emerged eleven seats ahead of the Labor party's forerunner, the Alignment, in the Knesset elections of May 17, 1977. Long relegated to the opposition, the Likud shocked the dominant political forces inside the country with the surprise victory. As the results were announced on Israeli television, the news anchor Haim Yavin declared "Ladies and Gentleman—a revolution!"[11] Begin's rise was especially jarring in Washington, where the settlement issue had already become a point of contention with Rabin. Carter was deeply attuned to Israeli claims being made on the West Bank and Gaza Strip. He had warned Israeli leaders of the dangers of land seizures and settlement expansion before the election.[12]

This opposition to settlement building was even more relevant after the Likud victory. On May 18, Secretary of State Cyrus Vance received a memo from the State Department reporting on the "stunning defeat" of the ruling Labor-Alignment with the projection of Likud's large electoral success. The Tel Aviv embassy reported on the "uncertainty" of U.S.-Israeli relations as a major factor in the left's poor showing: "The Israeli electorate foresees hard times ahead and has prepared to batten down the hatches by taking a strong swing to the right."[13] Officials in Washington feared that the results of the election would herald the end of Carter's comprehensive peace plan for the region. After the news of the political realignment reached the White House, NSC Middle East advisor William Quandt recommended a policy review. "Much of our strategy toward the Arab-Israeli conflict has been predicated on the assumption that a strong and moderate Israeli government would at some point be able to make difficult decisions on territory and on the Palestinians," Quandt told Brzezinski. "The Arabs will no doubt read the Israeli election results as signifying an end to the chance of getting to Geneva this year, and possibly the end of any hope for a political settlement . . . all in all, the short-term looks rather bleak in the Middle East."[14]

Rather than turn their backs, Carter's Middle East advisor argued that the administration should engage with the new government. The best course of action was to withhold any outward disappointment with the Likud's victory, stick to the plans for Geneva, and invite Begin to Washington in the event he was chosen as prime minister. Nevertheless, Quandt wrote, "Israeli voters should know that a hard-line government will not find it easy to manage the U.S.-Israeli relationship. Intransigence must be seen to carry a price tag, but we should not be seen as the bully. Begin should be allowed to make his own mistakes."[15] Sounding a note of optimism, Quandt suggested that American public support for a Likud government would be less than their support for earlier governments, giving the U.S. government "room for maneuver."[16]

Carter adopted this cautious approach to the Israeli elections in his conversations with allies. He told British prime minister James Callaghan that regardless of the change in Israel's administration, the United States would continue to pursue efforts for a comprehensive peace. If the Likud government was intransigent, Carter told Callaghan, the United States might have to move away from a commitment to Israel.[17] Callaghan discussed the possibility of internal splits within British and American Jewry over the election, mentioning Jewish leaders with whom he regularly consulted, adding that he "rather kept away from them this week whilst they are suffering from shock."[18] Carter agreed, noting similar dynamics in the United States: "If it became obvious that there was a choice between Begin and an unpopular government on the one hand and the security of Israel on the other there is no doubt that they would go with the security of Israel."[19] A fault line seemed to be opening up between supporters of centrist Israeli leaders and the new right-wing government, although this gap may have been less pronounced than Carter surmised. Internal discussions among domestic American Jewish leaders reveal discontent over Begin's victory but ultimately a calculated decision to support Israel's newly elected leader despite the troubling policies he began to espouse.[20]

Carter and Callaghan, whose relationship was warm and trusting, spoke of mutual concerns over Begin's political views and compared their respective plans to speak with the new prime minister. Callaghan had met Begin in 1974 and found him "extremely charming" yet "extremely hard line." Recalling the era of the British Mandate in Palestine, Callaghan told Carter that Begin had "fought very bitterly against us and has the respect that old enemies have." Carter voiced concern over Begin's more recent "unwarranted" statements about settlements in the West Bank ("or Judea as he calls it"). "He could at least have kept his mouth shut for a few weeks," Carter remarked. Callaghan's response was revealing. "But it is unrealistic to expect him to do so. He has been saying this for 30 years . . . I don't think he will modify that policy unless you can apply some leverage."[21] The British leader's comments were an early indication to Carter that U.S. aspirations for a shift in policy toward the Arab-Israeli conflict would require exercising active American pressure where it had not been heavily applied before. In contrast, discussing Arab leaders, Carter told Callaghan he was "favourably impressed . . . they may be wonderful con artists but my impression is that they genuinely want to make some progress." Callaghan agreed.[22]

The British and American concerns over Israeli territorial aims and settlement building were prescient. In his first speech to the Israeli Knesset as prime minister on June 20, Begin declared "the government will plan and establish and encourage settlements, both rural and urban, on the land of the homeland."[23] Among Palestinian leaders in exile, Begin's initial moves merely substantiated their deep antipathy. In Beirut, the editors of the PLO Information Bulletin wrote that Begin's election was "a confirmation of the long-held PLO line that unmasks the fascist and aggressive nature of the Zionist entity." The editors' diagnosis of Begin suggested impatience with international rhetoric about Israeli policy in the territories. "It proves the rightness of the PLO's attitude, that Zionist expansionism and aggression cannot be deterred by mere words," they concluded.[24]

Formulating a Negotiating Position

The extent of the Begin government's position on the Jewish right to settlement in the territories and cultural autonomy for Arabs would become clear as Carter continued his efforts to lay the groundwork for negotiations at a Geneva Conference. In proceeding with Middle East discussions, the president sought the help of other regional powers who might provide a mediating influence. Saudi Arabia's Crown Prince Fahd was welcomed to the White House on May 24. Fahd was considered the de facto leader during the reign of his half brother King Khalid, who ascended the throne in 1975 after the assassination of King Faisal. Given his financial support for the PLO and Arab leaders, Fahd was seen as the linchpin of any American-led peace process, someone who had the ability to set a moderate regional agenda.[25] The president had been encouraged by Brzezinski and Vance to indicate a willingness to work with the Saudi leader on efforts to reach a settlement, providing security guarantees and attesting to U.S. friendship with the Gulf monarchy.

Fahd himself was a great advocate of closer U.S.-Saudi ties and sought to capitalize on emerging Saudi leadership in the Arab world.[26] Only a few years after the 1973 oil crisis and OPEC embargo, the kingdom had flexed its political and economic muscle. As the largest oil exporter to the United States, Saudi Arabia had become a regional and global power.[27] During their opening discussions, the U.S. president stressed the close alignment between the two countries, telling Fahd "there is no other country with whom we have closer or more friendly relations than Saudi Arabia."[28] Fahd articulated the Saudi position on the Arab-Israeli conflict and stressed his willingness to follow the U.S. lead in negotiations. He explained, however, that Saudi Arabia and the other Arab states would not agree to a joint Palestinian entity with Jordan, rather favoring an actual homeland.[29] In their private conversation the next day, Fahd agreed to "induce the PLO to endorse United Nations Resolution 242," which would be a prerequisite for U.S. discussions with the PLO. The Saudi Crown Prince reiterated his commitment to the pursuit of a comprehensive settlement in the months ahead.[30]

Fahd's departure from the United States concluded the administration's extensive outreach to Arab leaders in the first half of 1977. In early June, U.S. officials began to strategize domestic outreach for promoting a comprehensive peace. "The case must be carried to the American people as a whole, including the Jewish community," Brzezinski advised the president. "This means stressing not only that a settlement is good for Israel, but also emphasizing explicitly that the *national interests* of the United States require a settlement."[31] For Carter's Middle East policy to work, he would need the support of American Jews, who remained skeptical of his intentions since the president's Palestinian "homeland" remark. Brzezinski's advice underscored the need to frame the entire undertaking in terms of the national interest, appealing to American Jewish patriotism and allegiance, rather than driving a wedge between their support for Israel and for the United States.

As the Carter administration planned its next steps, the Israeli Foreign Ministry was assessing the American approach for the new government in Jerusalem.[32] Begin announced a set of fifteen guidelines for his government's approach to key issues, revealing his commitment to settlement in the entirety of Israel and the territories.[33] Begin's guidelines asserted that "the right of the Jewish people to the Land of Israel is eternal and inalienable" and called for an increase in the "setting up of defense and permanent settlements, rural and urban, on the soil of the homeland."[34] At the same time, Begin's points included agreement to attend the Geneva Conference and an invitation to Israel's neighbors "to conduct direct negotiations for the signing of the peace treaties between them."[35] This dual approach emerged as a hallmark of Israeli diplomacy under Begin. On the one hand, it expressed a willingness to negotiate bilaterally with Arab states, albeit without the Palestinians. At the same time, it premised these negotiations on the assertion of Israeli sovereignty in the occupied territories and allowance for expanded settlement building. The approach was cleverly designed, and fundamentally at odds with the U.S. and Arab positions.

To dispel any criticism of the Israeli strategy, Begin deployed his close confidant Shmuel Katz and Israel's ambassador to the United States, Simcha Dinitz, to meet with Brzezinski and other advisors in the White House.[36] Katz was a founder of the right-wing nationalist Herut party, the forerunner of the Likud. He was also a cofounder of the Movement for Greater Israel in 1967, a group that advocated for permanent settlement in the occupied territories.[37] Dinitz had been a political advisor to former prime minister Golda Meir and was ambassador to the United States during the 1973 War, when he coordinated weapons shipments to Israel with Secretary of State Henry Kissinger. In their meeting with Carter's representatives, the gap between Israeli and American views was clearly articulated. Katz affirmed Begin's position on abiding by

UN Security Council Resolutions 242 and 338, although he took issue with the notion that the question of a Palestinian homeland or refugee compensation fell under these resolutions. This claim was an early indication that the Begin government did not accept the applicability of resolution 242 to the West Bank, disputing that "withdrawal from territories" signified a need to leave "Judea and Samaria" and ensuring a collision with his American interlocutors.

The logic of the new Israeli government was challenged on the issue of settlements. Brzezinski explicitly asked about their status, and Katz restated the Likud position "on the basic right of the Jewish people to Western Palestine as a whole."[38] He invoked international law, arguing that the rejection of the 1947 partition plan by the Arabs "restored the full legal basis" for Israeli claims to the territories. This inherent contradiction, claiming to abide by 242 and believing in the basic right of the Jewish people to Western Palestine, reflected a core element of the right-wing government's approach to the settlements: explicit and unapologetic.[39]

Katz stressed that Israel's position would not preempt negotiations, while at the same time insisting that settlement building would continue. Brzezinski asked him about building in areas populated by Arabs, and Katz acknowledged that there was some controversy on this matter. He stressed that the Likud government was hoping to persuade Arabs not to force an Israeli withdrawal. "If I can give you the vision that I have, after forty years of contacts with the Arabs," Katz remarked, "I would try to convince the Arabs in Western Palestine that their greatest chance for security and prosperity, without loss of their cultural identity and with local autonomy, lies in a unitary state under an Israeli government, with the right to citizenship for those who want it, or they can remain Jordanian citizens." The notion of a political solution to Palestinian aspirations was an anathema to Begin's envoy. "If an Arab entity of any kind is formed west of the Jordan River, it would be a threat to Israel."[40]

In essence, Katz had provided the Americans with a recipe for a one-state solution to the Israeli-Palestinian conflict: an Israeli state in full control of territory and inhabitants on both sides of the Green Line. Brzezinski pushed Katz to explain how such a vision squared with the demographic reality of a possible eventual Arab majority over Jews. Katz spoke of the hopes among the Likud for mass immigration "so that we could at least keep the ratio in our favor." He refused to accept any proposition that a mere Israeli withdrawal to the 1967 lines would yield peace with the Arabs. "We believe that the 1967 borders constitute a death trap."[41] Rather than concede that peace required giving up land, Katz reinforced the notion that Israel would emerge more vulnerable, lecturing his American interlocutors about the conflict, which he argued "stems from the Arab refusal to recognize our existence in any area." "You know," Katz concluded, "100 years ago Palestine was almost empty. Most of the Arabs came after the Zionists already made the area livable. There was no such thing as an Arab-Palestine that existed for 1,300 years before we came."[42] It was the clearest statement yet of a divergence between American and Israeli views about the causes and possible outcomes of the conflict.

Despite these irrefutable warnings of the Begin government's ideological shift and overt commitment to settlement expansion, Carter believed he had to try to bring the Israeli leader into his own political orbit. The president sent a warm note of congratulations to Jerusalem and invited Begin to the White House in July 1977. "I would welcome your ideas on how progress towards peace can best be achieved," Carter wrote. "I believe it important that we meet at an early date to establish a personal relationship and exchange views on the negotiation of a peace settlement and on other matters of mutual concern."[43] U.S. officials worked on a strategy to keep the focus of the meeting on elements of a comprehensive solution, seeking a clear Israeli endorsement of Security Council Resolution 242 along favorable lines as well as restraint on settlement building.[44] They also reached out to President Sadat of Egypt to encourage public statements reaffirming his commitment to a comprehensive peace with Israel.[45] Several U.S. senators endorsed Carter's approach, issuing a bipartisan letter signed by the likes of Robert Byrd, Abraham Ribicoff, and Edward Kennedy.[46]

As a means of shoring up domestic support, Carter, Vice President Mondale, Vance, and Brzezinski gathered with Jewish leaders in July, ahead of Begin's visit. Mondale had been a senator from Minnesota before Carter selected him as a running mate, and he was viewed as more sympathetic to Israel than other members of the administration. He often led discussions with pro-Israel lobbyists and was a favored conduit with the leader of AIPAC.[47] In the meeting, which was reported in full by the administration to Israeli Embassy officials in Washington, Vance provided updates of his discussions with Arab leaders while Brzezinski affirmed three underlying principles in the U.S. approach. "1. We will not deceive Israel nor the Jewish community; 2. We will not betray the fundamental moral problems Israel faces; and 3. We will not compel or threaten Israel's security."[48] The necessity of reiterating these points was a function of growing anxiety among Jewish leaders. Rabbi Alexander Schindler, attending as the head of the Conference of Presidents of Major Jewish Organizations, spoke of a perception of the "erosion of America's commitment to Israel."[49] Carter tried to reassure the participants that the United States would not impose a settlement and that he would personally work with Begin when he came to Washington later that month. While the administration worked to implement its foreign policy in the Middle East, domestic pressures from American Jews were a clear factor that had to be accounted for. The lack of parallel pressure from Arab Americans was a function of a less developed lobbying arm, although their own political voice had begun to take shape as well.[50]

Begin Visits Washington

On July 19, 1977, Menachem Begin arrived at the White House for his first face-to-face meeting with President Carter. During their morning discussion in the cabinet room, Carter laid out the central principles of the U.S. approach to the Middle East conflict, which included a comprehensive peace based on UN resolutions 242 and 338, a resolution of territorial boundaries, and the question of the refugees. "We have said a homeland tied into Jordan," Carter told Begin, "but we have no plan."[51] This was not entirely accurate, given the well-developed and confidential plan that had been laid out in February. But the president did not seek to preempt the parties themselves. Carter accordingly concluded his opening remarks with a reflection on the American role: "I am sure that not every side completely trusts us. We will try to act as best as we can. We will be eager to see you and your own neighbors negotiating directly. We have no desire to be intermediaries."[52]

The Israeli prime minister used the occasion of this first bilateral meeting to launch into a swift historical review of the Jewish fight for Palestine, typical of his grandiose rhetorical style. He first recalled the Israeli victory in 1948, during which time he was a leader of the Irgun militia, the group responsible for the infamous wartime atrocity at Deir Yassin. While the massacre was seen as a primary driver of forced Palestinian migration, Begin characterized the consequences of the violence quite differently. "It is true that some 450,000 Arabs left," he told Carter. "We did not want them to go. I myself wrote a pamphlet appealing to the Arabs not to flee. Their leaders told them to leave, promising them that they would take over Tel Aviv once the Arab victory had been won."[53] As with most historical work on the 1948 War, the afterlife of the massacre was subject to clashing interpretations, a reflection of unsettled questions about the causes and consequences of the Palestinian refugee crisis. Historians generally agree, however, that at least seven hundred thousand Palestinian refugees were either forced out of their homes by Jewish fighters or fled as a result of violence and fear of transfer during the course of the war.[54]

Begin also recalled the feeling of existential threat followed by a rapid Israeli victory in the June 1967 War, leaving President Carter a small map outlining the short distance between the Green Line and Israeli population centers. It was Begin's way to illustrate the "mortal danger" of his country returning to the pre-1967 borders. "Such a restored situation could mean the mutilation of our country," Begin remarked.[55] Choking up as he continued reviewing the history of Jews unable to defend themselves, Begin added, "This is our concept of national security, Mr. President. Our fathers and mothers got killed because they were Jews. We don't want our grandchildren to suffer the same fate."[56]

Carter, sidestepping the emotional aspects of the discussion, was encouraged by Begin's apparent willingness to proceed to a Geneva Conference for broader diplomatic talks on the basis of UN resolutions 242 and 338. Such a position seemed to open the door for Egypt's Anwar al-Sadat and Jordan's King Hussein to participate in regional negotiations. Yet Carter also saw major differences that would have to be resolved, most notably on the question of continued settlement expansion. "As far as you and your people are concerned,"

Carter told Begin, "the question of the West Bank is going to be important as an open subject for discussion." Israel's divergence from the U.S. position was openly acknowledged. "The attitude of your government at permitting new settlements—these very well might prevent the peace conference itself," Carter continued. "One of the acute concerns here has been the attitude of you and your government to the West Bank that almost closes off future negotiations."[57]

Another central point of contention remained the role of the PLO. Carter explained to Begin that he had notified the PLO through Arab leaders "that if they would fully endorse the UN resolutions and acknowledge Israel's right to exist, we would begin to talk and listen to their positions." "This is a very difficult thing for us," Carter added, "it is our impression that the Israeli people would be prepared to talk to them if the PLO acknowledged Israel's right to independence."[58] Carter's vision for PLO recognition was not a fanciful wish. In the weeks prior to Begin's visit, PLO chairman Arafat relayed a message to President Carter "implying the PLO's willingness to live in peace with Israel." His condition was a "U.S. commitment to the establishment of an independent Palestinian 'state unit entity.'"[59] Although the form of such an entity remained a matter of fierce disagreement, the principle of Palestinian diplomatic engagement was clear. Begin, however, would not countenance PLO involvement in Carter's Geneva initiative.

Carter suggested instead that perhaps the Palestinians would not be invited to the opening of Geneva "but that the question of the refugees be put on the agenda." Begin, invoking the plight of Jews who had been forced out of the Arab world in 1948 as a counterweight, quickly added, "Both the Arab and the Jewish refugees." The president replied he had no objection.[60] Like Rabin before him, Begin agreed to a Jordanian delegation representing Arab inhabitants of the West Bank as long as PLO members did not participate. "We too are Palestinians," Begin said. "We are prepared to agree that in the Jordanian delegation there should be Palestinian Arabs. We will not investigate their private credentials—but not the PLO."[61]

The Israeli prime minister then invited his advisor Shmuel Katz to discuss the Palestinians and the refugee question. Turning to Carter and his advisors, Katz pulled out a large map of the Arab states and Israel. "Every child in the Arab states is taught from an early age (now there are new text books recently surveyed) that this triangle (Israel) must as a patriotic duty and a moral imperative be eliminated as a decisive and immoral element in the Arab world."[62] This was a markedly charged tone in Israeli messaging about the fate of the Palestinians. It was the start of a public relations offensive that would recur with great frequency in meetings between Likud politicians and their American counterparts.

The new Likud leadership worked to reframe their views about Israel's internal conflict with the Arabs as part of their diplomatic offensive at the Carter White House. In the working dinner that evening, Begin's toast was a reflection of his deep-seated belief in the shared values between Israel and the United States. "We are a guardian of human liberty and democracy in the Middle East," Begin proclaimed, marveling at the peaceful transition from his predecessor in a region where such shifts were so often marked by violence. The Israeli prime minister summed up his view of why there was still no peace: "It is an historical conflict. It is not a territorial problem." He expanded on this point, emphasizing the lack of peace that existed between 1948 and 1967, before Israel's territorial expansion. "We came there. We have come there by right of our ancestors. But it was not recognized and time and again attempts were made to destroy us."[63]

The clear distinction between historical and territorial conflict enabled Begin to situate the Palestinians as merely "Arab inhabitants of Judea and Samaria," neither a nation nor a people in their own right. It was a radically different postwar vision than the collective rights of self-determination that the Palestinians demanded and the Americans had begun to recognize by the late 1970s. Begin concluded his toast by returning to his earlier theme about the Arab displacement in 1948. "We don't hate our neighbors," he told Carter. "We don't want to humiliate them at all. We never wanted to defeat them. We never wanted to wrong them. But we had to defend ourselves."[64]

Territorial Retention

In light of the Begin government's position, what might the territorial contours of a Palestinian political solution include? Before Carter and Begin began formal talks on the morning of July 20, the president and Secretary Vance relayed their initial negotiating position to the Israeli prime minister via Connecticut senator Abraham Ribicoff. Any territorial withdrawal, the president and his secretary of state explained, would have to consist of "mutually agreed and recognized borders on all fronts," and a settlement would have to include "provisions for a Palestinian entity." Such an entity would not be militarized, just as the administration's secret February study had recommended, and provisions should be made for "an open and economic and social relationship with Israel." The Carter administration was even more specific on the makeup of this entity. "Means should be sought to permit self-determination by Palestinians deciding their future status," the U.S. position conveyed, "like trusteeship for five years in which Israel would be co-trustee with Jordan of West Bank along lines of functional plan [sic] suggested by Dayan."[65]

General Moshe Dayan had joined Begin's government as foreign minister after a long association with the Israeli left. His functional plan for the West Bank had emerged in response to the Allon Plan of 1967, conceived in the aftermath of the war by Israeli minister and Labor politician Yigal Allon. The Allon Plan mandated a redrawing of the map of Israel to extend Israeli sovereignty in much of the occupied territories. In order to secure a permanent Israeli presence in the Jordan Valley, Latrun Salient, and the southern Gaza Strip (as well as the Golan Heights and Rafah approaches), Allon suggested annexing a large chunk of this territory and returning the remaining populated parts of the West Bank to Jordan or creating autonomous Palestinian enclaves.[66] Beyond the stated security concerns, the plan was premised on demographic considerations. Israel would acquire further territory without the Arab inhabitants who threatened to undermine the Jewish majority of the state.

Dayan, unlike Allon, felt there should be a greater degree of Palestinian autonomy in West Bank municipalities, and his plan called for shared administrative responsibilities between Israel and Jordan with more territory under Israeli sovereignty. The specifics of any such arrangement had not been fully outlined, and Carter and Vance suggested that a plebiscite should be held after five years to determine the specifics and "how to relate to Jordan and Israel."[67]

The introduction of a conditional model of trusteeship and a plebi-scite was a means to defuse some of the thorniest aspects of Arab demands and account for the Israeli ideas already in circulation. While these elements of a possible settlement accounted for Pal-estinian aspirations in political terms, it was a model that neces-sitated the deferral of actual sovereignty.

Although Begin may have signaled a degree of flexibility about Geneva in his meetings with Carter, his stated territorial position tells a more intransigent story. Declassified Israeli records reveal that on July 13, Begin sketched out his "peace principles," which he delivered privately to Carter during their initial meeting at the White House and in writing to Secretary Vance. The Israeli prime minister indicated a clear willingness to withdraw forces substantially in the Sinai as part of a peace deal with Egypt and seemed prepared to withdraw forces from the Golan Heights in the context of a peace treaty with Syria.[68] But the West Bank and Gaza were not ever part of his negotiations. "Concerning Judea, Samaria and the Gaza Strip our position is that we shall not place them under any foreign rule or sovereignty on the basis of two factors," Begin explained. "One, our people's right to the Land; it is our Land as of right. Two, our national security, which concerns the defensive capability of the State and the lives of our civilian population."[69]

After his private meeting with Begin on July 19, Carter made notes about Begin's approach to territory and expansion. "He will try to accommodate us on settlements," Carter wrote. "Wants to carry out Mapai plan at least," the president continued, referring to the ideas of Dayan and Allon. But Begin was reluctant to delay his expansion plans. Carter therefore suggested that Begin wait until after the Geneva talks and "restrict new settlers to existing settle-ments." The president was clearly aware of the diverging views. "This *is* difficult for him—Will stay on Golan. I told him Syria won't agree. W Bank, Gaza, Jerusalem. 'no foreign sovereignty'—Sinai— 'Substantial withdrawals.'"[70] Given these clear parameters by Begin on the possible Israeli negotiating position at Geneva, any diplo-matic endeavor spearheaded by the United States would have to address a central dilemma: What to do about the West Bank, Gaza Strip, and East Jerusalem?

In spite of a clear divergence, U.S. officials agreed not to publicly discuss their concerns over the fate of the territory itself. Carter seemed to think he could keep Begin and the Israelis in play as negotiating partners. During the final meeting between U.S. and Israeli officials on the morning of July 20, Carter announced that he had agreed not to talk openly about Israeli withdrawals to "the 1967 lines with minor adjustments" before checking with Begin. As they discussed preparations for their joint press conference, Carter asked that Begin mention UN resolutions 242 and 338. "As far as our agreement that I will not mention minor modifications in the 1967 lines, I hope that you will not say that you have my commitment not to talk about that."[71] Carter was in essence offering Begin his silence on the inviolability of the 1967 border in exchange for some Israeli movement on other issues. In spite of their clear differences, the visit had encouraged the U.S. president, who wrote in his diary that he found Begin to be "quite congenial, dedicated, sincere, and deeply religious." This was in contrast to Rabin, who, Carter simultaneously wrote, was "one of the most ineffective persons I've ever met."[72] Begin's visit had managed to assure the U.S. administration that there was some room for diplomatic maneuver.

Two days after Begin's trip, Carter was therefore shocked to hear that the Israeli prime minister had returned home and legalized three West Bank settlements, declaring them "permanent." Secretary Vance sent a critical telegram to Dayan, who had been working with the White House on this issue. "Particularly coming at this time," Vance wrote, "any new settlements, wherever located, would tend to confirm the fears of the Arabs that the new Israeli government intends to pursue an essentially annexationist policy with regards to the West Bank."[73] Vance reiterated the U.S. belief, as Carter told Begin, "there should now be a moratorium on any Israeli settlements in the occupied territories."[74] Responding to a public barrage of questions about this provocative move at a press conference, Carter was forthright in his approach: "I let Mr. Begin know very clearly that our government policy, before I became President and now, is that these settlements are illegal and contravene the Geneva Conference terms. Mr. Begin disagrees with this."[75] Deftly trying to steer away from an outright break with Israel, Carter posited that

FIGURE 2.1. "Prime Minister Menachem Begin Is Welcomed by Children of Elon Moreh."
Minister Ariel Sharon on the left. February 27, 1981. Herman Chanania,
courtesy of Israel's Government Press Office.

Begin was continuing the policy of earlier Israeli governments and expressed his hope that this shift was not "insurmountable."[76]

The American desire to reconcile views on territory with Israel belied all the strong indicators of an inevitable collision. Begin had a very clear idea of his ceiling on withdrawal. At no time during his subsequent discussions with Carter or eventually Egyptian president Anwar al-Sadat did the Israeli prime minister ever relent on his basic stated principle of "no foreign sovereignty" for the West Bank, Gaza Strip, and Jerusalem. It was a position he had taken for many years, well before the 1977 election that brought him to office. His government's declaration of permanence secured subsidies for the settlements, further legitimizing Israeli claims in the territories.[77] The PLO was acutely aware of this growing threat, taking heed of Begin's decisions in official communications.[78]

Secretary of State Cyrus Vance later explained how the American and Israeli divergence on territory amounted to a conceptual as well as political split.

Our approach is from point of view that Israel must ultimately turn over West Bank to Arab sovereignty, once borders, security arrangements and political status are agreed.

Israeli approach is from point of view that it does not agree to ultimate Arab sovereignty, even as part of Jordan. It sees West Bank as permanent self-governing colony.

Fundamentally, what is needed is for Israel to relinquish *now* its claim to sovereignty and refocus issue on security (which would require fundamental reversal of Begin's political ideology).[79]

This clear explanation lay bare the core difference between the U.S. and Israeli positions on sovereignty. Vance understood that any attempt at resolving the Palestinian question as part of a comprehensive peace initiative would ultimately fail if the issue of control were left in dispute. Carter's negotiating style evinced a strong conviction that he could assess Israel's opening position and gradually work to bring the sides closer together. Both the president and Vance clearly understood the challenge of reconciling Begin's views with their own comprehensive ideas. But a crucial element of possible success was the timing and nature of U.S. mediation and the degree to which the administration would exercise pressure to achieve its goal. In the absence of such external pressure, the Israeli plans would continue apace.

A Bumpy Road to Geneva

Against the backdrop of Begin's July 1977 visit to the White House, the Carter administration continued to hammer out a set of draft principles for a revival of the Geneva Conference. Secretary Vance traveled once again to the Middle East to meet with Arab and Israeli leaders in August. He intended to finalize discussions at the UN General Assembly in New York in September and issue invitations for a conference to convene before the end of 1977.[80] Vance carried with him five draft principles. These included a comprehensive settlement based on UN resolutions 242 and 338; the establishment of peaceful relations between Israel and the Arabs; phased withdrawal "to secure and recognized borders with mutually agreed security arrangements"; and a "non-militarized Palestinian entity with self-determination by the Palestinians."[81] Before even leaving Washington, Ambassador Dinitz visited the secretary of state at Begin's request to inform him that the prime minister had agreed to resolution 242 but "did not accept that this required *withdrawal* on all fronts." Vance was "furious" at what he perceived as "backsliding" and surmised correctly that the Israelis wanted the United States to refrain from mediating with the Arab states in a manner that exposed Begin's disagreements on substance and procedure.[82] The acceptance of the logic underlying the UN resolutions that had been negotiated after the 1967 and 1973 wars—a variant of "land for peace"—would be a difficult pill for the Begin government to swallow.

During early stops in Egypt, Syria, Jordan, and Saudi Arabia, Vance sought Arab agreement on the Palestinian question, an issue of particular concern to U.S. officials. The U.S. secretary of state had been examining various perspectives on Palestinian self-determination and the status of the occupied territories.[83] In discussions with Arab leaders, he introduced the idea of a "transitional arrangement," which was intended as an alternative to outright statehood "so that the Palestinians could demonstrate whether they were prepared to govern themselves and live peacefully beside Israel."[84] Removing the word "trusteeship" from his proposal after Syrian and Lebanese leaders expressed their distaste for a term that harkened back to colonial rule, Vance secured support from King Hussein of Jordan and Prince Fahd in Saudi Arabia for an arrangement that would defer self-determination in favor of an interim solution on the road to a more permanent outcome.[85] This idea gained traction and became an early influence on the autonomy provision of Camp David, ostensibly offering a temporally circumscribed period that could prepare Palestinians in the occupied territories for self-rule.

The PLO still had to be convinced of such an arrangement, alongside the more immediate concern of participating in the Geneva process and resolving an ongoing debate over the acceptance of UN resolution 242. Palestinian leaders strongly objected to the resolution on the grounds that it said nothing explicit about Palestinian national rights or the guarantee of a homeland. Yet the organization's thinking had evolved in a more accommodating direction. As early as June 1974, PLO officials had adopted a "Ten Point Program," which implicitly accepted the principle of partitioning Palestine into two states, one Arab and one Jewish.[86] This was a crucial step on the road to embracing a diplomatic solution alongside Israel, but it did not have the full support of all the PLO factions. Many within the national movement denounced the program, leading to a split within the PLO. This dynamic made it a sensitive moment for considering U.S. diplomatic initiatives.

Saudi Arabia acted as the conduit between the PLO Executive Committee and Vance in his attempts to further engage the national movement. The secretary of state suggested that an official dialogue with the organization would be possible if they accepted 242 "with a reservation that it did not deal adequately with the Palestinian issue."[87] During his meeting with Saudi officials in the city of Taif, Vance offered specific language for a reserved endorsement of 242 to be passed on to the PLO. "If the PLO would accept this language," Vance told the Saudis, thereby publicly acknowledging "Israel's right to exist, we would have met our commitment under the Sinai II agreement and would be willing to meet with the PLO immediately." He added that while his goal was to achieve a Palestinian homeland on the West Bank, he could not offer such a guarantee. The Saudis shared this offer with PLO chairman Yasser Arafat directly, as the Executive Committee of the PLO was meeting the same evening that Vance was in Saudi Arabia. After vigorous debate, the PLO Executive Committee voted against such an endorsement of 242. The result was due to strong opposition among hard-line factions who would not give up a chief bargaining tool, namely conceding the acceptance of Israel without the assurance of a Palestinian homeland in return.[88]

Official U.S. discussions with Arab parties on the inclusion of the PLO were leaked to the press before the secretary of state arrived in Israel. Prime Minister Begin was adamantly opposed to these efforts, and he "lectured" Vance on the 1975 U.S. commitment not to recognize or negotiate with the organization. Begin read out sections of the PLO covenant to Vance that called for the destruction of Israel, and he "questioned the morality" of the American position. The leading American diplomat stood his ground and defended his pursuit of an opening with the PLO on the condition they accepted 242, which would have superseded the PLO covenant had Arafat and the Executive Committee agreed. Clearly PLO objections deferred certain diplomatic options, but the Americans were also constrained by the straitjacket of Kissinger's earlier commitment to Israel.[89]

Begin's strong opposition to the PLO revealed a deeper hostility, one that extended beyond political grievance. Vance was accompanied to the Middle East by his wife, Grace, who kept a detailed diary of the visit, which provides a sense of how Israeli officials conceived of the Palestinian national movement. After being taken to settle in at the King David Hotel by Foreign Minister Dayan and his wife, Grace was brought to Yad Vashem, Israel's Holocaust museum and memorial. Her guide was Gideon Hausner, the lead prosecutor in the trial of the notorious Nazi official Adolf Eichmann. Hausner took Mrs. Vance through the Avenue of Righteous Gentiles, marking non-Jewish heroes who had saved Jews during the war. She was shown photographs and documents of the Nazi killing of Jews and the overall plans of Adolf Hitler's Final Solution to exterminate the Jewish people. Grace wrote that she "was told two times by Hausner and later by Mrs. Dayan that Israel can never again be taken in by enemies—that Nazis and PLO both dedicated to the destruction of Israel. Therefore, no compromises can be made." She recalled being "drained" by the visit, "too sad to comment on whole period." "But," she added, "did feel that [I] was leaned on heavily re PLO problem through visit to this memorial."[90]

At a Knesset dinner in honor of Secretary Vance that evening, Grace was seated between Dayan and Begin, and she described the Israeli prime minister as "his usual pleasant dinner self, rather pixie, from time to time." Her reflections quickly shifted. "When he rose to his feet to make toast, surprise, surprise. Had with him copy of PLO manifesto vowing destruction of Israel, which he read aloud with appropriate comments—then Sec. 242, with appropriate comments; compared PLO to Nazis, swore eternal opposition to those who would destroy Israel."[91] Begin's continuum linking the PLO with a broader history of anti-Semitism had been asserted in earlier meetings with Carter at the White House. The secretary of state's official visit only drove home the ideological gulf separating

American and international perspectives on the future of Palestinian nationalists, compared to the derisive attitude of the Begin government in Jerusalem. In condemning the PLO as a successor organization to the Nazis, Begin conflated genuine Israeli concern over terror attacks in the 1970s with existential fear of Palestinians. This distortion of a historical analogy served to elide Palestinians as a national group while linking Israeli political aims with a lachrymose reading of the Jewish past.[92]

The Origins of Autonomy

In his visit to Israel, Vance reported on his meetings with Arab leaders to Begin and continued to search for a way to bring the Palestinians into the process. He mentioned the suggestion of a "transitional administrative regime" to facilitate Palestinian self-determination, along with a plebiscite and other options to deal with the relationship between an eventual Palestinian entity and its neighbors.[93] Begin rejected this idea; his uppermost concern remained the content of the PLO charter and the organization's opposition to the creation of Israel, as well as the violence of the PLO. "We unhesitatingly call this organization 'genociders,'" exclaimed the prime minister. "Their aim is to destroy our country, our people, and their method is to kill civilians." The Israeli prime minister entirely ruled out the PLO's involvement at a Geneva gathering but made a non-national distinction. "We agree to the participation of Palestinian Arabs. This is the proper expression; not Palestinians, because we are all Palestinians," Begin insisted.[94]

Among the other topics that surfaced during Vance's time in Jerusalem was the increasingly vexing issue of settlements. In his meeting with the U.S. secretary of state, Begin, whose government adopted an entirely different line than the United States on settlement legality, asked Aharon Barak, Israel's attorney general, to read out a memo asserting his position. Barak explained that the provisions of international law only dealt with the forced transfer and removal of a population in occupied territories caused by movement of population into the territories, which he argued was not the case in the building of Jewish settlements. The attorney general argued that Article 49 of the Fourth Geneva Convention, which was widely seen by international jurists as applicable to the territories occupied in the wake of the 1967 War, did not apply to Jewish settlements. "Article 49 must be understood against the background of World War II," Barak told Vance. "It was aimed in part against such horrors at the barbarous extermination camps in occupied Europe to which Jews and others were taken by the Nazis and in part against the displacement of the local population with a view to making room for the German invaders." In light of this context and particular history, Barak asserted, "it is clear that the situation envisaged by Article 49 does not apply to the Jewish settlements in question. No Arab inhabitants have been displaced by Jewish settlements or by these peaceful villages and townships."[95]

The United States did not see this issue in the same light. After hearing the Israeli position articulated by Barak, Vance replied, "Our legal advisers have come to a different conclusion." Begin interjected a final word before a brief adjournment of the meeting: "Perhaps one day we have a meeting between our legal advisers and your legal advisers and there is no doubt they will reach a disagreement." The verbatim text notes that the collective response from the assembled delegations was "laughter."[96] In the official U.S. report on Vance's visit, NSC member Gary Sick recalled the increase in settlement activity that surfaced in the discussions, including Begin's legalization of three settlements and indication he would limit activity to another "'six or eight' settlements to be established on land within present military bases or on government-owned land." Dayan assured the Americans that these settlements might be closer to the center of the West Bank, posing no problem to an eventual peace settlement since they could be moved. "From all indications," Sick wrote, "Dayan believes there will be no real difficulties so long as present inhabitants are not displaced."[97]

The report of a private meeting about settlements between Vance, U.S. ambassador to Israel Samuel Lewis, Begin, and Dayan on the morning of August 10 expands on the content of these sensitive bilateral discussions. As Dayan explained, "We cannot stop settlements altogether, or even suspend new settlements for any substantial period of time. Such an effort would not be sustainable, just as the British effort to limit or suspend immigration into Israel during the Mandate period never proved enforceable or sustainable."[98] In explaining Israeli policy, Dayan promised that the settlements were located within twenty-five kilometers of the Green Line near Jerusalem, not in populated Arab areas. Vance asked for an explanation of why this was necessary, and Begin invoked historic arguments and referred to the "wonderful youth generation," especially religious Israelis, "determined to till their historical lands." He also explained that unlike his Labor party predecessors, he would not wink at illegal squatters but was being "straightforward" and "honest." "What we ask for," Begin told Vance, "is not your blessing but your understanding. Now you know what we intend to do. Please talk to President Carter and explain our position." Vance assured Begin he would talk to Carter when he returned, "but I said that the President already understands this problem but is deeply convinced that any new settlements will greatly complicate the peace-making process."[99]

While making the Israeli case for continued settlement building, Dayan asserted that these policies were compatible with long-term U.S. efforts toward Geneva. The foreign minister provided a flat assurance that no settlement would be an impediment to a peace agreement, promising that the Israeli government would move such a settlement. This logic served as a justification for building while negotiations were ongoing, rooted in official practice since 1967. "There had never been an Israeli government which did not authorize new settlements, that the ongoing settlement process of the land is and will remain a fundamental principle for the Jewish state," Dayan concluded. All the vocal criticism, he assured Vance, was focused on the "taking of new lands from Arab hands, and that no such thing would be occurring."[100]

Dayan's defense of the settlements emanated directly from the office of the legal advisor to the Israeli Ministry of Foreign Affairs, Meir Rosenne.[101] To justify their logic, Israeli legal experts like Rosenne navigated a series of High Court decisions about the settlements and formulated an alternative reading on the Geneva Conventions and the status of the occupied territories under international law.[102] This approach came into sharper focus during future negotiations over Palestinian autonomy and would be endorsed by neoconservative U.S. legal scholars in the Reagan White House. But the discussions in 1977 demonstrate how the initial articulation of these ideas was presented to the Americans and further developed in the months that followed.

This Israeli official consensus on settlements was inextricably linked with an emerging conception of limited autonomy for Palestinians, a dual approach to the contested sovereignty of the territory itself and the political rights of the inhabitants who lived there. The suggested status of the inhabitants in the territories, as Begin explained to Vance in Jerusalem, was "complete cultural autonomy, municipal and religious autonomy, not to interfere with their lives at all." Rather than force citizenship upon them, the option of Israeli citizenship and voting in the Knesset elections would be extended. "It would be completely on the basis of equality of rights," Begin explained, comparing those Arabs who did not take citizenship to Jewish residents in Israel who were also non-citizens. "So it will be complete equality of rights of Arabs and Jewish residents or Arab and Jewish citizens," the prime minister told Vance.[103]

By situating the Palestinian question as a national minority issue, Begin was stripping away claims of collective self-determination in favor of a narrow focus on the individual as a loyal citizen to the state of Israel, like the Arab citizens within the 1967 borders.[104] His attitude toward the Arabs was reflected in an interview he gave to the Israeli newspaper *Yedioth Ahronoth* in early September. "I want to say that I have a profound respect for the Arab nation. The Arab nation made a very great contribution to human culture. . . . In my opinion, the past decade has seen a growing rapport between the Arabs living in Israel and ourselves. Unpleasant incidents from time to time notwithstanding, I believe that the two people can live side by side in mutual respect based on understanding, peace, economic and social progress, and the building up of this country to a state of glory."[105] This benevolence toward Arabs writ large, rather than Palestinians as a distinct national group, underpinned Begin's insistence on the possibility of coexistence within a Jewish state with Arabs as a minority. It was not clear what would happen if all the Palestinians took on Israeli citizenship and shifted Israel's demographic a different way, or how such an arrangement could be sustained in the occupied territories.

To understand the emerging Israeli view of autonomy, Begin's perception of the Palestinians—as distinct from the PLO—is therefore instructive. For the Israeli prime minister, the PLO was Israel's "implacable enemy" while the problem of Jews and Arabs living together and "the human problem of the refugees" was another matter. He explained his views to Vance by returning to the consequences of the fighting during the 1948 War. "We would like that wound which was opened in 1948, not as a result of our guilt whatsoever—Their leaders asked them to flee and promised them to come victoriously to Tel Aviv. We didn't want to create that problem of refugees, but we know that in cruel wars, such problems always arise, and this should be healed."[106] The distancing of Israel's leadership from guilt over the creation of the refugee problem enabled Begin to present the Palestinians in a humanitarian light, rather than in national terms.[107]

As a minority in need of protection, Begin suggested, the Palestinians in the territories should be provided with economic opportunities and housing, but not political rights. He singled out Gaza as a model. "We want to solve the problem and we did quite a lot in the Gaza Strip for the humane solution of this problem," Begin emphasized. "Now they have proper houses, permanent jobs, have an income. Of course, we know that there are refugees on the other side; so the Arab countries should take care of them."[108] Dayan added that the refugees from Gaza were working in Israel and increasingly tied together with the Jewish population: "We don't like this business of the Gaza Strip with refugees and everything. I can't see any other way but being combined with Israel, providing them with work and surrounded with Israeli settlements."[109] To further emphasize the benevolent character of Israel's control of the territory, Begin told Vance, "If you go via Judea and Samaria, perhaps you won't see for miles on end one Israeli soldier. We don't interfere in their lives."[110] Despite popular recollections about the ease of travel for Jewish Israelis to cheap weekend markets in Gaza and the West Bank in the 1970s and 1980s, the experience of Palestinians was very much affected by the military presence.[111]

After leaving Israel, Vance had further consultations with President Sadat of Egypt and stopped in London to coordinate regional policy with the British prime minister.[112] In discussions with Carter back in Washington, Vance reviewed his trip and told the president that if there were no serious movement to Geneva by September, the U.S. strategy of bringing all the parties together for comprehensive negotiations would falter.[113] Carter agreed, and was especially encouraged by the consensus emerging from the Arab states. He was aware of the divergent position of the Israeli government on the key issues, however, writing in his diary that "the Israelis are going to be typically recalcitrant, but the more we go public with a reasonable proposition the more difficult it will be for them not to make an effort."[114] This underlying frustration with the Begin government characterized much of the administration's private correspondence, evincing impatience with the ideology of the ruling Likud party in light of U.S. efforts to work toward a significant diplomatic achievement.[115]

The Question of Sovereignty

Even as the Carter administration worked to find ways of bringing Palestinians to the negotiating table, the Israeli and Egyptian leadership were consulting secretly to advance their own bilateral interests. Foreign Minister Moshe Dayan, disguised with a wig, mustache, and dark glasses, flew to Morocco and met with Sadat's deputy prime minister, Dr. Hassan Tuhami, at King Hassan's palace on September 16. Tuhami, a confidant of the Egyptian president, presented Sadat's precondition for peace, which was the "evacuation of Arab occupied territories."[116] This would be the only condition for Sadat meeting Begin. The Palestinians, Tuhami stressed, "should be left to Egypt and the Arab nations," who would see to it they were not radicalized. Sadat's emissary was confident that the two parties could reach an agreement independently, barring Israeli retention of the territories. "Places are negotiable. Administration is negotiable. But sovereignty is not," Tuhami said.[117] This was the central principle of the Arab states in discussions about the West Bank and Gaza Strip, as well as the other territories captured by Israel in 1967.

The Israelis were operating under altogether different expectations. In his draft peace treaty prepared for Vance that month, Dayan had already provided the basic position of his government on the occupied territories in relationship to Jordan.

A) In Judea and Samaria equal rights and full coexistence should be ensured between Jew and Arab.

B) No part of this area should be subject to any foreign rule or sovereignty.

C) Any settlement should take Israel's security needs fully into account. In this context our position is that Israel's security on the eastern border should be based on the Jordan River.[118]

In asserting Israeli security needs as the basis for continued control of all territory west of the Jordan River, a collision on the place of Palestinian aspirations and the negotiation of a comprehensive peace was inevitable.

Dayan traveled to Washington shortly after meeting Tuhami to discuss modalities toward Geneva and the settlements with Vance and Carter. His positions in the draft peace treaty were questioned, and Dayan responded that there were no "musts" in Israel's paper; rather, it served as a basis for exploration.[119] Dayan explained that while Israel "would avoid discussing sovereignty" it would only construct settlements in places where there were "security concerns." He hoped to work with local Palestinians, like mayors not affiliated with the PLO, to determine what the population wanted. Jordan, Dayan believed, would one day be Palestinian, and they would rule both sides of the river. While not specifying Israeli sovereignty for the area, he preferred that the issue be deferred until practical questions would be answered on the ground, like "who will repair the roads."

Vance wondered if leaving this question of sovereignty unresolved might be possible through the introduction of a local administration. As Dayan suggested in response to Vance, "Israel would have military posts, but these posts would not interfere in the daily life of the population of the West Bank." This idea of a nominal occupation was presented along with the assertion that "settlements would also not interfere." In Dayan's view, the situation on the ground would be one of mutual interest. "Arabs could work in Israel or not, as they want, and Israelis could travel to the West Bank, as they want. Israel would not run the West Bank schools, providing the schools were not used for inciting terrorism," Dayan remarked. He assured the Americans he would ask West Bankers "what kind of autonomy they themselves want." "A Palestinian state is out of the question," Dayan concluded, "but otherwise we would consider their desires."[120]

U.S. ambassador to Israel Samuel Lewis sensed the inconsistencies in this approach and pushed Dayan farther. The perceptive diplomat posed a hypothetical scenario of a terrorist attack on an Israeli military installation in the mountains of the West Bank that was found to be the work of a terrorist cell based in Nablus. "What would Israel do?" Lewis asked. Dayan responded that Israel would search for the cell and get them. "This means Israelis retaining security responsibilities?" Lewis replied. "Theoretically if the local forces would do it we would leave it to them," Dayan responded, "but in practice they won't. It would be farfetched to think that they would."[121] The Israeli delegation was suggesting a different modus vivendi for the West Bank, neither a Palestinian state nor control by Jordan. This would provide Israel with de facto control over security, a position that would serve to solidify a non-national outcome for Palestinians in the occupied territories.

In Carter's subsequent discussion with Dayan about these issues, the president reaffirmed the U.S. view that settlements were illegal. At the same time, he acknowledged that Dayan's promise of limited expansion in only six existing settlements would be preferable to Israeli minister of agriculture and settlement czar Ariel Sharon's plan for more extensive building.[122] This back-and-forth discussion, which characterized so much of the Israeli-American meetings over the course of 1977, never fully resolved the status of the territories themselves.[123] As Carter's questions and follow-ups to Dayan made very clear, the Israeli foreign minister sought to defer any real consideration of the future of the West Bank. Instead Dayan suggested models of splitting off the territorial question from joint discussion of the refugees or returning to the status of the West Bank at a later date.

William Quandt, in his role as NSC analyst on this issue, prepared a short study for interim rule in the West Bank and Gaza that highlighted the risk of not addressing their future directly.[124] The American concern about the status of the territories remained consistent in broad policy discussions as well as private meetings with the Israelis. Before concluding his meeting with Dayan, Carter again raised the problem of Israeli settlement policy: "How the settlement issue is handled in public causes me concern. If Hussein and Sadat want peace, and I assume that they do, it is hard for them to listen to your talk about thousands of new settlers, about no foreign sovereignty over the West Bank, and about the West Bank being part of Israel." In Carter's view, this approach "almost forecloses the chance of a Geneva Conference." The president told Dayan, with great frustration, "I was really angry watching [Ariel] Sharon on television saying that there would be hundreds of settlers, maybe in the millions. That is not what Prime Minster Begin had told me, or what you have said."[125] A rift had opened between the United States and Israel on the road to Geneva and pointed to more systemic differences over the fate of the territories and the Palestinians themselves.

The opaque nature of Israeli policy on the question of sovereignty within the territories was clear to Carter and members of his administration, as well as Arab interlocutors. In conversations that Secretary Vance held with senior Jordanian diplomats some days later, Dayan's proposal of continued Israeli control in the territories was heavily criticized. "It would amount to helping Israel achieve its goal of staying in the West Bank," argued Abdul Hamid Sharaf, the minister to the Royal Jordanian Court.[126] Sharaf suspected the Palestinians would therefore come to Jordan, since they held Jordanian nationality and would not want to stay in the West Bank. The Israelis, in Sharaf's view, would talk about negotiations being open, but they would never be prepared to seriously talk about the fate of the territories.

Menachem Begin's ascent to power in 1977 threw a wrench in Carter's plans for a comprehensive peace. The United States had worked to promote a revival of the Geneva Conference, meeting with key Arab leaders, and even tried to secure PLO acceptance of UN resolution 242. But there was a fundamentally different political vision offered by the Begin government, predicated on continued Israeli settlement in the occupied territories and adamantly opposed to the PLO or Palestinian statehood. The Israeli prime minister had a very different idea for limited Arab autonomy, which was rooted in his view of the Palestinians as a national minority rather than a self-determining collective, a vision that was clearly at odds with the Carter administration's view of self-determination.

The failure to address these differences regarding self-determination meant that the status of the occupied territories themselves remain unresolved. The rhetoric of the Israeli leadership toward the 1967 land acquisitions, first under Rabin and then under Begin, was in clear opposition to foreign sovereignty in the occupied territories. The Israeli position stood in direct contrast to the U.S. stance and Arab demands, and it was clear and consistent throughout Begin's time in office, specifically when it came to the West Bank, Gaza Strip, and East Jerusalem, where territorial withdrawals were precluded from the start. The return of the Sinai Peninsula to Egypt was a different case, as the turn to bilateral negotiations with Egypt would soon underscore.

CHAPTER THREE

Egypt's Sacrificial Lamb

"PEOPLE CALL ME A POLITICIAN, but I am a revolutionary—a realist who believes in facts," PLO chairman Yasser Arafat told a visiting journalist in the summer of 1977. "There is a limit to my moderation," the Palestinian leader continued. He was willing to make a deal with the American government, but not without certain guarantees. "Please tell [Roy] Atherton and [William] Quandt I have a red line," Arafat instructed his guest, referring to Carter's Middle East advisors. In comments that Arafat knew would be conveyed back to American officials, he spoke of the PLO's legitimacy and willingness to accept 242, as long as it dealt with Palestinians "as a people with national rights and aspirations," not simply as refugees. This was an alternative vision to that of the Israeli government, which was premised on the denunciation of the PLO and the suppression of Palestinian nationalism that had intensified in the wake of Menachem Begin's victory. Arafat was cautious of U.S. entreaties to concede diplomatic recognition of Israel without securing something in return, just as the Palestinian national movement was consolidating its diplomatic strategy. "Maybe Carter can solve the problem," Arafat surmised, "but settling the problem without the Palestinians is like cooking something without leaving it to stew."[1]

The PLO leader spoke just months after the thirteenth gathering of the organization's highest policymaking body, the Palestine National Council (PNC). Meeting in Cairo, the PLO's legislative arm had explicitly called for an "independent national state" for the first time. This crucial March 1977 declaration did not refer to "total liberation," signaling a major advance in the acceptance of the idea of national independence in only part of historic Palestine.[2] Factional infighting about the form and content of possible political configurations for the future reflected a dramatic internal transformation within Palestinian nationalism. The PLO was gradually accepting the reality of partition and giving up on earlier commitments to a singular democratic Palestinian state, suggesting a "growing readiness to come to terms with Israel."[3] Such a shift can easily be obscured by a sole focus on terror attacks in the late 1970s, which were often carried out by dissident factions who rejected this move toward accommodation. Without ignoring the violence, it is possible to highlight a strategic rethinking of Palestinian national aims and motivations that was underway on the eve of crucial Arab-Israeli negotiations.

At the end of 1977, this diplomatic effort within the Palestinian national movement was thwarted as the PLO's political project hit up against countervailing forces. Backlash by Cold War conservatives and pro-Israel American Jews over a joint communiqué with the Soviet Union halted the U.S. advance toward a comprehensive peace at Geneva, while Egyptian unilateralism and Sadat's surprise visit to Jerusalem severely undercut the PLO's advances. These twin developments were formative in halting Palestinian efforts at a national solution to their plight, underscoring their precarious global position and the need for support from external parties, including the United States and Arab allies.

Secret Talks with the PLO

Arafat's message to the visiting American journalist indicated that while the earlier effort undertaken by Secretary Vance and the Saudis to engage the PLO through an agreement on UN Security Council Resolution 242 had not succeeded, there was still room for further negotiation. The U.S. secretary of state continued to pursue PLO recognition via a secret back channel with the Palestinian leadership in August, this time through the mediation of Walid Khalidi, a prominent Palestinian academic.[4] Vance conveyed that Carter had spoken openly of his support for a Palestinian "homeland," in effect recognizing "that the Palestinian question is not just a refugee issue but one involving the political status of the Palestinians." The secretary of state wanted Khalidi to communicate to the PLO that the U.S. government was committed to self-determination, and that even with the reservations over 242's elision of the Palestinians, the United States would open official contacts if the PLO accepted the resolution. Vance also warned Khalidi of the consequences of inaction. If the PLO did not accept 242, "it will risk seriously overplaying its hand and may end up with nothing and find itself on the outside looking in while the negotiating process goes forward."[5]

PLO officials remained deeply hesitant about the acceptance of 242 without a guarantee of substantive promises in return. At the same March 1977 PNC meeting in which they had endorsed an independent state, the PNC members had also rejected 242 and any diplomatic action taken on its basis, declaring that "Security Council Resolution 242 ignores the Palestinian people and their inalienable rights."[6] Alongside U.S. pressure to reconsider, the PLO was also navigating the demands of several other parties. Saudi Arabia, Egypt, and the Soviet Union were pushing the leadership to accept 242, while the Syrians were strongly advising against such a move. The Palestinians, Arafat argued, had already demonstrated a great deal of moderation by agreeing to establish their national authority on a small piece of land, "23 percent of Palestine."[7] What would they get in return for Vance's offer? Although endorsing 242 would allow the PLO to talk with the United States, it would still leave their political future up in the air. In mediating between the United States and the PLO, Khalidi tried to clarify the specifics of Vance's promise. Would there be the possibility of American support for a Palestinian state? In response, Khalidi was told that the United States would not endorse a particular solution, although Carter had spoken of his commitment to the principle of Palestinian "self-determination."[8]

After debating Vance's offer a second time—only a few days after he had made his first attempt from Saudi Arabia—the PLO Executive Committee decided against acceptance of 242 for the time being.[9] Rather than countenance Begin's offer of limited autonomy without collective political identity, Arafat was insisting on the assertion of national rights of Palestinians. The PLO leader still wanted to pursue avenues with the United States, even with his lingering suspicions of American diplomatic intentions, but he had very little room to maneuver. Internally, there were disagreements between Fatah factions who wanted to begin a dialogue and other factions who were opposed, often fueled by external Syrian pressure.[10] Yet attempts to meet the American requirements were ongoing, and Carter remained informed of the PLO's internal discussions.[11] The U.S. administration still hoped that movement on 242 might provide an opening toward Palestinian representation at a Geneva Conference.[12]

The administration's secret talks with the PLO continued in September, this time via Landrum Bolling, another trusted back channel between the Carter White House and Arafat. Bolling had been a journalist and president of Earlham College, a Quaker institution in Indiana. He held extensive conversations with the PLO leadership in Beirut, sending summaries and full notes back to Washington.[13] In one meeting with Arafat and senior PLO leaders at the apartment of Arafat's secretary, Um Nasser, Bolling was told that the organization did *not* reject UN resolution 242 but that there had been a great deal of pressure to do so.[14] The Palestinian leadership voiced frustration at the shifting U.S. position on a Geneva Conference, first offering a dialogue and participation on the basis of support for the creation of a Palestinian state, then promising only dialogue and a trusteeship "over a disarmed, vague Palestinian 'entity.'" The Palestinian leadership viewed such a plan as a "scheme to destroy rights [*sic*] of Palestinians."[15]

Bolling's mediation made clear that Arafat was being pulled in multiple directions. When the American intermediary pushed Arafat in this meeting to publicly support 242, the PLO chairman gave a "lengthy" and "tortured" explanation, admitting that he was "suffering from Arab blackmail." He was referring to Syrian and other hard-line pressures, fearful that he would be denounced for making concessions by leaders who try to be "more Catholic than the Pope . . . more Palestinian than Arafat."[16] The PLO leadership was working on a new formulation to satisfy the Americans and promised to report on developments to Bolling. As one of his "moderate" contacts, who was close to Arafat, told Bolling, "If only the Americans will promise they will give their support to our claim to a state, we will give them anything they want from us."[17]

Arafat's own position focused on the vagueness of the U.S. assurance to the Palestinians and the shifting language being employed. "What do the terms mean: 'homeland,' 'national rights,' 'self-determination,' 'entity?'" Arafat asked. "The United States should make up its mind what *its* policy is on the question."[18] He also wanted Bolling to understand the pressure of navigating critics who denounced any move toward the recognition of Israel and raised the possibility that some Arab leaders might go it alone with the Israelis. The PLO leader doubted this, having spoken with Sadat and Assad and King Khalid of Saudi Arabia: "The truth is the Arab governments are stuck with us and they cannot leave us if they wanted to. That, of course, is the scheme the Israelis are counting on, but it won't work."[19]

PLO exclusion from international diplomacy in the late 1970s was not solely the result of external pressure from Israel or fitful American promises. There was also a great deal of internal inconsistency within the national movement, as the range of voices hampered the emergence of a unified PLO stance on negotiations. Among the most revealing aspects of Bolling's meeting with the PLO was the window offered into the fierce contestation inside the organization, which Arafat described as a "true democracy." There was room for many different views, including moderates like Issam Sartawi, who had reached out to Jewish progressive forces with PLO authorization. Sartawi, who was later assassinated by the virulently anti-PLO Abu Nidal organization, was bitterly attacked by more extreme members of the PLO and certain Arab states. "Certainly," Arafat told Bolling, "we have our rejectionist elements in the PLO and they are free to express their views. I do not try to suppress them, but they do not control the PLO."[20] The exchange highlighted an inherent problem with PLO operations, as Bolling pointed out to Arafat: "If you allow such glaring contradictions to be expressed with regard to crucial policy matters, you should not be *surprised* if you are misunderstood."[21] The multitude of voices served in part to undermine Palestinian policy formulation.

Bolling worked to convey this internal complexity to the Carter administration. "A great deal of Arafat's time and energy goes into efforts to keep everybody on the reservation," Bolling wrote. "An outsider has to wonder: Why bother? By the very structure of the P.L.O, the assorted extremist groups get representation in the various organs of the P.L.O. out of proportion to their numbers. By the free-wheeling 'democratic' tradition of the P.L.O., each faction has extraordinary freedom to go its own way in setting policy, committing acts of violence, and interpreting the P.L.O. to the world. It is a mad, mad situation."[22] There was not a viable alternative to the organization, Bolling explained, and there were also doubts and apprehensions voiced among some Palestinians, who "fear that Arafat and his team may not be quite up to the leadership role that would be required of them if independence should come." These critics worried that "extremists attached to the P.L.O. will do more foolish things that will produce consequences for the Palestinians under Israeli occupation," Bolling concluded, while at the same time they "doubt that the Israelis will ever willingly leave the West Bank on any terms whatever."[23] The limits and strategic missteps of the PLO were clearly evident in the secret dialogue with the United States, but so were the very real constraints and contradictions of the Carter administration, especially regarding the true meaning of self-determination.[24]

Domestic Pressures and the U.S.-Soviet Joint Communiqué

Alongside the unsuccessful U.S.-PLO secret discussions over the adoption of 242 and the organization's inclusion in Geneva, domestic American pressures were also mounting from two influential constituencies at great odds with the Carter administration's pursuit of comprehensive peace. The first was the leadership of the American Jewish community, which remained anxious about the administration's policy toward the Middle East while moving decisively closer to supporting the Begin government. The second were Cold War conservatives, who bitterly opposed détente and dismissed Carter's new focus on human rights in his foreign policy. This latter group railed against the inclusion of the Soviet Union in U.S. negotiations, a stance that bolstered the growing migration of hawkish Democrats into the Republican camp and fueled the strength of an emerging neoconservative ideology in foreign policy circles.[25] Preparations for the Geneva Conference lay at the crux of this dual-fronted domestic opposition and highlighted the degree of political capital that Carter was expending in his efforts.

From the moment the results of the Israeli election had been announced in May 1977, the leadership of mainstream American Jewish political institutions grappled with the question of whether to support Menachem Begin as prime minister. After the early ambivalence of many American Jews toward Zionism, communal organizations aligned with Israel's Labor-led governments, especially in the aftermath of the 1967 and 1973 wars. American Jewish leaders felt comfortable with Golda Meir and Yitzhak Rabin at the helm of the Israeli state, as their worldviews seemed to underscore the linkage between domestic liberalism in the United States and the kibbutz-inflected Zionism of the Israeli state's early years. Even with the evolution of American Jewish politics in response to upheaval in the Middle East during the late 1960s and early 1970s, the affinity for a liberal politics remained intact.[26]

This balance was upended by the rise of the Likud and Menachem Begin to power, as more particularistic communal instincts took hold. Through a process of extensive internal deliberation, a decision was made to support Begin and rally behind his government as a means of bolstering American Jewish support for Israel regardless of who was in power. Rabbi Alexander Schindler, the leader of the Reform movement and chairman of the Conference of Presidents of Major American Jewish Organizations, explained this rationale. "We were never pledged to a Party as American Jews," Schindler told an interviewer in 1977. "We were not members of the Labor alignment by any manner of means. We were pledged to a cause—the cause of Israel's security. We were motivated by a love for the people of Israel. But it is impossible to express that support by fighting the leader of that country. At that point Begin was the only Prime Minister Israel had."[27]

The clear shift to support Begin was a risky move, bound to alienate more liberal voices within the community. As one authority on the history of American Jewish politics explained, "Instead of publicly differing with Begin's policies, they [Jewish leaders] began to circle the wagons to defend against Jimmy Carter's policies."[28] Alongside contrarian voices in the wider public, several leaders of major Jewish institutions were also critical of this move, signaling a growing fracture in the nature of domestic support for Israel.[29] The approach of supporting the ruling government at any cost emerged in the late 1970s as the blueprint for American Jewry's future relationship with both Israel and the U.S. executive branch.[30] It was part of a pattern that led communal politics in more conservative political directions into the 1980s.[31]

Frustration among American Jewish leaders toward the administration's Middle East policy had been mounting over the summer. In a September memo for Carter's chief of staff Hamilton Jordan and White House Counsel Robert Lipshutz, two Jewish leaders warned of a "growing crisis over Israel policy which is boiling just below the public political surface."[32] The primary concern was the attempt by the Carter White House to reach a formula with the PLO and initiate contacts with the organization. Invoking the 1975 Kissinger agreement, critics worried that there had been too much movement toward a possible official dialogue: "The Palestinians appear to be far more popular in the Administration than in the country at large."[33] Furthermore, these critics argued, the administration was too vocal on the settlement issue and was developing "an image of harshness towards Israel." "Starkly put," the authors concluded, "despite its rhetoric on human rights, [the Carter administration] is seen as less friendly to the Israeli democracy than its predecessors."[34]

The simmering discontent gave way to visceral outrage over a joint U.S.-Soviet Communiqué intended to guide the Geneva Conference, which was issued in New York City on October 1, 1977. In Cold War terms, given the broader geopolitical landscape of the 1970s, such a communiqué was a very significant departure for both the United States and the Soviets. It was the first joint statement on the Middle East by the two powers. While it had been suggested that the Soviet Union would be kept out of pre-Geneva discussions, Brzezinski felt they should be consulted to launch the Geneva Conference before the end of the year. Vance echoed this sentiment, reporting to Brzezinski that the Soviets had moderated their position and were not insisting on a separate Palestinian state but rather something closer to the vague political entity the Americans had in mind.[35]

Most of the language in the communiqué emanated from resolution 242, but it went farther in articulating a future for Palestinians.

The United States and the Soviet Union believe that, within the framework of a comprehensive settlement of the Middle East problem, all
specific questions of the settlement should be resolved, including
such key issues as withdrawal of Israeli Armed Forces from territories
occupied in the 1967 conflict; the resolution of the Palestinian question, including ensuring the legitimate rights of the Palestinian people;
termination of the state of war and establishment of normal peaceful
relations on the basis of mutual recognition of the principles of sovereignty, territorial integrity, and political independence.[36]

For the first time, the United States was officially calling for Israeli
territorial withdrawal while asserting the importance of the "legitimate rights of the Palestinian people." It also stressed the need to
deal with sovereignty, which was at the heart of a resolution to the
Palestinian question, even as the particular mechanism for fulfill-
ing self-determination remained vague.

Arab states reacted rather favorably to the joint communiqué.
Advocates for engagement like Egypt saw the implied reference to
the legitimacy of the Palestinian claims of sovereignty as a move
by the Carter administration toward "recognition of a Palestinian
state."[37] The PLO expressed genuine excitement over the communiqué and its bearing on Geneva, across political factions.[38] There
was even hope of a new resolution that might be passed by the UN
Security Council, one that would combine the main points of 242
with renewed demands for Palestinian self-determination.[39] Critics, like Syria and Iraq, remained skeptical of the possibility that
Israel would ever participate in a Geneva Conference given what
the content of the declaration implied.

The Israeli government was extremely displeased with the announcement.[40] The opposition extended well beyond Begin's Likud
party. Yitzhak Rabin, who was now a Knesset member in the opposition, told an Israeli interviewer that the statement reflected a shift in
gravity between the United States and Israel that "we have not experienced since the end of the 6-Day War."[41] He felt Israel was being co-
erced into a political solution, undermining all the diplomatic efforts
since 1967. Rabin blamed both the Carter administration and the
Likud government for policies that would lead to the imposition of
an external solution, denouncing a move to Geneva on these terms.[42]

An advance copy of the statement was provided to Israel's foreign minister, Moshe Dayan, who did not immediately raise any criticisms. In his memoirs, Dayan argues that Carter had assured him that he would be careful to use the term "entity" and not "state" in the context of addressing the future of the Palestinians.[43] Neither term was used, but the formulation exceeded the limited Israeli vision for the conference. In talks with Carter a few days after the statement, Dayan focused on Israeli opposition to a Palestinian state, again revealing the extent of his government's ongoing claim to sovereignty in the occupied territories. "For us it is unthinkable to withdraw from the West Bank and Gaza, and turn those areas over to the Palestinians, even if they are in federation with Jordan," Dayan explained. "We must come to terms with the Palestinians who live there, and we must keep some of our military installations and some of our settlements, and we must continue to be able to buy land."[44] For Dayan, even the most flexible arrangements with the Palestinians were predicated on the continuation of an Israeli presence in the same geographic space.

In reacting to the communiqué, Dayan invoked the language of security to justify Israeli fears of a PLO presence on its borders. He impassionedly sought Carter's guarantee not to endorse a national outcome for the Palestinian question: "We do not say the Palestinians have nothing to say about their future. We have to come together. But if we have to pull out our military installations, that would be unacceptable. We will not negotiate over a Palestinian state." Dayan opposed pulling out of the territory and yet claimed he was not asking for Israeli control or annexation. "We want to live together in the territories and we don't want to give them back."[45] He was both telling the Americans that Israel's basis for negotiations at Geneva rested on the fundamental premise of continuing de facto control over the very space that was being contested and seeking an American endorsement of such a position. Like the tactical avoidance of negotiating the fate of the territories after 1967, Israeli leaders were in fact proffering comprehensive negotiations as a means to maintain indefinite political sovereignty over the territories.

The Israeli position on the communiqué was mirrored by an outcry among American Jewish leaders. AIPAC widely distributed a scathing critique of the document, claiming it disregarded U.S. commitments to Israel and undermined prospects for a negotiated settlement.[46] Mark Siegel, the White House liaison with the American Jewish community, wrote of its "devastating effect" and told Hamilton Jordan that it had "driven Jimmy Carter's stock in the American Jewish community substantially below any U.S. President since the creation of the State of Israel."[47] During discussions with Vice President Mondale and Hamilton Jordan, Hyman Bookbinder, the Washington representative of the American Jewish Committee, targeted the phrase of "legitimate rights," which had until then not been part of the formal American foreign policy lexicon. "Obviously you do not apparently really understand what those words mean," Bookbinder told the administration officials. "The mistake you make is you go to the dictionary to ask what those words mean. That's not where you look up that phrase. That phrase is not in the dictionary. The individual words are. Those words in context are: Palestinian rights means to the Jewish community the destruction of Israel. And by being willing to leave those words in the document you betrayed an insensitivity and a lack of awareness, and you've just got to make up for it."[48]

Bookbinder's insistence that the articulation of rights for Palestinians signaled the destruction of Israel formed the core of a deeply rooted fear of Palestinian nationalism among American Jews. Such an instinctive inability to see the Palestinians as anything other than a threat to Jewish national interests was bolstered by successive incidents of Palestinian militancy in Israel and abroad in the 1970s. But it also tapped into a more pervasive cultural milieu of suspicion and existential fear that propagated myths that denied Palestinian existence as a collective. Communal anxieties, as expressed by Bookbinder, also fit within the idiom of Cold War national security concerns, linking Jewish political interests with neoconservative priorities in the Middle East. One Jewish Democratic activist remarked that Jews feel Carter is "using Israel as a bartering tool to get concessions from the Soviet Union on much broader issues, like arms limitations and trade and so on. At this moment, most Jews hope he'll be a one term President."[49]

The joint communiqué outraged American conservatives as well, who decried a shift in U.S. policy to include the Soviets in negotiations. The right flank of the Democratic Party, along with their Republican colleagues, saw the statement as an indication of détente's weakness. It signaled a partial reentry of the Soviets into the Middle East. These critics included Eugene Rostow, a founder of the anti-Soviet Committee on Present Danger, which opposed Soviet military expansion.[50] The communiqué seemed of a piece with Carter's broader policies around arms reduction, which Rostow and his colleagues discussed with the president over the summer.[51] The group suspected they were being "used" to bolster Carter's claim of speaking with hawks, and they were not favorably impressed by the president's performance. "The President[']s personality and style came through as pathetic, almost pitiful," Rostow wrote in a personal account, referring to the meeting as "claptrap." This lingering perception that Carter was soft on communism and was staffed "almost entirely by pronounced doves" would trail the president in the midterm elections and into the 1980 campaign.[52]

In spite of these criticisms from American Jewish leaders and Cold War conservatives, the joint statement of the United States and the Soviet Union underscored the fundamental difference between Carter's foreign policy and that of previous administrations. It also fit with Carter's May statement about a Palestinian "homeland" and sustained attempts to reformulate U.S. policy toward Israel and the Palestinians. Given the domestic ramifications, these were bold moves with serious electoral repercussions. But they did not always remain in place. With time, and political heat, Carter's statements on the Palestinians became more "circumspect," eventually replacing vocal support for a homeland with opposition to an independent Palestinian state.[53]

Sadat's Unilateral Move and the Demise of Geneva

During the UN General Assembly in New York in late September 1977, Secretary Vance continued to hash out the points of contention over the possibility of Geneva in negotiations with the Arab states and Israel.[54] In a discussion with Dayan, Vance reiterated the U.S. belief in a Palestinian entity (not a state) preferably linked with Jordan as the best option, a position still at odds with Israel's. To find a way out of this contradiction, Dayan suggested that parties refrain from defining the specific political formation under consideration: "The subject can be mentioned . . . and each side can interpret it as it sees fit." Vance agreed this was a constructive idea. Such a tactical move on Dayan's part deferred discussion of the most divisive issues to a meeting in Geneva itself, which was the opposite of the prior agreement that Egyptian president Sadat had hoped for.[55]

Dayan's Geneva working paper, developed in meetings with the Americans on October 5, 1977, called for the "negotiation and completion of peace treaties" between Israel and Egypt; Israel and Jordan; Israel and Syria; and Israel and Lebanon. The language for the territories, however, signaled a move away from political treaties: "The West Bank and Gaza issues will be discussed in a working group to consist of Israel, Jordan, Egypt and the Palestinian Arabs."[56] The paper quickly secured Israeli cabinet approval.[57] Rather than seek to resolve the fate of the territories, they would be subject to a discussion, which deferred the West Bank and Gaza territorial question from consideration. The mechanics of diplomacy had already begun to prevent the possibility of settling the Palestinian question in political terms.

Sadat watched these maneuvers with growing frustration. Ever since his country's acceptance of the Rogers Plan for Arab-Israeli peace in 1970, Egypt's leader had been looking to the United States as a regional patron. Carter's active interest in securing a comprehensive settlement had encouraged Sadat, and the two had developed a close working relationship. But the Egyptian president did not like the petty procedural debates around Palestinian representation and format of a hopeful summit. His apprehension over the preparatory discussions about Geneva between Carter, Begin, and the Arab leaders mounted in the wake of the joint communiqué.[58] Wary of jeopardizing the possibility of peace with "endless bickering over procedural issues," Sadat proposed an international summit for peace in the Middle East to be held in Jerusalem in December, before the meeting in Geneva.[59] This gathering would include the Soviet Union, China, France, the United Kingdom, the United Nations, and Yasser Arafat as the head of the PLO. Such an international effort, Sadat believed, would constitute the bold gesture that was needed for peace. Carter disagreed, expressing his concern that it would lead to a public rejection.[60]

Instead of making an announcement about a new summit, Sadat's speech to the People's Assembly in Cairo on November 9 contained an altogether different yet no less dramatic promise. The Egyptian leader vowed in emotional terms to "go to the Knesset itself" in order to secure Israeli withdrawal from the territories and legitimate rights for the Palestinians.[61] PLO chairman Yasser Arafat, whom Sadat described as the "sole legitimate representative of the Palestinian people," was sitting in the audience next to Vice President Hosni Mubarak. It was a stunning and unexpected remark.[62] As U.S. ambassador to Egypt Hermann Eilts wrote from Cairo, Sadat's offer to go to the Knesset was the first for an Arab leader, but should be seen "as his way of dramatizing lengths to which he prepared to go to achieve peace, not as a serious possibility."[63] The Americans had fundamentally misread Egyptian motivations.

Sadat's rationale for a dramatic announcement about his willingness to travel to Jerusalem is not easy to discern. In part, it reflected the decisive strategy he had pursued since the early 1970s. By moving away from the Soviet orbit toward the American sphere of influence, the Egyptian president sought out Western backing for internal reforms and the modernization of Egypt's economy. He was also navigating an internal rivalry with the military, which had consumed Egypt since the 1952 revolution. At the same time, he carried the mantle of serving as Nasser's successor, projecting Egypt's regional strength and continued patronage of the Palestinian cause.[64] This required decisive regional action, most notably achieved with the launching of the 1973 War. But it also required diplomatic follow-up like the convening of a regional peace conference under American guidance. Without movement in this direction, the U.S. ambassador to Egypt argued, "Sadat may find he has gotten out uncomfortably far beyond his Arab brothers."[65] In this light, Sadat's decisive shift away from the Geneva Conference and the international protections it offered was a risky gambit that undermined his stated aims and left the Palestinian question vulnerable to Israeli designs.[66]

Ten days later, Sadat defied the expert assessments and mounting criticism with an unprecedented trip to Jerusalem. The official visit, which began on Saturday evening November 19, came after Begin extended a formal invitation.[67] In breathless American and

Middle Eastern media coverage, Egypt's leader was praised for boldness on the one hand but accused of betraying the Arab world's stance toward Israel on the other. Sadat's trip generated tremendous internal dissent in Egypt, leading to the resignation of Foreign Minister Ismail Fahmy and his deputy, Mohammad Riad.[68] The visit was met by wide disapproval across the Arab world, with especially strident opposition emerging from Syria. The PLO view, as reflected in the organization's Beirut-based mouthpiece, was to condemn Sadat's decision. Officials believed it would only strengthen Begin's hand, "a useless step which will give the Israelis prestige and recognition."[69] Beyond the symbolism, critics wondered, what exactly would Sadat be able to secure from Begin?[70]

The sheer visual power of an Arab leader landing at Ben Gurion airport, greeted by a retinue of Israeli officials—including redoubtable military rivals—captured global attention. An honor guard carried Egyptian and Israeli flags, both national anthems were played, and Sadat even interacted warmly with former prime minister Golda Meir.[71] Sadat's entourage was driven up to Jerusalem, where the Egyptians spent the evening in the King David Hotel. After attending Eid al-Adha prayers in Jerusalem's Al-Aqsa mosque on Sunday morning, Sadat made his way to the Church of the Holy Sepulchre and then joined Begin for a visit to the Holocaust memorial of Yad Vashem.

In a remarkable speech delivered in Arabic in front of the Knesset that afternoon, Sadat spoke of a "durable and just peace." While he did not mention the PLO by name, he stressed "there can be no peace without the Palestinians."

> The cause of the Palestinian People and their legitimate rights are no longer ignored or denied today by anybody. . . . Even the United States, your first ally which is absolutely committed to safeguard Israel's security and existence, and which offered and still offers Israel every moral, material and military support—I say—even the United States has opted to face up to reality and facts, and admit that the Palestinian People are entitled to legitimate rights and that the Palestinian problem is the core and essence of the conflict and that, so long as it continues to be unresolved, the conflict will continue to aggravate, reaching new dimensions.[72]

In focusing so centrally on the Palestinian question, the Egyptian leader had reintroduced the concept of a permanent home into Israeli and broader public consciousness.[73]

Alongside the public gesture toward comprehensive peace, the trip did not yield a substantive indication of how it would be achieved.[74] During their working meetings in Jerusalem, Sadat reiterated Egyptian impatience with procedural issues around Geneva and evinced a desire for substantive talks with the Israelis. Both the Egyptian and Israeli delegations worked on a joint communiqué that was issued at a press conference by the two leaders at the Jerusalem Theatre. Praising Sadat's "sincere and courageous move," the statement proposed further dialogue between the two countries and movement toward negotiations, "leading to the signing of peace treaties in Geneva with all the neighboring Arab states."[75] As Sadat described the main motive of his visit, it was "to give the peace process new momentum and to get rid of the psychological barrier that, in my opinion, was more than 70 percent of the whole conflict, the other 30 percent being substance."[76] Looking at the content of Sadat's private conversations with Begin, however, it is clear that the differences in Israeli and Egyptian positions on the purpose of Geneva and the prospects for peace were no less contradictory than they had been before Sadat landed in Israel.

Tensions remained between Sadat's stated desire for a comprehensive peace and his unilateral actions, which undercut the support of other Arab states and shifted political developments in more troubling directions. During a meeting after Sadat's visit with Prime Minister Begin and Foreign Minister Dayan, U.S. ambassador Samuel Lewis asked for a report of their conversations in Jerusalem. Both Begin and Dayan stressed Sadat's disinterest in the procedural issues around Geneva, at the same time claiming he did not want to reach a separate deal. For Sadat, "the Palestinian question comes first," Dayan explained.[77] The Egyptian motivation for boldly coming to Jerusalem, Dayan continued, was not the return of the Sinai Peninsula and the city of Sharm el-Sheikh. "Sharm is desert and it won't change the economy of Egypt. Their real target is to improve the economy of the country. In this connection much depends on America." Begin concurred, and added what Sadat told him in private about the state of the Egyptian economy: "He said the problem was horrible and he complained about the military expenditure."[78] In light of these concerns, the Israelis anticipated that plans for a comprehensive peace might actually be falling to the wayside.

Part of the Israeli assessment on shifting priorities relied on a reading of the regional atmosphere toward Egypt. Dayan explained to the U.S. ambassador that for Sadat, diplomatic momentum "does not lead directly to Geneva." "I feel," Dayan continued, "that Sadat is less anxious to go to Geneva with Syria, the Russians and the PLO. He is obviously very hurt by their attitude. They call for his blood."[79] Lewis, in his report to Carter, concurred that from Begin's account "it looks as though our Geneva scenario has been considerably modified and the new track has, obviously, a heady odor of Israeli-Egyptian bilaterals."[80] The Americans nevertheless decided to stick with their more ambitious plans for a comprehensive peace, even as a conference in Geneva looked increasingly unlikely.[81]

Amid all the global attention given to Sadat's trip to Jerusalem, there was mounting concern that the Palestinian question could fall to the diplomatic wayside. Sadat conceded as much privately very soon after he returned to Cairo. He told Ambassador Eilts that he sensed "the concept of an independent Palestinian state did not appeal to Begin or [Defense Minister Ezer] Weizman." As a compromise, Eilts reported, the Egyptian president was "toying" with the idea of turning the West Bank over to the United Nations Emergency Force (UNEF) established after the 1956 Suez Crisis. It could be for a period of five years, and a plebiscite could be arranged "for self-determination." Alongside the West Bank, Sadat proposed that the Gaza Strip become the "main weight" of a Palestinian state, to which he would even give part of the Sinai, including Egyptian Rafah and the settlement of Yamit.[82] Subsequently, while explaining what self-determination would mean in this context, Sadat said "merely a plebiscite on the question of federation or confederation with Jordan." Upon further reflection, he said West Bankers "should also be given the option of independence," but it was not a real option as the PLO was losing ground.[83]

This stark retreat of the Egyptian leader from a staunch position as defender of a Palestinian state drew fury from other Arab countries. Leaders from the PLO, Libya, Syria, Algeria, and Southern Yemen met in Tripoli on December 2 to take action after Sadat's visit.

Rather than enact economic and diplomatic sanctions, the group formed a "resistance front," issuing the Tripoli Declaration of December 5. Egypt, in response, broke diplomatic relations with the four states.[84] The major sticking point in this roiling internal Arab debate was Sadat's seeming willingness to cede the West Bank in favor of a bilateral peace. Egypt, it seemed, had sold out the Palestinians for Sadat's internal gain. Ismail Fahmy, who had resisted Sadat's Jerusalem trip from the start, later remarked that it was a "shock to the Egyptian people, the Arab world and the Palestinians." In Fahmy's view, the trip "certainly destroyed Egypt's crucial role in helping the Palestinian people to regain their own land and statehood."[85]

These fears were not overstated, given the signals that were being conveyed in private diplomatic discussions. In reports from various Middle Eastern capitals, a number of U.S. ambassadors spoke of this sudden shift toward bilateralism and the threat to the Palestinians in light of Israeli aims.[86] Ambassador to Israel Samuel Lewis explained that "the key obstacle to moving beyond a bilateral agreement with Egypt is the current Israeli position regarding the West Bank."[87] In the opinion of the U.S. ambassador to Lebanon, Richard Parker, "something well short of the PLO maximum demands could eventually be sold to Palestinians," but Parker saw "no signs that the Israelis [were] going to meet even minimalist demands."[88] As part of a bid to help Sadat face his mounting critics, Carter actually urged Begin to make a public statement showing Israeli willingness to withdraw in principle from lands occupied in 1967 and to resolve the Palestinian question.[89] Begin was of course unwilling to offer such a statement, but he was thinking about an entirely different plan for the West Bank. It had started to emerge in Dayan's meetings with the Americans throughout 1977 and was reiterated in Morocco during a secret conversation with Sadat's confidant, Dr. Hassan Tuhami. There would not be an Israeli withdrawal, Dayan told Tuhami, but a new proposal was being prepared in Jerusalem.[90]

The Autonomy Offer

This proposal, Menachem Begin's "home rule for the Palestinian Arabs," was officially unveiled on December 16, 1977. Begin personally presented the plan to Carter in Washington after mentioning it to Secretary Vance in Jerusalem a few days earlier. "I hope the President will accept my plan," Begin told Vance. "It is not a Palestinian state but it is a dignified solution for the Palestinian Arabs. It is home rule of the inhabitants, by the inhabitants, for the inhabitants."[91] Begin's plan was a sophisticated piece of statecraft, perfectly timed to neutralize the Palestinian issue after Sadat's trip had called into question the ambitious U.S. approach to a comprehensive peace. There was a diplomatic vacuum that the Israelis were eager to fill on more favorable terms, and the presentation of autonomy fully reflected the political aims of the Begin government.[92] It stemmed from ideas about limited individual rights for "Arab inhabitants of Judea and Samaria" that Begin had been contemplating ever since the 1967 War.

Begin's approach was distinct from a collective or national solution to the Palestinian predicament and would not require Israel to relinquish control over the territory itself. He prefaced his presentation to Carter by reiterating that he envisioned an Administrative Council representing Arab inhabitants that "will be able to deal with all the problems of daily life."[93] Israel, however, would have to have the "right to deal with public order." He acknowledged the open-ended question of sovereignty and Sadat's rhetorical safeguarding of Palestinian rights, even as the Egyptian leader had privately sacrificed them. "We do claim sovereignty over Judea, Samaria and Gaza. We think this is the right of our people but Sadat says that the Arabs also claim sovereignty. So there are two claims and we will leave the issue open. It cannot be solved for now."[94] This was a formidable innovation in his negotiating tactic, helping to stymie Palestinian national demands.

In Begin's mind, it was better not to contest sovereignty in negotiations, for neither side would budge. Rather, Israel should offer ideas to make peace a possibility, which in his view could deal with "human beings." He saw that Arab populations were living under oppressive conditions and believed Israel was poised to alleviate their situation, a shift that he thought could be achieved with mechanisms of local rule. In terms of citizenship, Begin proposed that inhabitants could have freedom of choice where the situation remained unclear, like Jerusalem. "In Judea and Samaria, the Palestinian Arabs are already Jordanian citizens. This will not be changed." Begin, like Dayan, framed his position into terms of security. "If there are Arab guns on the green line, all of our civilians will be in mortal danger."[95] The ingenuity of the offer was to portray restrictive designs in a benevolent light.

The evening before Begin's presentation, Vance and Quandt recommended that Carter not endorse such a proposal but rather tell the Israelis to introduce it during formal negotiations as their opening position on the Palestinian issue.[96] Begin nevertheless read out the twenty-one articles of his proposal to Carter (see box on page 100).

In his proposal, the prime minister was promising local authority for elected Arab officials to guide decisions in areas like commerce, education, health, and transport. But Israel would maintain control of security over the territory, and residents within Israel would be "entitled to acquire land and settle in the areas of Judea, Samaria and the Gaza district" as well. In a direct challenge to the PLO's political vision and the claims of Palestinian nationalists, Begin's plan was predicated on Israel retaining the territories acquired in 1967 rather than returning them in the context of a negotiation.

President Carter responded in detail to Begin's extensive presentation. He invoked UN Security Council Resolutions 242 and 338, which called for Israeli withdrawal from occupied territories in exchange for secure borders and permanent peace. While acknowledging the Israeli view that withdrawal was not a total withdrawal, the president understood that Begin was intent on keeping the West Bank and Gaza Strip. He therefore asked the Israeli leader three questions. The first dealt with Israel's commitment to withdrawal from the West Bank, even with minor adjustments. The second question dealt with Palestinian Arabs from other countries, and the third question with sovereignty.

Begin responded by repeating his concern about security and the incompatibility of the Green Line as a defensible border. "If we withdraw to the 1967 lines, there will be permanent bloodshed," the prime minister insisted. "The 1967 line did not constitute a border." Begin intimated that Israeli state sovereignty would end at the 1967 line, but security would extend to the Jordan River.[97] Brzezinski, sensing the political problem that this position caused, then addressed the question of sovereignty. Begin insisted that it was

Proposal

December 15, 1977

Proposal Subject to the Confirmation of the Government of Israel

HOME RULE, FOR PALESTINIAN ARABS, RESIDENTS OF JUDEA, SAMARIA AND THE GAZA DISTRICT

1. The administration of the Military Government in Judea, Samaria and the Gaza district will be abolished.
2. In Judea, Samaria and the Gaza district administrative autonomy of the residents, by and for them, will be established.
3. The residents of Judea, Samaria and the Gaza district will elect an Administrative Council composed of eleven members.
4. Any resident, 18 years old and above, without distinction of citizenship, or if stateless, is entitled to vote in the election to the Administrative Council.
5. Any resident whose name is included in the list of the candidates for the Administrative Council and who, on the day the list is submitted, is 25 years old or above, is entitled to be elected to the Council.
6. The Administrative Council will be elected by general, direct, personal, equal and secret ballot.
7. The period of office of the Administrative Council will be four years from the day of its election.
8. The Administrative Council will sit in Bethlehem.
9. All the administrative affairs of the areas of Judea, Samaria and the Gaza district, will be under the direction and within the competence of the Administrative Council.
10. The Administrative Council will operate the following Departments:

    a. The Department of Education;
    b. The Department of Religious Affairs;
    c. The Department of Finance;
    d. The Department of Transportation;
    e. The Department for Construction and Housing;
    f. The Department of Industry, Commerce and Tourism;
    g. The Department of Agriculture;
    h. The Department of Health;
    i. The Department for Labor and Social Welfare;
    j. The Department of Rehabilitation of Refugees;
    k. The Department for the Administration of Justice and the Supervision of the Local Police Forces;

    and promulgate regulations relating to the operation of these Departments.

11. Security in the areas of Judea, Samaria and the Gaza district will be the responsibility of the Israeli authorities.
12. The Administrative Council will elect its own chairman.
13. The first session of the Administrative Council will be convened 30 days after the publication of the election results.
14. Residents of Judea, Samaria and the Gaza district, without distinction of citizenship, or if stateless, will be granted free choice (option) of either Israeli or Jordanian citizenship.

15. A resident of the areas of Judea, Samaria and the Gaza district who requests Israeli citizenship will be granted such citizenship in accordance with the citizenship law of the State.

16. Residents of Judea, Samaria and the Gaza district who, in accordance with the right of free option, choose Israeli citizenship, will be entitled to vote for, and be elected to, the Knesset in accordance with the election law.

17. Residents of Judea, Samaria and the Gaza district who are citizens of Jordan or who, in accordance with the right of free option will become citizens of Jordan, will elect and be eligible for election to the Parliament of the Hashemite Kingdom of Jordan in accordance with the election law of that country.

18. Questions "arising from the vote" to the Jordanian Parliament by residents of Judea, Samaria and the Gaza district will be clarified in negotiations between Israel and Jordan.

19. Residents of Israel will be entitled to acquire land and settle in the areas of Judea, Samaria and the Gaza district. Arabs, residents of Judea, Samaria and the Gaza district will be entitled to acquire land and settle in Israel.

20. Residents of Israel and residents of Judea, Samaria and the Gaza district will be assured freedom of movement and freedom of economic activity in Israel, Judea, Samaria and the Gaza district.

21. These principles may be subject to review after a five-year period.

Reproduced from Attachment to *FRUS*, Doc. 177.

merely a legal issue to be sorted out and that a local administrative council could manage complex questions like land expropriation and immigration. These issues, as Begin saw them, were also caught up with security: "We could only accept new immigrants up to the point where our own security would not be affected." Vance interjected: "So this would be dealt with by the Administrative Council, subject to Israel's view on possible security problems. The Council would not have total authority." Begin agreed.

The Israeli attorney general, Aharon Barak, interceded on the question of sovereignty, arguing that the military governor of the West Bank and Gaza would "delegate authority to the Council in order for it to act," rather than the Israeli state, to avoid implications that Israel claimed sovereignty. Vance followed up, asking if the military governor reserved the right to revoke these powers. Barak said "in principle, yes." Brzezinski responded that this would then mean Israeli sovereignty ("at least, de facto," Vance added). Barak defended Begin's position, saying that the military governor was "not the sovereign authority," a position the U.S. delegation sought to clarify further. From a legal standpoint, the attorney general's argument rested on the notion that the territories were not occupied in the first place, undermining any claim that Arab residents would be under military rule. It was a tautological position, one that enabled Israel to claim both control and non-annexation of the territories, a position that had been refuted by Israel's legal counsel in the wake of the 1967 War.[98]

Begin planned to present his autonomy proposal in full to President Sadat during an impending trip to Sadat's private residence in Ismailia, Egypt. He added that autonomy's success depended on collective Egyptian, American, and British concession that there would be no Palestinian state. Before adjourning for the Sabbath, Begin provided hard copies of his plan to Brzezinski, Carter, and Vance.[99] Brzezinski asked Begin why Bethlehem and not East Jerusalem would be the seat of the Legislative Council. Begin's response revealed the ideological certitude that animated his plans and the contradiction of claiming to resolve the Palestinian question along more equitable lines. "It cannot be East Jerusalem, because Jerusalem is the capital of Israel," Begin explained. "And it cannot be Nablus either. Bethlehem is the best. There cannot be two capitals in Jerusalem. They should have their own proper capital. Bethlehem is the center of communications."[100] Begin's approach to Jerusalem, like his view on settlements and Jewish claims to sovereignty, remained consistent. Palestinians were not viewed as a collective people seeking national rights but a minority population in need of individual attention, with adaptable outcomes that the Israeli prime minister believed could placate more robust demands for self-determination. It explains why the U.S. government found Begin to be a frustrating negotiator, as he rarely retreated from these views in his baseline assertions.[101]

Israel's definitive attitude toward the Palestinians concerned Carter, who wanted to protect Sadat diplomatically in the wake of his Jerusalem trip and the breakdown of Geneva. If the autonomy plan were misread in the public sphere, Carter felt, it would undermine all of Sadat's goodwill. He told Begin after the Sabbath that the plan could appear positive but also it could very well appear empty, given Begin's comments about the military governor and restoring Israeli control at will. "We believe that how these proposals are cast, and how your well-constructed ideas are interpreted, will be crucial."[102] The intimation that Israeli state sovereignty would be limited to the 1967 borders, for example, with security extending up to the Jordan River, seemed promising to Carter. It could be subject to negotiations between Jordan, Egypt, and Palestinian Arabs "on a time scale commensurate with your development of a sense of security and trust in the Arabs." Carter was "gratified" by Begin's apparent "flexibility" on this matter.[103] But the president remained concerned that the interpretation of Begin's plan could be negative and jeopardize Sadat's reputation.

Broader regional engagement was a necessity in light of the reaction to Egypt's sudden shift. In Carter's view, if Begin and Sadat could agree, King Hussein would join the discussions, but Syrian president Assad only much later. The Palestinians themselves remained excluded from the possible negotiations over their fate. Despite the secret back channels, Carter was deeply skeptical of the PLO in his comments to Begin, remarking that they had been "absolutely negative, and I see no role for them to play in the present peace negotiations."[104] Although they did not agree to 242, the PLO was still integral to Sadat's legitimacy, so the president's remarks may have assuaged Begin but they denoted a newfound hostility toward the organization.[105]

The autonomy proposal that Begin brought to Carter was a highly consequential blueprint for Israel's diplomatic strategy toward the Palestinians, and its imprint extended far beyond the 1970s. Several areas helped set in motion dynamics that perpetuated the condition of statelessness Arafat had feared. Most notably, Begin was inflexible on the status of the West Bank. He would not agree to foreign forces, like the United Nations, guaranteeing protection in the territories as Sadat had suggested in November. He invoked the German Jews of the Middle Ages, Schutzjuden, who paid for external protection. "We do not want to be protected Jews," Begin declared. "We are disciples of Jabotinsky. We don't want to be a Schutzjuden-Staat. We want to sustain our independence and to end the persecution of Jews. People used to pity Jews. We want to live as a normal nation."[106] In linking his foreign policy to maudlin readings of Jewish history, Begin codified Israeli national priorities in existentially woeful terms. Ideologically, such a view echoed the Likud's long-standing attachment to the "Greater Land of Israel."

The position was absolute when it came to the West Bank, even if there was more willingness on the return of the Sinai Peninsula.

In a further indication of how clearly the autonomy plan would undercut Palestinian claims, Begin reiterated Israel's dismissal of the Palestinian refugee question. For the Israeli leadership, the return of refugees into the territories would threaten Jewish claims on the land. "Israelis have the right to go to the territories. It is inconceivable that we can give the same right to the others," explained Attorney General Barak.[107] As for the question of settlements, Begin did not see them having a special status, as Arabs lived in Israel and Jews lived in the territories. "There is no problem. Of course, there are settlements, but we have a principle of symmetric justice. The residents of Israel can buy land in Judea, Samaria, and Gaza, and Arabs can get land in Israel. There will be reciprocity. They can come to Tel Aviv and buy land and build homes."[108] These logics of exchange, functioning on a basis that accepted the population transfers of 1948 and 1967 and equated them with Jewish settlement in the territories, cohered in Begin's mind as a just solution to the political reality that had taken root in the West Bank and Gaza. Begin was shaped by his intellectual mentor, Ze'ev Jabotinsky, in propagating a distinct view of the Arabs as a minority with rights living under the dominance of Jewish-majority rule.[109]

The Carter administration's reaction to the autonomy plan seemed to embolden Begin, and he remained buoyant about his reception during a stop in the United Kingdom on his way back to Israel. At the Chequers Estate in Buckinghamshire, the Israeli prime minister met with Prime Minister Callaghan and Foreign Secretary David Owen. He boasted to them that his plan for the West Bank had met with "wholehearted, even enthusiastic acceptance." Although Carter had initially been hesitant, after a tête-à-tête, Begin reported, he "accepted the plan for Judea and Samaria without qualification, except for a few problems with its judicial aspects." Several senators and congressmen, ex-president Ford, Secretary Kissinger, and leading members of the Jewish community all supported the Israeli plan, Begin asserted.[110] After he had reiterated the main points of the proposal, Callaghan told Begin that his approach was "remarkable and imaginative." While disagreeing with Begin's positions on security, and explaining that Sadat could not accept it straightaway, the British prime minister and his advisors saw it as a good starting point to the negotiations over the Palestinian question. This flexibility highlights the Callaghan government's sympathy toward Begin, a clear departure from previous British policy and an indication of a permissive stance that may have actually enabled Israeli actions in the West Bank.[111]

Inwardly, U.S. government officials were skeptical of the Israeli plans, but they too entertained the possibility of building on some of these ideas in addressing the Palestinian issue. In his memoir, Secretary of State Cyrus Vance reflected on the emergence of the Israeli negotiating model, which deferred this possibility of Palestinian self-determination: "Despite our differences with the Israelis on how to solve the Palestinian problem, the president and I shared their concerns about a radicalized Palestinian state. We concluded that some form of transitional arrangement was needed so that the Palestinians could demonstrate whether they were prepared to govern themselves and live peacefully besides Israel, while remaining under international supervision to ease Israel's fears." Vance's own initial ideal was transitional, a "UN trusteeship under joint Israeli-Jordanian administration, leading to a plebiscite and Palestinian self-determination after several years." While such a concept was to undergo "considerable revision and development," Vance wrote that it was "one of the roots of the Camp David arrangement for Palestinian autonomy during a transitional regime."[112]

In outlining such a transitional agreement, Vance drew on a longer history of external powers mediating the Palestinian question. Like the British approach to the Arabs in the Mandate era earlier in the century, the United States would promote a time-bound solution that would have the Palestinians "demonstrate whether they were prepared to govern themselves and live peacefully beside Israel."[113] The central problem with this approach—an outdated colonial model that would prove ineffectual in the aftermath of decolonization—was the powerful hold of the Israeli state on the territories since 1967. Conceivably, under the Labor settlement plan, or even Moshe Dayan's conception of Palestinian self-rule, it might have been plausible to prepare the West Bank and Gaza for a political solution outside the realm of Israeli control. But the stance of the Likud, and Begin's clear pronouncements on continued

Israeli military and political dominance of the territories, ensured that the emergence of any autonomy arrangements would have to be predicated on the prevention of non-Israeli sovereignty.

Begin in Egypt

"This is perhaps the first time we sit together since Moses crossed the waters not very far from here," Anwar al-Sadat proudly told his guest. "Let us here teach the world a new way of facing problems between two nations let us tell them that sincerity, honesty, goodwill and, above all, love can solve any problem." It was Menachem Begin's first trip to Egypt, and Sadat's warm welcome underscored its historic nature. "When Moses took us out of Egypt, it took him 40 years to cross the Sinai desert," a reverent but jovial Begin told his Egyptian counterpart. "We did it in 40 minutes."[114] The Christmas Day visit to Sadat's presidential residence on the banks of the Suez Canal in Ismailia provided the Israeli prime minister with a chance to formally present his autonomy plan to the Egyptians after its announcement to American and British leaders.

FIGURE 3.1. "Prime Minister Menachem Begin Gives Tourist Guidance to President Sadat, Beer Sheva." May 27, 1979. Sa'ar Ya'acov, courtesy of Israel's Government Press Office.

Begin sought out Sadat's approval for his approach to the Palestinian question, as distinct from the broader discussions over the Sinai Peninsula. After first laying out the Israeli position on withdrawal from the Sinai, the Israeli leader turned to his proposal for "self-rule for the Palestinian Arabs." He opened with the issue of sovereignty, which he acknowledged neither Israel nor Palestinians were willing to cede. Rather, by dealing with human beings and leaving the question of sovereignty open, Begin described the essence of his idea. "We give the Palestinian Arabs self-rule and the Palestinian Jews security." He read out the details of his proposal, which Sadat said he would take into consideration, pleased to have moved from procedural concerns to substantive negotiations.[115]

Later that evening, having reviewed the Israeli proposals, Sadat returned to the second meeting with the Israelis and was more critical. On the question of the Sinai, Sadat opposed any restrictions on Egyptian sovereignty. He rejected Begin's suggestion to keep airfields or Jewish settlements behind after a withdrawal. "If I tell my people that my friend Begin said there will be settlements in Sinai and some defense force to defend them, they will throw stones at me." As for the Palestinian question, Sadat continued, it was "a step, a real step. . . . But it is not sufficient as yet." He went on to describe the aspirations of Palestinian moderates for independence and the tight spot Egypt found itself as their defender in the Arab world given all the opposition to his trip to Jerusalem. The two leaders agreed this difference was a "problem." In revising the joint statement to the public about their meeting, Begin raised the issue of invoking 242 and withdrawal from the territories, which he could not sign onto given his divergent interpretation of the resolution. He also objected to the word "self-determination," if it signified a state. "This is the mortal danger of which I speak. We can use the word 'self-rule.'"[116]

Despite Sadat's rhetorical support for the Palestinians, his talks with Begin revealed a great deal of Egyptian antipathy toward the PLO and Palestinian nationalists. Begin expressed fears about security and the growing influence of the PLO on Israel's borders, framing his explanation in Cold War terms and appealing to Sadat's hostile view of the Soviet Union. "Some of the PLO men are Soviet agents," Begin remarked. "All of them," Sadat replied. The Egyptian president nevertheless upheld his commitment to representing Palestinian aspirations. "Still I must lead the Arab world. It is the leadership of Egypt historically that has always prevailed. It is in your interest as well as ours." [117]

The symbolic claims of leadership belied Sadat's narrower interests and willingness to concede to Begin in private, which Egypt's newly appointed foreign minister later criticized.[118] In concluding their talks, both leaders returned to the concept of self-rule, and Begin reiterated his opposition "to a Palestinian state of Arafat and [Fatah leader] Kaddumi." Sadat agreed, "As you know I have always been in favor of a link with Jordan—a federal or a confederal— would be decided before Geneva." It was a startling and crucial admission, paving the way for significant concessions in future negotiations.[119] Begin was relieved to hear it, and insisted the final Ismailia declaration only mention "self-rule" from the Israeli point of view. "We will not wound them by saying anything else," Begin added. "Self-determination means a state and that we cannot accept." Sadat again agreed, "But tomorrow I will be accused of having sold the Palestinian Arabs to Mr. Begin." Begin assured him it would not happen. "We must have the courage of decision," the Israeli prime minister concluded.[120]

Both the Israelis and the Egyptians were flatly dismissive of the Palestinian national movement and the existing leadership in the occupied territories. Dayan stressed that neither side wanted a Palestinian state, nor were there existing leaders in the territories that could make one. If either side committed in public to statehood, Dayan emphasized, Arafat would seek to come back to the territories, and the refugees would be transferred to Jericho, "a first stage for an attack on Israel." Sadat again concurred, having his own doubts about elements within the PLO: "I quite agree with you about the question of security and that the extremists should not be permitted, since they will cause trouble for all of us, especially after the Tripoli Conference. There is Arafat and that fanatic [George] Habbash [sic]. He has declared himself a Marxist-Leninist." In the same breath as he dismissed Palestinian hard-liners, like the head of the Popular Front for the Liberation of Palestine, Sadat was clearly conflicted given his role as a nominal protector of

Palestinian rights. "The difficulty is for me that I have to solve the Palestinian problem by self-determination."[121]

Aware of Egypt's discomfort with the PLO, the Israelis saw an opening. They pressed Sadat to negotiate the Palestinian problem independently with the Jordanians and the "Palestinian Arabs" in a manner that avoided self-determination. "We always speak with candor," Begin remarked. "All of us understand that self-determination means a state. Therefore, we shall suggest self-rule or home-rule or autonomy." In the context of a first official visit to Egypt, the Israeli prime minister was seeking out an alliance on the Palestinian question. He wanted Sadat to agree to a statement "in general terms about a just settlement of the Palestinian Arab problem" without specifying further.[122] Dayan added that Sadat could tell the Palestinian Arabs that Egypt would fight for self-determination as a face-saving mechanism. After further consultations, a decision was ultimately made to announce two different views of the Palestinian problem at the closing press conference and hold further meetings in Cairo and Jerusalem led by Egypt's new foreign minister, Mohammed Kamel.

Sadat's acquiescence to Israel's firm agenda for dealing with the Palestinians at Ismailia was a telling indicator of his overall approach to the elements of the negotiations that did not concern Egypt's bilateral interests. His mirroring of Israeli language and open use of Begin's term for the West Bank was clear in the public statements the next morning: "The position of Egypt is that in the West Bank and the Gaza Strip a Palestinian state should be established. The position of Israel is that Palestinian Arabs in Judea, Samaria and Gaza should enjoy 'self-rule.' We have agreed that because we have differed on this issue it should be discussed in the political committee of the Cairo Preparatory Conference."[123] In settling the Palestinian question via committee, while preparing bilateral Egyptian-Israeli negotiations at a subsequent conference in Cairo, the two parties had agreed to disagree on the question of Palestinian self-determination, deferring a decision but also giving Begin effective room to push forward with his own plans. Sadat's own advisors were appalled at the discussions, as well as Begin's relentless style. In his memoirs, Kamel later wrote with disdain how he watched the Israeli prime minister "bargaining and bartering (like a petty shopkeeper), dealing with things that did not belong to him in the first place, just as if the offer of a comprehensive, just and lasting peace were a passing summer cloud!"[124]

The Egyptian diplomat may not have liked his style, but Begin was deeply committed to his vision for the Palestinians. Returning to Jerusalem, he announced "Israel's Peace Plan" to the entire Israeli Knesset on December 28, 1977.[125] Begin's final version, like the earlier "home-rule" proposal presented to the Americans, British, and Egyptians, was nonterritorial, stressing autonomy through the election of administrative councils by Arab inhabitants of the territories. Begin was steadfast in his belief that such a vision would provide a solution in its own right, unlike American and Egyptian conceptions that imagined autonomy as a means to some greater form of Palestinian self-determination.

In his Knesset speech announcing the plan, Begin implored, "We have a right and a demand for sovereignty over these areas of *Eretz Yisrael* [the Land of Israel]. This is our land and it belongs to the Jewish nation rightfully." The prime minister opposed any engagement with the PLO, emphasizing that "we do not even dream of the possibility—if we are given the chalice to withdraw our military forces from Judea, Samaria and Gaza—of abandoning those areas to the control of the murderous organization that is called the PLO. . . . This is history's meanest murder organization, except for the armed Nazi organizations."[126] Begin's visceral opposition to the PLO, which was a recurring theme in all his public and private discussions, shaped his strong rejection of a Palestinian state.[127] As the plan emphasized, foreign and military policy would remain under Israeli control, ensuring that any rights granted to the Arab inhabitants of the territories would be of an extremely limited nature.

Begin's pretense of providing the local population with cultural and economic autonomy drew on an older colonial discourse of limited self-determination for native inhabitants. Simultaneously, the prime minister asserted that Israeli citizens maintained the right to purchase land and settle in the occupied territories. Begin's handwritten "unilateral declarations" appended at the bottom of his original draft plan made the collective impact of these limitations very clear.

A) Under no circumstances will Israel permit the establishment in Judea, Samaria and the Gaza District a "Palestinian State." Such a state would be a mortal danger to the civilian population of Israel and a grave peril to the free world.

B) After the end of the transitional period of five years Israel will claim its inalienable rights to sovereignty in the areas of Eretz Israel: Judea, Samaria and the Gaza District.[128]

These declarations contradicted the positions of both the Americans and the Egyptians in meetings with the Israeli prime minister before the Knesset announcement.

For Begin, the autonomy plan was a benevolent means to curtail Palestinian self-determination. He believed he had found a solution for the challenges that emerged after the conquest of 1967, one that could both bypass direct annexation of the territories and uphold liberal claims of protecting a national minority. It was a clear political vision, an alternative to the global struggle being waged by the PLO. Begin outlined his views with great conviction to *Time* magazine. "What is wrong with a Jewish majority living together with an Arab minority in peace, in human dignity, in equality of rights?" he wrote. "I believe that we can live together. It is not an occupied country as people understand that horrible term. We let them live in their homeland."[129]

From Tehran to Aswan

U.S. negotiators attempted to mediate between Sadat and Begin via third parties, trying to find a viable middle ground between the autonomy plan that Begin had articulated and a fully sovereign Palestinian state. Carter spent New Year's Day 1978 in Iran, where he was visiting the Shah as part of a nine-day tour of six nations. At the Pahlavi dynasty's Sa'dabad Palace in Tehran, he met with King Hussein of Jordan, who was also visiting the Iranian capital.[130] Hussein was dismayed by the autonomy plan, and skeptical of Carter's efforts after Sadat's trip. He feared the emergence of a separate peace between Egypt and Israel, and the discussions led to a sharp decline in U.S.-Jordanian relations.

Carter opened the discussion with the question of the West Bank, and Hussein agreed to accept "a disarmed and demilitarized" Palestinian entity, with possible UN presence, as part of an overall settlement. Carter presented the U.S. position, preferring "self-determination which does not involve a completely independent state." Hussein said based on the territorial withdrawal and a resolution to the Palestinian problem, he could agree to participate in negotiations, but he also stressed his increasingly isolated position in the Arab world. "As soon as you raise the West Bank," one of Hussein's advisors added, "the entire Palestinian question becomes an issue." "Jordan cannot absorb all the Palestinian problems," the advisor continued. "Their opponents would say that Jordan is talking for other Arabs without permission."[131] Signaling Hashemite fears of being co-opted by Israeli territorial designs, the exchange also underscored how the Palestinians themselves had been stripped of real agency to represent their own positions.

The growing disconnect between Begin's view of autonomy and the limits of Egyptian and Jordanian legitimacy in representing the Palestinians was laid bare in Carter's subsequent meeting with King Khalid of Saudi Arabia in Riyadh. Carter shared with King Khalid the content of his discussion with King Hussein and the overall progress in the Egyptian-Israeli discussions.[132] The Saudi monarch was more receptive to the idea of a Palestinian state, even one with international guarantees like Cyprus, and Carter stressed that the views he outlined about a Palestinian homeland related to Jordan was just a starting point. If the parties involved negotiated something closer to the Saudi view, the United States would not object. For now, Carter stressed, regional pressures constrained King Hussein. Since the 1974 Rabat Summit had led to a decision asserting the PLO as the sole representative of the Palestinian people, Jordan was not in a position to contradict the official PLO leadership. Carter believed the Palestinians in the West Bank and Gaza might accept such a plan as well but said that "he could not speak for the Palestinians."[133] Yet he would at least try to clarify, even rhetorically, American support for their political rights and claims to self-determination.

On the way back to Washington, the U.S. president stopped in the Egyptian city of Aswan to meet with Sadat and bolster the

Palestinian aspect of the peace negotiations. Carter would show his support for the increasingly beleaguered Egyptian president and discuss the principle of self-determination. In his remarks to the press after the meeting in Aswan, Carter addressed the Palestinian question directly: "There must be a resolution of the Palestinian problem in all its aspects. The problem must recognize the legitimate rights of the Palestinian people and enable the Palestinians to participate in the determination of their own future."[134] Relaying the rationale of his remarks to Vice President Mondale, who was meeting with Begin in Jerusalem at the time, Vance explained Carter's logic. The statement in Aswan was meant "to strengthen Sadat's hand against his Arab critics," in a manner that reflected both the U.S. position and some evolution in American thinking "without prejudging the self-determination question in any significant way." "It is not a viable position," Vance wrote to Mondale, "to insist that the Palestinians should have no say whatsoever in their future status, given the general acceptance in world opinion of the concept of self-determination."[135]

While the Aswan language was a powerful interjection on behalf of the Palestinians, the practical implications for a solution to their political plight were less clear. Even while acknowledging the necessity of engagement with the Palestinians in political terms, the Carter administration would still not speak directly with the PLO and was publicly critical of the organization. The efforts that Vance had initiated with Arafat on 242 were eclipsed by domestic debates over Soviet involvement, Sadat's unilateral trip to Jerusalem, and Begin's autonomy plan. In spite of these intervening developments, Yasser Arafat was pleased with the Aswan statement and he attempted once more to impress upon Carter his commitment to diplomatic engagement. At a meeting with congressional members of the House International Relations Committee in Damascus, including Congressman Paul Findley, Arafat and his PLO aides provided a message to Carter stressing a desire to maintain a moderate line, defending Carter's policies against hard-liners. Although there was no mention of the PLO at Aswan, Arafat professed a "glimmer of hope" in the statement.[136]

In his message to Carter, Arafat underscored his wider attempts at moderation within the PLO. He suggested that this was happening not only at the level of the leadership "but also among the rank-and-file of the Palestinians."[137] The PLO leader offered himself as a pragmatist who could work with the United States. After all the pressures of the previous months, he hoped that Carter "will not further push me into a corner because I would like to maintain my moderate balance. Otherwise, I have nothing to lose but my *Kufiyah* (Arab headdress)." Arafat's message was "self-serving," Brzezinski told Carter, "but may also contain a grain of truth." Either way, the NSC advisor noted, "our current posture of ignoring the PLO while concentrating on the Palestinian issue and encouraging moderate Palestinian voices to make themselves heard is the appropriate position for now."[138] This deliberate isolation of the main nationalist arm of the Palestinians was crippling for the Palestinian vision of statehood. In choosing to sideline the PLO, the United States was in effect signaling that the Israeli and Egyptian pursuit of bilateral peace could proceed without resolving competing claims over the occupied territories.

By the end of 1977, U.S. efforts had pivoted from the comprehensive vision for a regional settlement at a revived Geneva Conference to the much narrower bilateral negotiating track between Egypt and Israel. The PLO's struggle for self-determination was sacrificed in the process. After intensive American efforts to engage with the organization via intermediaries and secret channels in order to secure acceptance of UN resolution 242, barriers remained: the PLO was internally divided on the mechanisms of diplomacy, refusing to concede recognition of Israel without guarantees of a state in return. The worries were well-founded, as statehood was not ever fully on the table, and the language of self-determination and a "homeland" lacked the specificity to accommodate political control. In turning down the American entreaties but vowing to continue engaging diplomatically, the PLO was both signaling a red line and asserting its ongoing receptivity to negotiations.

The constraints under which the PLO operated were multi-faceted. Domestically, the backlash against Carter's inclusion of the Soviet Union in the Geneva track revealed a conservative Cold War opposition that was unhappy with the direction of American foreign policy in the aftermath of détente. There was also, however, a more visceral backlash from within the American Jewish political leadership about the possibility of Palestinian statehood. Strident antagonism toward the PLO was driven in part by the organization's commitment to armed struggle but also by a deeper discomfort with Palestinian claims to self-determination only a decade after the conquest of 1967. The American Jewish alignment with the Likud government fueled the hostility toward the PLO, given Begin's refusal to recognize Palestinian collective rights. His alternative commitment to the limited individual rights of "Arab residents of Judea and Samaria" was premised on a very different conception of Israel's presence in the territories, which was legitimated on ideological and national grounds as the exclusive purview of the Israeli state.

To mitigate critics who demanded action on the Palestinian question, Begin instead presented a sophisticated autonomy scheme as a benevolent solution. In reality, it was premised on continued Israeli control of the West Bank and Gaza Strip, as well as the assertion of a right to build settlements in the same space Palestinians were claiming self-determination. This was a clear repudiation of legal jurists who had explicitly advised the Eshkol government that these settlements were illegal under international law.[139] Yet the Israeli government's introduction of autonomy, and the somewhat benign reaction of American and British interlocutors who accepted that it could be a starting point for negotiations over the territories, served to embolden Prime Minister Begin in his pursuit of an alternative vision for the Palestinian future.

Crucially, Begin's advance would have been impossible without the concessions of Egyptian president Anwar al-Sadat. More than the other factors, Sadat's unilateral trip to Jerusalem—whether for domestic economic reasons, strategic interests, frustration with Geneva, or a desire for the grand gesture that would secure the return of Sinai once and for all—served as a major stumbling block for the PLO. Beyond the clear embrace of a bilateral track with Israel, Sadat's opening of a dialogue without clarity on the fate of the Palestinians set in motion a process of their political exclusion. His hostility toward the PLO and indication of support for a federation with Jordan in conversations with Begin at Ismailia encouraged Israeli designs in the West Bank and undercut Arafat at a crucial juncture in the Palestinian struggle for national independence.

President Carter's own approach to Palestinian aspirations was not always clear. While he had an aversion to outright statehood, he was sympathetic to the realization of Palestinian political rights and wanted to find a middle ground that could accommodate a comprehensive peace. Even as the PLO was marginalized, Carter's trip to Aswan indicated a commitment to adjudicating Palestinian demands with promises about "the legitimate rights of the Palestinian people." This could be clarified along divergent lines, however, from outright territorial self-determination to transitional arrangements that assumed Palestinians were not quite ready to govern themselves, as Secretary Vance had suggested.[140]

While Sadat's turn to bilateral talks with Israel had come as a surprise to the Americans, Carter continued to believe that a regional peace deal was possible and felt the United States was the ideal broker between the parties. In his memoir, the president noted that Egypt and Israel could not independently resolve basic problems like the Palestinian question, Israeli territorial withdrawal, and regional peace without American assistance. "The process was breaking down again," Carter wrote, "it remained necessary for the United States to continue playing a leading role in resolving the basic Middle East questions."[141] This U.S. role as mediator would reach its height with the emergence of the Camp David talks a few months later. But well before the summit had even begun, American aims at evenhandedness had already been compromised. With the introduction of autonomy, Sadat's concessionary negotiating, and the U.S. sidelining of the PLO, Palestinian aspirations were swiftly losing out to Israel's alternative vision for the territories.

CHAPTER FOUR

Camp David and the Triumph of Palestinian Autonomy

ON MARCH 11, 1978, Palestinian commandos from Yasser Arafat's Fatah wing of the PLO landed on the shore north of Tel Aviv. They had planned to seize a luxury hotel in Israel's coastal city and take hostages, but the arrival boats had missed the original destination. After killing an American photographer, the militants hijacked a taxi and then an Egged bus along the coastal highway.[1] The ensuing gunfight led to the killing of over thirty civilians, including thirteen children, and was characterized at the time as "the worst terrorist attack in Israel's history."[2] The attack, known in Israel as the "Coastal Road Massacre," had been planned by Fatah leader Khalil al-Wazir (known as Abu Jihad) and was aimed in part at scuttling the peace talks between Sadat and Begin and retaliating for the Mossad assassination of PLO leaders in Lebanon in 1973.[3] Fatah's actions were also partly intended to assert the centrality of the national movement as it was being marginalized, with the ebb and flow of militant action highlighting deep struggles within the PLO over its diplomatic strategy.[4]

In response to the Coastal Road Massacre, the Israeli government launched Operation Litani three days later.[5] The Begin government targeted PLO bases in South Lebanon with over 25,000 soldiers, subjecting a large area up to the Litani River to heavy bombardment with shelling and air strikes. The incursion led to the deaths of at least 1,000 Palestinian and Lebanese civilians.[6] The Carter administration, seeking to limit regional escalation, pushed back against this operation, but the damage was extensive.[7] Aside from civilian casualties, Israel's actions pushed the PLO northward from their bases and increased tensions in the Lebanese civil war that had started three years earlier. It also led to the internal displacement of at least 100,000 people from South Lebanon and the establishment of a "security zone" in the south patrolled by the South Lebanon Army (SLA). Carter was deeply involved in ending the violence in Lebanon by spearheading a UN resolution that led to the establishment of the UN Interim Force in Lebanon (UNIFIL). The violence served as a precursor to the much larger invasion of Lebanon that would follow in 1982 and signaled Israel's intention to fight the PLO across border areas.

Both the terror attack and the Litani incursion coincided with a difficult period of U.S. engagement with the wider region. A series of domestic debates had erupted over aircraft sales to Egypt and Saudi Arabia in February, part of a "package deal" that ultimately passed through Congress. Carter expended a great deal of political capital to push these deals forward, resulting in weakened domestic support and reduced chances for a comprehensive peace in the Middle East.[8] With a midterm election approaching in November, it would not be easy for the Carter administration to confront the unresolved questions raised by Sadat and Begin's bilateral talks.

After clashing directly with Begin on the issue of settlements in late March, Carter struggled through the summer to advance negotiations over the Middle East. Through internal discussions, the president decided to invite the Israeli and Egyptian leaders to join him for a presidential summit in September, hoping that a bilateral framework could provide an opening toward a comprehensive regional peace. The agreements reached at Camp David fell short of these aims. While successfully negotiating the first treaty between Israel and an Arab state, the summit also enabled the Begin government to secure Israel's hold over the occupied Palestinian territories with the formalization of a separate autonomy track. The concurrent expansion of the settlement project and the onset of negotiations over self-rule for the Palestinians (without their participation) signaled the triumph of an influential idea that would halt any political or diplomatic progress toward meaningful self-determination for the Palestinian people.

The Emergence of Camp David

The Begin government had argued for months that UN resolution 242 did not apply to the West Bank. On the eve of a trip that Begin was making to the United States in March, his minister of agriculture and settlement czar, Ariel Sharon, announced an increase in the number of settlements. The move ignited fierce domestic opposition in Israel. Defense Minister Ezer Weizman, visiting Washington ahead of Begin, telephoned the prime minster and threatened to resign. "If you do not stop those settlements," Weizman shouted, "I will personally come back and do so."[9] Weizman had been engaged in a bitter fight with hard-line members of the ruling party, who were suspicious of his diplomatic efforts with Egypt.[10] Even some American Jewish leaders spoke out about the settlement announcement, as divisions inside the Jewish community deepened around the Lebanese incursion. One prominent Jewish philanthropist, Laurence Tisch, criticized the Israeli government's policy publicly. "If Begin insists on pressing the settlements issue, he will lose every last American. There is no justification for this position," Tisch remarked.[11]

On March 22, a heated meeting between Begin and Carter at the White House underscored the growing policy differences between the two leaders.[12] The Israeli prime minister's dismissive attitude toward UN resolution 242 particularly angered the Americans, and "Carter was clearly in a fighting mood." The president delivered scathing remarks to Begin, telling him that he was "not willing to stop expansion or the creation of new settlements." In private meetings, pro-Israeli senators like Jacob Javits and Clifford Case wholeheartedly agreed with the president that Begin should be taken to task for his irresponsible policies in the occupied territories.[13] Even with the forceful reaction, Carter had limited capital to expend on a direct confrontation with the Israeli government over settlements. Vance described the tension that framed the meeting, and the impact of the terror attack, which strengthened Begin's hand. "The possibility of getting Begin to alter his positions on the West Bank and Palestinian questions," Vance later wrote, "was virtually eliminated."[14] Instead, Begin promoted his autonomy plan, insisting once again that UN resolution 242 did not apply to all the territories.

While Sadat had broken off negotiations with Begin in January 1978 over this very issue, his stance began to soften by the spring. In a weekend meeting between Presidents Carter and Sadat and their wives, Rosalynn and Jehan, at Camp David in February, the beginning of a significant shift in priorities had become evident to American officials. Rather than work toward a comprehensive peace that would include the Palestinian issue, Sadat appeared increasingly willing to settle for a bilateral agreement to ensure the return of the Sinai. Despite the rhetoric and appearance of defending the Palestinian right to self-determination, there was little substantive Egyptian commitment to offering clear alternative proposals on the future of the West Bank and Gaza.[15]

This was a stark departure from the approach articulated in Sadat's November 1977 Jerusalem speech. An overriding desire to secure U.S. backing for arms and economic aid, as well as an aversion to detail in countering Begin's restrictive autonomy proposal, chipped away at the Egyptian leader's firm position on resolving the Palestinian question and left officials in the United States considering new avenues to break the diplomatic stalemate between the two countries. As one NSC official explained to Carter in May, "The central idea that he [Sadat] is now working with involves a virtual abandonment on his part of the concept of Palestinian self-determination or Palestinian statehood in return for an explicit Israel commitment to withdraw from the West Bank/Gaza."[16] This sidelining of substantive discussions over the meaning of Palestinian self-determination generated a great deal of internal dissent among Sadat's advisors, as well as wider Arab anger.[17]

The Egyptian president's flexibility impressed the Americans, who gradually understood that Sadat would moderate his demands in order to achieve a viable settlement with Israel. Carter's legal counsel, Robert Lipshutz, had long been questioning the insistence of Sadat and fellow Arab leaders on Palestinian statehood. "They all fully recognize that it's in their worst interest to see that happen," Lipshutz told an interviewer in February 1978. "I think their public posture is in their judgment required for the time being because of their own inter-Arab relationships."[18] In his own private assessment, Carter's counsel argued that "the best outcome of all that is to end up in a federation of some type with Jordan."[19] While other U.S. officials focused on a transitional regime in the West Bank and Gaza, there was clear movement toward the deferral of a decision on the fate of the territories "while the parties experimented with self-rule in the West Bank and Gaza."[20] The United States would gauge the respective positions of Egypt and Israel, and then consider introducing specific parameters for negotiations.

In July 1978, Vance hosted the Egyptian and Israeli foreign ministers at Leeds Castle in Kent. This was a critical meeting on the road to Camp David, as the U.S. secretary of state reframed the nature of the American role. Rather than mediate between the parties, the Carter administration would offer a proposal "for a comprehensive settlement, including arrangements for peace between Egypt and Israel and an autonomy process of the West Bank." As Vance later explained, U.S. officials drafted a document that eventually became "the basis of the Camp David framework."[21] In a bid to break the Egyptian-Israeli negotiating impasse, Vance then flew to the Middle East to privately invite both leaders to the United States on behalf of the president.[22] Sadat and Begin readily accepted Carter's invitation, hoping to cobble together a mutually beneficial agreement for Egypt and Israel. Preparations were made for a September summit, which would attract a great deal of global and domestic attention.

Immediately after the summit was announced, White House advisors began to reconfigure their comprehensive peace plan in order to focus on specific aspects of an agreement between Egypt and Israel. They still spoke, however, of tackling interrelated issues like the West Bank and Gaza, the status of the settlements, UN resolution 242, and the fate of the Palestinians. In his formulation of a negotiating strategy for Camp David, National Security Advisor Brzezinski told Carter that he would "have to persuade Begin to make some substantive concessions, while convincing Sadat to settle for less than an explicit Israeli commitment to full withdrawal and Palestinian self-determination."[23] Beyond an agreement between Israel and Egypt, Brzezinski stressed the need for "general self-government for the Palestinians."[24] Brzezinski also urged the president to get both leaders to accept the "Aswan language on Palestinian rights," a reference to Carter's statement in Egypt that January recognizing "the legitimate rights of the Palestinian people" and calling for "Palestinians to participate in the determination of their own future."[25]

American preparatory memos for Camp David clearly established the desire for Israeli territorial withdrawal from the West Bank and Gaza Strip, a genuine settlement moratorium, and an adjudication of the Palestinian question. By combining the Aswan formulation with other priorities, U.S. officials worked to solidify a viable approach to resolving regional conflict, but it promised considerably less than the comprehensive elements of the February 1977 position laid out soon after Carter entered office. Alongside the reality of the Begin election and Israel's vision for autonomy, Sadat's trip to Jerusalem had served to undercut those ambitious plans. Washington had not fully abandoned the rhetorical commitment of securing a wider settlement, but the impact of the preceding months was unmistakable. Just before leaving for the United States, Begin reiterated his precondition for negotiating, which included "no withdrawal to the 1967 borders" and continued Israeli "military control of the West Bank and Gaza under any interim agreement."[26] It was clear that his vision for a settlement remained aimed at Egypt alone.

The Meaning of the Accords

Thirteen days of meetings took place between the Egyptian and Israeli delegations in the presidential retreat at Catoctin Mountain Park in Maryland from September 5 to 17, 1978. While shielded from the public eye, there are numerous accounts of the dramatic proceedings and the fraught moments of tension from a wide array of participants.[27] At its core, however, Camp David's objectives were cast before it even began, and were broadly in line with Israeli strategic thinking. Vance and Brzezinski both hoped that "Carter could persuade Begin to make some concessions on the Palestinian

FIGURE 4.1. "Anwar Sadat, Jimmy Carter and Menachem Begin at the Camp David Accords Signing Ceremony." September 17, 1978. White House Staff Photographers Collection at the Jimmy Carter Library.

question" in order to secure Sadat's agreement on peace with Israel. In the view of NSC advisor William Quandt, the American president actually had in mind the narrower objective of reaching an Israeli-Egyptian agreement, "with or without much of a link to the Palestinian issue."[28] Rather than seek the restoration of the 1967 borders, Carter and his team focused on the return of the Sinai Peninsula to Egypt. This "more Israel-friendly objective," as one recent account explains, ultimately brought together "a Sinai agreement with an understanding over the West Bank and Gaza that built on Begin's autonomy scheme."[29] It may not have looked that way on the eve of the summit, Quandt later reflected, but Carter understood what animated Sadat. Despite his vocal insistence on a comprehensive peace, Sadat "would not continue to insist on much for the Palestinians, at least not at the expense of recovering Egyptian territory."[30]

The announcement of the final Camp David Accords, after nearly two weeks of discussion, reflected the bottom line of each party. While Begin first stonewalled on the demilitarization of the Sinai Peninsula and the return of Jewish settlements to Egyptian control (nearly derailing the negotiations as Sadat rushed to leave), the Israeli prime minister conceded on relinquishing Israeli airfields and agreed for the Knesset to vote on the evacuation of Sinai settlements. This yielded *A Framework for the Conclusion of a Peace Treaty between Egypt and Israel*, the second of the two core provisions signed at the summit's conclusion. It laid out the path to a bilateral peace agreement premised on the phased return of the Sinai Peninsula to Egypt in exchange for the normalization of relations with Israel as well as the opening of the Suez Canal to Israeli ships. This was the core of the final agreement signed in March 1979, providing Sadat with the territory Egypt had lost in 1967, but also securing the U.S. backing he had long sought to achieve. For Israel, the first formal recognition from an Arab state was a milestone achievement, and it neutralized any military threat from the southwest. Since it was not dependent on broader linkage with progress on other fronts, it also provided the Begin government with an opportunity to consolidate Israel's territorial hold on the remaining areas acquired in 1967: East Jerusalem, the West Bank, the Gaza Strip, and the Golan Heights.

The first of the two agreements, *A Framework for Peace in the Middle East*, built directly on Begin's autonomy plan and focused on the West Bank and Gaza Strip. Largely sidestepping broader regional relations, the framework called on "Egypt, Israel, Jordan and the representatives of the Palestinian people" to "participate in negotiations on the resolution of the Palestinian problem in all its aspects."[31] Exactly what this meant in political or territorial terms was left intentionally vague, instead calling on the parties to decide on a process guaranteeing full autonomy to Palestinians within a period of five years.[32] In the interim, the framework contained a provision for negotiations to establish an autonomous Self-Governing Authority (SGA) in the West Bank and Gaza Strip. What sort of entity might emerge was unclear, as was the extent of an Israeli withdrawal from the territories. Rather than restore the pre-1967 borders in line with Carter's comprehensive plans of 1977, the Americans had turned away from a fight over broader territorial withdrawal at Camp David. Under severe pressure from Begin and his negotiating team during the talks, the United States backed down from a confrontation over the precise application of UN Security Council Resolution 242 to the West Bank and Gaza

Strip.[33] Through deliberately ambiguous language in crafting this text, Carter and his advisors were able to secure Sadat's and Begin's support in the waning hours of the summit.[34]

Begin kept his eye firmly on the red lines he had outlined throughout his talks in 1977 and 1978: there would be no withdrawal from the West Bank and Gaza Strip, and no Palestinian state. While the first of the two frameworks included specific language to "recognize the legitimate rights of the Palestinian people and their just requirements," this lacked substantive meaning.[35] Explicitly, the accords did not include any reference to self-determination: the result of the diplomatic effort Begin and his advisors had made to secure the term's exclusion. He also did not have to accept the application of UN resolution 242 "to all fronts of the conflict," and he did not retreat on Israel's claim to sovereignty in Jerusalem. The autonomy provisions that Begin had introduced as a "solution" to the Palestinian issue in 1977 were incorporated in the final Camp David framework as a necessary concession to safeguard the success of a bilateral agreement and preserve Israel's hold on the territories. While Sadat had spoken openly of a resolution of the Palestinian question in the West Bank, Begin and his advisors successfully dislodged the issue from the agreement on bilateral relations. In this manner, the pursuit of a peace deal with Egypt had also become a means to avoid peace with the Palestinians.[36]

Critics of the Camp David Summit gradually recognized this outcome, speaking out forcefully against Sadat's perfidious behavior toward the Palestinians.[37] His own advisors dissented from the final accords, with his foreign minister, Mohammed Kamel, boycotting the signing ceremony and resigning from office.[38] In brief remarks prior to the official signing on September 17, President Carter reiterated the importance of an agreement on some form of Palestinian self-determination. He reminded his audience "of the hopes and dreams of the people who live in the West Bank and Gaza Strip."[39] During his warmly received address before a special joint session of the U.S. Congress on September 18, Carter expanded on the "painful human question of the fate of the Palestinians," suggesting another way forward. "The Camp David agreement guarantees that the Palestinian people may participate in the resolution of the Palestinian problem in all its aspects," Carter told the assembled lawmakers. "Israel has agreed, has committed themselves, that the legitimate rights of the Palestinian people will be recognized."[40] But how exactly would those rights be secured? What did the phrasing mean in practical terms?

While the Camp David Accords represented the first moment since the establishment of Israel that Palestinians were promised some form of "rights," the specifics were never spelled out. In the context of the PLO's wider struggle for global recognition, Carter's promise could be viewed as a great rhetorical advancement for the perennially stateless people.[41] But while this semantic recognition of Palestinian "rights" seemed a mark of progress, it did not in any practical way satisfy Palestinian aspirations for independence. This gap between the rhetoric of a political solution and a reality on the ground was acutely apparent to the Palestinians themselves. The PLO Executive Committee announced its "total rejection" of the accords soon after they were signed, and leaders from the territories declared that the idea of autonomy was an "open plot" against Palestinian rights, especially self-determination.[42] PLO chairman Yasser Arafat warned that any supporters of Sadat would "pay a high price," later describing the autonomy idea as "no more than managing the sewers."[43]

The PLO had reason to worry about Camp David. As had been the case before the summit, neither the Israelis nor the Americans would support a PLO-run Palestinian state or self-determining entity. This called into question the tangible outcome of the peace agreement beyond Egyptian-Israeli normalization. While the significance of such a bilateral agreement should not be diminished—it served to neutralize regional hostilities and the immediate threat of war, inaugurating a new era of relations between Israel and Egypt— the peace came at a great cost. Sadat had sacrificed Palestinian rights, which he had so vocally defended months earlier. U.S. officials understood the "free hand" Israel had gained over the occupied territories. In his assessment of Camp David, NSC advisor William Quandt suggested that while Israel gave up territory captured from Egypt in 1967, they secured retention of the West Bank: "For Begin, Sinai had been sacrificed, but Eretz Israel had been won."[44]

One of the major sources of friction to emerge in the immediate aftermath of the summit confirmed Palestinian fears. This was the status of settlement building in the occupied territories, which Carter had assured the joint session of Congress would end. "After the signing of this framework last night and during the negotiations concerning the establishment of the Palestinian self-government," Carter told the assembled lawmakers, "no new Israeli settlements will be established in this area."[45] Contrary to Carter's assertion, settlements would burgeon soon after. Prime Minister Begin, insisting he only agreed to a three-month freeze, had never actually conceded the Israeli "right" to build in the West Bank.[46]

Several days after the signing of the Camp David Accords, the Israeli prime minister proclaimed on American television that Israel would remain in the West Bank indefinitely and would continue its settlement program. This declaration flew in the face of the proposed five-year transition period and attempts to reach a settlement moratorium discussed in an early draft of the agreement. But Begin had only agreed to a more limited side letter. At the time, Carter saw the settlement setback as a secondary problem in light of the agreement that had been achieved. He therefore largely bowed out of a confrontation with the prime minister over this matter, declaring it "just an honest difference of opinion."[47] Two weeks later, the president was asked about the inflexibility of the Israelis, and he reaffirmed that the settlements were indeed "illegal" and "an obstacle to peace." He did not believe that "this one issue, if unresolved expeditiously, would prevent the peace treaty between Israel and Egypt."[48]

Forging an Egyptian-Israeli Peace

In the six months that followed the September summit, diplomats from Egypt and Israel worked toward the implementation of the Camp David Accords. Sadat tried to secure a linkage between Egyptian-Israeli peace and movement on Palestinian autonomy, but the Israelis were not amenable to his proposals. The Egyptian leader was the subject of caustic anger and boycott from Arab states, including Syria, Iraq, and Libya.[49] Carter was under increasing pressure to finalize the negotiations, especially as the Iranian Revolution had broken out in January 1979. The turmoil led to the downfall of Mohammad Reza Shah, Carter's close ally, and the rise of Grand Ayatollah Ruhollah Khomeini to power in February. It was not a hospitable time for continuing the Middle East negotiations.

It was also not the time for direct engagement with the Palestinians. At a White House cabinet meeting in January 1979, Secretary Vance raised the possibility of establishing relations with the PLO to generate substantive movement in the talks. Zbigniew Brzezinski recounted that Vice President Walter Mondale, a strong ally of Israel, was furious, while "[political advisor] Ham[ilton] Jordan—always mindful of the influence of the Jewish community in U.S. domestic politics—cheerfully quipped that perhaps one of us might want to be the first U.S. Ambassador to the West Bank, because in two years we would all be unemployed."[50] When two administration officials mentioned offhandedly to a congressional subcommittee that the United States might seek to engage with the organization, Begin drafted a cable to Vance denouncing the idea: "I would naturally assume, that the United States Government, even without consulting us, would wish to refrain from having any contact with this terrorist organization whose method is the murder of innocent civilians, women and children, and whose purpose is the destruction of the state of Israel."[51]

Regional upheaval in 1979 compounded the difficulties facing implementation of the peace treaty. Brzezinski, who focused on this unfolding geopolitical context, voiced concern that a broader strategy had been lost in the negotiations. Carter's National Security Advisor concluded that peace negotiations should relate more directly to the unfolding developments in Iran and new alignments in the Arab world, which included a weakening Saudi Arabia.[52] For Egypt, these new alignments added to Sadat's troubles. Increasingly isolated and besieged by Arab denunciations of Camp David, the Egyptian president sent his prime minister, Mustafa Khalil, to the White House. In a meeting with President Carter and Israeli foreign minister Dayan on February 25, Khalil warned of the delay in the implementation of the accords: "Unless we conclude an agreement now it will be difficult to do so in a month and impossible in two or three. Our region is threatened." The specter of an Arab summit before the conclusion of a peace treaty was worrying to Sadat and his advisors. Their concern over Iranian and

Arab reaction had further minimized the Palestinian issue. "We cannot isolate ourselves from the Arab world," Khalil remarked in the White House. Carter agreed, and pushed for swift action on the peace treaty with Israel. "Once it is done the other Arab countries cannot reject Egypt."[53]

The Israelis were also mindful of regional tensions. On March 2, Israeli prime minister Begin met with President Carter at the White House to discuss the final stages of the negotiations with Egypt. "The world is in turmoil and the Soviets are taking over by proxy," Begin told the U.S. president, referring in part to the Iranian Revolution. Begin also pointed to internal military developments in Iraq and the presence of Soviet advisors in Damascus, which he claimed had put Israel in a precarious position. "We see this as an awakening of Islamic fanaticism, just as in the Middle Ages. It could be contagious," Begin exclaimed. The Israeli prime minister, invoking a refrain that would be repeated with increasing frequency in the 1980s, continued, "The United States has only one stable ally in the Middle East, and this is Israel, whose stability is inherent because it is a democracy." By appealing to his U.S. interlocutors as the guarantors of regional stability, Begin linked Israeli strategic aims with American regional interests. "Israel can do whatever is necessary to prevent Saudi Arabia from being taken over by Communism," the prime minister promised. "We cannot lose Saudi oil to Communism."[54]

Turning his attention to the substantive disagreements over the negotiations with Egypt, Begin also emphasized the central role of Palestinian autonomy in the treaty's delay. The provision over Palestinian self-rule had become a point of disagreement between Egyptian and Israeli negotiators, and remained the core obstacle to Begin's movement on the implementation of a bilateral peace treaty with Sadat. Israel's prime minister stressed his fear that a Palestinian state might emerge from the autonomy provisions he himself had introduced. "People go around in Judea and Samaria and say to the Arabs that they should accept autonomy since it is only a first step towards a Palestinian state," Begin explained to Carter. "We know this from reliable sources. Had we thought that out of autonomy a Palestinian state would arise we would never have suggested it. We will not accept a Palestinian state." Instead, after a five-year interim period, the prime minister argued, "we shall claim our sovereign right over those areas."[55]

Begin also invoked broader regional changes as a basis for his deep opposition to statehood. The PLO had openly backed the Iranian Revolution, which was a direct blow to Israel's long-standing alliance with the Shah. Arafat and a large delegation flew to Tehran soon after the revolution, and in a welcome ceremony they were handed the keys to the former Israeli Embassy, remade as the local office of the PLO. Prime Minister Mehdi Bazargan's cabinet broke off relations with Israel, ordering diplomats and citizens to leave the country.[56] "What is a Palestinian state?" Begin asked Carter rhetorically. "Arafat was in Tehran. He took over our embassy. He raised a flag. He said: 'I feel now I am near Jerusalem.'" This development was a nonstarter for the prime minister. "We must have ironclad guarantees that there will be no Palestinian state. I believe, Mr. President, that you have said so in public."[57]

In Begin's reading of the Camp David Accords, the notion of autonomy was never intended to apply to the territory itself. The Israeli leader was deeply concerned that the United States would attempt to secure territorial control for Arabs in the West Bank and Gaza Strip by agreeing to a more expansive view of autonomy. "If the self-governing authority provides full autonomy to the West Bank, this means that the territory has full autonomy, and Israel will have no right to be there. But we do have that right, because this is the land of Israel."[58] A heated back-and-forth ensued between Israeli negotiators and their U.S. counterparts in the White House Cabinet Room over the exact meaning of the accords. "No one is trying to trick Israel by slipping in a word here or there," an exasperated Carter replied. "We are not scheming against Israel; we are not trying to hurt you; and neither is Sadat."[59] The negotiations over Camp David's regional framework had hit up against two divergent views of the territory on which to enact some provision of self-rule for the Palestinians. In Israel's configuration, which Begin worked to reify, the land itself was reserved for Jewish settlement and therefore separated from any autonomy arrangement.[60]

As part of a final effort to secure the peace treaty with Egypt, the U.S. president traveled to Cairo and Jerusalem several days later.

Carter's March 11 discussion with Begin and Ariel Sharon underscored his growing concern that Israel's concept of Palestinian autonomy provided cover for burgeoning settlement expansion in the occupied territories. Sitting in the prime minister's office, Carter told the Israelis of his worry that the discussions over autonomy were advancing without Palestinian or Jordanian participation, which signaled, "in effect, that almost in perpetuity Israel can retain complete control over the West Bank area." He added the concern that Sharon, with Begin's explicit support, indicated he would put "a million Jewish settlers on the West Bank," which would make it "impossible" for the Palestinians to participate in the discussions. "I have no way of looking into your hearts and souls and see how deeply you want to proceed with the self-government that the Prime Minister himself proposed," Carter told Sharon and Begin. "But something has to be done to assure those who live on the West Bank and Gaza."[61]

The Israeli prime minister responded with a robust defense of his vision for autonomy, reinforcing the notion that it was compatible with settlement expansion and insisting it could not lead to a state. "I believe it is one of the most beautiful, human ideas ever proposed by Zionism and Judaism, because we were a persecuted people and we understand another people, and we want not to interfere in their daily affairs." In using this rhetoric, Begin posited the quotidian needs of Palestinian residents as apolitical, in contrast to the more politically expansive, temporally dynamic, and developmental needs of Israel. These needs also rested on an argument of security, which cohered in Begin's mind with Jewish settlements: "What we need is security, and may I respectfully say that if my friend, the Minister of Agriculture [Ariel] Sharon spoke about a million Jews in Judea and Samaria, he didn't mean any wrong, Mr. President. The number of Jews living in Judea and Samaria is not an obstacle to the autonomy for the Arab inhabitants." By invoking a benevolent image of coexistence, Begin sought to justify Israeli national dominance over Palestinians. "Why can't Jews and Arabs live together?" Begin asked. "In Haifa they live together; in Nazareth they live together. This is the idea: to live together. But the Arabs will have autonomy. We will not interfere with their affairs. We want to make sure that there is security and there is no Palestinian state."

Sharon, the architect of Israel's settlement expansion in the Likud government, reinforced Begin's point. Drawing on a long-standing trope that denied Palestinian national identity in a particular geographic space, Sharon asserted that Jordan was the Palestinian state. "We want the autonomy; we are ready to go very far, but there will never be a second Palestinian state, and I think it is important to make it clear now, in order to prevent misunderstanding in the future."[62] Equating the settlers with Palestinian Arabs in Israel, Sharon asked Carter how he could prevent Jews from settling beyond the 1967 borders, given the number of Palestinian Arabs within Israel itself. "Altogether in this part of the world, I don't see any possibility whatsoever to draw any geographical line which can divide between Jewish population and Arab population, because we live here together." Such logic of equivalence between settlers and the Palestinian citizens of Israel suggested a retroactive justification of population exchange and the simultaneous denial of an inter-state occupation beyond the 1967 borders.

As the driver of the settlement project, Sharon did not shy away from his boastful prediction of one million Jewish settlers in the territories: "Believe me, Mr. President, when I use this figure of one million, saying that in 20–30 years I hope that one million Jews will live there, Mr. President, I can assure you, they will live there. There's nothing to do about it." Sharon did not distinguish between areas of the West Bank or East Jerusalem either. "They will live there and if we said that we believe that in Jerusalem, what we call the Greater Jerusalem, it is a crucial problem for us, to have one million Jews, they will live there. . . . We were very careful to settle Jews," Sharon concluded, "and that is what we are doing now."[63] The exchange of views highlights how Israel successfully delineated the limits of its position on Palestinian autonomy while asserting the centrality of settlement expansion in the context of negotiations over a peace treaty with Egypt. Carter had long opposed these settlements but also sought to avoid confrontation with Israel in order to secure the signing of the treaty. In part, the pressure to complete the deal amid a difficult domestic and regional context served to leave these boasts unchallenged.

The American president understood that the Egyptian-Israeli negotiations had exposed two competing political projects and that the Israeli view was far more restrictive when it came to autonomy. Yet he reminded Begin and Sharon that the Americans had played a mediating role that had worked in their favor. "I think you would agree that we have never put any pressure on Israel. We have never forced or encouraged Israel in any way to sign an agreement that was detrimental to the best interests of your own country."[64] With these words of assurance, Carter warned Begin not to drag out the Knesset debate about the final language of the treaty or to get bogged down in the autonomy issue, because it would weaken Sadat. In the president's words, "My belief is that the whole agreement might very well come apart."[65]

On the following morning, Carter was offered the chance to meet the full Israeli cabinet to secure approval for the peace deal. Begin, flanked by his ministers, used the opportunity to reiterate his narrow view of autonomy: "It should be clear to everyone that a so-called Palestinian state is out of the question for us. What we decided on at Camp David is autonomy, full autonomy for the Arab inhabitants." Once again, the prime minister portrayed his support for autonomy as a benevolent act. "I will say today in the Knesset to my colleagues and my opponents that I believe it is a fine concept of Judaism and Zionism, which proves our liberal approach to the problems of another national group."[66]

This "liberal" approach rested on a very particular definition of Palestinian Arabs. "We recognize the Arab nationality in our country, as you know," Begin explained. "In our identity cards, it is written Nationality: Jew, or Arab. We recognize the Arab nationality as such. And therefore it is no problem for us to recognize the rights of the Palestinian Arabs." At the same time, Begin was quick to assert Israeli Jewish rights "in Judea and Samaria and the Gaza Strip," adding "this is what we wrote in the Camp David agreement."[67] For Begin, there was no Palestinian identity specific or indigenous to historic Palestine. Rather, Palestinians ("Arab inhabitants") were a minority group in an Israeli nation that was entirely sovereign over all the territory between the Mediterranean and the Jordan River. Israel's occupation would both expand its borders and serve as the definitive means to prevent the emergence of a Palestinian state.

Carter soon flew to Egypt and got Sadat's agreement on the final language of the treaty. Many of the Egyptian leader's initial demands on Palestinian self-rule were scuttled or ignored, with little substantive protest. The decision was made to ratify the peace agreement and fulfill its comprehensive aspects regarding the Palestinian issue by starting autonomy negotiations within one month. This was affirmed in a side letter negotiated in Jerusalem before Carter's departure and eventually signed by Begin and Sadat.[68] While Carter was in Egypt, Begin gave an interview with Israel Radio on the evening news expressing his optimism about the signing of a treaty and the prospect of autonomy, reminding his listeners of his long-standing position: "There will be no border through Eretz Israel."[69]

On March 26, Carter hosted the peace treaty signing between Sadat and Begin in Washington on the White House lawn. It formalized the bilateral peace agreement between Egypt and Israel and reiterated the language for autonomy talks. Egypt had secured U.S. backing and left the orbit of the Soviet Union, flush with American military and economic aid and no longer bogged down in regional discord with Israel. While the deal was welcomed across the United States and in Israel, the PLO leadership was bitterly opposed. Speaking to a group of military recruits in Beirut's Sabra refugee camp on the day of the signing, as effigies of the three leaders burned in front of him, Arafat vowed to loud applause to "chop off the hands" of Carter, Sadat, and Begin.[70] The PLO's official statement noted that Sadat "sold Palestine to the Israelis under the cover of 'self-rule' for the Palestinians living under occupation while neglecting the Palestinians living in the refugee camps for 30 years. Sadat sold himself, his people, the Palestinian People and the Arab lands in return for a mere 1.8 billion U.S. dollars. . . . It is in fact not a peace treaty at all but a military pact between Egypt, Israel and the USA which has endeavored to recognize the region after the loss of Iran."[71] Drawing loud applause in his Beirut speech, Arafat declared, "I shall finish off American interests in the Middle East."[72]

The Egyptian-Israeli peace agreement spurred a wider geopolitical realignment. There was widespread Arab denunciation, and the Arab League severed relations with Egypt and moved their headquarters from Cairo to Tunis.[73] The Soviet Union, which had moved closer to the PLO in the aftermath of Camp David, was also furious with the signing of the treaty. In a personal letter to the U.S. president, Soviet leader Leonid Brezhnev outlined in some detail his deep antipathy toward the separate settlement between Israel and Egypt. Part of the reaction related to Cold War rivalry, as Brezhnev accused Carter of "solving questions on the sly, bypassing the Soviet Union."[74] But Brezhnev's most pointed criticisms concerned the fate of the Palestinians.

> Let us face the truth. All what is happening now means an actual departure from a solution of the Palestinian problem. It was simply drowned in various political maneuvers which may appear subtle to someone but in fact are not in any way tied—neither from political nor from humane viewpoints—to the legitimate demands of the Arab people of Palestine. What kind of peace is that if more than three million people who have the inalienable right to have a roof over their heads, to have their own even a small state, are deprived of that right. This fact alone shows how shaky is the ground on which the separate agreement between Israel and Egypt being imposed by the United States is built.[75]

Brezhnev's warning indicated a more assertive stance on behalf of the Palestinians, which reflected the consolidation of Soviet support for a range of PLO factions, along with existing backing for Syria and Iraq. The expanding role of the Soviets and their special relationship with the PLO alerted Cold War hawks, who viewed the deepening relationship as a threat to U.S. interests in the Middle East, particularly the Gulf.[76]

After concluding the treaty, the Israeli-Palestinian conflict moved out of focus while Carter's foreign policy team tried to manage the debilitating crisis that had stemmed from the overthrow of the Shah in Iran. The president sent his advisors to Saudi Arabia and Jordan to try to smooth over criticism of the Egyptian-Israeli agreement, and he reduced his visibility in Arab-Israeli affairs considerably by appointing Democratic operative Robert Strauss as his lead negotiator for the upcoming autonomy talks.[77] The president did not want to suffer through more of the gritty debates on the Middle East or expend further domestic political capital, already in short supply.

Secretary of State Vance was bothered by the diminished attention given to the region and Strauss's new role. At a foreign affairs breakfast with his top advisors later that summer, Carter suggested that Strauss take full control in implementing the Camp David treaty in order to mitigate political fallout and reduce Vance's direct involvement. Vance's angry response conveyed a sense that the president had largely given up on his comprehensive vision for Middle East peace: "There is Lebanon, there is the Palestinian question, there is the question of the U.N. Do you want me literally to do nothing? Mr. President, I am not going to be a figurehead for you. If you don't want me to do this, I am going to resign as Secretary of State."[78] Carter rebuffed the resignation threat, telling Vance that he needed Strauss up front "as a political shield" to counter domestic pressures on the administration.[79] Vance remained in office, and the autonomy talks were launched at a distance from direct White House involvement.

Preparing for Autonomy Talks, Expanding the Settlements

The completion of the peace treaty in March 1979 did not slow Israeli settlement expansion, which continued even as preparation was underway for the start of the autonomy talks that May. Several days after the peace treaty was signed, the head of Begin's government office replied on his behalf to a critic of Camp David from the northern city of Safed. "The Prime Minister believes that we have the right of sovereignty over Judea, Samaria and Gaza and to fulfill that right. We left this question open to allow for the completion of the Peace Treaty," Begin's advisor Yechiel Kaddishai explained. "Our stance is that our army will remain in Judea, Samaria and Gaza," Kaddishai added. His final line underscored the Israeli government's position on settlements: "We acknowledge that we will expand existing settlements and establish new settlements. We are standing on this promise."[80]

A series of secret meetings were convened at the Israeli Defense Ministry in Tel Aviv to formalize the government's position on Palestinian autonomy in the weeks after the accords were reached.[81] Several defense officials and Begin's highest-ranking aides worked on an implementable autonomy plan, which excluded the possibility of a Palestinian legislative body and maintained Israel's military government in the territories. The *Washington Post* reported on the emerging formula, which stressed the overriding principle that autonomy "not include the right to eventually create an independent

Palestinian state."[82] The *Post* explained how Israel was claiming special water, land, and settlement rights, and emphasized that the plan followed Begin's precept that "individual Arabs on the West Bank and Gaza Strip should be given autonomy, but that the areas themselves should not be allowed to become collectively autonomous in the sense of constitutional democracies."[83]

There were also extensive back-door negotiations within the Israeli government to secure settlement expansion plans in the West Bank and Gaza Strip. These new settlements were planned in a manner that would ensure Israeli control of the territories regardless of any peace deal or agreement on Palestinian autonomy.[84] Ostensibly held to devise bargaining positions on the future of the 1967 lands, the settlement committee (also known as the "Ben-Elissar Committee" after the leading role played by Begin's director general, Eliyahu Ben-Elissar) made several recommendations to Prime Minister Begin that evolved into actual policies implemented in 1979 and the early 1980s.[85] These included the territorial retention of 250,000 acres of "state land" in the West Bank, continued control of underground water resources, and special jurisdiction for Jewish settlers in the territories.[86]

In the week before the first autonomy meeting began in late May, the Israeli ministerial committee in charge of negotiations deliberated on its opening position paper. This report, approved by the full cabinet, stated explicitly that sovereignty for any proposed autonomous council should "derive from the Israeli military government in the occupied territories."[87] The position paper included two declarations that mirrored Begin's first draft of the autonomy plan from 1977: (1) no establishment of a Palestinian state, and (2) an Israeli claim to sovereignty over the territories at the end of the period of autonomy.[88] While Egypt and the United States hoped to use autonomy as an interim means and transition period to more permanent negotiations over borders and sovereignty, the Israelis clearly signaled that autonomy was an end in itself and sovereignty would ultimately rest with the State of Israel.[89] Begin also mandated that the military government in the occupied territories would remain the source of any authority, assuring settler leaders that expansion would continue after the ninety-day freeze he had promised Carter at Camp David.

Ben-Elissar, who would soon become Israel's first ambassador to Egypt, later confirmed Begin's dedication to personal rather than territorial autonomy in the Camp David process. He explained that both the Egyptian and Israeli leaders got what was "most important" to them. "One got Sinai, and the other got the exercise of single sovereignty, Israeli sovereignty, over the territory between the Mediterranean and Jordan."[90] As the articulation of the official Israeli position, Ben-Elissar's statement is a testament to the underlying intentions and outcomes of the autonomy negotiations. It reveals how the conception of limited individual Arab rights by Israel was incongruous with the national sovereignty of Palestinians in the West Bank and Gaza Strip, cementing de facto Israeli control and effective sovereignty beyond the Green Line as a central component of the Camp David Accords. This contradiction was the core reason for the stalled negotiations over Palestinian autonomy, which extended from 1979 until 1982.

British and American Premonitions

Members of the British Foreign Office and officials at the U.S. State Department closely observed Israeli planning in the early months of 1979. The British ambassador in Tel Aviv wrote to his colleagues that while many in Israel believed the West Bank and Gaza were "inalienably their heritage," some had recognized that they were "operating a hated colonial regime in the West Bank and Gaza, and that the hatred is likely to grow."[91] At the same time, the ambassador explained, "four months after Camp David, there is today virtually no one in this country [Israel] of any political persuasion who believes that the autonomy plan agreed there either could or should be implemented on the West Bank."[92] Britain's consul general in Jerusalem reported on the popular reaction among Palestinians, who viewed autonomy as a "threat" rather than a political solution. "The dismal fact is when Presidents Sadat or Carter speak comfortable words about the Palestinians and autonomy, their voices sound impotent and far away," he wrote to the Foreign Office. "When Begin speaks the Master's voice is clear, and as far as the West Bankers are concerned, his police and soldiers seem all too soon to arrive and carry out his threats."[93]

British sentiments signaled a deeper recognition of the passage of decolonization in the 1950s and 1960s, suggesting an inevitable reckoning with Israel's language and practice of colonial expansion well into the 1970s.[94] In the view of the head of the Near East Directorate of the Foreign Office, Begin "rejects the whole concept of a Palestinian people precisely because the existence of such people would, if acknowledged, call into question some of the moral ground for Zionism."[95] He therefore doubted that the Palestinian issue would be resolved through territorial compromise.[96] The consul general in Jerusalem noted the dejection of Palestinians, who "gloomily take refuge in the feeling that the Jews are rowing against the tide of history and that someday they will be carried off downstream like Rhodesia, Taiwan, Iran and so on."[97] Although under no illusion that Israel would end its territorial occupation without external pressure, Foreign Office officials still concluded that the Camp David Accords might give the United States "a better lever to apply to Israeli policy" and help start a move toward multilateral negotiations.[98]

UK diplomats were not alone in voicing concerns about the fate of the Palestinians after Camp David. A series of cables from the American embassy in Tel Aviv were sent to officials in Washington and diplomats stationed throughout Europe and the Middle East, analyzing the Israeli objectives ahead of the autonomy talks. The first, just after the Egyptian-Israeli agreement was signed in March, tackled the Israeli position on water. "There is little inclination here to share even partial control of water sources with West Bankers," wrote Richard Viets, a political officer at the U.S. Embassy.[99] Viets recounted past efforts of Palestinians to drill new wells, which were summarily refused. "Pre-1967 Israel has continued to expand its exploitation of the aquifer layer shared by Israel and most of the West Bank. While Arab water use in the West Bank has been frozen by Israeli authorities. . . . The GOI [Government of Israel] conveniently ignores the fact that Israeli occupation policy for the last 12 years prevented West Bankers from expanding their utilization."[100] It was possible, Viets argued, that joint decision making could lead to joint control of water sources, or some form of Israeli custodianship over water sources during the proposed transitional period, but such a body "must be more than a sham which the Israelis use to cover their sole control of decisions."[101]

The core issue of contention in the autonomy talks would not be water, however, but a dispute over the proprietorship of land and settlements in the West Bank and Gaza Strip. American diplomats were fully aware that the settlement project had become a central component of the Likud government agenda and had no expectation of a complete moratorium on building at the onset of negotiations.[102] Instead they outlined the "optimum compromise" they believed could be achieved:

—Retention of almost all existing settlements, with a heavy price for removal of a symbolic few;
—De facto freeze on new settlements;
—Settlements to be exempt from jurisdiction of SGA [Self-Governing Authority] and directly linked to GOI [Government of Israel];
—In order to permit thickening of existing settlements some sort of shared GOI-SGA responsibility for allocation of public lands, with the Israelis having the final say.[103]

Such a low ceiling toward the outcome of the negotiations did not augur well for the possibility of an agreement on Palestinian autonomy that might ensure sovereignty and self-determination for the Arabs in the occupied territories, which the Israelis had in any case already neutralized.

The overarching U.S. view of the settlement project underscored the challenge over territory that awaited the participants in the autonomy talks. During the ten-year phase of Labor's settlement building after the 1967 War (1967–1977), government coalitions had established thirty-eight settlements in the West Bank and four in the Gaza Strip.[104] On the grounds that a Jewish communal presence existed in parts of the West Bank before 1948, the Etzion Bloc and Kiryat Arba (Hebron) were included as areas marked for settlement growth. But the government had opposed settlements in areas of "dense Arab population," which Labor politicians argued would be returned to Arab sovereignty under a final peace deal. The Likud victory had changed the calculus for Israel. As Viets explained, Begin and his ministers saw the conquest of the West Bank and Gaza Strip "as a fulfillment of Israel's historic destiny."[105] Undeterred by the heavy Arab presence in the West Bank highlands, the Likud sought to solidify the territorial gains even further. In its first nine months in office, the government set up fourteen new settlements in the West Bank, mostly in the "Heart of Samaria," which had hitherto been off limits, and two in Gaza. Despite a year's break (as the American diplomat described, "to catch its breath") and a three-month settlement freeze after Camp David, planning and building quickly resumed.[106] While many Israelis opposed settlement in the heart of the West Bank, and even Labor leader Shimon Peres hinted that if his party were negotiating over autonomy, it would be prepared to abandon the settlements in the West Bank highlands, U.S. officials asserted that there would still be "strong public reaction to removing them."[107]

Israel's mastermind behind this new phase of settlement expansion was Ariel Sharon, the minister of agriculture in the Begin government. In his reporting on the unfolding Israeli plans, Richard Viets made it clear that Sharon intended to increase building substantially.[108] The World Zionist Organization, which had a settlement department working alongside official government channels, submitted its own "master plan" for a similar model of expansion along these lines.[109] Viets noted in his cable to Washington superiors at the State Department that the Gush Emunim settler movement and its allies in the National Religious Party (NRP) were pressuring Prime Minister Begin to provide "iron-clad assurances that settlement activity would continue during negotiations and under autonomy" as a means of securing their support for the peace treaty with Egypt.[110]

In addition to maintaining the right to expand settlements and control water resources, the Israeli negotiating position was further premised on the maintenance of Israeli troop presence in the West Bank.[111] This derived from stated security concerns about the external threats of Arab countries across Israel's eastern border and the internal threat of Palestinian nationalist groups.[112] The opening Israeli negotiating position in the autonomy talks, Viets surmised, required "the legal right of Israeli security forces to operate in the West Bank and Gaza." Such a prerequisite was premised on Israel's "ultimate control over public order, political activity, political assembly and censorship . . . control over immigration . . . control of the prisons; and control over the return of refugees."[113] In taking this approach, the Israeli government linked its claims of sovereign control with the necessity of developing the territory itself. As Viets expanded in another cable, Begin's point of departure in the talks "conceives of autonomy as a permanent regime for territories under Israeli control, if not sovereignty."[114] Sharon, Viets concluded, "is committed to the permanent retention of Israeli control over the West Bank and Gaza, which he believes can only be assured by immediate and massive settlement of those territories."[115]

British diplomats confirmed and expanded on Viets's conclusion, explaining the mechanism by which Israeli sovereignty would operate in the settlements that Begin and Sharon were developing: "Jewish settlements are to have police force of their own. Jewish residents with license to carry arms will be able to do so throughout the autonomous region. The Ministry of Communication is to control entire communications infrastructure: the administrative council will not be authorized to set up radio or television stations or to issue stamps." These were critical vestiges of sovereignty that Israel would extend to areas settled beyond the Green Line. "Overall planning and control of water resources in whole area west of the Jordan will be in Israeli hands," the Foreign Office explained.[116] Like their American counterparts, British diplomats were fully aware that the Israeli version of autonomy would necessitate the retention of full political sovereignty in the territories. Such an outcome would cement Israeli control and undercut the possibility that Palestinians would achieve any real sovereignty on the ground.[117]

Settlement Legality

Israel's consistent position on settlement expansion and continued sovereignty in the territories was bolstered by the advice of a leading U.S. legal scholar, Eugene Rostow. Rostow, a neoconservative who had criticized the Carter administration for its Soviet policy and would later join the Reagan administration as its highest-ranking Democrat, was the Sterling Professor of Law at Yale University.[118] In publications that provided ongoing justification for Israeli control of the territories, Rostow repudiated U.S. acceptance of the Fourth Geneva Convention in the case of the West Bank.[119] The arguments were in complete alignment with earlier presentations of this issue to the Carter administration in 1977 by Israeli attorney general Aharon Barak.

Like Barak, Rostow argued that the original postwar provisions against occupied territory were only intended for the case of Germany and its neighbors, but "Israeli administration of the areas [West Bank and Gaza] has involved no forced transfer of population or deportations."[120] In Israel's—and Rostow's—view, the West Bank and Gaza Strip were "still unallocated territories of the Palestinian Mandate," and "Israel's legal position with regard to its right of settlement in the West Bank is impregnable."[121] Rostow had a personal investment in these questions, at one point dismissing the Carter administration's "enthusiasm for the so-called 'Palestinian' cause."[122] The rationale he provided on the legal question of settlements sustained an alternative argument for expansion that would shape Israeli and American policy for decades.[123]

American diplomats who were preparing for the autonomy negotiations in May conceded from the outset that a longer settlement freeze was unlikely. Under the best of circumstances, they admitted, the negotiations would still give Israel final say on retaining the right to expropriate disputed land from Arab owners. Characterizing the views of local West Bank residents, career diplomats at the American Consulate in Jerusalem expounded on growing local fears. "Many Palestinians look at the future through the experience of the past and see the possibility of these Jewish settlers slowly transforming the West Bank bit by bit into Jewish controlled entity; first the Jerusalem suburbs, Jordan Valley, Etzion Bloc and Kiryat Arba, then the other close-in planned towns like Givon, Ma'aele Adumim, Ofra," foreign service officers explained. These residents envisioned "a process of nibbling away at the remaining bedrock of Arab Palestine, splitting it with Israeli-built roads connecting Tel Aviv with the Jordan Valley, engulfing the area from Bethlehem to Ramallah and half way to Jericho, and eventually ghettoizing the Arab population centers such as Nablus and Hebron." "This may indeed be a far-fetched fear," the diplomats continued, "but such fears and paranoia are rampant and affect the general mood of the West Bank." Lamenting that for twelve years the United States had been opposing settlement activity as "illegal" and "an obstacle to peace," the consulate reported that this was "ignored or rejected" by Israel.

"The Palestinian Arab instead sees the U.S. as apparently unwilling or unable to put the force of our policy behind these strong words and, to the contrary, pouring more and more economic and military aid into the country which flaunts our strictures."[124]

There were also leading Israeli politicians who looked upon this expansion in the West Bank with dismay. In discussing the views of Foreign Minister Moshe Dayan, the U.S. Embassy in Tel Aviv described his insistence that negotiations should *not* be a period of "grab" to establish settlements "where we do not think a permanent settlement is necessary," but rather they should enable a final policy to be determined on those existing settlements already built. Dayan's vision, however, was not in alignment with the dominant view of the Begin government, and he was excluded from the autonomy negotiating team.[125]

Despite the systemic problems that they outlined, U.S. diplomats offered little in the way of an alternative. Officials in Jerusalem reminded Washington "there is no Palestinian negotiating partner." The Camp David process, in their view, would remain subject to strong opposition by West Bankers, along with the PLO, Jordan, and the wider Arab world.[126] Even the most cooperative Palestinian leaders remained skeptical of the autonomy negotiations. In an interview with the *New York Times* columnist Anthony Lewis, Gaza mayor Rashid al-Shawa noted deep reservations about the process that was unfolding. "Mr. Begin tells the world that the state land must be theirs, that they can settle wherever they want, that the autonomy is of people and not land, that there will never be a Palestinian state. With all this, what am I going to negotiate about?" the Gaza mayor told Lewis. "I understand going and talking about details if the principle is right. But when you deny me the principle—self-determination—what is there to discuss?"[127]

As a preview of what negotiations ultimately wrought, al-Shawa's concerns—along with other premonitions—underscored a fundamental incompatibility: the negotiation over Palestinian autonomy was bound to exclude meaningful sovereignty and would be tied up with the Israeli retention of land and the expansion of settlements.[128] The Israeli position put forward at Camp David had provided a clear road map for territorial consolidation. In articles attacking Begin's promotion of administrative autonomy, Israeli journalist Amnon

Kapeliouk argued that "South African Bantustans have more pre-rogative and wider margin of maneuver." Kapeliouk criticized his government for establishing administrative councils exclusively for the settlements, enshrining occupation and separation.[129]

The First Round

Egyptian and Israeli delegations met in the southern Israeli city of Beersheba on Friday afternoon May 25, 1979, for the first round of autonomy talks. Early that morning, the Israeli army evacuated the northern Sinai town of El-Arish in coordination with the Egyptian army, completing an agreement to begin negotiations one month after the exchange of the instruments of ratification of the Egyptian-Israeli peace treaty.[130] Dr. Joseph Burg, Israel's minister of interior, and General Kamal Hassan Ali, the Egyptian defense minister, led their respective delegations in the talks, held at Ben Gurion University. King Hussein of Jordan did not accept the invitation to participate, as Jordan was fiercely critical of the Camp David Accords.[131] U.S. secretary of state Cyrus Vance and Carter's special envoy to the Middle East, Robert Strauss, headed the American delegation.

Strauss, who had been chairman of the Democratic National Committee and successfully completed the 1973–1979 Tokyo Round of Multilateral Trade Negotiations as U.S. trade representative, was a political figure deeply sympathetic to Israel.[132] According to an internal Israeli memo, Strauss's belief in Israel's conception of its own security would ensure his loyalty on matters as sensitive as the fate of Jerusalem: "He is the man who will go to the President [Carter] close the door behind him and say the city will not be divided into two, and we must find an acceptable solution to the problem. He will do this, of course, after he hears and discusses Israel's position and feeling on the topic."[133] Burg, the leader of Israel's National Religious Party, was selected in part to safeguard Begin's coalition allies but also as a signal that the prime minister viewed the autonomy issue as an internal Israeli domestic problem, not a matter for the Foreign Ministry to deal with.[134]

Moshe Dayan, stung by his exclusion from the committee, tendered his resignation in October. His resignation letter cited Israel's relations with Arabs in the territories as the cause. For the final two years of his life, Dayan worked to promote unilateral autonomy for Palestinians while ending Israeli military control in the West Bank.[135] As Dayan recalled in his memoirs, "I . . . did not believe that Israeli sovereignty could be imposed on these Arabs against their will."[136] Dayan's preference was not territorial compromise or the creation of a Palestinian state but a more robust definition of full autonomy for Arabs than Begin was offering, in connection with either Israel or Jordan. He refused to advocate for Israeli annexation of the territories and disagreed with members of the government who supported the appropriation of Arab land.[137] It was a curious position for the general who had convinced Israelis after the 1967 War that they could somehow retain the territories without compromising the democratic character of the state.

Speaking on behalf of Egyptian prime minister Mustafa Khalil, who was unable to attend, General Ali opened the meeting. He invoked President Sadat, who "has emphasized repeatedly that the Palestinian problem is the heart and crux of the entire conflict." Ali articulated guidelines to underpin the talks, emphasizing the need for Palestinian participation in determining their own future: "Only the Palestinians themselves can make such a decision, for self-determination is their God-given right. Our task is merely to define the powers and responsibilities of the self-governing authority with full autonomy and the modalities for electing it."[138] In a method parallel to the Israeli use of autonomy, the Egyptians thereby deployed an abstract concept of self-determination, which was emptied of politically decisive meaning.[139] This tactic served their immediate agenda as benevolent protectors of Palestinian rights, even as Sadat had all but cast the Palestinians aside in signing a bilateral treaty with Israel.

The absence of Palestinian participation in the autonomy meetings, which continued until their conclusion in 1982, was noted from the inception.[140] U.S. diplomats, despite their continuing public pronouncements on the importance of Palestinian economic and political rights, in fact privately supported Palestinian exclusion from the negotiations. In one secret conversation between Israeli minister Burg and U.S. ambassador Strauss, the two men agreed to proceed without Palestinian representation.

BURG: Sadat said perhaps we can go ahead for the moment without
Palestinians. In the world Palestinians means PLO and this is
poison for us . . .

STRAUSS: As far as we are concerned we agree that for the moment,
for the next few months, we can get along without Palestinians. . . .
We must put the dowry together and assume that we will find the
bride.[141]

Although Vance stressed the American belief that "governments
derive their just powers from the consent of the governed," such
consent was markedly absent in the case of the occupied Palestinians. "We believe that the Palestinian people must have the right for
themselves and their descendants to live with dignity and freedom,
and with the opportunity for economic fulfillment and political expression," Vance had remarked in his opening speech. He had also
accounted for the Palestinian diaspora. "We must make a start to
deal with the problem of Palestinians living outside the West Bank
and Gaza. They too must know that an accepted and respected
place exists for them within the international community."[142] Like
much of the Carter administration's rhetoric and approach to
human rights, it was, in the words of one critic, "more apparent
than real."[143]

As vacuous as the Egyptian and American endorsements of Palestinian self-determination may have been, they were met with an
overwhelmingly negative Israeli response. In his opening speech,
Burg remarked that at the heart of autonomy "lies the conviction
that the Palestinian Arabs should and must conduct their own
daily lives for themselves and by themselves." But he stressed a
conceptual distinction. "What I must make clear and what must
be understood from the outset is that autonomy does not and cannot imply sovereignty . . . we must, by definition, reject a-priori
an independent Palestinian statehood. Israel will never agree, and
indeed, totally rejects the propositions, declarations or establishment of a Palestinian state in Judea, Samaria and the Gaza District."[144] Israel's overarching priority, as successive rounds made
clear, was to keep the talks in motion and embed a hegemonic
definition of autonomy without enabling Palestinian sovereignty
or statehood.

Burg's position throughout the talks rested on a dramatic narrative of Israel's security needs: "No hostile element or agent or force dare control the heartland of this land to threaten the lives of its city dwellers and villagers and thereby hold a knife to the jugular vein of Israel."[145] In Israeli diplomatic parlance, Palestinians often denoted the PLO, and as Begin himself would tell Strauss, "The PLO is beyond the pale of human civilization."[146] Until the conclusion of the negotiations, then, no Palestinians would participate in a discussion about their own future, nor would a joint Jordanian delegation that might mitigate concerns about PLO involvement. A confidant of Burg at the time, American Jewish leader Henry Siegman, later recalled discussions during which the Israeli minister of interior admitted the mere existence of the talks was a mechanism for "shooting the dog" of Palestinian autonomy.[147]

Egyptian Enablement

Israel's views of autonomy were well known and unsurprising, unlike the critical legitimacy conferred on the talks by Egypt. To mark the one-year anniversary of the signing of the Camp David Accords, the Egyptian government sent its vice president, Hosni Mubarak, to Washington to meet with President Carter and Israeli representatives. In a private conversation, Mubarak and Egyptian ambassador Ashraf Ghorbal gathered with President Carter, Secretary Vance, National Security Advisor Brzezinski and Ambassador Strauss to discuss Egypt's economic, military, and political concerns. Mubarak's priority was economic; in light of Egypt's isolation from the Arab world since Camp David, the country was relying on the United States for hard currency and extensive wheat imports. Listing items like maize, animal fats, rice, and chicken, the Egyptian vice president outlined a "crisis" facing his country, which was now dependent on American aid. "It is the food of the people. If Egypt could buy it elsewhere it would do so, but it can't," Mubarak stressed.[148]

Cognizant of resurgent Cold War concerns, the Egyptian leader was clear in emphasizing allegiance to the United States and antipathy toward Egypt's former Soviet patrons. Mubarak warned of the growing threat from Soviet influence in the Middle East and the attendant risks of Egypt's marginalization in the wake of Camp

David. The country needed more military equipment, including Phantom jets, to ensure continued stability against neighbors like Libya. Mubarak also asked for destroyers and more naval equipment to bolster his country's power and the position of its primary patron: "Egypt is keen to keep the image of the United States in good shape . . . a worsening image would be detrimental to both of us." Linking Egypt's fate with America's regional influence, Mubarak then turned to the ongoing autonomy talks, imploring the Americans to reach a "precise conclusion." In Mubarak's view, Sadat felt the United States had to convince Begin to move, "so that the Arab world (the Saudis and other moderates) would know something is being done."[149]

Carter was mindful of Israel's dominance over the autonomy talks and stressed to Mubarak the need for a more coordinated Egyptian position. "Sometimes it is difficult . . . to be more forceful— [as in] protecting Palestinian rights, promoting the autonomy talks, preventing settlements—than [is] Sadat. It is hard when we take a strong position, and Sadat is more accommodating." It was clear from Carter's remarks that the Egyptian stance in the negotiations had demanded even less from Israel than the United States. "Begin is stubborn and courageous. He will say no if he means no; yes if he means yes. On several occasions, we [the United States] have been more forceful in carrying out the Camp David accords than has Egypt," Carter warned. On the difficult issues like the fate of Jerusalem, settlements, and the Palestinian question, Carter felt Egypt and the United States had to align their approach. "We both need to be forceful, in public and in private. Jews in America constantly say: why are we tough when Sadat doesn't care?" Egypt, in Carter's view, seemed to abdicate responsibility on a number of the broad issues emanating from Camp David. Referring to a recent Israeli cabinet decision permitting Israelis to buy Arab land in the West Bank, Carter turned to Mubarak. "What is the Egyptian position? We don't know." Mubarak simply agreed.[150]

Egypt's acquiescence on the central issues confronting the future of the Palestinian question extended to the level of more minute debates in the autonomy negotiations. During the sixth round of talks held at the San Stefano Hotel in the Egyptian coastal city of Alexandria in September 1979, Prime Minister Mustafa Khalil got into a disagreement with his Israeli interlocutors over the mechanisms for implementing autonomy on the ground. Egypt believed that any Self-Governing Authority should have legislative, executive, and judicial powers, while the Israeli position was limited to budgetary and regulatory powers. The Israelis also insisted on inserting language that emphasized autonomy was only for *inhabitants* of the West Bank and Gaza "and not to territory." Khalil knew this was a ruse to strip autonomy of all meaning, arguing that in the Camp David Accords "it was never mentioned that it [will] apply to inhabitants and not territory." Yet despite his reservations, Khalil acceded to the Israeli interpretation of Camp David, particularly on the question of Palestinian statehood. "We have to be careful in our phrases," Khalil remarked to Burg. "I cannot come and say powers and responsibilities that could lead to forming an independent Palestinian state." Burg quickly replied, "On this I would go along with you. This is the point." It was a clear indication that even for Egypt, the outcome of the autonomy talks cohered with Israeli and American priorities to avoid the possible emergence of a Palestinian state.[151]

Khalil was aware of the perception his acquiescence would generate outside the negotiating room. "We don't like that this will grow out and leak and then the Palestinians will say, well you have already accepted the thesis that the Self Governing Authority and the responsibilities and so on will apply only to the inhabitants and not to the land."[152] This acknowledgment that autonomy would preclude the creation of a Palestinian state matched the position of Sol Linowitz, the lead U.S. negotiator who replaced Ambassador Strauss in later rounds of negotiations. In a private letter to one critic of the ongoing talks, Linowitz stressed, "Both Egypt and the United States have emphatically stated to Israel that they (and we) view such an autonomy as precluding the creation of an independent Palestinian state."[153] Notwithstanding Sadat's strong talk about self-determination at Camp David, the bilateral treaty with Israel was more important than investing the political and diplomatic capital necessary for a viable outcome to the autonomy negotiations that followed. This lack of commitment explained why so many of Sadat's advisors had already resigned and why there was growing protest in Egypt over the outcome of Camp David.[154]

The PLO and American Jews Respond

For the PLO leadership, following the talks from a distance in Lebanon, the implications were distressingly clear. Arafat conveyed his views to the U.S. government via a secret back channel, like he had with the debate over UN Security Council Resolution 242.[155] The PLO chairman described the Camp David Accords as nothing more than "meaningless negotiations about some permanent colonial status for the Palestinians under Israeli rule." Arafat warned of the "massive build-up of U.S. arms to both Israel and Egypt, and preparations for another Arab-Israeli war which Begin is doing everything to provoke through his attacks on South Lebanon. That is not a treaty for peace—it is a treaty for war."[156]

Arafat was equally dismissive of autonomy, which he called "a farce," instead suggesting an alternative path. "If there is a clear platform for serious, comprehensive peace negotiations," Arafat remarked to U.S. officials, "we will of course take part." In Arafat's view, that platform should include three major points.

1) Human rights for the Palestinians;
2) The principle of the right of return for the Palestinians;
3) The right of the Palestinians to have our own state.[157]

In the wider context of an emerging discourse on human rights in the 1970s, the PLO demands echoed similar political struggles around the globe. The organization's attempts at a diplomatic track with the United States had continued after the setback of Camp David. American congressman Paul Findley, an Illinois Republican and critic of U.S. failures to negotiate with the PLO, met frequently with Arafat to try to parlay the organization's views into a diplomatic opening. His attempts were unsuccessful, not quite crossing the threshold to reverse the 1975 ban on dialogue.[158]

As a means of furthering inroads beyond the United States, the PLO also turned to engagement with Europe. On July 6, 1979, Arafat arrived in Vienna for extensive meetings with Austrian chancellor Bruno Kreisky and West German chancellor Willy Brandt. The PLO leader asserted that Camp David had destroyed the possibility of a regional peace conference or any chance for a comprehensive settlement.[159] Israeli foreign minister Moshe Dayan told Kreisky,

FIGURE 4.2. *Camp David Treacherous Accords* by Hosni Radwan, 1979.
Courtesy of Liberation Graphics and the Palestine Poster Project Archives.

who was Jewish, that the meeting was "a demonstrative act against the State of Israel and the Jewish people," and the Israeli cabinet pulled its ambassador from Austria.[160] But the Arab League welcomed the Kreisky talks, and the PLO issued a bulletin stating that the meeting "represents an increasing European awareness of the failing of U.S. policy in the Middle East."[161] Arafat's diplomatic success in Austria bolstered his international standing, and reports of the PLO chairman's "cheerful and hopeful mood" circulated in the Carter White House.[162]

U.S. officials were not entirely unsympathetic to Arafat's criticism of the Camp David process and the ongoing autonomy discussions. There was a desire to soften the PLO's opposition to the talks, which would also alleviate pressure on the Egyptians. While the PLO did have allies inside the administration, efforts to reverse Kissinger's ban on engagement that summer ended badly. State Department officials had explored a UN resolution that would reaffirm the applicability of 242 to the territories and assert Palestinian self-determination, which they hoped might elicit PLO acceptance and satisfy conditions for opening a dialogue. Carter approved the UN initiative and through intermediaries managed to secure a Palestinian delay in bringing a more adversarial text to a vote in the General Assembly. But as a result of dueling pressures from Saudi Arabia and Israel, as well as Egyptian opposition, he soon revisited his plans.[163]

Andrew Young, Carter's ambassador to the United Nations and a prominent African American civil rights leader, had been part of the attempt to delay the PLO's harsher text. The United States was hoping "to explore a compromise that could encourage Palestinian participation in the Camp David peace process" and sought out a more amenable draft resolution.[164] At the apartment of the Kuwaiti ambassador to the United Nations, Young met secretly with the PLO representative to the organization, Zehdi Labib Terzi, to discuss it. The Mossad leaked a transcript of the brief meeting to Begin, and the details were published more widely, contradicting Young's initial statements on the meeting and forcing his resignation from the post. The ambassador had breached standing U.S. policy on non-engagement, and had not secured prior permission from the State Department, angering Vance.[165]

Carter's press secretary "wept" when he read the resignation letter to the media. Carter himself was sympathetic to Young, writing in his diary that it was "absolutely ridiculous that we pledged under Kissinger and Nixon that we would not negotiate with the PLO."[166] Young's untimely departure was particularly delicate because of his track record as a prominent civil rights leader, widening an unpleasant schism between American Jews and African Americans.[167] Vernon Jordan, then the president of the National Urban League in New York, felt that Jewish institutions had rashly criticized Young, unfairly contributing to his firing.[168] Young was an iconic symbol within the black community, and feelings of despair over his untimely departure ran deep. An African American cleaning lady in Jordan's building tearfully exclaimed, "I just do not understand. I don't understand diplomacy and I don't understand foreign policy or international relations. But the one thing I do understand is that we always get screwed. And Andy Young got screwed because he was black."[169]

The impression that Israel's supporters in America "had gotten him, you know, had gotten black America's spokesman in American government," gained a lot of currency among those critical of the Jewish community's influence on U.S. policy toward Israel and the Palestinians.[170] Mark Siegel disputed the assertion made by Carter's press secretary, Jody Powell, that "it's going to be terrible how this is going to affect blacks and Jews in America, how blacks are going to blame Jews for getting rid of Andy Young."[171] American Jewish leader Hyman Bookbinder, however, did see a link between Jewish outrage over Young's communication with the PLO and his immediate release. "Even though there was no explicit Jewish request or demand that he go," Bookbinder explained, "the decision to let him go at this time in honesty technically requires that we acknowledge . . . that the Administration said, 'My God, we are going to have a lot of trouble with the Jews on this one.'"[172]

Young's untimely departure underscored the trap of nonengagement with the PLO at the very moment it was seeking out (and securing) international legitimacy. Each time U.S. diplomats spoke openly about the possibility of reform or engagement with the organization, the Israelis invoked Henry Kissinger's commitments not to recognize or negotiate with them, and domestic supporters of Israel followed suit. It was a diplomatic straitjacket that constrained U.S. officials throughout the 1970s. Carter later explained that "accepting the resignation of Andrew Young was one of the most heart wrenching decisions I had to make as president. He was a close and intimate friend, and the prohibition against meeting the PLO was preposterous, as this group was a key to any comprehensive peace agreement."[173]

Carter's constrained position on autonomy was compounded by the looming 1980 U.S. election and heightened American Jewish communal concerns about the direction of the autonomy talks.[174] In his chairman's report to the Conference of Presidents of Major Jewish Organizations, the umbrella group of American Jewish political life, Theodore Mann voiced concerns about the Begin government's rigid stance. He noted the signs of an "annexationist cabinet" coming to power, one whose ultimate goal would be extending Jewish sovereignty in the occupied territories. Mann voiced worry that this would divide American Jewry, spawning fights over settlements, "essentially a peripheral issue." Rather, Mann wrote, "Jews should—must—debate fundamental religious and moral issues, and issues that bear on their survival as a people . . . the issue on which all other issues hinge, is whether Jews regard sovereignty over Judea, Samaria and Gaza as being in their interest."[175]

In Mann's view, which he shared with other Jewish leaders, this was not a question of Israel's *right* to sovereignty in the West Bank: "I think most of us—all of us—would agree that Israel's right is as good or better than anyone else's . . . the issue rather is whether it is good for the Jewish people . . . to attempt to achieve such sovereignty." The chairman was rather open to the competing positions on sovereignty, with many Jews invoking a religious right to the territories, while others felt it should be "abjured because of the equally deep religious view that Jews should not rule over 1,200,000 Arabs who do not wish to be ruled by them, no matter how benignly." The underlying hesitancy voiced by Mann concerned the wisdom of airing such a divisive debate in public, which he felt would be taken advantage of "by the President, the State Department, and Congressmen who are critically important to Israel."[176]

The decisive choice of the American Jewish leadership to avoid a public conversation over Israel's occupation of the territories stemmed from its potential impact on the autonomy negotiations: "Our very success in having helped to create such a remarkable ally for that beleaguered nation of Israel, is what imposes restraints upon us in speaking out."[177] Ultimately, the calculus of Mann and his fellow communal leaders contributed in part to a silencing of dissent and the rightward shift already distinguishing American Jewish political life at the end of the 1970s. This trend directly affected the Palestinians and the fate of their possible self-determination in subsequent years.

Autonomy into the 1980s

Ambassador Linowitz continued to work diligently to reconcile the central divisions between Egypt and Israel in a bid to achieve some tangible results for the Palestinians.[178] During a meeting in Cairo in January 1980, the Egyptian and Israeli delegations presented Linowitz with varying models of autonomy to break the deadlock over the permissible degree of Palestinian self-rule. Israel's model was entirely functional— the establishment of what was called a "Self Governing Authority (Administrative Council)" for Palestinians to deal with shared issues, while residual sovereignty remained with Israel. This functionalism reflected a persistent employment of autonomy as a political and discursive tool to diminish the possibility of sovereignty. Egypt's autonomy model, however, was based on the mode of civil administration used by the Israeli military government and was intended to provide Palestinians with actual power for self-rule, in the form of exclusive authority over land *and* inhabitants. Conceptually, the Egyptian model was akin to a mandate for the development of an eventual independent state after an interim waiting period.[179]

Linowitz selected the Israeli model as the basis for continuing negotiations, and the Egyptians reluctantly agreed. Secret documents reveal prior meetings between the U.S. and Israeli delegations to prepare and adopt the Israeli position paper, with U.S. ambassador James Leonard telling Israeli representatives, "We will ask you, and even suggest to you, some formulations in conformity with what you gave to us."[180] Egypt's acquiescence reflected Sadat's underlying personal trust in the U.S. ability to extract concessions from Israel during the course of the negotiations. Leading members of Sadat's delegation at Camp David had, however, attacked this confidence. Egypt's foreign minister, Mohammed Ibrahim Kamel, warned Sadat about the autonomy provisions of Camp David just before resigning in protest on the final day of the September 1978 summit: "We are only deceiving ourselves if we say this project will end in the realization of a just solution to the Palestinian cause, for Israel will use it as an instrument and a source of support to liquidate the issue in accordance with its expansionist intentions."[181]

Kamel's warnings evoked the skepticism of other critics like Brezhnev, but in the months after Camp David, Sadat was primarily concerned with achieving a peace deal with Israel and with securing U.S. backing for internal reforms in his country. He believed Egypt in the post-Nasser era was "encumbered with worries and problems" and that its public utilities were "in a state of collapse."[182] These domestic concerns fueled Egypt's turn away from Soviet patronage in the wake of the 1973 War and culminated in Sadat's decision to pursue the bilateral agreement with Israel. The Egyptian president did become increasingly vocal about Begin's intransigent stance toward implementing the Camp David Accords. In conversations with Carter during the summer of 1980, Sadat demanded the Israeli prime minister agree that "Jerusalem is negotiable, stop the settlements, and take care of the human rights of the Palestinians." Recording this conversation in his diary, Carted noted: "I don't believe he [Begin] will do any of these things, and has dug himself a hole very damaging to Israel."[183] Sadat was not entirely honest in defense of the Palestinians. As declassified CIA analysis of his evolving position on autonomy reveals, "Sadat does not want a fully independent Palestinian state in the West Bank. He fears such a state would be pro-Soviet and a threat to regional stability."[184] As had been clear from Sadat's approach when negotiations with Carter first began, Egypt could not plausibly defend the interests of Palestinian nationalists.

While the autonomy talks continued that spring, it was clear that Israeli de facto control in the territories had been secured. Moreover, U.S. negotiators were often present and participating in discussions with the Israeli leadership when this jurisdiction over settlements and the wider West Bank was boldly asserted.[185] This tense diplomatic environment and Sadat's domestic preoccupations contributed to a feeble Egyptian stance in the negotiations. In a further indication of the increasingly asymmetrical nature of the autonomy talks, the Egyptians were often excluded from key meetings between the Israeli and American delegations. Records of these bilateral meetings highlight a pattern by which Palestinian concerns were rendered subsidiary to Israeli priorities. Among these priorities was ensuring that negotiations over possible Palestinian autonomy did not undermine the physical expansion of settlements in the occupied territories.

One example of what this linkage enabled was revealed in a meeting between U.S. ambassador Linowitz and the full Israeli delegation in Jerusalem on September 2, 1980. Turning to the rapid expansion of Israeli settlements in the occupied territories, Linowitz asked Ariel Sharon to explain the status of settlement development and the rationale of expansion in light of their sensitive role in the autonomy talks. "We are finishing the skeleton," Sharon answered, anticipating the announcement of four further settlements. In one of the clearest expressions of what these settlements were intended to achieve, Sharon then outlined his aims:

> You have to take into consideration, and again I am saying why I believe we have to hurry, why I believe that we have to finish it before the coming elections in Israel: the facts that were created in the areas, the skeleton, the map that exists practically in the area now does not allow any more and will not enable in the future any territorial compromise. I don't see any possibility of territorial compromise. There are many possibilities of political answers or, let's say modifications, but I cannot see any territorial compromise. I don't see now any area that can be handed to anybody having this skeleton practically in the area.[186]

The "skeleton" Sharon helped design and implement on occupied Palestinian land was a means to ensure none of the territory could ever be ceded to the Palestinian inhabitants. This framework of the settlement project, and its deployment as a prerequisite even for diplomatic discussion of autonomy, was explicitly meant to prevent any cession of territory by Israel, or the creation of a Palestinian state. Throughout the autonomy talks, PLO representatives watched these developments with biting criticism: "The Palestinian people are not in a hurry. We waited thirty-one years and we can wait more. They can continue building settlements with U.S. dollars, they can set for their Judaization schemes for the Palestinian cities and towns as they are doing now in Hebron; but Palestine will remain ours."[187]

Carter's Defeat

Succumbing to foreign policy missteps and economic troubles at home, Carter lost the 1980 presidential election to former California governor Ronald Reagan.[188] Clashes with the American Jewish community over Israel and the Palestinian question, which had contributed to Carter's defeat in the New York Democratic primary against Edward Kennedy, drove a larger number of Jewish voters than ever to the Republican Party.[189] Carter's campaign staff was immensely frustrated by this abandonment of the president, a reversion to the suspicions that many American Jews had harbored in 1976.[190] Events in the Middle East had also contributed to Carter's defeat, including the hostage crisis in Tehran and the outbreak of a major war between Iraq and Iran in September.

Linowitz, with the encouragement of both Carter and president-elect Reagan, returned to Israel in December 1980 for another round of talks over autonomy. He held several private meetings with Begin, imploring the Israeli prime minister to work harder for a resolution, but there was no progress.[191] In a final report on the state of the negotiations, Linowitz assessed the prospects of their success in a new administration. He told Carter that much had been achieved in the talks, aside from five core issues: "1) Source of power; 2) Water and land rights; 3) Jewish settlements; 4) Security; and 5) East Jerusalem."[192] Given the effort that had been expended in dozens of meetings, this extensive list underscored the effectiveness of Israeli tactics in negotiating autonomy along such narrow lines. There was a slim possibility that these issues would be tackled anew in the shifting ideological context of the Reagan White House.

Carter, who had sacrificed a great deal of political capital by offering limited support for some form of Palestinian self-rule during his tenure, was bitterly disappointed with the failure of the autonomy talks. During his final meeting with Israel's ambassador to the United States, Ephraim Evron, the outgoing president lamented the state of affairs: "I don't see how they [Israel] can continue as an occupying power depriving the Palestinians of basic human rights, and I don't see how they can absorb three million more Arabs into Israel without letting the Jews become a minority in their own country. Begin showed courage in giving up the Sinai. He did it to keep the West Bank."[193] It was a clear-eyed assessment, borne out by the rhetoric and policies of the Israeli government throughout the negotiations, both of which had been condoned by the acquiescent mediation of Carter's own administration.

The emergence of the Camp David Accords and the negotiations over peace with Egypt that followed reflected the triumph of Begin's vision for the post-1967 era. The territory captured from Egypt could plausibly be returned for peace and recognition, neutralizing the possibility of Arab aggression in the southwest and satisfying some form of resolution 242's premise of "land for peace." Even while Begin drew criticism from the more extreme elements of his government who did not want to withdraw Jewish settlements from the Sinai Peninsula, he never had to compromise on his claims to the West Bank, the Gaza Strip, East Jerusalem, and the Golan Heights. The progress toward a peace treaty with Egypt went hand in hand with settlement building elsewhere, deliberately planned and protected by legal cover provided in part by conservative American allies.

Begin's visceral hostility toward the PLO, bolstered by visible attacks like the Coastal Road Massacre, further marginalized Palestinian nationalists at the very moment Arafat was seeking to improve relations with Europe and the United States. The conflicting impulses of Palestinian factions, which shifted between armed struggle and diplomacy, in part reflected the rhythm of Egypt's inroads with Israel and the recognition that a bilateral peace had emerged at the expense of Palestinian self-determination. Efforts within the Carter administration to engage the PLO were constrained by the strictures of Kissinger's 1975 ban but also by the need for a diplomatic success in the Egyptian-Israeli negotiations and the growing domestic pressures on Carter that in part guided his strategy at Camp David. The president understood the limits of Begin's willingness to negotiate beyond Egypt and Sadat's flexibility in achieving a bilateral peace at the expense of the Palestinians.

Even while the accords themselves contained provisions for launching autonomy negotiations and addressing broader regional concerns, the autonomy talks that began in May 1979 reflected the Israeli interpretation of autonomy for individuals but not sovereign control over the territory itself. The exclusion of the PLO was a natural outcome of this architecture, given the elision of any provision for "self-determination" and the conceptual and legal limits of Israeli views on autonomy. More surprising was the American role in these talks, which shifted from mediation to effective collaboration as the talks extended into 1980. The enabling behavior of the Egyptians helped fuel this dynamic, and there was little political capital that Carter or his administration expended to reverse the drift toward Begin's favored outcome. The attempts to bring the PLO back in, as the Andrew Young affair demonstrated, only exacerbated domestic tensions in the months before Carter's critical reelection campaign.

The election of Ronald Reagan solidified many of the trends already unleashed by Camp David, particularly Begin's political victory over the PLO. Like the revival of Cold War concerns already evident in American defense strategy under Carter, a growing neoconservative influence on U.S. policy in the Middle East marked the start of the 1980s. Israel was cast as a strategic ally and the PLO as a Soviet proxy, paving the way for a deadly military intervention in Lebanon. What began largely as a political battle to defeat Palestinian nationalism—one that Begin had waged successfully through the Camp David Accords and the autonomy talks—would move to the streets of wartime Beirut. The restraining role of the United States in the late 1970s, whether fitfully promoting a resolution of the Palestinian question through diplomacy or speaking against the settlement project and Begin's restrictive autonomy, gave way to a more permissive White House and a new way of thinking about the Middle East.

CHAPTER FIVE

Neoconservatives Rising

REAGAN AND THE MIDDLE EAST

"I'VE BELIEVED MANY THINGS IN MY LIFE, but no conviction I've ever held has been stronger than my belief that the United States must ensure the survival of Israel."[1] When it came to the Middle East, as his memoirs reflect, President Ronald Reagan's abiding affinity was for Israel. During an early campaign meeting about the Middle East, one participant remembers the candidate talking fondly about *Exodus*, a wildly popular movie based on the novel by Leon Uris that celebrated the miraculous victory of Israel over the Arabs in 1948. Reagan's approach during the campaign was an extension of this worldview.[2]

His speeches and the election pamphlets distributed by the newly organized pro-Israel Coalition for Reagan-Bush focused on the missteps of Jimmy Carter's Middle East policy for American Jews.[3] On September 3, 1980, Reagan addressed a Jewish American group at the B'nai B'rith Forum in Washington, D.C. His remarks that day were revealing as a harbinger of Middle East policy in the initial months of his administration: "While we have since 1948 clung to the argument of a moral imperative to explain our commitment to Israel, no Administration has ever deluded itself that Israel was not of permanent strategic importance to America. Until, that is, the Carter administration, which has violated this covenant with the past."[4] Reagan's extensive repudiation encompassed his predecessor's pursuit of a comprehensive settlement between Israel and the Arabs, the inclusion of the Soviet Union in the negotiations, and U.S. arms sales to Jordan and Saudi Arabia. He took aim at the "ambiguities" of the autonomy talks that followed the Camp David Accords between Egypt and Israel, suggesting that Jordan should act as a sovereign state to oversee the implementation of Security Council resolutions 242 and 338 rather than allow for indigenous Palestinian self-determination. This criticism was reflected in the pages of the staunchly pro-Israel *Commentary* magazine, an intellectual home for many of Reagan's foreign policy advisors. The magazine characterized Carter's hands-on approach to resolving Israel's conflict with the Arab world as appeasement.[5]

In positioning his administration's foreign policy as an antidote to his predecessor's struggle in the wider Middle East, Reagan and his advisors reverted to a Cold War vision of the region as a primary site of a global power struggle with the Soviet Union. To win this struggle, Reagan officials believed, a doctrine that combined a fight against terrorism and Soviet proxies and the bolstering of traditional allies was necessary. The intensification of a strategic alliance with Israel was at the heart of this shift, and it would be formalized with a Memorandum of Understanding between the two allies shortly after Reagan entered the White House. In the early months of the new administration, the PLO was cast as both a hardcore terrorist group and an agent of Soviet influence, which fit well with the suppression of nationalist movements in the Global South during Reagan's time in office. A newly permissive approach to Israeli settlements indicated a change in legal thinking that empowered the Israeli government to substantially expand building in the West Bank and Gaza Strip. This was linked with greater alignment between U.S. diplomats and the Begin government on the pursuit of restrictive autonomy for Palestinians, thereby enshrining Israel's vision for political state prevention.

The Reagan Revolution

The specter of a Cold War revival was at the heart of Reagan's pro-Israel leanings, with the country seen as part of an anti-communist struggle that would keep Soviet influence in the Middle East at bay. In preparing to run for the presidency, Reagan described Israel as an asset against the Soviet Union. "Without this bastion of liberal democracy in the heart of the area," the former governor of California wrote in the *Washington Post* in 1979, "the Kremlin would be confined to supporting militant regimes against pro-American conservative governments which would not be able to divert the attention and energy of the radicals away from themselves by using the 'lightning rod' of the 'Zionist state.'" Reagan's approach would therefore end up supporting "conservative" governments like Saudi Arabia, apartheid South Africa, and Latin American dictatorships, framing an initial sharp turn away from Carter's rhetoric of human rights. Explaining this policy in the Middle East, Reagan wrote that "our own position would be weaker without the political and military assets Israel provides."[6]

Reagan's November 1980 victory over Carter signaled a transformation in American domestic politics, one that had been roiling the Republican Party since Barry Goldwater's 1964 presidential defeat.[7] But in addition to staking out his successful campaign in staunch opposition to big government, Reagan vowed to renew the American fight against communism.[8] Conservatives had seized on the expansion of Soviet influence, especially their December 1979 invasion of Afghanistan, as proof of the Cold War's full-blown revival, targeting Jimmy Carter in the campaign and drawing committed advocates of anti-communism away from the Democratic Party. A large part of the growing unease with existing foreign policy stemmed from the heated debates over the lessons of the Vietnam War, with liberal Democrats arguing that it had been needlessly prolonged, and critics on the right seeing the American withdrawal and subsequent collapse of South Vietnam as an "indication of détente's cowardice."[9]

Alongside more muscular Democrats like Senator Henry "Scoop" Jackson and a retinue of budding neoconservatives that included Paul Wolfowitz and Richard Perle, President Reagan "transformed détente from a badge of honor to a political expletive."[10] Liberal Democrats succumbed to these charges of weakness from the right, ultimately leading to the destruction of a centrist American foreign policy and the intensification of military intervention that would soon follow.[11] This "Return to Militarism" in U.S. foreign policy, which in part grew out of Carter's defense budgeting, had implications that extended well beyond the 1980s and the end of the Cold War.[12] A rethinking of U.S. economic policy alongside deep-seated social and cultural shifts marked the 1980s as a decade of conservative resurgence at home, while Reagan's stance abroad inaugurated interventionist policies in the Middle East.

The president and his advisors began to promote a global struggle against communism, recasting regional conflicts as proxies of the Cold War. Democratic hawks like Elliot Abrams and Jeane Kirkpatrick joined the new administration, disillusioned with Carter's perceived weakness when it came to foreign policy.[13] On the Israeli-Palestinian front, Israel would now be positioned as an ally in contrast to the Soviet-backed Palestinians.[14] Such an approach appealed to Reagan, especially after the humiliation of the Iranian hostage crisis, which had generated a desire for leadership that could speak out forcefully against threats to U.S. interests. Under the growing influence of these staunch anti-communists, Reagan's worldview reconstituted the Middle East as a site of contestation between the United States and the Soviet Union.

Strong ideology, however, did not always make for good governance. Allies and critics alike have described Reagan's White House and his foreign policy team as "dysfunctional" during the first six years of the administration.[15] Early concerns about infighting between advisors were often papered over by Reagan's admirers, but in the view of one expert on the National Security Council, "when it came to the management of the foreign policy apparatus of the U.S. government, Reagan's record is almost certainly the worst of any modern President."[16] Among the initial group of foreign policy aides appointed in 1981, Richard Allen was chosen to lead the National Security Council but was soon replaced by Judge William P. Clark Jr., a trusted confidant of the president. General Alexander Haig, who had been chief of staff in the Nixon White House and Supreme Allied Commander of NATO in Europe, was chosen as the first secretary of state, and Caspar "Cap" Weinberger, a former vice president of the Bechtel Corporation and Nixon appointee, was named secretary of defense.[17] Reagan preferred a backseat approach to policymaking and trusted this inner circle to articulate his views on international affairs. Yet they often disagreed on questions relating to the Middle East, with Haig voicing consistent support for Israel, while Weinberger pushed for engagement with moderate Arabs and resisted the use of military force as a tool of foreign policy.[18] These divisions would prove to be a serious impediment to decision making early on in Reagan's tenure.[19]

As secretary of state, Haig pursued a radical rethinking of American priorities in the Middle East, which he called "strategic consensus." To address concerns about the Soviet Union and the "fear of Islamic fundamentalism" in the wake of the Iranian Revolution and the Soviet invasion of Afghanistan, he argued that the United States should pursue policies with the dual aim of fighting communism and bolstering moderate Arab states, while upholding Israel's security.[20] The logic of Haig's new order necessitated that the U.S. government oppose Soviet allies like Syria and the PLO.[21] Haig's policy was a piece of the larger "Reagan Doctrine," an overarching statement of U.S. foreign policy aims that abetted a revival of a global Cold War struggle. Through military interventions and the arming of anti-communist resistance movements in the effort to "roll back" Soviet-supported government in Latin America, Africa, and Asia, the Reagan White House embarked on what one scholar of the period has called an "anti-revolutionary offensive in the Third World."[22]

In the Middle East, this approach played a central role in the administration's retreat from dealing with the question of Palestinian self-determination. Hermann Eilts, the U.S. ambassador to Egypt at the time, explained how this "different sense of priorities" affected regional diplomacy. "The whole idea of autonomy talks that flowed from Camp David was given short shrift," Eilts later recalled, "and the Reagan administration, it seemed, really didn't care. It had strategic consensus and the Soviets on its mind."[23] For career officers in the State Department, this was troubling. Nicholas Veliotes, Reagan's assistant secretary of state for Near Eastern and South Asian Affairs, remarked that there was "a determination to globalize everything in the Middle East." "In part," Veliotes explained some years later, "if your analysis of the Middle East always started from the East-West focus, you could obscure the regional roots of the problem."[24] In oversimplifying regional complexities and positioning Israel as a key asset early on in the first term,

Reagan represented a clear departure from Carter's approach to comprehensive peace in the region.

Israel: A Strategic Ally

To strengthen the U.S.-Israeli relationship along Cold War lines, Alexander Haig made his first trip to Egypt and Israel as secretary of state in April 1981. Reports had already surfaced of Reagan's plans for a military presence on the ground in the Persian Gulf and the prevailing view in Washington that "subordinates the regional quarrel between Arabs and Israelis to the global rivalry between the Soviet Union and the United States."[25] At his opening meeting with Israeli prime minister Menachem Begin and senior advisors, Haig articulated such an approach in addressing the rising tensions in the Lebanese city of Zahle, close to the Syrian border. Syrian aggression against the Christians living in the town, a subset of the civil war that had been raging throughout the country since 1975, was portrayed as part of a broader Soviet struggle for increased influence in the region.[26]

This worldview was not limited to regional struggles but shaped discussions over the Palestinian question as well. Begin was eager to draw on the Cold War framework as justification for enshrining his well-developed views about limited autonomy, reminding Haig that he had already spoken on several occasions of a promise of "autonomy, not sovereignty." Haig agreed. Begin then reminded the secretary of state of Israel's deep opposition to a Palestinian state, invoking Soviet influence elsewhere in the region. "It would be a mortal danger to us," Begin implored. "It would be a Soviet base in the Middle East, after all the Soviets achieved: Mozambique, South Yemen, Ethiopia, invading Afghanistan," the prime minister emphasized. "Unavoidably the Judea, Samaria and Gaza District and those settlements would be taken over by the PLO and the PLO is a real satellite of the Soviet Union."[27] The inclusion of the PLO into the Soviet orbit solidified the link between Palestinian state prevention and shared U.S.-Israeli foreign policy goals in the Cold War. Secretary Haig's official toast at a dinner that evening underscored this interdependence. Turning to his Israeli hosts at Jerusalem's King David Hotel, Haig praised the country for playing "an essential role in protecting our mutual strategic concerns against the threats of the Soviet Union and against the threats of its many surrogates."[28]

Such mutual interest between the United States and Israel was encapsulated by Haig's effort to initiate a strategic dialogue beyond existing military channels. The secretary of state presented this idea during his meeting the next morning, part of an effort to develop a regional strategy in the Middle East. Haig suggested that key State Department personnel, including Robert McFarlane and General Vernon Walters, act as liaisons with the Israelis.[29] They would meet with their Israeli counterparts in Washington and Jerusalem, under the cover of relations with other local and European powers. Haig said that the "interrelationship" must be "carefully guarded, but it must be launched with an attitude of mutual confidence between the two of us."[30] These meetings, which continued throughout the summer and fall of 1981, culminated in the formalization of a strategic alliance between the two countries.[31]

The start of formal discussion about this alliance coincided with Begin's first official visit to the Reagan White House in September 1981. At the welcome ceremony on the South Lawn, Reagan delivered solicitous opening remarks that echoed the new approach of his administration. "We know Israelis live in constant peril. But Israel will have our help. She will remain strong and secure, and her special character of spirit, genius, and faith will prevail," the president assured his guest. "The security of Israel is a principal objective of this administration," Reagan concluded, telling Begin "we regard Israel as an ally in our search for regional stability."[32] Since taking office, Reagan had also courted domestic supporters of Israel, outwardly embracing the same constituency he courted during the election.[33] The Office of Public Liaison, led for several years by future senator Elizabeth Dole, expended considerable energy reaching out to Jewish communal leaders and listening to their concerns. Dole outlined a "Jewish Strategy" for the administration and sought to capitalize on the historically disproportionate number who voted for Reagan in the election.[34]

Some observers cautioned Reagan not to embrace the Likud government in pursuing pro-Israel policies. In the lead editorial on the morning of Begin's visit, the *Washington Post* warned Reagan

FIGURE 5.1. "President Ronald Reagan and Prime Minister Menachem Begin
Sharing a Laugh at the White House in Washington." September 10, 1981.
Sa'ar Ya'acov, courtesy of Israel's Government Press Office.

to be wary of an "endorsement of [Begin's] evident goal of annexing the West Bank."[35] A *New York Times* editorial earlier that week spoke of the forgotten promise of the Camp David Accords to provide self-rule for Palestinians: "Guaranteeing Israel's security is not the same as underwriting an annexation of the West Bank."[36] Both newspapers pushed for engagement with the Palestinian question and greater political rights in the occupied territories. The political leadership in Israel and the United States, however, was disinclined to focus on what they deemed an internal Israeli matter.

During their first extended meeting on September 9, the American and Israeli delegations agreed to launch a written document outlining strategic cooperation. The remarks by Defense Minister Ariel Sharon reflected an expansive vision of Israel's Cold War strategic value to the United States in the Middle East: "Israel can do things, Mr. President, that other countries cannot do. We have the stability of a real democracy. We are on the Mediterranean. Israel is a country positioned from which we can both act in the Mediterranean theatre and in Africa. We are capable of embarking upon cooperation immediately." Sharon also invoked covert Israeli actions, including the raid on Entebbe Airport in July 1976 to free hostages and the secret June 1981 airstrike on Osirak, an Iraqi nuclear reactor that was being built near Baghdad. "We have American equipment which we can put at your disposal in the shortest time. We have the needed infrastructure, including military industry, other industries, airfields and so forth. We have a long arm strategic capability, as for example, Entebbe and Baghdad," Sharon added.[37]

One American participant recalled seeing Secretary Weinberger "blanch visibly" at Sharon's presentation, which outlined Israeli military assistance as far east as Iran and as far north as Turkey. Weinberger had pushed for engagement with moderate allies in the region and was wary of any sign that the United States was turning away from key Arab states, particularly the Gulf countries. "Everyone on the American side was shocked by the grandiose scope of the Sharon concept for strategic cooperation," observed U.S. ambassador to Israel Samuel Lewis. "It even included use of Israeli forces to assist the U.S. in case of uprisings in the Gulf emirates."[38] The gap between the Israeli concept of strategic cooperation and the tempered enthusiasm of some U.S. officials was linked to competing interests across the Middle East. One of the primary beneficiaries of U.S. Cold War strategy in the region was now Saudi Arabia, a country that defense officials like Weinberger hoped would move closer toward the West as Egypt had done at Camp David. This duality bred a great deal of tension. Israeli leaders and American Jewish organizations vocally opposed the sale of F-15 fighter jets and Airborne Warning and Control Systems (AWACS) to Riyadh, threatening to undermine an emerging regional constellation of power. Reagan insisted to Begin that Saudi Arabia could be "brought around" to the U.S. orbit, fearing that they would otherwise turn to the Soviet Union. The president promised that he had Israel's interests in mind while pursuing the arms sales. "If not," he added, "we will take corrective action."[39]

Against the backdrop of these strategic discussions, Israeli leaders gave a great deal of thought to their presentations in Washington that dealt with autonomy. Begin's advisors encouraged those traveling to the United States to refrain from dealing with debates over sovereignty in the West Bank or Jerusalem: "The United States should be urged (only for the purpose of deferring these difficult matters) to adopt positions consistent with those of Israel."[40] During a breakfast meeting between the two delegations on September 10, the Israelis followed this line precisely. Dr. Joseph Burg, the head of the Israeli autonomy delegation, told Reagan about the "philosophy" of the autonomy talks, which ranged between two extremes. "We do not want to be absolute rulers of more than one million Arabs and secondly, we cannot afford a Palestinian state. It would be a communist state, irredentist, and a danger to our lives." Burg recounted the Israeli conception of self-government and the progress on technicalities in the talks he convened with the Egyptians. "We did not make progress on one important matter and I can put that into a mathematical formula," Burg explained to the U.S. president. "Autonomy is not sovereignty. Sovereignty minus x is autonomy. Our problem was to determine the size of x. For Egypt, autonomy was seen as a corridor to an Arab state and for us, instead of an Arab state, a substitute for an Arab state."[41] In presenting the Israeli view of progress on autonomy, Burg invoked the U.S. role in facilitating an advancement of the talks. Haig remarked that he found Burg's presentation "very helpful," and that "what Dr. Burg has said is very close to our thinking."[42]

On the PLO, Begin's advisors voiced concern about possible indirect U.S. engagement on matters relating to Lebanon and encouraged the idea that the links between the organization and the Soviet Union be emphasized: "P.L.O. statements promising Soviet bases in a Palestinian state, supporting Soviet positions, and attacking the United States, cannot be repeated too often."[43] It was an opportune moment to push the line of greater Soviet-Palestinian cooperation, as the diplomatic links between the two had grown in the wake of Camp David, with the Kremlin on the verge of upgrading the PLO's diplomatic status to allow for an embassy in Moscow.[44] This alignment was framed in a manner that would highlight Israel's role as an ally in the global anti-communist struggle, which appealed to Reagan's own thinking. Concluding his talks with the Israelis, Reagan summed up the American view on the Palestinians: "We will never negotiate with them until they recognize the right of Israel to exist and abandon the present position. Until then, we shall never negotiate with the Palestinians."[45] This position reflected the ascendant view at the White House, pleasing Israeli diplomats immensely.[46]

On November 30, 1981, Reagan officials signed a U.S. government Memorandum of Understanding with Israel, promoting strategic cooperation to deal with the Soviet threat. It encompassed joint military exercises and preventative threat measures, emphasizing the importance of a unified front against communism.[47] While leading supporters of Israel like Secretary Haig were pleased to formalize a strategic relationship, conservative critics like Weinberger worked to strip it of real content. As Lewis recalls, "Weinberger managed to have it signed in the basement of the Pentagon without any press present, so that it didn't get any attention. The Israeli press was fully briefed and made a big thing out of it, but there were no photographs of Weinberger signing this document with Sharon—they might have been used in the Arab world to undermine his position."[48]

In forging this alliance, the Reagan administration turned a blind eye to the more troubling aspects of the Begin government's agenda, such as ongoing settlement expansion in the West Bank. They also put aside strident arguments that had emerged over Israel's bombing of Iraq's Osirak nuclear reactor that summer.[49] But not long after the signing of the memorandum, a major crisis erupted in December. Prime Minister Begin decided to extend Israeli law to the Golan Heights through implicit annexation.[50] Critics of Israel in the administration were furious, with Weinberger exclaiming, "How long do we have to go on bribing Israel? If there is no real cost to the Israelis, we'll never be able to stop any of their actions."[51] Reagan took decisive action by suspending the agreement and the millions in potential arms sales, infuriating the Israeli prime minister. Begin responded directly to Ambassador Lewis. "Are we a state or vassals of yours? Are we a banana republic?" he exclaimed. "You have no right to penalize Israel. . . . The people of Israel lived without the memorandum of understanding for 3,700 years, and will continue to live without it for another 3,700 years."[52] This angry reaction did in fact reveal the existence of some underlying tension in the U.S.-Israeli relationship in the early Reagan years.[53]

Despite these disagreements, Israel emerged in the early 1980s with a new strategic rationale to entrench its global Cold War standing and solidify its regional position in the Middle East.[54] This bilateral alliance also helped the Begin government counter Palestinian demands for self-rule by dismissing the PLO as a Soviet proxy and denying them political standing in the process. Furthermore, the relationship enabled intensified settlement building in the occupied territories, solidifying Israel's internal hold over the West Bank and Gaza Strip.

Excluding the PLO

In January 1980, Jimmy Carter's National Security Advisor, Zbigniew Brzezinski, had commissioned an in-depth study titled "US Relations with the Radical Arabs." The top-secret document was sent to select officials in the Carter White House, including the president and Secretary of State Cyrus Vance. Written in the wake of the Iranian Revolution and at the time of the Soviet invasion of Afghanistan, the memo outlined the ways in which America could improve its relations with the Islamic world. The Brzezinski study pointed out that U.S. "relations with the radical Arabs are in large measure a function of our attitude toward the Palestinians and their most widely recognized representative, the PLO." Carter's advisors argued that "as long as we maintain our present position on the PLO and as long as the Palestinians do not see an independent state in their future, progress on these other fronts is likely to be limited."[55]

The new administration was not receptive to this stance.[56] When Reagan was asked during the campaign whether he thought the PLO was a terrorist organization, he answered affirmatively while also making an important distinction: "I separate the PLO from the Palestinian refugees. None ever elected the PLO."[57] His views were connected to broader conservative antipathy toward the violence of anticolonial movements in the 1960s and 1970s. "We live in a world in which any band of thugs clever enough to get the word 'liberation' into its name can thereupon murder schoolchildren and have its deeds considered glamorous and glorious," Reagan had said in his B'nai B'rith speech. "Terrorists are not guerrillas, or commandos, or freedom-fighters or anything else. They are terrorists and should be identified as such. If others wish to deal with them, establish diplomatic relations with them, let it be on their heads. And let them be willing to pay the price of appeasement."[58] He vowed to uphold the 1975 U.S. agreement with Israel concerning PLO non-engagement until the organization met conditions for a dialogue and became "truly representative of those Arab Palestinians dedicated to peace and not to the establishment of a Soviet satellite in the heart of the Middle East."[59]

Although the PLO was shifting from military resistance to a diplomatic track in the 1970s, there were still important fissures within the constituent factions of the Palestinian national movement. Several terror attacks in the early 1980s reaffirmed the administration's belief that there was no negotiating partner among the Palestinians. European governments, in contrast, saw a complex organization undergoing an internal transformation and challenged such a broad indictment by advocating engagement with the official arm of Palestinian nationalists. In one meeting with Jewish leaders, British foreign secretary Lord Carrington noted that he "personally opposed terrorism but for the past two years has spent more time negotiating with 'so called' 'terrorists' (or 'freedom fighters, depending on who is describing them') than he has with non-terrorists."[60] It was rejectionist factions and splinter groups the Europeans deemed responsible for persistent violence. One such group, the notorious Abu Nidal organization, was formed in 1974 after a split in the PLO. The faction was supported by Baathist Iraq in a highly visible and destructive terror campaign against Israel and western targets, as well as PLO members who pursued a diplomatic track. Officials in the Reagan White House often blurred this distinction.[61]

Richard Allen, Reagan's National Security Advisor, was a central figure in articulating the administration's policy toward the PLO and was vocal in dismissing countervailing influences within the organization. During an interview on the ABC news program 20/20, Allen labeled the group a "terrorist organization" until "it provides convincing evidence to the contrary."[62] According to Allen, moderate factions within the organization had little bearing on the administration's overall stance: "I've heard descriptions that identified Arafat as a moderate. But we're certainly wanting in hard proof that this is the case. One man's moderate is another man's terrorist." Asked about Soviet influence in the region, Allen remarked, "It's difficult to assess the relationship with the PLO because there are various component parts. . . . But, overall, I think it's fair to say the Soviet Union is supporting the main aims of the PLO."[63]

Douglas J. Feith was another ideological opponent of the PLO working in the National Security Council. In a largely redacted memo concerning U.S. relations with the Palestinians, Feith suggested an uncompromising approach that aligned with the administration's global Cold War aims. The administration should take action that would demonstrate the "coherence" of three "chief foreign policy promises and themes: 1) to combat international terrorism; 2) to counter the Soviet Union's use of subversive proxies; and 3) to bolster our friends and stand down our enemies."[64] Feith pointed to a section of Secretary of State Alexander Haig's Senate confirmation testimony, where Haig singled out the PLO as a "pretty tough hardcore group of terrorists."[65] An unsigned memo appearing alongside Feith's analysis recommended a "multifaceted campaign against the PLO," including diplomatic marginalization of the organization through a campaign to "ostracize" the group, an emphasis on the Soviet connection, and the closure of the PLO information office in Washington. The second suggested element of an American campaign against the PLO was labeled "Force," with the first recommendation suggesting a "'Green light' to Israel to destroy the PLO's military capabilities."[66]

There were White House officials who understood that the situation was complex and attempted to offer more nuanced assessments. Raymond Tanter, an NSC staffer focusing on Middle East issues, wrote to Richard Allen in November, "The President should not brand all of the PLO organizations as terrorists since the PLO includes a number of social and political institutions."[67] He cited the CIA's *Palestinian Handbook*, which recognized non-terrorist entities like the PLO Research Center and the Palestine Red Crescent Society. Tanter composed a primer on this issue for a presidential press conference, highlighting the distinction between individual humanitarian agencies and the PLO as a whole. In it, he emphasized that there would be no negotiations until relevant UN resolutions were accepted alongside an affirmation of Israel's right to exist.[68] Congressman Paul Findley, who had pushed for engagement with the PLO under Carter, continued to argue that the long-term interests of American policy in the region necessitated a dialogue with the PLO, but officially the administration stood its ground.[69]

Unofficially, there is ample evidence of direct low-level contact between the American government and moderate members of the PLO. A series of newspaper articles in the summer of 1981 revealed ongoing talks since Henry Kissinger's time in office, which Reagan's contacts primarily facilitated through the CIA and the American embassy in Beirut.[70] The administration also had less formal contacts with PLO members through interlocutors like John Mroz, the director of Middle East Studies at the International Peace Academy in New York. Mroz's congenial relationship with Isam Sartawi, a leading Palestinian voice of engagement, is clear from letters provided directly to Geoffrey Kemp, senior director for Near East and South Asia Affairs at the National Security Council. Sartawi had passed along to Mroz official PLO documents distributed by Arafat, which were then given to Kemp at the White House in their original Arabic.[71]

Internal executive branch discussions further reveal a more nuanced understanding of the PLO and its moderating elements than Allen's public remarks or Feith's internal recommendations would imply. In an August memo to Kemp, Landrum Bolling outlined a more realistic view of the complicated Palestinian situation. Bolling, who was the important back channel contact with the PLO under Carter, underscored the growing rift between Palestinians in the West Bank and the PLO in Beirut. He noted that the sense among West Bankers was that "there is still no coherent, unified Palestinian strategy for ending the occupation and bringing peace."[72] They blamed a quarreling leadership in Lebanon for stunting political progress and criticized cross-border terrorism because it provided justification for the ongoing Israeli occupation. There was, however, a consensus position that backed the PLO as the legitimate voice of the Palestinian people, seeing it as the kernel of an independent state. Bolling, unlike Allen, stressed these positive developments: "Palestinians accept Israel as a permanent fact in the Middle East. They know that Israel is here to stay, and they are prepared to live with it. Almost no Palestinian thinks or talks anymore about the abolition of the State of Israel."[73]

Palestinian factions in Beirut took note of the hostile atmosphere in Washington, which was reflected in the active Arabic press at the time. One leading weekly, *Al-Hadaf* (The Target), was unrelenting in its critique of what it characterized as American neoimperial aspirations in the Middle East, as well as the failure of Arab states that were seen as having sold out the Palestinian cause. The newspaper, founded by the acclaimed Palestinian writer Ghassan Kanafani, was the mouthpiece of the Marxist-leaning Popular Front for the Liberation of Palestine (PFLP).[74] The PFLP served as a strong counterweight to the dominant Fatah party of Yasser Arafat; the sentiments expressed in its official publication reflected the view of many grassroots leaders in Lebanon who remained wary of calls for engagement along U.S.-dictated lines.

Reagan himself, in the eyes of *Al-Hadaf*, was restoring the use of force as the primary tool of American foreign policy in the region. Along with Secretary of State Haig, the president was portrayed as a radical departure from Carter and the U.S. human rights agenda with his strident anti-Soviet approach.[75] From the perspective of Palestinian activists in the Global South, Reagan offered little hope for improving America's standing abroad. The reports in *Al-Hadaf* reflected the atmosphere of Reagan's first few months in office, when attention to regional conflict was replaced by a reinscription of Cold War strategies. By mid-February 1981, the paper was forcefully attacking the new president for ratcheting up military pressure in the region and resorting to ideological positions that situated the Soviet Union as the prime antagonist in the Middle East.[76] The brunt of *Al-Hadaf*'s fury, however, was directed at Israel and Prime Minister Menachem Begin. Under a grotesque cartoon of Begin, face deformed, blood dripping from his hands, and a dagger at the ready, the paper attacked Israeli settlement policy in the West Bank and Begin's undermining of Palestinian national identity.[77]

Enabling Settlements

The linkage between Begin's settlement expansion and the Reagan administration was evident in the changing U.S. position toward the legality of ongoing building projects in the West Bank. Throughout Carter's presidency, U.S. policy on the settlements had been "clear and consistent."[78] They were considered illegal under international law and detrimental to the peace process, and the administration opposed both new settlements and expansion of those already built. During the 1980 campaign, Reagan took a very different stance. In an interview with *Time* magazine on June 30, 1980, the California governor was asked whether he would "try to persuade Israel to stop settling on the West Bank." His response underscored a clear difference with Carter. "Frankly, I don't know the answer to that. Under U.N. Resolution 242, the West Bank was supposed to be open to all, and then Jordan and Israel were to work out an agreement for the area." In light of these terms Reagan argued, "I do not see how it is illegal for Israel to move in settlements."[79]

In the week after his inauguration, Reagan would expand on this new position after lawmakers in Jerusalem approved three new West Bank settlements. When asked about the expansion during a press conference, Reagan replied: "As to the West Bank, I believe the settlements there—I disagreed when the previous administration referred to them as illegal, they're not illegal. Not under the UN resolution that leaves the West Bank open to all people—Arab and Israeli alike, Christian alike." Reagan was drawing on an argument promoted by neoconservatives within the administration who disputed the prevailing interpretation of UN resolution 242, but the international community was in agreement that the text clearly deemed the settlements illegal. The president admitted, however, that further building was not astute: "I do think now with this rush to do it and this moving in there the way they are is ill-advised because if we're going to continue with the spirit of Camp David to try and arrive at a peace, maybe this, at this time, is unnecessarily provocative."[80] While recognizing that settlement expansion might be detrimental to fully implementing Camp David, the president was careful not to preclude Jewish presence in the area. A congressional letter requesting clarification of Reagan's exact policy received a noncommittal note of appreciation.[81] A more pointed inquiry about the policy shift from the chairman of the Palestine Congress of North America was shuffled to the Office of the Public Liaison.[82]

Egyptian officials were furious that the Israeli government was claiming to negotiate a solution to the Palestinian question while pursuing a "ruinous policy" of "settlements and more settlements."[83]

Israel's expansion into the territories in early 1981 directly affected the fate of the autonomy talks, drawing the ire of the Egyptian minister of foreign affairs, Kamal Hassan Ali. In a letter to Israel's minister of foreign affairs and future prime minister Yitzhak Shamir, Ali invoked the understanding reached at Camp David about a settlement moratorium while negotiations were ongoing. In Ali's view, it was both "illegal and inconceivable to use this illegitimate and trumped up anachronism in the name of so-called Israeli security, as a pretext to cover up Israel's policy of annexation." As the lead Egyptian diplomat explained, this was "an incitement to hatred, a provocation, and an added source of tension among the Palestinian and Arab population."[84] In such an atmosphere, the shift in the American position away from long-standing assertions of settlement illegality proved to be damaging and consequential.

The Begin government pushed the Americans to endorse their expansion by asserting the settlements as part of a broader security arrangement for Israel. During Secretary Haig's April 1981 visit to Israel, Ariel Sharon laid out his conception of Israel's security needs in a series of slides. His explanation was rooted in the retention of the occupied territories for defensive purposes. "I want to emphasize that the West Bank, the Judean and Samarian mountains and the Golan Heights are the backbone of the State of Israel as far as its defense is concerned, not only for the deployment of troops but for its early warning capability, command and control capability and anti-air defense system," Sharon told Haig. "As long as we have our military troops posted there we can adopt a defensive strategy."[85] Haig was sympathetic to this argument, and it contributed to the administration's legitimizing stance on the question of legality.

At the National Security Council, Middle East advisor Raymond Tanter wrote a vigorous defense of the Reagan administration's new approach in August 1981.

> The settlements *are legal*, but the issue is properly a *political* question, *not* a *legal* question. The *USG* [United States Government] *has recognized no country's sovereignty* over the West Bank *since Britain* controlled the area under the Palestine Mandate. The issue of sovereignty is open and will not be closed until the actual parties to the conflict *formally consent* to a peace agreement. In the meantime, there is

no law that bars Jews from settling in the West Bank. No one should be excluded from an area simply on account of nationality or religion. An ambiguous response concerning the legality of settlements inadvertently causes more press interest than either: 1) a finding that settlements are legal or 2) a statement that the legal question is irrelevant.[86]

Tanter's position reflected the rationale of the earliest statements that Reagan made about settlements during the campaign. The justification was formulated several months after the president took office, by which time government officials had become fully aware of the extensive damage caused by the settlements and yet "remained mute" on the matter.[87]

Despite mounting evidence of the settlements' detrimental effects, there was a strong neoconservative influence on the political and legal approach to the issue in the White House. Douglas Feith had previously denounced Carter's insistence that settlements were an obstacle to peace, arguing that the problem was Arab intransigence. "If the Jews have a claim to Judea-Samaria at least as rightful as that of the Arabs and if the purpose of the Israeli settlements there is to stake this claim," Feith wrote in the Heritage Foundation's journal *Policy Review*, "then it may be that Israel's stand on the West Bank is not irrational after all."[88] Significantly, Feith deliberately used the biblical names for the occupied territories, "Judea and Samaria," the default parlance of religious nationalists and Likud party politicians in Israel. This united a strategic argument with a neoconservative legal one.

When it came to prevailing discourse around the Israeli-Palestinian conflict, a rightward turn had suffused the intellectual currents of American politics and foreign policy during the late 1970s and early 1980s.[89] It was a time when the Democratic senator from New York, Daniel Patrick Moynihan, publicly rejected the application of the Geneva Conventions to the settlements. In a noted article for *Commentary* at the beginning of 1981, Moynihan lambasted the United Nations for its condemnation of Israel. Singling out U.S. support for a Security Council resolution that had reaffirmed the applicability of the Geneva Conventions to the West Bank, Moynihan argued that the treaty was intended to criminalize deportation and territorial occupation in Nazi Germany, and its invocation in this case "played, of course, perfectly into the Soviet propaganda position."[90] Moynihan's formative role in emboldening neoconservatives with his activism around anti-Zionist resolutions at the United Nations in the mid-1970s set the stage for these debates in the early 1980s.[91]

This rightward drift also took hold in Israeli political life. Begin narrowly won a second election on June 30, 1981, with forty-eight seats going to the Likud, forming the nineteenth government of Israel. As demonstrated in his earlier interactions with Carter and Sadat, the Israeli prime minister had a very clear and consistent view of continued territorial control by Israel on all the land west of the Jordan River. He never hid his views from the public, speaking about them at an annual ceremony held at the gravesite of Ze'ev Jabotinsky on the day of his second electoral victory: "Western *Eretz Yisrael* is all under our control. She is no longer divided. No piece of territory will pass to non-Jewish control, to foreign sovereignty."[92] Begin's position on continued sovereignty and settlement expansion was bolstered by the writings of vocal defenders like Moynihan and the advice of Eugene Rostow, who had already published legal arguments along these same lines as a faculty member at Yale and was serving in the Reagan administration as the newly appointed director of the Arms Control and Disarmament Agency. The consequence of this semantic and legal shift was borne out in practical terms by the rapid pace of Israeli expansion through the 1980s. Since the Likud victory in 1977, the settler population outside of the Jerusalem area had quadrupled from about 5,000 to 20,000, and in the Gaza Strip the number of settlements had doubled. In the summer months of 1981 alone, 7,000 settlers had moved into the West Bank.[93]

In February 1982, Reagan's ambassador to Israel Samuel Lewis cabled an urgent memo about these developments to Washington and more than a dozen American embassies and consulates throughout the Middle East and Europe. He wrote a detailed account explaining how "settlement activity goes on at an accelerated pace, although in new and potentially more serious directions."[94] In a sober and matter-of-fact style, Lewis recounted the method of land appropriation that had taken over nearly a third of the West Bank, describing the process by which Jerusalem's municipal boundaries were being extended southward over the Green Line toward Gush Etzion, now one of the largest settlement blocs in the West Bank. He also outlined the manner in which Israel's Ministry of Defense "pre-settlements" were transformed into permanent civilian settlements, a process that bypassed any earlier pledge of a slowdown by Begin. Lewis reported on plans by the World Zionist Organization to increase the Israeli settler population to 130,000 within five years by expanding existing settlements rather than building new ones from scratch. He highlighted how such an increase was being organized in a cost-effective manner to create urban communities where settlers would work in Israeli cities and live in cheap spacious homes over the Green Line. Lewis also pointed to an important demographic transformation taking place, with the newest settlers moving for economic rather than ideological reasons.[95]

The most glaring section of the cable was the American ambassador's insights into the act of territorial acquisition itself, explaining how thousands of acres were being declared state-owned or Jewish-owned private land and "taken over de facto for settlement purposes." Encouraged by the exorbitant demands of settlers who had recently been evacuated from the Yamit region settlements in the Sinai as part of the Israeli-Egyptian peace deal, West Bank settlers were caught in a "land rush," often resorting to questionable methods in order to purchase land parcels. Few officials in Israel really knew the exact area under Israeli control, although the government had built a "massive infrastructure" of roads, power lines, military installations, and power systems "thoroughly locked into Israeli grids" that was intended to create a system of dependence on Israel proper.[96]

Lewis captured the ultimate aim of this entire settlement endeavor in his cable. "The goal has been to create a matrix of Israeli control in the West Bank so deeply rooted that no subsequent Israeli government would be able to relinquish substantial chunks of that territory, even in exchange for peace," the ambassador explained. Concluding with an assessment of the growing support for these settlements among Israelis, Lewis decried the lack of protest and explained how announcements of new expansion are "met with virtual silence" and how "the majority of Israelis have come to accept the settlements in the occupied territories as a fact of life." Finally placing these developments alongside the stalled autonomy talks, the ambassador explained how the presence of a large number of Israeli settlers undermines the possibility of a "self-governing authority developing into an embryo government of an independent PLO-state-in-the-making."[97] It could not be more evident to U.S. officials that any resolution of the Palestinian question was impossible under these circumstances.

Reagan himself was personally aware of the consequences of this expansion. In his diary entry on February 14, 1983, the president wrote: "Valentine's Day. Had a brief on the West Bank. There can be no question but that Israel has a well thought out plan to take over the W.B. [West Bank]."[98] In his memoirs, Reagan later wrote that settlements were a "continued violation of UN Security Council Resolution 242."[99] This was contrary to his statements during the campaign and at odds with his actions while in office. As late as 1988, upon hearing that Israel was planning new settlements, all Reagan could muster was "We are going to try and talk them out of that."[100] In actuality, the Reagan administration played a crucial role in enabling expansion, and the Israelis were acutely aware of this permissive approach.

In the course of a fact-finding meeting with Israeli officials on January 28, 1982, Secretary of State Haig raised the matter of land acquisition directly with Israeli minister Joseph Burg and the autonomy committee in Jerusalem. He invoked the suspicions mounting in the Arab world and among Palestinians "that what is underway is de facto annexation," proffering the possibility of thickening existing settlements rather than building new ones: "Camp David does not say that annexation is the objective, just as it does not say, very clearly, that there is any hope or any objective of a Palestinian state. But you can't have it both ways." Israeli officials countered with a deep commitment to settlement building both as a security mechanism to safeguard Israel proper and as a long-standing right inherent in the Zionist return to the land in their response. For Burg, the head of the autonomy committee, Israeli settlements were an insurance policy "to prevent partition of this country." Limiting growth, Burg argued, would lead to a process of "degeneration" and "national despair." He disputed Haig's characterization of Jewish settlements as annexation, invoking his own experience living in Prague during the German annexation of Sudetenland. "I know what is annexation [*sic*]. Living in part of Eretz Israel is not annexation."[101]

Other Israeli officials pushed back against Haig from alternative directions. Yitzhak Shamir, the minister of foreign affairs, argued that the status of territory could be separated out from the political rights of the individual. This arrangement, in practice, yielded a reality where territorial sovereignty was transformed while the inhabitants remained disenfranchised.[102] In the fall of 1981, confronting an earlier political impasse during the autonomy talks, Shamir explained his government's position during an interview with Israeli radio: "The purpose of the autonomy scheme, that we have proposed, is not to create a state for a stateless people, and not to give a home to a homeless people." Shamir was adamant that Palestinians were not entitled to self-determination. "The Palestinian Arab people is not a stateless people and is not a homeless people. They already have their state, they already have their home and their country—it is called now Jordan. Jordan is a Palestinian Arab state. Its population is of Palestinian origin. Its culture, language and its mentality are all Palestinian."[103] For Shamir, like Begin, autonomy served as a mechanism to deal with the Palestinian Arabs in the territories of the West Bank and Gaza along non-national lines.

Ariel Sharon, the leading architect of the expansion, focused on conveying the importance of security to Haig by depicting the settlements as integral to Israel's defense. "Settlements have been always part of our national security concept, and I am a great believer in this concept, being born myself on one of those settlements, and I can tell you that my mother—she is 82 years old—still sleeps with a gun under her pillow and that's normal here. Everyone knows exactly his task. That is the immediate contribution of the settlements to Israel's security." Sharon also justified building across the 1967 borders as a natural outcome of displacement and migration, while linking settlements directly with Palestinian state prevention. "These settlements are perhaps the strongest barrier that we have against any possibility of forming in the future a second Palestinian state, and by doing that, by having these settlements, that is the contribution, as I said, to the rest of the world." He also added his

Cold War concerns about Soviet expansion in the Middle East, depicting the settlements as a solution both to the Soviet "danger" in the long term and in short-term confrontations with Arab states.[104]

More than all his colleagues, Prime Minister Begin offered Reagan's secretary of state the definitive Israeli response. He excitedly told Haig and his delegation that the legal debate over settlements was "finished." Begin recalled the first time he met President Carter in the Cabinet Room, and Carter told Begin "we consider your settlements to be illegal and an obstacle to peace." He had seen Carter more than ten times, and at each meeting, Carter repeated the message, "illegal and an obstacle to peace." But Begin disagreed. "I answered: legal and not an obstacle to peace. He didn't tire; I didn't tire." As Begin asserted, "Mr. Ronald Reagan, put an end to that debate. He said, the settlements are not illegal. A double negative gives a positive result. In other words, they are legal or legitimate." For Begin, who had long championed the expansion of the Jewish presence beyond the 1967 borders, settlements were not an obstacle to peace with the Palestinians. "On the contrary," he added, "they are a great contribution to peaceful relationships between the Jews and the Arabs in Judea and Samaria and the Gaza District." Without them, PLO fighters would come down from the mountains to the plains of Israel and carry out attacks on Jews. "If there are no settlements there, they can just come down."[105]

Haig had been informed that the situation in the West Bank was generating "paranoia" among Palestinians. "I can tell you the paranoia is just mind-boggling," the secretary of state replied to his Israeli counterparts. "Mostly they are fed incorrect facts and they get that from the PLO . . . but one thing they say they know, and one thing they fear is that this is a formula—autonomy under the current arrangements, as they believe them to exist—that the land will all be gone."[106] Yet Begin painted an idealistic view of Palestinian relations with the settlers. "They visit each other. They help each other. There's never been a problem. The only place in which there are clashes from time to time is in Hebron—the only place." Invoking a mythological trope about the lack of cultivation before the arrival of Zionist pioneers, the prime minister recalled the rocky land in which settlements were built. "It was desert, untilled for so many years, but, of course, you can do something and we do something, in the pioneering spirit which you know so well from your own history and, therefore, sometimes the grey color turned into green." Sharon deceitfully added that these areas had little or no inhabitants, "the population is very small or doesn't exist at all." It was also the case, Sharon noted, that these hilltops were state-owned land. "I had tremendous difficulties when I tried to expropriate private land," Sharon told the Americans, in light of the Begin's government's legal dispute over certain areas of the West Bank.[107] As for the issue of credibility around the world, Sharon concluded, "If I will have to choose—I know it is a hard decision—between credibility and security—I will take security."[108] In articulating their positions in such a direct and forceful manner, Israeli officials took full advantage of sympathetic American interlocutors and the forgiving attitude of the Reagan administration. The U.S. secretary of state expressed his appreciation for the substantive talks, admitting that he spoke with "uncharacteristic bluntness," a function of the "mutual confidence" between both Israel and the United States.[109]

Autonomy's Demise

Haig traveled to Jerusalem to seek a way out of the impasse around autonomy, as the United States continued to mediate successive rounds of discussions between Egypt and Israel into early 1982. After the successful implementation of the Egyptian-Israeli peace treaty, the focus on the Palestinian dimension of the Camp David talks received far less attention. This was compounded by a political transition in Cairo. Egyptian president Anwar al-Sadat was gunned down on October 6, 1981, during the annual Egyptian victory parade to mark the Egyptian army's performance in the 1973 War. The assassins, led by the Egyptian army officer Khaled Al-Islambouli, were members of Egyptian Islamic Jihad. Their motivations grew out of domestic unrest in Egypt and disaffection over Sadat's treatment of Islamists inside the country.[110] While Sadat's passing did not jeopardize the Camp David Accords (his vice president, Hosni Mubarak, worked to safeguard them), it did highlight the increasingly deadlocked discussions over autonomy.

In a final attempt to advance these discussions, Haig convened a meeting of Israeli officials in Jerusalem that January, nearly two years since Sol Linowitz had made the last serious effort under Carter. Among the topics that had bedeviled the talks was the debate over sovereignty, with the Egyptians demanding the relinquishment of Israeli control and Israel asserting it should be maintained. Elyakim Rubinstein, Israel's legal advisor, offered the official view: "The source of authority, legally speaking, is sort of in the shadows but is under us in the five years, and, of course, it would have some practical implications with the security things, with the Jewish settlements and so on." He did not want to bother with international agreements or treaties. "Who needs them? This is something which just would waste the time and there is no problem, real problem, that necessitates it." Likewise, Rubinstein argued, there should not be a separate Palestinian currency or other symbols of sovereignty. Haig, who was sympathetic to the Israeli point of view, could not see why the Egyptians raised objections. "I must say, I don't feel that we have a problem with this thing [autonomy]. It's sort of an airbag; the more you punch it, the less is there."[111]

Although sovereignty had been at the heart of the debate over the Palestinian political future at Camp David, it was now an afterthought. Dr. David Kimche, the director general of the Israeli Ministry of Foreign Affairs, agreed that it was a "non-issue": "I mean, on no account are the Palestinian Arabs going to be represented by anybody in the UN or in foreign capitals, neither by us or anybody else." For Kimche, the real practical issue was security, and that was worth the effort of continuing the negotiations. Without the participation of Egyptian diplomats, let alone the Palestinians affected by new arrangements in the territories, Haig expressed sympathy for securing Israeli military guarantees. He envisioned a police force that would deal with day-to-day law enforcement, while wondering about the introduction of arms into the territories. The discussion foreshadowed future debates over security control in the West Bank and Gaza Strip, which would confront Palestinian negotiators seeking an independent hold over the territory themselves. Israeli officials would not cede the right to operate freely in these areas. "The fight against terrorism would be our responsibility, whatever it would include," one Israeli official explained, underscoring the commitment to maintaining full control as the security forces saw fit. "We are not going to freeze things," added Rubinstein.[112]

State Department and NSC officials who accompanied Haig to Jerusalem later reported to the director of the CIA that there was no "give" on the Israeli position, including the size of Israeli military presence in the territories.[113] There was also no substantive push by the Americans toward the baseline position of Egypt or even the minimum of what Palestinians would demand, with the secretary of state merely gauging Israel's position without leveraging pressure in return. Just as Begin had laid out years earlier in his original autonomy plan to Carter, reiterated once again to Reagan administration officials, it was a clear vision to ensure a system of control whereby Arab inhabitants in the West Bank and Gaza Strip might accrue more individual rights, but in which sovereign control over their territory remained with the Israeli government.

In concluding his discussions with Ariel Sharon, Haig voiced concern with the ultimate fate of the autonomy talks, about which he was "pessimistic." There was a growing feeling in both Egypt and Israel that autonomy was unachievable, and this was a "very dangerous attitude to develop." Haig again specified Egyptian criticism, namely "that things are happening on the West Bank and continue to happen that are creating a de facto annexation." While the secretary of state himself did not believe it, he told Sharon, "I think we have to be very, very sensitive to it . . . I would urge you to look very carefully on whether or not you could take some additional steps." These steps related to free transit in the West Bank, particularly with mayors and journalists. The Egyptians were hearing concerns from local Palestinians about a "deterioration" and Haig wanted Sharon to alleviate the pressure. "I think you ought to have a look and see what you could do in good conscience, without unacceptable risks, that will improve the climate . . . I am offering this advice as good offices, not claiming to know better than you do." But at the same time, Haig assured Sharon that the Israeli model would succeed in the end. "I must tell you that my discussion in Cairo on the subjects of security led me to believe they are very comfortable with what I think your own thinking is," Haig remarked to Sharon, "and I don't think it will be a problem in [the] autonomy category."[114]

Sharon understood the favorable environment in which autonomy was being negotiated. He assured Haig he was ready to present the Israeli view and was impatient to secure a deal. "I believe one

can achieve autonomy," Sharon asserted, "to every American representative who came here to this country, I have repeated again and
again that we could have achieved that already." Sharon was eager
to see the autonomy talks advance on Israeli terms and told Haig he
had taken steps to enable implementation, including the replacement of military personnel in the territories with a more amenable
civilian administration. The primary concern, as Israeli officials
had long warned, was anything resembling statehood. "We will not
allow a situation that in Judea, Samaria and Gaza there will be a
second Palestinian state or a corridor to a second Palestinian state,
and we will not accept terrorist activity," Sharon emphasized. "If I
could have advocated to the Arabs, I would have told them: people,
take this autonomy; you have never been offered anything better
than that." He underscored the benevolent advantage of Begin's
concept: "You were under first Iraqi occupation, then Jordanian
and Egyptian, for 19 years. You were never offered anything like
that, take it, you are going to run your own lives." To bolster his
argument, Sharon even pointed to dissenters who sought cooperation with Israel, suggesting that autonomy was a wedge to break
the PLO's hold over the territories.[115] In the Israeli view, reiterated
throughout Haig's visit, autonomy was a means both to accommodate alternatives to the PLO and to avoid self-determination.

On the morning of his departure from Jerusalem, the U.S. secretary of state attempted to summarize the status of the negotiations
and reach a conclusive end before the imposed April 1982 deadline.
While the discussions were restricted to U.S. and Israeli officials
without any Arab participation, they clearly reflect the trajectory
of diplomatic efforts in the wake of Camp David and the triumph
of Israel's political vision for the occupied territories. "I recognize
that this is the real autonomy group," Haig humorously said to the
large room of participants, "and as somebody said when we came
in, it appears to be becoming the largest industry in Israel." He reviewed the status of the talks since the departure of Carter's envoy
Sol Linowitz, and the stops and starts that followed on the heels
of Sadat's assassination. Egypt had hardened its position, Haig explained, demanding that any agreement be "acceptable" to the Palestinians and the Arab world. In practice, this signaled a return to
the principle of self-determination, which Sadat had first presented

when the discussion of the Palestinian question was raised in 1977. Haig told the Israelis that he had rejected this, since "Camp David and the Peace Treaty were not arrived at under such a conception." Sadat's successor, Egyptian president Hosni Mubarak, eventually agreed to abandon his position "in practice" and renew efforts on the talks.[116]

Haig shared Israel's desire to keep the autonomy talks in motion and conclude an agreement, while cognizant of the regression that had set in after Sadat's death. There were practical reasons that the issue had come to a stalemate, but also deep-seated cultural differences between the two parties that had made it difficult to see eye to eye. He urged his Israeli hosts "to remember the differences in society" between Israel and Egypt. "You have a very sophisticated, educated, enlightened, communicative society. Everybody knows and understands what is going on. They may not draw the same conclusions from this fact. But that is not true in Egypt; never has been; never will be." Haig's was a derisive view of the Egyptians, reflecting the secretary of state's internal biases and greater comfort with the Israelis, but also the natural manifestation of a U.S.-Israeli relationship under Reagan that was rooted in perceived shared interests and a sense of common values. The secretary of state hoped the Israel would adapt accordingly, even with the reservations that had been expressed. "We are not looking for concessions. What we are looking for is ingenuity, to enable us to settle questions," Haig explained. "We have been at this for years. There isn't an awful lot that is mysterious and I basically believe it is doable."[117] Such an approach captured the prevailing atmosphere of permissiveness and mutuality that shaped American engagement with autonomy under the new administration.

In a follow-up letter to Reagan after Haig had departed, Begin stressed his compliance with the Camp David Accords but rejected any possibility that self-determination for Palestinians would be on the table. He recalled Sadat's contravening attempts during the Camp David negotiations and again invoked Carter's acquiescence that it would be "totally unacceptable" to the United States. "There is no 'self-determination' there, there is no Palestinian state there, there is no participation of the PLO there. There is autonomy, full autonomy, for the Arab inhabitants of Judea, Samaria (generally but mistakenly called 'West Bank') and the Gaza District." The Egyptians were trying to return to the pre–Camp David model, and this was "impossible" for Begin. If such a position had succeeded, he told Reagan, "there would not have been a Camp David Accord."[118]

Begin's view derived from his clear understanding of the agreement signed with Sadat in September 1978, which remained constant and had been reiterated to all U.S. officials who had attempted to negotiate on the Palestinian question since that time. There were clear limits to the Israeli position, which even Middle East analysts at the CIA understood.

> Prime Minister *Begin asserts that the CDA [Camp David Agreements] rule out the emergence of a Palestinian state.* In Begin's view the agreements "guarantee that under no condition" can a Palestinian state be created. In practice, Begin affectively rules out any exercise of Palestinian self-determination except one that continues Israel's permanent position in the West Bank. . . . Begin's view is that the SGA [Self-Governing Authority] should be a *solely administrative authority* regulating the affairs of the Arab inhabitants and leaving control of the territory and all key security issues with Israel. In sum, *autonomy is for people not territory* and therefore does not prejudice Israel's territorial claims to the West Bank.[119]

This distinction between autonomy for people as opposed to territory undergirded the entire Israeli approach to the Palestinian question in the late 1970s and early 1980s, whether in discussions with Robert Strauss, Sol Linowitz, or Alexander Haig. The autonomy talks did not represent a diplomatic dead end for Israel but rather served as an integral means of enshrining the Camp David Accords along Begin's lines. In Egypt's feeble response and explicit countenancing of the Israeli notion that autonomy would preclude rather than facilitate Palestinian statehood, Cairo had enabled the breakthrough on bilateral peace at Camp David to thwart a political solution for the Palestinians.

U.S. diplomats understood that the autonomy negotiations they were tasked with mediating had buried the possibility of meaningful Arab sovereignty in the occupied territories. In his memoirs, Sol Linowitz reflected on how Begin's rationale drove the underlying logic of the negotiations: "Part of the problem with the concept of 'full autonomy,' which was his, was the fact that it was only a concept, a large and principled gesture that would have to be limited, of course, by the reality of Israeli interests." In Linowitz's account, those interests were predicated on the distinction between Palestinian inhabitants and the sovereign status of the territories. "The philosophical roots of the concept," Linowitz explained, "lay tangled in Begin's distinction between autonomy for inhabitants of the land (which was what he claimed he meant) and autonomy on the land itself."[120] These inconsistencies were immediately apparent, yet they inhered in the U.S. approach to successive rounds of negotiations. Fully aware of Israeli intentions on settlements, security, and other key aspects of life in the occupied territories, American diplomats went into the autonomy talks thinking they might be able to mediate between the parties. But instead, U.S. involvement served to legitimize a profoundly consequential political discussion about the fate of Palestinian self-rule in the territories while the possibility of their territorial rights and sovereignty had already been ruled out by Israel.

Reagan's victory over Carter heralded a new alignment between U.S. neoconservatives and the Likud government in Israel. The tenor of the presidential campaign and the ideological influences on the new administration's foreign policy underscored that an alternative framing of events in the Middle East was ascendant. After repeated confrontations over the possibility of a comprehensive peace and the meaning of a political solution to Palestinian demands in the late 1970s, the revival of a Cold War footing in the early 1980s was a boon to the Begin government. It led directly to the signing of a Memorandum of Understanding to formalize the strategic alliance between the United States and Israel, while Palestinian nationalists were marginalized as agents of Soviet influence. In the fight against communism, Israel could position itself as providing necessary assistance to the United States while the Palestinians were seen as an impediment, abetting terror and threating the "Strategic Consensus" that Secretary Haig sought to implement. Some defense officials understood the risks of such an approach to wider U.S. regional strategy, especially in the Gulf, recoiling at contentious decisions like Israel's 1981 Golan Heights Law and the bombing of Iraq's Osirak nuclear reactor. But Reagan grafted his global view onto local events, eager in these early months to accommodate a stalwart friend in the region.

At this decisive juncture in the international history of the Middle East, following the Iranian Revolution in 1979 and the outbreak of the Iran-Iraq War in 1980, Reagan's policies aggravated Arab attitudes toward the United States and further underscored the troubling consequences of Camp David for the Palestinians. The stinging critique of the accords among neoconservatives within the new administration inaugurated a new U.S. approach to international law with regard to settlement building in the West Bank and Gaza Strip. For Israeli leaders in Jerusalem, this welcome shift enabled the continuation of a robust expansion plan in the occupied territories, while also empowering Israel to assert sovereignty in the context of the autonomy talks. As the final series of those discussions in 1981 and early 1982 made clear, the transition from Carter to Reagan had accelerated the erosion of a diplomatic solution to the Palestinian question. By rejecting Carter's approach to self-determination and acquiescing to the restrictive interpretations of Israel, the new U.S. administration sealed the fate of the Palestinian autonomy talks in Begin's favor. While Egyptian diplomats protested this pattern, they had in fact legitimated the discussions, serving as rather poor and undesignated agents of Palestinian demands while countenancing an outcome that precluded statehood and further marginalized the PLO.

Collectively, these developments fit with a broader ideological shift away from the human rights emphasis of the late 1970s toward the global Cold War revival of the early 1980s. In practical terms, the link between Reagan's worldview and the intentions of the Begin government served to deny the Palestinians substantive political standing. It also presaged more explicit support for Israel's military aims across its northern border. There were already murmurings of a large-scale military operation against the PLO in Lebanon. The means of Palestinian state prevention were moving swiftly to a military track, and a deadly battle to destroy Palestinian nationalism was now headed for Beirut.

CHAPTER SIX

The Limits of Lebanon

ON FRIDAY SEPTEMBER 17, 1982, four Israeli soldiers in full battle dress knocked on the door of the Beirut home of Shafiq al-Hout, the PLO's official representative in Lebanon. Al-Hout was in hiding, a target of several assassination attempts for his leadership of the Palestinian resistance inside the country. The soldiers forced their way into the residence and began questioning Shafiq's wife, Bayan, while searching for valuable documents. One officer found al-Hout's old Palestinian passport, from his childhood in Jaffa, where he was born and raised during the British Mandate. The soldiers were amazed as they looked through its pages. "Your reaction is no surprise to me. I am sure you have never seen such a document," Bayan told them. "As you can see, the text is written in all three languages: Arabic, English, and Hebrew. It comes from the time when Palestine had enough room for everyone, regardless of his religion or sect." The soldiers confiscated the cherished passport, despite Bayan's attempts to get it back, as she recounted tearfully to her husband when they were reunited some days later. In his memoirs, al-Hout recounts the incident with obvious pain, conveying a message from the story, "that the Zionists' perpetual objective is the elimination of Palestinian national identity. Why else would they insist on continuing to eradicate all physical, spiritual, and cultural trace of our presence in Palestine?"[1]

Coming on the heels of political efforts to prevent Palestinian self-determination in the autonomy negotiations with Egypt, the 1982 Israeli war against the PLO in Lebanon was understood by

Palestinians as an outright assault on their national identity. Under the leadership of Prime Minister Menachem Begin and Minister of Defense Ariel Sharon, the Israeli government launched an invasion in June under the pretext of stopping militant rocket fire on the Galilee region. The PLO had relocated to Lebanon from Jordan after armed confrontation with King Hussein's army in 1970. This shifted the center of nationalist politics to the Palestinian refugee camps in Lebanon. Israeli leaders were increasingly anxious about the power of the PLO and the growing links between Palestinians inside the occupied territories and in the Arab diaspora. By targeting the PLO inside Lebanon and forcing its withdrawal, strategic thinkers in Israel believed Palestinian national aspirations for a homeland could be quashed and a pliant Maronite state could be established as an ally to the north.[2]

Surveying the plausible outcomes of the Israeli invasion soon after it began, American intelligence suggested that the fighting would likely weaken the PLO. At the same time, the war would undermine U.S. relations with moderate Arab states and strengthen Begin's hand in the autonomy negotiations. Egypt had temporarily withdrawn from these discussions after the invasion, removing the pressure on Begin to be more conciliatory to the Palestinians. If autonomy talks were restarted, U.S. analysts wrote, "Begin will press hard for the resumption of the talks on his terms, in part because he believes that the demise of the PLO as a military force in Lebanon will reduce pressures on West Bank and Gaza Palestinians to refuse to 'cooperate' with the Israeli administration there."[3]

Israel's hope that newly sympathetic figures in the West Bank and Gaza Strip would materialize was misplaced. Instead, events in Lebanon strengthened the call for self-determination in the occupied territories. As it turned out, internal divisions in Lebanon were far more complex than Israeli leaders grasped, and the decision to intervene militarily led to a large-scale war that quickly drew in the United States. The ensuing violence resulted in the death of at least five thousand Lebanese and Palestinian civilians in the midst of a brutal civil war.[4] Even after the heaviest fighting ended, a prolonged Israeli occupation of the south of the country lasted until 2000, reshaping regional politics well into the twenty-first century. The fighting in Lebanon fundamentally undercut Israeli and American influence in the Middle East, while transforming perceptions of both Zionism and Palestinian nationalism around the globe.

Despite the war's longevity and broader impact, historical treatment of it remains sparse. Most of the extant writing has been left to journalists and the partisan memoirs of participants.[5] Scholarly accounts of the war are largely sequestered within national or quasi-national frames, alternating between a critique of Israeli overreach,[6] a focus on PLO actions during the summer siege of 1982,[7] the Phalange-led massacre in the Sabra and Shatila Palestinian refugee camps,[8] and the shattering of American naiveté with the bombings of the U.S. Embassy and Marine barracks in Lebanon's seaside capital.[9] Few studies have managed to synthesize these various perspectives by situating the war in its local, regional, and international contexts.

Part of the reason these disparate elements have not easily been drawn together is a wider legacy of willful amnesia. For the Lebanese, the events of 1982 are a subset of a broader civil war that extended from 1975 to 1990. The lack of a unified narrative about this period stems from an aversion to implicating segments of the ruling political class in the violence or in facilitating the Israeli invasion. "We should recognize the traumas that we experienced and inflicted upon each other during the war," explained one scholar of contemporary Lebanon, "and the traumas that we continue to experience through the imposed silence of the 'post civil war' era."[10] It is largely to the credit of an entire generation of postwar Lebanese artists and filmmakers—rather than historians—that the silence has been challenged.[11] Among Israeli scholars, the 1982 War is also described in traumatic terms, with one historian noting that many of his fellow citizens "prefer to deal with it by suppressing and forgetting it."[12] The Lebanon War exists as a cultural touchstone but also a historical black box, lacking the sustained scholarly attention that marks other aspects of the Israeli past.[13] This view was somewhat altered during the thirtieth anniversary, as newspapers, conferences, and TV coverage offered more critical examinations of the war. But there exists a deep silence and denial around the events in Lebanon. It is an exonerated war, and for some who selectively remember a formative military experience of early youth, it has even become a war of pride.[14]

With the availability of new sources on 1982, it is possible to challenge this amnesia by examining the important linkages between diplomatic efforts at preventing Palestinian sovereignty and the impact of the war itself. While the Camp David Accords had obstructed the quest for Palestinian statehood in political terms, they helped pave the way for a military intervention after Reagan took office. Against the backdrop of PLO marginalization and the deepening U.S. alliance with Israel, Lebanon emerged as a nexus of Cold War contestation in the Middle East. The convergence would challenge U.S.-Israeli relations and dominant regional politics, leaving the Palestinians vulnerable in dramatic new ways.

The Palestinians in Lebanon

After the 1967 War, Palestinian nationalists had used Jordan as a base for attacks against Israel, threatening the stability of the Hashemite Kingdom and leading to the outbreak of the Jordanian civil war in 1970.[15] In the wake of the violence, the PLO leadership sought to regroup under more favorable circumstances. Lebanon was an obvious choice. Yasser Arafat and the Lebanese army had brokered the Cairo Agreement in November 1969, which authorized actions on behalf of the Palestinian national liberation struggle and guaranteed Palestinian civic rights in Lebanon.[16] Through mass mobilization, paramilitary training, and the control of services, the PLO bolstered its local standing in their new host country and effectively created a "state within a state."[17] It was not a welcome development among many Lebanese factions, who were balancing demographic and political considerations to maintain control in a young and weak confessional democracy. External powers had long sought influence inside the country, from French colonial rulers to neighbors like Syria. The United States was also heavily invested in the country, and a brief but formative intervention by President Eisenhower in 1958 had demonstrated the precarious nature of local Lebanese control.[18]

Growing PLO influence on the ground in the 1970s encroached upon Lebanese sovereignty, and a weak Lebanese army was eventually forced to renounce its control of certain areas in the country. These developments increased tension between the Lebanese and the Palestinians, with the PLO solidifying its hold in south Lebanon, venturing outside refugee camp strongholds and creating alliances with various Muslim groups. In 1975, open clashes with Lebanese Christian forces broke out in the southern city of Sidon and quickly spread all over Lebanon, helping to ignite a fifteen-year civil war.[19] The fighting involved an array of factions that pitted Christians against Muslims, Palestinians and Lebanese leftists against right-wing Christian Phalangist militias, and various Christian and Muslim factions against one another. There was also a crucial external role played by Syria, which first intervened militarily in 1976.

For the Shia Muslim population in the south of Lebanon, the dual impact of the PLO presence and the rise of cross-border skirmishes with Israel was profoundly dislocating. Many had borne the brunt of the earlier 1978 incursion by Israel up to the Litani River in south Lebanon, fleeing the countryside to cities farther north. Long impoverished and politically disenfranchised, the Shia found their land appropriated by Palestinian refugees and the entire region transformed into a land bridge for the "reconquest of Arab Palestine" as the Palestinian liberation struggle swiftly took precedence over local concerns.[20] Unable to cope with the Palestinian presence, growing Shia discontent fomented the rapid rise of the Amal Movement, which formed the basis for the subsequent emergence of Hezbollah.[21]

The violence in the south also affected border towns in northern Israel, with the exchange of rocket fire from PLO members leaving residents in Israel's Galilee region exposed. UN mediation in 1978 had led to the establishment of the UN Interim Force in Lebanon (UNIFIL), which acted as a peacekeeping entity to restrain these cross-border skirmishes.[22] Violence broke out again 1981, and a cease-fire was put in place via the mediation of President Reagan's Special Envoy in Lebanon, Ambassador Philip Habib.[23]

Prime Minister Begin and Defense Minister Sharon both sought to take advantage of the new Cold War mind-set in Washington. An emerging decision to militarily target the PLO grew out of the stalled Palestinian autonomy talks that had been ongoing since the spring of 1979. In Sharon's view, the lack of a diplomatic solution to the Palestinian question after the Camp David Accords invited a display of force that would somehow defeat Palestinians in their Lebanese stronghold. More ambitious than Begin, the defense

minister aimed to destroy the PLO military infrastructure throughout Lebanon and undermine the organization as a political entity
in order to "break the backbone of Palestinian nationalism" and
facilitate the absorption of the West Bank by Israel.[24]

With members of the Reagan administration viewing the PLO
as a Soviet proxy, there was greater support for Israeli desires to
target the Palestinian national movement militarily than had existed under Carter. To garner Reagan's support in reviving Israel's
military agenda in the border area, Prime Minister Begin promoted
a strategic Cold War argument while emphasizing humanitarian
dimensions as well. Drawing on decades of a close Zionist alliance
with the Maronite Christian community of Mount Lebanon, Begin
saw himself as the savior of a besieged minority and promoted the
view that the Maronites were the "Jews of the 1980s." As he told
the Israeli cabinet in April 1981, "Israel will not allow genocide to
happen."[25] In his sweeping presentation, Begin was referring to accounts of Christians killed and threatened by Palestinian groups,
like the notorious 1976 massacre in Damour. He promised to act as
a protector to his Maronite interlocutors.

In a meeting with Ambassador to Israel Samuel Lewis, Begin
expanded on his approach to Lebanon. "Under no circumstances
will Israel allow the Christians of Lebanon in the 80s [to] become
the Jews of Europe in the 40s. We cannot countenance it because
we are a Jewish state." Appealing to the protection of religious free-
doms, Begin stressed, "The Maronites are one of the most ancient
Christian groups in the Middle East. It is inconceivable that we
would stand by and allow the Christians to be destroyed." Asserting
his own leadership role against a historical backdrop of Jewish persecution, Begin remarked, "Today I am a proud Jew. We were once
helpless and massacred and now by divine providence we have the
means to help other people whose destruction is being connived by
a brutal enemy."[26]

A U.S. Green Light

As defense minister, Ariel Sharon was eager to move beyond Begin's
rhetoric with substantive action and developed the plans needed
to implement Israeli war aims. Convinced of Lebanese Christian

political strength, based on Israel's Mossad intelligence, Sharon sought to establish a Maronite-led government in Lebanon, headed by the Lebanese Phalange party leader Bashir Gemayel.[27] Sharon envisioned the eventual signing of a peace treaty between the two countries, as well as the expulsion of the Syrian army from Lebanon.[28] To achieve these aims, Sharon conceived two military plans with the code names of "Little Pines" and "Big Pines." The former, intended for the Israeli army to go up to forty kilometers inside Lebanon, would target PLO installations. The latter was predicated on an invasion up to the Beirut-Damascus highway, just outside the capital, linking Israel's troops with Maronite forces.

Prime Minister Begin first presented "Big Pines" to the Israeli cabinet on December 20, 1981, but the majority of ministers rejected it. Sharon and the army's chief of staff, Rafael Eitan, realized that there was no chance of persuading the cabinet to approve a large-scale operation. Instead, they adopted a tactic to implement an operation in stages by securing a smaller incursion first.[29] This avoided the need to persuade lawmakers, whom Begin and Sharon felt were "weak-kneed, lily-livered faint hearts," as Ambassador Samuel Lewis later recounted. Instead, Sharon reframed the operation, convincing Begin "that the Israelis needed only to project their force fifty kilometers into Lebanon to clean out the PLO artillery and Kaytusha rockets." This led the cabinet to discuss "a much smaller and less frightening operation," Lewis explained, appearing merely as "an incursion, slightly larger than the one that took place in 1978."[30]

Sharon did not hide his broader ambitions in conversation with American allies. The Israeli defense minister first revealed the extent of his military plans during a meeting with Ambassador Habib in December 1981 at the Israeli Foreign Ministry. Habib's assistant, Morris Draper, recalled this meeting during a ten-year retrospective on American involvement in Lebanon. U.S. officials hoped to solidify a "de facto cease-fire" in the south, but Sharon "rather lost his temper and threw cold water over the plans." He described a much wider incursion, alarming the Americans, who warned President Reagan when they returned to Washington. Habib described "in graphic detail" to Secretary of State Haig and other State Department officials what would happen. "We were going to see American-made munitions being dropped from American-made aircraft over Lebanon, and civilians were going to be killed, there was going to be a hell of a big uproar, and the United States—which didn't look very good in the Middle East anyway at the time, for being so inactive—was going to take a full charge of blame," Draper recalled.[31]

Samuel Lewis corroborated Draper's recollections, adding that "Habib and everybody else was thunder-struck by Sharon's plan, although I think our Embassy staff were not quite as surprised, except for the fact that Sharon was being so open about his views."[32] Habib reportedly asked Sharon what Israel would do with the thousands of Palestinians in the country, and Sharon allegedly replied, "We'll hand them over to the Lebanese. In any case, we expect to be in Lebanon only for a few days. The Lebanese Christians will take care of them."[33]

Sharon's revelation of expansive war aims, as Lewis noted, was intended "to prepare the Reagan administration for a large Israeli operation in Lebanon which was likely to occur."[34] It did not take much convincing. A few days before the invasion, Sharon came to Washington and explained in greater detail to Secretary Haig what he was planning. The notebooks of Charles Hill, a top State Department aide who attended the meeting, clearly indicate that an American "green light" was given for Israel's actions.[35]

Tuesday May 25

ARIEL SHARON: Lebanon: . . . We see no alternative to entering and destroying terrorist bases. Don't want war with Syria. Don't want you to be taken by surprise. Tomorrow or three weeks, we just don't know . . . I see no alternative.

ALEXANDER HAIG: On Lebanon, we understand your difficulties. I thought you intended deep, lasting attack. Now I sense a departure from that. We can't tell you not to defend your interests. But we are living with perception. Must be a recognizable provocation. Once a resort to force, everything changes. Like the Falklands. Hope you'll be sensitive to the need for provocation to be understood internationally.

So we have to work this Lebanon problem. Make every effort to avoid it. We want Syria out of Lebanon more than you. It is a Soviet proxy. . . .

SHARON: We are aware of your concern about size. Our intent is <u>not a</u>
<u>large operation. Try to be as small and efficient as possible.</u>
HAIG: Like a lobotomy.
[C. H. notation: A GREEN LIGHT FROM HAIG ON LIMITED
OPERATION][36]

While Israel waited for a "recognizable provocation" to begin a military incursion, Charles Hill noted that Haig had given a "green light" for a "limited operation" denoting clear American support for such action before the war began.[37]

"Operation Peace for Galilee"

Leaving the side door of the Dorchester Hotel across from London's Hyde Park on the evening of June 3, 1982, Israeli ambassador Shlomo Argov strolled down Park Lane toward his waiting car. As he bent to enter the back seat, an assassin's bullet hit him in the head. The attack, which would leave him brain-damaged and confined to a hospital bed for the remaining twenty-one years of his life, provided the final pretext for Israel's invasion of Lebanon three days later.[38]

Israeli intelligence had information that the violently anti-PLO Abu Nidal group was behind the attack, but this distinction was inconsequential as Prime Minister Begin proceeded to order an attack on the PLO in Beirut.[39] The Argov assassination attempt provided the internationally recognized provocation that Haig had insisted Sharon needed to initiate military action against the organization. Even before Israeli troops crossed the border, the Israeli air force had attacked PLO targets in Beirut and southern Lebanon. After securing Israeli cabinet approval for operation "Little Pines" on June 5, Israeli troops moved into Lebanon across the northern border and made sea landings near the southern coastal city of Sidon.[40]

"Operation Peace for Galilee" formally began on Sunday, June 6, 1982. The Begin government's official war aim was to ensure the immediate cessation of cross-border violence.[41] But the invasion quickly expanded well beyond the forty-kilometer line Sharon had suggested in his operation "Little Pines," as Israeli troops headed toward Beirut, linking up with Maronite forces. The Israelis promised the Americans that they had no intention of staying in Lebanon and occupying the country, simply asserting they would not tolerate a return to the status quo of PLO shelling in the Galilee region.[42]

While condoned by Haig, Israeli actions were not fully accepted by the U.S. administration. On June 8, two days after the invasion, Prime Minister Begin and Ambassador Habib met to discuss Israeli war aims. Habib was one of the U.S. diplomats most concerned with Israel's mounting bombing campaign in Beirut. Along with Ambassador Samuel Lewis, the Americans argued with Begin that the PLO was not responsible for the assassination attempt against Argov and that the Israelis were exceeding the promise to stop at the forty-kilometer mark of the invasion.

> HABIB: I have received a message from our embassy in Beirut. The city has no electric power, no gas. Men without uniforms are moving about with arms. It is a city of two million people. What I wish to ask is, can you stop the bombing of Beirut?
>
> BEGIN: Did we bomb Beirut?
>
> HABIB: Yesterday.
>
> BEGIN: We bombed the PLO headquarters and we do not know if Arafat survived it. He is a little Hitler. Those days are gone forever. Now we rely on our own strength.
>
> HABIB: What I am suggesting is that the bombing in that area be stopped. I know you bombed the headquarters but people get hurt and damage to property is inflicted. I know how you feel about hurting civilians.[43]

Begin's rhetoric, invoking comparisons between the PLO and the Nazis, isolated the Palestinian question in a larger historical frame of global anti-Semitism. This conflation, an inaccuracy that the Israeli prime minister would repeat throughout his time in office, served to exclude Palestinian lives as a dehumanized entity only capable of evil toward Jews. By targeting the Palestinian question in this way as a problem to be solved militarily, the Israeli government dismissed any viable claim the Palestinians might have to national self-determination. Yet, as Habib's protestations made clear, some officials were beginning to recognize that their close alignment with

Israel posed problems for U.S. Middle East policy more broadly. There was a growing fear in Washington that the Arab world would view American silence as a sign of complicity, or even a signal that the United States had helped initiate the Israeli violence.[44]

Restraining an Ally

In the days immediately following the invasion, American officials continued to debate the extent to which the administration should endorse Israel's "lobotomy." Secretary Haig and Reagan's ambassador to the United Nations, Jeane Kirkpatrick, felt that Israel should be left to destroy the PLO, which they saw as a proxy of the Soviet Union. The more cautious trio of Secretary of Defense Caspar Weinberger, White House Chief of Staff James Baker, and National Security Advisor William Clark favored holding Israel to a more limited operation.[45] Despite Begin's assurances in the Knesset that Israel was not seeking a war with Syrian troops inside Lebanon, a major clash erupted on June 9. More than a hundred Israeli jets swept over the Bekaa Valley, attacking surface-to-air missile installations and shooting down Syrian MiGs. The conflict had grown considerably.[46]

The Israeli prime minister was fully aware that U.S. support for his country's actions was subject to internal debate, and the disagreements intensified on the eve of Begin's preplanned visit to Washington in June 1982.[47] President Reagan's first meeting with Begin about Lebanon was a tense forty-five minutes in the White House on June 21 with just the two leaders and their note-takers present. The meeting opened with the U.S. president's assertion that the invasion, with its incursion toward Beirut, had exceeded its stated goals of responding to PLO attacks. America, Reagan implored, could not offer unconditional support to a "military operation which was not clearly justified in the eyes of the international community." Even in light of the terrible attack on the Israeli ambassador in London, Reagan argued, "Israel has lost ground to a great extent among our people. . . . They cannot believe that this vile attack—nor even the accumulation of losses that Israel has suffered from PLO terrorist activity since last summer—justified the death and destruction that the IDF brought to so many innocent people over the past two weeks."[48]

Within his overarching anti-Soviet agenda, Reagan believed—correctly or mistakenly—that the United States could simultaneously manage its long-standing friendship with Israel and its important alliances with wealthy anti-communist Arab states. But to succeed, Reagan and his advisors needed Israel's cooperation. "Your actions in Lebanon have seriously undermined our relationship with those Arab governments whose cooperation is essential to protect the Middle East from external threats and to counter forces of Soviet-sponsored radicalism and Islamic fundamentalism now growing in the region," Reagan told Begin. "U.S. influence in the Arab world, our ability to achieve our strategic objectives, has been seriously damaged by Israel's actions."[49]

Begin, using the same Cold War logic he deployed before the invasion, responded that America would benefit if Israel drove the PLO out of Lebanon. Detailing the stockpiles of Soviet weaponry found in the south of the country, Begin told Reagan, "We now realize that this area has been turned into a Soviet base, the principal center of Soviet activities in the Middle East. It was a true international terrorist base." Reagan, however, pushed Begin to account for the civilian casualties, which Begin replied were an exaggeration by a media "biased against Israel." The meeting between the leaders ended abruptly, a clear signal that the two countries' interests were diverging and that America would not remain silent in the face of Israeli aggression.[50]

The Israelis soon lost a close ally after Alexander Haig was forced to resign in the midst of the June fighting in Lebanon.[51] The secretary of state had overextended his reach inside the administration, undercutting Reagan. George Shultz, a former Nixon cabinet official and executive at the Bechtel Corporation, replaced Haig on July 16. Growing tension in the U.S.-Israeli relationship increased markedly in late June and July 1982.[52] As Ambassador Samuel Lewis explained, "The sympathy of the administration, which up to early July, had been strongly pro-Israel, increasingly shifted towards the Palestinians."[53] Primarily, the shift was a response to the Israeli siege on Beirut, intended to "eradicate the PLO quasi-government" from the capital. Combining powerful military force and psychological warfare, Israeli forces inflicted heavy casualties in the city, bombarding Palestinian positions from land, sea, and air, while occupying the international airport.[54]

Reagan was intensely disturbed by the barrage of TV images coming from Beirut as the Israeli army heavily shelled the Lebanese capital. As he wrote in his diary one evening in late July, "Calls and cables back and forth with Lebanon. U.N. with us supporting voted 15 to 0 for a ceasefire and U.N. observers on the scene. Israel will scream about the latter but so be it. The slaughter must stop."[55] Despite the president's personal revulsion and mounting international criticism, the Israelis ignored the cease-fire and the bombardment of Beirut intensified during the first week of August.

Secretary Shultz sent Philip Habib to Beirut to negotiate an end to the fighting and facilitate a peaceful evacuation of PLO fighters from the city to neighboring Arab states. Yasser Arafat had signaled that he and his men were willing to withdraw with requisite guarantees of security for Palestinian civilians and Lebanese supporters who remained behind.[56] Habib worked on an arrangement whereby Palestinian and Syrian forces would withdraw and the Lebanese government would take back control of Beirut. Throughout the summer of 1982, the PLO leader had stood his ground in Lebanon, longer than was expected. In early July, as he shared with his close colleague Shafiq al-Hout the letter he had drafted for the PLO's exit, Arafat sounded a wistful note about the departure: "Beirut has given Palestine what no other Arab capital has. It has given and given, without asking for anything in return. And it never would ask. Nor should we make it ask. We should pay it back of our own free will."[57]

On Wednesday morning, August 4, the entire U.S. National Security Council convened in the White House Situation Room. Present at the meeting were Reagan, Vice President Bush, Shultz, Secretary of Defense Weinberger, CIA director William Casey, the members of the Joint Chiefs of Staff, UN ambassador Kirkpatrick, Ambassador to Israel Samuel Lewis, Assistant Secretary of State for Near Eastern Affairs Nicholas Veliotes, and a retinue of West Wing advisors.[58] An all-out Israeli assault on West Beirut had begun the night before, and Shultz was concerned with the claim of de-escalation being made publicly by the Israelis in comparison to what Special Envoy Philip Habib was actually witnessing on the ground.

Shultz recommended drafting a Security Council Resolution that might condemn Israel, while developing a strongly worded letter to Prime Minister Begin expressing anger over the lack of cooperation, possibly suspending arms shipments and enacting unilateral sanctions. Weinberger clarified that Israel had acted first against the PLO, and Lewis reported that the air assault was even worse than the ground incursion in terms of damage. But Kirkpatrick dissented sharply: "The group should not lose sight of the fact that the PLO is not a bunch of agrarian reformers. They are international terrorists who are working against U.S. interests and committing acts of violence throughout the world, supported by the Soviet Union. We want them out and the U.S. should not throw away the possibility of getting rid of the PLO by taking measures against Israel which will inhibit, if not eliminate, the prospects of achieving our objectives. Clearly, once we have removed the PLO from Lebanon we can make fast progress in the peace process."[59]

Kirkpatrick's impassioned views resonated partially with the president, who was inclined to see events in the Middle East through such a Cold War lens, but at the same time he was viscerally affected by the impact of the violence. Weinberger was a cautious realist, and he "agreed with Ambassador Kirkpatrick regarding just who the PLO is." But, he argued, "the U.S. must let Israel know of the cost to Israel of its nightly activities." In recounting the meeting, Nicholas Veliotes remembered how "Jeane Kirkpatrick said to President Reagan that the Israeli victory in Lebanon represented the greatest strategic turnaround in the West since the fall of Vietnam. And the meeting broke up shortly after because she had successfully pressed Ronald Reagan's buttons."[60]

As the meeting ended, a decision was nevertheless made to draft a strongly worded letter to Begin, which the president worked on for several minutes. Reluctantly agreeing to change the language from his customary "Dear Menachem" to "Dear Mr. Prime Minister," Reagan concluded, "There must be an end to the unnecessary bloodshed, particularly among innocent civilians. I insist that a cease-fire in place be reestablished and maintained until the

PLO has left Beirut. The relationship between our two nations is at stake." The president instructed his assembled advisors that the PLO should receive equal emphasis in public statements of blame and implored them not to "tee-off only on Israel." At 10:02, Reagan closed the meeting, "stating that he was extremely tired of a war whose symbol had become a burn baby [*sic*] with no arms." As Nicholas Veliotes recalls, "Reagan wasn't a simpleton. Reagan was going to defend Israel's right to defend itself. Reagan was violently anti-terrorist. He was very sympathetic to Israel. But he also abhorred senseless bloodshed."[61]

On August 10, Israel received a draft agreement from Habib signaling that American and multinational forces would help supervise the PLO evacuation. Sharon had grander plans for a political agreement in Lebanon "and was fearful that American soldiers would get in his way." He therefore ordered a "saturation bombing" of Beirut.[62] On August 12, an intense daylong bombing of West Beirut by the Israelis inflicted over five hundred casualties in what would be the last day of the summer siege on the Lebanese capital.[63] Reagan's diary reveals the depth of his anger and a growing rift between two stalwart Cold War allies.

> Met with the news the Israelis delivered the most devastating bomb & artillery attack on W. Beirut lasting 14 hours. Habib cabled—desperate—has basic agreement from all parties but can't arrange details of P.L.O. withdrawal because of the barrage. King Fahd called begging me to do something. I told him I was calling P. M. Begin immediately. And I did—I was angry—I told him it had to stop or our entire future relationship was endangered. I used the word holocaust deliberately & said the symbol of his war was becoming a picture of a 7 month old baby with its arms blown off. He told me he had ordered the bombing stopped—I asked about the artillery fire. He claimed the P.L.O. had started that & Israeli forces had taken casualties. End of call. Twenty mins. later he called to tell me he'd ordered an end to the barrage and pled for our continued friendship.[64]

Alongside the growing strain between the American and Israeli leaders, Begin's trust in Sharon eroded significantly as a result of the escalation, and the Israeli cabinet stripped the defense minister of key powers.[65]

Ambassador Habib eventually negotiated a cease-fire, and PLO leader Yasser Arafat agreed to the withdrawal of PLO combatants from Lebanon.[66] The first contingent of men left on August 21, and Arafat and leading PLO officials departed on a Greek shipping vessel to Tunisia on August 30. Over ten thousand fighters departed Lebanon by sea and land routes, launching the PLO into exile once more.[67] Israeli troops remained in Beirut, with Sharon determined to forge a peace treaty with the Lebanese government. In side letters to Arafat during the arduous negotiation, Habib had guaranteed the protection of Palestinian civilians remaining behind after the armed PLO guerilla fighters were evacuated.[68] But these promises were blatantly ignored—with calamitous results—in the weeks that followed.

The Reagan Plan

As part of the agreement brokered between the Government of Lebanon, Israel, and the PLO, a multinational force (MNF) was to be deployed to assist in the PLO's evacuation.[69] On August 25, eight hundred U.S. Marines began to arrive in Beirut as part of this MNF, equipped for a non-combat role of assisting the Lebanese Armed Forces alongside French and Italian military personnel to aid in the withdrawal. The mandate of the MNF was limited in scope, not intended to last more than thirty days. Reporting on the deployment to congressional leaders, President Reagan wrote, "I want to emphasize that there is no intention or expectation that U.S. Armed Forces will become involved in hostilities. . . . Our agreement with the Government of Lebanon expressly rules out any combat responsibilities for the U.S. forces."[70] Acutely aware of domestic political pressure and congressional opposition to military deployments abroad, the president was wary of overextending the Marine mission and firmly rejected Israeli ambitions for grander designs in Lebanon.[71]

Events in Lebanon had forced a reckoning with the very questions that Reagan had sidestepped when entering office. Secretary Shultz encouraged him to launch a diplomatic initiative to deal with the Palestinian question. On September 1, 1982, the president announced a formal peace plan from his "Western White House" in

FIGURE 6.1. U.S. Marines leave a utility landing craft during landing operations at the port. Beirut, September 1, 1982. Courtesy National Archives, photo no. 330-CFD-DN-SN-83-05661.

Santa Barbara, California. This was Reagan's first and only major speech on the Arab-Israeli conflict during his eight years in office. Building on Jimmy Carter's Camp David framework, Reagan acknowledged that movement on implementing the Camp David Accords had been slow even as Israel had completed its withdrawal from the Sinai. Noting that the "opportunities for peace in the Middle East do not begin and end in Lebanon," Reagan recognized that "we must also move to resolve the root causes of conflict between Arabs and Israelis." In the president's view, the central question was "how to reconcile Israel's legitimate security concerns with the legitimate rights of the Palestinians."[72] Secretary Shultz had already underscored the importance of a "solution to the Palestinian problem" in a meeting with Defense Minister Ariel Sharon several days before Reagan announced his plan.[73]

To expand on the foundations of Camp David, Reagan called for a transitional period of Palestinian self-government in the West Bank and Gaza to prove that autonomy posed no threat to Israeli security. Reagan's plan, like Carter's at Camp David, still fell short of statehood for Palestinians, but it explicitly countered Israeli claims of sovereignty. As the president remarked, "It is clear to me that peace cannot be achieved by the formation of an independent Palestinian state in those territories, nor is it achievable on the basis of Israeli sovereignty or permanent control over the West Bank and Gaza."[74] Rather, Reagan called for negotiations based on the principles of land for peace enshrined in UN resolution 242. The president added a guarantee that "the United States will oppose any proposal—from any party and at any point in the negotiating process—that threatens the security of Israel. America's commitment to the security of Israel is ironclad. And, I might add, so is mine."[75]

In one of the most surprising elements of the speech, Reagan singled out the expansion of Israeli settlements over the Green Line. It was an issue that would emerge as the most contentious element of his proposal. "The United States will not support the use of any additional land for the purpose of settlements during the transitional period," the president clarified. "Indeed, the immediate adoption of a settlement freeze by Israel, more than any other action, could create the confidence needed for wider participation in these talks. Further settlement activity is in no way necessary for the security of Israel and only diminishes the confidence of the Arabs that a final outcome can be freely and fairly negotiated."[76] The president made it clear that while the United States would "not support the establishment of an independent Palestinian state in the West Bank and Gaza . . . we will not support annexation or permanent control by Israel." When it came to Israeli settlements, Secretary Shultz later explained, "Their ultimate future must be determined in the course of the final negotiations. We will not support their continuation as extraterritorial outposts."[77]

This middle ground—between the curtailment of Israel sovereignty and the prevention of Palestinian statehood—reflected the new U.S. position on the fate of the settlements. In explanatory cables to world leaders, Shultz expanded on the central elements of the plan, particularly the issue of Palestinian autonomy. "The term 'self-determination' has, in the Middle East context, become a codeword for the formation of a Palestinian state," explained the secretary of state. "We will not support this exclusive definition of self-determination. Nevertheless, the President is totally committed to the proposition that the Palestinians must have a leading role in determining their own future." Rather than statehood, American policymakers envisioned a joint association of the West Bank and Gaza with Jordan, "a realistic and fair solution."[78] One of the architects of the Reagan plan, Assistant Secretary of State Nicholas Veliotes, later explained that no career experts working on it believed the Begin government would accept the plan; rather the hope was to get PLO-Jordanian acceptance and put pressure on Israel to face an election and bring a more amenable Labor government to power.[79]

Growing directly out of Carter's diplomatic blueprint, the Reagan Plan was a startling departure for a president who had so strongly opposed his predecessor's approach. The shift betokened recognition that there would be a price to pay for a lack of engagement on the Israeli-Palestinian front. Israel's invasion of Beirut was viewed as a turning point. As Reagan himself concluded, "If we miss this chance to make a fresh start, we may look back on this moment from some later vantage point and realize how much that failure cost us all."[80]

Israeli Reactions

Menachem Begin was on a rare vacation in the north of Israel when Ambassador Samuel Lewis hand delivered a draft of Reagan's speech.[81] Lewis viewed Reagan's initiative as a return to Camp David but found it abysmally timed.[82] He recalled the prime minister's anger as he read the new peace agenda issued by the White House. With little time to savor his victory over the PLO after their expulsion from Lebanon, Begin was shocked as he read through the plan. Beyond Lebanon, the prime minister recognized its implications for the Israeli interpretation of Camp David, in particular the questions of autonomy and settlements. While agreeing to consult with his cabinet about the U.S. initiative, the prime minister "became increasingly angry as he talked. . . . He took on an aggrieved mood of bitterness and of being treated unfairly."[83] Begin's hope for a regional transformation along expansive Likud lines had been dashed.

In a furious reply to Reagan's speech, Begin lambasted the president's characterization of settlements.

> What some call the West Bank, Mr. President, is Judea and Samaria and the simple historic truth will never change. . . . Millennia ago, there was a Jewish kingdom of Judea and Samaria where our kings knelt to God, where our prophets brought forth a vision of eternal peace, where we developed a rich civilization which we took with us in our hearts and in our minds on our long global trek for over eighteen centuries and with it we came back home. King Abdullah [of Jordan] by invasion conquered parts of Judea and Samaria in 1948 and in a war of legitimate self defense in 1967 after having been attacked by King Hussein we liberated with God's help that portion of our homeland. . . . The Palestinian state will rise itself the day Judea and Samaria are given to Jordanian jurisdiction; then, in no time, you will have a Soviet base in the heart of the Middle East. . . . For Zion's sake, I will not hold my peace, and for Jerusalem's sake, I will not rest. (Isaiah, chapter 62)
> —Menachem[84]

Begin convened his cabinet on September 2, and they adopted a formal resolution that detailed several major points of opposition to Reagan's speech. Israeli officials categorically rejected the Reagan Plan, offering a limited return to the moribund autonomy talks.[85] The grounds on which they would reconvene these autonomy negotiations disputed the rights of Palestinians in East Jerusalem to vote in any West Bank or Gaza election and precluded the possibility of Palestinian autonomy over land and water resources.[86]

American intelligence officials had already warned that any initiative by the administration to revive the autonomy component of Camp David would be met by Israeli rejection.[87] The talks had run aground earlier in the year, after Alexander Haig's visit to Israel. Egyptian and Israeli differences over Palestinian self-determination were too entrenched and the events in Lebanon had further buried the discussions. Egypt, like much of the Arab world, was shocked by the scope of Israeli actions in Lebanon and would recall their ambassador from Tel Aviv, freezing the process of normalization in preference for a "cold peace."[88]

The Reagan administration was much firmer in its stance on Camp David with the announcement of the Reagan Plan. While outlining the features of the September 1 address for Prime Minister Begin, Reagan had Lewis reiterate U.S. support for the Camp David Accords while also expanding on transitional measures that the American government would now directly support. These measures, intended to transfer authority from Israel to the Palestinian inhabitants of the territories, included a definition of full autonomy "as giving the Palestinian inhabitants real authority over themselves, the land and its resources." Such a position on the issue of autonomy went well beyond the ceiling imposed by Begin's interpretation of Camp David's autonomy provisions.[89] The Americans also articulated support for Palestinian participation in the elections of a West Bank–Gaza authority, a real settlement freeze, and Palestinian responsibility for internal security.

Israel's contrary effort to curtail Palestinian political sovereignty was twinned with the continued insistence on settlement building on the territory itself. In rejecting the Reagan Plan, the Israeli ministers argued that the Camp David Accords had only prevented expansion of settlements during a three-month transition period with Egypt that ended on December 17, 1978. "Since then," Israeli cabinet ministers argued, "many settlements have been established in Judea, Samaria and the Gaza District without evicting a single person from his land, village or town. Such settlement is a Jewish inalienable right and an integral part of our national security. Therefore, there shall be no settlement freeze. We shall continue to establish them in accordance with our natural right." The officials closed by citing President Reagan himself, who "announced at the time that 'the settlements are not illegal.'"[90]

This defiant stance on settlements persisted throughout the 1980s, without any direct or substantive American intervention after the announcement of the Reagan Plan. The Carter administration had faced similar intransigence after the Camp David Accords, and Begin and Sharon had elicited sharper words from U.S. officials over settlement expansion. But the gap between the rhetoric in Washington and the reality on the ground in the West Bank underscored the weak nature of the opposition to what by the early 1980s had become an "irreversible" phenomenon of settlement expansion.[91]

U.S. officials tried to coax Begin into a more amenable stance on sovereign control of the occupied territories. The official directive that Lewis delivered to Begin re-stated American opposition to the dismantling of existing settlements but also outlined clear opposition to Israeli control of the territories: "It is our belief that the Palestinian problem cannot be resolved through Israeli sovereignty or control over the West Bank and Gaza." At the same time, Lewis assured Begin that statehood was not in the cards for the Palestinians and clarified the meaning of self-determination along narrower lines: "We believe that the Palestinians must take the leading role in determining their own future and fully support the provisions in Camp David providing for the elected representatives of the inhabitants of the West Bank and Gaza to decide how they shall govern themselves consistent with the provisions of their agreement in the final status negotiations."[92]

This fine line between an outright endorsement of Palestinian statehood and the restrictive Israeli approach to Palestinian autonomy was the direct by-product of the struggle over the Camp David negotiations. The announcement of the Reagan Plan threatened the Israeli position on the accords, with officials in Jerusalem worried that the United States had "jeopardized" its earlier stance. Ambassador Lewis defended his government's more assertive approach. The United States, he explained, "is no longer a mediator, to broker ideas back and forth. We are now asserting our own ideas anchored in what we believe in the Camp David Accords. Even at Camp David we were not a broker. We had our own ideas." Israeli officials were dismayed with this apparent turn. Elyakim Rubinstein, a leading Israeli diplomat who was present at Camp David, told Lewis that his more expansive understanding of the accords "pushes up the Palestinian issue, and we do not like it."[93]

The Sabra and Shatila Massacre

The prospects of the Reagan Plan's success were short-lived, as a result of both Israeli opposition and the unfolding events in Lebanon. After meeting Begin to present the contours of the Reagan Plan, Ambassador Lewis did not know that the Israeli prime minister departed for a secret rendezvous with Bashir Gemayel, the Lebanese president-elect and close ally of the Israeli government. Still furious over the Reagan Plan, the Israeli prime minister greeted Gemayel "brusquely" and began to demand the signing of a peace treaty between Lebanon and Israel. As Lewis was told later, "Begin told Gemayel that Israel had now won him the Presidency and had ridden his country of the PLO fighters; it was therefore time to sign a peace treaty." The Israelis believed that Gemayel would comply, but his domestic position was precarious. He tried to tell Begin "that such a treaty would need time" and that "he had to proceed cautiously" given all the "political fence mending that he had to undertake." As Lewis later recounted, this position "got under Begin's skin; he became furious." Begin spoke to Gemayel "in very demeaning and authoritarian terms; he was obviously very upset that his Lebanese allies were not being compliant." The Israeli prime minister felt "betrayed" given what Israel had done for the Phalangists and the Christians. "That session in Nahariyya changed Gemayel's views of the Israelis," Lewis explained. "He viewed them as much more sinister than he had before. All the Lebanese were shocked by Begin's behavior to their new President."[94]

Bashir Gemayel's time as president-elect did not last very long. On September 14, Gemayel was assassinated in a massive bomb explosion at the Phalange headquarters in East Beirut's Ashrafieh neighborhood. The man who detonated the bomb, Habib Shartouni, was affiliated with the Syrian Social Nationalist Party (SSNP). Shartouni and the SSNP saw Gemayel as a traitor who had sold their country to Israel. The close involvement of the Syrian intelligence services in the assassination shattered any remaining Israeli grand plans for the emergence of a Lebanese state remade under the leadership of a strong Christian ally. Syrian involvement in the civil war had further complicated the Israeli goals, as Syria had maintained the support of important Lebanese factions after intense fighting in the early weeks of the war. These alliances were deftly employed against the Israelis and the United States in 1982, generating opposition to the prolonged occupation of the country.

Defense Minister Sharon, a close confidant of Gemayel's, reacted to his assassination by pushing forward into West Beirut with IDF units. Although the PLO had already departed Lebanon for other Arab countries, Israeli troops had remained and were now entering the capital. Prime Minister Begin explained to the Americans that this was a limited precautionary measure and that "the main order of the day is to keep the peace. As long as peace is kept, the people can be brought together to talk. Otherwise, there could be pogroms."[95] That same afternoon, in Washington, Israeli ambassador to the United States Moshe Arens was called to meet with Secretary of State George Shultz about Israeli actions in West Beirut. With information that had been procured by Charles Hill, Shultz's executive assistant, the Americans had intelligence that Sharon had moved his troops into the city. Shultz told Arens that this "appears to be a provocative act" and "is counterproductive." U.S. credibility was "being eroded," and the secretary concluded "we are upset but we have been quiet until now." Arens insisted the Israelis did not want to deceive the Americans and that these were merely precautionary measures, as Israel "did not have ambitions in Beirut, not in the West, not in the East, and not in Lebanon at all." Shultz responded tersely: "Your activity in West Beirut will engender a situation where Israel is controlling an Arab capital." There would be "psychological" consequences.[96]

Arens, toeing the line of military strategists in the field, replied that Israel was already in control of Sidon and Tyre without such consequences: "What is the alternative to our actions?" The U.S. secretary of state was adamant that Israeli control over a city like Beirut was a "major" issue. "We know that for you [Bashir's] assassination is painful, perhaps more than it pains us, but you are obligated to act for the quiet of Beirut." To avoid the appearance of a "provocation," Shultz demanded from Arens that the Israelis "pull your forces back . . . the Lebanese have to deal themselves with their problems." But as Arens insisted, "In West Beirut there are 2,000 militants from al-Murabitun," referring to a left-wing militia that had helped defend the PLO, "it seems that there also remains the murderers of Bashir."[97] The Israelis were convinced that the Lebanese army was not capable of acting in their place to keep the peace. Shultz was not moved, adding that PLO members were no longer posing a challenge in Beirut and reiterated his strong sentiments to Arens.[98]

With Shultz meeting Philippines president Ferdinand Marcos the next day, September 16, U.S. undersecretary of state Lawrence Eagleburger continued the tense discussions with the Israelis over their consolidation of forces in West Beirut. Eagleburger read from

talking points that described Israeli behavior as "contrary to a series of assurances" made by the Begin government, stressing that
"Israel's credibility has been severely damaged here in Washington by recent Israeli actions in West Beirut." Eagleburger told the
Israelis that they must pull back and conveyed U.S. support for a
Security Council resolution opposing Israel's actions: "I want to reiterate strongly that the occupation by Israel of an Arab capital is a
grave political mistake with far-reaching symbolic and concrete implications of the most dangerous sort." Arens contested the American claim of Israeli deception and defended the IDF's moves as a
prerequisite for maintaining order after Gemayel's assassination.
"Our common objectives are attainable," Arens stressed, "but we've
got to work together and not at cross-purposes. We should avoid
this openly confrontational mode. If you think this will scare us,
you're wrong."[99]

For the Israeli ambassador, the U.S. approach to the Middle East
was only conflating Lebanon's complexities with the Palestinian
question. "Before the Palestinian problem can be addressed we've
got to clear up the situation in Lebanon. First things first! Rather
than tying these two things in a package we should take them one
by one," Arens insisted, attempting to disentangle the two. "Cou-
pling the Lebanese situation with the future of Judea, Samaria and
Gaza may get you some short-run success, but in the long run we
won't get anywhere.[100] In situating the events in Beirut as distinct
from Reagan's approach to the peace process, Arens was hoping to
isolate the Palestinian question, when in fact the invasion centered
on a military solution to the power of the PLO.

Immediately after the PLO's departure, Secretary of Defense
Weinberger had ordered the U.S. Marines back to their ships, as
he had been anxious for the military to leave the country. Deeply
cautious in the wake of the Vietnam War, the U.S. defense establishment resisted wars with no definitive end, a central tenet of
Weinberger's Pentagon leadership.[101] The departure of the Marines
also precipitated the rapid withdrawal of French and Italian forces,
both of which had intended to stay longer. In this ensuing vacuum,
Christian Phalangist militias—reeling from the assassination of
their leader Bashir—were free to terrorize Palestinian civilians who
remained behind after the PLO's evacuation. The United States

had guaranteed the safety of the civilians as part of the withdrawal agreement and yet was unwittingly complicit in the massacre that followed.

Between the evening of September 16 and the afternoon of September 18, Christian Phalange militiamen launched an attack on defenseless Palestinian civilians in the Israeli-controlled Sabra and Shatila refugee camps. Marshaled at the Beirut airport, a major Israeli staging point, these forces were ushered through Israeli lines into the camps, which were surrounded by Israeli forces. Under the command of Elie Hobeika, the Phalange militiamen raped, killed, and dismembered at least eight hundred women, children, and elderly men while Israeli flares illuminated the camps' narrow and darkened alleyways.[102] The Israeli cabinet had met on the evening of September 16 and officials were informed that Phalange fighters were entering the Palestinian camps. Israel's deputy prime minister, David Levy, worried aloud about the consequences of Phalange actions in the wake of Gemayel's assassination: "I know what the meaning of revenge is for them, what kind of slaughter. Then no one will believe we went in to create order there, and we will bear the blame."[103] Sharon himself told cabinet members of the Phalange movements, stressing that "the results will speak for themselves . . . let us have the number of days necessary for destroying the terrorists."[104] This insistence that only "terrorists" were to be found in the camps belied the actual reality of those who had remained after the PLO evacuation.

News of civilian deaths in the camps began to filter out to Israeli military officials, politicians, and journalists overnight. The following day, on September 17, Israeli foreign minister Yitzhak Shamir hosted a meeting with Habib's assistant Morris Draper, Sharon, and several Israeli intelligence chiefs. Shamir reportedly heard of a "slaughter" in the camps that morning, but he did not mention it to those assembled. Instead, the discussion focused on the Israeli insistence that "terrorists" who stayed behind in Beirut needed "mopping up." Sharon browbeat Ambassador Draper, who demanded the IDF pull back from the areas it occupied in West Beirut so the Lebanese National Army could take over. Sharon exploded at Draper's suggestion: "I just don't understand, what are you looking for? Do you want the terrorists to stay? Are you afraid that somebody will think that you were in collusion with us? Deny it. We denied it." Draper was insistent and pushed for definitive signs of an Israeli withdrawal. Sharon cynically told him, "Nothing will happen. Maybe some more terrorists will be killed. That will be to the benefit of all of us."[105]

Draper warned Sharon that this prolonged presence would enable the Lebanese to "go and kill the Palestinians in the camps." Sharon replied: "So, we'll kill them. They will not be left there. You are not going to save them. You are not going to save these groups of the international terrorism [*sic*]." Draper, swept up in Sharon's rhetorical onslaught, responded, "We are not interested in saving any of these people." Mr. Sharon declared, "If you don't want the Lebanese to kill them, we will kill them." Draper caught himself and backtracked, reminding the Israelis that the United States had painstakingly facilitated the PLO exit from Beirut "so it wouldn't be necessary for you to come in." He told Sharon, "You should have stayed out." Sharon exploded again: "When it comes to our security, we have never asked. We will never ask. When it comes to existence and security, it is our own responsibility and we will never give it to anybody to decide for us." Draper acquiesced to a delayed withdrawal after a forty-eight-hour period, since the Jewish holiday of Rosh Hashanah was starting that evening. U.S. diplomats effectively provided Israel cover as the Phalange fighters remained in the camps, slaughtering civilians until the following morning.[106]

According to the transcripts of the once secret conversations, which took place after the PLO withdrew from Beirut and guarantees had been made to protect the civilians left behind, there was an unceasing denunciation by Israeli military strategists of "terrorists" circulating in Beirut's refugee camps. Like Begin's invocation of the Nazis when speaking of the PLO, a similar pattern of dehumanization had surfaced with the Sabra and Shatila massacre. The transcripts demonstrate how the Israelis misled the U.S. diplomats about the events in the city with deceptive claims about the nature of those remaining behind, even as the Americans knew that the armed militants had been evacuated and there were civilians in the camps. As the Sharon-Draper exchange underscores, imprecise language helped forestall the deployment of Lebanese forces to the refugee camps, enabling a prolonged massacre to continue.[107]

The rhetoric of terrorism and security had long underpinned the Israeli justification for taking direct military action against Palestinians, with no distinction made between PLO fighters, who had already been evacuated, and innocent civilians who remained in the camps. In the broader sweep of Israel's approach to the Palestinians, the 1982 invasion served to blur this distinction even further, linking a diplomatic approach to sidelining the Palestinian question that had taken hold at Camp David with the military approach of quashing Palestinian identity in a more permanent fashion. America's role in abetting this process, as the new evidence from 1982 now reveals, was both a moral stain and a strategic disaster, undercutting U.S. influence in the region and precipitating further military involvement in the Lebanese civil war.[108]

Implications of the Massacre

Sabra and Shatila was a turning point in the war, and it radically altered global perceptions of Israeli and U.S. actions in Lebanon, and the very nature of the Palestinian question. Many supporters of Israel abroad were paralyzed by the invasion of Lebanon and its aftershocks, and Sabra and Shatila intensified these feelings. Begin had described the invasion as a "war by choice," which was an anathema to the defensive ethos of the dominant Zionist narrative that animated Jewish support for Israel abroad.[109] "It was shameful, it was shocking," explained Rita Hauser, a prominent lawyer and Republican Jewish activist who had served as U.S. ambassador to the UN Human Rights Council. "People were really horrified, they were shocked at it. Many Israelis were. It's simply something that Jews, Israelis are not supposed to do."[110]

Other leaders of the Jewish community rallied to Israel's defense. "The history of the Jewish people is too full of massacres and pogroms, and the injunctions of Jewish law are too powerful a force in Jewish consciousness to have permitted or even countenanced a Jewish role in this awful incident," wrote Julius Berman, the chairman of the Conference of Presidents of Major Jewish Organizations, in a press release soon after the massacre. "Any suggestion that Israel took part in it or permitted it to occur must be categorically rejected."[111] This defensive stance fit within a post-1967 frame that absolved Israel of agency in instances of diplomatic or military overreach, especially in connection with the Palestinians.[112] But for some modern Jewish historians, as well as revisionist Israeli scholars, the global reaction to the war raised piercing questions about the nature of Jewish power and the meaning of political Zionism in the modern age.[113]

The war also affected the broader context in which the Palestinian question was viewed. The Palestinian quest for self-determination was in fact rendered visible once again on a global scale, despite Israeli hopes that it would disappear.[114] In the view of one Fatah activist close to Yasser Arafat, Sabra and Shatila was a "wake up call." It was a reminder "that you are dealing with a people. You are not dealing with a bunch of terrorists."[115] Strategically, it also served to bolster Palestinian politics. An authority on Palestinian security affairs later observed that the massacre signaled "a crack in the shield of Israel's moral authority, a crack in the shield of Israel's military prowess." In the wider sweep of Palestinian national politics, "the net result was a liberation for the PLO."[116] This shifting perception was evident in the American media, where Israel found itself derided for overstepping a moral red line. The major Jewish organizations registered complaints with the White House about the use of Nazi imagery in U.S. newspapers to criticize Israeli behavior, including cartoons of Begin plotting a "final solution" to end the Palestinian refugee problem.[117]

Internally in Israel, public anger at the government's involvement in Lebanon and role in Sabra and Shatila brought four hundred thousand demonstrators to rally in Tel Aviv on September 25.[118] Begin was accused of a lackluster response to the violence, and he appointed a commission to investigate Israeli responsibility in the massacre. Yitzhak Kahan, the Chief Justice of Israel's Supreme Court, was appointed to lead the independent board of inquiry. The Kahan Commission issued its findings in early February 1983, exonerating the Israeli government of immediate responsibility but finding particular leaders indirectly responsible for allowing the Phalangists into the camps.[119] Begin, Shamir, and Chief of Staff Rafael Eitan were censured, and Defense Minister Ariel Sharon, as well as the director of Military Intelligence Yehoshua Saguy and the Division Commander in charge of Beirut, Amos Yaron, were either forced out of their posts or briefly removed from operational roles. The Kahan Commission report excoriated Sharon's conduct in Lebanon, in particular his negligence in the massacre, a criticism that Sharon bitterly contested for the rest of his life.[120]

Sharon insisted that his actions were in line with long-standing Israeli policy toward the Christians in Lebanon. He told a meeting of the Defense and Foreign Affairs Committee of the Knesset on September 24 that it was hypocritical to blame him for Sabra and Shatila when the Labor government knew about a Christian massacre of Palestinians in the Tel al-Zaatar camp in 1976 and still supported them in 1982. "We (the Likud party) did not criticize you (Labor) for supporting the Christians. I am talking about the moral aspect. You kept on supporting (the Christians) even after the (Tel Za'ater) massacre. The information about the massacre and its cruelty was in everybody's possession," Sharon told member of the Knesset Yitzhak Rabin. "We had already known what they have done with the weapons we supplied and the forces we helped them build. However, we did not criticize you." He turned to Shimon Peres, the opposition Labor party leader, and told him that after Tel al-Zaatar, "you have no monopoly on morality." "The Phalangists murdered in Shatila and the Phalangists murdered in Tel Za'ater. The link is a moral one: should we get involved with Phalangists or not. You supported them and continued to do so after Tel Za'ater."[121] Sharon's primary defense was to blame the Phalange militiamen, and not the IDF, who remained outside the camps during the massacre. But new evidence from the Kahan Commission report, drawn from its unpublished appendices, paint a more incriminating picture of Sharon and wider Israeli official eagerness to invite the Phalange militia into Beirut. This was part of Israel's long-standing discussions with Maronite leaders to "clean the city out of terrorists" as part of the political agenda in Lebanon.[122]

Critically, these plans were not limited to PLO fighters, as evident from statements concerning Palestinian refugees as well. The refugees were first discussed at the end of a secret meeting with Bashir Gemayel, Chief of Lebanese Military Intelligence Johnny Abdu, and leading Israeli and Lebanese officials at Sharon's Negev ranch late on the evening of July 31. Sharon explained that he would be insisting on a peace agreement with the Lebanese government and had to address the question of the Palestinian refugees left behind in Beirut. Bashir told the Israelis, "We'll take care of everything and we'll let you know soon." Yehoshua Saguy, the Israeli intelligence chief, responded, "The time has come for Bashir's men to prepare a plan to deal with the Palestinians. I understand you are getting ready to deal with it and you need to prepare a plan." Sharon added a final note: "The Jews are weird but you must agree about the issue—we don't wish to stay there and take care of the issue."[123]

By discussing the fate of Palestinians in such a manner, Sharon and the other Israeli officials invited Gemayel and the Phalange to do Israel's bidding in the refugee camps of Beirut. This pattern of countenancing violence and even possibly instigating a refugee exodus by destroying their homes extended back to early July, when, during a meeting between Sharon and Bashir Gemayel at the Lebanese Forces headquarters in Beirut, Gemayel asked the Israelis "whether we would object to him moving bulldozers into the refugee camps in the south, to remove them, so that the refugees won't stay in the south." According to notes on the meeting, "the DM [Sharon] responded by saying that it was none of our business. We do not wish to handle Lebanon's internal affairs."[124] Yet such open talk of driving out Palestinians through violence and expulsion recurred in discussions just before the massacre. In a crucial meeting with Gemayel on September 12, two days before his assassination, Bashir told Sharon that "conditions should be created which would lead the Palestinians to leave Lebanon."[125]

Excerpts from the restricted testimonies of the Kahan Commission underscore that members of the Israeli military and intelligence organizations knew in advance what the Phalange were intending to do to the Palestinians. According to the testimony of Colonel Elkana Harnof, a senior Israeli military intelligence officer, the Phalange revealed that "Sabra would become a zoo and Shatila Beirut's parking place." Harnof added details about acts of brutality and massacres relayed to Defense Minister Sharon as early as June 23.[126] On that same day, a report was passed to Foreign Minister Shamir and Defense Minister Sharon attesting to the Christians "terminating" five hundred people in the evacuation of West Beirut. Mossad director Nahum Admoni and others met with Bashir Gemayel and the description of the meeting contains harrowing evidence of what was intended for the Palestinians throughout Lebanon.

According to the notes of the meeting, "Bashir [Gemayel] adds it is possible that in this context they will need several 'Dir Yassins,'" referring to the notorious massacre of Palestinians by Jewish Irgun fighters in the 1948 War that sowed fear and dispersal. But, the meeting notes continue, "N.[ahum] Admoni stresses that as long as the IDF is around, the Christians will have to refrain from this type of action. Bashir explains once again that he will act at a later stage since a Christian state would not be able to survive if the demographic aspect will not be dealt with."[127] As Admoni explained to the Kahan Commission, "Bashir had a very spontaneous speaking style. He was preoccupied with Lebanon's demographic balance, and discussed it a lot. When he (Bashir) talked in terms of demographic change—it was always in terms of killing and elimination."[128]

The invocation of Deir Yassin was an apt metaphor for the behavior of those who disliked the Palestinian presence in Lebanon and wanted to see them disappear. From the evidence available, Sharon and other Israeli military and intelligence officials may have assumed Gemayel's forces would circulate through the refugee camps to engage in some form of indiscriminate violence, resulting in the exodus of Palestinian civilians from the camps and the razing of their dwellings to the ground. It is unclear whether the scale of the violence intended was even greater than what actually occurred, or where these refugees were expected to go, if they survived such an onslaught. Jordan was one clear destination, and Sharon himself had voiced hopes to see the Hashemite Kingdom collapse and turn into a Palestinian state as a result of an influx of Palestinians from Lebanon, relieving pressure on Israel to withdraw from the West Bank.[129] An indication of Phalange intentions was offered to a staff member of the Kahan Commission by the father of one militia member involved in the massacre who testified that before entering the camps the fighters were briefed by Elie Hobeika and "the men understood that their mission was to liquidate young Palestinians as a way of instigating a mass flight from the camps—in accordance with Bashir's vision of the final act of the war in West Beirut."[130]

A closer focus on Sabra and Shatila sheds light on a line of thinking about Palestinian identity that extended from the late 1970s through the autonomy negotiations, reaching tragic ends through the destruction wrought in Beirut. Israeli officials were attuned to the link between internal concerns over the Palestinian question and the external struggle for regional influence. But they did not want to pay the moral price for a strategic alliance with the Maronites. When pressed by Chief Justice Kahan about Phalange intentions with regards to Palestinian civilians, Mossad chief Yitzhak Hofi explained the Israeli reply to Gemayel: "We told him we thank him very much, but that we have no intention that the solving of the Lebanese Palestinian problem would be made at the expense of the State of Israel."[131] In light of these testimonies, and the nature of Israeli-Phalange relations during the war, the events of 1982 fit within a much wider attempt to vanquish the Palestinians, diplomatically and militarily, since the planning of Camp David.

An Ephemeral Peace

Even after the violence of September was revealed, American and Israeli officials continued efforts to claim victory in Lebanon. Defense Secretary Casper Weinberger's critics blamed him for enabling the violence by withdrawing the Marines, and Ambassador Habib would later admit that the United States had failed to keep its word in not protecting Palestinians left behind following the PLO's evacuation.[132] The situation had turned into the quagmire Reagan's advisors initially feared. In the aftermath of the massacre, an acute sense of moral obligation spurred an immediate shift in the president's view, and he was newly willing to intervene with a more substantive MNF force.[133] Sabra and Shatila had compelled the American government to redeploy U.S. Marines to Beirut, leaving them exposed without a clear mission in the midst of the civil war.

Notwithstanding the deteriorating events on the ground, the Israeli security establishment maintained its belief that a peace agreement with the Maronites was possible. Before his resignation, Sharon spoke often of normalization with the Lebanese and of free Israeli civilian entry into Beirut. Ambassador Habib protested these suggestions as unseemly given the context of the war. "I know you want to go to the Hotel Commodore and have a cup of coffee," he told the minister of defense, referring to the buzzing journalist mainstay in West Beirut. "It's a lousy hotel, but you want to go there and have a cup of coffee, and I say wait a little while, please. This is not a time for tourism."[134] Sharon's efforts at normalization built on a longer history of secret Israeli-Maronite negotiations, which continued throughout Israel's military invasion of Lebanon.

David Kimche, an Israeli diplomat and Mossad recruitment officer, traveled to the Gemayel family compound in the Bikfaya hills in January 1983 to meet with Sheikh Pierre Gemayel. Pierre was the father of both the slain Bashir and his brother Amin, the new Lebanese president. Pierre had founded the Phalangist party after his participation in the 1936 Summer Olympics in Berlin, where he was heavily influenced by German and Spanish fascism, serving as a strange counterpart to his Mossad visitor. But the elder Gemayel was optimistic that a new Lebanon could still be built with their help. He told Kimche to "tell Mr. Begin and Mr. Sharon that the relations between you and us are like marriage bonds. This is a deep bond for a lifetime, like a Maronite wedding." Gemayel explained the analogy: "You have physical power and we have political power. We can open doors on your behalf in the Middle East."[135]

In spite of the setbacks of the war, and the assassination of his elder son, Gemayel maintained confidence in his cause: "Once we thought we would not be able to build Lebanon like we dreamed of. But today that looks possible. The Muslims are beginning to understand us and we are a bit optimistic. We have the possibility to now build a new Lebanon and begin to live together like we want and hope. Give us time."[136] Like Begin's rhetoric defending the Maronites, Gemayel's assurances fueled unrealistic expectations about the possibilities opened up by the war, with disastrous results for the country and its inhabitants. During an interview decades after his own involvement as the Israeli government's coordinator in occupied Lebanon, the former diplomat Uri Lubrani acknowledged this overreach. Lebanon is like a "piano," Lubrani remarked, and "one has to play all the various octaves." "Some of the Mossad were captivated by the Maronites, who played on their egos with nice food and hospitality." But they also knew how to manipulate their Israeli interlocutors, who failed to account for competing forces. The legacy of the invasion, Lubrani concluded, is that "Israel had no business trying to manage the internal affairs of the Lebanese."[137] It was a lesson learned too late.

During the early part of 1983, the United States continued to back secret Israeli negotiations for a peace treaty with the Lebanese government.[138] The talks were held while Lebanon was subject to both Israeli and Syrian occupation, and U.S. diplomats often solicited Israeli negotiating positions before seeking approval from Beirut.[139] The Israelis wanted open borders with Lebanon and the establishment of diplomatic missions that would lead to a full peace. Lebanese negotiators were far more circumspect, initially attempting to limit the discussions to military matters. They viewed the negotiations as a joint effort with the United States, imposed as the only means of securing Israel's withdrawal.[140]

There were also broader political aims driving Israeli efforts to force an unsustainable treaty on a reluctant and shaky Lebanese government.[141] In a declassified CIA intelligence analysis prepared for the agency's director, William Casey, on February 9, 1983, the CIA's Near East and South Asian experts provided the rationale for these negotiations: "Beirut believes—probably correctly—that Tel Aviv is deliberately dragging them out to scuttle the Reagan initiative." The regional analysts surmised that a peace treaty with Lebanon would divert American attention from pushing the president's September 1982 peace plan, which had directly challenged the narrow Israeli view of Camp David and the Palestinian issue, eliciting so much anger from Prime Minister Begin. The CIA analysts also took stock of the domestic consequences of the invasion, which had driven the negotiations: "Israeli political leaders, including Prime Minister Begin, probably have more reason than ever to secure major concessions on security and normalization now that the Sabra-Shatila massacre report is in. They need to prove the Lebanese invasion was a profitable political gamble for Israel."[142]

Lebanon's government, led by Amin Gemayel, signed the peace agreement with Israel on May 17, 1983.[143] Primarily, as a leading study explains, the agreement declared an "end to the state of war between Lebanon and Israel, forbade the presence of forces hostile to one in the territory of the other (implicitly, Syria and the PLO in Lebanon), established an American-led 'Joint Liaison Committee' to oversee the normalization of relations; and called for a 'security region' along the shared border."[144] Gemayel was a weak leader and was compelled to sign in order to end Israel's military intervention. Yet Israel did not achieve the full normalization it sought, and its efforts via a side letter from the Americans to link the IDF withdrawal with a Syrian pullout "explicitly" handed Syrian president Hafez al-Assad an "unexpected veto." He had opposed the Israeli peace agreement from the start and was unwilling to give up any of Syria's newfound regional influence gained during the war. Habib, who had negotiated the agreement on behalf of the United States as Reagan's trusted lead regional diplomat, did not attend the signing ceremony and later remarked the accords "weren't worth the paper they were written on."[145] He swiftly lost the confidence of the Syrians after the negotiations and resigned from his post.

Begin's Departure

The Israeli public continued to debate the efficacy and morality of the Lebanon War, with the peace movement growing in strength after the massacre at Sabra and Shatila.[146] Begin's initial effort to present the military intervention in humanitarian terms— appealing to the rescue of Israel's Christian brethren—had also linked Israel's Cold War foreign policy with the reassertion of Jewish power and a highly nationalist interpretation of communal solidarity. This approach implicated support for Israel with a right-wing Likud worldview.[147] During the war, Begin was widely maligned for yielding to Sharon's aggressive agenda and for the moralizing tone in which he presented Israeli aims.[148] The Israeli prime minister, whose own parents were killed by the Nazis, invoked the Holocaust and the suffering of Jews as a justification for his actions in Lebanon.[149] In response, the Holocaust scholar Ze'ev Mankowitz excoriated Begin for his misuse of Jewish history. In a scathing letter to the Israeli liberal daily newspaper *Haaretz*, Mankowitz wrote that "Begin has lost touch with reality and is punishing phantoms born in the greatest tragedy that ever befell our people. Whatever its final outcome, the epitaph to be place upon the war in Lebanon will read: Here lies the international stature and moral integrity of a wonderful people. Died of a false analogy."[150]

Beset with grief over the recent death of his wife, Aliza, and the terrible outcome of the Israeli invasion, Begin resigned from office in August 1983. Reagan, in a most gracious cable to his dear friend "Menachem," wrote the departing leader that "few men have so rightly worn the mantle of peacemaker as you . . . a half a century at the center of history is an extraordinary achievement."[151] The Israeli leader—a fixture of public and political life since before the birth of the state in 1948—was rarely seen in public again.[152] The Likud Central Committee selected Yitzhak Shamir to succeed Begin as prime minister. Shamir was also a disciple of the Revisionist Zionist Ze'ev Jabotinsky and a former leader of the Stern Gang, who had a "reputation for extremism and violence." Shamir was even more intransigent than Begin, having opposed the Sinai withdrawal, and was "generally unreceptive to the idea of bargaining and compromise."[153] Moshe Arens, the ambassador to the United States and also a member of the right-wing Herut party, was appointed defense minister to replace Ariel Sharon.[154] The new leadership was even less inclined to push forward on the political front, in particular when it came to the Palestinians.

Alongside these political implications, the cultural consequences of Lebanon left an indelible mark on Israeli society.[155] For committed Zionists, the impact of the 1982 War was devastating. "In Lebanon the grandeur that started in 1967 was exploded," remarked the American Israeli scholar and rabbi David Hartman to the *New York Times*. "The early naiveté of the pioneers, all that is gone now. We have to find a way to reinstitute into Israeli society a sense of joy and vision now that we have gained some anchorage in reality. Israelis need music," Hartman concluded, and "there is no music in the air now. There is just this invasion of reality."[156] Amos Oz, a leading Israeli writer and public intellectual, reflected some years later how the experience of the war shaped the nation's psyche.

> After Lebanon, we can no longer ignore the monster, even when it is dormant, or half asleep, or when it peers out from behind the lunatic fringe. After Lebanon, we must not pretend that the monster dwells only in the offices of Meir Kahane; or only on General Sharon's ranch,

or only in Raful's carpentry shop, or only in the Jewish settlements in the West Bank. It dwells, drowsing, virtually everywhere, even in the folk-singing guts of our common myths. Even in our soul-melodies. We did not leave it behind in Lebanon, with the Hezbollah. It is here, among us, a part of us, like a shadow, in Hebron, in Gaza, in the slums and in the suburbs, in the kibbutzim and in my Lake Kinneret.[157]

For Oz, like many others who witnessed and wrote about the events of 1982 and its aftermath, the war represented a moment of rupture. Yet it also tended to direct attention inward, in some ways distancing Israeli society from reckoning with the Arab victims of state violence. The persistence of rhetoric and tactics articulated during the war—often under the guise of humanitarian imperatives—continued to animate the logic of military action and state policy toward Palestinians living under Israeli control well after it ended.[158]

Searching for a Middle East Policy

By the fall of 1983, the debilitating lack of movement in Lebanon, fraying relations with Jordan, and stalled negotiations over the fate of the Palestinians raised major concerns within the Reagan administration. There were serious challenges facing U.S. policy in the Middle East. George Shultz outlined his worries to the president: "We need to take a hard look at emerging signs of serious danger for us and for our friends in the area." Shultz was especially concerned about policies "toward settlements on the West Bank, and toward the human condition of Palestinians both in the occupied territories and in Lebanon."[159] Shultz's warnings coincided with a series of important NSC meetings and critical administration directives that attempted to provide a new coherent policy for the region.

The resulting strategy emphasized the prevention of Soviet hegemony and the protection of adequate U.S. access to Gulf oil reserves as the primary objectives of American policy in the Middle East.[160] Another major concern was ensuring the security of Israel and obtaining a resolution of the Palestinian problem, and Reagan believed that the United States was well suited for both tasks. But the president's accompanying statement on cooperation with Israel once again threw into relief the inevitable dilemma that would result from his approach. "I acknowledge that our ability to defend vital interests in the near East and South Asia would be enhanced by the resolution of the Arab-Israeli conflict," Reagan affirmed. "Nevertheless, in recognition of Israel's strategic location, developed base infrastructure, and the quality and interoperability of Israeli military forces, we will undertake to resume cooperative planning with Israel expanding on the work begun earlier."[161] In choosing to renew strategic cooperation with Israel, Reagan understood that he could further undermine America's credibility with Arab states, as Lebanon had so clearly demonstrated.

The president's National Security Advisor, William Clark, stressed the importance of fully restarting strategic cooperation with Israel and saving face with the Arab world. Under the rubric of collaborating to defeat Soviet aggression, Clark believed Israel would not question U.S. "latitude on issues where U.S. and Israeli interests do *not* coincide," namely equipping "moderate Arab states" as part of parallel strategic alliances.[162] The approach demonstrated the paramount importance of the Soviet threat, which remained the dominant prism through which Reagan viewed the Middle East. But the flawed logic of such an arrangement was clear in Lebanon, where a strengthened U.S.-Israel alliance did not coexist with support from Arab states. The ongoing Israeli occupation of the country had in fact engendered a great deal of opposition in the region, growing swiftly in the wake of the May 17 agreement, which had enabled a security region along the border.[163]

Any gain from the short-lived calm that had been brokered in the Lebanese-Israeli peace treaty soon gave way to further violence. As predicted, Israeli forces began to leave the Shouf Mountains above Beirut in the fall of 1983, triggering a power vacuum. U.S. troops remained in place, exposed to attacks near the airport and drawn into the fighting alongside Lebanon's Christian militias. Local opposition among Lebanon's disaffected Shia population led to targeted strikes against American installations. These attacks were mostly the work of an emergent paramilitary group, Hezbollah. In April 1983, a suicide bomber killed sixty-three people, including several key CIA operatives, soldiers, and Marines, in a targeted attack on the U.S. Embassy in Beirut.[164]

On October 23, 1983, in the single deadliest attack against the U.S. Marine Corps since World War II, an enormous explosion ripped through the U.S. Marine barracks at the Beirut International Airport, killing 241 American servicemen.[165] Minutes later, a second suicide bomber hit the French military barracks in the "Drakkar" building, killing 58 paratroopers in France's single worst military loss since the Algerian War. These attacks led to open warfare with Syrian-backed forces and, soon after, the rapid withdrawal of the Marines and multinational forces to their ships, accelerating the end of U.S. and European involvement in Lebanon. Despite Reagan's pledge to retaliate against the perpetrators, and not withdraw until the mission was complete, American troops departed within months.[166] In the words of U.S. ambassador Samuel Lewis, America left the country "with our tail between our legs."[167]

The possibility of Lebanese unity quickly crumbled as the Syrian army filled the void left by the departing multinational forces, which evacuated by March 1984. Soon after, Amin Gemayel abrogated the May 17 agreement that had been signed with Israel and turned to Syria for support. Israeli forces partially withdrew twenty-five miles north of Israel's border with Lebanon, using General Saad Haddad's South Lebanon Army (SLA) as a proxy to control the area alongside its own forces. This marked the onset of a "prolonged de facto partition of Lebanon" between Israeli and Syrian spheres of influence. The regional implications of this partition, as CIA analysts predicted in a prescient report, affected the Palestinians as well. Ultimately, as the CIA argued, "a prolonged stalemate in Lebanon will tend to detract attention from other Levantine issues, particularly the Palestinian problem."[168]

For Israeli leaders, despite the setbacks of the invasion, there was interest in keeping the Palestinian question isolated from developments in the territories themselves. But this could not prevent the transformation of the Lebanese occupation into a recurring source of violent conflict as well as political dissent within Israel. Israeli military forces continued to occupy a large swath of south Lebanon until May 2000, when Hezbollah forced a withdrawal.[169] Despite the lofty rhetoric of Israeli leaders and the Cold War aspirations of the Reagan White House, the invasion of Lebanon had facilitated Syria's regional ascendency and adversely impacted America's strategic position in the Middle East by inviting further Soviet influence. Syria was able to maintain direct influence over Lebanon for more than twenty years, only forced out by the "Cedar Revolution" in the aftermath of Lebanese prime minister Rafik Hariri's assassination in 2005.

One year after the initial Israeli invasion, CIA analyst Graham Fuller explained the growth of such a close Syrian-Soviet alliance. "Syria can derive considerable satisfaction from the flow of events in Lebanon which strengthen Assad's conviction that things are going his way," Fuller suggested. "Syria will take efforts to avoid sparking Israeli attacks against itself, especially while the pace of events is moving strongly against national reconciliation and in favor of confessionalism and partition. *Syria can live happily with partition*, confident that it remains the dominant power in Lebanese politics. *The USSR's* interests are closely linked to Syria's. The Soviets support Syrian opposition to any U.S.-sponsored peace plan in the area."[170] Given the political dynamics that have inhered since the Syrian army's formal departure from Lebanon in 2005, and Russian influence in sustaining the Syrian civil war that began in 2011, this particular legacy of the intervention should not be ignored.[171]

The war in Lebanon also served as an incubator of other important regional transformations, especially in light of the 1979 Iranian Revolution and its influence among Lebanon's Shiite population. Hezbollah grew into a highly organized paramilitary organization and political force in the midst of the 1982 War, resisting the Israeli intervention and targeting American and European forces who had joined the fray. "Israel's myopic obsession with destroying the Palestinian resistance spawned a far more dangerous enemy," one historian of the period has noted. "American Cold War naiveté opened the door for Iran in Lebanon."[172]

While the signing of a strategic agreement between Begin's Likud government and the Reagan White House in 1981 may have marked the formal onset of a strategic alliance between the United States and Israel, the 1982 Lebanon War and the legacy of the Israeli and U.S. intervention was a crack in the dominant narrative of abiding friendship between stalwart allies. Israel's leaders were motivated by overly ambitious regional aims, blind to the internal realities of a fractured Lebanese state, and their military invasion compromised relations with the United States. But in enabling a new strategic rationale to underpin bilateral ties, the Reagan administration had also empowered Israel to intervene and shut down political horizons in the occupied territories. The U.S.-Israel alliance and the unchecked hostility toward Palestinian nationalism in Jerusalem fueled the 1982 invasion and implicated the United States in the tragedy of the war.

The foundations of this shift were rooted, however, in Carter's success at Camp David. To a large extent, it was the assurance of bilateral peace with Egypt and the failure of a comprehensive regional settlement that paved the way for more ambitious Israeli intervention beyond the West Bank and Gaza Strip. In a revealing interview some years after the PLO expulsion, Yasser Arafat told a researcher in Tunis, "We knew that the invasion of Lebanon would not have taken place if there had been no Camp David agreement and without the Iran-Iraq war. Because of Camp David, Egypt was absent; Iraq was completely preoccupied; and the Syrians accepted the cease-fire after about four days."[173] When asked whether he partly blamed the United States and its support for the Camp David Accords for what happened in Lebanon, Bethlehem's mayor Elias Freij told NBC's *Meet the Press* the following: "I am blaming the United States for what has befell the Arab women and children and civilian people in Lebanon, the Palestinians and the Lebanese, and the destruction of West Beirut, the obliteration of the Palestinian refugees' camps in Tyre, Sidon, Damour, and other places."[174]

Lebanon, and the siege of Beirut, endured as a touchstone of the Palestinian struggle for self-determination, drawing renewed global attention to the Palestinian issue and reviving the quest for statehood. During a historic interview in Beirut with veteran journalist and peace activist Uri Avnery—his first with an Israeli— Arafat appealed to world opinion for a greater understanding of the Palestinian reality.[175] "I am not worried. I am not worried at all about the future despite this extensive invasion of Lebanon," Arafat told Avnery. "I turn to every human being in the world to come here and see this great power, the Israeli Army, what it did against the Palestinians, to our refugees, to our women and children. . . . History is not made of battles." The PLO leader was adamant that his fight was against the Israeli army, not the Jewish people. "We want to live with all the Jews. We are not against the Jews! . . . The Jews are a religious people, people sticking to religion. The Israeli military regime damages the whole course of life, and damages, in a very disgraceful way, the Jewish spirit." This distinction between Judaism as a religion and the political impact of Zionism and the Israeli state had long characterized PLO writings about Israel, and the war in Lebanon had thrown these distinctions into greater relief.[176] Before Avnery left, Arafat asked if he was going back home the same day, which he was. "You think you have the right to go back there, and I don't have the same right?" Arafat asked Avnery. "Simply, I am a human being! To where? Apart from my native country? I want to return to my homeland."[177]

Throughout the summer siege, Palestinian leaders continued to assert the PLO's willingness to accept binding UN resolutions and the possibility of a negotiated settlement. In the aftermath of the PLO's evacuation from Beirut in August, ABC News hosted an episode of *This Week with David Brinkley* on the situation in the Middle East, inviting Bassam Abu Sharif of the Popular Front for the Liberation of Palestine (PFLP) to discuss the political repercussions of the departure. The prominent PLO factional leader, who had been involved in several militant actions against Israel and was injured in a Mossad assassination attempt a decade earlier, was asked whether he would be satisfied with a Palestinian state in the West Bank and Gaza. Abu Sharif remarked that it was "satisfactory" to have a state on "any part of Palestine." In a follow-up, he was asked, "Does that mean that the Palestinians, in your view, the PLO, in your view, can accept the simultaneous existence of Israel as a Jewish state?" Abu Sharif replied, "This is the PLO program. It was very clear . . . it is to establish a Palestine independent state on any part of Palestine." Brinkley asked if such an outcome were to materialize, "would that be the end of your hostility to Israel?" Abu Sharif replied that "this would be probably a start for simultaneous cooperation between Palestinians and Jews."[178]

Failures among the PLO leadership were also more evident after the summer of 1982, as the locus of the national struggle shifted from the external leadership to political activists inside the West Bank and Gaza Strip.[179] The unintended consequence was to strengthen calls for a national solution to the Palestinian question.

Contrary to Israel's aims, the invasion had in some crucial ways emboldened the Palestinian cause. The fighting revealed the persistence of PLO military strength and political commitment despite the organization's forced departure from Lebanon.[180] A special National Intelligence Estimate prepared by the CIA in the aftermath of the war described this altered climate: "Israel has been surprised to discover that its military victory has not produced the expected political dividends and seems to have strengthened its antagonists' political hand."[181] This analysis cohered with the view of one Israeli Knesset member, who remarked, "In Beirut, we created a Palestinian state."[182] A formative link can be traced from the Palestinian presence in Lebanon prior to the 1982 Israeli invasion and the advancement of the PLO's statist agenda after the organization's expulsion.[183]

But the war in Lebanon, like the diplomacy around Camp David, also highlighted the danger ascribed to the Palestinian national struggle. Just as the motivation for a shift from the political prevention of sovereignty to military targeting of the PLO was clear with the invasion, the pendulum now swung back the other way. As the PLO leadership regrouped in exile, Israel redoubled efforts to solve the Palestinian question in non-statist terms. A revival of Palestinian nationalism ultimately forced Israel's reluctant reckoning with the Palestinian question on rather different grounds than the prior decade.

CHAPTER SEVEN

Alternatives to the PLO?

THE SHIP THAT CARRIED YASSER ARAFAT away from Beirut was called the *Atlantis*. Two destroyers escorted it on the journey to Athens, from where PLO leaders would travel onward to Tunis. One of the passengers on the journey in late August 1982 was the Lebanese photographer and visual artist Fouad Elkoury, who was invited aboard by the PLO spokesman and disguised himself as a fighter to get on the ship. He later described the atmosphere of the journey as "heady with contemplation and a certain thoughtlessness." In Elkoury's photographs, one can see a smiling Arafat, flashing a victory sign as the ship left the Lebanese port. But there are more intimate images, of exhausted *fedayeen* fighters lying on deck chairs, Arafat and his commanders looking out to sea, several smiling children, and one passenger kneeling for the afternoon prayer. As the *Atlantis* pulled into the Athens port, the Greek prime minister awaited its arrival. Elkoury's camera captured the welcome ceremony on shore, including a line of onlookers dressed in traditional Palestinian embroidery, carrying the Palestinian flag alongside Arafat's portrait.[1]

Elkoury's photographs are a jarring reminder of the split between the leadership of the national movement and the reality of exile; the struggle between politics on the inside and the external quest for self-determination that continued far away from historic Palestine. Arriving in Tunis, the PLO was deprived of the infrastructure it had developed in Arab states like Jordan and Lebanon.[2] In the new headquarters that Arafat established in the Hotel

Salwa, his office staff gathered in silence and shock to watch an Italian documentary about the Sabra and Shatila massacre in Beirut. Fighters living in isolated PLO camps were "demoralized and dispirited," with others dispersed across Yemen, Algeria, Syria, Sudan, and Iraq.[3] In these far-flung locations, the PLO worked to reconstitute the national movement in exile, having understood the necessity of political engagement in the wake of Lebanon.

Yet for Israel and the United States, the aftermath of the war led to a series of efforts to bypass the PLO and find alternative modes of engagement with the Palestinians. Some of these attempts built on the leadership within the occupied territories, while other ideas turned to the Jordanians as a desired address for resolving the Palestinian question. These economic and political efforts ultimately failed, and the outbreak of the first Intifada in 1987 forced a reckoning with Palestinian nationalism on its own terms. As the Reagan administration moved to engage diplomatically, the PLO returned to the center of the political stage, while still disconnected from the realities of life inside the West Bank and Gaza Strip. The recognition of the national movement and the onset of an official dialogue at the end of the 1980s was a pivotal development for the United States and Israel. It was also a milestone for the PLO, which had fully embraced a statist platform after years of an internal struggle over national aims.

Bypassing the National Movement

While many factions within the PLO had decisively shifted from armed struggle to political engagement in the 1970s, there were still a host of disagreements about tactics and strategy in the wake of the exile from Beirut. At the February 1983 gathering of the Palestine National Council (PNC) in Algiers—the first PNC meeting after the 1982 War—the national movement took stock of the new reality. In his account of the gathering, the PLO's representative in Lebanon, Shafiq al-Hout, offered a critical assessment of these discussions. "I was not alone in believing that we had not 'won' the war in Lebanon," al-Hout recalled, but the meeting was "not commensurate with the huge blow which the Palestinian movement had just received. . . . The conference was hollow, celebratory." There was a central question that had not been answered, al-Hout explained. "What now after the departure from Beirut?"[4]

Underneath the surface appearance of a "festival of resistance," Algiers represented a failure of self-criticism about the limits of the national struggle and where the Palestinians might be headed. While the events in Lebanon had emboldened the PLO's fighting force, it also revealed a great deal of Arab opposition to the Palestinian struggle. Al-Hout addressed these glaring issues in an acerbic speech, singling out the lack of national unity among various factions. "Each Palestinian faction has its own flag, its own spokesman, its own military forces and celebrations," he told the conference. "All that's missing is an exchange of ambassadors!" What was the PLO's political strategy? How much progress could be made in the diplomatic realm? What of military resistance? The final conference communiqué did not provide much clarity on these questions. "It was like one of those crossword puzzles where you can read from right to left or left to right, and from top to bottom or vice versa," al-Hout wrote. "Every person could interpret it his own way and find nothing offensive in it."[5] On a range of issues, from a discussion of the Reagan Plan to compromises over relations with Egypt and Jordan, another senior PLO official described the council decisions as "saying yes and no at the same time."[6]

The equanimity at Algiers did not hold for very long. Dissidents within the Fatah movement rebelled against Arafat for what they characterized as his abandonment of armed struggle, given his openness to consider diplomatic alternatives. This newly formed "Rejection Front" strongly opposed a negotiated settlement with Israel, drawing on deeper discontent that had plagued Fatah for many years. Critics singled out diplomatic consideration of the Reagan Plan, which still did not recognize a Palestinian state, as well as internal discussions over a possible confederation with Jordan.[7] There were also further internal splits over Arafat's meeting with Egyptian president Hosni Mubarak in December 1983, drawing condemnation from the Popular Front for the Liberation of Palestine (PFLP), the Democratic Front for the Liberation of Palestine (DFLP), and members of Fatah itself.[8] These divisions served to marginalize the exiled organization as it pursued broader international initiatives, drawing attention to the activism of Palestinians inside the occupied territories.

The PLO's marginalization was further exacerbated by the persistence of violence within various corners of the national movement. In October 1985, a splinter group called the Palestine Liberation Front hijacked the Italian cruise ship *Achille Lauro* and carried out the cold-blooded killing of Leon Klinghoffer, a Jewish wheelchair-bound tourist.[9] While out of sync with the political direction of the PLO, these factions committed highly visible and egregious acts of terror against Israeli and Jewish targets around the globe. A string of plane hijackings and deadly shootings at the Rome and Vienna airports further strengthened anti-engagement views, and outrage over Palestinian violence mounted. In the United States, the Reagan administration, which was confronting a rash of worldwide terrorist attacks throughout the 1980s, had little tolerance for the PLO's violence on the international scene.[10]

American and Israeli officials instead undertook parallel efforts to find an alternative address for resolving the Palestinian question that bypassed the national movement. The Israeli government remained determined to avoid the prospect of Palestinian self-determination inside the occupied territories. Before the autonomy talks had ended in April 1982, the Israeli civil administration in the territories had begun developing "Village Leagues" that were intended to provide alternative sources of leadership to the PLO in the West Bank.[11] Officials sought out figures not aligned with the Palestinian national movement to head Leagues that would be granted a degree of authority over the Arab population. This was assumed to be a mechanism that would remove direct Israeli control over certain aspects of daily life, enabling a form of indirect rule over the territories not unlike colonial models of governance in other contexts.[12] The concept of local control over municipal governance via pliable non-PLO Palestinian leaders had first emerged under Moshe Dayan's tenure in the occupied territories. After Likud's rise to power, Begin and Sharon expanded this effort, looking for rural leadership to counter the political influence of Palestinian nationalists. Non-urban figures were seen as more reliably "quietist" and "amenable to collaboration" than city dwellers, and the Israeli architects of the Leagues believed they could successfully pit the two against each other.[13]

Israel's attempt to institute these Village Leagues was short-lived, with widespread Palestinian resistance in 1981 and 1982

bringing about a swift end to this effort amid riots and civil dis-
obedience, highlighting the effect of mass mobilization that as one
important study explains "cut across class and clan."[14] The Village Leagues also failed as a result of Jordanian opposition, which
joined in with PLO efforts to discredit the project. This deprived
Begin and Sharon of the possibility of finding local partners for
their autonomy plans, alienating non-PLO and pro-Hashemite
urban leaders.[15] When asked why he did not participate in this initiative, for example, Bethlehem mayor Elias Freij told NBC's Martin
Fletcher, "There are no talks going with anybody. The Israelis have
created these creatures. They're protecting them just as symbols.
And these symbols or collaborators will simply sign a blank check
for Israel." Freij compared the efforts on the part of the Israelis to
pursue Village Leagues as akin to the failed autonomy talks. Those
talks, Freij explained, were devoid of content. "Israel is not giving
us anything whatsoever. Israel wants the land. It is talking of an autonomy where Mr. Begin says will never lead to self-determination,
will never lead to statehood." Harkening back to the language of
Camp David, the Bethlehem mayor insisted that the real meaning
of the agreement was "full autonomy" for Palestinians, akin to the
Egyptian formula suggested during the autonomy negotiations,
not the model being proffered by Israel. "We have not fought for
60 years to accept a very limited, powerless administrative council
without doing anything," Freij declared.[16]

The Jordanian Option and Quality of Life Initiatives

A search for alternative approaches to the Palestinian question
also featured in Washington. Reagan had won reelection handily
in 1984, and the administration deemphasized a return to comprehensive diplomacy in the region during his second term. At a news
conference in the spring of 1985, the president was asked pointedly
about the seeming lack of interest in restarting the peace process.
Having unveiled an ambitious peace plan in September 1982, Reagan now seemed to have stepped back. He responded by insisting
it was not a policy of "disengagement." "Our proposal, in the very
beginning, was that we did not want to participate in the negotiations," Reagan explained. "It wouldn't be any of our business to do

so but that we'd do whatever we could to help bring the warring parties together and, in effect, you might say, continue the Camp David process."[17] Instead of reviving a full-scale peace initiative, U.S. policymakers focused on more limited programs to alleviate hardships in the West Bank and Gaza Strip, repositioning the Palestinian issue in humanitarian terms. Diplomatically, U.S. officials also explored what was known as the "Jordanian Option," an effort to conduct peace talks with King Hussein over the fate of the Palestinians. This was intended to circumvent the PLO and build a moderate Palestinian infrastructure under the aegis of an Israeli-Jordanian arrangement.[18]

Reagan's electoral victory in 1984 coincided with a political realignment in Israel, where a standoff between the Labor and Likud parties had resulted in a unity coalition with a rotation in the premiership. Shimon Peres, the Labor leader, served as prime minister until 1986, and then the Likud leader Yitzhak Shamir completed the term. Peres had grown in popularity for withdrawing troops from Lebanon and successfully managing the struggling economy. He too believed that diplomatic engagement with Jordan could perhaps lead to "a kind of condominium over the West Bank and Gaza at the expense of the PLO."[19] To shift the focus away from Palestinian nationalists, Peres launched a series of secret meetings with King Hussein of Jordan that began in July 1985. Israeli and U.S. officials agreed to move forward in stages, beginning with a joint Jordanian-Palestinian delegation meeting with the U.S. assistant secretary of state for Near Eastern Affairs, Richard Murphy. This would ostensibly be followed by PLO acceptance of the U.S. conditions for dialogue and the start of negotiations. American officials wanted to strengthen Peres's position against the Likud and Shamir. But the divisions within Israel's national unity government over the inclusion of PLO members in the Murphy meeting derailed it from the start. Reagan backed away at the final moment, minimizing strains in the U.S.-Israel alliance by reiterating his refusal to deal with the PLO.[20]

PLO leaders also debated the value of reconciling with Jordan from their exile in Tunis, as they sought to further ties with Palestinians in the occupied territories.[21] The organization opted to adopt an interim strategy to access the West Bank through Jordan, in order to shift the center of gravity back to the West Bank. In a February 1985 communiqué, the PLO formulated a joint position in support of a confederation with the Hashemite Kingdom.[22] By the fall, however, relations between King Hussein and Arafat had deteriorated, as the PLO's failure to rein in violent factions and Hussein's political vulnerabilities undercut the alliance.[23] In a scathing address on February 19, 1986, King Hussein announced the end of the initiative with the PLO.[24] He blamed the Palestinian leadership for continued intransigence in not accepting UN resolution 242, and in the view of his biographer, the remarks signaled "the end of an era in which Jordan was the leading actor in the search for a peaceful solution to the Middle East conflict."[25] Reflecting on this emblematic return "to where we had started," George Shultz described his "deep frustration" with the overriding climate of failure. "I knew that without a peace process, a dangerous vacuum existed that would likely be filled by violence," the secretary of state concluded. "We would need a new model. We would not give up."[26]

Shultz's influence in the White House had grown steadily since his appointment to replace Haig in the summer of 1982. He sought a different approach to the Middle East after the challenges of Lebanon, although much of Reagan's second term was overshadowed by the explosive revelations of the United States trading arms for hostages as part of the Iran-Contra scandal.[27] King Hussein visited the White House in the summer of 1986, after he had severed the PLO initiative. In a memo ahead of the monarch's arrival, Shultz outlined the American commitment to a continuation of the strong alliance between the two countries, which Hussein was beginning to doubt after a failed Jordanian arms sale and lingering strains in the relationship with the United States in the wake of Camp David.[28] The secretary of state saw a meeting with Hussein as an opportunity for reassurance, while also encouraging a "more active Jordanian role" in the West Bank.[29] In a closed-door discussion, the president told Hussein that he supported "an alternative Palestinian leadership" and wanted to move forward on "quality of life" issues in the occupied territories.[30] Later that afternoon, Reagan's National Security Advisor John Poindexter also met privately with Hussein and reiterated his shared "frustration with

Arafat," agreeing that the PLO leader was unlikely to join the peace process.[31]

In the weeks following the visit, NSC official Dennis Ross helped prepare the groundwork for this initiative. Ross had served under Paul Wolfowitz at the State Department's Policy Planning staff, and was put in charge of Near East and South Asia Affairs at the NSC in June 1986.[32] In a cable composed by Ross, Poindexter encouraged Secretary Shultz to help King Hussein in his effort to "close all doors" to Arafat and provide money to build a "moderate Jordanian position on the West Bank." Poindexter sensed there could be problems with this approach. "I realize supporting the King's efforts to undermine Arafat and nurture an alternative leadership may be controversial. Some may feel that the King will fail or that there can be no alternative to Arafat," Poindexter wrote. "I am concerned that if we look lukewarm in our support we will guarantee his failure, and I am convinced that Arafat is incapable of ever negotiating peace with Israel."[33] Even though other policymakers and external critics had repeatedly stressed the importance of dealing with the PLO leadership directly, the NSC chief had other ideas. Advancing the notion that the PLO could be shut out of the peace process by going along with Jordan alone, the administration ignored many of its own critical assessments over the previous years.

Jordan mirrored the American approach to the Palestinians. In a coda to the cessation of Jordanian-PLO relations, King Hussein closed down the PLO office in Amman in July 1986. Prime Minister Shimon Peres and Defense Minister Yitzhak Rabin, who had returned to the leadership and was now responsible for the occupied territories, met secretly with Hussein at his holiday house in Aqaba that same month. They traveled by speedboat from Eilat for a four-hour discussion. Hussein was deeply critical of the PLO and "said he would try to cultivate moderate leaders from the occupied territories as an alternative." The leaders also discussed a five-year plan for "economic development" in the West Bank.[34] In August, the king tried to strengthen his support among Palestinians in the territories by launching a West Bank Development Plan to improve their economic conditions. Israel expressed its support for this initiative in the hope of further undermining the PLO and possibly asserting its own claim to the West Bank.[35]

While Jordan and Israel were in agreement to weaken the PLO with American help, U.S. financial support for King Hussein's plan was less forthcoming than the Jordanian monarch had hoped, with senior policymakers reluctant to dole out funding.[36] But the NSC continued pushing the idea of alternative leadership to the PLO. In talking points prepared by Dennis Ross for a discussion with Saudi ambassador Prince Bandar bin Sultan, Poindexter criticized the Saudi government for continuing to give money to Arafat, who "has failed every test that's ever been put to him to show he is committed to making peace." Poindexter stressed that "the King [Hussein] has given up on Arafat and we think for good reason. He is now trying to build an alternative Palestinian leadership. A leadership that is committed to negotiating peace, and we support that effort." Poindexter, who would later be convicted for his role in Iran-Contra, told Bandar that "in our judgment, your continued financial support for Arafat undermines the King's [Hussein's] efforts to build a credible alternative Palestinian leadership and is counterproductive to the peace process." The NSC advisor proceeded to ask Bandar to "at least reduce" Saudi support for Arafat if he couldn't end it, by making payroll deductions for all Palestinian workers in Saudi Arabia "optional."[37]

Poindexter also outlined a more activist approach for the Saudis, encouraging them to support moderates in the West Bank and contribute to "developmental projects" in the territories. He sought "small investments—$25 to 30 million in institutional and infrastructure projects"—as a counter to the growth of radical forces. This was all done "under the rubric of improving the quality of life for the Palestinians in the West Bank—and giving them some hope in the process."[38] The NSC continued pushing this idea through October. Reviewing an invitation list to an administration Middle East meeting, Ross suggested to the president's assistant that Dr. Martin Indyk, a founder of the Washington Institute for Near East Policy, be invited. "I include Martin because he represents a think tank that can do much to build the intellectual underpinnings of support in important Jewish and political circles for increased investments in Jordan and the West Bank," Ross explained.[39] Having recently flexed their political muscle against the arms sale to Jordan, domestic supporters of Israel remained opposed to any form of aid for the Jordanians. Indyk and his organization could potentially circumvent these concerns, a sign of growing influence by outside lobbyists in the 1980s.

The "Quality of Life" initiative was an uphill battle. In December, Ross prepared a brief study of King Hussein's West Bank development plan for the National Security Council. Describing the bleak situation on the ground, he outlined several reasons for America's involvement in the initiative. With 60 percent of the Palestinian population under the age of fifteen, the younger generation had no memory of association with Jordan and didn't identify with King Hussein. In Ross's view, "They have been socialized by more radical ideologies," including "the imagery of radical Shiite success" when it came to the Israeli withdrawal from Lebanon. This ideological shift "convinced many that the answer to Israeli occupation is fundamentalism and armed struggle."[40] King Hussein, fearing the long-term survival of the Hashemite monarchy, was seeking to stem the tide of this perceived radicalism by delivering on economic relief.

The assumptions undergirding American policy drew on reactions to the 1979 Iranian Revolution and an uncertainty about how to approach the Israeli government's actions in the occupied territories. If extremism took root in the West Bank, Ross argued, it would prompt Israel to act, "making it more likely that Sharon, Eitan and others will gain more clout and pursue their objective of de-populating the West Bank of Arabs." Sensing the threat this would pose to Jordan's stability, Ross wrote, "Hashemite rule in Jordan is probably not sustainable in a circumstance where the Palestinians on the West Bank move to the East Bank and fundamentally alter the demographic balance in the country." Reestablishing Jordanian influence in the area, Ross argued, "will ensure that Palestinians in the West Bank stay put, and it may in time also create a more moderate constituency prepared to join with the King in negotiations with Israel." Ross acknowledged that this might be a long shot but felt that the "Quality of Life" initiative was still well worth the investment of American funds and "could have a profound effect."[41]

Ross concluded his assessment with a premonitory note: "The monies involved may not be great, but their effects could be. And these effects should be measured not only in terms of what they positively produce but also in terms of the negative developments that they prevent." The NSC staffer was paying attention to the rumblings in the territories themselves. "If Hussein fails," Ross concluded, "we will surely face an explosion in the West Bank—with long term consequences for the prospects of Arab-Israeli peace."[42] The memo predated the outbreak of the Intifada by a year, underscoring U.S. recognition that the status quo was enormously damaging to Palestinians in the West Bank and Gaza Strip. Yet efforts to address the situation were premised on the exclusion and marginalization of the Palestinian national movement, an echo of the ill-fated Village Leagues promoted years earlier. In parallel fashion, both approaches also evoked Menachem Begin's original autonomy vision.

Incrementalism

The administration's disengagement from comprehensive peace initiatives during the mid-1980s was framed as a logical step away from diplomacy that had not yielded tangible results. "We're interested in negotiations that produce outcomes," wrote the newly appointed National Security Advisor Frank Carlucci in early 1987. "The U.S. does not need more unrealized expectations or perceived failures in the Middle East.[43] On February 13 of that year, senior members of the administration gathered for a National Security Planning Group meeting with President Reagan in the Situation Room.[44] Carlucci, using talking points prepared by Dennis Ross, presented the "Building Blocks of Strategy" for a new U.S. approach to peacemaking in the region. In Carlucci's view, the "hallmark of our approach right now should be incrementalism. We need to develop a systematic, tempered approach to rebuilding credibility. . . . We should move in a low-key way on the peace-seeking process." The Middle East required U.S. involvement that was measured but substantive in nature. Frustrated with a pattern of inaction, Carlucci called for more "momentum" in order "to counter an image of drift" on the Palestinian issue.[45]

To assess the state of U.S. policy at the time, the president issued a National Security Study Directive, which was sent off to the State Department, the Department of Defense, and the CIA. Among the series of questions posed to Middle East staffers, one in particular concerning Jordan revealed the shift in Reagan's thinking. "How can we strengthen Jordan's role in the peace process and its efforts to assert leadership on the Palestinian question? What further steps could we take, e.g., in the Quality of Life area or in the bilateral relations, to strengthen the King's hand?"[46] Reagan, at the behest of his advisors, was approaching Jordan as the primary interlocutor for arbitrating the Palestinian issue. He was suggesting a continued shift away from U.S. involvement in a political solution that might yield self-determination, an extension of Begin's successful efforts to rule out statehood at Camp David. The new Israeli government was only too pleased with this marginalization.

Reagan's incremental approach was also unfolding against the backdrop of steady settler population growth in the occupied territories. In February 1987, Israeli prime minister Yitzhak Shamir arrived at the White House for his first official meeting since taking over the premiership from Peres in October 1986. Shamir was a staunch territorial maximalist in the mold of Menachem Begin. As one Israeli political observer would write years later, "Shamir is not a bargainer. Shamir is a two dimensional man. One dimension is the length of the land of Israel, the second, its width. Since Shamir's historical vision is measured in inches, he won't give an inch."[47] In contrast to Peres and the Americans, Shamir was far less invested in pursuing negotiations with Jordan. Members of the administration understood their attempts with Hussein might be compromised after Shamir assumed office. "How do we move ahead and make progress in the coming year? How do we show that moderates can deliver?" aides asked ahead of a briefing between Shamir and Shultz. "Quality of Life is the one concrete thing we have going in the peace-seeking process. Settlements will undo it and again we want Shamir to leave with that clear impression," Reagan's advisors wrote. "We also want Shamir to leave knowing that partnership requires sensitivities to each other's needs, something that means Israel should be mindful of our need to support Arab moderates resisting radicals and fundamentalists."[48] U.S. officials were clearly aware that the continued Israeli opposition to the arming of moderate allies as well as the expansion of settlements would ultimately undermine American policy in the region.

There was also a domestic American context the administration needed to account for, in light of the earlier battles with pro-Israel advocates over arms deals with Arab states. In the one-on-one meeting with Shamir, Reagan emphasized strengthened cooperation between America and Israel but made it clear that the United States "will provide limited arms sales to Arab friends. Don't expect you agree; but do expect *no campaign* against us."[49] The president stressed positive developments with King Hussein and then concluded the brief meeting with a most astonishing compliment to Shamir: "Impressed you have been able to hold line on new settlement activity against political pressure. Tell me your secret. New settlements would only undercut promising developments on West Bank and with Hussein and cause problems between us."[50] There was no big secret; the reality on the ground flew in the face of Reagan's false praise. Between 1985 and 1990, fourteen new settlements were built in the West Bank, and the number of total settlers doubled from 46,000 to 81,600. The only decline in growth was a result of economic recession that adversely affected Israel's construction industry rather than opposition by the Shamir government.[51]

Shamir himself confirmed his maximalist position in an interview with the Israeli newspaper *Maariv* after his electoral defeat in 1992. "It pains me greatly that in the coming four years I will not be able to expand the settlements in Judea and Samaria and to complete the demographic revolution in the land of Israel," the departing prime minister stated. "I know that others will now try to work against this. Without this demographic revolution, there is no value to the talk about [Palestinian] autonomy, because there is a danger that it will be turned into a Palestinian state. What is this talk about 'political settlements?' I would have carried on autonomy talks for ten years, and meanwhile we would have reached half a million people in Judea and Samaria."[52] Despite Reagan's claims to the contrary in his personal meeting, Shamir was among the most active agents of settlement expansion in Israeli history.

In light of the dire warnings about the consequences of settlement expansion going back to the Carter White House, Reagan's continued neglect of this issue was startling. The problem had been recurring throughout his presidency, and leading members of the administration had been attentive to the issue. One of the strongest voices against Israeli settlement expansion in the 1980s was Reagan's vice president, and the future president, George Herbert

Walker Bush. As early as August 1983, in a meeting with Israeli ambassador to the United States Meir Rosenne, Bush criticized Rosenne's claim that Jews should be permitted to live in "Judea and Samaria." "You will have a hard time selling your position here," Bush told Rosenne. "The U.S. is the most moderate in the world in its position on settlements, the President is a friend of yours, but he thinks settlements are not conducive to peace."[53]

During this same meeting, Israel's Deputy Chief of Mission and future prime minister, a young Benjamin Netanyahu, argued with Bush that settlements were not the real issue: "There's a disparity between Arab rhetoric on settlements and the real interests of the Arab neighboring states. The real difficult decision that they have to make is to accept that Israel is a 'fait accompli.'" Bush was skeptical of Netanyahu's hyperbolic warnings. "Even the nuttiest Arabs like Kaddafi [*sic*] recognize that Israel is here to stay. The P.L.O. are dumb not to change their charter to strike out their call for the 'elimination of the Zionist entity.' If they did so, we would talk to them. They are like those in Taiwan who still talk of liberating the mainland." Netanyahu disagreed. "Israel's survival," he told Bush, "would be in grave doubt if we relinquished control of Judea and Samaria. The settlements there are a sign of Israel's presence."[54]

Bush was not impressed, pushing the Israelis to admit how many more settlements they would be establishing. Rosenne avoided the question and spoke of Arab mistreatment of the Palestinians. "The Arabs, indeed, have been brutal in their treatment of the Palestinians," Bush shot back. "The U.S. gives more aid to the Arab refugees than the Arab states do. Nevertheless, the settlements are not conducive to peace. Is there any country in the world which supports your settlements policy?" he asked Rosenne. "We support the peace treaty, but we do oppose settlements. Don't be under any misapprehension about it," Bush continued. "You are up against a stone wall in trying to change the views of the President on this issue. The main question remains, what can be done for the Palestinians, for they at present have no place to go. What is the Israeli solution to the problem of the Palestinians?" Rosenne argued that if they would have "sat down and negotiated on Camp David," Israel would have established an autonomy council, "but they have refused to do so."[55] Given Shamir's open admission of his own views concerning autonomy, it is difficult to believe that Rosenne's stance reflected any genuine desire to resolve the Palestinian question beyond a restricted version of autonomy. Begin's political vision still triumphed, even in the face of critics who understood that its underlying aim was to suppress Palestinian self-determination.

Israeli Alternatives

Although Shamir continued voicing opposition to direct talks with Jordan, Israel's efforts to engage the Hashemite Kingdom diplomatically remained in play. King Hussein met secretly with Peres in his new role as foreign minister, and they finally reached an agreement in London on April 11, 1987. The "London Document" outlined the basis of an international conference to coordinate bilateral negotiations between Israel and Jordan based on UN resolutions 242 and 338, shutting out the PLO in the process.[56] Shamir, excluded from the talks by Peres, rejected the document out of hand.[57] King Hussein was embittered by the internal Israeli disagreements and the lack of U.S. support, leading to his complete disengagement from diplomacy on the Palestinian question.

Ironically, Likud politicians were more willing to engage with the Palestinians directly than Labor party leaders. Secret discussions in 1987 suggested that there were alternative voices advocating for direct contact with the PLO rather than attempting efforts with Jordan. Moshe Amirav, a Likud member close to Prime Minister Shamir, held ten meetings with prominent Jerusalem-based Palestinian nationalist leaders Sari Nusseibeh and Faisal Husseini in his Jerusalem home in the summer of 1987.[58] They were the first Palestinians to meet with members of the Israeli right-wing government. Amirav sought out the possibility of a historic agreement between Israel and the PLO, asserting "the right of both people to the land" in his report to Shamir. "The injustice done to both peoples in our terrible and bloodstained history requires redress via the following equation: security and peace for the Jewish people, self-determination on part of the land and redress of the injustice done to the refugees of the Palestine people," Amirav explained. "The sole official representative of the Palestinian people in any settlement is the PLO without whose participation there is no point in reaching any settlement," Amirav continued. "Likewise, in Israel there is no point in reaching any settlement without the Likud."[59]

The Likud member's proposal suggested the "establishment of a region of Palestinian self-administration" in the West Bank and Gaza Strip, a total of five thousand square kilometers with a capital in East Jerusalem. Amirav wrote that this "interim agreement" would "guarantee Israel's security and enable it to maintain its settlements in Judea and Samaria at a fixed and unchanging level." Suggesting that such an arrangement could advance the establishment of Palestinian self-administration "which would wield powers approaching those of a state" within one year, Amirav also left open the possibility of "halting negotiations and leaving the situation as it stands." His proposal for an interim solution included a Palestinian flag, anthem, stamps, and currency. In outlining the conditions for these negotiations, which were to be held in secret and hosted by Egypt, the Likud member's proposal included provisions for the recognition of the right of Palestinian people "not as refugees, but as a people," to statehood; recognition of the PLO "as the representative of the Palestinian people"; and "cessation of any further Israeli settlement" in the territories. In turn, the PLO would have to recognize "Israel's existence within the 1948 borders," meaning pre-1967, and call for a "cessation of all hostile or terrorist actions everywhere."[60]

As a bookend to the decade-long diplomatic effort initiated under Carter, the Amirav Plan contained some promising elements. Primarily, Amirav recognized the centrality of resolving the Palestinian question with statehood: "Attempts to reach a settlement that do not include the Palestinians as a major partner to the negotiations or whose outcome is not the establishment of an independent Palestinian state are doomed to failure."[61] But Amirav also put forward some of the more limiting principles of the autonomy negotiations, like an interim arrangement and the option of formalizing the status quo, as well as overall Israeli sovereignty in the occupied territories and Jerusalem.

Amirav planned to travel to Geneva to present the working paper to Yasser Arafat, but on the eve of his trip, Israeli air force jets bombed the Lebanese Palestinian refugee camps in Saida's Ain el-Hilweh district, killing fifty of Arafat's supporters. Faisal Husseini was arrested for "pro-PLO activities" and jailed without trial.[62] The main conduit for the talks suspected that Defense Minister Yitzhak Rabin of the Labor Party, who favored the Jordanian initiative, was responsible. Amirav backed out of the trip to Geneva and a peace activist went in his place, but Arafat would only accept an official overture. The story broke in the Israeli press and upset King Hussein, who believed Israel had promised to "quash pro-P.L.O. Palestinians." Several days later, masked men on Bir Zeit University's campus clubbed Nusseibeh, while Husseini was re-arrested, and hard-line Likud members moved to expel Amirav from the party. In discussing the outcome of these talks, Nusseibeh told the *New York Times* that political dogmas "have become like a religion, and anyone who deviates from them is a heretic."[63] Efforts with Jordan were as futile as efforts with the PLO: a resolution to the Palestinian question was simply not a necessity for the Israeli government. This stasis would not last much longer.

The Intifada Ignites

On December 8, 1987, an Israeli army vehicle crashed into a truck carrying Palestinian workers, killing four from the Gaza Strip's Jabalia refugee camp. This incident set off spontaneous protests that spread to the West Bank. Demonstrators unfurled Palestinian flags, burned tires, and threw stones and Molotov cocktails at Israeli cars, and the Israeli security forces responded with force. The first Intifada had erupted. This largely nonviolent and unarmed mass protest, which lasted through the early 1990s, fundamentally altered the landscape of Palestinian politics and the PLO's relations with Israel as well as the United States. It shattered any illusion that the Palestinian national movement could be sidestepped.[64]

After twenty years of military occupation, Palestinians had reached a breaking point. The situation in the Gaza Strip, in particular, was intolerable. Yitzhak Rabin, Israel's defense minister, publicly sanctioned "a policy of beatings and breaking of bones," and the evening news was filled with images of young Palestinians savagely beaten by Israeli soldiers.[65] Footage of the Intifada reframed the international perception of Palestinian aspirations for self-determination. People around the world watched in disbelief as the territories erupted in predominantly peaceful protest, which was met with a harsh Israeli military response.

The mass protests in the occupied territories came five years after the Israeli invasion of Lebanon, which had considerably altered the global image of the Palestinians. "If Sabra and Shatila was the first notice to Israel that you were dealing with a national movement," explained one PLO confidant, "then this came to remind them you are dealing with people who have national aspirations. You can break their bones, but you can't bring them down to surrender their national feelings and you cannot break their spirit."[66] The Israeli journalist Amos Elon, a leading voice of the left, described the events this way: "Twenty years of shortsighted Israeli policies lie battered in the streets of the West Bank, Gaza, and East Jerusalem. The writing was on the wall for years, but most Israelis never bothered to read it."[67]

PLO leaders were taken aback by the uprising, which was entirely generated from within the West Bank and Gaza Strip. The Tunis exiles had long realized that in order to safeguard their leadership role of the Palestinian struggle, they would need to do so through the occupied territories. Abu Jihad, the head of the Fatah movement's armed wing, had argued along those lines well before the 1982 War. He recognized that there was no future for guerilla warfare or a para-state in Lebanon, and the center of gravity had to move to the West Bank. From his base in Amman and then in Tunis, Abu Jihad had worked to rebuild the infrastructure for a popular unarmed uprising through grassroots organizing of Fatah cells. His cadres exported the revolutionary movement into the occupied territories even after Israeli commandos assassinated him in April 1988.[68] Hamas, the Islamic Resistance Movement, was also established with the outbreak of the Intifada to act as a counterweight to the PLO.[69]

Seeing an opportunity to capitalize on popular discontent, the PLO began to play an active role alongside the newly formed Unified National Command inside the territories.[70] Among the fourteen demands outlined by West Bank and Gaza Palestinian leaders on January 14, 1988, was a call to abide by the Fourth Geneva Convention, a demand for the cessation of settlement activity and land confiscation, and the removal of restrictions on political contacts between inhabitants of the territories and the PLO, "in order to ensure a direct input into the decision-making processes of the Palestinian Nation by the Palestinians under occupation."[71] The central political platform that emerged from these protests was a call for self-determination and the establishment of an independent Palestinian state.

Israeli leaders remained opposed to granting Palestinians political rights and continued to undermine their collective efforts during the Intifada.[72] Defense Minister Rabin, convinced he could end the uprising through military means, ordered the IDF to crack down even more forcefully. Thousands of Palestinians were arrested, but the uprising persisted. Some officials gradually began to rethink the government's approach to the Palestinians. In an attempt to quell the unrest, Foreign Minister Peres floated a "Gaza First" idea to dismantle settlements and embark on a peace settlement, but Shamir was adamantly against territorial concessions and rejected the initiative.[73] The prime minister later wrote in his memoirs that the Intifada "changed nothing in our basic situation" and "proved to me once more that the conflict was not over territory but over Israel's right to exist." He defended the government's response as a necessary means of protection, observing that "no one in Israel was more aware of the moral and physical dilemmas involved than the young soldier patrolling the alleys of camps, interrogating frightened inhabitants, subduing rioters, helping to haul thousands off to detention, shooting only when he had to, and facing trial himself if he erred and shot too soon."[74]

Supporters of Israel abroad, reeling from the images on nightly television, struggled to articulate a unified response to the unfolding events. The detrimental impact of the occupation, which had largely failed to penetrate the consciousness of most Israelis and their supporters in the United States, was now indisputably apparent.[75] As one Israeli journalist wrote, the occupation "has held 1.5 million Palestinians as pawns, or bargaining chips, and as a source of cheap menial labor, while denying them the most basic human rights. The pawns have now risen to manifest their frustration, their bitterness and their political will."[76] Many American Jews were shocked to see the proverbial David and Goliath image of Israel and the Arabs turned so blatantly on its head.[77]

Several prominent leaders of the community spoke out against Israeli prime minister Yitzhak Shamir on the eve of another visit with Reagan in an open letter to the *New York Review of Books*.

Shamir was deeply opposed to negotiations with the Palestinians and remained a strong advocate of Israeli settlements in the occupied territories. Even the mounting protests did not diminish his commitment to this agenda. The critical language of the open letter reflected an American Jewish fracturing that had started in the wake of Prime Minister Menachem Begin's election in 1977: "By our own choice, and by the world's insistence, we Jews are one family. We therefore say to you, the most highplaced of our brothers, that your ideology about the 'undivided land of Israel' is harmful to the Jewish people. It makes peace negotiations impossible. It casts the Jews in Israel, and those who care about them all over the world, in the impossible position that the Jewish state can live only by forever repressing the Palestinians."[78]

Jewish leaders had hit upon the central fault line animating the relationship between their respective communities and the Israeli state. They described a mounting division, which had a global reach: "We are divided at this moment between the proponents of ideological intransigence and those who believe in moderation. The majority of Jews in the world belong to the moderate camp. May we respectfully remind you, Prime Minister Shamir, that you are coming to Washington these fateful days not as party ideologue but as the representative of the whole house of Israel."[79] Claiming both membership in the "family" of the "Jewish people" and "belonging to the moderate camp," these communal representatives publicly voiced the dissonant feelings that had been growing steadily since the first victory of the Likud party over Labor in 1977. Confronting the Intifada and the Shamir government's intransigent reaction to the violence underscored the impossibility of such a position ten years later. How might they and their constituents reconcile support for the state of Israel with an increasingly reactionary government and the demands of the Palestinian national movement?

Shultz's Gamble

The political crisis around the Intifada was not limited to Israelis or the Jewish diaspora. U.S. policymakers were increasingly concerned about the impact the uprising was having on American interests in the region as well. Initially, the unrest in the territories was met with a tempered call in Washington for reengagement with diplomatic negotiations. In a one-page fact sheet for the president on the "West Bank and Middle East Peace Process," Dennis Ross wrote of the disturbances and the growing Palestinian frustration with Israeli occupation. "Our approach to the peace process has been guided by the principle that we must give the Palestinians a reason for hope, not despair." In Ross's view, "The violence in the territories may create a new sense of urgency and give us a reason to try to energize the process."[80] By February 1988, the U.S. government began moving in this direction. In a briefing for former U.S. presidents, Ross explained how the administration was reengaging after a year of peace process discussions "dominated by arguments about procedure," making it clear that "it's time to address substance and the specific issues involved in the negotiating process."[81]

Secretary of State Shultz, by this time firmly in control of Reagan's foreign policy, had also recognized the damaging nature of the status quo. He flew to the region several times in early 1988, meeting with Israeli and Arab leaders but not the PLO in a final bid to resuscitate America's role as a broker to the conflict.[82] The resulting Shultz initiative of March 4, 1988, was seen as the "most important" proposal since the Reagan Plan, and it attempted to address some of the gaps in the earlier proposal.[83] Drawing on the Camp David Accords, the Shultz initiative called for a comprehensive peace through direct, bilateral negotiations. Wary of the time lag in Carter's earlier attempts at a settlement, Shultz's idea was to explicitly speed up the interval between a transitional period and final status implementation utilizing a negotiating tactic called "interlock." In order to address the Palestinian issue directly, the talks would be preceded by an international conference at which all participants would have to accept UN resolutions 242 and 338. Shultz expended a lot of time traveling around the region to sell his initiative, but he was greeted with fierce criticism from Prime Minister Shamir, who was adamantly opposed to an international conference and unreceptive to the exchange of territory for a peace agreement. The Palestinians were disappointed as well, sensing that they were being treated as appendages to the Jordanians.[84]

But it was King Hussein, heavily courted by Shultz to accept the initiative, who ultimately brought about its demise. At the end of

July 1988, Hussein announced Jordan's disengagement from the West Bank: "Jordan is not Palestine; and the independent Palestinian state will be established on the occupied Palestinian land after its liberation, God willing."[85] The king refused to negotiate in place of the PLO, relinquishing legal and administrative ties with the West Bank and leaving Israel to deal with the territories.[86] This crucial development forced the United States and Israel to deal solely with the PLO, a prospect that had been unthinkable in the late 1970s. The disengagement meant that Jordan would no longer be the address for dealing with the Palestinian issue, cutting out the fiction of an intermediary. For the Israelis, Hussein's announcement signaled the demise of the ill-conceived "Jordanian Option" and forced an eventual reckoning with a national movement that had for decades been denied recognition.[87] Jordan's disengagement also marked the failure of American "Quality of Life" initiatives, reenforcing the necessity of direct engagement with the PLO leadership, whether or not U.S. policymakers welcomed the idea. The half-hearted schemes to build a pliable alternative Palestinian leadership could not substitute for political negotiations with the PLO.

Amid this opening, senior figures within the PLO publicly endorsed negotiations with Israel. Bassam Abu Sharif, who was expelled from the PFLP and become an advisor to Yasser Arafat, was a leading voice for engagement. In a statement circulated to the Arab League Summit in Algiers in June 1988, and published in part as an op-ed in the *New York Times*, Abu Sharif wrote that the PLO should talk to the Israeli government in the context of a peace conference. "The Palestinians would be making a big mistake if they thought they could solve their problem without talking directly with Israel," he wrote.[88] As the paper's foreign affairs columnist Anthony Lewis argued, it was "the most explicit and articulate endorsement so far by the Palestinian mainstream of a two-state solution: a Palestinian state living in peace alongside Israel."[89] Hard-line factions within the PLO denounced the statement, while Arafat himself did not endorse or condemn it. Israeli prime minister Shamir dismissed the remarks as "nothing new."[90] Yet a group of fifteen prominent American Jews welcomed Abu Sharif's remarks, calling the statement "the clearest expression thus far, by any Palestinian official, of a readiness to negotiate peace between Israel and the Palestinians."[91]

Algiers-Stockholm-Geneva

As the Intifada raged on in the West Bank and Gaza Strip, local leaders of the uprising worried that their moment of national unity might pass without tangible results. They pressured the PLO leadership in Tunis to formally accept the idea of a negotiated two-state settlement, a position that was still being challenged by extreme factions within the organization. But Jordan's disengagement had empowered moderates within the PLO, who recognized the shifting center of political gravity. "Pressed by these external forces," explained one analyst of nationalist thinking, "the Palestinians were galvanized to cut through their initial ambiguities and to move definitively beyond the struggle between what they believed was *just* and what they realized was *possible*."[92]

The decisive move to embrace a negotiated settlement came in Algeria that fall. At the November 1988 Palestine National Congress in Algiers, Yasser Arafat won a majority of votes for the historic decision to accept relevant UN resolutions 242 and 338.[93] The poet Mahmoud Darwish crafted a Palestinian Declaration of Independence, and it proclaimed an independent Palestinian state alongside Israel on the basis of UN resolution 181, which had enshrined the idea of partition in 1947. According to a leading historian of Palestinian nationalism, "this was the first official Palestinian recognition of the legitimacy of the existence of a Jewish state and the first unequivocal, explicit PLO endorsement of a two-state solution to the conflict."[94] The notion that a state of Palestine could exist side by side with a state of Israel, near heresy in the 1970s, had emerged as the preferred Palestinian position at the close of the 1980s.

In light of these developments, U.S. officials slowly entertained an official dialogue with the PLO. Like Reagan's reversal when it came to dealing with the Soviet Union, this shift was a striking turn for an administration so adamantly opposed to engagement since its first months in office.[95] The process was complicated by the approaching November election and Reagan's imminent departure from office. It was also subject to internal debate, which included Secretary Shultz's denial of Yasser Arafat's request for a visa to travel to the UN General Assembly in New York to deliver an address about engagement. Shultz was nervous about provisions calling for Palestinian self-determination, as the United States moved closer to endorsing political rights but would not cede the idea of a state.[96] The arguments that had first confronted Carter in the late 1970s persisted a decade later.

Swedish government officials spearheaded the initiative that ultimately bridged the gap between the United States and the PLO. In the spring of 1988, Swedish foreign minister Sten Andersson reached out to a small group of prominent American Jews and arranged meetings with PLO leaders to formulate a statement demonstrating the Palestinian commitment to a peace deal with Israel. These leaders included Rita Hauser, the New York lawyer who had served as ambassador to the UN Human Rights Council, Stanley K. Sheinbaum, an economist and human rights activist, and Drora Kass, the director of the International Center for Peace in the Middle East.[97] Initially, the Swedish initiative was focused on Israel, but the Shamir government's negative reaction led to Andersson's realization that the way to engagement was through the United States. Hauser, who was instrumental in the talks, recounted Andersson's desire for American Jews to act as a bridge between the United States, Israel, and the PLO. "When I talked to Sten," Hauser recalled, "the only way to break this would be if the Americans recognized the PLO, then the Israelis would have to follow suit. It was ridiculous! It should have been the other way around. But that's the way it was."[98]

Andersson was deeply affected by the violence of the Intifada, having traveled to Israel and the Palestinian territories in March 1988. Austria's former chancellor, Bruno Kreisky, who had engaged extensively with Arafat and the PLO, also encouraged Andersson's efforts. The Swedish foreign minister wrote a letter of condolence to Arafat after the Mossad's assassination of Abu Jihad, Fatah's military commander and Arafat's chief deputy. In the note, Andersson recalled sending his son to an Israeli kibbutz in the 1960s, an experience that opened his eyes to the plight of the Palestinians.[99] After Arafat's positive response and thanks, Andersson wrote again telling the PLO leader of his interest in facilitating a dialogue with members of the American Jewish community as a means of securing U.S. engagement with the organization.

The ensuing meetings between American Jewish figures and the PLO leadership in Stockholm proved crucial in paving the way for Secretary of State Shultz to develop an American position on substantive discussions with the organization. Rita Hauser later described her own evolving perception of the PLO in the course of the secret talks: "At two o clock in the morning my phone would ring, and I would joke to my husband 'oh, it's the PLO.' The first time that they came on I was a little frightened. At this point the PLO was seen as a terrorist organization, all that kind of stuff. And they were, you know, nice enough guys, human beings, and wanting to move in this direction, very much so."[100] Hauser and her fellow Jewish leaders were subject to withering criticism in the course of the Stockholm talks, most notably from the Israeli government and staunch supporters of Israel in the United States. Yet they persisted in their meetings.[101]

Shultz's requirements for opening a dialogue included the PLO's acceptance of UN resolutions 242 and 338, recognition of Israel, and the renunciation of terrorism, conditions that would meet the requirements of Kissinger's non-engagement promise of 1975. The Swedish foreign minister was in constant contact with Shultz, who gave the "green light" for this endeavor, unbeknownst to the participants at the time.[102] They served as the necessary interlocutors to smooth the way for an official PLO dialogue and acceptance of the organization by the U.S. government.

As it turned out, Shultz's stipulations were not a simple requirement to meet. Traveling to Geneva instead of New York to deliver his highly anticipated General Assembly address, Yasser Arafat publicized the political decisions first taken by the Palestinian National Council in Algiers. He affirmed UN resolutions 242 and 338, calling for the establishment of a state of Palestine "based on international legitimacy embodied in UN resolutions since 1947 and the ability of the Palestinian people to enjoy the rights of self-determination, political independence, and sovereignty necessary over its land."[103] As for renouncing terrorism, Arafat said the following:

> As the leader of the Palestine Liberation Organization, I declare one more time: I condemn terrorism in all its forms. At the same time I salute all those I see before me in this hall, whose interrogators and occupiers accused them of terrorism during the battles to liberate their countries

from the fires of colonialism. They are all honest leaders of their peoples and faithful to the principles and values of freedom and justice.[104]

Shafiq al-Hout, the leading PLO official in Lebanon and a close advisor of Arafat, described the enthusiastic applause that broke out around the hall: "It seemed to me as if a great weight had been lifted from his [Arafat's] chest. As far as he was concerned, it left no excuse for the United States to keep the PLO on its list of terrorist organizations."[105]

Arafat's speech reflected a deep-seated tension within anti-colonial movements of the twentieth century. The use of violence for political ends had limited currency after the age of decolonization. In al-Hout's view, the Geneva address was therefore a monumental development. It "reflected very clearly the political turn that the *intifada* had brought about by transforming the Palestinian struggle from a national liberation movement into a national independence movement."[106] While reactions at the United Nations were exceedingly positive, the U.S. delegation and American media were more circumspect. According to al-Hout, "What we had considered to be a miracle breakthrough for the leadership—recognition that a solution should be founded on international law to establish two states on the land of Palestine—was received by the United States as if it were simply a maneuver by the PLO to play with words and hide behind obfuscation."[107]

Rita Hauser publicly endorsed Arafat's speech and vouched for his sincerity. Reagan administration officials still demanded a rewording of the pledge. Having failed to repeat verbatim the "magic words" of Shultz's precise statement on renouncing terror rather than condemning it, Arafat finally met the American conditions in a follow-up press conference on December 14, 1988.[108] Palestinian interlocutors were divided on whether to issue a restatement meeting Shultz's demands. Several Palestinian businessmen worked quickly to provide the PLO leader with a replica of the text prescribed by the U.S. State Department, assisted by Andersson's Swedish aides.[109]

At the Geneva press conference, Arafat read out a statement before the cameras as Shultz and his advisors watched live from the State Department. "Self-determination means survival for the

Palestinians," Arafat explained, "and our survival does not destroy the survival of the Israelis, as their rulers claim." The insistence on a possible future for both Palestinians and Israelis was the culmination of efforts toward a two-state solution that had been extended for more than a decade. "As for terrorism," Arafat continued, "I renounced it yesterday in no uncertain terms, and yet, I repeat for the record, I repeat for the record that we totally and absolutely renounce all forms of terrorism, including individual, group and state terrorism."[110] The PLO leader responded directly to critics who continued to marginalize or dismiss the national movement, insisting that the remaining matters should be discussed "around the table" at an international conference. "Let it be absolutely clear that neither Arafat, nor any [one else] for that matter, can stop the intifada, the uprising," concluded the PLO leader. "The intifada will come to an end only when practical and tangible steps have been taken towards the achievement of our national aims and establishment of our independent Palestinian state."[111]

Arafat's insistence on statehood, however, was a one-sided pledge. Israeli and American officials remained opposed to such an outcome, a reminder that the quest for self-determination did not inevitably lead to national sovereignty. Secretary Shultz and President Reagan both affirmed the onset of a PLO dialogue as a step toward direct negotiations with Israel and a comprehensive peace in the Middle East. But statehood was explicitly not endorsed. "Nothing here may be taken to imply an acceptance or recognition by the United States of an independent Palestinian state," Shultz declared. "The position of the United States is [that] the status of the West Bank and Gaza [Strip] cannot be determined by unilateral acts of either side, but only through a process of negotiations. The United States does not recognize the declaration of an independent Palestinian state."[112] Reagan added assurances to Israel in his remarks, noting "the United States' special commitment to Israel's security and well-being remains unshakeable. Indeed, a major reason for our entry into this dialogue is to help Israel achieve the recognition and security it deserves."[113]

The leading Palestinian interlocutor with the United States, the Palestinian American academic Dr. Mohamed Rabie, was bitterly disappointed by these official reactions. He saw the statements as "in violation of both the letter and the spirit of the Stockholm agreement" and felt they undercut efforts he had undertaken with former NSC advisor William Quandt to start a meaningful dialogue.[114] In Rabie's view, the statements "reinforced PLO suspicion and deepened its mistrust of U.S. intentions."[115] Others were more upbeat about the developments. Mahmoud Abbas, the leading PLO proponent for negotiations, recalled the recognition with pride in his memoir: "An important victory was won. We had surmounted an obstacle that had been placed in our path by Henry Kissinger fourteen years previously."[116] For Abbas, the onset of a dialogue with the United States was vital: "It meant that we, the PLO, had definitely become an official and integral part of any dialogue on the Middle East conflict. If America was serious about achieving a comprehensive peace settlement then Israel would recognize our existence, one way or another."[117]

Shultz designated the U.S. ambassador to Tunisia, Robert Pelletreau, as the authorized lead channel for the official dialogue with the PLO. On December 15, Pelletreau called the British ambassador in Tunisia to ask for the organization's telephone number. The following day, members of the PLO Executive Committee met with the American delegation at a guest palace in Carthage. Pelletreau welcomed the start of the dialogue, although substantive issues would be postponed until a new U.S. administration took office on January 20, 1989.[118] After so many years of officially shutting out the PLO, even as secret talks and coordination in Lebanon had bypassed Kissinger's ban, the U.S. government had finally legitimated the national vanguard of a leading revolutionary movement. In handwritten notes from a meeting with President Reagan soon after the dialogue had started, National Security Advisor Colin Powell scribbled, "Reaction to PLO decision: American Jewish community—resigned to it. Israelis unhappy— Shamir bitter & sad."[119] It was a sober reminder of just how much distance had been traveled from Carter's earliest efforts to engage the Palestinians, followed by Reagan's own strong opposition to the PLO throughout the 1980s.

By the end of 1988, the PLO had achieved the international recognition that had eluded the national movement for so long. The failed attempts to bypass Palestinian nationalism in the 1980s had actually served to legitimate the organization and force Israel, the United States, and the wider Arab world to reckon with their quest for national self-determination. This recognition was also the culmination of years of diplomatic efforts, armed struggle, and back-channel negotiations. After a decade of internal debate, the PLO had managed to reposition itself at the forefront of the national struggle, reconciling warring factions and garnering official status from the U.S. government.

It was a great surprise that such a shift took place in the last months of a Republican administration ideologically opposed to Palestinian nationalism, viewing the PLO as a Soviet proxy. Reagan himself had a lingering aversion to the entire region, which he recounted in his memoir: "Although we had moments of progress, and at times we managed to bottle up at least temporarily the savagery that forever lies beneath the sands of the Middle East, the region was still an adders' nest of problems when I moved out of the White House eight years later. And along the way it had been the source of some of my administration's most difficult moments."[120] In the wake of war in Lebanon, the U.S. government had in fact contributed handsomely to the region's problems, particularly Israel's conflict with the Palestinians.

Despite multiple Israeli and American plans to circumvent the PLO through Jordan or via local alternatives in the occupied territories, the Intifada served to redirect attention back to the national movement itself. The shift was abetted by changing domestic perceptions of the PLO among American Jews and secret efforts at engagement involving European diplomats as well. But PLO recognition did not denote the national movement's attainment of political sovereignty, and the form and content of a possible Palestinian political future remained unclear after Arafat's Geneva concession. It was only with the end of the Cold War and the onset of the Madrid Talks in 1991 that such a future was more sharply delineated. Reagan's departure from the scene and a new U.S. administration foregrounded a different set of priorities and considerations.

CHAPTER EIGHT

A Stillborn Peace

"BY NOW, IT SHOULD BE PLAIN TO ALL PARTIES that peacemaking in the Middle East requires compromise," explained a triumphant President George Bush, in an address to a Joint Session of Congress on March 6, 1991. "We must do all that we can to close the gap between Israel and the Arab states—and between Israelis and Palestinians." Operation Desert Storm had just ended with a victory for the United States and coalition forces, which defeated Saddam Hussein's army after Iraq's invasion and annexation of neighboring Kuwait. The first Gulf War elevated American regional influence, and Bush sought to leverage the opportunity for a diplomatic push that would resolve the Palestinian question. "A comprehensive peace must be grounded in United Nations Security Council Resolutions 242 and 338 and the principle of territory for peace," Bush asserted. "The principle must be elaborated to provide for Israel's security and recognition and at the same time for legitimate Palestinian political rights. Anything else would fail the twin test of fairness and security."[1]

Echoes of the earlier failed efforts by Carter and Reagan could be discerned in Bush's speech, but global circumstances had changed considerably in the forty-first president's favor. When Bush took office in January 1989, the Cold War between the United States and the Soviet Union was ending. Ronald Reagan and Mikhail Gorbachev had laid the groundwork in their bilateral summitry. George Bush proved an adept leader through a succession of pivotal events that followed.[2] Soviet support for the United States in the context of Saddam Hussein's aggression underscored a new spirit of cooperation and marked an auspicious moment for renewed American engagement in the Middle East.[3] Without the tension of a geopolitical rivalry that had at times undermined earlier efforts to resolve the Arab-Israeli conflict, Bush had a chance to focus anew on diplomacy.

Together, the end of the Cold War and the victory in the Persian Gulf provided the White House with a reservoir of political capital to reengage in Israeli-Palestinian negotiations. The early 1990s was a period marked by a flurry of diplomatic activity, characterized by renewed efforts for a comprehensive peace summit at Madrid. This gathering was followed by extensive talks over the fate of Palestinian self-determination in negotiations between Israelis and Palestinians convened by the Bush administration in Washington. Substantively, however, these talks remained constrained by the limits of the Camp David framework, as Begin's autonomy model intruded on the efforts to address the core question of territorial sovereignty. Unbeknownst to the negotiators in Washington, the PLO leadership in Tunis was simultaneously convening secret talks with the Israeli government in Oslo. Arafat and senior members of the PLO sought recognition and a return to the occupied territories, goals that were ultimately secured in exchange for the very concessions that had been demanded by the Israelis in the Camp David process.

Baker's Challenge

Bush's secretary of state, James A. Baker III, was centrally involved in the efforts to restart a comprehensive peace plan for the Middle East. Even before the Gulf Crisis had started, Baker was exploring options on the Arab-Israeli front. At the behest of Defense Minister Yitzhak Rabin and Foreign Minister Moshe Arens, the government of Israeli prime minister Yitzhak Shamir began to develop more substantive ideas on addressing the Palestinian question.[4] Shamir put forward an initiative to his cabinet on May 14, 1989, invoking "the principles of the Camp David Accords" while simultaneously opposing the establishment of an "additional Palestinian state." He ruled out negotiations with the PLO, and also clarified that "there will be no change in the status of Judea, Samaria and Gaza other than in accordance with the basic principles of the Government."[5] Shamir's plan called for elections in the West Bank and Gaza Strip without PLO participation, a means to creating an interim agreement for self-government.[6]

Secretary Baker was willing to consider this Israeli initiative as an opening, but he would not cede the principle of territorial withdrawal. At the annual American Israel Public Affairs Committee (AIPAC) conference on May 22, Baker spoke in a startlingly forthright manner about the ideology of the Israeli right in the context of the ongoing Intifada: "Now is the time to lay aside, once and for all, the unrealistic vision of a greater Israel. Israeli interests in the West Bank and Gaza—security and otherwise—can be accommodated in a settlement based on Resolution 242. Forswear annexation. Stop settlement activity. Allow schools to reopen. Reach out to the Palestinians as neighbors who deserve political rights."[7] The fiercely pro-Israel audience was thrown off guard by the candid speech as they confronted an administration that was blunt and businesslike after the Reagan administration's warm embrace.

Baker's rhetoric was followed by efforts to "redesign" the Shamir Initiative into something more palatable for the Palestinians, to ensure their inclusion in the dialogue directly. Yet Baker's attempts were debilitated as a result of constraining influences within the Likud Central Committee and an Israeli plan to move a large number of new Jewish immigrants from the Soviet Union into the occupied territories.[8] President Bush had closely followed the settlement issue from his time as vice president, and he and Baker did not appreciate Shamir's obstinacy on the issue, viewing his settlement policy as "a deliberate attempt to foil U.S. peacemaking."[9] This clash erupted into a particularly bitter debate as the American government refused to grant Israel loan guarantees of $10 billion in light of ongoing settlement expansion. At a hearing in front of the House Foreign Affairs Committee, Baker publicly recited the number of the White House switchboard to draw Israeli attention: "When you're serious about peace, call us."[10]

Alongside his efforts with the Shamir government, Baker attempted to bring the Palestinians into the discussions as well. The Bush administration had been empowered to engage directly with the national movement after the onset of the official U.S.-PLO dialogue at the end of Reagan's term in office. As part of these efforts, Baker worked to persuade the PLO to allow talks to begin with nonofficial representatives, in order to secure Israeli participation.[11]

Early stages of the talks had been fitful, and Egyptian president Hosni Mubarak stepped in to offer his own ideas and a direct channel to Arafat. This effort yielded a formula for including Palestinians in the negotiations, which was a departure from the long pattern of exclusion and Egyptian representation on their behalf. But a series of violent incidents in 1990 forestalled the official dialogue, beginning with a shooting by a disturbed Israeli soldier of seven Palestinians, followed by the June landing of the renegade Iraqi-backed Palestine Liberation Front on a beach outside Tel Aviv. While the attackers were neutralized, the head of the group, Abu Abbas, was still a member of the PLO Executive Committee and had also been responsible for the *Achille Lauro* hijacking. These outbursts of violence compelled President Bush to suspend the discussions between the United States and the PLO.[12]

The context of regional relations was also a crucial factor in the upending of the nascent U.S.-PLO relationship. Soviet patronage in the Arab world had ceased with the end of the Cold War and was accompanied by a rise of anti-American sentiment in Baghdad. Iraqi leader Saddam Hussein launched increasingly vocal attacks on the United States and Israel, and also made inroads with PLO leader Yasser Arafat, who frequently visited the Iraqi capital after the suspension of the dialogue with the United States. In the wake of the August 1990 invasion and annexation of Kuwait, Saddam attempted to link his actions with Israel's occupation of Arab territories, eliciting support from many in the Arab world.[13] The PLO's support for Iraq in the ensuing Gulf War was particularly damaging to Arafat's position, compromising the political gains that had been achieved in the Intifada. Despite acrimony with the PLO, Baker made several trips to the Middle East in the wake of the coalition victory, seeking to transform U.S. military alliances into a platform for an international peace conference to revive his previous efforts on the Arab-Israeli front.

The Madrid Conference

The venue for restarting Arab-Israeli peace talks was to be in Madrid, Spain, at a major conference cosponsored by the United States and the Soviet Union between October 30 and November 1, 1991.

It was the first official face-to-face gathering that included representatives from Israel, Lebanon, Syria, Jordan, and the Palestinian Territories. Saddam's defeat in the Gulf War and the end of the Cold War had reshaped regional politics, leaving Soviet clients like Syria without an interlocutor to counter American influence. The Palestinians attended as part of a joint Jordanian delegation that was coordinating closely with the PLO leadership in Tunis. While the Gulf War had discredited the PLO, the leadership acquiesced to a diminished role and used the Jordanian umbrella to exert its own influence behind the scenes.[14] Local officials in the occupied territories, who had gained political influence and popularity over the course of the Intifada, joined with leading figures in the Palestinian diaspora to continue constructive engagement with the Bush White House, which had been ongoing since 1989.[15] In turn, these new figures, including Faisal Husseini as coordinator of the joint delegation and Hanan Ashrawi as the public spokesperson, helped project what one Madrid observer called "a new image of Palestinian nationalism."[16]

For the first time since Israel's creation, the Madrid Conference served as a forum in which the Palestinians were included in substantive discussions over their political fate.[17] In an American "Letter of Assurance to the Palestinians," written a few weeks before the Madrid Conference opened, the U.S. position on the "legitimate political rights of the Palestinian people" and belief in "an end to Israeli occupation" was clearly stated.[18] The negotiations, Secretary Baker wrote, would be conducted in phases, moving from interim self-government arrangements to permanent status talks.[19] In the Madrid "Gameplan" prepared for the Palestinian delegation, a warning of potential Israeli political gambits at the conference included their presentation of "fully fledged autonomy plans."[20]

President Bush and Soviet president Mikhail Gorbachev cochaired the direct multilateral negotiations, which were redolent with symbolism. The head of the Palestinian delegation, the Gaza-based physician Haidar Abdel Shafi, spoke eloquently about the impact of the occupation. "What requiem can be sung for trees uprooted by army bulldozers?" he asked, seeking a restoration of Palestinian land as the basis of two viable states.[21] Israeli prime minister Yitzhak Shamir was more reluctant to join in the talks, and one attendee described his attitude during the meeting as "defiant" and "truculent."[22] At the behest of the American organizers, all the parties sat around one large table, the picture of hope for a region that had just emerged from a full-scale war.

Substantively, however, the impact of the Madrid gathering was limited.[23] The conference was to be followed by bilateral negotiations between Israel and Jordan, Lebanon, Syria, and the Palestinians in Washington, as well as multilateral negotiations in Moscow. One of the most important procedural legacies of the conference was the idea of reaching an interim agreement between Israel and the Palestinians, an approach that deferred final status issues like the refugee question and the fate of Jerusalem to permanent status talks. A similar mechanism had been suggested as part of the transitional phase of the autonomy negotiations, which served as a way for the Israeli government to maintain security assurances and residual sovereignty for an undefined period of time. Palestinians, as well as Egyptian interlocutors negotiating their future after Camp David, had long contested this absence of real sovereignty. Among Palestinian delegates to Madrid, deep suspicion of interim measures and the autonomy model that had been suggested over a decade earlier remained palpable.[24]

Several days after the conference ended, the Palestinian delegation made it clear in a letter to the Soviet foreign minister, Eduard Shevardnadze, that any return to Camp David was not acceptable. "We would like to emphasize that we do not view these negotiations in any way as a continuation of the Camp David talks," the delegates explained. "Nor do we perceive them as parallel to or an extension of previous Israeli-Egyptian negotiations. Thus, in substance, scope, and priorities, we reserve our right to decide on our own approach and principles based on our political program and our own definitions of the nature of the transitional phase and its requirements." They also raised the issue of intensified activity in the occupied territories, conveying "serious concern and grave alarm at Israel's escalation of its settlement activity in a calculated attempt at the de facto annexation of Palestinian land and resources." Seeking to move past the Carter- and Reagan-era debates over the status of settlements, the Palestinians argued that they were inherently illegal "and must not be made an agenda item or the subject of negotiations."[25] This powerful assertion of Palestinian concerns about the Madrid process made it very clear that the shadow of Begin's earlier diplomatic triumph still loomed over the fate of their struggle for self-determination.

The Washington Talks

U.S. negotiators were also aware of the pitfalls that carried over from the Camp David process. In Baker's invitation to all the parties to formally begin bilateral negotiations in Washington, the U.S. secretary of state warned of the past missteps on the question of an interim self-government. "Having experienced several years of negotiations on these issues in the late 1970s and early 1980s," Baker wrote, "it is our considered view that both Israel and Palestinians should avoid as much as possible a protracted debate on such principles as the 'source of authority,' 'nature of the interim self-government authority,' and the like."[26] Recognizing that the self-governing models Israelis and Palestinians would present were bound to diverge, Baker nonetheless saw the negotiations as an opportunity to clarify starting points around the powers and responsibilities that would be assumed by the Palestinians in the transitional period.

Rather than provide a model for achieving sovereignty, this architecture actually served as a constraining mechanism. By focusing the discussion on "interim self-government arrangements," which the Shamir government had insisted upon, "final status" issues were deferred to later talks. These included the end of the military occupation, the settlements, the status of Jerusalem, the refugees, control of land and water, and the question of sovereignty. Unlike the bilateral tracks that had started in the wake of Madrid with Syria, Lebanon, and Jordan—intended to resolve final status issues between the parties—the Israelis and joint Palestinian delegation began a prolonged discussion over interim arrangements. Before the discussions even began, Palestinians expressed concern over the imbalance in this architecture. "It appears that Israel is attempting to carry out unilateral steps to impose its own version of a de facto autonomy," the Palestinians wrote to the Madrid cosponsors. "Such moves are seriously prejudicial to the process itself and seek to predetermine the outcome of the negotiations."[27]

For the Shamir government, a prolonged discussion over interim arrangements worked to its advantage. Israeli negotiators could focus on temporary measures that might possibly lead to greater local jurisdiction and alleviate pressure in the territories, rather than discuss territorial withdrawals or the possibility of Palestinian sovereignty. There was a stark parallel with Begin's offer of limited autonomy to the Arab inhabitants of the land while continuing to assert territorial control and an insistence on the Jewish right to settle in "Judea and Samaria." As one advisor to the Palestinian delegation in Washington later explained, he and his colleagues found themselves in a "straitjacket," "only permitted to quibble over the details of the 1978 interim self-government autonomy plan."[28] Like Camp David, the bilateral discussions excluded the core issue of Palestinian acquisition of sovereignty over the occupied territories. This time, however, Palestinians were participating in the process itself and had a foreboding sense that the outcome had been foreclosed. As Hanan Ashrawi remarked to U.S. diplomats in one early meeting, "We do not want to be frozen in autonomy."[29]

There were many reasons why sovereignty remained off the table in the Washington talks, from Israeli concerns over security to American unease with the possibility of actual statehood. Yet the deferral of this central issue was not merely a theoretical point of debate. During the early 1990s, the territory upon which such sovereignty might be achieved was simultaneously being transformed by the occupation itself. Settlement expansion, which had grown exponentially since the Camp David Accords, continued in the wake of Madrid. Palestinian negotiators raised the issue of the Shamir government's ongoing activity directly with the Americans in the Washington talks, pointing to the impact of further building on water rights, transportation, and infrastructure needs. As the Palestinian delegate Ghassan Khatib told U.S. negotiator Alan Kreczko, it would be "impossible" to deal with the future Palestinian authority "while settlements are expanding." Kreczko's reply, echoing the sentiment of many U.S. diplomats who had negotiated before him, was to focus on the realm of the possible: "This is a political point, not a practical point. A couple more settlements won't make a difference."[30] Palestinian participants begged to differ. One told the Americans that they must "freeze the status of the disputed property before new *fait[s] accomplis* are created," while another added that "this is the ABC of good faith and fair dealing. We would have to negotiate about settlement while they colonize the land. At the end of 12 months there might be no water and no land."[31]

U.S. diplomats, presented with a compelling explanation of how Israeli territorial acquisition was undercutting the Palestinian position in the negotiations for the first time from the Palestinians themselves, responded that it would be best to deal with this issue as part of an agreement, "rather than only focusing on a single lump which causes problems." Kreczko affirmed to the Palestinians that the United States opposed the settlements, but it was "difficult to get Israel to stop." He suggested they not put themselves in a corner by defining a "red line" that halts negotiations, recalling the extensive autonomy talks. "The Egyptians called for a settlement freeze, but went ahead with negotiations," Kreczko suggested. Yet as Dr. Haidar Abdel Shafi, the head of the Palestinian delegation to Madrid, explained to the Americans, "The Egyptians negotiated when there were few settlements, after their peace treaty with Israel. It is now too late to go back to what you are suggesting. The situation is very grave."[32] American officials were sympathetic to the Palestinian concerns, but strategically, they felt a freeze would not be obtainable. Shamir had successfully dislodged the loan guarantee debate from the settlement issue, redoubling expansion efforts in the face of internal pressure from smaller parties on his right. The Bush administration instead looked to the possibility of the Israeli prime minister's defeat or forced coalition with Labor in the upcoming Israeli elections.[33]

In part, Menachem Begin's earlier red lines on withdrawal from territory occupied in 1967 shaped the structural constraints of the bilateral talks in Washington. One of the advisors to the Palestinian delegation, Sari Nusseibeh, spoke of the challenge raised by the direct negotiations under these conditions: "We are being led into [a] lion's den to agree, in view of the asymmetry of power. We feel it is dangerous. We are willing to enter direct negotiations, and work things out with Israel, but the U.S. position has to be translated into something concrete." Even as senior American officials spoke out against the settlement issue with the Israelis, the bilateral discussions had their own logic. As another member of the U.S.

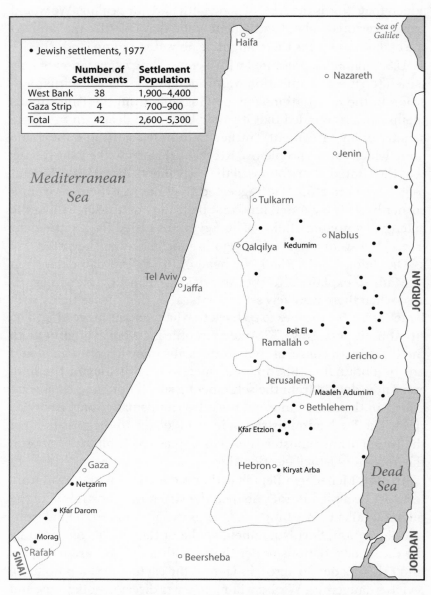

• Jewish settlements, 1977	Number of Settlements	Settlement Population
West Bank	38	1,900–4,400
Gaza Strip	4	700–900
Total	42	2,600–5,300

FIGURE 8.1. Map of settlements and settlement population in the West Bank and Gaza Strip, 1977 and 1992. Courtesy of Shane Kelley. The information on the tables is drawn from the Foundation for Middle East Peace; Peace Now and Hagit Ofran;

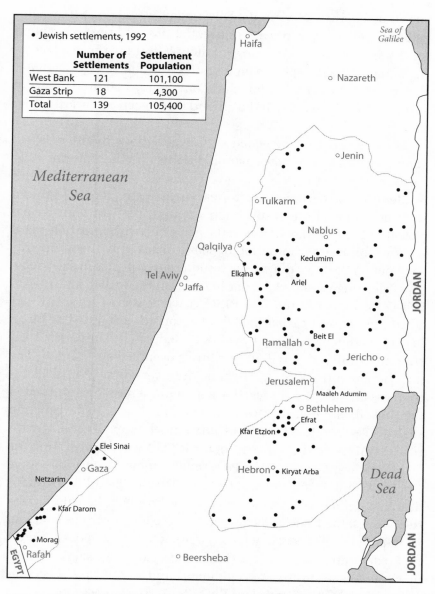

	Jewish settlements, 1992	
	Number of Settlements	**Settlement Population**
West Bank	121	101,100
Gaza Strip	18	4,300
Total	139	105,400

Sea of Galilee

Haifa

Nazareth

Mediterranean Sea

Jenin

Tulkarm

Nablus

Qalqilya

Kedumim

Tel Aviv
Jaffa

Elkana

Ariel

JORDAN

Ramallah Beit El

Jericho

Jerusalem

Maaleh Adumim

Bethlehem
Efrat

Kfar Etzion

Elei Sinai

Gaza

Netzarim

Hebron Kiryat Arba

Dead Sea

Kfar Darom

Morag

EGYPT
Rafah

Beersheba

JORDAN

FIGURE 8.1. (*cont.*) Shaul Arieli; Gordon, *Israel's Occupation*; and Israel's Central Bureau of Statistics. The number of Jewish residents in East Jerusalem was 26,000 in 1977 and 141,000 in 1992. See *The Statistical Yearbook of the Jerusalem Institute* (1983, 1992).

delegation remarked, "THE KEY IS AN AGREEMENT. Land is a sub-issue." In the U.S. view, the Palestinians would do well to delineate the issues, move forward in negotiations, and then movement on the settlements would surely follow.[34] But for those advocating actual statehood—or even a limited form of self-government that was less than a state but that nonetheless had ingredients of sovereignty—the reality on the ground made such a political future hard to imagine.

The Palestinians proceeded with negotiations in any case, assuming that they possessed national rights and that interim measures were a means to independence. Israeli officials did not see residents of the occupied territories possessing national rights and were not entertaining a sovereign outcome after the transitional period.[35] This divergence was at the heart of the incompatible plans laid out for an interim period of self-government. Two proposals were put on the table during the second round of talks in early 1992. The Palestinians offered the outline of what they called an "Interim Self-Government Authority" (PISGA), which was a very significant advancement over earlier models of autonomy suggested by Begin in conjunction with Camp David. Although only a temporary measure, the PISGA covered all territories occupied since 1967. "The jurisdiction of the PISGA," the final draft version noted, "shall encompass all these territories, the land, natural resources and water, the subsoil, and their territorial sea and air-space. Its jurisdiction shall also extend to all the Palestinian inhabitants of these territories." As an entity, the authority of the PISGA was derived "from the fact that it was elected by the Palestinian people. No outside source invests it with its authority." The provisions for the PISGA's establishment delineated clear transfers of authority to the Palestinians themselves, the basis of meaningful sovereignty over the land and its inhabitants.[36] Secretary Baker, writing to the head of the Palestinian delegation to the Peace Conference, Faisal Husseini, saw this document as a "positive development" and reconfirmed his commitment and that of President Bush "to see this process through to its required objective, namely, a comprehensive settlement."[37]

As the Washington talks progressed, Husseini recounted for Baker how the Israelis utilized procedural methods to disqualify certain Palestinian delegates from leaving the country, forcing some Palestinians to travel without others. Baker was sympathetic: "There is nothing we can do about a practice that we do not approve of, or about administrative detention. The only way to progress on these issues is through the peace process, and with self-governing authority for you . . . I can't wave a wand and stop the settlements. I can't wave a wand here and stop the administrative detentions." Baker was adamant that the Palestinians forge ahead with substance but that they needed to be strategic to preserve the self-governing arrangements. "If you insist on settlement first," Baker told Husseini, "that is dumb, because you won't get a settlement freeze."[38] The Palestinian delegation had little room to maneuver, constrained by Israeli actions on the ground, the demands of intensive diplomacy in Washington, and the need to maintain credibility with their own populace. But however narrow a space in which they were operating, the Washington talks underscored the necessity of direct participation by the Palestinians themselves, as agents attempting to secure a viable political future.

A Return to Autonomy

The Israeli proposal on self-rule, delivered on February 20, was a world away from the Palestinian document. It was a startling return to Begin's autonomy plan. Revealingly titled "Ideas for peaceful coexistence in the territories during the interim period," the draft spoke of the "establishment of interim self-government arrangements for the Palestinian Arab inhabitants of the territories." The territory itself, like Begin's initial plan, was not up for discussion, and the Israelis included a clause for "keeping the established links between Judea, Samaria, Gaza district and Israel intact" as well as maintaining traditional ties between the Palestinian Arab inhabitants and Jordan." Once again, "residual powers" and the "sole responsibility for security in all its aspects" were reserved by Israel, and just as Begin had written in his original autonomy plan, "Israelis will continue, as of right, to live and settle in the territories."[39]

In a letter to the Palestinian delegation outlining the Israeli plan, lead negotiator Elyakim Rubinstein elaborated on the flaws of the Palestinian proposal, "which basically represents a Palestinian state in all but name, considered by Israel a mortal security threat." As Rubinstein argued, the Israeli interim self-government arrangements "should be fair to the Arab population but not hamper the rights of Jews," a position that undergirded Begin's very clear proposal more than ten years earlier. The Israelis would not countenance a proposal that suggested the foundations of a future Palestinian state. In returning to Begin's approach at Camp David, Rubinstein spelled out the continuity. "Israel's basic approach to the arrangements is founded in principle [*sic*] developments since 1978." These arrangements, Rubinstein explained, would be based on a "functional-administrative approach, not to include state-like powers."[40] Aside from the direct involvement of Palestinians in the discussions, it was hard to see what had changed in the fundamental Israeli view to prevent the emergence of a Palestinian state.

During a heated meeting at the State Department in which the Palestinians responded to this proposal, Palestinian negotiator Hanan Ashrawi said the Israeli proposal was a "reorganization of the occupation . . . it confirms the occupation and legitimizes the annexation of land." When asked by U.S. ambassador Edward Djerejian whether this really was the case, Ashrawi shot back, "Either they're playing games, or they're not serious about the transfer of authority to the Palestinians. This is totally unacceptable." Faisal Husseini added that "what the Israelis gave us is less than Camp David and less than what we have now." The frustration with the Israeli position was on full display during the discussions. Ashrawi asked how long Palestinians could participate in a "charade." "This has been an exercise in futility. Our credibility with our people is diminished. Things are worse on the ground."[41]

American officials took issue with the Palestinian portrayal of events. U.S. diplomat Daniel Kurtzer told Ashrawi she was "posturing" and that as long as the Palestinians were in negotiations, "see what's there. They [Israel] won't put a position on the table you like. Just argue against it." Elias Samber, one of the Palestinian representatives, protested that the problem was that "land is completely absent from their presentation." Kurtzer stated, "So make it present. . . . Work on a way you can effectively exercise authority over the land." The constraints under which Baker was operating continued to play a central part in the U.S. approach. The secretary of state was treading carefully, mindful of looming Israeli elections and the possibility the Likud government would be replaced by a more reasonable Labor alternative. "If it is perceived in Congress that the Secretary has played into a Palestinian strategy to stop settlements and to get a settlement freeze, he's finished," Kurtzer explained. Ashrawi interjected, "Conversely, if we negotiate with the settlements continuing, we're finished."[42]

At the end of the meeting, frustrated by the narrow Israeli position and the demands of the U.S. negotiators, Ashrawi articulated one of the core elements of her opposition to the Israeli proposal: "Their position is racist. We start with the premise that we are human beings. Israelis only talk about Israeli interests, and say they can stay under conditions of coexistence under their own terms." Kurtzer urged the Palestinians to work on responding to the Israeli proposal, despite the impossibly difficult odds. He recalled Faisal Husseini remarking "there has never been a case with a people who have been able to negotiate their own way out of occupation." Somehow, Kurtzer urged, the Palestinians had to build a bridge, one that they might not be able to complete with the Israelis. "But you need the foundation for a bridge . . . I still say that you may be able to negotiate your own way out of occupation. The grist for the mill may be laid in the foundation."[43] In light of the dueling Israeli and Palestinian conceptions of a political outcome since the 1970s—the race between a clear vision of state prevention and an aspiration for meaningful self-determination—it was a tall order to achieve.

The subsequent Washington meetings, extending into 1993, were far less heated and increasingly productive sites for negotiating these foundations, including issues like the nature of interim self-governance and land policies.[44] With a political transition in Israel from Shamir's Likud-led government to the return to power of Yitzhak Rabin and the Labor party in the summer of 1992, Israeli negotiators gradually moved away from a strictly functional approach toward the territorial model developed by the Palestinians. This was a modest but highly significant historical shift from the narrower positions first espoused at the autonomy negotiations.[45] Room seemed to be opening to convince the Israelis and Americans that such a territorial approach cohered with "reasonable Israeli concerns on security and settlers" and was compatible with the initial terms of reference. As the Palestinians wrote in a highly confidential memo, "This MAY be an opportunity for us to achieve progress along the lines of our own proposals, for the first time. We should not waste this limited opportunity, nor minimize it, nor exaggerate it."[46]

Oslo's Faustian Bargain

The brief window that opened at Madrid and continued in Washington may have eventually paved the way to a just and equitable solution to the Palestinian question, but events quickly shifted in alternate directions. President Bush was preoccupied with the November election, where he faced Arkansas governor Bill Clinton. Floundering in the polls, Bush pulled Secretary Baker from the State Department to take over as chief of staff in August. The talks in Washington continued, but without the leadership of Baker and with the looming vote, U.S. mediation was lacking.[47] Clinton's victory brought a presidential transition and a new party into office, coinciding with rising violence between Israelis and Palestinians as well as the formative deportation of Hamas activists into Lebanon. This decision by Rabin generated a tremendous amount of international criticism and led to the suspension of Palestinian participation in the Washington talks. It also served to establish crucial links between Hamas members and the Lebanese militia Hezbollah.[48]

In January 1993, without the knowledge of the Palestinian delegates or American mediators who had been meeting in Washington, secret negotiations between the PLO leadership and the Israelis began outside Norway's capital. Yasser Arafat was not pleased with his continued exclusion from the Washington talks, and he turned to direct contacts with the Israelis, first informally and then with official representatives of Prime Minister Rabin and Foreign Minister Shimon Peres. Rabin and Peres, along with Deputy Foreign Minister Yossi Beilin, had contrasting views of engagement with the PLO, but they believed that an unofficial avenue would be a means to break the deadlock. Two Israeli academics, Dr. Ron Pundak and Dr. Yair Hirschfeld, began the meetings with the PLO treasurer, Ahmed Qurei (Abu Alaa), a close Arafat confidant. They were joined by Uri Savir, the director general of the Foreign Ministry, and Joel Singer, an Israeli attorney who had worked as a legal advisor in the military. Together the group worked to conceptualize a framework for an Israeli-PLO accord in conjunction with Arafat and his deputy, Mahmoud Abbas (Abu Mazen).[49] The United States was nominally informed as the talks proceeded, but when Peres and the Norwegian foreign minister, Johan Jørgen Holst, informed Clinton's secretary of state, Warren Christopher, of the final agreement in August, he was taken by surprise.[50]

President Clinton nevertheless hosted the official signing of the Oslo Accords on the south lawn of the White House on September 13, 1993, lending the agreement a U.S. imprimatur. In certain respects, the Oslo Accords were a clear advance over earlier efforts like Camp David.[51] The agreement signified the formal Israeli recognition of the PLO as the representative of the Palestinian people. It also included provisions to transfer territory in Gaza and Jericho to direct PLO control, providing Arafat with a base from which to organize the development of a possible political entity. In the minds of Oslo's architects, this innovation was a decisive breakthrough that might plausibly lead to further Israeli withdrawals and more territory for Palestinians to control. Uri Savir, the chief Israeli negotiator, later wrote that Oslo's central achievement was clarifying "that the land would ultimately have to be shared by two states."[52]

But what if the agreement helped enshrine something far less for the Palestinians? In crucial ways, the Oslo Accords were nowhere near as picture perfect as the famous handshake between Israeli prime minister Yitzhak Rabin and PLO chairman Yasser Arafat suggested. Like Camp David, Oslo proffered an interim five-year transitional period before discussing final status issues including borders, sovereignty, and refugees. A Palestinian police force would be brought in to maintain internal security in Gaza and Jericho, but Israel maintained responsibility for external control. Most glaringly, the agreement allowed for an Israeli clause that would enable ongoing settlement expansion before permanent status negotiations. This formal "Declaration of Principles on Interim Self-Government Arrangements" (DOP) suggested a process that might set in motion the end of Israeli rule over the territories but also left the specifics to be discussed at a later stage.[53] Such an approach meant a deferral of the very same issue that had undermined the discussions in

Washington, reifying the notion of limited self-rule under Israeli occupation. In signing the DOP, PLO negotiators "fell into traps" that the Palestinian delegation in Washington had been working to avoid, argued one advisor to the Washington delegation.[54] The agreement mirrored many of Begin's original autonomy ideas presented in 1977 and the more restrictive notions of autonomy that had been debated in the wake of Camp David.[55]

The logic of the interim agreement and the implementation talks that followed in Taba and Cairo served to maintain Israeli dominance over Palestinian movements in key areas of the territories and over land crossings to Egypt and Jordan. It paved the way for enclaves of Palestinian self-rule in a sea of Israeli control, while respecting the autonomy of individual enclaves.[56] This bred a condition that the forensic architect Eyal Weizman has incisively called "prosthetic sovereignty."[57] The blueprint for a subsovereign Palestinian entity that had been introduced by Begin fifteen years earlier was now the universal template for the Israeli and American concept of what the Palestinians could or should achieve in political terms. Moreover, Yasser Arafat and the PLO Executive Committee—the embodiment of the Palestinian national struggle—approved the template.[58]

It is no surprise that many of the Palestinian negotiators in Madrid and Washington felt betrayed by Arafat's acceptance of the Oslo Accords on far narrower terms than they had initially sought out.[59] Their earlier talks had been characterized by a fundamental clash of political visions that the PLO negotiators had simply bypassed in Oslo. In the Washington talks, Israel sought an interim agreement to offset the violence in the occupied territories. The Israelis believed it was possible to foster a "moderate leadership" within the context of the same five-year transitional arrangement suggested at Camp David and defer final status issues and the question of sovereignty. Palestinians, by contrast, were committed to the pursuit of statehood via an empowered PLO, seeking to end the Israeli occupation and settlement building. As the leading analyst of the peace process explains, "The Americans firmly sided with the Israelis, insisting that small practical steps needed to be taken first (confidence building measures), to be followed by agreement on a transitional period, and only later on the final status issues that were uppermost in the minds of the Palestinians."[60] The dynamic shifted somewhat with the start of the Rabin government, and Palestinians were able to drive harder on sovereignty. While it remains unclear how far the Palestinians might have been able to push forward their vision had the talks continued in Washington, the secret talks in Norway stopped this progress dead in its tracks.

Unlike the position of Palestinian negotiators in the Madrid process who opposed an interim agreement that would constrain sovereignty, the PLO agreed precisely to such an outcome in Norway. There are several reasons that have been offered as to why the PLO leadership signed on to the Oslo Accords, ranging from a desire to restore legitimacy and financial solvency after a decade languishing in the Arab diaspora to a total disconnect from the reality of life under Israeli occupation.[61] Arafat and his coterie of senior advisors had no experience living alongside settlements and under Israeli control, and were therefore less aware of the real consequences that an unfavorable set of interim conditions would pose. After the decision to side with Iraq in the Gulf War, the leadership had little credibility. A return to the territories was seen as a development that might place the PLO back at the heart of the national struggle. Yet it remained unclear how exactly such a return would enable the leadership to overcome the inevitable limitations Israel would place on them.[62]

In September 1995, Arafat and Rabin signed the Interim Agreement on the West Bank and Gaza Strip, known as Oslo II, establishing the Palestinian Authority (PA) and dividing the West Bank into three separate zones of control. Palestinian cities were declared "Area A" and placed under full Palestinian civilian and security control. Surrounding towns and villages and their adjacent land were designated "Area B," placed under Palestinian civilian control and Israeli security authority. "Area C" comprised the remaining 60 percent of the West Bank and all the Israeli settlements, which was left under full Israeli control.[63]

This agreement granted the PA limited self-government for an interim period of time over certain areas, providing the vestiges of statehood without actual content. The Oslo process lulled its proponents into the false belief that real issues like Jerusalem, refugees' right of return, settlements, and security would also eventually be dealt with. Rather, as a leading scholar of the occupation has argued, "a new indirect method of Israeli rule was put into place."[64]

For the Israeli leadership, Oslo was in many ways a legacy of Begin's opposition to Palestinian statehood. It formalized the ceiling of Palestinian self-rule. Rabin himself made this clear in a speech to a special session of the Israeli Knesset convened to ratify Oslo II on October 5, 1995. He explained the nature of a permanent solution for the existence of Israel alongside a "Palestinian entity": "We want this entity to be less than a state that will manage independently the lives of the Palestinians under its authority. The borders of the State of Israel at the time of the permanent solution will be beyond the lines that existed before the Six-Day War. We will not return to the lines of June 4, 1967."[65] Rabin never considered sovereign statehood outright, although a top advisor had suggested that it was an inevitable outcome to a real self-governing authority for Palestinians.[66]

Yet critics on the Israeli right strongly denounced negotiations with the PLO or the possibility of their achieving independence, adamantly opposing Oslo at every turn. During the Knesset vote to approve the original accord, Benjamin Netanyahu, who had succeeded Shamir as leader of the Likud, promised to cancel the agreement if his party came to power. He compared Oslo to Neville Chamberlain's appeasement of Adolf Hitler, telling Foreign Minister Peres, "You are even worse than Chamberlain. He imperiled the safety of another people, but you are doing it to your own people."[67] The frenzy of anger directed at Rabin intensified after Oslo II, with Netanyahu speaking at an opposition rally in Jerusalem at which demonstrators displayed an effigy of the Israeli prime minister in a Nazi SS uniform.[68] On November 4, 1995, Rabin attended a large peace rally in Tel Aviv held in support of his government's policy. Returning to his waiting car, he was shot in the back at close range by Yigal Amir, an extremist from the national religious camp who sought to derail the peace process by assassinating the Israeli leader.[69]

Among the PLO factions, there was mounting dissent and internal opposition to the Oslo Accords. Mahmoud Darwish, who had written the Palestinian Declaration of Independence in 1988, resigned from the PLO Executive Committee. "We have taken two generations to their death in the project of liberation and independence," exclaimed the national poet. "It now appears as if we are abandoning them completely, leaving them to the winds of the wilderness."[70] There was also enormous skepticism toward Arafat's move in the Arab world. He was seen as selling out meaningful Palestinian sovereignty for the sake of his own return to the West Bank and Gaza Strip, where he was eventually elected president of the PA in 1996. In the rush to secure greater global legitimacy, the PLO leadership sacrificed the basic principles of national self-determination, acquiescing in part to the earlier notions of autonomy put forward during the Egyptian-Israeli-American negotiations. This decision to embrace limited self-rule as an entry point back into the territories facilitated the emergence of a local authority largely subject to Israeli control. Such an arrangement deferred meaningful sovereignty, fostering the performance of independence without substantive political content.

The Consequences of State Prevention

"VICTORY IS AT HAND," Yasser Arafat declared in front the UN General Assembly. "I see the homeland in your holy stones. I see the flag of our independent Palestine fluttering over the hills of our beloved homeland."[1] The image of a Palestinian state described by the leader of the PLO in his breakthrough 1988 address remains unfulfilled, well after the national movement that he led achieved international recognition. West Bank hilltops are even denser with Jewish settlements in 2018, as the Israeli government's fifty-year celebration in Gush Etzion recedes swiftly from view.

Arafat's vision of a state appears increasingly distant as one surveys recent developments. To explain why, this book has described the process by which the emergence of meaningful Palestinian sovereignty was prevented by a confluence of forces at the very moment when it first seemed attainable. After the 1967 War brought the territory of the West Bank, Gaza Strip, and East Jerusalem under Israeli control, the Palestinian question was thrust into the diplomatic limelight, nearly two decades after being sidelined by Arab nationalist politics in the wake of 1948. The renewed strength of the PLO, which had been created at the behest of Egypt in 1964, found its independent footing in the aftermath of the 1967 and 1973 wars, as nationalists drew common cause with other anticolonial movements to render Palestinian demands visible around the globe. Yet that struggle did not end in statehood, even as the fight for self-determination was framed as the pursuit of national independence.

As early as 1973, PLO officials were steadily moving toward diplomacy rather than armed struggle, which had shaped the resurgence of the movement in its early years. They were attentive to the shifting international climate and cognizant of the challenging reality that confronted them in exile, first in Jordan and then in Lebanon. There was a sense of disconnect from the Palestinians who remained in Israel and the occupied territories, cut off from the Arab world and newly exposed to the military control of the Israeli state. Although the PLO's political legitimacy in the Middle East and Europe grew steadily throughout the 1970s, the United States remained deeply opposed to the tactics and substance of Palestinian demands for independence. Both the Nixon and Ford administrations sought to bypass the Palestinian question in favor of regional solutions to the Arab-Israeli conflict. Secretary of State Henry Kissinger formalized the PLO's marginalization with a 1975 ban on official engagement with the PLO that demanded an end to violence and the acceptance of UN resolutions that recognized Israel.

Political currents were moving in favor of the Palestinians by the second half of the decade. Jimmy Carter's 1976 election brought a new U.S. administration to power that was far more sympathetic to addressing their demands for self-determination. Carter's electoral victory and arrival in Washington was a break in both style and substance from his predecessors. The administration's approach was premised on abandoning Kissinger's bilateralism, which had been aimed at removing Egypt from the conflict rather than pursuing a comprehensive peace that included the Palestinians. Carter's stance was fueled by a deliberate turn to human rights rhetoric and away from the entrenched patterns of the Cold War. Such a position enabled the circulation of new ideas about Palestinian national aspirations. It was also coupled with a growing global awareness of the PLO as a legitimate vehicle for waging diplomatic struggle, a direct consequence of successful decolonization across the Global South.

Carter's consultations with Middle Eastern leaders in the early months of 1977 underscored this premise. Not long after the inauguration, the White House proposed a comprehensive regional peace plan that would build on the Geneva Conference, a gathering of key parties that had met briefly in the aftermath of the 1973 War. This Geneva meeting, which was intended for the second half of 1977, would include the Soviet Union and revive negotiations on the basis of United Nations Security Council Resolutions 242 and 338. It would also address the issue of Palestinian representation, through a joint delegation with other Arab states or a measure of PLO participation that was the subject of intensive deliberations. Yet Geneva never came to pass. The domestic backlash from Cold War conservatives and leaders of the American Jewish community who opposed Carter's vision was a major factor in derailing this comprehensive approach. While Israel and the Arab states agreed to work toward a gathering, their divergent positions on the key issues of contention resulted in a far more limited outcome. In the process, the Palestinian question was effectively removed from viable diplomatic consideration. Along with the impatience of Egyptian president Sadat, these pressures forced a return to a bilateral Egyptian-Israeli track, the very by-product of Kissinger's "shuttle diplomacy" that Carter had sought so eagerly to replace.

While these global and regional developments were unfolding between Washington and the Middle East, important local dynamics were also taking hold in Jerusalem and the occupied territories of the West Bank and Gaza Strip. Having solidified control of these areas in the June 1967 War, successive Labor governments in Israel had inaugurated a process of settlement expansion that started in the Golan Heights. Yitzhak Rabin's resignation and the triumph of the Likud party in the May 1977 elections brought Menachem Begin to power, a figure deeply opposed to meaningful Palestinian sovereignty or statehood. Much to Carter's dismay, the new Begin government sought to firmly entrench territorial gains and expand settlements for a combination of economic, political, and ideological reasons. Palestinian political sovereignty, long at the heart of both PLO and Arab demands, would have no place in such an emerging Israeli constellation.

Begin was a shrewd diplomat and political visionary, whose image of the Palestinian future was rooted in the belief that they were not a collective people or nation deserving of a state but a minority group of Arabs living in the greater Land of Israel and deserving of individual rights. This was completely at odds with the view of Palestinians themselves, as well as a growing number of Western powers and Arab states. Critical accounts of the U.S. relationship with Israel during the Carter administration point to personal animus between the president and the Israeli prime minister, criticizing the tough American stance toward an ally.[2] Yet much of the Carter administration's frustration stemmed from the substance of the interactions with the Israeli leadership and the divergent vision of a political outcome. Begin was determined not to cede control over the territories or halt settlement expansion, instead introducing the concept of autonomy for Arab inhabitants as an alternative.

Carter recognized that the Israeli position was intended to undermine the very principles on Palestinian self-determination that he articulated when he first arrived in office, even as he himself did not countenance a Palestinian state. At a news conference on March 9, 1978, the U.S. president would clarify that "we do not and have never favored an independent Palestinian nation, but within that bound of constraint, how to give the Palestinians who live in the West Bank, Gaza Strip some voice in the determination of their own future, is an issue still unresolved."[3] His stance highlighted the contested nature of sovereignty and self-determination in the 1970s, a decade in which a host of anticolonial struggles using resurgent rights-based language found limited backing around the globe.

While this was not a conducive environment for Palestinian diplomatic advances, the PLO itself also helped undermine the possible emergence of a sovereign, independent nation-state. In examining the PLO's strategy and actions in this period, it is clear that the national movement was making the unprecedented concession of accepting a state within the limits of the 1967 boundaries, a radical departure from its earliest political platform. At the same time, the organization's internal reticence to accept UN resolution 242 at several crucial early junctures—even with reservations—served to bolster critics of engagement and led U.S. officials to bypass the PLO for nonrepresentative alternatives. The flux within PLO decision making was an understandable reflection of the danger of conceding recognition of Israel without a guarantee of meaningful sovereignty in return. Yasser Arafat attempted to maintain a large umbrella organization that was populated by a range of factions, cognizant of the wider Arab political forces that influenced various corners of the movement, including uncompromising voices demanding continued military action. Therefore, although Palestinian nationalists had largely turned away from armed struggle by the mid-1970s, the persistence of violence by individual factions indicated that the organization was far from a unitary actor.

The constraints the PLO was facing were well known to U.S. officials. Yet Carter also faced domestic opposition to engagement, and he ultimately deferred substantive talks with the PLO as he pursued a more limited agenda. Instead it was Egypt that took the most active role in the U.S. diplomatic track. Anwar al-Sadat eagerly sought a peace agreement with Israel and American financial and military backing, while nominally speaking for the Palestinians along the way. The incongruity of an Arab leader seeking to withdraw from the Arab-Israeli conflict—a process the Egyptian president had started years earlier, without success—while a core element of that conflict remained unresolved was not lost on Israel, the Palestinians, and the wider Arab world. U.S. and Soviet leaders were also attuned to the pivotal Egyptian role, with the United States eager to secure a regional ally, while the Soviets had been losing influence in the Middle East since the 1967 War. The protracted discussions over Geneva solidified Sadat's move to the American camp, and his decision to travel to Jerusalem and focus efforts on bilateral negotiations with Begin was a further indication of Egypt's new stance. Although the path-breaking trip shattered Israeli anxieties about Arab intentions, it also had the effect of shifting negotiations back to Kissinger's bilateral approach, further eliding a national outcome for the Palestinians.

As U.S. diplomats slowly got behind Sadat's efforts, the emergence of the Camp David Summit was the final opportunity to keep the Palestinian question under consideration. In preparing for the talks and negotiating between Egypt and Israel, Carter and his advisors quickly realized that the fate of the Palestinians was tied to Begin's narrow conception of autonomy. While the United States questioned these motives, and raised pointed criticism of the Israeli vision of limited sovereignty, Sadat was willing to proceed along narrower lines. Carter's expansive planning for a regional settlement ultimately gave way to the much narrower—albeit significant—bilateral peace treaty between Egypt and Israel. Sadat's approach during the subsequent negotiations over the bilateral peace treaty sacrificed meaningful Palestinian self-determination for a watered-down notion of self-rule promoted by the Begin government. As his lead advisors protested and quit in succession, the Egyptian president stood his ground, believing he could represent Palestinian interests despite his antipathy toward the PLO and Israeli designs over the occupied territories. Partly a by-product of his domestic considerations and Egypt's desire to secure Western backing, this headstrong stance flew in the face of wider Arab concerns and left Egypt marginalized in the region. Internally, it was coupled with growing anger at the peace treaty with Israel and deeper discontent over the leadership of Sadat himself.

In the wake of the Egypt-Israel peace treaty of 1979, diplomatic efforts to address the Palestinian issue shifted to a series of smaller meetings devoted to autonomy. These autonomy talks, as they came to be known, were convened by the United States, Egypt, and Israel without Palestinian participation. They were the first sustained political consideration of Palestinian self-determination after 1948. They were also the most consequential. Israel's clear vision of autonomy was dependent on the extension of state sovereignty throughout the occupied territories, a mechanism of "de facto annexation" that blurred political boundaries and perpetuated conflict with the Palestinians.[4] Later iterations of Palestinian models for self-rule, such as the Palestinian Authority that emerged from the Oslo Accords, emanated from this central premise. A change in status for Arab inhabitants in the territories would be dependent on the continuation of Israeli settlements and some degree of Israeli security control west of the Jordan River.

During the autonomy talks, in their negotiating tactics and overall stance, the American and Egyptian diplomats often acquiesced to the Israeli view of limited sovereignty, serving to thwart the possibility of a meaningful political outcome for the Palestinians. As the Israeli concept was further clarified, and as Arab and Palestinian opposition grew, the logic and momentum of negotiations superseded warnings that the outcome might favor the Begin government. What then explained their continuation into the early 1980s? The Carter administration confronted domestic pressures and other pressing concerns in the Middle East, sustaining the discussions out of necessity as a marker of progress on the Palestinian front while having run out of political leverage to affect a meaningful outcome. For Sadat, the negotiations sustained the image that bilateral peace was connected to a broader settlement, drawing attention away from more hard-line critics who had opposed Camp David for the very reason that it undermined Palestinian aspirations. Without halting ongoing settlement expansion or providing substantive authority to local residents of the occupied territories, the autonomy talks further prevented Palestinian self-determination in the West Bank and Gaza Strip. Autonomy, as a political, diplomatic, and conceptual tool utilized to manage the Palestinian question, became the ground upon which the Israeli government cemented indefinite control over the occupied territories without any expiration date or formal annexation.

Beyond the particularities of the Palestinian question, historians of decolonization, human rights, and U.S. internationalism in the 1970s might consider the pursuit of Egyptian-Israeli peace in light of Carter's broader ambitions. Some have revisited the Carter era with increasing sympathy for the constraints under which the U.S. president governed and his accomplishments abroad. Camp David is often singled out as his greatest success. The Carter administration, it is argued, broke with decades of U.S. inaction by seizing on the terms of the debate over the Middle East, often unintentionally, overhauling them to fit with an alternative conception of the region. In this respect, the Carter administration was certainly the first to place the Israeli-Palestinian conflict at the center of regional affairs. Yet the failure matters as much as the success. At a moment when the rhetoric of human rights and self-determination were poised to undo the carefully managed script of Kissinger's détente, the Palestinians presented a formative example where the rhetoric of human rights fell short. A focus on the autonomy talks in particular illustrates the narrow extent to which the contours and possible solutions of Israel's conflict with the Arab world were circumscribed by Camp David and the troubling consequences that metastasized in its wake.

The role of domestic politics was also a formative impediment to Carter's broader ambitions. In their opposition to engagement with the possibility of Palestinian self-determination and with their crucial embrace of the expansionist Begin government, the outspoken activism of American Jewish leaders provides an important window into the growing role of interest groups and ethnic politics in the making of Middle East policy during the 1970s. The degree to which American Jewish leaders collectively constrained Carter's pursuit of a comprehensive peace is difficult to discern, but lobbying along restrictive Likud party lines became more evident in Congress, in the media, and within the American Jewish community. At the same time, important voices of dissent were visible and influential, breaking with a hostile view of the Palestinian question into the 1980s. Domestic opposition also came from anti-Soviet hawks, whose unrest indicated deeper discontent with Carter's departure from Cold War priorities around the globe. The emergence of a foreign policy anchored by an appeal to human rights bolstered the claims of neoconservative critics who worried that the United States had given ground to the Soviet Union. These concerns would grow more acute as other foreign policy challenges arose, particularly the Iranian Revolution in 1979 and the Soviet invasion of Afghanistan that year.

A potent backlash against Carter would drive many Democrats to support California governor Ronald Reagan in his quest for the White House. Carter's defeat in the 1980 election and the rise of the Reagan administration accelerated developments set in motion by Camp David and repositioned the Israeli-Palestinian conflict as a subset of the Cold War. The formal introduction of a strategic U.S. alliance with Israel was matched by the marginalization of the PLO as a Soviet proxy. Even as some U.S. officials warned of the danger in this approach, neoconservative ideologues dominated in the early years of Reagan's first term and found a natural ally in the Likud government of Israel. Most consequentially, the Reagan administration aided Israeli officials in the transition from a diplomatic attempt to suppress Palestinian nationalism toward a military intervention that targeted the PLO in its Lebanese stronghold. By green-lighting Israel's June 1982 intervention in Lebanon, U.S. officials helped exacerbate a broader civil war that had already been raging since 1975.

As the 1982 War and its aftermath demonstrated, the Israelis overestimated their own capabilities and the possibility of a political alliance with the Maronites. In the process, the Begin government sowed regional upheaval and drew the United States into its largest quagmire since the Vietnam War. The extent of the invasion, and the prolonged occupation of Lebanon, fomented violent resistance and drew in other Arab states to exacerbate a host of internal rivalries. Although American officials were divided in their view of Israeli actions over the summer of 1982, acute failures by the U.S. administration in the aftermath of the PLO evacuation from Beirut left innocent Palestinian refugees distressingly vulnerable in Sabra and Shatila. The deployment of U.S. Marines after the ensuing massacre was a further tragedy, highlighting the regional backlash against American intervention and support for Israeli war aims. The United States suffered incomparable damage in the Lebanese imbroglio, in terms of both human lives and regional influence. Many of the legacies of intervention in the 1980s still haunt U.S. foreign policy in the Middle East.

Such a reordering of America's position in the region during this period highlights U.S. internationalism at a moment of transition. The aftermath of Camp David and subsequent events in Lebanon were a crucial component of the American turn to military force in the region. While international historians are only recently beginning to turn their attention toward the Reagan era, it clearly had a far-reaching impact on the Global South, especially the Middle East.[5] The earlier insistence on a bifurcated Cold War/post–Cold War periodization scheme for organizing the late twentieth century is now seen as eliding the critical role of the United States in fomenting and exacerbating regional violence.[6] Rather than peripheral to events elsewhere, the Middle East was a central site of Reagan's interventionist foreign policy in the closing years of the Cold War. In this regard, *Preventing Palestine* tempers any triumphalist narrative of U.S. foreign relations in the Reagan era.[7]

From Latin America to Africa, historians have become more explicit about the need to locate the genesis of contemporary social and political problems within a period of ostensible American triumph.[8] Scholars of the global Cold War in particular have forced a necessary reckoning with histories of the periphery, but even they have neglected the Israeli-Palestinian conflict.[9] A move away from Carter's regional focus to the globalist approach of Reagan can be traced directly through this arena, with consequences that continue to underpin U.S. diplomacy toward the region. Although the Cold War mattered to Arab-Israeli relations in the late 1970s and 1980s, its impact was far less than might be expected, certainly in light of internal developments. As a framing and periodizing device, however, it helped situate those developments along a global axis. The rhythms and logic of Israeli and Palestinian concerns drew selectively and instrumentally upon strategic Cold War reasoning when it suited particular policy initiatives in both the Carter and Reagan administrations.

Lebanon was the nexus of these local and global forces, revealing the consequences of a violent encounter between dueling ideologies and armed intervention in the early 1980s. The country has long been a battleground for regional power rivalries, and was also the site where Israel's ambitious national agenda and the diplomatic fallout of Camp David collided in unexpected and damaging ways. In pursuing the PLO militarily, and working to defeat Palestinian nationalism via faulty alliances with the Lebanese Christian minority, Israel found itself implicated in a massacre and a wider war that undercut the entire edifice upon which a carefully cultivated ethos of defensive Zionism had been resting. Even alongside the creation of the Palestinian refugee problem in 1948 and military failures in 1956 and 1973, the 1982 War endures as one of the darkest episodes in Israeli history, to say nothing of its resonance in Lebanon. While the Israeli invasion was a formative proving ground for subsequent attempts to suppress Palestinian nationalism, the lessons of overreach were never quite absorbed by the political establishment at the time.

The PLO's expulsion from the country and the failure of the Israeli-Lebanese peace accords triggered new forms of regional resistance and the resurgence of the Palestinian question in the occupied territories themselves. A shift from political efforts to curtail Palestinian self-determination toward the military intervention in Lebanon further exposed the national movement to violence and exile. But it also enabled a regrouping and rearticulation of the national struggle in conjunction with Palestinians who remained inside the West Bank and Gaza Strip, reviving the quest for statehood that the Israelis had worked so diligently to suppress. Attempts to restart negotiations on the Palestinian front without PLO engagement yielded little in the way of meaningful political progress. Israel promoted its own alternatives like the ill-fated Village Leagues and "Quality of Life" initiatives to improve economic conditions in the territories via Jordanian channels. The primary goal of Israeli leaders—from Shamir to Peres—remained the suppression of Palestinian nationalism in the occupied territories and the prevention of any PLO influence. U.S. officials actively backed these ideas, although a short-lived plan to increase Hashemite control across the Jordan River gave way to King Hussein's renunciation of his country's influence over the West Bank. Far from bypassing the possibility of self-determination, these attempts fed into the outbreak of the first Intifada in 1987. Through largely nonviolent action, the mass uprising brought the national movement decisively in from the cold and renewed global attention to demands for statehood.

After an extended blanket policy of exclusion, the move toward recognition of Israel and a two-state settlement at the Palestinian National Council in Algiers, as well as a secret dialogue with American Jewish leaders under Swedish mediation, prompted formal PLO recognition and the beginning of an official dialogue in the final weeks of Reagan's presidency. The administration's belated recognition that the Palestinian issue had to be dealt with on its own terms, and via the PLO, was in many ways a return to the same principles articulated by Carter years earlier. This reversal occurred as the administration's sweeping anti-communist rhetoric gave way to growing accommodation with the Soviet Union during Reagan's second term in office. While the immediate catalyst for the reversal was the unrest in the occupied territories and Arafat's Geneva statement in which he renounced terrorism, a much longer history of U.S. efforts to contend with Palestinian national aspirations runs through this book.

By revisiting the years prior to PLO recognition, it emerges that the deferral of a political solution to Palestinian demands—from as early as Kissinger's 1975 ban—served to prolong the possible attainment of political sovereignty by the Palestinians. What was the cost of this deferred recognition? Could things have turned out differently had the ban not been in place? As this account has suggested, the complex relations between the United States, the PLO, Israel, and transnational actors in the intervening years adversely shaped a much wider set of policies toward the Palestinian question. Carter's ambitious plans for Geneva and then more modest achievements in Camp David both excluded the PLO, postponing a reckoning with the central question of political sovereignty in the occupied territories that had been articulated in the mid-1970s. Egypt helped legitimate this exclusion, and Reagan's ideological turn further marginalized the national movement as the war in Lebanon unleashed its own violent outcome. But the crushing military and political blow delivered by Israel did not actually defeat the national movement.

The contest between two divergent political projects—an Israeli vision of limited autonomy and a Palestinian vision of self-determination—was generally resolved in favor of the side that could better withstand its own pyrrhic victory at any given moment. But the international context was crucial. In the waning years of decolonization, Israel was able to withstand the postwar vision of anticolonial movements that had been arguing for the creation of sovereign, independent nation-states. While the PLO had drawn on the example of movements like the FLN in Algeria, an alignment with other struggles across the Global South lost its valence by the mid-1970s, supplanted by the rise of human rights discourse. Israel's position as an ally of the United States in the Cold War and joint rejection of efforts in bodies like the United Nations was solidified in the Reagan era, thereby helping to embed an alternative view of the PLO as a Soviet proxy and Palestinians as undeserving of statehood. The end of the Cold War and the U.S. victory in the Persian Gulf challenged this trend, facilitating the Bush administration's move to begin substantive negotiations in 1991.

The Madrid Conference and the Washington talks finally allowed the Palestinians to sit at the negotiating table, even under the severe political constraints that had been set in motion by Camp David. While the Palestinian delegation worked to secure greater sovereignty in these talks, Arafat's secret move to pursue the Oslo channel with the Rabin government led to a breakthrough agreement that did not actually address core demands. In securing the PLO's return to the West Bank and Gaza Strip with the signing of the Oslo Accords, Arafat's acceptance of limited self-rule through the establishment of an interim Palestinian National Authority diluted the central elements of the Palestinian national struggle, bumping up against the ceiling of autonomy first laid out by Begin in 1977. It also virtually guaranteed Israel's continued settlement expansion in the territories, further eroding the basis of what might emerge as a sovereign, independent nation-state.

Settlements, in this regard, remain a central actor in any wider story of this period. Carter's limited attempt to push Prime Minster Begin on settlement expansion, followed by Reagan's shift on their legality, would enable years of unchecked Israeli building in the occupied territories. This legacy tends to be obscured by a focus on peace between Egypt and Israel, an agreement that should be understood as contingent in Begin's mind on avoiding a resolution of the Palestinian issue. As the comprehensive track eroded, movement on settlement building continued apace, and took off in the 1980s. The settlements had become the mirror and negation, in effect, to the possibility of Palestinian sovereignty. About four thousand Jewish settlers lived in the West Bank and Gaza Strip when Begin entered office in 1977, and over one hundred thousand by the end of 1992, on the eve of the Oslo Accords. In the interim, commuter towns and bypass roads for Jewish residents bisected the actual ground upon which Palestinian sovereignty could be achieved, as a matrix of Israeli control was consolidated that by some accounts would prove irreversible.[10]

The Legacy of the 1970s and 1980s

Critics of the U.S., Israeli, and Palestinian roles in the peace process have long lamented the destructive impact of the 1990s and early 2000s. But new evidence deepens and complicates an understanding of the missteps that actually began far earlier. The Camp David process was the first diplomatic discussion of Palestinian self-determination, and also the most formative. For as damaging as the exclusion of actual Palestinians from the Egyptian-Israeli negotiations and the autonomy talks may have been, the impact on subsequent discussion of their political fate has also been crippling. By conditioning Palestinian political rights on a narrowly functionalist and nonterritorial definition of autonomy alongside continued

Israeli settlement expansion in the occupied territories, the earlier talks undercut the possibility of Palestinian sovereignty long before the "peace process" of the 1990s had begun. Begin's autonomy plan, as both records from his time in office and later discussions make clear, became the basis for the U.S. and Israeli negotiating positions—and the birth of the Palestinian Authority—in the years that followed.

The link between Camp David, the autonomy talks, and the Oslo Accords is almost entirely absent from studies of the peace process. But in the view of former Israeli Knesset member and political scientist Naomi Chazan, Camp David "indirectly curtailed . . . the prospects of territorial compromise in the West Bank and Gaza." "By decoupling peace from territories," Chazan explains, "they actually encouraged Israeli settlement."[11] In continuing with the post-1967 "decision not to decide" on the fate of the territories and deferring substantive negotiations over the Palestinian question in an autonomy process explicitly designed to prevent sovereignty, Camp David actually enabled the triumph of an Israeli vision intent on suppressing the demand for self-determination. This highly consequential strategy was a defining feature of Begin's statecraft, often lost in the broader picture of the peace treaty with Egypt.

A focus on the 1970s and 1980s also reveals a great deal about the nature of Israel's expansion beyond the 1967 borders and the diplomacy that sustained it. The very idiom in which early negotiations were rooted—autonomy not sovereignty, limited self-rule—exacerbated conditions on the ground and dismantled the political mechanisms for a just resolution to the Palestinian question. Even more restrictive than the notion of self-determination that featured in the mandate system after World War I, autonomy for the local inhabitants of the occupied territories was diluted to a point where it signaled indefinite Israeli control of the territories rather than a means to eventual self-government. Unlike the mandate system, which was premised on the assumption that the occupiers might one day leave, Israel's occupation has lasted twice as long, without an end in sight. The context of Israel's rule over the West Bank and Gaza Strip, which began well after the end of empire, the mandates, and the major waves of decolonization, can shed new light on the relationship between late twentieth-century occupation and the persistence of prolonged statelessness. In large measure, the blueprint for the limited degree of Palestinian sovereignty that might ever be reached in a negotiated settlement was first sketched out by Begin, Burg, Sharon, and members of the Israeli negotiating team, as well as through the acquiescence of U.S. and Egyptian diplomats working alongside them.

While historians of Palestine, Zionism, and Israel have looked anew at the emergence of communal and religious tensions in the late Ottoman context, and they have turned their attention to British Mandatory rule as an incubator of national divisions during the age of European colonialism, they have largely ignored the formative impact of the post-1967 era. Alongside the renewed focus on the contradictions that plagued Israeli state formation and the dichotomous treatment of Arab citizens in the 1940s and 1950s, as well as the transformative nature of occupation in the West Bank and Gaza Strip following the 1967 War, there is a need to fortify the link between Israeli territorial expansion and the ongoing condition of Palestinian statelessness.[12] The conjoined moment of Israeli state formation and the onset of the Palestinian Nakba in 1948 underscores the importance of positioning the imbricated history of Israel and Palestine in direct conversation with one another.[13]

By recovering post-1967 developments, the rationale and political-conceptual dynamics animating Israel's treatment of Palestinians in the territories become clearer, as does the tacit, and often explicit, acceptance and encouragement of this behavior by other actors. In emphasizing individual rights and de-territorialized autonomy, rather than allowing for collective self-determination after Camp David, the Israeli government and their compliant U.S. and Egyptian counterparts helped solidify a non-national, non-statist arrangement for Palestinians. More broadly, in rejecting a postwar vision of national self-determination leading to the creation of a sovereign state, the treatment of the Palestinian question links up with other contested struggles over sovereignty in the 1970s and 1980s. From East Timor to Kurdistan, occupying powers and great power supporters posited that groups demanding rights were neither a nation nor a people, and whatever political rights they might have inhered in them as individuals rather than a collective on the territory they occupied. Palestine is therefore an ideal test case for understanding the global deprivation of political rights to certain national movements and the uneven trajectory of self-determination in the postwar era.[14]

Like other unmet promises in Latin America and Southeast Asia, the events recounted in this book highlight the wide gulf that separated the benevolent rhetorical intentions of U.S. policymakers and their actual conduct as mediators. In the words of former U.S. ambassador to Israel Samuel Lewis, who discussed his own role as a leading Middle East diplomat in this era, "I think, we perhaps tried to play this role of honest broker, mediator, catalyst, participant, partner, whatever you'd want to describe it—we wanted to play it only with carrots."[15] As the role of U.S. appointed envoys like Robert Strauss and Sol Linowitz attest, Israeli negotiators asserted the limits of their respective positions and secured American support in the process.

Looking back on this period from the contemporary vantage point of a fractured Palestinian polity, we can more clearly discern the historical absence and active prevention of sovereignty and how it endures as a primary obstacle to Palestinian self-determination and statehood. *Preventing Palestine* does not suggest that the foreclosure was inevitable or that alternatives might not still be possible. Rather, it attempts to chart the actions by Israel, the United States, Egypt, regional Arab states, domestic actors, and many others between the late 1970s and early 1990s, thereby elucidating a historical moment that abetted the prevention of Palestine. In place of offering a totalizing view of early diplomatic efforts as deliberately destructive, this book suggests a fluid unfolding of events, constrained by domestic factors, various ideologies, the structure of negotiations, and the individual choices of Israelis, Palestinians, and a wide range of Middle Eastern and transnational actors. This delicate interplay captures a contingent history of state prevention in the late twentieth century.

In exploring how diplomatic practices interacted with existing governing structures and various forms of conceptual and political thinking, the period between Camp David and Oslo casts new light on the divergent meanings ascribed to words like "autonomy," "self-rule," and "sovereignty."[16] By pulling the frame away from a saturated focus on the post-Oslo era, I have attempted to explain how international political developments, the articulation of ideas and policies in the diplomatic arena, domestic politics in the United States, and transformations on the ground in the region itself during the late 1970s and 1980s produced (and constricted) the possible conditions under which the Palestinian question could be negotiated after U.S. recognition of the PLO in 1988. William Quandt, one of the Carter administration's advisors on the Arab-Israeli conflict, and the leading expert on the peace process, has argued, "On balance, Israel and its neighbors were no closer to agreement in 1988 than they had been in 1980. Perhaps the most one can say is that things had not deteriorated beyond repair."[17] But greater distance and the new sources uncovered in this book suggest that the contours of a just settlement may actually have eroded significantly during these interim years, adversely impacting the prospect of any successful negotiation in the 1990s and beyond.

Historians are not frequently in the business of asking counterfactuals, focused instead on how events, ideologies, and structural forces unfold and interact over a discrete period of time.[18] One must wonder, however, if things might have turned out differently had Carter's pursuit of a comprehensive peace moved forward, or Sadat held off on his trip to Jerusalem, or the Reagan Plan was taken seriously in the midst of the Lebanon War, or the Madrid and Washington process had reached a conclusion before the secret agreement in Oslo. Perhaps possibilities would have presented themselves in the last two and a half decades that are hard to imagine today. But given the history recounted in this book, a more troubling question remains: Was the legacy of Camp David so deeply entrenched—both conceptually in terms of preventing Palestinian statehood and physically in terms of the territorial transformation in the West Bank and Gaza Strip—that the peace process in the 1990s was bound to fail from its inception? Can Palestinians, as one leading U.S. diplomat suggested, really "negotiate their own way out of occupation"?[19]

State Prevention into the Twenty-First Century

Throughout 2017, several Israeli politicians could be heard lamenting the missed opportunity of Menachem Begin's autonomy plan, which they believe would have maintained Israel's Jewish character and circumvented international pressure to withdraw from the oc-cupied territories.[20] Naftali Bennett, the right-wing education min-ister and leader of the National Home Party, has been a leading advocate of a political solution for the Palestinians that dispenses with the idea of two separate states.[21] Instead, he has called for "autonomy on steroids" in its place. In a December 2017 interview, Bennett laid out his vision in great detail. "I have no desire to oc-cupy, govern and control the 2 million Arabs that live in Judea and Samaria. I remember what it was like during the First Intifada, and I don't want to control their education, their sewage system and their quality of life." Instead, Bennett suggested a "Stability Plan" that would "provide full civilian self-governance to the Palestin-ians so they can elect themselves, pay their taxes, and control those areas that are theirs." In particular, he called for the application of Israeli sovereignty in Area C of the West Bank. This would in-tegrate Palestinians who live there (about eighty thousand in his view) into Israel with an offer of full Israeli citizenship, including voting rights, or residency. Palestinians living in Area A and Area B, Bennett explained, "will govern themselves in all aspects bar-ring two elements: overall security responsibility and not being able to allow the return of descendants of Palestinians refugees."[22] The echoes of Prime Minister Begin could not be clearer.

As for how this "autonomy on steroids" might materialize, Ben-nett was open to ideas: "It could be a confederation with Jordan, or local municipalities, or a central government. It would encompass full freedom of movement, massive infrastructure investment, the creation of a tourism zone so Christians can enter Haifa, Nazareth, Nablus, Ramallah, Jerusalem and Hebron without going through road blocks." The elements of such a plan would not require the cooperation of the Palestinians themselves, Bennett argued, or the international community. It would also make life better in the oc-cupied territories, ensuring a continued Israeli presence across the Green Line. "It's a bottom-up economy-based peace solution and the Palestinians don't accept any other options. . . . My approach brings a much better horizon for Palestinians and Israelis be-cause right now the only quiet place in the Middle East is in Judea and Samaria and it's because we're there." When asked whether his vision would provide self-determination for the Palestinian population in the West Bank, Bennett demurred. "It's unrealistic. Self-determination also depends on democracy so that the people are able to *determine* what they want. Almost none of [*sic*] neighbours enjoy democracy and if they did they would cease to be. So The Stability Plan is only partial self-determination but in the real world you have to make compromises."[23]

Bennett's twenty-first-century resuscitation of Begin's political vision of autonomy and the attendant questions this book has raised can in part be traced to the impact of the second Intifada between 2000 and 2005. The violence contributed to the intensification of a right-wing shift in Israel, further engendering widespread opposition to the notion of a fully sovereign Palestinian state. But this opposition has far deeper roots, predating the Oslo Accords and the accompanying public debate about limited territorial withdrawal. Even Likud prime minister Benjamin Netanyahu—who denounced Oslo's supporters as countenancing appeasement, calling them "worse than Chamberlain"—claimed to embrace a "two-state" model to ending the conflict, before making clear that relinquishing control of the West Bank was not an option. He has spoken instead of a "state minus" for Palestinians, suggesting some form of limited self-rule with Israeli security control west of the Jordan River.[24] Netanyahu, it should be recalled, began his service in the Israeli government during the Begin era. He was deeply attuned to the arguments around autonomy and the debates over settlements, self-determination, and the meaning of sovereignty.

Israel's "decision not to decide" on the fate of the territories after 1967 has in fact given way to a de facto policy of annexation in certain areas and public calls for formal annexation in others. Despite rhetorical support for a negotiated settlement, many Israeli politicians have regressed to an even harsher stance than that of Menachem Begin himself. Such a trend is not limited to the right-wing political parties, as parallels can also be found among centrists and the Labor left. Rather than withdraw from the West Bank, or abandon the settlements, there is talk of interim measures and slow separation that ensures continued Israeli security control of the territories. The idea of a Palestinian state—even a demilitarized one— has receded from view. Competing political visions that circulate in its place are not necessarily premised on the attainment of equal rights, individual or collective, in either two states or one.

We ignore these trends at our peril. The return to the 1970s and 1980s serves as a reminder that the contemporary debates over the Israeli-Palestinian conflict, as well as U.S. and international involvement in its resolution, are in many ways a twenty-first-century revival of earlier iterations. A central claim of this book is that political catastrophes do not just appear out of the blue; they are the product of decisions taken at particular moments in time. If we widen our lens to explain how earlier histories of the Mandate period as well as state formation and dispossession in 1948 extend forward to the post-1967 era, the broader dynamics of the Palestinian question become more evident, as do the discrete periods in which diplomatic practices prevented its resolution in the late twentieth century and continue to obstruct a viable outcome in the twenty-first. Camp David and its aftermath loom large over recent discussions about how to address Palestinian sovereignty claims. The political formation through which they might ultimately be exercised cannot be separated from the underlying principle of self-determination at the very heart of Palestinian demands.

ACKNOWLEDGMENTS

THIS BOOK GREW out of a formative political encounter that challenged me to interrogate personal beliefs and communal expectations, while also opening new avenues of historical understanding and intellectual discovery. My greatest debt is to my parents, Don and Enid Anziska, who supported me every step of the way, absorbing my inquisitiveness and provocations with love and acceptance. Together with my siblings, Evan, Suzanne, Nina, and Zachary, they offered a home where ideas could be debated (loudly) and deeply held assumptions could be reexamined in a more critical light. That openness nurtured my own learning and enabled me to travel farther afield, while a growing family including Alison, Avi, and all my nieces and nephews pulled me back and grounded me amid the research trips and transatlantic moves.

Without the mentorship and guidance of my teachers, I would have been lost trying to make sense of the questions themselves. Seth Taylor, Geoff Cahn, and Harriet Levitt ignited an early love for history and politics and set me on my way. As an undergraduate, Hillery Hugg, Lavinia Lorch, Peter Pazzaglini, Janaki Bakhle, and Ann Douglas helped me start looking for answers. The earliest seeds of this research began under the attentive eye of Elizabeth Blackmar, who taught me how to be a historian. Her dedication to imparting a craft and engagement with her students is a model to strive for in any classroom. Rashid Khalidi invited me into a conversation about the Middle East that has been ongoing for over fifteen years, with abiding curiosity and excitement. Unfailing in his support and encouragement as an advisor, he provided the strongest possible academic base for undertaking this project. The friendship and warmth he and Mona have extended enriched my time in New York and well beyond Morningside Heights.

At St. Antony's College, Oxford, Eugene Rogan and Avi Shlaim were expert supervisors in the history and international relations of the Middle East; both read multiple drafts of chapters that made their way into this book and have remained supportive colleagues and friends. Margaret MacMillan took the time to read through an unwieldy draft that became part of the book as well, providing invaluable suggestions and framing at an early stage of this project. At Columbia University, Mark Mazower and Sam Moyn helped me think through diverse fields within international and global history and served as sounding boards while the project took shape, and Michael Stanislawski and Rebecca Kobrin each offered expertise and insight from Israeli and Jewish history. Ira Katznelson brought political science into rich dialogue with American history and pushed me to sharpen my analytical argument, measure my tone, and consider contingency and intent. Anders Stephanson upended my approach to the study of foreign relations, forcing me to confront conceptual challenges with pointed and constructive feedback, always with the welcome relief of his piercing humor and clear sense of what is at stake. Ron Zweig provided research advice, critical reactions to my work, and an intellectual community in which to research Israel and Palestine at New York University's Taub Center. I am grateful to him and the Israel Institute for enabling me to spend a fellowship year at NYU working on this book and to Shayne Figueroa for making it such a productive stay. Daniel Kurtzer sat for an early interview and served as an outside reader; his comments and insights were invaluable in mediating between the mode of the historian and the reality of the policymaker.

Generous institutional and financial support made this book possible. It is my pleasure to acknowledge Columbia University's Middle East Institute, Institute for Israel and Jewish Studies, and Center for Democracy, Toleration, and Religion; Oxford's Near and Middle Eastern Studies Grant, the Carr and Stahl Funds of St. Antony's College, and the British Society for Middle Eastern Studies Masters Scholarship; the Wexner Foundation Graduate Fellowship in Jewish Studies; the Boren NSEP Graduate Fellowship for International Study at the American University of Beirut (AUB) and AUB's Center for Arab and Middle Eastern Studies for a visiting fellowship; a Foreign Language and Area Studies Fellowship at the Hebrew University of Jerusalem; the Columbia-GSAS International Travel Fellowship and Columbia-LSE Research Exchange Fellowship in International History; and the Society for Historians of American Foreign Relations Dissertation Completion

Fellowship, renamed in blessed memory of the late Marilyn Young, who was an early advocate for this project, offering vital ideas and encouragement.

I am indebted to the archivists, librarians, and researchers who helped me locate material across multiple locations. In Jerusalem, Helena Vilensky, Galia Weissman, Louise Fischer, and Arnon Lamfrom provided assistance at the Israel State Archives and answered every query with pleasure and forbearance; Ziv Rubinovitz, Rami Shtivi, Dror Bar Yosef, Iris Berlatzky, Ori Rub, and Moshe Fuksman-Sha'al did the same at the Menachem Begin Heritage Center. In Atlanta, Keith Shuler, Brittany Parris, and Amanda Pellerin assisted at the Jimmy Carter Library; in Simi Valley, Kelly Barton and Shelly Williams assisted at the Ronald Reagan Library; and at Stanford, Carol Leadenham assisted at the Hoover Institution Archives. I am also grateful to Mary Curry at the National Security Archive and Patrick Kerwin and Ernest Emrich at the Library of Congress in Washington, D.C.; Laura Russo and Katelynn Vance at the Howard Gotlieb Archival Research Center at Boston University; Mary Marshall Clark at Columbia University's Center for Oral History; Shelley Helfand at the JDC Archives in New York; and Patrick Salmon and Richard Smith at the Foreign and Commonwealth Office in London. In Beirut, Jeanette Serouphim and Mona Nsouli offered invaluable help at the Institute for Palestine Studies. A chance visit to the Arab Image Foundation as well as a tip from Maral Mikirditsian led to a discovery and meeting with Akram Zaatari that proved fortuitous in researching and writing about 1982, pushing me in exciting new directions.

Numerous colleagues and friends offered invaluable assistance on various aspects of this project—often from their own areas of expertise or works in progress—a constant reminder that no researcher works in isolation. They provided crucial insight and feedback, shared additional documents and source suggestions, facilitated key introductions, and invited me to present parts of this work in venues that helped me make sense of what I found and figure out what I wanted to say. I am tremendously grateful to Andrew Arsan, Nigel Ashton, Bernard Avishai, Laila Ballout, Nadim Bawalsa, Steven Bayme, Peter Beinart, Omri Ben Yehuda, Maher Bitar, Rosie Bsheer, John Chalcraft, Paul Chamberlin, George Chauncey,

Helena Cobban, Sylvain Cypel, Ahmed Dailami, Sidra DeKoven Ezrahi, Raffaella Del Sarto, Andrea Dessì, Khaled Fahmy, Dina Fainberg, Samuel Freedman, Fawaz Gerges, Moti Gigi, Natasha Gill, Amos Goldberg, Ron Gregg, Jonathan Gribetz, Judith Gurewich, Dotan Halevy, Shaun Halper, Amira Hass, Shay Hazkani, Susannah Heschel, Sara Hirschhorn, Jonathan Hunt, Anne Irfan, Gail Israelson, Simon Jackson, Hazem Jamjoum, Jennifer Johnson, Charlie Keiden, Linda Kerber, Osamah Khalil, Kristine Khouri, Nathan Kurz, Lior Lehrs, Daniel Levy, Gideon Lichfield, Kristen Loveland, Ian Lustick, Liz Marcus, Jessica Marglin, Lenore Martin, Victor McFarland, Tom Meaney, Nancy Mitchell, Dirk Moses, David Myers, Zev Nagel, Jacob Norris, Derek Penslar, Mezna Qato, Jon Randal, Avi Raz, Shira Robinson, Aaron Rock-Singer, Doug Rossinow, Daniel Sargent, Tehila Sasson, Suzanne Schneider, Noa Schonmann, Rona Sela, Olivia Sohns, Steven Spiegel, Sophia Stamatopoulou-Robbins, Rebecca Steinfeld, Eli Stern, Rafi Stern, Simon Stevens, Dan Strieff, Salim Tamari, Hagai and Judith Tamir; Laura van Waas, Vanessa Walker, Stephen Wertheim, Lawrence Wright, Yael Zerubavel, Daniel Zoughbie, and the late Tony Judt.

Since joining the faculty at University College London (UCL) in the fall of 2015, all of my colleagues in the Department of Hebrew and Jewish Studies and across UCL have made me feel welcome and provided an academic home that manages to be both intimate and expansive in reach. Along with my students, they have afforded me an opportunity to discuss and present material within wider contexts, as well as the time and space to complete this book, especially during the final dash to submission.

Well before the project was even finished, Fred Appel expressed enthusiasm and offered expert guidance, shepherding the proposal and manuscript through review with keen insights and suggestions of his own that have enhanced the clarity and argument of the text. The entire team at Princeton University Press has been a delight to work with, and I am grateful to Thalia Leaf for her swift editorial assistance, Nathan Carr for his nimble production work, and Jenn Backer for her exceptional copyediting while meeting a tight deadline. The detailed feedback and constructive recommendations from the peer reviewers were more than any author could expect. It was especially heartening that two individuals who later disclosed their involvement were Salim Yaqub and Brad Simpson, given how much I have benefited from their respective scholarly contributions and professional example.

Alongside her camaraderie and hospitality, a one-on-one writing group with Victoria Phillips helped me through the painful chapter revision process. Gershom Gorenberg has been a dedicated guide into the history of Israel and the settlements as well as a teacher of narrative writing, making his reactions to the preface and introduction particularly useful. After sitting for an interview that lasted far more hours than he bargained for, Henry Siegman brought me into the U.S./Middle East Project, and he and Susan Eisenstat took me under their wing, with a striking depth of mutual understanding that provided a sounding board while I was writing and thoughtful feedback on various sections. With generous and incisive readings of the full manuscript, Ahmad Khalidi and Gershon Shafir provided dual anchors in Palestinian and Israeli politics and history. At a very late stage and with remarkable speed, William Quandt carefully combed through the text and offered invaluable comments; he has been a tremendous resource in other ways, not least as a practitioner and scholar of this period.

One of the great joys of working on contemporary history has been the opportunity to interview many of those who participated in or witnessed the events under examination and to call upon them in weighing oral history against the written record. I am eminently grateful to all those who gave of their time and agreed to my interview requests, sharing their recollections with frankness and detail, opening new avenues of inquiry, and providing context and texture where it was lacking. Like all those who assisted with this book, I alone am responsible for any errors or faults of interpretation that may have resulted.

For their kind cooperation in facilitating permission for photographic reproduction, I am grateful to the Palestine Poster Project Archives and Liberation Graphics (Dan Walsh and Amer Shomali); the Jimmy Carter Library (Sara Mitchell); Israel's Government Press Office (Ilana Dayan); and the National Archives. Shane Kelley worked seamlessly to create precise maps, with statistical details and crucial information provided by Hagit Ofran of Peace Now, Lara Friedman of the Foundation for Middle East Peace, Shaul

Arieli, Aliza Peleg of Israel's Central Bureau of Statistics, and Yair Assaf-Shapira of the Jerusalem Institute for Israel Studies.

I published partial findings on the Sabra and Shatila massacre discussed in chapter 6 in the *New York Times* as "A Preventable Massacre" (September 16, 2012), alongside key documents obtained from the Israel State Archives. Sasha Polakow-Suransky and Sewell Chan were peerless advocates and editors in pursuit of publication and have remained stalwart supporters as I worked on the book. Material from other previously published articles has been reprinted or incorporated with permission from the University of Pennsylvania Press, the University of California Press, and the Foreign Policy Association.

Several devoted friends accompanied me along this project, understanding when I vanished and when I needed to be pulled away from my desk. Brook Armstrong was there from the start, helping me find my footing; Chanani Gillers and Rebecca Klein were mainstays in New York; Daniel Altschuler, Ariana Berengaut, Marc Grinberg, Shadi Hamid, Florian Hoffmann, Lea Neubert, and Nahid Siamdoust coalesced in Oxford and spread far beyond; Josh Hersh and Ramzi Mezher appeared in Lebanon; and Sally Davies, Virginia Forbes, Lisa Jepson, and Jill Waters in London. Fred Meiton read and reread more versions of this book than he should have ever agreed to, enduring the highs and lows with stoic assurances, ample needling, and wit. Natasha Wheatley was a cherished roommate and brilliant interlocutor during countless formative moments in the life of this text and its grateful author.

On the eve of an exploratory research trip to the Middle East, an e-mail introduction changed the course of my life. Tareq has opened my eyes to the world in ways I am still coming to appreciate, showing me the meaning of empathy with infinite patience and grace. Along with a great deal of laughter, his intuitive ability to navigate through the hardest terrain drew me away from the study of historical and political misfortune into the bracing adventures of the present.

IN THE FIRST STAGES of the research for this book, I was often asked if it was too early to write histories of the 1970s and 1980s. Relatively assured at the time that it wasn't, I have become ever more certain of the importance and reward of investigating this recent past. The availability of a wide array of sources, much of it untapped by researchers, makes clear that there is a great deal yet to be discovered. One of the main challenges I have faced is the sheer volume of material and the opportunities—as well as clear limits—afforded by digitization.

For the U.S. perspective on Israel and the Palestinian question in this period, the publications of the Carter administration *FRUS* volumes on the Arab-Israeli dispute have been invaluable. The availability of additional volumes on North Africa, the Arabian Peninsula, and relevant themes like human rights provides further areas of exploration for the wider Middle East. The CIA's Records Search Tool (CREST) in College Park, Maryland, a revealing archive that had only been available onsite, is now accessible online. The Carter Presidential Library in Atlanta has a wide range of crucial material, and a great deal more was released to me in the course of Mandatory Review. Reagan-era *FRUS* volumes on the Middle East have not yet been released, but the Reagan Presidential Library in Simi Valley, California, provides ample material on many relevant topics and further releases via Mandatory Review as well. The limits of American documents are well known, given the severe backlog in release schedules and the widespread use of redactions on material relating to national security, broadly defined. But FOIA and Mandatory Review requests yield results, even several years after submission, creating a wider source base and additional opportunities for future researchers.

Though I was not initially expecting to find the most sensitive documents from this period, the Israel State Archives in Jerusalem turned out to be a treasure trove. Among the revelations were files scattered across newly opened collections on the Camp

David negotiations, the autonomy talks, U.S.-Israel relations, Jewish diaspora politics, and the 1982 Lebanon War. In particular, the generous declassification policy and excellent records from the Prime Minister's division and the Ministry of Foreign Affairs, in both Hebrew and English, provide a rich (and unredacted) source base, often including replica copies of American documents and verbatim Israeli transcripts of conversations that will not be opened in the United States. Many official meetings were conducted in English, although side meetings and bilateral discussions between Israeli and American diplomats were often recorded in Hebrew, along with legal memoranda and internal ministry discussions that are also available in Hebrew.

While this is a remarkable source base and covers a broad range of topics, not only related to Israel and the Palestinians, a word of caution is in order. A recent move to digitize the Israel State Archives and attendant debates over declassification and redaction have made physical access to the documents more difficult. The clear limits to digitization are also evident when coupled with the inability of researchers to rifle through boxes and files where meaningful adjacencies can be discovered, leading to new lines of inquiry that are simply not possible via computer alone. There have also been notable instances of sensitive material being reclassified. This is not to mention the broader structural challenge of researchers being denied access into Israel on the basis of political views or ethnicity as well as restrictions on movement for Palestinians in the West Bank and Gaza Strip seeking material (often about their own history) located inside Israeli archives. In this vein, the heroic work and online publication of relevant material by Akevot, the Institute for Israeli-Palestinian Conflict Research, as well as the struggles over access and declassification waged by individual researchers, must be noted. In Jerusalem, I also examined the private papers of Prime Minister Menachem Begin held at the Menachem Begin Heritage Center. These records include copious correspondence, policy formulations, and detailed exchanges between Begin's advisors. In Tel Aviv, the Jabotinsky Institute contains records of the Herut movement and the Likud.

At a crucial stage in my research, I was given access to sensitive documents from the unpublished appendix of the Kahan

Commission of Inquiry into the Sabra and Shatila massacre. The documents were provided by William Quandt, Professor Emeritus of Politics at the University of Virginia and staff member of the National Security Council during the Administration of President Jimmy Carter. In the course of Ariel Sharon's libel lawsuit against *Time* magazine, Quandt served as a consultant to *Time* and received the documents from the magazine's lawyers after the lawsuit had been resolved. As I state on page 375, note 104, experts who have seen them, including Israeli sources who are familiar with such documents, recognize them as the authentic text of the Kahan Commission Report unpublished appendix. The revelations these documents yield are discussed in chapter 6. For further information related to this material please visit the book's website at https://press.princeton.edu/titles/13225.html.

In tracing the perspective of Egyptians and the PLO, historians must confront a more limited primary source base, a result in part of the asymmetrical nature of negotiations over the Palestinian question. This disparity is also the result of restricted Egyptian access for government material on this period and the absence of state institutions and a national archive in the case of the Palestinians. Key Palestinian collections were also captured or destroyed by Israel in the 1982 Lebanon War. Nevertheless, PLO traces within U.S. diplomatic records as well as Palestinian private archives and official publications can yield a far more complete account of events. Some crucial Egyptian records were also provided to the Palestinian delegation ahead of the Madrid Conference talks, and these have been consulted via access generously granted by Rashid Khalidi, a Palestinian advisor and later participant in the Madrid and Washington negotiations. A portion of the records have been uploaded to the website of the Institute for Palestine Studies as an open source archive. When drawing upon the documents, I have cited them as Papers of the Palestinian Delegation to the Palestinian-Israeli Negotiations (PPD) and included links for those available online.

To recover the broader political voice of Palestinians, I examined archival material available exclusively in Lebanon, at Beirut's Institute for Palestine Studies (IPS). This essential archive contains extensive documents, newspapers, and bulletins published in Arabic and English by various Palestinian factions throughout this period. The IPS also holds a full series of the PLO's WAFA news agency reports, issued daily during the height of the Lebanese civil war and an invaluable source for understanding how Palestinians navigated the Israeli and American military presence in Lebanon. Online, *The Palestinian Revolution* is a newly available digital archive with a growing collection of primary sources, visual material, and oral history interviews on this period, and the Palestine Poster Project Archives contains further visual material as well. Lebanese archives consulted include the Arab Image Foundation in Gemmayze, Beirut, and the UMAM Documentation and Research Center in Harat Hreik, Beirut, both of which hold vital photographic and archival material.

For international context and a non-American perspective on Israel, the Palestinians, and the wider Middle East, I drew on newly opened files at the National Archives of the United Kingdom in Kew, London. These include the papers of British prime ministers James Callaghan and Margaret Thatcher (PREM) and the extensive files of the Foreign Office (FCO). Several crucial documents were released to me by Freedom of Information request as well. For the domestic influence of a key interest group in the United States, I consulted the collections of leading American Jewish organizations, including the Dorot Division of the New York Public Library, the American Jewish Congress papers at the American Jewish Historical Society, and the archives of the American Jewish Committee and the Joint Distribution Committee in New York City.

Across this period, I also consulted a range of donated collections at Boston University's Howard Gotlieb Archival Research Center, Stanford University's Hoover Institution Archives, Yale University's Manuscript Division, the Library of Congress Manuscript Division, and the National Security Archive in Washington, D.C. Access was also kindly granted to the personal papers of Henry Siegman, the former head of the American Jewish Congress (1978–1994), and Professor Ian Lustick, who was an analyst at the State Department's Bureau of Intelligence and Research during the autonomy negotiations.

Lastly, I conducted over thirty oral history interviews with retired diplomats, politicians, communal leaders, and military veterans across the United States, United Kingdom, Israel, Palestine, and Lebanon. While not all the interviews have been quoted directly, several served as background for pursuing various avenues of archival research. I also consulted existing oral history collections in many of these locations, including the Liddell Hart Centre for Military Archives at King's College London, the Avraham Harman Institute of Contemporary Jewry at the Hebrew University of Jerusalem, Columbia University's Center for Oral History, and several online repositories.

CCOH Columbia Center for Oral History Archives

CREST Central Intelligence Agency Records Search Tool

DDRS Declassified Documents Reference System

FRUS *Foreign Relations of the United States*

HIA Hoover Institution Archives

IPS Institute for Palestine Studies

ISA Israel State Archives

JCL Jimmy Carter Library

KCD Kahan Commission Documents

LOC Library of Congress

MBC Menachem Begin Heritage Center

MERIP *Middle East Research and Information Project*

NARA National Archives and Records Administration

NSA National Security Affairs

NSC National Security Council

PHE Papers of Hermann Eilts

PPD Papers of the Palestinian Delegation to the Palestinian-Israeli Negotiations

PPPJC *Public Papers of the Presidents: Jimmy Carter*

PPPRR *Public Papers of the Presidents: Ronald Reagan*

RRL Ronald Reagan Library

UKNA United Kingdom National Archives

YUL Yale University Library

NOTES

Preface: The Road from Gush Etzion

1. Jacob Magid, "Marking 50 Years of Settlements, PM Vows They Will Never Be Uprooted," *Times of Israel*, 27 September 2017, https://www.timesofisrael.com /marking-50-years-of-settlements-pm-vows-they-will-never-be-uprooted/; Yotam Berger, "Netanyahu at Settlement Jubilee Ceremony: There Will Be No More Uprooting," *Haaretz*, 27 September 2017, https://www.haaretz.com/israel-news/1.814667; "Netanyahu Vows Settlements Are Here to Stay at West Bank Ceremony," *Jewish Telegraphic Agency*, 28 September 2017, https://www.jta.org/2017/09/28/news-opinion /israel-middle-east/netanyahu-vows-settlements-are-here-to-stay-at-west-bank -ceremony.

2. Morris, *Righteous Victims*, 214; David B. Green, "This Day in Jewish History/ Reestablishing a Kibbutz," *Haaretz*, 25 September 2012, http://www.haaretz.com /jewish/features/this-day-in-jewish-history-reestablishing-a-kibbutz-1.466709.

3. See Gershom Gorenberg, "Israel's Tragedy Foretold," *New York Times*, 10 March 2006, http://www.nytimes.com/2006/03/10/opinion/israels-tragedy-foretold.html.

4. Shafir, *A Half Century of Occupation*, 68; Yotam Berger, "How Many Settlers Really Live in the West Bank?" *Haaretz*, 15 June 2017, https://www.haaretz.com/israel -news/.premium-1.794730.

5. Jonathan Lis, "Israel to Commemorate Six Day War in Event at West Bank Settlement of Gush Etzion," *Haaretz*, 6 April 2017, https://www.haaretz.com/israel -news/.premium-1.781878.

6. Ibid.

7. See Inbari, *Messianic Religious Zionism Confronts Israeli Territorial Compromises*, 72–80; David B. Green, "A Yeshiva Head and Settler Who Had a Change of Heart Is Born," *Haaretz*, 31 October 2014, https://www.haaretz.com/jewish/features /.premium-1.623687.

8. See his address "On the Assassination of Prime Minister Rabin Z"L," 6 November 1995, reprinted in *Alei Etzion*, vol. 4, Yeshivat Har Etzion, http://www.haretzion .org/torah/yeshiva-publications/154-alei-etzion.

9. See Hirschhorn, *City on a Hilltop*, 98–142.

10. Magid, "Marking 50 Years of Settlements."

Introduction

1. Jimmy Carter, "America Must Recognize Palestine," *New York Times*, 28 November 2016, https://www.nytimes.com/2016/11/28/opinion/jimmy-carter-america-must -recognize-palestine.html.

2. For the corrosive influence of the occupation, see Shehadeh, *Palestinian Walks*. On legal efforts to confront the consequences, see Sfard, *The Wall and the Gate*.

3. Jimmy Carter, "The President's News Conference," 12 May 1977, *Public Papers of the Presidents: Jimmy Carter, 1977–1981* (hereafter *PPPJC*), accessed in Gerhard Peters and John T. Woolley, *The American Presidency Project*, http://www.presidency.ucsb.edu/ws/?pid=7495.

4. See Stein, *Heroic Diplomacy*; Wright, *Thirteen Days in September*; Podeh, *Chances for Peace*, 137–56; Golan, *Israeli Peacemaking since 1967*, 29–56; and Galia Golan, "Sadat and Begin: Successful Diplomacy to Peace," in Hutchings and Suri, eds., *Foreign Policy Breakthroughs*, 121–47.

5. The leading accounts of Camp David, discussed in chapter 4 (note 27), tend to focus exclusively on the summit or the immediate events surrounding it and rely predominantly on U.S. sources. This work draws on an international source base with access to newly available records extending from the 1970s into the 1990s.

6. On the meaning of sovereignty and its "indeterminancy" as a central feature of legal contestation, see Koskenniemi, "The Many Faces of Sovereignty." The implications for Palestinian political aspirations are worth considering in this context. For an investigation of the concept's role in Jewish and Israeli discourse, see Yadgar, *Sovereign Jews*.

7. On nationalist and messianic impulses, see Leibowitz, *Judaism, Human Values, and the Jewish State*; and Ravitzky, *Messianism, Zionism, and Jewish Religious Radicalism*. On secular fervor, see Laor, "The Last Chapter."

8. On 1967, see Laron, *The Six-Day War and the Breaking of the Middle East*; Louis and Shlaim, *The 1967 Arab-Israeli War*; and Segev, *1967*. On voices of dissent, see Shapira, *The Seventh Day*; and Gili Izikovich, "The Seventh Day: Censored Voices from the 1967 War," *Haaretz*, 7 June 2015, http://www.haaretz.com/israel-news/1.659923.

9. On the fiftieth anniversary of the war, the Israel State Archives released detailed minutes of the discussions. For the digital version, see http://www.archives.gov.il/en/publication/cabinet_sixdaywar-en/. On the vexed role of the West Bank in illuminating the differences in state policy before 1967 and after, see Rubin, *The Limits of the Land*.

10. Raz, *The Bride and the Dowry*, 44. Menachem Begin used this precise phrase in a cabinet remark on 10 September 1967. See Raz, *The Bride and the Dowry*, 301n101. In his incisive and groundbreaking study, Raz documents the Israeli treatment of Palestinian refugees after 1967 and demonstrates that there was a deliberate attempt to appropriate the captured territories (the "dowry") while permitting as few Arab inhabitants as possible to remain (the "bride"). The implications of this broader Israeli strategy in the Arab world are examined by Shlaim in "The Iron Wall Revisited."

11. For the authoritative account of the origins of the settlement project and its growth during this period, see Gorenberg, *The Accidental Empire*. On early American reactions to construction in the Johnson White House, see Ben-Ephraim, "Distraction and Deception." On the initial development of Israel's civilian and economic

policies in the territories, see "The Committee of Directors-General: Meeting Minutes, 1967–1977," available online via Akevot, the Institute for Israeli-Palestinian Conflict Research, http://akevot.org.il/en/article/directors-general-committee-1967 -1977/. On the secular—not religious—origins of the settlements, see Gorenberg, "Settlements: The Real Story," *The American Prospect*, 26 June 2017, http://prospect .org/article/settlements-real-story. For the wider history of the settlements, see Zertal and Eldar, *Lords of the Land*; Gazit, *Trapped Fools*; and Benvenisti, *The West Bank Data Base Project*.

12. For background on Gush Emunim and their role in the settlement project, see Zertal and Eldar, *Lords of the Land*; Feige, *Settling in the Hearts*; Sprinzak, *The Ascendance of Israel's Radical Right*; Pedahzur, *The Triumph of Israel's Radical Right*; Friedman, *Zealots for Zion*; Lustick, *For the Land and the Lord*; and Newman, *The Impact of Gush Emunim* and "From Hitnachalut to Hitnatkut."

13. On the history and practices of the occupation, see Shafir, *A Half Century of Occupation*; Weizman, *Hollow Land*; Gordon, *Israel's Occupation*; and Azoulay and Ophir, *The One State Condition*.

14. On 1948, see Sa'di and Abu-Lughod, *Nakba*; Khalidi, *All That Remains*; and Morris, *The Birth of the Palestinian Refugee Problem Revisited*. U.S. policymakers, for example, focused exclusively on the humanitarian needs of Palestinian refugees rather than the political dimension of their dispossession. This approach was reflected in the extensive support for the refugee resettlement work of the United Nations Relief Works Agency (UNRWA).

15. For the leading periodizations of Palestinian political history, see Sayigh, *Armed Struggle*; Baumgarten, "The Three Faces/Phases of Palestinian Nationalism"; Khalidi, *The Iron Cage*; and Dakkak, "Back to Square One."

16. See Ahmad Samih Khalidi, "Ripples of the 1967 War," *Cairo Review of Global Affairs*, Spring 2017, https://www.thecairoreview.com/essays/ripples-of-the-1967 -war; the chapters by Pearlman, Khalidi, and Gerges in Louis and Shlaim, eds., *The 1967 Arab-Israeli War*; and al-Hout, *My Life in the PLO*, 119–30. On Arab intellectual self-critique after 1967, see Kassab, *Contemporary Arab Thought*.

17. On Palestinian nationalism and the PLO, see Quandt, Jabber, and Lesch, *The Politics of Palestinian Nationalism*; Rubin, *Revolution until Victory?*; Gresh, *The PLO*; Cobban, *The Palestinian Liberation Organization*; and al-Hout, *My Life in the PLO*.

18. See Chamberlin, *The Global Offensive*. This had a reverse dynamic as well, with the Palestinian question a constitutive part of regional decolonization. See Harrison, *Transcolonial Maghreb*. On the history of decolonization, see Jansen and Osterhammel, *Decolonization*.

19. Quandt, "Forty Years in Search of Arab-Israeli Peace," 25. On Johnson and 1967, see Sohns, "Lyndon Baines Johnson and the Arab-Israeli Conflict." I have also drawn on Anziska, "Israel and the U.S." in this introduction.

20. On the making of resolution 242, see Ashton, "Searching for a Just and Lasting Peace?"

21. See Chamberlin, *The Global Offensive*. On the wider history of the Palestinian armed liberation struggle, including revolutionary practice and thought, see the

extensive resources compiled in Karma Nabulsi and Abdel Razzaq Takriti, *The Palestinian Revolution*, 2016, http://learnpalestine.politics.ox.ac.uk/.

22. See Muslih, *Toward Coexistence*; and Sela, "The PLO at Fifty."

23. See Christison, *Perceptions of Palestine*; Khalil, "Pax Americana"; McAlister, *Epic Encounters*; and Saunders, *The Other Walls*, 9.

24. On Sadat, see Hirst and Beeson, *Sadat*; and Sadat, *In Search of Identity*.

25. See Daigle, *The Limits of Détente*. For the domestic Egyptian background and consequences, see Kandil, *Soldiers, Spies, and Statesmen*, 113–74.

26. On 1973, see Rabinovich, *The Yom Kippur War*; Kipnis, *1973*; and Ginor and Remez, *The Soviet-Israeli War*.

27. For the text of the resolution, see Laqueur and Rubin, *The Israel-Arab Reader*, 152.

28. On the Agranat Commission, see Molchadsky, "History in the Public Courtroom," 119–64. On Meir, see Klagsbrun, *Lioness*.

29. See Salim Yaqub, "The Weight of Conquest: Henry Kissinger and the Arab-Israeli Conflict," in Logevall and Preston, eds., *Nixon in the World*, 227–48; and Fischer, "Turning Point on the Road to Peace." On Rabin, see Rabinovich, *Yitzhak Rabin*.

30. See Chamberlin, *The Global Offensive*, 218–56.

31. "Interim Agreement between Israel and Egypt (Sinai II)," United Nations Peacemaker, https://peacemaker.un.org/egyptisrael-interimagreement75.

32. See Hanhimäki, *The Flawed Architect*, 302–31.

33. See Yaqub, "The Weight of Conquest."

34. For detailed analysis of this agreement and its historical context, see Khalil, "Oslo's Roots."

35. On the U.S. relationship with the Global South during this period, see Byrnes, "The United States in Opposition."

36. See Sargent, *A Superpower Transformed*; and Schulman and Zelizer, *Rightward Bound*. The rise of human rights in the 1970s is a burgeoning subfield. For crucial framing, see Moyn, *The Last Utopia*, 120–75; and Eckel and Moyn, *The Breakthrough*. On the domestic U.S. context, especially the role (and limits) of the Carter presidency, see Keys, *Reclaiming American Virtue*. For a regional critique, see the roundtable by Allen et al., "Problematics of Human Rights and Humanitarianism."

37. This would carry into his presidency. See Glad, *An Outsider in the White House*; Kaufman, *Plans Unraveled*; and Mitchell, *Jimmy Carter in Africa*.

38. Committee on House Administration, U.S. House of Representatives, *The Presidential Campaign 1976*, vol. 1, part 1, 217.

39. See Carter, "The President's News Conference," 12 May 1977. On the limits of self-determination in Carter's mind, see Nemchenok, "'These People Have an Irrevocable Right to Self-Government.'"

40. Morris, *Righteous Victims*, 488. See also Shlaim, *The Iron Wall*, 391–93; Quandt, *Peace Process*, 237–40; and Tessler, *A History of the Israeli-Palestinian Conflict*, 518–20. Others who have written about the autonomy talks did so without access to the primary records of the negotiations, which have only recently been opened to

researchers. See Gazit, *Trapped Fools*; Newman and Falah, "Bridging the Gap"; Sicherman, *Palestinian Autonomy, Self-Government and Peace*; Peleg, *Begin's Foreign Policy*; Plascov, "The 'Palestinian Gap' between Israel and Egypt"; Kieval, *Party Politics in Israel and the Occupied Territories*; and Bruzonsky, "America's Palestinian Predicament." One important study of autonomy's ideological underpinnings, based on Israeli sources, is Rubinovitz and Steinberg, "Menachem Begin's Autonomy Plan." In several crucial articles published soon after his stint in the State Department's Bureau of Intelligence and Research dealing with autonomy, political scientist Ian Lustick provided contemporaneous accounts that outlined the U.S. role in the talks. See Lustick, "Saving Camp David: Kill the Autonomy Talks"; Lustick, "Israeli Politics and American Foreign Policy"; and Lustick, "Two-State Illusion," *New York Times*, 15 September 2013.

41. See, for example, Ross, *The Missing Peace*; Miller, *The Much Too Promised Land*; Indyk, *Innocent Abroad*; and Kurtzer et al., *The Peace Puzzle*. A similar dynamic plays out with Israeli chroniclers. See Hirschfeld, *Track-Two Diplomacy*; Savir, *The Process*; and Rabinovich, *The Lingering Conflict*.

42. See Pressman, "Explaining the Carter Administration's Israeli-Palestinian Solution."

43. See Anziska, "Neither Two States nor One."

44. See the discussion of these records and Egyptian enablement in chapter 4, esp. notes 151–53.

45. That fateful year also saw the escalation of further global conflict, from revolution in Nicaragua to the revelation of a Soviet brigade in Cuba. A strong case for rethinking historical periodization in the Middle East around that year can be found in Bozarslan, "Revisiting the Middle East's 1979." See also Caryl, *Strange Rebels*.

46. Revisionist accounts of the Carter administration argue that the thirty-ninth president played an influential role in increasing American defense spending and formulating a more aggressive stance toward the Soviet Union. See, for example, Olav Njølstad, "The Carter Legacy: Entering the Second Era of the Cold War," in Njølstad, ed., *The Last Decade of the Cold War*, 196–225; Auten, *Carter's Conversion*; Sargent, *A Superpower Transformed*, 261–95; and Nancy Mitchell, "The Cold War and Jimmy Carter," in Leffler and Westad, eds., *The Cambridge History of the Cold War*, vol. 3, *Endings*, 66–88.

47. On the Carter Doctrine, see Stork, "The Carter Doctrine and U.S. Bases in the Middle East." On the shifting U.S. posture into the 1980s, see Crist, *The Twilight War*; Njølstad, "Shifting Priorities"; Odom, "The Cold War Origins of the U.S. Central Command"; and Davidson, "Visions of Political Islam and the American Military Presence in the Middle East." For evidence of continuities with the muscular approach of the Reagan years, see Gardner, *The Long Road to Baghdad*; and Grandin, *Empire's Workshop*.

48. While several scholars and journalists have drawn attention to the broader international history of the region during the twentieth century, the 1970s and 1980s remain understudied. For leading examples of the region's international history, see Schayegh, *The Middle East and the Making of the Modern World*; Ferris, *Nasser's Gamble*; Makdisi, *Faith Misplaced*; Yaqub, *Containing Arab Nationalism*;

Connelly, *A Diplomatic Revolution*; Alvandi, *Nixon, Kissinger, and the Shah*; Polakow-Suransky, *The Unspoken Alliance*; Bass, *Support Any Friend*; Byrne, *Mecca of Revolution*; Citino, *Envisioning the Arab Future*; Khalil, *America's Dream Palace*; Stocker, *Spheres of Intervention*; Gendzier, *Dying to Forget*; Bacevich, *America's War for the Greater Middle East*; Tyler, *A World of Trouble*; Little, *American Orientalism*; Daigle, *The Limits of Détente*; Jacobs, *Imagining the Middle East*; Hahn, *Caught in the Middle East*; Khalidi, *Sowing Crisis*; and Migdal, *Shifting Sands*. For recent work on the 1970s, see Chamberlin, *The Global Offensive*; and Yaqub, *Imperfect Strangers*.

49. Some leading examples are Berda, *Living Emergency*; Hajjar, *Courting Conflict*; Kretzmer, *The Occupation of Justice*; Ophir, Givoni, and Hanafi, *The Power of Inclusive Exclusion*; and Shehadeh, *Occupier's Law*. Ra'anan Alexandrowicz's 2011 documentary film, *Shilton Ha'Chok* [The law in these parts], painstakingly reconstructs the development of the legal regime in the territories during this period. On the question of the occupation's visibility, see Hochberg, *Visual Occupations*.

50. In addition to offering a critical assessment of the concept of "self-determination," the Palestinian question clearly illustrates the limits of the nation-state framework within postwar historical writing. It also highlights the complex interplay between sovereignty and liberalism in U.S. internationalism. For a discussion of this theme, see Ryan M. Irwin, "Decolonization and the Cold War," in Kalinovsky and Daigle, eds., *The Routledge Handbook of the Cold War*, 91–104. On the travails of statehood, see Kamrava, *The Impossibility of Palestine*; and Nusseibeh, *What Is a Palestinian State Worth?*

Chapter One: Jimmy Carter's Vision

1. *The Presidential Campaign 1976*, vol. 1, part 1, 216–17. See also Charles Mohr, "Carter Gets an Ovation after Assuring Jews in Jersey on His Religious Views," *New York Times*, 7 June 1976, 22.

2. Two prominent Jewish political activists involved with the campaign affirmed this sentiment. See Reminiscences of Stuart Eizenstat (1977), 4–8 and Reminiscences of Rita Hauser (1978), 16, both in *Ethnic Groups and American Foreign Policy Project*, Columbia Center for Oral History Archives, Rare Book & Manuscript Library, Columbia University in the City of New York (hereafter CCOH). See also Tivnan, *The Lobby*, 98–99.

3. Reminiscences of Stuart Eizenstat (1977), 5, CCOH.

4. *The Presidential Campaign 1976*, vol. 1, part 1, 216–17.

5. Sympathy toward Jewish aspirations for statehood was far more widespread in the United States than an understanding of Arab concerns. See Grose, *Israel in the Mind of America*; Mart, *Eye on Israel*; and Christison, *Perceptions of Palestine*.

6. *The Presidential Campaign 1976*, vol. 1, part 1, 216–17.

7. Ibid., 220.

8. "Israel's Survival Key to Real Peace: Carter," *Southern Israelite*, 11 June 1976, http://dlg.galileo.usg.edu/israelite/id:asi1976-0424.

9. Closed interview, background only (1977), 3, CCOH.

10. Carter, *Keeping Faith*, 281. For Carter's religious motivations, see Merkley, *American Presidents, Religion, and Israel*, 87–148; Balmer, *Redeemer*; and McDonald, "Blessed Are the Policy Makers." Also see Carter's own religiously inspired work on this conflict, *The Blood of Abraham*.

11. See Christison, *Perceptions of Palestine*, 157–94; and Janice J. Terry, "The Carter Administration and the Palestinians," in Suleiman, ed., *U.S. Policy on Palestine from Wilson to Clinton*, 163–74.

12. Carter, *Keeping Faith*, 282.

13. Mitchell, *Jimmy Carter in Africa*, 11–13.

14. Carter, *Keeping Faith*, 284.

15. Carter's position shifted drastically after he left office. See Carter, *Palestine: Peace Not Apartheid*; and Quandt, "Palestine, Apartheid, and Jimmy Carter." For his critics, see Joseph Lelyveld, "Jimmy Carter and Apartheid," *New York Review of Books*, 29 March 2007; and Stein, "My Problem with Jimmy Carter's Book."

16. On the Carter administration's strategic view of Palestinian rights, see Nemchenok, "'These People Have an Irrevocable Right to Self-Government.'" On the complicated U.S. relationship to self-determination, see Simpson, "The United States and the Curious History of Self-Determination."

17. Memo from Zbigniew Brzezinski, Richard Gardner, and Henry Owen to Governor Jimmy Carter, 3 November 1976, Box 9, Folder 19, Cyrus R. and Grace Sloane Vance Papers (MS 1664), Manuscripts and Archives, Yale University Library (hereafter YUL).

18. Ibid.

19. Brzezinski, *Power and Principle*, 6.

20. On Brzezinski's statecraft, see Gati, *Zbig*.

21. On Carter's approach and the role of human rights, see Clymer, "Jimmy Carter, Human Rights, and Cambodia"; Schmitz and Walker, "Jimmy Carter and the Foreign Policy of Human Rights"; Schmidli, "Institutionalizing Human Rights in U.S. Foreign Policy"; Mitchell, "The Cold War and Jimmy Carter"; and Sargent, *A Superpower Transformed*, 250–60.

22. See "Memorandum of Conversation," 20 November 1976, Plains, Georgia, Box 8, Folder 6, Vance Papers, YUL.

23. Brzezinski, *Power and Principle*, 84.

24. Members of the Brookings Study Group consisted of policy advisors, academics, and communal leaders. See *Toward Peace in the Middle East*. See also Jensehaugen, "Blueprint for Arab-Israeli Peace?"

25. Reminisces of Rita Hauser (1978), 9–10, CCOH; interview by author, New York, 11 January 2006.

26. *Toward Peace in the Middle East*, 2. One author of the report recalled a clear consensus that the national aspirations of the Palestinians had to be addressed, regardless of the exact terminology used. William Quandt, phone interview by author, 16 March 2006.

27. Reminiscences of Rita Hauser (1978), 20.

28. Christison, *Perceptions of Palestine*, 165.

29. Brzezinski, Duchêne, and Saeki, "Peace in an International Framework."

30. Memorandum of Conversation between Dayan and Brzezinski, Washington, 31 January 1977, 2:30–3:00 PM, *Foreign Relations of the United States, 1977–1980* (hereafter *FRUS*), vol. 8, Arab-Israeli Dispute, January 1977–August 1978, Document 2 (hereafter Doc.).

31. Ibid.

32. Ibid.

33. Ibid. See also Bar-On, *Moshe Dayan*.

34. Vance remains an understudied figure in the history of U.S. diplomacy. For recent exceptions, see Sexton, "The Wages of Principle and Power"; and Mitchell, *Jimmy Carter in Africa*.

35. Vance, *Hard Choices*, 164.

36. Ibid., 160.

37. Yaqub, *Imperfect Strangers*, 22.

38. Chamberlin, *The Global Offensive*, 14–16. For extensive biographies of the Palestinian leader, see Hart, *Arafat*; and Aburish, *Arafat*.

39. Yaqub, *Imperfect Strangers*, 22–23.

40. For an extensive examination of these internal tensions, see Sayigh, *Armed Struggle*; and Chamberlin, *The Global Offensive*. On Arafat's role, see Khalidi, *The Iron Cage*, 142–43; and Hussein Agha and Ahmad Samih Khalidi, "Yasser Arafat: Why He Still Matters," *The Guardian*, 13 November 2014, https://www.theguardian.com/news/2014/nov/13/-sp-yasser-arafat-why-he-still-matters.

41. Muslih, *Toward Coexistence*, viii–ix.

42. For the PLO's shift toward diplomacy after 1973, see Chamberlin, *The Global Offensive*, 218–56. Trial balloons toward compromise were launched during this period, which included a November 1973 article by PLO representative Said Hammami in the London *Times*, calling for the creation of a Palestinian state. See Hammami, "The Palestinian Way to Middle East Peace," *The Times*, 16 November 1973.

43. Yaqub, *Imperfect Strangers*, 163–65.

44. The idea of a state was spoken about frequently within the discourse of Palestinian politics, but it was not always embraced. For a representative but skeptical analysis in 1976, see Agha, "What State for the Palestinians?"; and in 1978, Khalidi, "Thinking the Unthinkable."

45. "Twelve Years . . . Palestine Lives," editorial, *Palestine: PLO Information Bulletin* 3 (January 1977): 4–5. All copies of *Palestine* were accessed in the library of the Institute for Palestine Studies, Beirut, Lebanon (hereafter IPS).

46. "1977: The Year of Giving and Revolutionary Dignity," *Palestine* 3 (January 1977): 6–7.

47. "Contacts with the PLO," confidential memo, Roger Tomkys, 14 January 1977, "Status of the PLO in the UK," FCO 93/1134, United Kingdom National Archives, Kew, London (hereafter UKNA).

48. Ibid.

49. In June 1980, the nine-member economic committee of the European Economic Community (EEC) would agree to acknowledge the Palestinian right to self-determination and PLO involvement in any peace initiative as part of the Venice Declaration.

50. On the emergence of Kissinger's pledge, see Chamberlin, *The Global Offensive*, 253–56.

51. For the introduction of the term by U.S. policymakers in the mid-1970s, see Saunders, *The Other Walls*, 36; and Quandt, *Peace Process*, 1. For a critique, see Khalidi, *Brokers of Deceit*.

52. The authoritative account of post-1967 efforts is Quandt, *Peace Process*.

53. They included Roy Atherton as assistant secretary for Near East and South Asia Affairs and Harold Saunders as director of intelligence and research and later Atherton's successor in the Near East Department. Both men had been involved in Arab-Israeli affairs for over fifteen years.

54. "The Israel/U.S. Relationship," Mason to White, 12 January 1977, "Political Relations between Israel and the USA," FCO 93/1151, UKNA.

55. Brzezinski, *Power and Principle*, 87.

56. Ibid., 88 (emphasis in original).

57. Proposal, "Possible Elements of a Middle East Settlement," February 1977, Zbigniew Brzezinski Collection, Geographic File, Jimmy Carter Library, Atlanta (hereafter JCL). This February 1977 document, nearly fifty pages long and likely authored by Harold Saunders with input from the Bureau of Intelligence and Research (INR), was circulated by William Quandt and contains extensive handwritten notes by Carter. It was released to the author in the summer of 2013 after a Mandatory Review request (MR-NLJC-2010-022) and further context was provided by Quandt, email to author, 26 August 2013.

58. "Israel-Egypt Introduction," in ibid.

59. For a brief window in 1949, secret negotiations were conducted between the Israeli leadership and Husni Al-Zaim for a peace treaty that would include the resettlement of Palestinian refugees in Syria and the delineation of a permanent border. See Shlaim, "Husni Zaim."

60. "Israel-Syria Introduction."

61. "West Bank, Gaza and the Palestinians: Introduction," in "Possible Elements of a Middle East Settlement."

62. Ibid.

63. Ibid.

64. Ibid.

65. "Jerusalem Summary," in "Possible Elements of a Middle East Settlement."

66. This would apply for Jerusalem and Hebron.

67. "Jerusalem Summary." The report added that "the idea of abandoning them would probably reduce to near zero the already slender chances of Israel agreeing to any solution of this sort."

68. The number suggested was ten thousand a year.

69. Carter's handwriting in "West Bank, Gaza, and the Palestinians Summary."

70. Cover note, Carter's handwriting, "Possible Elements of a Middle East Settlement."

71. Newlin to Vance, "Is Peace Achievable? A View from Jerusalem," Consulate Jerusalem to Department of State, Telegram 00206, 10 February 1977, 1977JERUSA00206, Central Foreign Policy Files, 1973–1979/Electronic Telegrams, RG 59: General Records

of the Department of State (GRDS), National Archives and Records Administration (hereafter NARA), 2, http://aad.archives.gov/aad/createpdf?rid=32004&dt=2532&dl =1629.

72. Ibid.

73. Rabinovich, *Yitzhak Rabin*, 98. For Rabin's first tenure as prime minister, see pp. 97–140.

74. Memorandum of Conversation, Jerusalem, 16 February 1977, 12:30 PM, *FRUS*, Doc. 7. Rabin did not believe that Israel should hold the bulk of the West Bank, in line with other Labor politicians at the time, and he was skeptical of those clinging to the entirety of the land even as he supported settlement building in certain areas. When asked by a settler about compromising the territory of the Etzion Bloc, for example, Rabin replied, "It won't be terrible if we go to Kfar Etzion with a visa." See Rabinovich, *Yitzhak Rabin*, 100, 122–27; and Rabin, *The Rabin Memoirs*, 331–34.

75. Telegram from Secretary of State Vance to the Department of State, 17 February 1977, 0101Z, *FRUS*, Doc. 8.

76. For critical appraisals after his death, see Tom Segev, "Shimon Peres: Not Just a Man of Peace," *New York Times*, 30 September 2016; and Hanan Ashrawi, "Shimon Peres: The Peacemaker Who Wasn't," *New York Times*, 3 October 2016.

77. For a sense of how this stance unfolded, see Gorenberg, *The Accidental Empire*, 129–62.

78. Telegram from Secretary of State Vance to the Department of State, 17 February 1977, 0101Z, *FRUS*, Doc. 8.

79. Memorandum of Conversation, Cairo, 17 February 1977, 12:30–2:30 PM, *FRUS*, Doc. 9.

80. See Bird, *The Good Spy*; Khalil, "The Radical Crescent"; and Stocker, "A Historical Inevitability?"

81. Memorandum of Conversation, Cairo, 17 February 1977, 12:30–2:30 PM, *FRUS*, Doc. 9.

82. Memorandum of Conversation, Cairo, 17 February 1977, 7:00–8:45 PM, *FRUS*, Doc. 10.

83. On Sadat's rise, see Kandil, *Soldiers, Spies, and Statesmen*, 99–174.

84. As Craig Daigle argued in *The Limits of Détente*, 1973 was Sadat's effort to break the logjam of détente.

85. Memorandum of Conversation, Cairo, 17 February 1977, 7:00–8:45 PM, *FRUS*, Doc. 10.

86. Telegram from Secretary of State Vance to the Department of State, Cairo, 17 February 1977, 2356Z, *FRUS*, Doc. 11.

87. Ibid.

88. Ibid.

89. For summaries of the meetings with King Hussein of Jordan and President Sarkis of Lebanon, see *FRUS*, Docs. 12–13.

90. Memorandum of Conversation, Damascus, 20 February 1977, *FRUS*, Doc. 15.

91. Vance recounted this private conversation, of which there is no record, at the 23 February NSC meeting discussed below.

92. Handwritten notes, 20–21 February 1977, Hotel Meridien Damas, Box 11, Folder 30, Vance Papers, YUL.

93. Minutes of a National Security Meeting, 23 February 1977, 9:00–9:35 AM, *FRUS*, Doc. 16.

94. Ibid.

95. Ibid. On Helsinki, see Snyder, *Human Rights Activism and the End of the Cold War*.

96. Memorandum from Brzezinski to Carter, "Follow-up on NSC Meeting on the Middle East," 23 February 1977, *FRUS*, Doc. 17.

97. See ibid., and corresponding footnotes 4 and 5 (emphasis in original).

98. Memorandum of Conversation, Washington, 7 March 1977, 11:00 AM–12:30 PM, *FRUS*, Doc. 18.

99. Ibid.

100. Ibid. See also Vance, *Hard Choices*, 170.

101. Memorandum of Conversation, Washington, 7 March 1977, 11:00 AM–12:30 PM, *FRUS*, Doc. 18.

102. Memorandum from Brzezinski to Carter, 7 March 1977, *FRUS*, Doc. 19.

103. Quandt, *Camp David*, 48.

104. Ibid., 43. Also see Vance, *Hard Choices*, 171. This had driven American diplomats to try to get the PLO to accept resolution 242.

105. Memorandum of Conversation, Washington, 8 March 1977, 10:35–11:30 AM, *FRUS*, Doc. 20.

106. Ibid.

107. Ibid.

108. See Brzezinski, *Power and Principle*, 90–91; Carter, *Keeping Faith*, 286–88; Rabin, *The Rabin Memoirs*, 292–300; Vance, *Hard Choices*, 168–73; and Quandt, *Camp David*, 46–51.

109. Rabin, *The Rabin Memoirs*, 294.

110. Ibid., 296.

111. Ibid. On Rabin's stance toward Carter, see also Rabinovich, *Yitzhak Rabin*, 136–39.

112. Notebooks of Stuart Eizenstat, 17 March 1977, Box 2, Stuart Eizenstat Papers, Manuscript Division, Library of Congress, Washington, DC (hereafter LOC).

113. Memorandum of Conversation, Washington, 9 March 1977, 6:45 PM, *FRUS*, Doc. 21.

114. For the most thorough account of the origins of the Conference of Presidents, clearly tracing it to the aftermath of the Qibya massacre, see Rossinow, "'The Edge of the Abyss.'"

115. Jimmy Carter, "Clinton, Massachusetts Remarks and a Question-and-Answer Session at the Clinton Town Meeting," *PPPJC*, 16 March 1977.

116. The issue remained a topic of conversation two months later, at a subsequent meeting of American Jewish leaders in the White House. See Memorandum of Conversation, 16 May 1977, 3:15–4:15 PM, *FRUS*, Doc. 34.

117. "Carter, the World and the Jews," *Time*, 27 June 1977, 9.

118. See the crucial "eyes only" memo by Hamilton Jordan to President Carter, "Politics and Foreign Policy," June 1977, *FRUS*, Doc. 38. This document lays out an incisive, well-reasoned, and comprehensive diagnosis of American Jewish political attitudes toward Israel, congressional voting trends, responses to Carter's approach, and recommendations for the easing of Jewish communal anxieties by the White House.

119. On Siegel's background, see Judy Bachrach, "The Man Who Walked out the White House Door," *Washington Post*, 24 March 1978, https://www.washingtonpost .com/archive/lifestyle/1978/03/24/the-man-who-walked-out-the-white-house-door /e9c1e5ad-ce89-4919-bc6c-4456732a8669/?utm_term=.887830e6ca07.

120. See Mark Siegel, "Jewish Identity, Zionism and Israel," 13 November 1978, Office of the Chief of Staff Files, 1977–1980, JCL, http://research.archives.gov/description /142156.

121. Ibid.

122. On the early role of these organizations in building the postwar liberal American state and the subsequent shift away from liberalism, see Svonkin, *Jews against Prejudice*; Dollinger, *Quest for Inclusion*; and Staub, *Torn at the Roots*.

123. See Kenen, *Israel's Defense Line*; Melman and Raviv, *Friends in Deed*; O'Brien, *American Jewish Organizations and Israel*; and Tivnan, *The Lobby*. For more critical views of the pro-Israel lobby, see Curtiss, *Stealth PACs*; Findley, *They Dare to Speak Out*; and Mearsheimer and Walt, *The Israel Lobby and U.S. Foreign Policy*. The 1953 Qibya massacre was an early moment of galvanization for American Jewish leaders around Israel and has been situated as the pivotal origin point of the Israel lobby. See Rossinow, "'The Edge of the Abyss.'"

124. Brzezinski, *Power and Principle*, 91.

125. Tivnan, *The Lobby*, 104.

126. *PPPJC*, 16 September 1977.

127. Brzezinski, *Power and Principle*, 91. Both Carter and Vance ignore the Clinton town hall remarks altogether in their memoirs.

128. In William Quandt's view, Carter was "impatient with fine diplomatic distinctions, with the taboos surrounding certain 'buzzwords,' and with the unimaginative and repetitive nature of many of the discussions of the topic." See Quandt, *Camp David*, 50.

129. See, for example, the controversy over Joan Peters and her claims about the Palestinians in *From Time Immemorial*; and Said and Hitchens, *Blaming the Victim*.

130. M. S. Weir to Private Secretary, 10 March 1977, Middle East, PREM 16/1370, UKNA.

131. "The Palestinian Homeland," *Palestine* 3 (May 1977): 3.

132. Ibid. By 1977, the organization had moved away from using the term "homeland" in favor of the phrase "independent national state."

133. Henry Tanner, "Why Not a Homeland or a State for the Palestinian Refugees?" *New York Times*, 10 April 1977, E1.

134. Ibid.

135. "Weekly National Security Report #7," Brzezinski to Carter, 1 April 1977, Box 41, Brzezinski Donated Collection, JCL.

136. Ibid.

137. Memorandum of Conversation, 4 April 1977, 11:10 AM–12:30 PM, *FRUS*, Doc. 25.

138. Ibid.

139. Egypt's minister of economy raised these concerns in discussions the following day. See Memorandum of Conversation, 5 April 1977, 10:45–11:45AM, *FRUS*, Doc. 27. On domestic transformations in Egypt, see Hinnebusch, *Egyptian Politics under Sadat*; and Meital, *Egypt's Struggle for Peace*.

140. Memorandum of Conversation, 25 April 1977, 11:05AM–12:15 PM, *FRUS*, Doc. 30.

141. See Shlaim, *Lion of Jordan*.

142. Memorandum of Conversation, 25 April 1977, 11:05AM–12:15 PM, *FRUS*, Doc. 30.

143. Minutes of a Policy Review Committee Meeting on the Middle East, 19 April 1977, 3:00–4:40 PM, *FRUS*, Doc. 28.

144. Memorandum of Conversation, Geneva, 9 May 1977, 3:50–7:00 PM, *FRUS*, Doc. 32.

145. This was also the case in British meetings with the Egyptian leadership. See "Record of a Discussion between the Foreign and Commonwealth Secretary and the President of Egypt at the Barrage, Nile Delta, 26 April 1977," PREM 16/1370, UKNA.

146. Chamberlin, *The Global Offensive*, 246. See also Sela, "The PLO at Fifty," 307–10.

147. See Rabinovich, *Yitzhak Rabin*, 132–36; and William E. Farrell, "Rabin Stuns Israel," *New York Times*, 8 April 1977, http://www.nytimes.com/1977/04/08/archives /long-island-opinion-rabin-stuns-israel-by-canceling-his-candidacy.html.

Chapter Two: Menachem Begin's Reality

1. Carter, *Keeping Faith*, 295.

2. On Jabotinsky and his influence, see Stanislawski, *Zionism and the Fin de Siecle*; Heller, *Jabotinsky's Children*; and Rubin, "The Future of the Jews." On Begin, see Shilon, *Menachem Begin*; and Peleg, *Begin's Foreign Policy*.

3. For Begin's ideological worldview toward settlement in Israel and across the Green Line, see Goldstein, "Menachem Begin and 'The Whole Land of Israel' until the Six Day War"; Naor, "'A Simple Historical Truth'"; and Shelef, "From 'Both Banks of the Jordan' to the 'Whole Land of Israel.'"

4. Minutes, cabinet session, 19 June 1967, A-8164/8, Israel State Archives, Jerusalem (hereafter ISA).

5. In particular, he was drawn to the ideas of Giuseppe Garibaldi and Giuseppe Mazzini. See Shindler, *The Triumph of Military Zionism*, 12; and Mazzini, *A Cosmopolitanism of Nations*.

6. He refined the idea that "the Arab minority will have cultural autonomy." Cited in Rubinovitz and Steinberg, "Menachem Begin's Autonomy Plan," 8.

7. This often masked true intentions. See Raz, "The Generous Peace Offer"; and Shlaim, *The Iron Wall*, 267–358.

8. See Gorenberg, *The Accidental Empire*.

9. "We cannot give up Judea and Samaria," interview with Menachem Begin, undated, Private Papers of Menachem Begin, PM20, Menachem Begin Heritage Center, Jerusalem (hereafter MBC).

10. "Extracts from Likud's Election Programme," Private Papers of Menachem Begin, PM20, MBC. "Eretz Israel" in this context means the entirety of the biblical "Land of Israel," including all of Israel and the Palestinian territories. Autonomist thinking had a rich precedent in Jewish history, as a vehicle for a cohesive minority group to organize itself culturally and politically, albeit with limited sovereignty. See Shumsky, "Brith Shalom's Uniqueness Reconsidered" and "Leon Pinsker and 'Auto-emancipation!'" On its roots in late imperial Russia, see Rabinovitch, *Jewish Rights, National Rites*.

11. This event is known as the *mahapach* in Hebrew. See Dowty, "Zionism's Greatest Conceit"; and Cohen and Leon, "The Mahapach and Yitzhak Shamir's Quiet Revolution."

12. Memo, Brzezinski to Carter, 16 May 1977, "Israeli Settlement at Mes'ha and Vance-Allon Meeting," reproduced in Declassified Documents Reference System (hereafter DDRS) (Farmington Hills, MI: Gale 2015); and memorandum, "President's Meeting with Ambassador Samuel Lewis," Brzezinski to Carter, 4 May 1977, Brzezinski NSA Material, Country File-Israel, Box 34, JCL.

13. Telegram from the Department of State to Secretary of State Vance in Geneva, 18 May 1977, 0531Z, *FRUS*, Doc. 35.

14. Memo, William B. Quandt to Zbigniew Brzezinski, 18 May 1977, Brzezinski NSA Material, Country File-Israel, Box 34, JCL.

15. Ibid.

16. Ibid.

17. "Text of a telephone conversation between the Prime Minister and the President of the United States of America on Saturday 21 May 1977," PREM 16/1370, UKNA.

18. Ibid.

19. Ibid. Brzezinski also encouraged Carter along these lines, making what he termed a "perverse" observation: "The electoral outcome may not be actually all that bad. . . . Begin, by his extremism, is likely to split both Israeli public opinion and the American Jewish community." NSC Weekly Report #13, 20 May 1977, Brzezinski Donated Material, Box 41, JCL.

20. See, for example, the minutes of the executive committee of the American Jewish Congress after the 1977 election and subsequent discussions over the role of AIPAC. American Jewish Congress, records, I-77; Box 833, Folder 27; and Box 624, Folder 14, American Jewish Historical Society, New York.

21. "Text of a telephone conversation between the Prime Minister and the President of the United States of America on Saturday 21 May 1977."

22. Ibid.

23. Memo, Zbigniew Brzezinski to Jimmy Carter, 20 June 1977, DDRS.

24. *Palestine* 3 (June 1977): 3.

25. On preparations for Fahd's visit, see "Your Meeting with Crown Prince Fahd," Brzezinski to Carter, 17 May 1977, CIA Records Search Tool (hereafter CREST), NLC-128-6-15-1-6, JCL.

26. Vance's description of internal Saudi state development and the intensifying U.S.-Saudi relationship is revealing as an indicator of their growing influence in U.S. Middle East policy in the late 1970s, and in particular the role of oil pricing in this relationship. See ibid.

27. On the oil crisis, see McFarland, "Living in Never-Never Land"; and Wight, "The Petrodollar Era." On the domestic U.S. impact, see Jacobs, *Panic at the Pump*. On the relationship between anticolonial oil elites and decolonization, see Dietrich, *Oil Revolution*.

28. Memorandum of Conversation, Washington, 24 May 1977, 10:55 AM–12:30 PM, *FRUS*, Doc. 36.

29. Ibid.

30. Notes of a meeting, "Private Conversation between President Carter and His Royal Highness Prince Fahd Bin 'Abd Al-Aziz Al-Saud," 25 May 1977, *FRUS*, Doc. 37.

31. NSC Weekly Report #16, Brzezinski to Carter, 10 June 1977, Brzezinski Donated Collection, Box 41, JCL (emphasis in original).

32. See the secret memo, "Sedrat ha'mifgashim bein manhigei Arav v'nasi Carter" [Order of the meetings between Arab leaders and President Carter], 7 June 1977, MFA-5988/13, ISA.

33. For interviews that reveal Begin's thinking during his early months in office, see PM16, MBC.

34. NSC Memorandum, "Official Positions of Begin and Yadin," William Quandt and Gary Sick to Zbigniew Brzezinski, 8 June 1977, Brzezinski NSA Material, Country File-Israel, Box 34, JCL.

35. Ibid.

36. See Memorandum of Conversation, 10 June 1977, 4:00–5:00 PM, *FRUS*, Doc. 41.

37. He would later quit his job because of differences with Begin over the peace process in 1978.

38. Memorandum of Conversation, 10 June 1977, 4:00–5:00 PM, *FRUS*, Doc. 41.

39. On the use of the law for the expansion of the occupation, see Erakat, "Taking the Land without the People"; and Moses, "Empire, Resistance, and Security."

40. Memorandum of Conversation, 10 June 1977, 4:00–5:00 PM, *FRUS*, Doc. 41.

41. Ibid. On the tangled history of the phrase "Auschwitz borders," which Katz's phrase evokes, see Robert Mackey and Elizabeth A. Harris, "Israeli Settlers Reject the 'Auschwitz Borders' of 1967," *New York Times*, 19 May 2011, http://thelede.blogs.nytimes.com/2011/05/19/israeli-settlers-reject-the-auschwitz-borders.

42. Memorandum of Conversation, 10 June 1977, 4:00–5:00 PM, *FRUS*, Doc. 41.

43. Jimmy Carter to Menachem Begin, 20 June 1977, A-4155/1, ISA.

44. "Discussion paper for PRC meeting on Middle East," 22 June 1977, Brzezinski Donated Collection, Box 24, JCL; "Summary of Conclusions of a Policy Review

Committee Meeting on the Middle East," 25 June 1977, 9:30–11:15 AM, *FRUS*, Doc. 43; and "Summary of a Policy Review Committee Meeting," 5 July 1977, 3:30–5:15 PM, *FRUS*, Doc. 47.

45. Draft telegram from the Department of State to the Embassy in Egypt, undated, *FRUS*, Doc. 44.

46. Senate Leaders to Jimmy Carter, 28 June 1977, Brzezinski NSA Material, Country File-Israel, Box 35, JCL.

47. This was Morris Amitay, who confirmed in an interview he was skeptical of William Quandt, whom he characterized as "unhelpful" and "hostile" during earlier interaction over the Middle East. Phone interview by author, 4 April 2006.

48. "Memorandum for the Files of a Meeting with President Carter Re: Meeting with Jewish Leadership—6 July 1977," *FRUS*, Doc. 49. Carter's Jewish liaison Mark Siegel was very positive in conveying the contents to the Israelis. "Everyone said good things, including Brzezinski. The President was excellent and could not have been better." See Zvi Rafiah, "Divrei ha'Nasi bfgishato im hamanhigim hyehudim" [The president's remarks in his meeting with Jewish leaders], MFA-5988/13, ISA.

49. "Memorandum for the Files of a Meeting with President Carter Re: Meeting with Jewish Leadership—6 July 1977," *FRUS*, Doc. 49. See also Morris Abram's memo to Carter, "Why Portions of the American Jewish Community Are Concerned with the Present Posture of U.S./Israeli/Arab Relations," 5 July 1977, Brzezinski NSA Material, Country File-Israel, Box 35, JCL.

50. See Yaqub, *Imperfect Strangers*; and Pennock, *The Rise of the Arab American Left*.

51. Meeting between President Carter and Prime Minister Begin, 19 July 1977, 11:00 AM, A-4155/2, ISA, 2. For the U.S. account of the meeting, see Memorandum of Conversation, 19 July 1977, 11:15 AM–1:10 PM, *FRUS*, Doc. 52.

52. Meeting between President Carter and Prime Minister Begin, 19 July 1977, 11:00 AM, A-4155/2, ISA, 3.

53. Meeting between President Carter and Prime Minister Begin, 19 July 1977, 11:00 AM, A-4155/2, ISA, 6. On the massacre itself, see Khalidi, *Dayr Yasin*; and Morris, *Righteous Victims*, 207–9. For the historiographical debate, see Gelber, "Appendix II: Propaganda as History," in *Palestine 1948*.

54. See Morris, *The Birth of the Palestinian Refugee Problem Revisited*; and Khalidi, *All That Remains*.

55. Meeting between President Carter and Prime Minister Begin, 19 July 1977, 11:00 AM, A-4155/2, ISA, 8.

56. Ibid.

57. Ibid., 11.

58. Ibid., 12.

59. This was Arafat's phrasing. See Memorandum from Brzezinski to Carter, undated, *FRUS*, Doc. 51.

60. This issue of Jewish refugees from Arab lands would play a recurring role in the settlement of the Palestinian refugee question. On their political usage, see Shenhav, "The Jews of Iraq, Zionist Ideology, and the Property of the Palestinian Refugees of 1948"; and Zamkanei, "Justice for Jews from Arab Countries."

61. Meeting between President Carter and Prime Minister Begin, 19 July 1977, 11:00 AM, A-4155/2, ISA, 12.

62. Ibid., 13.

63. Begin-Carter toasts, U.S. Information Services, 21 July 1977, A-4155/2, ISA.

64. Ibid.

65. Memo, U.S. position conveyed to the Prime Minister via Ribicoff, 19 July 1977, 8:00 PM, A-4155/2, ISA.

66. See Allon, "Israel: The Case for Defensible Borders."

67. Memo, U.S. position conveyed to the Prime Minister via Ribicoff, 19 July 1977.

68. The extent of this withdrawal is unclear; the Hebrew and English handwritten documents, as well as the official translation prepared between 7 and 13 July, leave room for interpretation. See Hebrew and English versions of "Israel's Peace Principles: Conveyed Privately by P. M. Begin to President Carter, Washington 19.7.77; and in Writing to Vance," A-4313/1, ISA.

69. Ibid.

70. See Memorandum, Brzezinski to Carter, 19 July 1977, footnote 3, *FRUS*, Doc. 54 (emphasis in original).

71. Memorandum of Conversation, 20 July 1977, 10:05–10:40 AM, *FRUS*, Doc. 57. See also Carter's letter to Begin affirming he would not speak publicly on the 1967 lines, but if asked by Arab leaders for American views on borders, the United States would state them. Carter to Begin, 1 August 1977, PM72, MBC. This position, according to Vance, showed that even though the United States "would consult closely with Israel, we were not going to concert with it against the Arabs." Vance, *Hard Choices*, 186.

72. Carter, *White House Diary*, 71.

73. Telegram from the Department of State to the Embassy in Israel, 25 July 1977, 2330Z, *FRUS*, Doc. 59.

74. Ibid.

75. *PPPJC*, 29 July 1977.

76. Ibid.

77. Bernard Gwertzman, "Carter Asserts Step on Israeli Settlers Is Obstacle to Peace," *New York Times*, 29 July 1977, A1.

78. Begin's expansionist comments appeared on the cover of July's PLO Bulletin. See *Palestine* 3 (15 July 1977).

79. Undated handwritten note, "Notes: governmental and international meetings, daily priorities, and official matters," [1 of 4], 1977–1980, Box 10, File 24, Vance Papers, YUL (emphasis in original).

80. See Vance, *Hard Choices*, 184.

81. Memo, "Summary of Vance's Middle East Trip," Gary Sick to Zbigniew Brzezinski, 12 August 1977, CREST (NLC-6-50-3-7-0), JCL.

82. Vance, *Hard Choices*, 186.

83. Ibid., 185–86.

84. Ibid., 187.

85. Memo, Sick to Brzezinski, 12 August 1977, CREST (NLC-6-50-3-7-0), JCL. As Vance recalled in his memoir, "Syrian Foreign Minister Khaddam objected to

the term 'trusteeship' reminding us of the Arabs' experience with foreign rule under League of Nation mandates." See Vance, *Hard Choices*, 187.

86. While this earlier program still emphasized armed struggle, it did not exclude diplomatic means and in fact was the basis for the more explicit acceptance of partition and the emergence of the two-state model. For the text of the 1974 resolution, see Laqueur and Rubin, *The Israel-Arab Reader*, 162–63. On the significance of 1974, see Khalidi, *The Iron Cage*, 193–95; and Cobban, *The Palestinian Liberation Organisation*.

87. Vance, *Hard Choices*, 188.

88. Ibid., 188–89.

89. Ibid.

90. Diary of Grace Sloane Vance, 10 August 1977, "Trip to Middle East July 30, 1977–August 12, 1977," Box 17, Folder 1, Vance Papers, YUL.

91. Ibid.

92. On Begin's misuse of this history, see Zertal, *Israel's Holocaust and the Politics of Nationhood*.

93. Minutes of a meeting between Begin and Vance and delegations, 9 August 1977, 5:30 PM, Jerusalem, MFA-6862/2, ISA. In his memoir, Vance suggests that the idea of a "West Bank-Gaza transitional international regime" lodged itself into Begin's mind in some form, leading to the official Israeli presentation on autonomy in December 1977. See Vance, *Hard Choices*, 189–90.

94. Minutes of a meeting, 9 August 1977, 5:30 PM, Jerusalem, MFA-6862/2, ISA.

95. See full transcript of the Israeli version, "Memorandum of Conversation," 10 August 1977, 9:35 AM–11:00 AM, MFA-6862-2, ISA.

96. Ibid.

97. Memo, Sick to Brzezinski, 12 August 1977, CREST (NLS-6-50-3-7-0), JCL. See also the State Department report, "Telegram from the Department of State to the White House," 12 August 1977, 1310Z, *FRUS*, Doc. 89.

98. Telegram from Embassy in Israel to the Department of State, 17 August 1977, 1949Z, *FRUS*, Doc 82.

99. Ibid.

100. Ibid. As Vance later wrote, "I pointed out that even though he was suggesting putting civilians into already existing military bases, this too would violate international legal principles. It is the fact of moving *civilians* of one country into occupied territory that constitutes the legal violation." See *FRUS*, Doc. 89 (emphasis in original).

101. See "Jewish Settlements in Administered Territories" [Hebrew and English], 10 August 1977, MFA/6862/2, ISA.

102. For an extensive explanation of how this legal thinking developed, along with maps and transcripts of the High Court decisions to bolster the view of scholars claiming the legality of occupation, see the entire file, "Hitnachluyot: P'sak Hadin Hamaleh" [Settlements: The full ruling], 11/74–11/79, MFA-9336/10, ISA.

103. See meeting between Begin and Vance, 10 August 1977, 11:20 AM, MFA-6862/2, ISA.

104. On the troubled history of these citizens between 1948 and 1967, see Robinson, *Citizen Strangers*.

105. See interview with the Prime Minister by Rafael Bashan, 12 September 1977, PM16, MBC.

106. Meeting between Begin and Vance, 10 August 1977, 11:20 AM, MFA-6862/2, ISA.

107. This denial of responsibility for the making of the refugee problem fit with Begin's earlier discussion about 1948, even as leading figures like Yitzhak Rabin spoke openly in his memoir of the state's role in the creation of refugees. This section was censored but later released to the press. See Rabinovich, *Yitzhak Rabin*, 25-26. In her biography of David Ben Gurion, Anita Shapira also writes of his order of expulsion. See Shapira, *Ben-Gurion*, 171. On the shifting Israeli historical memory about the making of the refugees, see Shapira, "Hirbet Hizah: Between Remembrance and Forgetting"; and Yizhar, *Khirbet Khizeh*.

108. Meeting between Begin and Vance, 10 August 1977, 11:20 AM, MFA/6862/2, ISA.

109. Ibid.

110. Ibid.

111. See, for example, the footage in Amos Gitai's film of the occupied territories during the early 1980s, *Yoman Sadeh* [Field diary], 1982.

112. See Memorandum of Conversation with Sadat, 11 August 1977, 3:30–4:40 PM, *FRUS*, Doc. 87; telegram from Vance to Department of State and the White House, 11 August 1977, 1940Z, *FRUS*, Doc. 88; and "Note of a Meeting to discuss the Middle East," 13 August 1977, PREM 16/1371, UKNA.

113. Vance, *Hard Choices*, 190.

114. Carter, *White House Diary*, 83.

115. American Jewish leader Hyman Bookbinder noted this pattern in a report to the Israeli government. See "Report of Bookbinder meeting with Jordan" [Hebrew and English], 12 August 1977, MFA-6862/2, ISA.

116. "Highlights from Meeting of September 16, 1977," A-4313/4, ISA.

117. Ibid.

118. Dayan to Vance, 2 September 1977, MFA-6864/15, ISA.

119. "Memorandum of Conversation between the Secretary and Foreign Minister Dayan," 19 September 1977, 12:00–2:20 PM, *FRUS*, Doc. 105.

120. Ibid.

121. Ibid.

122. See both "President's Meeting with Foreign Minister Moshe Dayan of Israel, 19 September 1977, 3:30–5:00 PM," *FRUS*, Doc. 106 and "Meeting of Foreign Minister Dayan with President Carter, 19 September 1977," Brzezinski Donated Collection, Box 13, JCL.

123. The White House even prepared a draft "Aide Memoire" on the settlement question for the Israelis, reasserting the U.S. position on their illegality under Article 49 of the Fourth Geneva Convention and considering the West Bank and Gaza to be occupied territory to which UN resolution 242 applied. See Quandt to Brzezinski,

"Aide Memoire," 20 September 1977, Brzezinski NSA Material, Country File-Israel, Box 35, JCL. The relevant section of the text notes "the Occupying Power shall not deport or transfer parts of its own civilian population into the territories it occupies." See International Committee of the Red Cross, *The Geneva Conventions of August 12, 1949,* 172.

124. Memo, Quandt to Brzezinski, "An Interim Regime for the West Bank and Gaza," 9 September 1977, Brzezinski NSA Material, Country File-Israel, Box 35, JCL. This report, which called for new administrative structures and a settlement freeze, clearly anticipated the consequences of indefinite control of the territories. Quandt suggested a referendum on an eventual agreement in which Palestinians living in the territories could exercise self-determination, in line with the U.S. position.

125. "President's Meeting with Foreign Minister Moshe Dayan of Israel, 19 September 1977, 3:30–5:00 PM," *FRUS,* Doc. 106.

126. Memorandum of Conversation, 24 September 1977, *FRUS,* Doc. 112.

Chapter Three: Egypt's Sacrificial Lamb

1. The U.S. ambassador to Lebanon relayed the content of the meeting in a cable to the State Department. See Parker to Atherton, 19 August 1977, *FRUS,* Doc. 96.

2. Muslih, *Toward Coexistence,* 26–27.

3. Ibid., 28. Muslih calls the period between June 1974 and November 1988 the "Two-State Solution Phase" of the PNC; see Muslih, *Toward Coexistence,* 23–39. On the PLO's development of a diplomatic strategy in this period, see Sayigh, *Armed Struggle,* 410–23; al-Hout, *My Life in the PLO,* 119–30; and Abbas, *Through Secret Channels,* 11–18.

4. See telegram from Department of State to Embassy in Lebanon, 17 August 1977, 0153Z, *FRUS,* Doc. 93.

5. Ibid. For the PLO view of Vance's efforts, see "Palestine Is the Core," editorial, *Palestine* 3 (August 1977): 3. Israeli officials were deeply opposed. See Meir Rosenne's report, "The PLO's Stance in Relation to Resolution 242," 14 August 1977, MFA-6862/8, ISA.

6. "Resolutions of the Thirteenth Palestine National Council, Cairo, Issued March 21–25, 1977," reprinted in "Documents and Source Material," *Journal of Palestine Studies* 6.3 (1977): 188.

7. Parker to Atherton, 19 August 1977, *FRUS,* Doc. 96.

8. Yaqub, *Imperfect Strangers,* 245–50.

9. Salim Yaqub explains that this negative response "reflected growing doubts among Palestinians that the Americans were acting in good faith," driven in part by conflicting reports on the extent of Vance's offer and other ideas that had been floated by the U.S. secretary of state. Ibid., 247–48.

10. "Central Intelligence Agency Intelligence Information Cable," 20 August 1977, *FRUS,* Doc. 97.

11. Telegram from Embassy in Lebanon to the Department of State, 23 August 1977, 0930Z, *FRUS,* Doc. 98.

12. Memorandum, Brzezinski to Carter, 30 August 1977, *FRUS*, Doc. 99.

13. See memo from Brzezinski to Carter, 19 September 1977, *FRUS*, Doc. 104.

14. See Tab A, "Summary of Conversations with Arafat," 17 September 1977; and Tab B, Full Notes on Conversation with Arafat, 9–12 September 1977, *FRUS*, Doc. 103.

15. Tab A, "Summary of Conversations with Arafat."

16. Ibid.

17. Ibid.

18. Tab B, Full Notes on Conversation with Arafat, 9–12 September 1977, *FRUS*, Doc. 103.

19. Ibid.

20. Ibid. Bolling questioned Arafat about the Syrian control of Saiqa, a small group within the PLO that rejected Arafat's leadership. He explained that "they have to live with my leadership." On the effect of internal dynamics on Palestinian participation in negotiations, see Pearlman, "Spoiling Inside and Out."

21. Tab B, Full Notes on Conversation with Arafat (emphasis in original). Bolling was referring to public statements by hard-line factions opposed to negotiations or acceptance of 242.

22. Tab C, "Some Reflections on the Current Status of the P.L.O. and of Various Palestinian Attitudes and Opinions," 16 September 1977, *FRUS*, Doc. 103.

23. See ibid.

24. These contradictions comport with wider trends in the 1970s. For the Carter administration, self-determination often meant less than the sum of its parts. See Simpson, "Self-Determination, Human Rights, and the End of Empire in the 1970s."

25. See Vaïsse, *Neoconservatism*.

26. See Zeitz, "'If I am not for myself.'"

27. Reminiscences of Rabbi Alex Schindler (1977), 29, CCOH. One Israeli intellectual active in the peace movement confidentially remarked, "Just when American Jews should have been more critical of what was going on in Israel, a major American Jewish leader—a self proclaimed dove—throws his support to Begin. It was positively whorish." Tivnan, *The Lobby*, 112.

28. Tivnan, *The Lobby*, 111.

29. See Goldberg, *Jewish Power*, 210. On internal cleavages, see I. F. Stone, "Confessions of a Jewish Dissident," *New York Review of Books*, 9 March 1978; and Baruch A. Levine, "Israel and Dissidence," *New York Review of Books*, 4 May 1978.

30. See Tivnan, *The Lobby*, 175–77.

31. For a broader discussion of these tensions within the American Jewish community, and the rise of "The New Tribalism," see Barnett, *The Star and the Stripes*, esp. 155–94. On contemporary divisions over Israel, see Beinart, *The Crisis of Zionism*; and Waxman, *Trouble in the Tribe*.

32. See "Reasons Why the Jewish Community and Other Israeli Supporters Are Disturbed by Administration Actions and Inactions since the July 6 Meeting," memo, Edward Sanders and Roger Lewis to Hamilton Jordan and Robert Lipshutz, 19 September 1977, Hamilton Jordan Files, Box 35, JCL.

33. Ibid.

34. Ibid.

35. Brzezinski, *Power and Principle*, 108.

36. "Joint Statement by the Governments of the U.S. and the USSR, 1 Oct. 1977," full text in Lukacs, *The Israeli-Palestinian Conflict*, 16.

37. Marvine Howe, "Arabs Believe Israel Will Refuse to Join Geneva Talks," *New York Times*, 4 October 1977, 3.

38. See "PLO Welcomes Declaration," *New York Times*, 2 October 1977; and "U.S.-Soviet Communiqué," editorial, *Palestine* 3 (1 October 1977): 3.

39. See the comments of Farouk Kaddoumi, head of the PLO's political department, in "PLO Welcomes Declaration."

40. "Israel Reacts to Statement," *New York Times*, 2 October 1977. See also Summary of the President's Meeting with Foreign Minister Moshe Dayan, 4 October 1977, *FRUS*, Doc. 124.

41. "Rabin Reaction to U.S.-Soviet Statement," 2 October 1977, Hamilton Jordan Files, Box 35, JCL.

42. Rabin's efforts to forestall a comprehensive peace during the negotiations with Henry Kissinger after the 1973 War now seemed poised to collapse, with Israel being pushed back to the 1967 borders.

43. Dayan, *Breakthrough*, 64–74.

44. Summary of the President's Meeting with Foreign Minister Moshe Dayan, 4 October 1977, *FRUS*, Doc. 124.

45. Ibid.

46. "The United States, the Soviet Union and a Middle East Peace," October 1977, Hamilton Jordan Files, Box 35, JCL.

47. Siegel to Jordan, 3 October 1977, Hamilton Jordan Files, Box 35, JCL.

48. Reminiscences of Hyman Bookbinder (1977), 58–59, CCOH.

49. Terence Smith, "Growing Alarm among U.S. Jews Threatens Carter's Mideast Policy," *New York Times*, 30 October 1977, 34. See also "The Jews and Jimmy Carter," editorial, *New York Times*, 6 November 1977; and Letters to the Editor, 13 November 1977.

50. On Rostow and the roots of his campaign against détente, see Rosenberg, "The Quest against Détente"; and the biography of his brother by Milne, *America's Rasputin*.

51. Eugene Rostow, "Memorandum for the files, meeting with President Carter, Secretary of Defense Brown, and Zbigniew Brzezinski, National Security Advisor," 4 August 1977, Ascension 1985-M-004, Box 4, Eugene Victor Rostow Papers (MS 1024), Manuscripts and Archives, YUL.

52. Ibid.

53. Quandt, *Camp David*, 62.

54. See Memorandum of Conversation, 26 September 1977, 8:15 PM, *FRUS*, Doc. 113. Vance also discussed Egypt's emerging willingness to negotiate with Israel alone if Syria opted out of the Geneva Conference.

55. Yaqub, *Imperfect Strangers*, 252–53.

56. See "Working Paper on Suggestions for the Resumption of the Geneva Peace Conference," multiple drafts [Hebrew and English], 18 September–15 October 1977,

A-4313/1, ISA; and Working Paper, October 1977, Brzezinski NSA Material, Country File-Israel, Box 35, JCL. In meetings with the Americans, the Jordanians raised the question of sovereignty and pointed to ongoing efforts by the Israelis to promote local alternatives with Palestinians on the basis of narrow autonomy. Vance felt that Geneva would be different, "they were thinking of something more." See Secretary's Bilateral with Jordanian Court Minister Sharaf, 1 October 1977, *FRUS*, Doc. 121.

57. On attempts to encourage Dayan's role as a moderate alongside Begin, see "Peace Negotiations and Israeli Coalition Politics," 7 October 1977, Brzezinski NSA Material, Country File-Israel, Box 35, JCL; and memorandum for the president from Brzezinski, NSC Weekly Report #32, 14 October 1977, Brzezinski Donated Material, Box 41, JCL.

58. On the evolution of Sadat's thinking, see Sadat, *In Search of Identity*, 360–63; Yaqub, *Imperfect Strangers*, 252–56; Shemesh, "The Origins of Sadat's Strategic Volte Face"; Karawan, "Sadat and the Egyptian-Israeli Peace Revisited"; Safty, "Sadat's Negotiations with the United States and Israel"; and Indyk, *To the Ends of the Earth.*

59. Telegram from the Embassy in Egypt to the Department of State, 3 November 1977, 2255Z, *FRUS*, Doc. 141.

60. Telegram from the Department of State to the Embassy in Egypt, 5 November 1977, 0129Z, *FRUS*, Doc. 142.

61. Telegram from the Embassy in Egypt to the Department of State, 9 November 1977, 2120Z, *FRUS*, Doc. 144.

62. On the genesis of Sadat's remark and plans to visit Jerusalem, see Fahmy, *Negotiating for Peace in the Middle East*, 252–67. Fahmy explicitly disputes several accounts by Israeli officials and Sadat himself. Ibid., 1.

63. Telegram from the Embassy in Egypt to the Department of State, 9 November 1977, 2120Z, *FRUS*, Doc. 144.

64. For a persuasive read of Sadat's behavior from the vantage point of an "intraregime power struggle," see Kandil, *Soldiers, Spies, and Statesmen*, 156. For personal accounts of the decision and its aftermath, see Sadat, *In Search of Identity*, 365–72; Sadat, *A Woman of Egypt*, 367–409; and Fahmy, *Negotiating for Peace in the Middle East*, 2–3, 279–84.

65. Telegram from the Embassy in Egypt to the Department of State, 10 November 1977, 1540Z, *FRUS*, Doc. 145.

66. Salim Yaqub argues that Sadat "woefully underestimated Begin's determination" and sealed Geneva's fate in the process by ensuring bilateral negotiations with Israel despite rhetorical arguments otherwise. Yaqub, *Imperfect Strangers*, 254–56.

67. Begin to Sadat, 15 November 1977, A-4313/5, ISA. For detailed coverage of the lead-up to Sadat's visit and the trip itself, see the special publication and release of new documents by the Israel State Archives, "'No More War': The Begin Government's Initiative and Sadat's Visit to Jerusalem, November 1977," http://www .archives.gov.il/en/chapter/no-war-begin-governments-peace-initiative-sadats-visit -jerusalem-november-1977. See also the original materials of Begin's office file "Bikur Sadat B'Yisrael" [Sadat's visit to Israel], PM1103, MBC.

68. For Fahmy's caustic account of Sadat's decision and his resignation, see Fahmy, *Negotiating for Peace in the Middle East*, 274–84.

69. "Sadat's Visit," *Palestine* 3 (November 1977): 3.

70. Even Carter was worried about the benefits of the trip. During a telephone conversation with Begin, who informed the president of Sadat's visit, Carter told the Israeli prime minister, "There is the need for some tangible contribution for Sadat to take home. He has run high risks. There should be something tangible that he can take as a success." See Memorandum of Telephone Conversation between Carter and Begin, 17 November 1977, 3:53–4:00 PM, *FRUS*, Doc. 147. See also Vance's instructions to Ambassador Samuel Lewis in Tel Aviv, telegram from the Department of State to the White House, 18 November 1977, 1510Z, *FRUS*, Doc. 148.

71. Three thousand journalists and broadcasters in Israel covered the event. On the interaction with Meir, see Klagsbrun, *Lioness*, 680–81.

72. Sadat, "Statement to the Israeli Knesset," 20 November 1977, in Lukacs, *The Israeli-Palestinian Conflict*, 143–44.

73. It clearly altered discourse in the United States. Three months after Sadat's speech, the *New York Times* ran a three-part series on the front page titled "The Palestinians." James M. Markham, "Palestinians, People in Crisis, Are Scattered and Divided," *New York Times*, 19 February 1978, A1. New evidence reveals sharp divisions within Israeli military circles over the speech and Sadat's broader aims. See Ofer Aderet, "Israeli Military Archive Reveals Split among Generals over Sadat's Historic 1977 Visit," *Haaretz*, 25 February 2018, https://www.haaretz.com/israel -news/.premium-idf-archives-reveal-split-among-generals-over-sadat-s-1977-visit -1.5846713.

74. Mark Siegel, who was in Jerusalem representing the White House during Sadat's Knesset speech, recalled that Zbigniew Brzezinski was infuriated by Sadat's trip. The emphasis on a bilateral peace deal between Israel and Egypt flew in the face of the NSC advisor's plan for a comprehensive regional settlement in Geneva. Mark Siegel, phone interview by author, 31 March 2006.

75. "Transcript of Joint Press Conference including the Agreed Communiqué Issued upon the conclusion of President Sadat's Visit to Israel," 21 November 1977, Ben-Elissar Files, A-4155/5, ISA.

76. Ibid.

77. Top Secret Meeting of the Prime Minister and the Minister of Foreign Affairs with Ambassador Lewis, 23 November 1977, 6:00 PM, A-4155/5, ISA.

78. Ibid.

79. Ibid.

80. Telegram from the Embassy in Israel to the Department of State, 23 November 1977, 2150Z, *FRUS*, Doc. 157.

81. Memorandum from Secretary of State Vance to President Carter, 24 November 1977, *FRUS*, Doc. 158.

82. See Eilts's report on Sadat's visit and discussions, telegram from the Embassy in Egypt to the Department of State, 23 November 1977, 1606Z, *FRUS*, Doc. 155; and memorandum from Brzezinski to Carter, undated, *FRUS*, Doc. 164.

83. Telegram from Vance to the White House and the State Department, 11 December 1977, 0101Z, *FRUS*, Doc. 170.

84. Marvine Howe, "Arab Meeting Fails to Forge Joint Front against Sadat Moves," *New York Times*, 5 December 1977; Marvine Howe, "Hard-Line Arab Bloc Is Formed at Tripoli," *New York Times*, 6 December 1977.

85. Fahmy, *Negotiating for Peace in the Middle East*, 280. In his memoir, Fahmy is scathing about the long-term fallout from the trip, which undercut the efforts toward Geneva, removed the Soviets as a counterbalance to the United States, and left Israel with free reign "to manipulate the Palestinian issue as it saw fit." Ibid., 282.

86. Among the most embittered reactions was that of Jordan's King Hussein, who felt that real peace had been "derailed" by Sadat. He shared his gloomy assessment with U.S. ambassador to Jordan Thomas Pickering. See Ashton, "Taking Friends for Granted," 633–34.

87. Memorandum from Brzezinski to Carter, undated, *FRUS*, Doc. 164.

88. Ibid.

89. See Message from the White House to the Embassy in Egypt, 9 December 1977, 1525Z, *FRUS*, Doc. 166.

90. See the ISA publication and Mossad report (Hebrew) of Dayan's visit to Morocco on 2 December 1977, http://www.archives.gov.il/en/chapter/israel-egypt -open-peace-talks-marrakesh-december-1977/.

91. See Memorandum of Conversation, Secretary's Meeting with Prime Minister Begin, Jerusalem, 10 December 1977, 9:30–11:45 PM, *FRUS*, Doc. 168.

92. Summary of the President's Meeting with Prime Minister Begin of Israel, 16 December 1977, 9:00–10:00 AM, *FRUS*, Doc. 177. Stuart Eizenstat, who was in the room, noted that "Begin did almost all talking. Had maps. Seemed clearly pleased with his forthcoming position." Box 4, Folder 28, Stuart Eizenstat Papers, LOC. Begin's plan had been approved by Israel's Ministerial Defense Committee but awaited review by his cabinet. For the full Israeli minutes of these meetings, see A-4155/6 and MFA-6862/11, ISA.

93. Memorandum of Conversation, Washington, 16 December 1977, 9:00–10:00 AM, *FRUS*, Doc. 177.

94. Ibid.

95. Ibid.

96. Memo, Dennis Clift to the Vice President, CREST (NLC-133-109-3-25-3), JCL.

97. Memorandum of Conversation, Washington, 16 December 1977, 9:00–10:00 AM, *FRUS*, Doc. 177.

98. This was Theodor Meron, who rejected the government's argument about the land not being occupied. Subsequent arguments by Israeli lawyer and diplomat Yehuda Blum, and Attorney General and later Supreme Court Chief Justice Meir Shamgar, embedded a contrary opinion that became the basis for justifying settlement. See Meron's clear reiteration of his original opinion in "The West Bank and International Humanitarian Law."

99. This version is included in the text box on pp. 100–101.

100. Memorandum of Conversation, Washington, 16 December 1977, 9:00–10:00 AM, *FRUS*, Doc. 177.

101. For a critical U.S. analysis of Begin's autonomy plan, viewing it far less favorably in a report for Brzezinski, see Saunders cable, "Begin West Bank/Gaza Proposal," 21 December 1977, CREST (NLC-16-110-3-26-1), JCL.

102. Memorandum of Conversation, 17 December 1977, 7:05–8:35 PM, *FRUS*, Doc. 178.

103. Ibid.

104. Ibid. Carter made similarly cutting remarks to Arab American leaders two days earlier and publicly castigated the PLO without mentioning Arafat's efforts to engage diplomatically. See Yaqub, *Imperfect Strangers*, 259–61.

105. As Brzezinski told an interviewer a few weeks later, the administration's new view was "Bye-bye PLO." Yaqub, *Imperfect Strangers*, 261.

106. Memorandum of Conversation, 17 December 1977, 7:05–8:35 PM, *FRUS*, Doc. 178.

107. Ibid.

108. Ibid. Shortly after saying this, Begin notified Carter that Israel was not prepared to allow Palestinians to buy land in pre-1967 Israel. Note to author from William Quandt, 14 February 2018.

109. For more on the genesis of Begin's idea, see Rubinovitz and Steinberg, "Menachem Begin's Autonomy Plan." On Jabotinsky's wartime evolution from advocating multinational states toward an embrace of population transfer and ethnic Jewish statehood, as well as his understanding of the Arabs, see Rubin, "The Future of the Jews," esp. 87–134.

110. Record of a discussion between Callaghan and Begin, Chequers, 20 December 1977, PREM 16/1729, UKNA. In a subsequent report to the Americans, Callaghan told Carter of Begin's exuberance, stressing that he shared Carter's view, hoping the proposal would lead to a comprehensive approach. See cable, Jim Callaghan to Jimmy Carter, 21 December 1977, PREM 16/1729, UKNA.

111. For a recasting of the Callaghan government along these permissive lines, see Ashton, "'A Local Terrorist Made Good.'"

112. Vance, *Hard Choices*, 187.

113. Ibid.

114. Top Secret Meeting between Begin and Sadat at the President's Residence, Ismailia, 25 December 1977, 12 noon, MFA-6864-2, ISA.

115. Ibid.

116. Second session, 25 December 1977, 7:00 PM, MFA-6864-2, ISA.

117. Ibid.

118. See Kamel, *The Camp David Accords*, 21–27. Kamel was deeply skeptical of Sadat's approach at Ismailia and agreement to structure negotiations along Begin's lines.

119. Begin would later tell Ambassador Lewis he was "surprised and struck" by Sadat's agreement to his position that a Palestinian state was a threat. See telegram from the Embassy in Israel to the Department of State, 1454Z, 27 December 1977, *FRUS*, Doc. 180.

120. Second session, 25 December 1977, 7:00 PM, MFA-6864-2, ISA.

121. Ibid.

122. Ibid.

123. Press conference attended by President Sadat and Premier Begin, 26 December 1977, MFA-6864/2, ISA.

124. Kamel, *The Camp David Accords*, 31.

125. Reprinted in Laqueur and Rubin, *The Israel-Arab Reader*, 218–20. For the internal Israeli versions that were discussed and approved by the cabinet, see the multiple Hebrew and English iterations located in A-4313/6, ISA. The Hebrew version, as delivered, is "Tochnit ha'Shalom shel Yisrael" [Israel's peace plan], PM136, MBC.

126. Laqueur and Rubin, *The Israel-Arab Reader*, 219.

127. See, for example, his description of an attack by the PLO in Nahariya to U.S. ambassador Samuel Lewis. "Top secret meeting between Prime Minister Begin and Ambassador Lewis, Prime Minister's Office, Knesset, May 7, 1979, 7:30 PM," MFA-6915/11, ISA.

128. Cable, top secret, 3 May 1979, "Proposals for the Introduction of Full Autonomy for the Palestinian Arabs, Inhabitants of Judea, Samaria and the Gaza District and for the Preservation of the Rights of the Jewish people and Israel's Security in these Areas of Eretz Israel (Palestine)," MFA-6915/11, ISA. A copy of the original document on which Begin sketched his autonomy plan was donated by the deputy of his General Directorate to the archives at the Menachem Begin Heritage Center in Jerusalem. It shows a direct link between Begin's original ideas in 1977 and the accepted starting point of the Egyptian-Israeli negotiations that began two years later. See "Proposals for the introduction of full autonomy for the Palestinian Arabs, inhabitants of Judea, Samaria and the Gaza District, and for the preservation of the rights of the Jewish People and Israel's security in these areas of Eretz Israel (Palestine)." Handwritten copy (Hebrew and English), Nadav Aner Donation, MBC.

129. Quoted in Rubinovitz and Steinberg, "Menachem Begin's Autonomy Plan," 8–9.

130. President's meeting with King Hussein, 1 January 1978, 8:20–8:50 AM, *FRUS*, Doc. 182.

131. Ibid.

132. Memorandum of Conversation, 3 January 1978, 5:35–6:33 PM, *FRUS*, Doc. 183.

133. Ibid.

134. *PPPJC*, 4 January 1978.

135. Telegram from Vance to the Embassy in Israel, 5 January 1978, 0006Z, *FRUS*, Doc. 185.

136. Telegram from the Embassy in Syria to Embassy in Belgium, "Congressmen Meet Arafat and Receive Message for Carter," 6 January 1978, 1415Z, *FRUS*, Doc. 187. On Findley's role in engaging the PLO in the context of the ban, see Yaqub, *Imperfect Strangers*, 305–9.

137. "Message from Yasir Arafat," Brzezinski to the President, 10 January 1978, NSA Brzezinski Material, Collection 7, Box 49, JCL.

138. Ibid.

139. See Meron, "The West Bank and International Humanitarian Law."

140. On the Carter administration's indeterminate approach, see Christison, *Perceptions of Palestine*, 175–81.

141. Carter, *Keeping Faith*, 306.

Chapter Four: Camp David and the Triumph of Palestinian Autonomy

1. Moshe Brilliant, "Israeli Officials Say Gunmen Intended to Seize Hotel," *New York Times*, 13 March 1978; "Tragedy of Errors," *Time*, 27 March 1978.

2. See "A Sabbath of Terror," *Time*, 20 March 1978; and Kim Willenson, "Slaughter in Israel," *Newsweek*, 20 March 1978, 24. The attack included the prominent militant Dalal Mughrabi, who shot and killed the American photographer, Gail Rubin, the niece of U.S. senator Abraham Ribicoff.

3. These high-level leaders included Muhammad Youssef al-Najjar (Abu Youssef), Kamal Adwan, and Kamal Nasser.

4. See Sayigh, *Armed Struggle*, 424–41. On Palestinian objectives for the use of violence, see Sayigh, "Palestinian Armed Struggle."

5. For background on Operation Litani, see Morris, *Righteous Victims*, 501–5.

6. See Norton and Schwedler, "(In)security Zones in South Lebanon."

7. On the domestic debate over the use of American cluster bombs in the fighting, see Yaqub, *Imperfect Strangers*, 262–64.

8. On the sale and the domestic fallout, see Strieff, "Arms Wrestle." Mark Siegel, the domestic liaison with the Jewish community, quit his job in protest. See Terence Smith, "Carter Liaison Aide with Jews to Quit White House," *New York Times*, 9 March 1978, A9; and Reminiscences of Mark Siegel (1978), 258–59, CCOH. On the deeper American Jewish rifts that spring, see David Alpern, "Carter and the Jews," *Newsweek*, 20 March 1978; Arthur Samuelson, "The Dilemma of American Jewry," *The Nation*, 1 April 1978; Terence Smith, "Carter Leads a Drive to Mollify Jewish Opponents of Arms Deal," *New York Times*, 17 May 1978, A1; and "White House Denies 'Israeli Lobby' Insult by Hamilton Jordan," *New York Times*, 18 May 1978, A16.

9. Raymond Carrol, "Begin under Fire," *Newsweek*, 20 March 1978, 25.

10. See Weizman, *The Battle for Peace*, 282–84.

11. See Arthur Samuelson, "The Dilemma of American Jewry," *The Nation*, 1 April 1978, 361.

12. Terence Smith, "Talks Called Grim," *New York Times*, 23 March 1978; "The Middle East Impasse," *New York Times*, 24 March 1978. For the transcript, see *FRUS*, Doc. 232.

13. Brzezinski, *Power and Principle*, 246–47. There was a concerted effort to engage congressional leaders ahead of the Begin meeting. See Vance, *Hard Choices*, 207. Congress had been debating the settlements during hearings convened by the Senate Committee on the Judiciary and the House Committee on International Relations since the ascension of the Likud party to power in 1977. See U.S. Congress,

Israeli Settlements in the Occupied Territories; and U.S. Congress, *The Colonization of the West Bank Territories by Israel*.

14. Vance, *Hard Choices*, 209. White House officials had tried to modify Begin's proposal regarding Israel's presence in the West Bank and Gaza during a transitional period and by reaffirming resolution 242, working with Sadat to prepare a joint plan of action that would lead to a comprehensive American proposal. See Quandt, *Camp David*, 174–82.

15. For the Camp David meeting between Sadat and Carter, see "Memorandum of Conversation," 4 February 1978, 11:40 AM–1:20 PM, *FRUS*, Doc. 211. On Sadat's shifting stance throughout 1978, see Quandt, *Camp David*, 209–10.

16. Memo, David Aaron to Jimmy Carter, 22 May 1978, DDRS.

17. See Fahmy, *Negotiating for Peace in the Middle East*, 285–301; Kamel, *The Camp David Accords*, 124–44; and Boutros-Ghali, *Egypt's Road to Jerusalem*, 46–55.

18. Reminiscences of Robert Lipshutz (1978), 25–26, CCOH.

19. Ibid.

20. Vance, *Hard Choices*, 213.

21. Ibid., 216.

22. For the texts of the letters, and the reports of Vance's visit to Israel and Egypt, see *FRUS*, Docs. 283–89.

23. Memo, Zbigniew Brzezinski to Jimmy Carter, 1 September 1978, DDRS.

24. Ibid.

25. *PPPJC*, 4 January 1978.

26. Vance, *Hard Choices*, 217–18.

27. For a daily account based on American sources, see *FRUS*, vol. 9, Arab-Israeli Dispute, August 1978–December 1980. For the definitive study of Camp David from a U.S. perspective, see Quandt, *Camp David*. A compelling narrative based in part on Jimmy and Rosalynn Carter's private diaries is Wright, *Thirteen Days in September*. For recent and forthcoming works based on newly available U.S. and UK primary sources, see Strieff, *Jimmy Carter and the Middle East*; Yaqub, *Imperfect Strangers*, 264–75; Jensehaugen, *Arab-Israeli Diplomacy under Carter*; and Ashton, "Taking Friends for Granted." Memoirs by Egyptian, Israeli, and American participants include Kamel, *The Camp David Accords*; Fahmy, *Negotiating for Peace in the Middle East*; Boutros-Ghali, *Egypt's Road to Jerusalem*; Weizman, *The Battle for Peace*; Dayan, *Breakthrough*; Vance, *Hard Choices*; Brzezinski, *Power and Principle*; and Carter, *White House Diary*. Earlier studies by journalists and scholars include Haber, Schiff, and Yaari, *The Year of the Dove*; Telhami, *Power and Leadership in International Bargaining*; Sachar, *Egypt and Israel*; Friedlander, *Sadat and Begin*; and Stein, *Heroic Diplomacy*.

28. Quandt, *Camp David*, 213.

29. Yaqub, *Imperfect Strangers*, 265.

30. Quandt, *Camp David*, 213.

31. "A Framework for Peace in the Middle East," 17 September 1978, in Laqueur and Rubin, *The Israel-Arab Reader*, 223.

32. Quandt, *Camp David*, 215.

33. Yaqub, *Imperfect Strangers*, 265, 406n76.

34. For how this unfolded, see Quandt, *Camp David*, 250–55.

35. Ibid., 225. This was the precise phrase that had raised such fury in the joint U.S.-Soviet communiqué of 1977. Begin now accepted the words "without much argument," later telling his colleagues "they had little meaning in any event." Quandt, *Camp David*, 254.

36. See Quandt, *Camp David*, 263–65; and Bernard Avishai, "Begin vs. Begin," *New York Review of Books*, 31 March 1979. The Israeli position was not exclusively a product of Begin's thinking. The leader of the opposition, Shimon Peres, supported most of Begin's "red lines" on the eve of the summit, as revealed by newly declassified Israeli documents. See Gidi Weitz, "Secret 1978 Talks Lay Bare the Hawk That Peacemaker Peres Once Was," *Haaretz*, 11 October 2016, https://www.haaretz.com /israel-news/.premium-1.747031. On the deliberate nature of Israeli legal ambiguities on the Palestinian component, see Mayer Gabay, "Legal Aspects of the Camp David Framework for Peace in Relation to the Autonomy Proposal," in Dinstein, ed., *Models of Autonomy*, 255–59.

37. Among the most piercing critiques was Said, *The Question of Palestine*, 182–238. See also Mahmood, "Sadat and Camp David Reappraised"; Sayegh, "The Camp David Agreement and the Palestine Problem"; and Rashid Khalidi, "The Palestine Liberation Organization," in Quandt, ed., *The Middle East*, 261–78. On domestic Arab American reactions, see Yaqub, *Imperfect Strangers*, 267–68.

38. Kamel, *The Camp David Accords*, 361–82.

39. *PPPJC*, 17 September 1978.

40. *PPPJC*, 18 September 1978.

41. They had been promised it before in the 1939 White Paper and in UN General Assembly Resolution 181 in November 1947. See also Nemchenok, "'These People Have an Irrevocable Right to Self-Government.'"

42. See "Statement by the PLO Executive Committee on the Camp David Agreements, Issued in Beirut, 18 September 1978" and "Statement by the West Bank National Conference," *Journal of Palestine Studies* 8.2 (1979): 178, 195.

43. *Al Sharq al-Awsat*, 25 October 1978 and 25 May 1979, quoted in Sicherman, *Palestinian Autonomy, Self-Government and Peace*, 35.

44. Quandt, *Camp David*, 264.

45. *PPPJC*, 18 September 1978.

46. This point of contention has been a matter of some bitterness between Carter's and Begin's supporters. Carter asserted that his handwritten notes and those of Secretary of State Cyrus Vance prove Begin's deception, a claim that Israeli witnesses vehemently deny. The best explanation of what transpired can be found in Quandt, *Peace Process*, 200–203 and *Camp David*, 255–66. See also the oral history of Ambassador Samuel Lewis, Frontline Diplomacy, Manuscript Division, LOC.

47. *PPPJC*, 28 September 1978. See also Yaqub, *Imperfect Strangers*, 267.

48. *PPPJC*, 10 October 1978. On the domestic pressure Carter was facing, see Strieff, *Jimmy Carter and the Middle East*.

49. Yaqub, *Imperfect Strangers*, 268.

50. Brzezinski, *Power and Principle*, 278. In January 1979, Mondale would oppose contacts with the PLO on the grounds that it would "evoke a bitter public reaction from the American Jewish community" and make an Israeli-Egyptian peace treaty more difficult to achieve. See Mondale memo for Carter, "Proposed Contacts with Palestinians," 19 January 1979, National Security Affairs-Brzezinski Material, Subject File Palestinian Liberation Organization, 1/78–4/79, JCL (released via Mandatory Review [MR] request). For Vance's closely held memo on developing contacts with the Palestinians, see Vance to the President, eyes only (undated), Records of the Office of the National Security Advisor, Series 7, PLO, 1/78–4/79, container 49, JCL (released via MR request).

51. Letter to Secretary Vance, secret final draft, 29 April 1979, 2:00 PM, MFA-6915/11, ISA. The officials were Harold Saunders and Herbert Hansell.

52. Secret memo, Brzezinski to Carter, "Secretary Vance's Middle East Strategy Paper," 1 February 1979, Zbigniew Brzezinski Donated Collection, Subject File, Serial X, Box 36, JCL.

53. Secret Memorandum of Conversation, President Carter, Secretary Vance, Prime Minister Khalil, Foreign Minister Dayan, Brzezinski, The Oval Office, 25 February 1979, 2:03–2:45 PM, Zbigniew Brzezinski Donated Collection, Subject File, Serial X, Box 36, JCL.

54. "Summary of President's Meeting with Prime Minister Begin," 2 March 1979, 10:00 AM–12:40 PM, Zbigniew Brzezinski Donated Collection, Subject File, Serial X, Box 36, JCL.

55. Ibid.

56. Jonathan Randal, "PLO Chief, in Iran, Hails Shah's Fall," *Washington Post*, 19 February 1979.

57. Minutes of a meeting between Prime Minister Begin and President Carter at the White House, Washington, DC, Friday, 2 March 1979, 10:00 AM, A-4156/6, ISA.

58. "Summary of President's Meeting with Prime Minister Begin," 2 March 1979, 10:00 AM–12:40 PM, Brzezinski Donated Collection, Subject File, Serial X, Box 36, JCL.

59. Ibid.

60. This double process of de-territorialization and re-territorialization evokes the shifting forms of territorial control that characterized eastern Mediterranean border zones in the Mandate period, never fully resolved in the post-1948 West Bank. See Schayegh, "The Many Worlds of 'Abud Yasin."

61. "Meeting between the President of the USA, Mr. Jimmy Carter and delegation, and Prime Minister Menachem Begin and delegation, 11 March 1979, 11:30 AM, Prime Minister's Office, Jerusalem," MFA-6868/7, ISA.

62. These quotations are all from the 11 March 1979 meeting transcript in MFA-6868/7, ISA.

63. Ibid.

64. Ibid.

65. Ibid.

66. Ibid.

67. Meeting between Mr. Jimmy Carter, President of the United States of America, and delegation, and the Government of Israel-Prime Minister Begin, and the Entire Cabinet, Monday, 12 March 1979, 10:30 AM, Prime Minister's Office, Jerusalem, MFA-6868/7, ISA.

68. See "Secret draft letter of Sadat and Begin, 3PM, March 12, 1979" and "Letter, Carter to Begin, March 14, 1979," both in MFA-6868/7, ISA.

69. Begin interview with Israel Radio, Cable, MFA-6868/7, ISA.

70. "Palestinians, Reacting to the Pact, Go on Strike and Denounce Egypt," *New York Times*, 27 March 1979, 1.

71. "Sadat-Quisling of the Arab World," editorial, *Palestine* 5 (March 1979): 3.

72. "Palestinians, Reacting to the Pact, Go on Strike and Denounce Egypt," 10.

73. See "Arab League: Summit Communiqué (March 31, 1979)," in Laqueur and Rubin, *The Israel-Arab Reader*, 228.

74. Leonid Brezhnev to Jimmy Carter, 19 March 1979, DDRS.

75. Ibid.

76. On the PLO move toward the Soviets after Camp David, see Sayigh, "The Palestinians," in Sayigh and Shlaim, eds., *The Cold War and the Middle East*, 136–38; and Laskier and Bazov, *Teror be-sherut ha-mahepekhah* [Terrorism on behalf of the revolution], 85–104. On Soviet attitudes toward the accords, see Evgeni M. Primakov, "Soviet Policy toward the Arab-Israeli Conflict," in Quandt, ed., *The Middle East*, 387–409.

77. Among the points Carter wanted his National Security Advisor to emphasize to the skeptical Saudi and Jordanian leadership was "Palestinian rights." See handwritten note, Carter to Brzezinski, 15 March 1979, Brzezinski Donated Collection, Box 14, JCL.

78. Quoted in Brzezinski, *Power and Principle*, 438.

79. Ibid., 439.

80. Letter [Hebrew], Yechiel Kaddishai to Yedidya Yehuda, 1 April 1979, PM184, MBC. Kaddishai repeated the same message in Begin's name on 14 May to a settler from the Jordan Valley. See Kaddishai to Mrs. Oshrit Cohen, 14 May 1979, PM184, MBC.

81. See declassified Prime Minister material A-4181, Folders 9, 10, 17, ISA.

82. William Claiborne, "Israel Plans Narrow Arab Autonomy," *Washington Post*, 1 December 1978.

83. Ibid. A copy of the article, with handwritten comments affirming the reporter's extensive claims, can be found in the office files of Begin's director general, Eliyahu Ben-Elissar, who chaired the meeting and was likely the source of the story. See A-4182/7, ISA.

84. See "Commission to prepare for Judea, Samaria and Gaza negotiations, minutes of the first meeting, October 1, 1978" [Hebrew], A-4181/17, ISA; "Timetable for establishing self-government in Judea, Samaria and Gaza" [Hebrew], letter from Dr. Binyamin HaLevi to Prime Minister Begin, 19 November 1978, A-4181/9, ISA; and "Settlement plan in the areas of Judea, Samaria and the Gaza Strip" [Hebrew], letter from Shimon Ravid to Eliyahu Ben-Elissar, A-4181/12, ISA.

85. The Ben-Elissar Report was delivered on 28 December 1978.

86. See Claiborne, "Israel Plans Narrow Arab Autonomy."

87. Michael Pike, "Autonomy Negotiations," 22 May 1979, Document 18, FCO 93/2164, UKNA.

88. Ibid.

89. In discussions with the leading Israeli legal advisors to the autonomy talks, it was clear that this became a central issue of contention and was not fully resolved among the Israeli delegation. Ruth Lapidoth, interview by author, Hebrew University, Jerusalem, 13 February 2012; Robbie Sabel, interview by author, Hebrew University, Jerusalem, 22 February 2012. See also Lapidoth's writings on the talks, "The Autonomy Negotiations" and "The Autonomy Negotiations: A Stocktaking."

90. Quoted in Alterman, *Sadat and His Legacy*, 27.

91. John Mason to Roger Tomkys, 31 January 1979, Document 3, "Autonomy," FCO 93/2164, UKNA.

92. Ibid.

93. Confidential memo 014/6, Michael Hannam, British Consulate General in Jerusalem, to Roger Tomkys, Near East and North Africa Department, Foreign and Commonwealth Office (FCO), File 2164, 12 February 1979, "Autonomy in the Occupied Territories-1979," UKNA.

94. Even Prime Minister Margaret Thatcher, reluctant to support outright Palestinian statehood given her Cold War priorities, was troubled by developments on the ground and entertained arguments from the Foreign Office supporting engagement with the PLO. See PREM 19/295, "Situation in the Middle East: Part 2," 21 September 1979–9 May 1980 and FCO 93/2055, "The Palestinians: Palestinian self-determination," UKNA. For more on Thatcher's views, see Ashton, "Love's Labours Lost"; Lochery, "Debunking the Myths"; and Bermant, *Margaret Thatcher and the Middle East*.

95. Hannam to Tomkys, 12 February 1979, Document 5, FCO 93/2164, UKNA.

96. Ibid.

97. Ibid.

98. Hannam to Tomkys, 12 February 1979, FCO 93/2164, UKNA.

99. Viets to Washington et al., "Autonomy Negotiations: The Israeli Position on Water," 28 March 1979, Box 37, File 5, "Egypt-Political Material," Papers of Hermann Eilts, Howard Gotlieb Archival Research Center, Boston University (hereafter PHE).

100. Ibid.

101. Ibid.

102. Viets to Secretary of State et al., "Autonomy Negotiations: Israeli Position on Land and Settlements," 2 April 1979, Box 37, File 5, PHE.

103. Ibid.

104. See the map of 1977 settlements in chapter 8. Labor also established several settlements in the Golan Heights and Sinai Peninsula, the latter of which were evacuated as part of the Israeli-Egyptian peace deal.

105. Viets, "Autonomy Negotiations: Israeli Position on Land and Settlements," 2 April 1979, Box 37, File 5, PHE.

106. Ibid. At the time of writing his memo, Viets estimated fifty-five West Bank settlements with ten thousand settlers, and seven or eight Gaza settlements with less than one thousand. This did not include East Jerusalem.

107. Ibid.

108. Sharon had spoken of a "million Jews" in the West Bank by 2000; elsewhere it was reported that he told President Carter that he wanted not one million but two million. See American Consulate to Secretary of State, "Autonomy Negotiations: West Bank Attitudes Toward Land and Settlements," 9 April 1979, Box 37, File 5, PHE.

109. This was known as the "Drobles Plan." See Tessler, *A History of the Israeli-Palestinian Conflict*, 523–24.

110. Viets, "Autonomy Negotiations: Israeli Position on Land and Settlements," 2 April 1979, Box 37, File 5, PHE. See also the UK FCO report on internal pressure from an interview with Israeli education minister Zevulen Hammer, 3 April 1979, Document 10, FCO 93/2164, UKNA; and Kieval, *Party Politics in Israel and the Occupied Territories*.

111. Viets to Secretary of State, "Autonomy Negotiations: Israeli position on IDF withdrawal, deployments and security options on the West Bank," 13 April 1979, Box 37, File 5, PHE.

112. Viets to Secretary of State, "Autonomy Negotiations: The Israeli Position on Internal Security and Public Order," 25 April 1979, Box 37, File 5, PHE.

113. Ibid.

114. Viets to Secretary of State, "Autonomy and the Israeli Negotiating Team," 27 April 1979, Box 37, File 5, PHE.

115. Ibid.

116. "Israeli Position on Autonomy Cabinet Debate," 22 May 1979, Document 19, FCO 93/2164, UKNA.

117. Given this reality, the reflections of Israel's leading legal negotiator at the autonomy talks, Professor Ruth Lapidoth, deserve closer attention. In her extensive writings on autonomy, and in an interview conducted with her, Lapidoth insisted that the failure of the negotiations was the fault of the Palestinians for objecting. As she wrote in describing autonomy's successful elements, "A regime of autonomy should be established with the consent of the population intended to benefit from it. (Thus, due to the objection of the Palestinians, the autonomy negotiations between Egypt and Israel from 1979 to 1982 were doomed to failure)." In light of Israeli preconditions, and the structural premise of continued Israeli sovereignty underpinning the talks, her position is startling. See Lapidoth, "Elements of Stable Regional Autonomy Arrangements"; and interview by author, 13 February 2012.

118. Rostow, who had served in the Johnson administration as undersecretary of state for political affairs and helped draft UN Security Council Resolution 242, was viewed as an authority on the Arab-Israeli conflict.

119. Rostow, "'Palestinian Self-Determination.'" An abbreviated version of this argument appeared as "Israel's Settlement Right Is 'Unassailable,'" letter to the editor, *New York Times*, 19 September 1983. For the origins of Israeli legal thinking that justified expansion, see "Hitnachluyot: P'sak Hadin Hamaleh" [Settlements: The full ruling], 11/74–11/79, MFA-9336/10, ISA.

120. Rostow, "'Palestinian Self-Determination,'" 160. For a discussion of the inducement of Palestinians to leave and Israel's concerted effort to bar mass return that did in fact occur in the aftermath of 1967, see Raz, *The Bride and the Dowry*, 103–35.

121. Rostow, "'Palestinian Self-Determination,'" 162. Israel and supporters of the Begin government used this precise argument in meetings with British and American officials. See "Record of a Meeting between Mr. Hurd, Minister of State, and Dr. Josef Burg, Israeli Minister of the Interior, at the Knesset, Jerusalem, 11 December 1979," FCO 93/2164, UKNA; *Insight*, published by the Israeli Ministry of Foreign Affairs, 1.3 (14 July 1980), MFA-6969/3, ISA; and cable, "Language of ADL Decision on the Settlements" [Hebrew], A-4179/2, ISA. On the question of the legality of occupation with particular focus on Israel, see Benvenisti, *The International Law of Occupation*, 203–48; Dinstein, *The International Law of Belligerent Occupation*; and Shafir, *A Half Century of Occupation*, 22–30.

122. Rostow, "'Palestinian Self-Determination,'" 161.

123. In a detailed congressional letter to the president in March 1985, six U.S. senators would adopt wholesale Rostow's argument in opposing any peace initiative that involved a land exchange. See Senator Jesse Helms et al. to Ronald Reagan, 6 March 1985 and reply by J. Edward Fox, undated, case file 081477, CO001-07, WHORM: Subject File, Ronald Reagan Library, Simi Valley, CA (hereafter RRL).

124. See American Consulate to Secretary of State, "Autonomy Negotiations: West Bank Attitudes toward Land and Settlements," 9 April 1979, Box 37, File 5, PHE.

125. American Embassy Tel Aviv to Washington, "Dayan on Autonomy," 2 April 1979, Box 37, File 5, PHE. For the UK view on the makeup of the autonomy team, critical of Dayan's exclusion, see "Preparations for the Autonomy Negotiations," 17 April 1979, Document 11, FCO 93, UKNA.

126. "Autonomy Negotiations: West Bank Attitudes toward Land and Settlements," 9 April 1979, PHE.

127. Anthony Lewis, "Autonomy in Gaza?" *International Herald Tribune*, 10 April 1979.

128. There was strong evidence of ongoing dispossession of Arabs and expropriation of their land at the time. See American Consulate Jerusalem to Secretary of State, "Israeli Settlements and Dispossession of Arabs," 11 May 1979, Box 37, File 5, PHE.

129. See *International Documents on Palestine*, Folder "Feb.–April 1979," IPS.

130. This was agreed to in the joint Begin-Sadat letter of 26 March 1979 that accompanied the signing of the Israeli-Egyptian treaty.

131. See Al-Madfai, *Jordan, the United States, and the Middle East Peace Process*, 33–61; and Ashton, "Taking Friends for Granted."

132. In his diary, President Carter had remarked upon Strauss's initial selection: "If anyone can keep these negotiations on track and protect me from the Jewish community politically, it's Bob Strauss." See entry for 24 April 1979, Carter, *White House Diary*, 315. On Strauss, see McGarr, *The Whole Damn Deal*.

133. Letter [Hebrew], Zvi Rafiah to Israeli Ambassador to U.S., Washington, 26 April 1979, Subject: Bob Strauss, A-4339/6, ISA.

134. This is confirmed by Eliyahu Ben-Elissar, the director general of Begin's office, in his memoir, *Lo Od Milhamah* [No more war], 199.

135. Defense Minister Weizman resigned as well in May 1980, disillusioned with the direction of the autonomy talks and Begin's "pipe dreams." See Weizman, *The Battle for Peace*, 383–89.

136. Dayan, *Breakthrough*, 303.

137. Ibid., 305. On Dayan's approach to the Palestinian question, see Nathan Yanai, "Moshe Dayan on the Palestinian Problem," in Simon, ed., *The Middle East and North Africa*, 158–84.

138. "Meeting of Committee on Autonomy," Friday 25 May 1979, 2:45 PM, Ben Gurion University, Beersheba, A-4318/1, ISA.

139. On the contradictory uses and meanings of self-determination, see Simpson, "Self-Determination, Human Rights, and the End of Empire in the 1970s"; and "Denying the 'First Right.'"

140. Vance addressed it at the opening of the talks. See "Meeting of Committee on Autonomy," 25 May 1979, 2:45 PM, A-4318/1, ISA.

141. Excerpt from "Secret: Record of a meeting held on Tuesday September 11, 1979 between Dr. Burg and Mr. Robert Strauss," A-4316/7, ISA.

142. "Meeting of Committee on Autonomy," 25 May 1979, 2:45 PM, A-4318/1, ISA.

143. See Derek N. Buckaloo, "Carter's Nicaragua and Other Democratic Quagmires," in Schulman and Zelizer, eds., *Rightward Bound*, 248. On Carter's mixed human rights legacy, see Peterson, "The Carter Administration and the Promotion of Human Rights in the Soviet Union."

144. "Meeting of Committee on Autonomy," 25 May 1979, 2:45 PM, A-4318/1, ISA.

145. See the meeting minutes of 25 May 1979, in A-4318/1, ISA.

146. See Strauss-Begin talks, 12 September 1979, A-4316/7, ISA.

147. Henry Siegman, "Hurricane Carter," *The Nation*, 4 January 2007; and interview by author, Pound Ridge, NY, 14 January 2012. See also the sharp recollections of Burg's involvement by his son Avraham Burg, *In Days to Come*, 67–70.

148. Memorandum of conversation, "Mubarak meeting," The Cabinet Room, 17 September 1979, 1:38–2:30 PM, Brzezinski Donated Material, Box 36, JCL.

149. Ibid.

150. Ibid.

151. All quotes in this paragraph are from "Minutes of session 2, committee on autonomy, San Stefano Hotel, Alexandria, 26 September 1979, 6:45 PM," MFA-6897/5, ISA. For an Egyptian perspective on the Alexandria talks, see Boutros-Ghali, *Egypt's Road to Jerusalem*, 282–88. In a volume based on a January 1980 academic conference in Tel Aviv examining autonomy in comparative perspective, legal scholar Yoram Dinstein noted that "Israel is reconciled to the idea of autonomy as a conduit to drain Palestinian Arab nationalism and direct it to goals other than political independence. Egypt, on the other hand, adheres to the concept of autonomy only because it believes that it will serve as a channel to ultimate statehood." The minutes of the meeting actually demonstrate a gradual alignment with Israel. See Dinstein, *Models of Autonomy*, 302.

152. From the 26 September 1979 transcript in MFA-6897/5, ISA.

153. Ambassador Sol Linowitz to Esther Baruch, 4 April 1980, "Correspondence 1980, A-G," Box 51, Folder 12, Sol M. Linowitz Papers, LOC.

154. On domestic opposition to peace with Israel in Egypt, see Coldwell, "Egypt's 'Autumn of Fury.'"

155. Despite the ban on direct diplomatic communication with the PLO, the CIA maintained regular contact with members of the organization in Lebanon. See Bird, *The Good Spy.* For more on the 1979 back channel, see the records of U.S. ambassador to Lebanon John Gunther Dean, JCL. As Dean writes in the finding aid to his donated records, "What emerges from all these papers is that during the period 1979–1980, the U.S. authorities in Washington considered the PLO and Mr. Arafat valid interlocutors on matters pertaining to the over-all problems of the Near East and not only to security interests related to Americans in the region."

156. "Summary of two evenings of talk with Yasir Arafat—July 24, 25, 1979," undated report, NSA Brzezinski Material, Box 49, File 6, Palestine Liberation Organization 5/79–10/80, JCL.

157. See ibid.

158. On Findley's efforts, see Yaqub, *Imperfect Strangers,* 305–7.

159. *Haliyat,* Journal of the Center for Documentation and Research, Lebanon, 15 (1979): 278, IPS.

160. Ibid., 279.

161. Ibid., 280. See also "Chairman Arafat in Vienna," editorial in *Palestine* 5 (July 1979): 3. On 3 March 1980 French president Valery Giscard d'Estaing recognized the right of the Palestinian people to self-determination and was quickly backed by Great Britain as well.

162. See "Summary of two evenings of talk."

163. Yaqub, *Imperfect Strangers,* 307–9.

164. Don Oberdorfer, "Young Admits PLO Talks, Draws Rebuke from Vance," *Washington Post,* 15 August 1979; and Bernard Gwertzman, "Vance Chides Young for Holding Talks with P.L.O. Official," *New York Times,* 15 August 1979. See also Mitchell, *Jimmy Carter in Africa,* 615–22.

165. Young himself called the policy "ridiculous." See Don Oberdorfer, "Young Criticizes U.S. PLO Policy as 'Ridiculous,'" *Washington Post,* 20 August 1979; and Andrew Young, "Lessons from a Missed Opportunity," *Los Angeles Times,* 12 September 1993. On Young, see DeRoche, *Andrew Young.* Vance was particularly angry that Young had not informed him directly, and he instead learned about the meeting from the Israelis.

166. See Carter, *White House Diary,* 351–52. Carter instructed Brzezinski and Vance "not to make any more reassurances that we were not meeting with the PLO." Ibid., 352.

167. On the broader relationship between African Americans and Arab Americans in this period, see Yaqub, "'Our Declaration of Independence.'"

168. Reminiscences of Vernon Eulion Jordan Jr. (1980), 2, CCOH.

169. Ibid., 3.

170. Reminiscences of Mark Siegel (1979), 359–60, CCOH.

171. Ibid.

172. Reminiscences of Hyman Harry Bookbinder (1979), 127, CCOH. On the broader consequences of the Young resignation on black politics and relations with

Palestinians, see Yaqub, *Imperfect Strangers*, 309–15. On the reaction of black leaders, see Feldman, *A Shadow over Palestine*, 100–101.

173. This was in Carter's 2010 annotated notes to the diary. See Carter, *White House Diary*, 352.

174. Ibid., 361.

175. "Report of Theodore Mann to the Conference of Presidents, November 8, 1979," enclosure sent to Israeli ambassador Ephraim Evron, Washington, DC, 15 November 1979, A-4328/11, ISA.

176. Ibid. Some months after Mann's memo, Carter would write in his diary that "Begin is driving Israel into almost complete isolation among the nations of the world and even alienating a lot of American support that has been the salvation of Israel until now." Entry for 23 July 1980, Carter, *White House Diary*, 450.

177. "Report of Theodore Mann to the Conference of Presidents, November 8, 1979."

178. See, for example, Paul Hoffman, "Israel Debates Palestinian Self-Rule as Negotiations with Egypt Near," *New York Times*, 20 May 1979, 12; and "The 'Autonomy' Stall," editorial, *New York Times*, 18 April 1980, A30.

179. Sicherman, *Palestinian Autonomy, Self-Government and Peace*, 45. For the full record of all these crucial January meetings, see the verbatim transcripts in MFA-6897/6, ISA. In a sign of the significance of this contestation over the autonomy models in the meeting of the "Powers and Responsibilities" working group, excerpts of the discussion and the full model presented by the Israelis was provided to the Palestinian delegation at the Madrid talks in 1991. These were discovered in Rashid Khalidi's box files from the talks. See Papers of the Palestinian Delegation to the Palestinian-Israeli Negotiations, Private Collection of Rashid Khalidi (hereafter PPD); and for the original, "Meeting of Working Group on Powers and Responsibilities of the Autonomy Committee," 16 January 1980, 10:45 AM, Mena House, Cairo, MFA-6897/6, ISA. While both the Egyptian and Israeli models employed a waiting period, the Egyptian version suggested something akin to the process of the Permanent Mandates Commission (PMC) established by the League of Nations. Although the PMC had no coercive power, only the ability to convoke global attention and foster norms, parallels between the autonomy proposals and Class A mandates are worth considering. See Pedersen, *The Guardians*.

180. See "Record of a meeting which took place at the Minister of Interior on Sunday, January 27, 1980, at 5:00 PM," A-4316/10, ISA.

181. Kamel, *The Camp David Accords*, 366. When the Israelis first presented their version of a Self-Governing Authority model, it was "totally rejected" by Egyptian ambassador Ahmed Ezzat Abdel Latif, the leader of the Egyptian Working Group. "The underlying philosophy of such a plan, such a model, is the perpetuation of Israeli control on the West Bank and Gaza and the continuation of its illegal occupation, which is totally unacceptable to us . . . it makes mockery of Camp David." See "Meeting of Working Group on Powers and Responsibilities of the Autonomy Committee," 16 January 1980, 10:45 AM, Mena House, Cairo, MFA-6897/6, ISA.

182. Kamel, *The Camp David Accords*, 367.

183. Entry for 2 August 1980, Carter, *White House Diary*, 453.

184. See "Egypt: Sadat, Israel, and the U.S.: An Intelligence Memorandum, Secret," July 1981, CREST (CIA-RDP06T00412R000200340001-1), NARA.

185. See, in particular, the discussion between Carter and Begin and their delegations in the Cabinet Room on 15 April 1980, 10:31 AM–12:07 PM, Brzezinski Donated Collection, Box 37, JCL.

186. "Meeting between Ministerial Committee for Autonomy Talks and U.S. Special Ambassador, Mr. Sol Linowitz, Sept 2, 1980, 11:30 AM, Cabinet Room, Prime Minister's Office, Jerusalem," A-4316/14, ISA. On Sharon's role as "master builder" of the settlements, see Landau, *Arik*, 153–81.

187. "Autonomy Talks in Deadlock," *Palestine* 6 (February 1980): 3.

188. On the election, see Drew, *Portrait of an Election*.

189. Carter, who had managed to win about 70 percent of the Jewish vote in 1976, only mustered 45 percent in 1980, an all-time low for a Democrat. See Tivnan, *The Lobby*, 134; and Aaron Rosenbaum, "Woo and Woe on the Campaign Trail," *Moment*, January–February 1981. In his diaries, Carter displays frustration over those particular results in one postelection meeting with a liaison to the Jewish community. In his accompanying editorial notes from 2010 Carter adds, "I still have deep regrets about the fact that I alienated many American Jews during my time as president . . . when I pressed Israel, during and after my presidency, to withdraw from other occupied Arab territory as a necessary prerequisite to peace, I was considered by some Jewish Americans to be anti-Israel." Carter, *White House Diary*, 485.

190. See Drew, *Portrait of an Election*, 318.

191. Cable, Secretary of State to U.S. Embassy Tel Aviv, 16 December 1980, RAC Project Number (NLC-16-121-7-22-9), JCL.

192. Ambassador Sol Linowitz to President Jimmy Carter, "Progress in the autonomy negotiations," RAC Project Number (NLC-128-9-5-7-8), JCL. An alternate, sanitized version, withholding Linowitz's concerns about the future prospect of the autonomy talks under Reagan, was released to the public. See Box 10, Folder 5, January–July 1981, Sol M. Linowitz Papers, LOC. Linowitz himself had been shaped by the legal arguments of the Israelis, and possibly Rostow, noting in his memoir that the settlements were not "obviously illegal." Linowitz, *The Making of a Public Man*, 225.

193. Entry for 15 January 1981, Carter, *White House Diary*, 508.

Chapter Five: Neoconservatives Rising: Reagan and the Middle East

1. Reagan, *An American Life*, 410.

2. Rita Hauser, interview by author, New York, April 4, 2008. On the American embrace of Uris's novel, see Silver, *Our Exodus*.

3. Electoral pamphlet, Coalition for Reagan-Bush, undated, CO001-07, WHORM: Subject File, RRL.

4. Address by Ronald Reagan to the B'nai B'rith Forum, 3 September 1980, Folder "Israel Settlements 1981," Box 90494, Geoffrey Kemp Files, RRL.

5. See, among others, Podhoretz, "The Future Danger"; Milson, "How to Make Peace with the Palestinians"; and Tucker, "The Middle East: Carterism without Carter?"

6. Ronald Reagan, "Recognizing the Israeli Asset," *Washington Post*, 15 August 1979. On the role of Israel as a "strategic asset," see Ben-Zvi, *The United States and Israel*. On Reagan's global approach, and the role of human rights, see the forthcoming volume edited by Hunt and Miles, *Reagan's World*.

7. On the remaking of American conservatism, see Perlstein, *Before the Storm*; Perlstein, *Nixonland*; Perlstein, *The Invisible Bridge*; Decker, *The Other Rights Revolution*; Phillips-Fein, *Invisible Hands*; and Kruse, *White Flight*.

8. For Reagan's biographers, see Brands, *Reagan*; Morgan, *Reagan*; Cannon, *President Reagan*; and Morris, *Dutch*. For insight on Reagan's own thinking, see Reagan, *An American Life*; and Reagan and Brinkley, *The Reagan Diaries*. On his domestic impact, and the broader economic and cultural transformations of the 1980s, see Rossinow, *The Reagan Era*; and Rodgers, *Age of Fracture*.

9. Jeremi Suri, "Détente and Its Discontents," in Schulman and Zelizer, eds., *Rightward Bound*, 236. On Reagan's foreign policy, see Arquilla, *The Reagan Imprint*; Collins, *Transforming America*; Diggins, *Ronald Reagan*; Wilson, "How Grand Was Reagan's Strategy"; and Wilentz, *The Age of Reagan*.

10. Suri, "Détente and Its Discontents," 242. For an incisive study on how the domestic politics around détente paved the way for Reagan's 1980 victory, see Zelizer, "Detente and Domestic Politics."

11. See Julian Zelizer, "Conservatives, Carter, and the Politics of National Security," in Schulman and Zelizer, eds., *Rightward Bound*, 265–87. John Lewis Gaddis situates this transitional moment in containment's broader history in *Strategies of Containment*, 342–79.

12. Smith, *Morality, Reason, and Power*, 9. On defense policy, see Olav Njølstad, "The Carter Legacy: Entering the Second Era of the Cold War," in Njølstad, ed., *The Last Decade of the Cold War*, 196–225; and Auten, *Carter's Conversion*.

13. A leader of this disaffected group was referring to fellow dissident liberals as "neoconservatives" by 1982. See Norman Podhoretz, "The Neo-Conservative Anguish over Reagan's Foreign Policy," *New York Times Magazine*, 2 May 1982. For a neoconservative critique of Carter's foreign policy, see Kirkpatrick, "Dictatorships and Double Standards." On the history and intellectual roots of the neoconservatives and their impact on Reagan, see Vaïsse, *Neoconservatism*; Blumenthal, *The Rise of the Counter-Establishment*; Ehrman, *The Rise of Neoconservatism*; Halper and Clarke, *America Alone*; Mann, *Rise of the Vulcans*; and Norton, *Leo Strauss and the Politics of American Empire*.

14. Christison, *Perceptions of Palestine*, 198.

15. Rothkopf, *Running the World*, 211.

16. Ibid., 212. Others disagree; see William Inboden, "Grand Strategy and Petty Squabbles: The Paradox and Lessons of the Reagan NSC," in Brands and Suri, eds., *The Power of the Past*, 151–80.

17. For more background on their approach to foreign policy, see Rothkopf, *Running the World*, 210–28. Also relevant, but less reliable, are Haig, *Caveat*; Weinberger,

Fighting for Peace; and McFarlane, *Special Trust*. For a crucial study of the Weinberger Doctrine, see Yoshitani, *Reagan on War.*

18. Quandt, *Peace Process*, 247.

19. Howard Teicher, interview by author, 19 June 2013, Washington, DC.

20. See Haig, *Caveat*, 169–70; and Quandt, *Peace Process*, 248–49. For detailed attention to Haig's views on strategic consensus, see Peck, *The Reagan Administration and the Palestinian Question*; and Cobban, "The US-Israeli Relationship in the Reagan Era." For the Israeli view of Haig, see "Alexander Haig v'Hamizrach Ha'Tichon" [Alexander Haig and the Middle East], 27 January 1981, MFA-8467/4.

21. Crist, *The Twilight War*, 63–64.

22. See Odd Arne Westad, "Reagan's Anti-Revolutionary Offensive in the Third World," in Njølstad, ed., *The Last Decade of the Cold War*, 241–62. On the Reagan Doctrine, see Pach, "The Reagan Doctrine"; and Stanley Hoffmann, "Reagan Abroad," *New York Review of Books*, 4 February 1982.

23. Interview with Hermann Eilts, Frontline Diplomacy. For contemporaneous accounts of Reagan's impact, see Spiegel, *The Other Arab-Israeli Conflict*, 395–429; and Aruri, "The United States and Palestine."

24. Interview with Nicholas Veliotes, Frontline Diplomacy.

25. Joseph Kraft, "A New Middle East Approach," 5 March 1981, A-7383/10, ISA.

26. Meeting between Begin, Haig, and delegations, 5 April 1981, 4:45 PM, MFA-7083/12, ISA.

27. Ibid.

28. Toasts by FM Shamir and Secretary of State Haig after Dinner Hosted by FM Shamir, King David Hotel, 5 April 1981, A-4341/1, ISA.

29. See Meeting between Shamir, Haig and their delegations [Hebrew and English], 6 April 1981, 9:45 AM, Ministry of Foreign Affairs, Jerusalem, MFA-6890/2, ISA.

30. Ibid.

31. For full records of these top-secret meetings between McFarlane and Israeli officials, see A-7384/6, ISA.

32. "Remarks at the Welcoming Ceremony for Prime Minister Menachem Begin of Israel," *Public Papers of the Presidents: Ronald Reagan, 1981–1989* (hereafter *PPPRR*), 9 September 1981.

33. See the report of a meeting between Secretary of State Haig and Jewish leaders Howard Squadron, Max Fisher, David Korn, and Yehuda Hellman, 24 February 1981, 9:00 AM, A-4328/11, ISA.

34. The background, goals, and details of each leadership meeting can be found in the Folder "Jewish Strategy," OA 5456, as well as OA 6410 and OA 8120 in the Elizabeth Dole Files, RRL.

35. "Welcome, Mr. Begin," *Washington Post*, 8 September 1981.

36. "True Grit with Mr. Begin," *New York Times*, 6 September 1981.

37. "Top Secret Meeting between President Reagan and PM Begin at the White House," 9 September 1981, 11:10 AM, A-7384/9, ISA.

38. Interview with Samuel Lewis, Frontline Diplomacy. See also Crist, *The Twilight War*, 57.

39. "Top Secret Meeting between President Reagan and PM Begin at the White House," 9 September 1981, 11:10 AM, A-7384/9, ISA.

40. Memorandum, "Suggestions Regarding Begin Visit," September 1981, A-7384/9, ISA. See also "Talking Points in the U.S.A," September 1981, A-7384/9, ISA.

41. "Breakfast meeting between President Reagan and Prime Minister Begin at the White House," 10 September 1981, 9:10 AM, A-7384/9, ISA.

42. Ibid.

43. "Suggestions Regarding Begin Visit" and "Talking Points in the U.S.A," A-7384/9, ISA.

44. On the Soviet-PLO relationship in the early 1980s, see Laskier and Bazov, *Teror be-sherut ha-mahepekhah*, 104–13; and on the embassy, Ned Temko, "PLO's Arafat: What He Wants Is Embassy in US," *Christian Science Monitor*, 22 October 1981, https://www.csmonitor.com/1981/1022/102239.html.

45. "Breakfast meeting between President Reagan and Prime Minister Begin at the White House," 10 September 1981, 9:10 AM, A-7384/9, ISA.

46. The Israeli Ministry of Foreign Affairs North America division conducted extensive analysis of Reagan's views and noted the favorable departure from Carter. See ISA/MFA/8467/1, 4, 5, 15 and 8652/2, 3, 4.

47. For the full text of the memorandum, see Laqueur and Rubin, *The Israel-Arab Reader*, 238–39.

48. Lewis, Frontline Diplomacy.

49. Israeli archives now reveal that the Osirak attack elicited furious American opposition, even from neoconservatives like UN ambassador Jeane Kirkpatrick. See ISA/A/7384/4, 6. See also Begin's emotional letter to Weinberger on the suspension of arms supply after the attack, comparing Israel's preventative actions against nuclear weapons with the failure to stop Zyklon B poisoning during the Holocaust. Begin to Weinberger, 10 June 1981, A-7384/4, ISA.

50. For the administration's angry reaction, see Folder "Golan Heights 1982," Geoffrey Kemp Files, RRL.

51. Quoted in Haig, *Caveat*, 328.

52. Ibid., 329.

53. This strain is evident in a personal letter from Reagan to Begin after the suspension of the Memorandum of Understanding in the wake of the Golan Heights Law. See Reagan to Begin, 8 January 1982, A-4342/1, ISA.

54. Quandt, *Peace Process*, 289.

55. Memo, Peter Tarnoff to Zbigniew Brzezinski, "US Relations with the Radical Arabs," 16 January 1980, Folder 1, "Soviet and Middle East," Box 4, Dennis Ross Files, RRL.

56. On 23 April 1986, Dennis Ross, a young NSC analyst, received a copy of the report from his former boss, Paul Wolfowitz, then the ambassador to Indonesia. In the margins, Wolfowitz had scribbled a series of disparaging comments, calling the overall conclusion of the study "BS." See "US Relations with the Radical Arabs."

57. "Msibat Itonaim-Reagan" [Reagan's press conference], 6 November 1980, MFA-8652/3, ISA.

58. Address by Ronald Reagan to the B'nai B'rith Forum, 3 September 1980.

59. Ibid., 12–13.

60. See "Meeting with Lord Carrington," 28 February 1981, A-4338/11, ISA. The French were also dealing with the PLO. See "Meeting with Jean François-Poncet," A-4338/11, ISA.

61. See Seale, *Abu Nidal.*

62. Transcript of complete interview given by Richard Allen to *20/20: The ABC News Magazine,* 2 April 1981, Folder "PLO 1981," Box 90220, Geoffrey Kemp Files, RRL.

63. Ibid.

64. Memo, "U.S. Policy toward PLO," Douglas J. Feith to Norman A. Bailey, 28 August 1981, Folder "PLO 1981," Box 90220, Geoffrey Kemp Files, RRL.

65. Ibid.

66. This second unsigned document, "Subject: PLO," also appears in "PLO 1981," Box 90220, Geoffrey Kemp Files, RRL. It is possible that this approach to use "force" and the suggestion of a "green light" to target the PLO can be understood in connection with the 1982 Israeli invasion of Lebanon, discussed in chapter 6. I am grateful to Andrea Dessì for his insight on this point.

67. Memo, "The PLO and the President's Press Conference," Raymond Tanter to Richard V. Allen, 9 November 1981, "PLO 1981," Box 90220, Geoffrey Kemp Files, RRL.

68. Ibid.

69. Congressman Paul Findley to Richard V. Allen, 10 July 1981, Folder "PLO 1981," Box 90220, Geoffrey Kemp Files, RRL.

70. "U.S., PLO: 7 Years of Secret Contacts," *Los Angeles Times,* 5 July 1981, 1; "U.S., PLO Reportedly Have Custom of Secret Dealings," *Philadelphia Inquirer,* 6 July 1981, 1-A.

71. Isam Sartawi to John Mroz, 27 May 1981, Folder "PLO 1981," Box 90220, Geoffrey Kemp Files, RRL. For more on this secret channel, see Christison, *Perceptions of Palestine,* 205.

72. Memo, "Continuing Strains among the Palestinians," Landrum Bolling to Geoffrey Kemp, 14 August 1981, Folder "PLO 1981," Box 90220, Geoffrey Kemp Files, RRL.

73. Ibid. Bolling met continually with the PLO leadership after earlier efforts at engagement under Carter. See "Meeting with Yasir Arafat—April 13, 1979—Beirut," Records of the Office of the National Security Advisor, Series 7, PLO, 1/78–4/79, Container 49, JCL (released via MR request).

74. Kanafani was born in Acre and forced into exile in 1948, and was later recruited by Dr. George Habash into the Arab Nationalist Movement (ANM), a left-wing pan-Arab organization whose membership evolved into the PFLP. Although assassinated by the Israeli Mossad alongside his niece in a Beirut car bombing in 1972, Kanafani's influence on Palestinian letters was far-reaching. See Hilary Kilpatrick's introduction to Kanafani, *Men in the Sun.*

75. "Il-Rais Reagan yusalam risala muhima fi beit il-abyad" [President Reagan delivers important message in the White House], *Al-Hadaf* 12.522 (24 January 1981), IPS.

76. "Idarat Reagan tu'hadad" [The Reagan administration is threatening], *Al-Hadaf* 12.525 (14 February 1981), IPS.

77. "Hukumat Begin tas'ad min il-nisha't il-istitani" [Begin government increasing settlement activity], *Al-Hadaf* 12.524 (7 February 1981), IPS.

78. Peck, *The Reagan Administration and the Palestinian Question*, 11.

79. "An Interview with Reagan," *Time*, 30 June 1980.

80. "Excerpts from President Reagan's Answers in Interview with Five Reporters," *New York Times*, 3 February 1981.

81. Congressman Carl D. Pursell to Ronald Reagan, 25 February 1981; reply by Max Friedersdorf, 2 May 1981, FO, case file 007580, WHORM: Subject File, RRL.

82. Samih K. Farsoun to Ronald Reagan, 23 February 1981, ND 016, case file 007358, WHORM: Subject File, RRL.

83. Kamal Hassan Ali to Yitzhak Shamir, 19 February 1981, A-4182/17, ISA.

84. Ibid.

85. Meeting between Begin, Haig, and delegations, 6 April 1981, 10:50 AM, MFA-6890/2, ISA.

86. "Thoughts on Legality of Israel's West Bank Settlements," memo, Raymond Tanter to Richard V. Allen, cc: Douglas Feith, 3 August 1981, CO074, case file 037386, WHORM: Subject File, RRL (emphasis in original).

87. See David A. Korn, "U.S. Views on Israeli Settlements Have Shifted," letter to the editor, *New York Times*, 1 October 1991, www.nytimes.com/1991/10/01/opinion/l-us-views-on-israeli-settlements-have-shifted-684291.html.

88. Feith, "The Settlements and Peace," 29.

89. See Christison, *Perceptions of Palestine*, 223–41. The broader conservative shift in American politics is delineated in Schulman and Zelizer, *Rightward Bound*.

90. Moynihan, "Joining the Jackals."

91. For more on Moynihan's intellectual leanings on Israel and inspiration for neoconservatives, see Yaqub, *Imperfect Strangers*, 177–82. A flattering study of Moynihan can be found in Troy, *Moynihan's Moment*. For a critical read of Moynihan and the relation of his views on race and Zionism, see Feldman, *A Shadow over Palestine*, 43–57.

92. "Dvarim al kever rosh Beitar" [Words at the gravesite of Beitar's leader], 30 June 1981, PM136, MBC.

93. These are Samuel Lewis's numbers; for a slightly different count, see Zertal and Eldar, *Lords of the Land*, 99.

94. Cable, Sam Lewis to George Shultz et al., 2 February 1982, Folder "Israel Settlements, 1982," Box 90494, Geoffrey Kemp Files, RRL.

95. For an extensive analysis of the phases of expansion with particular attention to the 1980s, see Allegra, Handel, and Maggor, *Normalizing Occupation*; and Demant, "Israeli Settlement Policy Today."

96. Cable, Sam Lewis to George Shultz et al., 2 February 1982. On the evacuation of Yamit, see Feige, *Settling in the Hearts*, 196–211; and Hirschhorn, *City on a Hilltop*, 58–97.

97. Cable, Sam Lewis to George Shultz et al., 2 February 1982.

98. Reagan and Brinkley, *The Reagan Diaries*, 130.

99. Reagan, *An American Life*, 441.

100. Reagan and Brinkley, *The Reagan Diaries*, 577.

101. "Meeting between Committee on Autonomy, Chairman Dr. J. Burg, Minister of Interior and USA Secretary of State, Mr. Alexander Haig, 28 January 1982, 8:10 AM, Cabinet Room, Government Secretariat, Prime Minister's Office, Jerusalem," MFA-6898/8, ISA.

102. Ibid.

103. "Raayon Sar HaChutz" [The foreign minister's interview], *Kol Yisrael* [Voice of Israel], 24 October 1981, MFA-6898/6, ISA.

104. "Meeting between Committee on Autonomy."

105. Ibid.

106. Ibid.

107. The dispute centered around the Elon Moreh settlement, which was contested by Arab petitioners in front of the Supreme Court, who ordered the land returned in a ruling on 22 October 1979, which Begin accepted in deference to legal authority, while shifting toward a policy of settling on state lands in the West Bank. On the significance of the Elon Moreh ruling, and the Israeli judicial system's "contribution toward the Judaization of the West Bank" (in the words of Israeli historian Tom Segev), see the special publication (Hebrew and English) by the Israel State Archives, "The 'Elon Moreh' High Court Decision of 22 October 1979 and the Israeli Government's Reaction," http://www.archives.gov.il/NR/exeres/2256A595-10F5-458E-ACB8-7CDDBDF86634,frameless.htm?NRMODE=Published; Yaacov Lozowick, "What Are the Settlements For?" 6 November 2012, Blog of the Israel State Archives, http://israelsdocuments.blogspot.co.uk/2012/11/1979-what-are-settlements-for.html; and Tom Segev, "That Seventies Show: The Settlements Didn't Begin with Begin," *Haaretz*, 26 October 2012, http://www.haaretz.com/weekend/the-makings-of-history/that-seventies-show-the-settlements-didn-t-begin-with-begin.premium-1.472488.

108. "Meeting between Committee on Autonomy." U.S. officials were aware of Sharon's flagrant behavior years earlier. Reporting on land requisition in April 1979, Lewis noted that "the fact is that the GOI [Government of Israel], under the constant goading of Sharon and Gush Emunim, appears to be moving towards abandonment of its forbearance concerning seizure of private land for settlements." Gilbert Kulick to Secretary of State, "Land Requisition for Settlements," 27 April 1979, PHE.

109. "Meeting between Committee on Autonomy." Lord Carrington, the British foreign secretary, traveled to Jerusalem in March and covered much of the same ground with Begin, to no avail. Carrington was more insistent than Haig, telling Begin that "Palestinian nationalism won't go away" and autonomy would never accommodate the Palestinian question. "Meeting between Prime Minister Begin and Secretary of State for Foreign and Commonwealth Affairs, Lord Carrington," Jerusalem, 31 March 1982, A-7375/7, ISA.

110. See the detailed work on religious motivations by Kepel, *The Prophet and Pharaoh*; and military linkages by Kandil, *Soldiers, Spies, and Statesmen*; and Kandil, *The Power Triangle*.

111. Meeting between Minister of Foreign Affairs of Israel, Mr. Yitzhak Shamir and Secretary of State of U.S.A., Mr. Alexander Haig, 14 January 1982, 11:30 AM, Jerusalem, A-4342/1, ISA.

112. Ibid.

113. The two officials, Deputy Assistant Secretary of State Wat T. Cluverius IV and Geoffrey Kemp of the NSC, emphasized Sharon's position on this matter: "The continuing security role of the Israeli security forces, whether military or civilian, would continue in Sharon's definition to be widespread. This also contradicts the Egyptian and Palestinian conception, which envisages security responsibility largely reverting to local Arab police authorities." See "Memorandum for the Record. Cluverius and Kemp to the Director of Central Intelligence," 19 January 1982, CREST (CIA-RDP84B00049R001303220026-8), NARA.

114. Meeting of Sharon and delegation and Haig and delegation, King David Hotel, Jerusalem, 3:00 PM, 14 January 1982, A-4342/1, ISA.

115. Ibid.

116. "Meeting between the Minister of Interior, Dr. J. Burg, Chairman Committee on Autonomy and USA Secretary of State, Dr. Alexander Haig," 15 January 1982, 10:45 AM, MFA-7068/13, ISA.

117. Ibid.

118. Begin to Reagan, 18 January 1982, A-4342/1, ISA.

119. Redacted author, "Memorandum on U.S.-Israeli Differences over the Camp David Peace Process, 24 August 1982," declassified 24 September, CREST (CIA-RDP 84B00049R00160401004-1), NARA (emphasis in original). Private correspondence has confirmed the likely author was Robert Ames, the CIA's top Middle East analyst, later killed in the April 1983 bombing of the U.S. Embassy in Beirut.

120. Linowitz, *Making of a Public Man*, 227.

Chapter Six: The Limits of Lebanon

1. Al-Hout, *My Life in the PLO*, 167–71.

2. Shlaim, *The Iron Wall*, 406–11.

3. Interagency Intelligence Assessment: Likely Evolution of Lebanon Situation, 17 June 1982, CREST (CIA-RDP85T00153R000200050020-3), NARA. This aim has also been revealed in an Israeli intelligence study of the war. See Amir Oren, "Revealed: The Deceptions by Begin, Sharon and Eitan behind the First Lebanon War," *Haaretz*, 5 May 2014, https://www.haaretz.com/israel-news/.premium-1.588972.

4. This number might be as high as 20,000 but remains the subject of debate. See Khalidi, *Under Siege*, 200n5; and Gabriel, *Operation Peace for Galilee*. Over 650 Israelis were killed.

5. Among the best accounts by journalists are Schiff and Yaari, *Israel's Lebanon War*; Friedman, *From Beirut to Jerusalem*; Fisk, *Pity the Nation*; and Randal, *Going All the Way*. For memoirs, see Reagan, *An American Life*; Haig, *Caveat*; Shultz, *Turmoil and Triumph*; Tanter, *Who's at the Helm*; Teicher and Teicher, *Twin Pillars to Desert Storm*; Gates, *From the Shadows*; Salem, *Violence and Diplomacy in*

Lebanon; Avner, *The Prime Ministers*; Kimche, *The Last Option*; Eitan, *A Soldier's Story*; Gefen, *An Israeli in Lebanon*; Timmerman, *The Longest War*; Yermiya, *My War Diary*; Sharon, *Warrior*; Arens, *Broken Covenant*; al-Hout, *My Life in the PLO*; and Makdisi, *Beirut Fragments*. For regional perspectives, see Evron, *War and Intervention in Lebanon*; Rabinovich, *The War for Lebanon*; and Sayigh, "Israel's Military Performance in Lebanon, June 1982."

6. Naor, *Begin Ba'Shilton* [Begin in power]; Shilon, *Menachem Begin*; and Schiff and Yaari, *Israel's Lebanon War*.

7. Khalidi, *Under Siege*; Sayigh, *Armed Struggle*, 522–43; Sayigh, "Palestinian Military Performance in the 1982 War"; Brynen, "PLO Policy in Lebanon."

8. Al-Hout, *Sabra and Shatila*; Sayigh, *Too Many Enemies*; Kapeliouk, *Sabra and Shatila*.

9. Crist, *The Twilight War*; Tyler, *A World of Trouble*.

10. Maya Mikdashi, "Let Us Now Praise Murderous Men," *Jadaliyya*, 19 April 2014, http://www.jadaliyya.com/pages/index/17395/let-us-now-praise-murderous-men. On the role of memory around the Lebanese civil war, see Haugbolle, *War and Memory in Lebanon*.

11. For artists, see Zaatari, *The Earth of Endless Secrets, A Conversation with an Imagined Israeli Filmmaker Named Avi Mograbi*, and "Letter to a Refusing Pilot"; Raad, *The Atlas Group*; Elkoury, *Atlantis* and *Passing Time*; Joreige, *Objects of War*; and Adnan, *Sitt Marie Rose*. For films, see Nadine Labaki, *Wa'hala l'wein?* [Where do we go now?] (2011), Ziad Doueiri, *West Beirut* (1998) and *The Insult* (2017); and Al-Jazeera's documentary *Harb Lubnan* [The War of Lebanon] (2007).

12. Eyal Zisser, "The 1982 'Peace for Galilee' War: Looking Back in Anger—Between an Option of a War and a War of No Option," in Bar-On, ed., *A Never-Ending Conflict*, 208.

13. The war unleashed political and artistic upheaval in Israel. See, for example, Kenan, *The Road to Ein Harod*; Ravikovitch, *Hovering at a Low Altitude*; and the discussion in Glenda Abramson, "Oh, My Land, My Birthplace: Lebanon War and Intifada in Israeli Fiction and Poetry," in Harris and Omer-Sheman, eds., *Narratives of Dissent*, 221–40. For films, see Samuel Maoz, *Lebanon* (2009); and Ari Folman, *Waltz with Bashir* (2008).

14. On the evolution of memory around the war, see Asher Kaufmann, "Forgetting the Lebanon War? On Silence, Denial and Selective Remembrance in Israel of the First Lebanon War," in Ben-Ze'ev, Ginio, and Winter, eds., *Shadows of War*, 197–216.

15. Palestinians refer to the events in Jordan as "Black September." See Chamberlin, *The Global Offensive*, 108–41; and Sayigh, *Armed Struggle*, 262–81. For Israel's role in the fighting, see Rubinovitz, "Blue and White 'Black September.'"

16. Sayigh, *Too Many Enemies*, 30; al-Hout, *My Life in the PLO*, 75.

17. For background on the Palestinians in Lebanon, see Sayigh, *Too Many Enemies*; Rubenberg, "The Civilian Infrastructure of the Palestine Liberation Organization"; Cobban, *The Palestinian Liberation Organisation*; and Khalili, *Heroes and Martyrs of Palestine*.

18. On this earlier intervention, see Gendzier, *Notes from the Minefield*.

19. The clashes were with the army and internal security forces, and it was Maaruf Saad's local organization (allied to the Palestinians), rather than the Palestinians themselves, who were mainly involved. For more on the Lebanese Civil War, see, among others, Hiro, *Lebanon*; Khalaf, *Civil and Uncivil Violence in Lebanon*; Salibi, *A House of Many Mansions*; Stocker, *Spheres of Intervention*; and Khalidi, *Conflict and Violence in Lebanon*.

20. See Ajami, "Lebanon and Its Inheritors." Imam Musa al-Sadr, the prominent Iranian-born cleric who had revitalized Shia politics in the south by establishing Amal and empowering a passionate constituency of supporters, was a leading critic of these developments. While Musa al-Sadr had initially supported the Palestinian cause, shortly before his mysterious 1978 disappearance in Libya, he was quoted by Lebanese politician Karim Pakradouni as saying, "The Palestinian resistance is not a revolution; it does not seek martyrdom. It is a military machine that terrorizes the Arab world. With weapons Arafat gets money; with money he can feed the press; and thanks to the press he can get a hearing before world public opinion. . . . The Shia have finally gotten over their inferiority complex vis-à-vis the Palestinian organizations."

21. For an overview on the interrelated dynamics and separate trajectories of both, see Norton, *Hezbollah*. Ironically, both organizations were supported by the PLO at different times.

22. On UNIFIL and the role of peacekeepers in Lebanon, see Weinberger, "Peace-keeping Options in Lebanon."

23. Habib was a senior American career diplomat, born in Brooklyn, New York, of Lebanese Maronite ancestry. For more background, see Boykin, *Cursed Is the Peacemaker*.

24. Avi Shlaim explains this difference in outlook between Begin and Sharon. See Shlaim, *The Iron Wall*, 406–7. See also Benny Morris's review of the Hebrew volume on military decision making in 1982 published by Israel's Defense Ministry, "The Israeli Army Papers That Show What Ariel Sharon Hid from the Cabinet in the First Lebanon War," *Haaretz*, 2 March 2018, https://www.haaretz.com/life /books/.premium-the-idf-papers-that-show-what-sharon-hid-in-the-lebanon-war-1 .5867371.

25. Meeting between Prime Minister Begin and U.S. Ambassador Lewis, Jerusalem, 29 April 1981, 12:15 PM, A-7384/2, ISA. On the history of the Zionist-Maronite relationship, see Eisenberg, *My Enemy's Enemy*.

26. Meeting between Prime Minister Begin and U.S. Ambassador Lewis, A-7384/2, ISA. This line of argument about Maronite persecution at the hands of the Palestinians would continue after the invasion, with Begin sending Christian allies to meet with Ambassador Lewis at the U.S. Embassy in Tel Aviv in order to encourage the United States to help rescue Lebanon from Palestinians. As May El-Murr told Lewis about the PLO, "We simply have to cut off their head, like with a snake." See Meeting held at the Embassy of the United States in Tel Aviv, 6 July 1982, Ambassador Samuel Lewis, Mrs. May El-Murr and Mr. Freddie El Murr, A-4321/4, ISA.

27. On Israel's motivations in Lebanon, see Schulze, "Perceptions and Misperceptions"; Yaniv and Liber, "Personal Whim or Strategic Imperative?"; and Oren, "Revealed." For more on the Maronite connection, see Laurie Eisenberg, "History

Revisited or Revamped? The Maronite Factor in Israel's 1982 Invasion of Lebanon," in Karsh, Miller, and Kerr, eds., *Conflict Diplomacy and Society in Israeli-Lebanese Relations*, 54–78; Schulze, *Israel's Covert Diplomacy in Lebanon*; and Randal, *Going All the Way*.

28. See Shlaim, *The Iron Wall*, 406–18.

29. Ibid., 407.

30. Lewis, Frontline Diplomacy. See also Feldman and Rechnitz-Kijner, *Deception, Consensus, and War*.

31. Morris Draper, "Marines in Lebanon: A Ten-Year Retrospective: Lessons Learned," Quantico, VA, 1992 (courtesy of Jon Randal).

32. Lewis, Frontline Diplomacy.

33. Ibid. For more on Sharon's role in the 1982 War, see Benziman, *Sharon*; and Landau, *Arik*. On his early efforts to sow chaos in Lebanon prior to the invasion, see Bergman, *Rise and Kill First*, 240–47.

34. Lewis, Frontline Diplomacy.

35. While recent scholarship still upholds Haig's denial of having given Sharon permission, the minutes of the meeting prove otherwise. See Crist, *The Twilight War*, 109. For an earlier study on the green light, without access to Hill's notebooks, see Schiff, "The Green Light."

36. Handwritten meeting notes, 25 May 1982, Notebook #17, Charles Hill Papers, Box 76, Hoover Institution Archives, Palo Alto, CA (hereafter HIA; emphasis in original).

37. See Shlaim, *The Iron Wall*, 411–14.

38. Tyler, *A World of Trouble*, 271.

39. See Schiff and Yaari, *Israel's Lebanon War*, 97–99; and Bergman, *Rise and Kill First*, 248–50. See also Quandt, *Peace Process*, 250–54.

40. On the internal dynamics of Sharon's discussions with the cabinet, see Shlaim, *The Iron Wall*, 415–18; and Morris, "The Israeli Army Papers."

41. See Zisser, "The 1982 'Peace for Galilee' War," 193–210. Begin admitted that 1982 was a war of "option" and it would cure the "trauma of 1973" (Begin cited on pp. 194–95).

42. "Top Secret Meeting between Prime Minister Begin and Ambassador Philip Habib," Jerusalem, 7 June 1982, 5:00 PM, MFA-7080/3, ISA.

43. "Top secret meeting between Prime Minister and Foreign Minister with Ambassador Philip Habib," 8 June 1982, 5:45 PM, MFA-7080/3, ISA.

44. George J. Church, "The Shakeup at State," *Time*, 5 July 1982.

45. Detailed accounts of the administration's policy debate over Lebanon can be found in Quandt, "Reagan's Lebanon Policy"; and Tanter, *Who's at the Helm?*

46. Shlaim, *The Iron Wall*, 420–21.

47. See "Meeting of Ministerial Committee, Presided over by Prime Minister Begin, with Ambassador Philip Habib, The Prime Minister's Office, Jerusalem," 13 June 1982, 5:30 PM, MFA-7080/4, ISA.

48. Summary of the President's meeting with Prime Minister Menachem Begin of Israel, 21 June 1982, Folder "Near East and South Asian Affairs Directorate, NSC: Records," Box 91987, File 3, RRL.

49. Ibid.

50. For a detailed account, see "Summary of the President's Plenary Meeting" and "Summary of the Working Luncheon," 21 June 1982, both in Folder "Near East and South Asian Affairs Directorate, NSC: Records," Box 91987, File 3, RRL.

51. On Haig's resignation and conduct in Lebanon, see Stanley Hoffmann, "The Vicar's Revenge," *New York Review of Books*, 31 May 1984; and Haig, *Caveat*, 317–52.

52. See, for example, the letter exchange between Reagan and Begin on 8 July 1982, in A-4178/4, ISA.

53. Lewis, Frontline Diplomacy.

54. Shlaim, *The Iron Wall*, 422–23.

55. Ronald Reagan, diary entry, 7/31–8/1/82, in Reagan and Brinkley, *The Reagan Diaries*, 95.

56. Shlaim, *The Iron Wall*, 424; al-Hout, *My Life in the PLO*, 152; and Khalidi, *Under Siege*.

57. Quoted in al-Hout, *My Life in the PLO*, 151–52.

58. For the record of participants and detailed minutes, see "National Security Council Meeting," 4 August 1982, 9:10–10:02 AM, NSC 00057 [Lebanon Situation] in Records, Meeting Files, NSC Executive Secretariat, RRL.

59. Ibid.

60. Veliotes, Frontline Interview.

61. Ibid.

62. Shlaim, *The Iron Wall*, 425.

63. For details on the siege and a periodization of the fighting, see Khalidi, *Under Siege*.

64. Diary entry, 12 August 1982, Reagan and Brinkley, *The Reagan Diaries*, 98. In his memoir, Reagan aide Michael Deaver describes the impetus for the call and the outcome, which he witnessed in the Oval Office. See Deaver, *A Different Drummer*, 99–103.

65. Shlaim, *The Iron Wall*, 425.

66. For a detailed study of Arafat and his decision making during the war, see Rashid Khalidi, "Leadership and Negotiation during the 1982 War: Yasser Arafat and the PLO," in Kellerman and Rubin, eds., *Leadership and Negotiation in the Middle East*, 49–69.

67. Shlaim, *The Iron Wall*, 425; al-Hout, *My Life in the PLO*, 156–57.

68. See "Preface to the 2014 Reissue," in Khalidi, *Under Siege*.

69. On the negotiations of the withdrawal, see "Second Meeting between Minister A. Sharon, Mr. P. Habib, Mr. Draper, Mr. D. Kimche, and others, P.M, 8 August 1982," A-4317/4, ISA; "Meeting between Prime Minister and Ambassador Philip Habib, The Prime Minister's Office, Jerusalem," 11 August 1982, 10:00 AM, A-4317/5, ISA; and "Meeting between prime Minister Begin and Ambassador Philip Habib, The Prime Minister's Office," 15 August 1982, 8:30 AM, A-4317/5, ISA.

70. Ronald Reagan to Thomas O'Neil Jr., 24 August 1982, Countries (CO) 86, File 081440, RRL. A duplicate copy of this letter was sent to the President Pro Tempore of the Senate, Strom Thurmond, in ibid.

71. Shlaim, *The Iron Wall*, 427.

72. "Address to the Nation on United States Policy for Peace in the Middle East," *PPPRR*, 1 September 1982.

73. Top Secret, Meeting between Minister of Defense Ariel Sharon with George Shultz, 27 August 1982, 4:00 PM, A-4342/10, ISA.

74. "Address to the Nation on United States Policy for Peace in the Middle East," *PPPRR*, 1 September 1982.

75. This last phrase of assurance was composed right before delivery, as is evident from the president's handwriting on the original copy of the final draft. See draft copy, Presidential Address on the Middle East, 1 September 1982, 2:00 PM, File "Speechwriting: Speech Drafts," Box 49, RRL.

76. "Address to the Nation on United States Policy for Peace in the Middle East," *PPPRR*, 1 September 1982.

77. Cable, George Shultz to UN Secretary General, 2 September 1982, Folder "Arab-Israel Peace Process: Memos, September 1982," Box 90217, Geoffrey Kemp Files, RRL.

78. Ibid.

79. E-mail from Nicholas Veliotes, 8 March 2012; interview with Nicholas Veliotes, 17 March 2012, McLean, VA. Robert Ames was also a major contributor to the initiative. For an assessment of the Reagan Plan soon after it was announced, see Aruri and Moughrabi, "The Reagan Middle East Initiative." Within the PLO, Yasser Arafat initially agreed to work with King Hussein along these lines, but a subsequent PNC meeting in Kuwait voted down such a move.

80. "Address to the Nation on United States Policy for Peace in the Middle East," *PPPRR*, 1 September 1982.

81. See Reagan to Begin, delivered by Lewis, 31 August 1982, A-4342/7, ISA. The accompanying talking points sent to Begin by Reagan were published in the *New York Times*, 8 September 1982.

82. Interview with Samuel Lewis, 19 March 2012, McLean, VA.

83. Lewis, Frontline Diplomacy.

84. Reagan to Begin, 5 September 1982, A-4342/7, ISA.

85. See Dan Meridor to Begin, 5 September 1982, and Begin to Reagan, 5 September 1982 with attachments, both in A-4342/7, ISA.

86. Cable, "September 2 Israeli Cabinet Communiqué on President Reagan's Middle East Speech," Folder "Arab-Israel Peace Process: Cables, September 1982," Box 90217, Geoffrey Kemp Files, RRL.

87. See "U.S.-Israeli Differences over the Camp David Peace Process," 24 August 1982, CREST (CIA-RDP84B00049R001604010004-1).

88. Shlaim, *The Iron Wall*, 431.

89. "U.S. Positions to be conveyed to Prime Minister Begin on behalf of the President," 31 August 1982, A-4342/7, ISA.

90. Cable, "September 2 Israeli Cabinet Communiqué on President Reagan's Middle East Speech."

91. See Memorandum for the Director of Central Intelligence, "Israeli Policies in the West Bank," 28 October 1982, CREST (CIA-RDP84B00049R001202830034-4),

NARA. This CIA report discusses the work of Meron Benvenisti, former deputy mayor of Jerusalem, whose pioneering research warned of the new reality being created in the West Bank. Benvenisti, the CIA analysis explained, "argues that Israel is acting *not* as an occupier but as a power moving toward establishing *permanent sovereignty*" (emphasis in original). See Benvenisti, "The Turning Point in Israel," *New York Review of Books*, 13 October 1983.

92. "U.S. Positions to be conveyed to Prime Minister Begin on behalf of the President," 31 August 1982, A-4342/7, ISA.

93. "Meeting with U.S. Ambassador to Israel," 13 September 1982, 11:30 AM, A-4342/8, ISA.

94. Lewis, Frontline Diplomacy. This was confirmed to Rashid Khalidi in 1983 by former Lebanese prime minister Saeb Salam, who had met Gemayel after this meeting with Begin. Gemayel was very concerned and told Salam that he could not trust some of his closest aides, trained in Israel, fearing they were more loyal to Israel than to him. Rashid Khalidi, note to author, 10 March 2015. See also Shlaim, *The Iron Wall*, 426–27.

95. "Meeting between Prime Minister Menachem Begin and Ambassador Morris Draper," 15 September 1982, 11:30 AM, MFA-6875/11, ISA.

96. Cable from Israeli embassy-Washington to Jerusalem office [Hebrew], 15 September 1982, 6:30 PM, A-4317/3, ISA.

97. This militia, the Independent Nasserite Movement (INM), was a part of the left-leaning Lebanese National Movement (LNM), which helped defend the PLO from IDF attacks on southwest Beirut until the end of the 1982 siege.

98. Cable from Israeli Embassy, Washington, to Jerusalem office [Hebrew], 15 September 1982, 6:30 PM, A-4317/3, ISA.

99. "Pgishat Eagleburger-Arens" [Eagleburger-Arens meeting], 12:45 PM, 16 September 1982, A-4317/5, ISA. The note-taker at the meeting was Benjamin Netanyahu, who worked for Arens at the Israeli embassy. Netanyahu voiced concerns that U.S. claims of Israeli "deception" would end in a "shooting war with each other, and that's not good for either of us."

100. Ibid.

101. For Weinberger's own annunciation of the "Weinberger Doctrine" and its link to Vietnam, see Miller Center, "Interview with Caspar Weinberger," University of Virginia, 19 November 2002, 16–17, https://millercenter.org/the-presidency/presidential-oral-histories/caspar-weinberger-oral-history-secretary-defense.

102. The most thoroughly documented and reliable source, which contains the names of each victim, puts the number at over three thousand. See al-Hout, *Sabra and Shatila*; and Rosemary Sayigh, "Seven Day Horror," *Badil*, Spring 2001, http://www.badil.org/en/component/k2/item/1121-seven-day-horror. Testimonies from witnesses and survivors include Shahid, "The Sabra and Shatila Massacres"; Al-Shaikh, "Sabra and Shatila 1982"; Siegel and Barbee, "Inside and Outside the Hospital"; and Genet, "Four Hours in Shatila." For an authoritative account of the massacre from the Israeli perspective, see Schiff and Yaari, *Israel's Lebanon War*, 250–85. Other accounts include Thomas Friedman, "The Beirut Massacre: The Four Days,"

New York Times, 25 September 1982; Ménargues, *Les Secrets de la Guerre du Liban*; and the startling German documentary, *Massaker* (2004), produced by Monika Borgmann, Lokman Slim, and Hermann Theissen, which interviews the Phalange executioners.

103. Quoted in Kahan Commission of Inquiry, 18. For the full text of the report, see Doc. 104, "Report of the Commission of Inquiry into the Events at the Refugee Camps in Beirut," 8 February 1983, Israel Ministry of Foreign Affairs, Historical Documents, vol. 8, 1982–1984, http://www.mfa.gov.il/mfa/foreignpolicy/mfadocuments /yearbook6/pages/104%20report%20of%20the%20commission%20of%20inquiry %20into%20the%20e.aspx.

104. For Sharon's remarks at the cabinet meeting, during which he discussed the occupation of West Beirut and securing of the camp exteriors, see partial transcript, Kahan Commission Documents (hereafter KCD), 287. These documents comprise part of the unpublished appendix of the Kahan Commission Report, containing crucial information about the events around the massacre. They were made available to the defense team in the course of a trial between Ariel Sharon and *Time* magazine in the 1980s and subsequently provided to the author (please see "A Note on Sources," pp. 316–17, for further information). After close examination and corroboration by additional experts, I am satisfied with their authenticity and view them as essential and necessary contributions to the historical record, bearing in mind the balance between privacy of individuals, harm to reputation, and the public right to know about the events. The appendix is cited as "Notes Prepared by Kahan Commission Staff, Excerpts of Conversations, Testimonies, Cabinet Discussions, et al. [Hebrew and English], 328pp, Private Collection of Seth Anziska" (KCD). I am grateful to the late attorney Michael Kennedy for consulting on the legal dimensions of these documents: phone conversation, 29 June 2013. For more on the Sharon trial and an earlier discussion of this material, see David Margolick, "Sharon V. Time Inc.: Battleground Is the Courtroom," *New York Times*, 6 April 1984, https://www.nytimes.com/1984/04 /06/nyregion/sharon-v-time-inc-battleground-is-the-courtroom.html; Thomas L. Friedman, "Time Magazine and Sharon Settle the Libel Suit He Filed in Israel," 23 January 1986, https://www.nytimes.com/1986/01/23/nyregion/time-magazine-and -sharon-settle-the-libel-suit-he-filed-in-israel.html; and Julie Flint, "The Sharon Files," *The Guardian*, 28 November 2001, https://www.theguardian.com/world/2001 /nov/28/israelandthepalestinians.warcrimes.

105. See the transcript of the meeting between Shamir, Sharon, and Draper, 12:30 PM, 17 September 1982, A-4317/3, ISA. This account is based in part on the meeting minutes now available in the Israel State Archives and is adapted from Seth Anziska, "A Preventable Massacre," *New York Times*, 17 September 2012. On the reaction of Israel's chief archivist to the publication of these documents, see Yaakov Lozowick, "Sabra and Shatila: One of Israel's Darkest Hours," 19 September 2012, *Israel's Documented Story*, Israel State Archives, http://israelsdocuments.blogspot.com/2012/09 /sabra-and-shatila-one-of-israels.html.

106. Meeting between Shamir, Sharon, and Draper, 12:30 PM, 17 September 1982, A-4317/3, ISA.

107. On 15 September, Draper had in fact debated with Sharon about the number of armed militants remaining behind after the PLO evacuation, knowing it was "miniscule" and that there were civilians in the camps. See Anziska, "A Preventable Massacre"; and Schiff and Yaari, *Israel's War in Lebanon*, 258–60.

108. On the U.S. reaction to the revelations of the massacre, see "Arens-Shultz meeting," 18 September 1982, 8:30 PM, MFA-6875/11, ISA; and "Shultz/Arens conversation," 20 September 1982, 11:00 PM, A-4317/3, ISA.

109. This was in a speech to the Israeli National Defense College on 8 August 1982. See the entire Hebrew transcript of the address in document 181, *Menachem Begin: The Sixth Prime Minister* [Hebrew], 590–96. On the relationship between Zionism and military power, see Shapira, *Land and Power*.

110. Rita Hauser, interview by author, 4 April 2008.

111. See "Statement by Julius Berman, Chairman, Conference of Presidents of Major Jewish Organizations," 20 September 1982, MFA-6892/1, ISA.

112. Despite the trying consequences of the massacre among Jewish leaders in the United States, the atmosphere improved by early 1983, to the point where Shultz was assuring a range of Jewish leaders that there was no American shift "in dedication to Israel's security." See Kenneth J. Bialkin, "Memorandum of Meeting at State Department," 11 January 1983, A-4328/12, ISA.

113. See Biale, *Power and Powerlessness in Jewish History*. The emergence of Israel's "New Historians" was driven in part by the events in Lebanon. See Shlaim, "The Debate about 1948"; and Lockman, "Original Sin." Sharon himself spoke in grandiose terms of Jews learning to wield power in discussions with Pierre and Bashir Gemayel. "How to create power and how to convey its presence is the great test. We were 18 million, six million were exterminated. After 40 years we are close to 15 million. We learned how to use the power we have, but we are still not ourselves." See "Minutes of a Meeting between the Defense Minister and Pierre and Bashir Gemayel," 21 August 1982, KCD, 2–4.

114. See Christison, *Perceptions of Palestine*; and McAlister, *Epic Encounters*. Historian Paul Chamberlin situates the roots of this shift in the 1970s in *The Global Offensive*.

115. Hussein Agha, interview by author, 17 March 2008.

116. Ahmad Khalidi, interview by author, 17 March 2008.

117. The ADL complaint and accompanying cartoons can be found in Folder 3, Anti-Defamation League of B'nai B'rith, Michael Gale Files, RRL.

118. This was 10 percent of the population at the time. See Eisenberg and Caplan, *Negotiating Arab-Israeli Peace*, 69. On the history of the peace movement, see Herman, *The Israeli Peace Movement*.

119. On the reaction to the report and the government debate about accepting its findings, as well as the protests and violence that accompanied these debates, see Yaacov Lozowick, "Secrets from Israel's Archives," *Tablet*, 21 February 2013, http://tabletmag.com/jewish-news-and-politics/124809/secrets-from-israels-archives; and further releases at the Israel State Archives, "Israel's Cabinet Grapples with Sabra and Shatila," Israel State Archives Blog, 21 February 2013, http://israelsdocuments.blogspot.com/2013/02/israels-cabinet-grapples-with-sabra-and.html.

120. Sharon's defense began soon after the massacre, as is evident in his meeting with Habib: "Meeting of Minister of Defense Ariel Sharon and Ambassador Philip Habib," 23 September 1982, 6:30 PM, A-4317/3, ISA. See also Sharon's lawsuit against *Time* magazine for libel, Aharoni, *General Sharon's War against Time Magazine*; and the personal account by Sharon's confidant and lawyer Dov Weisglass, *Ariel Sharon: A Prime Minister*, 18–94.

121. See excerpts from Defense and Foreign Affairs Committee, 24 September 1982, protocol 118, 11–43 (222–28 in KCD).

122. KCD, 9–11. Other officials knew of the planned introduction of the Lebanese Forces into the refugee camps ahead of time. See ibid., 33.

123. See the minutes of the "Meeting between Bashir Gemayel and Johnny Abdu with the DM," 1 August 1982, Home of Ariel Sharon, KCD, 234–43.

124. See "Meeting between Defense Minister Sharon and Bashir Gemayel at the Lebanese Forces' Headquarters in Beirut, 8 July 1982," KCD, 294–95.

125. See "Was there awareness of the possibility of a massacre?" Notes of the staff of the Kahan Commission, KCD, 83. For more on this crucial meeting with Gemayel, see Sharon's testimony in ibid., 100–102.

126. See "Col. Elkana Harnof's testimony," 22 November 1982, KCD, 78.

127. See "A Report passed to the Foreign Minister, Defense Minister and others," 23 June 1982, KCD, 79.

128. Ibid., 80.

129. Shlaim, *The Iron Wall*, 407. For more on Israeli interests in triggering a mass exodus to Jordan, and the possible collapse of the Hashemite Kingdom in order to allow a "free hand" for ruling the West Bank, see the discussion in Eisenberg and Caplan, *Negotiating Arab-Israeli Peace*, 325n3.

130. Schiff and Yaari, *Israel's Lebanon War*, 261. Further details are discussed in Bergman, *Rise and Kill First*, 262–64. On Lebanese reckoning with the massacre and Hobeika, who was assassinated in January 2002 after agreeing to testify in the war crimes trial against Sharon, see Laurie King-Irani, "Detonating Lebanon's War Files," *MERIP*, 31 January 2002, http://www.merip.org/mero/mero013102.

131. Testimony of Yitzhak Hofi, 20 October 1982, KCD, 81–83.

132. See Boykin, *Cursed Is the Peacemaker*, 266–73; and Khalidi, *Under Siege*, 176.

133. Tyler, *A World of Trouble*, 282–84. Tyler recounts a revealing exchange between Reagan and his NSC staffer Philip Dur about the success of President Dwight Eisenhower's earlier intervention in Lebanon in 1958, which consisted of 19,000 troops compared to Reagan's 1,800.

134. See "Meeting of Minister of Defense Ariel Sharon and Ambassador Philip Habib," 23 September 1982, 6:30 PM, A-4317/3, ISA.

135. Meeting between Pierre Gemayel and David Kimche [Hebrew], 10 January 1983, MFA-6848/8, ISA. In a meeting with Sharon and the Mossad in August, Pierre told the Israelis, "God has sent you. During the last seven to eight years everybody has let us down. The Americans and the Europeans were afraid of burning their hands here. It was necessary for you to act the way you did. You've come and saved us." "Minutes of a Meeting between the Defense Minister and Pierre and Bashir Gemayel in Bashir's Office," 21 August 1982, KCD, 2–3.

136. Ibid.

137. Author phone interview with Uri Lubrani, 25 June 2012.

138. The U.S.-mediated discussions began in November 1982. See "Meeting between Minister of Foreign Affairs, Mr. Yitzhak Shamir and Ambassador Philip Habib," 24 November 1982, 4:35 PM, A-4317/11, ISA; letter exchanges, Shultz and Begin, 27 and 29 November 1982, A-4317/11, ISA; and "Top Secret Meeting between Prime Minister Begin and Ambassador Philip Habib at the Prime Minister's Office, Jerusalem," 16 December 1982, 6:00 PM, A-4317/11, ISA.

139. See, for example, the meeting between Begin and Habib, 9 February 1983, 5:00 PM, A-4317/12, ISA.

140. Eisenberg and Caplan, *Negotiating Arab-Israeli Peace*, 66–68.

141. For the treaty negotiations, see "Secret Agreement between Israel and Lebanon," 18 January 1983, A-4317/11, ISA; and *Milchemet Shalom HaGalil, Masa u'Matan Mamshelet Yisrael Mamshelet Levanon* [Operation Peace for Galilee, Negotiations between the Government of Israel and the Government of Lebanon], 4–10 January 1983, A-4317/9, ISA. See also the continuation in A-4317/10, 12, ISA; and Kimche, *The Last Option*, 162–85.

142. Secret talking points for DCI on Lebanon-Israel, 9 February 1983, CREST (CIA RDP85M00363R001202740017-2), NARA.

143. For the full text of the Lebanese-Israeli Agreement, see Laqueur and Rubin, *The Israel-Arab Reader*, 287–89. On its inherent limitations, see Eisenberg and Caplan, *Negotiating Arab-Israeli Peace*, 52–72.

144. Eisenberg and Caplan, *Negotiating Arab-Israeli Peace*, 67.

145. Ibid., 67, 70.

146. See Shindler, *A History of Modern Israel*, 147–97; and Shapira, *Israel*, 377–90. See also Thomas Friedman, "Israel's Dilemma: Living with a Dirty War," *New York Times*, 20 January 1985, http://www.nytimes.com/1985/01/20/magazine/israel-s-dilemma-living-with-a-dirty-war.html. Peace Now had been founded in March 1978 after Sadat's visit to Jerusalem and it expanded considerably in the wake of 1982.

147. See the comments of Rabbi David Hartman to Tom Friedman in "Israel's Dilemma: Living with a Dirty War," *New York Times*, 20 January 1985.

148. Begin has been the subject of rehabilitation by Israeli scholars, but the events of 1982 do not sit comfortably with some of the more hagiographic interpretations. A fawning account can be found in Gordis, *Menachem Begin*. For critical studies, see Weitz, "From Peace in the South to War in the North"; Ofira Seliktar, "Israel's Menachem Begin," in Kellerman and Rubin, eds., *Leadership and Negotiation in the Middle East*, 30–69; and Shilon, *Menachem Begin*. See also the special issues of *Haaretz Magazine*, "Rethinking Begin," 21 December 2007, and "The Man Who Transformed Israel," 24 February 2012; as well as the review essay by Avi Shilon, "Missing Menachem," *Jewish Review of Books*, 24 March 2014. A psychoanalytic read of Begin and his leadership is offered by Grosbard, *Menachem Begin*.

149. See the text of a published telegram Begin sent to Reagan invoking the memory of the Holocaust in Shlaim, *The Iron Wall*, 423.

150. Quoted in Sachar, *A History of Israel*, 913.

151. Cable, Ronald Reagan to Menachem Begin, 12 September 1983, Folder 3, "Prime Minster Begin Cables," Executive Secretariat, NSC: Head of State File, RRL.

152. Shlaim, *The Iron Wall*, 431–32.

153. Ibid., 432–33.

154. Quandt, *Peace Process*, 259; Shlaim, *The Iron Wall*, 429.

155. On the breakdown of Israel's cultural consensus in the wake of 1982, see Sidra DeKoven Ezrahi, "From Auschwitz to the Temple Mount: Binding and Unbinding the Israeli Narrative," in Lothe, Suleiman, and Phelan, eds., *After Testimony*, 291–313.

156. See Friedman, "Israel's Dilemma."

157. Oz, *The Slopes of Lebanon*, 23.

158. On the link between events in Beirut and Israeli military actions in the West Bank, see Gal and Hammerman, *From Beirut to Jenin* [Hebrew].

159. Memo, George Shultz to Ronald Reagan, 5 October 1983, Folder "NSPG 72," Box 91306, Executive Secretariat, NSC: NSPG, RRL.

160. See the entire Folder "NSDD 99: Security Strategy for Near East and South Asia," Box 91290, Executive Secretariat, NSC, RRL. On policy formulation within the administration, see Simpson, *National Security Directives of the Reagan and Bush Administrations*.

161. Memo, George Shultz to Ronald Reagan, 5 October 1983.

162. Memo, William P. Clark to Ronald Reagan, 11 July 1983, File 2, "NSDD 99: Security Strategy for Near East and South Asia," Box 91290, Executive Secretariat, NSC, RRL (emphasis in original).

163. Ibid., 70.

164. For a harrowing description of the bombing, and the death of key CIA operative Robert Ames, see Bird, *The Good Spy*.

165. Quandt, *Peace Process*, 258. On the end of American involvement in Lebanon, see Shultz, *Turmoil and Triumph*, 220–34. For an account of the Marine mission in Lebanon and the barracks bombing, see Hammel, *The Root*. On the intervention, see Bowditch, "Force and Diplomacy."

166. On Reagan's pledge to retaliate and remain, see "Transcript of President Reagan's News Conference on the Attack in Beirut," *New York Times*, 25 October 1983. On Reagan's about-face, see Micah Zenko, "Reagan's Cut and Run," *Foreign Policy*, 7 February 2014, http://foreignpolicy.com/2014/02/07/when-reagan-cut-and-run; and Crist, *The Twilight War*, 139–58.

167. Phone interview with Ambassador Samuel Lewis, 6 September 2012.

168. Secret talking points for DCI on Lebanon-Israel, 9 February 1983, CREST (CIA RDP85M00363R001202740017-2), NARA.

169. For more on the withdrawal, and the role of domestic Israeli critics, see Sela, "Civil Society, the Military and National Security."

170. Graham Fuller, Secret talking points for SSG meeting, Situation Room, "Syrian and Soviet options in Lebanon," NIO/NESA, 29 August 1983, CREST (CIA-RDP85M00363R00020034001-6), NARA (emphasis in original).

171. See Ryan Crocker, "Containing the Fire in Syria," *Yale Global*, 23 July 2013, http://yaleglobal.yale.edu/content/containing-fire-syria.

172. Crist, *The Twilight War*, 153.

173. Interview with Yasser Arafat by Zahid Mahmood, 11 March and 2 June 1986, *International Documents on Palestine*, IPS.

174. See Transcript, NBC's *Meet the Press*, 29 August 1982, CREST (CIA-RDP88-01070R000100330005-4), NARA.

175. See "Press Interview Statements by PLO Executive Committee Chairman Arafat," 2 July 1982, *International Documents on Palestine*, IPS. The interview with Avnery was conducted for the weekly *Ha'olam Haze*, which he edited. Avnery told Arafat, "I have been waiting for this interview for years . . . the one point that should be made completely clear in a way that every Israeli in the street can understand: that you want a solution of peace based on mutual understanding, mutual respect and recognition."

176. On PLO readings of Zionism, see Gribetz, "When *The Zionist Idea* Came to Beirut."

177. "Press Interview Statements by PLO Executive Committee Chairman Arafat." Israeli intelligence sought to assassinate Arafat and used Avnery's visit as an opportunity to attempt a strike, even agreeing to kill Israelis in the process. Arafat eluded this attempt, part of a broader astonishing tale called "Operation Salt Fish." The episode, recently brought to light by the Israeli journalist Ronen Bergman, is discussed in *Rise and Kill First*, 255–61, 267–76.

178. "Full Text: Middle East," *This Week with David Brinkley*, 29 August 1982, 11:30 AM, CREST (CIA-RDP88-01070R000100330006-3), NARA.

179. On post-1982 challenges, see al-Hout, *My Life in the PLO*, 172–81; and Sayigh, *Armed Struggle*, 545–606.

180. See Sayigh, "Palestinian Military Performance in the 1982 War."

181. Special National Security Intelligence Estimate, "PLO: Impact of the Lebanese Incursion," 8 November 1982, CREST (CIA-RDP85T00176R001100290014-5).

182. This was Shevach Weiss during a discussion of Sharon's role in Sabra and Shatila. See transcript of Knesset meeting, 22 September 1982, Abraham D. Sofaer Collection, Box 8, HIA.

183. This link is suggested most explicitly in Sayigh, *Armed Struggle*; and Brynen, *Sanctuary and Survival*. See also Yezid Sayigh, "The Palestinians," in Sayigh and Shlaim, eds., *The Cold War and the Middle East*, 125–55; and Thompson, *Justice Interrupted*, 239–74.

Chapter Seven: Alternatives to the PLO?

1. See Elkoury, *Atlantis*.

2. See Rashid Khalidi, "Palestinian Politics after the Exodus from Beirut," in Freedman, ed., *The Middle East after the Israeli Invasion of Lebanon*, 233–53; and Sahliyeh, *The PLO after the Lebanon War*.

3. Loren Jenkins, "Bitter Exile," *Washington Post*, 27 December 1982.

4. Al-Hout, *My Life in the PLO*, 177–78.

5. Ibid., 180–81.

6. Quoted in Thomas Friedman, "PLO Council Says Reagan's Proposal Is Not Acceptable," *New York Times*, 22 February 1983, http://www.nytimes.com/1983/02/22/world/plo-council-says-reagan-s-proposal-is-not-acceptable.html. For a partial text of the communiqué, see "Palestine National Council: Political Statement (February 22, 1983)," in Laqueur and Rubin, *The Israel-Arab Reader*, 277–80.

7. Khalidi, *The Iron Cage*, 170. For more on the PLO's "Dissident Rebellion," which was backed by Syrian forces in Lebanon, see Sayigh, *Armed Struggle*, 561–67; and Laqueur and Rubin, *The Israel-Arab Reader*, 290–93.

8. For an insider account of these internal splits, see al-Hout, *My Life in the PLO*, 202–9.

9. The group was led by Abu Abbas and had the support of the Iraqi Ba'athist regime. Abu Abbas also had a seat on the PLO Executive Committee, serving as a spoiler during the years in which the PLO sought American recognition.

10. For a description of Reagan's antiterrorism policy, with detailed reference to the Middle East, see Wills, *The First War on Terrorism*; Laham, *Crossing the Rubicon*; and Toaldo, *The Origins of the U.S. War on Terror*. See also Shultz, *Turmoil and Triumph*, 643–88.

11. On the Village Leagues, see the newly released files at the Israel State Archives, MFA-8415/18; as well as Flora Lewis, "How to Grow Horns," *New York Times*, 29 April 1982; Milson, "How to Make Peace with the Palestinians"; Litani, "'Village Leagues'"; Tamari, "In League with Zion"; Hirst, *The Gun and the Olive Branch*, 515–26; Cohen, "Village Leagues"; and Jamjoum, "The Village Leagues." Another non-PLO strategy was targeting local mayors in the occupied territories. See Ma'oz, *Palestinian Leadership on the West Bank*.

12. These figures included Mustafa Dudin for the Hebron League, Beshara Qumsiyeh for the Bethlehem League, and Yusif al-Khatib for the Ramallah League. Al-Khatib was assassinated in November 1981 by PFLP militants, after which other Village League personnel were armed by Israeli authorities. See Jamjoum, "The Village Leagues," 21–22.

13. Jamjoum, "The Village Leagues," 1.

14. Ibid., 16.

15. Ma'oz, *Palestinian Leadership in the West Bank*, 201. Israeli authorities then arrested several West Bank mayors in retaliation, replacing them with military officers. See Jamjoum, "The Village Leagues," 23.

16. Transcript, NBC's *Meet the Press*, 29 August 1982, CREST (CIA-RDP88-01070R000100330005-4), NARA.

17. "The President's News Conference," *PPPRR*, 21 March 1985.

18. Quandt, *Peace Process*, 271. On the early history of the Jordanian option's adoption by Israeli policymakers, see Pedatzur, "Coming Back Full Circle." On Jordan's broader role in the peace process, see Susser, *Israel, Jordan, and Palestine*; Abu-Odeh, *Jordanians, Palestinians, and the Hashemite Kingdom in the Middle East Peace Process*; and Al-Madfai, *Jordan, the United States and the Middle East Peace Process*.

19. Quandt, *Peace Process*, 262.

20. Shlaim, *The Iron Wall*, 446–47.

21. Khalidi, *The Iron Cage*, 148. On the internal dynamics of Palestinian political life in the West Bank and Gaza during the 1980s, see Ann Mosley Lesch and Mark A. Tessler, "The West Bank and Gaza: Political and Ideological Responses to Occupation," in Lesch and Tessler, eds., *Israel, Egypt, and the Palestinians*, 255–71.

22. For the full text, see Laqueur and Rubin, *The Israel-Arab Reader*, 298–99. Quandt, *Peace Process*, 260–65 covers related events during these years in some detail, and Bernard Avishai provides a perspective from Amman in "Looking Over Jordan," *New York Review of Books*, 28 April 1983, and "Jordan: Looking for an Opening," *New York Review of Books*, 27 September 1984.

23. Quandt, *Peace Process*, 260–65.

24. For sections of Hussein's three-and-a-half-hour address, see Laqueur and Rubin, *The Israel-Arab Reader*, 299–313.

25. Shlaim, *Lion of Jordan*, 433.

26. Shultz, *Turmoil and Triumph*, 462.

27. For more on the scandal and its impact on Middle East policy, see Quandt, *Peace Process*, 266–68; Shlaim, *The Iron Wall*, 453–57; and Byrne, *Iran-Contra*.

28. See Ashton, "Taking Friends for Granted."

29. Memo, George Shultz to Ronald Reagan, 5 June 1986, "Chronological File, June 1986," Box 5, Dennis Ross Files, RRL.

30. Talking points for the President's meeting with Jordan's King Hussein, 9 June 1986, Box 5, Dennis Ross Files, RRL.

31. Talking points for Poindexter's meeting with King Hussein, 9 June 1986, Box 5, Dennis Ross Files, RRL.

32. Ross, *The Missing Peace*, 50.

33. Draft cable, John Poindexter to George Shultz, 23 June 1986, Box 5, Dennis Ross Files, RRL.

34. Shlaim, *The Iron Wall*, 451–52.

35. This argument is suggested by Shlaim, *Lion of Jordan*, 433–35. For more on Israeli and Jordanian influence over the West Bank, see Melman and Raviv, *Behind the Uprising*.

36. See miscellaneous memos in Box 7, Dennis Ross Files, RRL.

37. Talking points for Prince Bandar, Dennis Ross for John Poindexter, Box 7, Dennis Ross Files, RRL.

38. Ibid. This approach persisted beyond the 1980s, in both U.S. efforts to support economic integration and alliances without a political settlement to the Palestinian question, and growing calls to abandon efforts for peacemaking and focus on improving daily life for Palestinians as a permanent solution to their political plight. See, for example, Danny Dayan, "Peaceful Nonreconciliation Now," *New York Times*, 8 June 2014, http://www.nytimes.com/2014/06/09/opinion/peaceful-nonreconciliation -now.html?hp&rref=opinion&_r=1; and the confirmation testimony of David Friedman as U.S. ambassador to Israel, 16 February 2017, available at https://www.c-span .org/. It has also been a feature of policymaking in the case of the Gaza Strip. See U.S. Special Representative for International Negotiations Jason D. Greenblatt, "Gaza

Conference Remarks," Washington, DC, 13 March 2018, https://www.state.gov/p
/nea/ci/pt/rls/prs/2018/279222.htm.

39. Handwritten note, Dennis Ross for John Poindexter, 3 October 1986, Box 5,
"Chronological File, October 1986," RRL. The Washington Institute was closely affiliated with AIPAC's leadership.

40. "Funding Development on West Bank," 15 December 1986, "Chronological
File, December 1986," Box 5, Dennis Ross Files, RRL.

41. Ibid.

42. Ibid.

43. Talking points, Frank Carlucci for National Security Planning Group
Meeting, 13 February 1987, "Chronological File, Feb. 1987," Box 7, Dennis Ross
Files, RRL.

44. Agenda, National Security Planning Group Meeting, 13 February 1987,
"Chronological File, Feb. 1987," Box 7, Dennis Ross Files, RRL.

45. Ibid.

46. National Security Study Directive Number 4-87, 22 January 1987, "Chronological File, Jan. 1987," Box 7, Dennis Ross Files, RRL.

47. Avishai Margalit, "The Violent Life of Yitzhak Shamir," *New York Review of
Books*, 14 May 1992.

48. Memo, Robert Oakley to Frank Carlucci, 17 February 1987, "Chronological
File, Feb. 1987," Box 7, Dennis Ross Files, RRL.

49. Talking points, meeting with Prime Minister Shamir of Israel, 18 February
1987, "Chronological File, Feb. 1987," Box 7, Dennis Ross Files, RRL (emphasis in
original).

50. Ibid.

51. Zertal and Eldar, *Lords of the Land*, 102–3.

52. Quoted in Shlaim, *The Iron Wall*, 517.

53. "Meeting at White House of Ambassador Rosenne with Vice President Bush,"
2 August 1983, A-4343/13, ISA.

54. Ibid.

55. Ibid.

56. For the full text of the document, see Laqueur and Rubin, *The Israel-Arab
Reader*, 313–14. For background, see Aruri, "The PLO and the Jordan Option."

57. The genesis and collapse of the London Agreement are covered in Shlaim,
Lion of Jordan, 440–52; and Shlaim, *The Iron Wall*, 457–65. For a firsthand account,
see Shultz, *Turmoil and Triumph*, 936–49. See also Eisenberg and Caplan, *Negotiating Arab-Israeli Peace*, 73–91.

58. The talks were conducted through the left-wing Israeli peace campaigner
David Ish-Shalom. Further details were provided during an author interview with
Sari Nusseibeh, 29 February 2012, Jerusalem. See also Abbas, *Through Secret Chan-
nels*, 39–43.

59. See "Report by Herut Party Member Amirav of Israel entitled 'Outline for
Advancement of Negotiations between the Likud and the PLO,'" Jerusalem, September 1987, *International Documents on Palestine*, IPS.

60. Ibid.

61. See "Report by Herut Party Member Amirav of Israel."

62. On the initiative and its failure, see Thomas Friedman, "Mideast Peace Bid Ends; Hope and One Arm Hurt," *New York Times*, 12 October 1987.

63. Ibid.

64. On the Intifada, see Schiff and Yaari, *Intifada*; Lockman and Beinin, *Intifada*; Melman and Raviv, *Behind the Uprising*; King, *A Quiet Revolution*; Siniora, "An Analysis of the Current Revolt"; Nusseibeh and David, *Once Upon a Country*; and Ashrawi, *This Side of Peace*.

65. Quandt, *Peace Process*, 274. In his biography of Rabin, Itamar Rabinovich examines the origin of this approach and its use "long after he [Rabin] had reached the conclusion that there was only one way to deal with the intifada, and that was through a political solution." See Rabinovich, *Yitzhak Rabin*, 157.

66. Hussein Agha, interview by author, 17 March 2008.

67. Amos Elon, "From the Uprising," *New York Review of Books*, 14 April 1988.

68. Ahmad Khalidi, interview by author, 8 November 2017. For a detailed account of Abu Jihad's assassination, based on startling testimony from many of the participants, see Bergman, *Rise and Kill First*, 297–323.

69. On the history of Hamas, see Baconi, *Hamas Contained*.

70. Shlaim, *The Iron Wall*, 466. For important statements and demands from the Palestinian leadership, see Laqueur and Rubin, *The Israel-Arab Reader*, 314–38.

71. Cited in Laqueur and Rubin, *The Israel-Arab Reader*, 319.

72. On the Israeli views of the Palestinian national movement and its evolution, see Sela and Maoz, *The PLO and Israel*.

73. Shlaim, *The Iron Wall*, 467.

74. Shamir, *Summing Up*, 182.

75. The Israeli novelist David Grossman captured this in devastating prose for both audiences. See Grossman, *The Yellow Wind*.

76. Elon, "From the Uprising."

77. Arthur Hertzberg, "The Uprising," *New York Review of Books*, 4 February 1988. See also Hertzberg's exchange with Elie Wiesel on 18 August 1988 as an example of how divisive the issue had become: http://www.nybooks.com/articles/archives/1988 /aug/18/an-open-letter-to-elie-wiesel/.

78. Kenneth J. Arrow et al., "An Open Letter to the Prime Minister of Israel," *New York Review of Books*, 31 March 1988.

79. Ibid.

80. Memo, Paul Schott Stevens to Nancy Risque, "One Page Fact Sheet for the President," undated, "Chronological File, January 1988," Box 8, Dennis Ross Files, RRL.

81. "Briefing to Ex-Presidents re: U.S. Initiative on Middle East Peace," 8 February 1988, "Chronological File, Feb. 1988," Box 8, Dennis Ross Files, RRL.

82. For Shultz's detailed account, see Shultz, *Turmoil and Triumph*, 1016–34.

83. Quandt, *Peace Process*, 275.

84. Ibid., 276. For Shamir's views, see *Summing Up*, 174–79.

85. "Disengagement from the West Bank," in Laqueur and Rubin, *The Israel-Arab Reader*, 340.

86. For more background, see Siddiqi, "From Liberation to Self-Determination," 93–98.

87. Shlaim, *Lion of Jordan*, 457–66.

88. See Ihsan A. Hijazi, "An Aide to Arafat Comes under Fire," *New York Times*, 22 June 1988. Abu Sharif was expelled from the PFLP in 1987 for deemphasizing armed struggle. For his personal account of this transformation, see Abu Sharif, *Arafat and the Dream of Palestine*.

89. Anthony Lewis, "A Chance to Talk," *New York Times*, 23 June 1988.

90. Elaine Sciolino, "P.L.O. Aide's Plan Has U.S. Intrigued," *New York Times*, 28 June 1988.

91. These leaders included Irving Howe, Philip Klutznick, and Nathan Glazer. See "Prominent U.S. Jews Hail P.L.O. Statement," *New York Times*, 2 July 1988. A more expansive list of signatories could be found in the *New York Review of Books* and included Theodore Mann, Seymour Lipset, Arthur Hertzberg, and Rita Hauser. See "Israel and the Palestinians," *New York Review of Books*, 18 August 1988, http://www.nybooks.com/articles/1988/08/18/israel-and-the-palestinians/.

92. Muslih, *Toward Coexistence*, 34 (emphasis in original).

93. See Abbas, *Through Secret Channels*, 22–23. For the full text of the PNC political resolution, see Laqueur and Rubin, *The Israel-Arab Reader*, 349–53. On the broader impact and significance, see Khalidi, "The Resolutions of the 19th Palestine National Council."

94. Khalidi, *The Iron Cage*, 194–95. The full text of the declaration is reprinted in Laqueur and Rubin, *The Israel-Arab Reader*, 354–58. Israel's right to exist was not explicitly recognized (that was a formulation that would come later), but 242 and 338 were endorsed. For a description of how this was seen in Jerusalem, see Nusseibeh, *Once Upon a Country*, 296–97.

95. On Reagan's shift toward the Soviets, see Fischer, *The Reagan Reversal*; and Mann, *The Rebellion of Ronald Reagan*.

96. On Shultz's mixed signals, see Rabie, *U.S.-PLO Dialogue*, 59; and Shultz, *Triumph and Turmoil*, 1035.

97. Rich details of the Stockholm mission are available in an unpublished chapter by Ed Harriman, Fifty Years War: Israel and the Arabs Television Documentary Archive, Box 10, Folder 10, Liddell Hart Centre for Military Archives, King's College, London (KCL). William Quandt recounts the evolution of the dialogue in some detail in *Peace Process*, 277–85. See also Kathleen Hendrix, "Mission to Stockholm," *Los Angeles Times*, 16 December 1988.

98. Rita Hauser, interview by author, 4 April 2008, New York. Further transcripts about this effort are available in the Fifty Years War Collection, KCL. See, in particular, interviews with Yasser Abed Rabbo, William Quandt, and George Shultz.

99. Rabie, *U.S.-PLO Dialogue*, 69.

100. Rita Hauser, interview by author, 4 April 2008.

101. Hauser recalled a particularly disappointing encounter with Yitzhak Rabin, who had been a close confidant for years prior: "He refused to shake my hand. 'Rita,' he said, words to the effect of 'you've been a traitor to the Jews,' etc. etc. I was very deeply both shocked and offended. And I remember saying to him, 'Yitzhak, you're wrong. At

some point, you will deal with the PLO, whether you like this guy you don't like him, they are the only game in town and nothing will ever happen if you don't deal with the PLO. And they have made their move, they are moving away from the extremist position.'" After the Oslo Accords, Hauser hosted Prime Minister Rabin and his wife, Leah, at the fiftieth anniversary celebration of the United Nations in New York. Yasser Arafat was sitting opposite them in the concert hall. As Hauser recalled, "Rabin had the decency to say to me, 'Rita, I owe you a real apology: he is my partner in peace.' . . . That is my last memory of him [Rabin], you were right we had to deal with the PLO, he is my partner in peace." A few days later, Rabin was assassinated in Tel Aviv.

102. See Rabie, *U.S.-PLO Dialogue*; and discussed with Rita Hauser, interview by author, 4 April 2008.

103. Al-Hout, *My Life in the PLO*, 238.

104. Ibid., 239.

105. Ibid.

106. Ibid., 237.

107. Ibid., 236.

108. On the "magic words" and the details of the press conference, see Rabie, *U.S.-PLO Dialogue*, 84–88; Quandt, *Peace Process*, 282–85; and Shultz, *Turmoil and Triumph*, 1043–45.

109. Rabie, *U.S.-PLO Dialogue*, 84–85. The businessmen were Hasib Sabbagh and Munib al-Masri.

110. For the text of Arafat's statement, see appendix I, Rabie, *U.S.-PLO Dialogue*, 180–81.

111. Ibid.

112. For the text of Shultz's statement, see appendix J, Rabie, *U.S.-PLO Dialogue*, 182.

113. For the full text of Reagan's statement, see appendix K, Rabie, *U.S.-PLO Dialogue*, 183.

114. Rabie, *U.S.-PLO Dialogue*, 86. Quandt was by that time a senior fellow at the Brookings Institution in Washington and was first approached by Rabie in August 1988. For his assessment of the initiative, see Quandt, *Peace Process*, 278–81.

115. Rabie, *U.S.-PLO Dialogue*, 87.

116. Abbas, *Through Secret Channels*, 33.

117. Ibid., 34–35.

118. Rabie, *U.S.-PLO Dialogue*, 99–100.

119. Handwritten note, 16 December 1988, File 3, "OA 92477," Colin Powell Files, RRL. Powell took over the position from Frank Carlucci, who replaced Caspar Weinberger as secretary of defense following Iran-Contra.

120. Reagan, *An American Life*, 407.

Chapter Eight: A Stillborn Peace

1. "Address before a Joint Session of the Congress on the Cessation of the Persian Gulf Conflict," *Public Papers of the President: George Bush, 1989-1993*, 6 March 1991.

2. For an overview of the schools of thought that have developed about the end of the Cold War, see Beth Fischer, "U.S. Foreign Policy under Reagan and Bush," in Leffler and Westad, eds., *The Cambridge History of the Cold War*, vol. 3, *Endings*, 267–88; Leffler, *For the Soul of Mankind*; Westad, *The Cold War*; Wilson, *The Triumph of Improvisation*; and Anders Stephanson, "Cold War Degree Zero," in Isaac and Bell, eds., *Uncertain Empire*, 19–50. On Bush and his role, see Engel, *When the World Seemed New*; Bush and Scowcroft, *A World Transformed*; and Sparrow, *The Strategist*.

3. Quandt, *Peace Process*, 302.

4. Shlaim, *The Iron Wall*, 482–83; Baker, *The Politics of Diplomacy*, 115–21.

5. "Israeli Prime Minister Yitzhak Shamir: Peace Plan," in Laqueur and Rubin, *The Israel-Arab Reader*, 359.

6. See Shamir, *Summing Up*, 194–206; Khalidi, "The Half-Empty Glass of Middle East Peace"; Baker, *The Politics of Diplomacy*, 121–23.

7. Quandt, *Peace Process*, 296.

8. Ibid., 297–98; Shlaim, *The Iron Wall*, 485. For the text of Baker's "Five Point Plan," see Laqueur and Rubin, *The Israel-Arab Reader*, 367–68.

9. Bar-Siman-Tov, "The United States and Israel since 1948," 256; Baker, *The Politics of Diplomacy*, 124–30.

10. "Baker Ultimatum to Israel: 'Call Us if You Really Want Peace,'" *Los Angeles Times*, 13 June 1990, http://articles.latimes.com/1990-06-13/news/mn-371_1_mideast-peace-talks. For the footage, see "James Baker and the White House Telephone," YouTube, https://www.youtube.com/watch?v=ADcALMO5wf4. On the loan guarantees, see Hadar, "High Noon in Washington."

11. Quandt, *Peace Process*, 297–98.

12. For the text of the suspension statement, see appendix P, Rabie, *U.S.-PLO Dialogue*, 189–90.

13. Quandt, *Peace Process*, 300–302. On PLO support for Iraq in the Gulf War, see also Thrall, *The Only Language They Understand*, 54.

14. On the background to Madrid, see Baker, *The Politics of Diplomacy*, 443–69, 487–513; Ross, *The Missing Peace*, 46–87; Kurtzer et al., *The Peace Puzzle*, 15–58; Quandt, *Peace Process*, 303–10; Ashrawi, *This Side of Peace*; Abbas, *Through Secret Channels*, 85–101; and Shlaim, *The Iron Wall*, 501–4.

15. For early discussions with Palestinian leaders over the creation of an actual peace process and content of the negotiations, see "Handwritten notes of a meeting between Hanan Ashrawi, Dennis Ross and Aaron David Miller, 30 October 1989"; "Handwritten notes of a meeting between John Kelly, Dan Kurtzer, John Hirsch, and Hanan Ashrawi, 30 October 1989"; and "Meeting with Dan Kurtzer and Hanan Ashrawi, 31 October 1989," all in PPD.

16. Shlaim *The Iron Wall*, 504.

17. The St. James Palace conference of 1939 could be viewed as one earlier instance prior to the establishment of Israel in 1948.

18. See "James Baker's Letter of Assurance to the Palestinians," 18 October 1991, http://www.usip.org/sites/default/files/file/resources/collections/peace_agreements/letter_of_assurance.pdf.

19. The interim arrangements would be completed within one year and would have a five-year life span. In the third year the parties would negotiate permanent status agreements. On the assurances provided (and not provided) to the Israelis, see "Memo of briefing by Dennis Ross, Madrid, 2 November 1991," PPD.

20. See "Gameplan, *Not Distributed*," undated, handwriting of Ahmad Khalidi, PPD (emphasis in original).

21. "Palestinian Delegation Leader Haydar Abd al-Shafi: Speech at the Madrid Peace Conference," quoted in Laqueur and Rubin, *The Israel-Arab Reader*, 396. See also the obituary for Haidar Abdel Shafi, *Economist*, 4 October 2007, http://www .economist.com/node/9898496.

22. This was the historian Avi Shlaim, who attended the conference and wrote about it subsequently in several accounts. See Shlaim, *The Iron Wall*, 501–9; and Avi Shlaim, "Changing Places," *London Review of Books* 14.1 (January 1992): 10–12. For Shamir's account, see Shamir, *Summing Up*, 236–42.

23. See "Baker to all parties," 22 November 1991, PPD, http://www.palestine -studies.org/sites/default/files/uploads/images/Baker%20letter%2022%20Nov_ %201991.pdf.

24. See "Memo of briefing by Alan Kreczko, Madrid, November 2, 1991," PPD.

25. See "Letter from the Palestinian Team to the Middle East Peace Process to U.S.S.R. Foreign Minister Eduard Shevardnadze, 25 November 1991," PPD.

26. See "Baker to all parties," 22 November 1991, PPD.

27. See "Letter from the Palestinian Team to the co-Sponsors of the Middle East Peace Process," Jerusalem, 15 November 1991, PPD.

28. See Khalidi, *Brokers of Deceit*, 36–37.

29. Quoted in a meeting between the Palestinian delegation to the Washington talks and U.S. diplomats on 8 December 1991. See "Memo on meeting with Alan Kreczko and T. Feifer, 8 December 1991, Washington," PPD,
http://www.palestine-studies.org/sites/default/files/uploads/images/Minutes %20Kreczko%2C%20Feifer%20meeting%208%20Dec_%2091.pdf.

30. "Memo on meeting with Alan Kreczko and T. Feifer, 8 December 1991, Washington." For an understanding of how these events are connected to earlier dynamics, see Khatib, *Palestinian Politics and the Middle East Peace Process*.

31. "Memo on meeting with Alan Kreczko and T. Feifer, 8 December 1991, Washington."

32. Ibid.

33. Shlaim, *The Iron Wall*, 514; Quandt, *Peace Process*, 312–13.

34. "Memo on meeting with Alan Kreczko and T. Feifer, 8 December 1991, Washington" (emphasis in original).

35. See Shlaim, *The Iron Wall*, 510; and Quandt, *Peace Process*, 326–27.

36. See Final Delivered Draft "Outline of Model of the Palestinian Interim Self-Government Authority (PISGA)," 14 January 1992, PPD, http://www.palestine -studies.org/sites/default/files/uploads/images/PISGA%20Jan%2014%2C%201992 %20%20p%201%2C2.pdf.

37. Baker to Husseini, 10 February 1992, transmitted via the U.S. Consulate General in Jerusalem, http://www.palestine-studies.org/sites/default/files/uploads/files/Baker%20letter%2010%20Feb_%201992.pdf.

38. "Meeting at the United States State Department with Secretary of State James Baker," 20 February 1992, PPD, http://www.palestine-studies.org/sites/default/files/uploads/files/Minutes%20Baker%20meeting%2020%20Feb_%2092.pdf.

39. See "Ideas for peaceful coexistence in the territories during the interim period," 20 February 1992, PPD, http://www.palestine-studies.org/sites/default/files/uploads/files/Israeli%20proposal%2020%20Feb_%201992.pdf. See also Elyakim Rubinstein to H. Abdul Shafi, 21 February 1992, PPD, http://www.palestine-studies.org/sites/default/files/uploads/files/Rubinstein%20to%20Abd%20al-Shafi%2021%20Feb_%2092.pdf.

40. Elyakim Rubinstein to H. Abdul Shafi, 21 February 1992.

41. "Minutes of the Meeting at the State Department," 26 February 1992, PPD, http://www.palestine-studies.org/sites/default/files/uploads/files/Minutes%20Djerejian%20Kurtzer%20meeting%2026%20Feb_%2092.pdf.

42. Ibid.

43. Ibid.

44. See, for example, "Draft Minutes: Meeting with U.S. State Department Officials," 13 May 1993, PPD, http://www.palestine-studies.org/sites/default/files/uploads/files/Minutes%20Kurtzer%2C%20Miller%20meeting%2013%20May%2093.pdf; "Draft Minutes Land Working Group, Session 1, Round 10," 17 June 1993, PPD, http://www.palestine-studies.org/sites/default/files/uploads/files/Minutes%20Land%20working%20group%2017%20June%2093.pdf; and "Minutes Concept Working Group," 23 June 1993, PPD, http://www.palestine-studies.org/sites/default/files/uploads/files/Minutes%20Concept%20working%20group%2023%20June%2093.pdf. In these latter two meetings, Suad Amiry and Rashid Khalidi's discussions with the Israelis about territoriality and sovereignty are crucial. See also the critical debate over security in "Draft Minutes Meeting with the Americans," 23 June 1993, PPD, http://www.palestine-studies.org/sites/default/files/uploads/files/Minutes%20Kurtzer%2C%20Miller%20meeting%2023%20June%2093.pdf. Khalidi discusses this in *Brokers of Deceit*, 50-65.

45. See "Highly Confidential Memo on Joint Concept/Land Working Group Meeting," 24 June 1993, PPD, http://www.palestine-studies.org/sites/default/files/uploads/files/Memo%20on%20Joint%20Concept-Land%20meeting%20June%2024%201993.pdf.

46. Ibid. See also Shlaim, *The Iron Wall*, 528-29.

47. Quandt, *Peace Process*, 315 -16.

48. Baconi, *Hamas Contained*, 28. In addition to European and international rights organizations invoking the Fourth Geneva Convention's prohibition against forced transfer, the U.S. State Department "strongly condemn[ed]" the move. See Clyde Haberman, "Israel Expels 400 from Occupied Lands; Lebanese Deploy to Bar Entry of Palestinians," 18 December 1992, *New York Times*, http://www.nytimes.com

/1992/12/18/world/israel-expels-400-occupied-lands-lebanese-deploy-bar-entry
-palestinians.html?pagewanted=all.

49. On Oslo, see Abbas, *Through Secret Channels*; Savir, *The Process*; Ross, *The Missing Peace*; Beilin, *Touching Peace*; Makovsky, *Making Peace with the PLO*; Qurie, *From Oslo to Jerusalem*; Hirschfeld, *Track-Two Diplomacy toward an Israeli-Palestinian Solution*; and Rabinovich, *Yitzhak Rabin*; on the internal tensions that Oslo instigated within the PLO, see al-Hout, *My Life in the PLO*, 270–81.

50. Quandt, *Peace Process*, 328; Shlaim, *The Iron Wall*, 534; and Abbas, *Through Secret Channels*, 206–7. On the Norwegian angle, see Waage, "Norway's Role in the Middle East Peace Talks" and "The 'Minnow' and the 'Whale.'"

51. For the text of the agreement, see Laqueur and Rubin, *The Israel-Arab Reader*, 413–25.

52. Uri Savir, "Oslo, 20 Years Later," *New York Times*, 29 August 2013.

53. On the ambiguity that resulted, the "Achilles's heel of the Oslo process," see Shafir, *A Half Century of Occupation*, 121–22.

54. Khalidi, *Brokers of Deceit*, 57–58. See also Shehadeh, *From Occupation to Interim Accords*.

55. In two separate interviews this link was conceded: first by Ruth Lapidoth, the Israeli Foreign Ministry's Legal Advisor to the Autonomy Negotiations in Jerusalem on 13 February 2012, and then by former Madrid Conference spokeswoman and now PLO Executive Committee member Hanan Ashrawi in Ramallah on 27 February 2012.

56. Shlaim, *The Iron Wall*, 541–42.

57. Weizman, *Hollow Land*, 155–59. On Oslo's method of control, see Gordon, *Israel's Occupation*, 169–96. For an explanation of this logic with regard to the Palestinian bid for statehood at the United Nations, see Darryl Li, "Preening Like a State," *MERIP*, 3 April 2014, http://www.merip.org/preening-state.

58. Palestinian analyst Mouin Rabbani has situated Oslo as part of Israel's wider attempt to co-opt Palestinians. Recalling arrangements like the Village Leagues, Rabbani argues that while "Israel's search for a native pillar in the occupied territories had been one of the most unsuccessful in the history of colonialism, it now seemed that Israel had recruited no less than the leadership of the national liberation movement as sub-contractor for its rule." See "In Honor of Titans," *Jadaliyya*, 10 December 2012, http://www.jadaliyya.com/pages/index/8903/in-honor-of-titans.

59. See Khalidi, *Brokers of Deceit*, 58–59, especially 145n55. Khalidi explains how Oslo helped to "formally consecrate" Begin's autonomy idea. See also Said, *The End of the Peace Process*; and critical reflections on Oslo's twentieth anniversary by Avi Shlaim, "It's Now Clear: The Oslo Peace Accords Were Wrecked by Netanyahu's Bad Faith," *The Guardian*, 12 September 2013.

60. Quandt, *Peace Process*, 326–7.

61. Khalidi, *Brokers of Deceit*, 59–62; Shafir, *A Half Century of Occupation*, 127–28.

62. Khalidi, *Brokers of Deceit*, 60. For a defense of Oslo from a leading proponent, see Abbas, *Through Secret Channels*, 199–224. On Oslo's achievements and limitations from an Israeli proponent, see Savir, *The Process*, 193–244.

63. Shafir, *A Half Century of Occupation*, 44.

64. Ibid.

65. Quoted in Rabinovich, *Yitzhak Rabin*, 212–13. In registering his own opposition to Palestinian statehood, right-wing Israeli minister Naftali Bennett invoked Rabin as a precedent. See the exchange on Bennett's Facebook page, 27 May 2017: https://www.facebook.com/NaftaliBennett/videos/1451696384852025.

66. See Yossi Beilin's comment in "Memo on meeting at home of Counselor of Embassy of Netherlands, Como Hubar, Herziliyya, 15 June 1992," PPD, http://www.palestine-studies.org/sites/default/files/uploads/files/Minutes%20Beilin%20meeting%2C%20Herzillyya%2015%20June%2092.pdf.

67. Quoted in Shlaim, *The Iron Wall*, 539.

68. Ibid., 571.

69. On Rabin's assassination, see Ephron, *Killing a King*; and Rabinovich, *Yitzhak Rabin*, 221–35. On Amir, see Michael Feige, "Yigal Amir," in LeVine and Shafir, eds., *Struggle and Survival*, 384–98.

70. "Mahmoud Darwish: Resigning from the PLO Executive Committee," in Laqueur and Rubin, *The Israel-Arab Reader*, 412. Shafiq al-Hout also resigned; see his account in *My Life in the PLO*, 270–81. On the opposition, see Sayigh, *Armed Struggle*, 653–62; and Shlaim, *The Iron Wall*, 539–40.

Conclusion: The Consequences of State Prevention

1. Quoted in Paul Lewis, "Arafat, in Geneva, Calls on Israelis to Join in Talks, *New York Times*, 14 December 1988.

2. See, for example, Stein, "My Problem with Jimmy Carter's Book," 6–8.

3. *PPPJC*, 9 March 1978.

4. See Lustick, "Israel and the West Bank after Elon Moreh" and "The Two-State Illusion."

5. See Coleman and Longley, *Reagan and the World*; and Hunt and Miles, *Reagan's World*.

6. See Douglas, "Periodizing the American Century"; and Stephanson, *"Simplicissimus."* Journalist James Mann also criticized this bifurcation in *Rise of the Vulcans*.

7. On works that attempt to rehabilitate the Reagan legacy, see Russell Baker, "Reconstructing Ronald Reagan," *New York Review of Books*, 1 March 2007. On triumphalism, see Schrecker, *Cold War Triumphalism*.

8. See, for example, Mamdani, *Good Muslim, Bad Muslim*; Gleijeses, *Visions of Freedom*; Grandin, *Empire's Workshop*; Khalidi, *Sowing Crisis*; Hogan, "The 'Next Big Thing'"; and Zeiler, "The Diplomatic History Bandwagon."

9. On histories of the periphery, see Westad, *The Global Cold War*; and Prashad, *The Darker Nations*. On approaching the broader region in the post-1945 era, see Chamberlin, "Rethinking the Middle East and North Africa in the Cold War."

10. For details of the growth, see the maps in chapter 8.

11. Naomi Chazan, "Domestic Developments in Israel, 1978–1988," in Quandt, ed., *The Middle East*, 155.

12. On the late Ottoman context, see Campos, *Ottoman Brothers*. For the Mandate era, see Norris, *Land of Progress*; Kelly, *The Crime of Nationalism*; Banko, *The Invention of Palestinian Citizenship*; and Meiton, "Electrifying Jaffa." On citizenship and exclusion in the early state years, see Rozin, *A Home for All Jews*; and Robinson, *Citizen Strangers*. On 1967 and the occupation, see Raz, *The Bride and the Dowry*; Gorenberg, *The Accidental Empire*; and Shafir, *A Half Century of Occupation*.

13. On writing conjoined histories of 1948, see Yazbak and Weiss, *Haifa Before and After 1948*. For a global reframing of 1948, see Khalidi, "1948 and After in Palestine" and the entire special issue of *Critical Inquiry* 40.4, titled "Around 1948." On situating 1948 in the context of forced migrations, see Confino, "Miracles and Snow in Palestine and Israel."

In considering my own approach and source base, I have also benefited from the growing field of Israel/Palestine studies. This amalgam of scholarly engagement in both Israeli and Palestinian history as well as Jewish-Arab relations before 1948 utilizes local sources and is keenly sensitive to the complex interplay of culture, society, politics, and language. See, for example, Levy, *Poetic Trespass*; Gribetz, *Defining Neighbors*; Klein, *Lives in Common*; Jacobson and Naor, *Oriental Neighbors*; Robinson, *Citizen Strangers*; Schneider, *Mandatory Separation*; Halperin, *Babel in Zion*; and Cohen, *Year Zero*.

14. See Simpson, "Denying the 'First Right'" and "The United States and the Curious History of Self-Determination." For an exploration of earlier cases in the twentieth century, see Manela, *The Wilsonian Moment*. Palestine is also an illustrative case of how the condition of statelessness is produced and sustained by state actors. On statelessness, see Bloom, Tonkiss, and Cole, *Understanding Statelessness*.

15. Lewis, Frontline Diplomacy. For more on Lewis's approach as a diplomat, see Craig Daigle and Tamara Wittes, "Peacemaking as Interstate Diplomacy: Samuel Lewis," in Fixdal, ed., *Ways out of War*, 33–52.

16. On conceptual history, see Reinhart Koselleck, "The Need for Theory in the Discipline of History," in *The Practice of Conceptual History*, 1–19.

17. Quandt, *Peace Process*, 286.

18. On historians and counterfactuals, see Evans, *Altered Pasts*; and Gaddis, *The Landscape of History*, 91–109.

19. This was Daniel Kurtzer, in "Minutes of the Meeting at the State Department," 26 February 1992, PPD.

20. See Anziska, "Neither Two States nor One"; and Yoav Kisch, "The Day After Obama: The Autonomy Plan of MK Yoav Kisch Based on the Principles of the Late PM Menachem Begin," January 2017, http://kisch.co.il/wp-content/uploads/2017/01/Autonomy-plan.pdf.

21. See Naftali Bennett, "For Israel, Two-State Is No Solution," *New York Times*, 7 November 2014. This trend gained further traction after the election of Donald J. Trump as U.S. president in 2016 and his formal recognition of Jerusalem as Israel's capital. See David M. Halbfinger, "As a 2-State Solution Loses Steam, a 1-State Plan Gains Traction," *New York Times*, 5 January 2018; and Chemi Shalev, "'Fire and Fury': Trump's Israel Policies Crafted by Ultra-Right Bannon-Adelson-Netanyahu Axis,"

Haaretz, 8 January 2018, https://www.haaretz.com/us-news/trump-s-israel-policies
-crafted-by-ultra-right-axis-1.5729683.

22. See Naftali Bennett, "My Stability Plan Offers Only Partial Self-determination
but Will Allow the Palestinians to Thrive," *Fathom*, Winter 2017, http://fathomjournal
.org/my-stability-plan-is-only-partial-self-determination-but-will-allow-the
-palestinians-to-thrive-naftali-bennetts-bottom-up-peace-plan/. On the growing call
for the application of Israeli sovereignty in the West Bank, see Pnina Sharvit Baruch,
"Implications of the Application of Israeli Sovereignty over Judea and Samaria," *Institute for National Security Studies* (INSS), Insight No. 1007, 8 January 2018, http://
www.inss.org.il/publication/implications-application-israeli-sovereignty-judea
-samaria/; and Chaim Levinson and Noa Landau, "Netanyahu: Annexation of West
Bank Settlements Being Discussed with U.S.," *Haaretz*, 12 February 2018, https://
www.haaretz.com/israel-news/netanyahu-settlement-annexation-being-discussed
-with-u-s-1.5810341.

23. Bennett, "My Stability Plan."

24. See Jodi Rudoren, "Netanyahu's Comments Cast Doubt," *New York Times*, 9
March 2015. On a "state minus," see "Netanyahu Says Palestinians Can Have a 'State
Minus,'" *Times of Israel*, 22 January 2017, http://www.timesofisrael.com/netanyahu
-says-palestinians-can-have-a-state-minus; and Allison Deger, "Netanyahu in DC: I
Don't Want Palestinian 'Subjects' but the West Bank Will Remain 'Militarily under
Israel,'" *Mondoweiss*, 7 March 2018, http://mondoweiss.net/2018/03/netanyahu
-palestinian-militarily/.

Archival Sources

ISRAEL

Avraham Harman Institute of Contemporary Jewry. Hebrew University, Jerusalem.
Israel State Archives. Jerusalem.
Jabotinsky Institute. Tel Aviv.
Menachem Begin Heritage Center. Jerusalem.

LEBANON

Arab Image Foundation. Beirut.
Institute for Palestine Studies. Beirut.
UMAM Documentation and Research Center. Beirut.

UNITED KINGDOM

Liddell Hart Centre for Military Archives. King's College, London.
National Archives. Kew, London.

UNITED STATES

American Jewish Committee Archives. New York.
American Jewish Historical Society, New York.
    American Jewish Congress Records.
American Jewish Joint Distribution Committee Archives. New York.
Central Intelligence Agency Records Search Tool.
Columbia Center for Oral History Archives, Butler Library, New York.
Dorot Jewish Division, New York Public Library.
Hoover Institution Archives, Stanford University, Palo Alto, CA.
    Charles Hill Papers.
    Abraham D. Sofaer Papers.
Howard Gotlieb Archival Research Center, Boston University.
    Hermann Eilts Papers.
Jimmy Carter Presidential Library. Atlanta, GA.
Manuscript Division, Library of Congress, Washington, DC.
    Stuart Eizenstat Papers.
    Sol M. Linowitz Papers.

Manuscripts and Archives, Yale University Library, New Haven, CT.
Eugene Rostow Papers.
Cyrus R. and Grace Sloane Vance Papers.
National Archives and Records Administration. College Park, MD.
National Security Archive. Washington, DC.
Ronald Reagan Presidential Library. Simi Valley, CA.

PRIVATE PAPERS

Kahan Commission Documents. Author's Collection.
Khalidi, Rashid. Papers of the Palestinian Delegation to the Israeli-Palestinian
Negotiations. New York.
Lustick, Ian. Papers. Philadelphia.
Siegman, Henry. Papers. New York.

ELECTRONIC ARCHIVES

Akevot. Institute for Israeli-Palestinian Conflict Research. https://akevot.org.il/en/.
The American Presidency Project, University of California, Santa Barbara. www
.presidency.ucsb.edu/ws.
Declassified Documents Reference System. Farmington Hills, MI: Gale Group, 2015.
http://galenet.galegroup.com/servlet/DDRS?locID=columbiau.
Frontline Diplomacy. Manuscript Division, Library of Congress. http://memory.loc
.gov/ammem/collections/diplomacy/index.html.
Israeli Ministry of Foreign Affairs. Historical Documents, Vol. 8, 1982–1984. http://mfa
.gov.il/MFA/ForeignPolicy/MFADocuments/Yearbook6/Pages/TABLE%20OF
%20CONTENTS.aspx.
Miller Center. University of Virginia, Presidential Oral Histories. https://millercenter
.org/the-presidency/presidential-oral-histories.
National Archives and Records Administration. Record Group 59: General Records of
the Department of State Central Foreign Policy File, 1973–79. http://aad.archives
.gov/aad/fielded-search.jsp?dt=2532&tf=X&cat=WR43&bc=,sl.
The Palestinian Revolution. http://learnpalestine.politics.ox.ac.uk.

Published Documents

Committee on House Administration, U.S. House of Representatives. *The Presidential Campaign 1976*. Washington, DC: US GPO, 1978.
Foreign Relations of the United States, 1977–1980. Vol. 8, Arab-Israeli Dispute, January 1977–August 1978. Ed. Adam M. Howard. Washington, DC: US GPO, 2013.
Foreign Relations of the United States, 1977–1980. Volume 9, Arab-Israeli Dispute, August 1978–December 1980. Ed. Alexander R. Wieland. Gen. ed. Adam M. Howard.
Washington, DC: US GPO, 2014.

International Committee of the Red Cross. *The Geneva Conventions of August 12, 1949.* Geneva, 1949.

Menachem Begin: The Sixth Prime Minister [Hebrew]. Jerusalem: Israel State Archives, 2014.

Toward Peace in the Middle East: Report of a Study Group. Washington, DC: Brookings Institution, 1975.

U.S. Congress. House. Committee on International Relations. *Israeli Settlements in the Occupied Territories: Hearings before the Subcommittee on International Organizations and on Europe and the Middle East.* 95th Cong., 12 and 21 September, 19 October 1977. Washington, DC: US GPO, 1978.

U.S. Congress. Senate. Committee on the Judiciary. *The Colonization of the West Bank Territories by Israel: Hearings before the Subcommittee on Immigration and Naturalization.* 95th Cong., 17 and 18 October 1977. Washington, DC: US GPO, 1978.

Interviews

Hussein Agha, 17 March 2008, London.

Morris Amitay, 4 April 2006, by telephone.

Hanan Ashrawi, 27 February 2012, Ramallah.

Amos Avgar, 22 July 2010, Jerusalem.

Bernard Avishai, 26 June 2012, Jerusalem.

Thomas Friedman, 28 April 2008, by telephone.

Ralph Goldman, 22 July 2010, Jerusalem.

Bernard Gwertzman, 15 March 2006, New York.

David Harman, 22 July 2010, Jerusalem.

Rita Hauser, 11 January 2006 and 4 April 2008, New York.

David Hirst, 18 July 2012, Beirut.

Loren Jenkins, 5 September 2012, by telephone.

Yechiel Kaddishai, 13 June 2010, Tel Aviv.

Ahmad Khalidi, 17 March 2008, London.

Rashid Khalidi, 25 March 2008, New York.

Daniel Kurtzer, 3 March 2008, Princeton.

Ruth Lapidoth, 13 February 2012, Jerusalem.

Samuel Lewis, 19 March 2012, McLean, VA; and 6 September 2012, by telephone.

Uri Lubrani, 25 June 2012, by telephone.

Sari Nusseibeh, 29 February 2012, Jerusalem.

William Quandt, 16 March 2006, by telephone.

Jonathan Randal, 23 May 2012, by telephone.

Meir Rosenne, 28 February 2012, by telephone.

Robbie Sabel, 20 February 2012, Jerusalem.

Yezid Sayigh, 25 July 2012, Beirut.

Gary Sick, 7 February 2006, New York.

Mark Siegel, 31 March 2006, by telephone.

Henry Siegman, 14 January 2012, New York.
Hanna Siniora, 24 February 2012, Jerusalem.
Hagai Tamir, 19 June 2010, Jaffa.
Howard Teicher, 19 June 2013, Washington, DC.
Roger Tomkys, 12 February 2013, Cambridge, UK.
Nicholas Veliotes, 17 March 2012, McLean, VA.

Newspapers and Periodicals

Al-Ahram Weekly
Al-Hadaf
The American Prospect
The Atlantic
Badil
Cairo Review of Global Affairs
Christian Science Monitor
Commentary
The Economist
Fathom
Foreign Affairs
Foreign Policy
The Forward
The Guardian
Haaretz
Haliyat
Jadaliyya
Jewish Review of Books
Jewish Telegraphic Agency
London Review of Books
Los Angeles Times
Middle East Research and Information Project (MERIP)
Moment
Mondoweiss
The Nation
The National Interest
Newsweek
New York Review of Books
New York Times
New Yorker
Palestine: PLO Information Bulletin
Philadelphia Inquirer
Politico
Southern Israelite
Tablet

Time
The Times (London)
Times of Israel
Washington Post

Unpublished Manuscripts

Bowditch, Thomas Anderson. "Force and Diplomacy: The American Failure in Lebanon, 1982–1984." PhD diss., University of Virginia, 1999.

Byrnes, Sean Thomas. "The United States in Opposition: The United Nations, the Third World, and Changing American Visions of Global Order, 1970–1984." PhD diss., Emory University, 2014.

Coldwell, Dominic. "Egypt's 'Autumn of Fury': The Construction of Opposition to the Egyptian-Israeli Peace Process between 1973 and 1981." MPhil thesis, University of Oxford, 2003.

Davidson, Ezra. "Visions of Political Islam and the American Military Presence in the Middle East: From Carter to Reagan." PhD diss., New York University, 2011.

Jamjoum, Hazem Mohammad. "The Village Leagues: Israel's Native Authority and the 1981–1982 Intifada." MA thesis, American University of Beirut, 2012.

McFarland, Victor. "Living in Never-Never Land: The United States, Saudi Arabia, and Oil in the 1970s." PhD diss., Yale University, 2014.

Molchadsky, Nadav. "History in the Public Courtroom: Commissions of Inquiry and Struggles over the History and Memory of Israeli Traumas." PhD diss., University of California–Los Angeles, 2015.

Rubin, Gil S. "The Future of the Jews: Planning for the Postwar Jewish World, 1939–1946." PhD diss., Columbia University, 2017.

Rubinovitz, Ziv, and Gerald M. Steinberg. "Menachem Begin's Autonomy Plan: Between Political Realism and Ideology." Paper presented at the annual meeting of the Association for Israel Studies, University of Haifa, June 2012.

Sexton, Mary DuBois. "The Wages of Principle and Power: Cyrus R. Vance and the Making of Foreign Policy in the Carter Administration." PhD diss., Georgetown University, 2009.

Siddiqi, Ahmad. "From Liberation to Self-Determination: The PLO's Move to the Two-State Solution, 1973–1988." MPhil thesis, Oxford University, 2009.

Sohns, Olivia Louise. "Lyndon Baines Johnson and the Arab-Israeli Conflict." PhD diss., University of Cambridge, 2014.

Wight, David. "The Petrodollar Era and Relations between the United States and the Middle East and North Africa, 1969–1980." PhD diss., University of California–Irvine, 2014.

Secondary Sources

Abbas, Mahmoud. *Through Secret Channels*. Reading: Garnet, 1995.

Aburish, Said K. *Arafat: From Defender to Dictator*. London: Bloomsbury, 1998.

Abu Sharif, Bassam. *Arafat and the Dream of Palestine*. New York: Palgrave MacMillan, 2009.

Abu-Odeh, Adnan. *Jordanians, Palestinians, and the Hashemite Kingdom in the Middle East Peace Process*. Washington, DC: United States Institute of Peace Press, 1999.

Adnan, Etel. *Sitt Marie Rose*. Trans. Georgina Kleege. Sausalito: Post-Apollo Press, 1982.

Agha, Hussein J. "What State for Palestinians?" *Journal of Palestine Studies* 6.1 (1976): 3–38.

Aharoni, Dov. *General Sharon's War against Time Magazine: His Trial and Vindication*. New York: Steimatzky, 1985.

Ajami, Fouad. "Lebanon and Its Inheritors." *Foreign Affairs* 63.4 (1985): 784–85.

Al-Hout, Bayan Nuwayhid. *Sabra and Shatila: September 1982*. London: Pluto Press, 2004.

Al-Hout, Shafiq. *My Life in the PLO: The Inside Story of the Palestinian Struggle*. London: Pluto Press, 2011.

Al-Madfai, Madiha Rashid. *Jordan, the United States and the Middle East Peace Process, 1974–1991*. Cambridge: Cambridge University Press, 1993.

Al-Shaikh, Zakaria. "Sabra and Shatila 1982: Resisting the Massacre." *Journal of Palestine Studies* 14.1 (Autumn 1984): 57–90.

Allegra, Marco, Ariel Handel, and Erez Maggor, eds. *Normalizing Occupation: The Politics of Everyday Life in the West Bank Settlements*. Bloomington: Indiana University Press, 2017.

Allen, Lori, Samera Esmeir, Keith David Watenpaugh, Ilana Feldman, Nefissa Naguib, and Nell Gabiam. "Roundtable: Problematics of Human Rights and Humanitarianism." *International Journal of Middle East Studies* 48.2 (2016): 357–86.

Allon, Yigal. "Israel: The Case for Defensible Borders." *Foreign Affairs* 55.1 (October 1976): 38–53.

Alterman, Jon B., ed. *Sadat and His Legacy: Egypt and the World, 1977–1997: On the Occasion of the Twentieth Anniversary of President Sadat's Journey to Jerusalem*. Washington, DC: Washington Institute for Near East Policy, 1998.

Alvandi, Roham. *Nixon, Kissinger, and the Shah: The United States and Iran in the Cold War*. Oxford: Oxford University Press, 2014.

Anziska, Seth. "Autonomy as State Prevention: The Palestinian Question after Camp David, 1979–1982." *Humanity: An International Journal of Human Rights, Humanitarianism, and Development* 8.2 (Summer 2017): 287–310.

———. "Israel and the U.S." In *Great Decisions 2014 Briefing Book*, 15–28. New York: Foreign Policy Association, 2013.

———. "Neither Two States nor One: The Palestine Question in the Age of Trump." *Journal of Palestine Studies* 46.3 (2017): 57–74.

Arens, Moshe. *Broken Covenant: American Foreign Policy and the Crisis between the U.S. and Israel*. New York: Simon and Schuster, 1995.

Arquilla, John. *The Reagan Imprint: Ideas in American Foreign Policy from the Collapse of Communism to the War on Terror*. Chicago: Ivan R. Dee, 2006.

Aruri, Naseer. "The PLO and the Jordan Option." *Middle East Report* 131 (March–April 1985): 3–9.

———. "The United States and Palestine: Reagan's Legacy to Bush." *Journal of Palestine Studies* 18.3 (Spring 1989): 3–21.

Aruri, Naseer H., and Fouad M. Moughrabi. "The Reagan Middle East Initiative." *Journal of Palestine Studies* 12.2 (1983): 10–30.

Ashrawi, Hanan. *This Side of Peace: A Personal Account.* New York: Touchstone, 1996.

Ashton, Nigel J. "'A Local Terrorist Made Good': The Callaghan Government and the Arab-Israeli Peace Process, 1977–79." *Contemporary British History* 31.1 (2017): 114–35.

———. "Love's Labours Lost: Margaret Thatcher, King Hussein and Anglo-Jordanian Relations, 1979–1990." *Diplomacy & Statecraft* 22.4 (2011): 651–77.

———. "Searching for a Just and Lasting Peace? Anglo-American Relations and the Road to United Nations Security Council Resolution 242." *International History Review* 38.1 (2016): 24–44.

———. "Taking Friends for Granted: The Carter Administration, Jordan, and the Camp David Accords, 1977–1980." *Diplomatic History* 41.3 (2017): 620–45.

Auten, Brian A. *Carter's Conversion: The Hardening of American Defense Policy.* Columbia: University of Missouri Press, 2008.

Avner, Yehuda. *The Prime Ministers: An Intimate Narrative of Israeli Leadership.* New Milford: Toby Press, 2010.

Azoulay, Ariella, and Adi Ophir. *The One State Condition: Occupation and Democracy in Israel/Palestine.* Stanford: Stanford University Press, 2013.

Bacevich, Andrew J. *America's War for the Greater Middle East: A Military History.* New York: Random House, 2016.

Baconi, Tareq. *Hamas Contained: The Rise and Pacification of Palestinian Resistance.* Stanford: Stanford University Press, 2018.

Baker, James A. III, with Thomas M. DeFrank. *The Politics of Diplomacy: Revolution, War and Peace, 1989–1992.* New York: G. P. Putnam's Sons, 1995.

Balmer, Randall. *Redeemer: The Life of Jimmy Carter.* New York: Basic Books, 2014.

Banko, Lauren. *The Invention of Palestinian Citizenship, 1918–1947.* Edinburgh: Edinburgh University Press, 2016.

Barnett, Michael N. *The Star and the Stripes: A History of the Foreign Policies of American Jews.* Princeton: Princeton University Press, 2016.

Bar-On, Mordechai, ed. *A Never-Ending Conflict: A Guide to Israeli Military History.* Westport, CT: Praeger, 2004.

———. *Moshe Dayan: Israel's Controversial Hero.* New Haven: Yale University Press, 2012.

Bar-Siman-Tov, Yaacov. "The United States and Israel since 1948: A 'Special Relationship?'" *Diplomatic History* 22.2 (1998): 231–62.

Bass, Warren. *Support Any Friend: Kennedy's Middle East and the Making of the U.S.-Israel Alliance.* New York: Oxford University Press, 2003.

Baumgarten, Helga. "The Three Faces/Phases of Palestinian Nationalism, 1948–2005." *Journal of Palestine Studies* 34.4 (2005): 25–48.

Beilin, Yossi. *Touching Peace: From the Oslo Accord to a Final Agreement*. London: Weidenfeld and Nicolson, 1999.

Beinart, Peter. *The Crisis of Zionism*. New York: Times Books, 2012.

Ben-Elissar, Eliahu. *Lo Od Milhamah* [No more war]. Or Yehudah: Sifriyat Ma'ariv, 1995.

Ben-Ephraim, Shaiel. "Distraction and Deception: Israeli Settlements, Vietnam, and the Johnson Administration." *Diplomatic History* 42.3 (June 2018): 456–83.

Ben-Ze'ev, Efrat, Ruth Ginio, and Jay Winter, eds. *Shadows of War: A Social History of Silence in the Twentieth Century*. Cambridge: Cambridge University Press, 2010.

Ben-Zvi, Abraham. *The United States and Israel: The Limits of the Special Relationship*. New York: Columbia University Press, 1993.

Benvenisti, Eyal. *The International Law of Occupation*. 2nd ed. Oxford: Oxford University Press, 2012.

Benvenisti, Meron. *The West Bank Data Base Project 1987 Report: Demographic, Economic, Legal, Social, and Political Developments in the West Bank*. Jerusalem: West Bank Data Base Project, 1987.

Benziman, Uzi. *Sharon: An Israeli Caesar*. New York: Adama Books, 1984.

Berda, Yael. *Living Emergency: Israel's Permit Regime in the Occupied West Bank*. Stanford: Stanford University Press, 2018.

Bergman, Ronen. *Rise and Kill First: The Secret History of Israel's Targeted Assassinations*. Trans. Ronnie Hope. New York: Random House, 2018.

Bermant, Azriel. *Margaret Thatcher and the Middle East*. Cambridge: Cambridge University Press, 2016.

Biale, David. *Power and Powerlessness in Jewish History*. New York: Schocken Books, 1986.

Bird, Kai. *The Good Spy: The Life and Death of Robert Ames*. New York: Crown, 2014.

Bloom, Tendayi, Katherine Tonkiss, and Phillip Cole, eds. *Understanding Statelessness*. London: Routledge, 2017.

Blumenthal, Sidney. *The Rise of the Counter-Establishment: From Conservative Ideology to Political Power*. New York: Times Books, 1986.

Boutros-Ghali, Boutros. *Egypt's Road to Jerusalem: A Diplomat's Story of the Struggle for Peace in the Middle East*. New York: Random House, 1997.

Boykin, John. *Cursed Is the Peacemaker: The American Diplomat versus the Israeli General, Beirut 1982*. Belmont, CA: Applegate Press, 2002.

Bozarslan, Hamit. "Revisiting the Middle East's 1979." *Economy and Society* 41.4 (2012): 558–67.

Brands, H. W. *Reagan: The Life*. New York: Doubleday, 2015.

Brands, Hal, and Jeremi Suri, eds. *The Power of the Past: History and Statecraft*. Washington, DC: Brookings Institution Press, 2016.

Bruzonsky, Mark A. "America's Palestinian Predicament: Fallacies and Possibilities." *International Security* 6.1 (Summer 1981): 93–110.

Brynen, Rex. "PLO Policy in Lebanon: Legacies and Lessons." *Journal of Palestine Studies* 18.2 (1989): 48–70.

———. *Sanctuary and Survival: The PLO in Lebanon*. Boulder, CO: Westview Press, 1990.

Brzezinski, Zbigniew. *Power and Principle: Memoirs of the National Security Adviser, 1977–1981*. New York: Farrar, Straus, Giroux, 1983.

Brzezinski, Zbigniew, François Duchêne, and Kiichi Saeki. "Peace in an International Framework." *Foreign Policy*, no. 19 (Summer 1975): 3–17.

Burg, Avraham. *In Days to Come: A New Hope for Israel*. Trans. Joel Greenberg. New York: Nation Books, 2018.

Bush, George, and Brent Scowcroft. *A World Transformed*. New York: Vintage, 2011.

Byrne, Jeffrey James. *Mecca of Revolution: From the Algerian Front of the Third World's Cold War*. New York: Oxford University Press, 2016.

Byrne, Malcolm. *Iran-Contra: Reagan's Scandal and the Unchecked Abuse of Presidential Power*. Lawrence: University of Kansas Press, 2014.

Campos, Michelle. *Ottoman Brothers: Muslims, Christians, and Jews in Early Twentieth- Century Palestine*. Stanford: Stanford University Press, 2010.

Cannon, Lou. *President Reagan: The Role of a Lifetime*. New York: Simon and Schuster, 1991.

Carter, Jimmy. *The Blood of Abraham*. London: Sidgwick and Jackson, 1985.

———. *Keeping Faith: Memoirs of a President*. New York: Bantam Books, 1983.

———. *Palestine: Peace Not Apartheid*. New York: Simon and Schuster, 2006.

———. *White House Diary*. New York: Farrar, Straus and Giroux, 2010.

Caryl, Christian. *Strange Rebels: 1979 and the Birth of the 21ˢᵗ Century*. New York: Basic Books, 2013.

Chamberlin, Paul Thomas. *The Global Offensive: The United States, the Palestine Liberation Organization, and the Making of the Post–Cold War Order*. New York: Oxford University Press, 2012.

———. "Rethinking the Middle East and North Africa in the Cold War." Roundtable, *International Journal of Middle East Studies* 43.2 (2011): 317–19.

Christison, Kathleen. *Perceptions of Palestine: Their Influence on U.S. Middle East Policy*. Berkeley: University of California Press, 2000.

Citino, Nathan. *Envisioning the Arab Future: Modernization in U.S.-Arab Relations, 1945–1967*. Cambridge: Cambridge University Press, 2017.

Clymer, Kenton. "Jimmy Carter, Human Rights, and Cambodia." *Diplomatic History* 27.2 (April 2003): 245–78.

Cobban, Helena. *The Making of Modern Lebanon*. Boulder, CO: Westview Press, 1985.

———. *The Palestinian Liberation Organisation: People, Power, and Politics*. Cambridge: Cambridge University Press, 1984.

———. "The U.S.-Israeli Relationship in the Reagan Era." *Conflict Quarterly* (Spring 1989): 5–32.

Cohen, Hillel. "Agudat Hakfarim: Kishalon Hamisgeret, Nizachon Hatfisa, V'hashalom Ha'ebud" [Village Leagues: Failed framework, conceptual victory, and the lost peace]. *The New East* (2014): 251–77.

———. *Year Zero of the Arab-Israeli Conflict 1929*. Waltham, MA: Brandeis University Press, 2015.

Cohen, Uri, and Nissim Leon. "The Mahapach and Yitzhak Shamir's Quiet Revolution: Mizrahim and the Herut Movement." *Israel Studies Review* 29.1 (2014): 18–40.

Coleman, Bradley Lynn, and Kyle Longley. *Reagan and the World: Leadership and National Security, 1981–1989*. Lexington: University Press of Kentucky, 2017.

Collins, Robert M. *Transforming America: Politics and Culture in the Reagan Years*. New York: Columbia University Press, 2007.

Confino, Alon. "Miracles and Snow in Palestine and Israel: Tantura, a History of 1948." *Israel Studies* 17.2 (2012): 25–61.

Connelly, Matthew. *A Diplomatic Revolution: Algeria's Fight for Independence and the Origins of the Post–Cold War Era*. Oxford: Oxford University Press, 2002.

Crist, David. *The Twilight War: The Secret History of America's Thirty-Year Conflict with Iran*. New York: Penguin Press, 2012.

Curtiss, Richard H. *Stealth PACs: How Israel's American Lobby Seeks to Control U.S. Middle East Policy*. Washington, DC: American Educational Trust, 1990.

Daigle, Craig. *The Limits of Détente: The United States, the Soviet Union, and the Arab-Israeli Conflict*. New Haven: Yale University Press, 2012.

Dakkak, Ibrahim. "Back to Square One: A Study in the Re-Emergence of Palestinian Identity in the West Bank, 1967–1980." In Michael Dumper, ed., *Arab-Israeli Conflict: Volume II, 1967–1991*. London: Routledge, 2009.

Dayan, Moshe. *Breakthrough: A Personal Account of the Egypt-Israel Peace Negotiations*. New York: Knopf, 1981.

Deaver, Michael K. *A Different Drummer: My Thirty Years with Ronald Reagan*. New York: Perennial, 2001.

Decker, Jefferson. *The Other Rights Revolution: Conservative Lawyers and the Remaking of American Government*. New York: Oxford University Press, 2016.

Demant, Peter. "Israeli Settlement Policy Today." *Middle East Report*, no. 116 (1983): 3–29.

DeRoche, Andrew J. *Andrew Young: Civil Rights Ambassador*. Wilmington, DE: Scholarly Resources, 2003.

Dietrich, Christopher R. W. *Oil Revolution: Anticolonial Elites, Sovereign Rights, and the Economic Culture of Decolonization*. Cambridge: Cambridge University Press, 2017.

Diggins, John P. *Ronald Reagan: Fate, Freedom, and the Making of History*. New York: W. W. Norton, 2007.

Dinstein, Yoram. *The International Law of Belligerent Occupation*. Cambridge: Cambridge University Press, 2009.

——, ed. *Models of Autonomy*. New Brunswick, NJ: Transaction Books, 1981.

Dollinger, Marc. *Quest for Inclusion: Jews and Liberalism in Modern America*. Princeton: Princeton University Press, 2000.

Douglas, Ann. "Periodizing the American Century: Modernism, Postmodernism, and Postcolonialism in the Cold War Context." *Modernism/modernity* 5.3 (1998): 71–98.

Dowty, Alan. "Zionism's Greatest Conceit." *Israel Studies* 3.1 (Spring 1998): 1–23.

Drew, Elizabeth. *Portrait of an Election: The 1980 Presidential Campaign*. New York: Simon and Schuster, 1981.

Eckel, Jan, and Samuel Moyn, eds. *The Breakthrough: Human Rights in the 1970s.* Philadelphia: University of Pennsylvania Press, 2013.

Ehrman, John. *The Rise of Neoconservatism: Intellectuals and Foreign Affairs, 1945–1994.* New Haven: Yale University Press, 1995.

Eisenberg, Laura Zittrain. *My Enemy's Enemy: Lebanon in the Early Zionist Imagination, 1900–1948.* Detroit: Wayne State University Press, 1994.

Eisenberg, Laura Zittrain, and Neil Caplan. *Negotiating Arab-Israeli Peace: Patterns, Problems, Possibilities.* 2nd ed. Bloomington: Indiana University Press, 2010.

Eitan, Raful. *A Soldier's Story: The Life and Times of an Israeli War Hero.* Trans. Eliot A. Green. New York: S.P.I. Books, 1991.

Elkoury, Fouad. *Atlantis.* 2012. Photographs. 9th Gwangju Biennale. http://www.fouadelkoury.com/install.php?id=25.

———. *Passing Time.* Beirut: Kaph Books, 2017.

Engel, Jeffrey A. *When the World Seemed New: George H. W. Bush and the End of the Cold War.* New York: Houghton Mifflin Harcourt, 2017.

Ephron, Dan. *Killing a King: The Assassination of Yitzhak Rabin and the Remaking of Israel.* New York: W. W. Norton, 2015.

Erakat, Noura. "Taking the Land without the People: The 1967 Story as Told by the Law." *Journal of Palestine Studies* 47.1 (2017): 18–38.

Evans, Richard. *Altered Pasts: Counterfactuals in History.* New York: Little Brown, 2014.

Evron, Yair. *War and Intervention in Lebanon: The Israeli-Syrian Deterrence Dialogue.* London: Croom Helm, 1987.

Fahmy, Ismail. *Negotiating for Peace in the Middle East.* London: Croom Helm, 1983.

Feige, Michael. *Settling in the Hearts: Jewish Fundamentalism in the Occupied Territories.* Detroit: Wayne State University Press, 2009.

Feith, Douglas J. "The Settlements and Peace: Playing the Links with Begin, Carter and Sadat." *Policy Review* 0.8 (1979): 25–40.

Feldman, Keith P. *A Shadow over Palestine: The Imperial Life of Race in America.* Minneapolis: University of Minnesota Press, 2015.

Feldman, Shai, and Heda Rechnitz-Kijner. *Deception, Consensus, and War: Israel in Lebanon.* Boulder, CO: Westview Press, 1984.

Ferris, Jesse. *Nasser's Gamble: How Intervention in Yemen Caused the Six Day War and the Decline of Egyptian Power.* Princeton: Princeton University Press, 2012.

Findley, Paul. *They Dare to Speak Out: People and Institutions Confront Israel's Lobby.* Chicago: Lawrence Hill Press, 1985.

Fischer, Beth A. *The Reagan Reversal: Foreign Policy and the End of the Cold War.* Columbia: University of Missouri Press, 1997.

Fischer, Louise. "Turning Point on the Road to Peace: The Government of Yitzhak Rabin and the Interim Agreement with Egypt (Sinai II)." *Israel Studies* 19.3 (2014): 55–80.

Fisk, Robert. *Pity the Nation: Lebanon at War.* 3rd ed. Oxford: Oxford University Press, 2001.

Fixdal, Mona, ed. *Ways out of War: Peacemakers in the Middle East and Balkans.* New York: Palgrave Macmillan, 2012.

Freedman, Robert O., ed. *The Middle East after the Israeli Invasion of Lebanon.* Syracuse, NY: Syracuse University Press, 1986.

Friedlander, Melvin A. *Sadat and Begin: The Domestic Politics of Peacemaking.* Boulder, CO: Westview Press, 1983.

Friedman, Robert I. *Zealots for Zion: Inside Israel's West Bank Settlement Movement.* New York: Random House, 1992.

Friedman, Thomas L. *From Beirut to Jerusalem.* Updated ed. New York: Anchor Books, 1995.

Gabriel, Richard A. *Operation Peace for Galilee: The Israeli-PLO War in Lebanon.* New York: Hill and Wang, 1984.

Gaddis, John Lewis. *The Landscape of History: How Historians Map the Past.* New York: Oxford University Press, 2002.

———. *Strategies of Containment: A Critical Appraisal of American National Security Policy during the Cold War.* Oxford: Oxford University Press, 2005.

Gal, Irit, and Ilana Hammerman, eds. *Mibeirut Lejenin: Milchemet Levanon, 1982–2002* [From Beirut to Jenin: The Lebanon War, 1982–2002]. Tel Aviv: Am Oved, 2002.

Gardner, Lloyd C. *The Long Road to Baghdad: A History of U.S. Foreign Policy from the 1970s to the Present.* New York: New Press, 2008.

Gates, Robert Michael. *From the Shadows: The Ultimate Insider's Story of Five Presidents and How They Won the Cold War.* New York: Simon and Schuster, 1996.

Gati, Charles, ed. *Zbig: The Strategy and Statecraft of Zbigniew Brzezinski.* Baltimore: Johns Hopkins University Press, 2013.

Gazit, Shlomo. *Trapped Fools: Thirty Years of Israeli Policy in the Territories.* London: Frank Cass, 2003.

Gefen, Israel. *An Israeli in Lebanon.* London: Pickwick Books, 1986.

Gelber, Yoav. *Palestine 1948: War, Escape and the Emergence of the Palestinian Refugee Problem.* 2nd ed. Brighton: Sussex Academic Press, 2006.

Gendzier, Irene L. *Dying to Forget: Oil, Palestine and the Foundation of U.S. Policy in the Middle East.* New York: Columbia University Press, 2015.

———. *Notes from the Minefield: United States Intervention in Lebanon and the Middle East, 1945–1958.* New York: Columbia University Press, 1997.

Genet, Jean. "Four Hours in Shatila." *Journal of Palestine Studies* 12.3 (Spring 1983): 3–22.

Gilmour, David. *Lebanon: The Fractured Country.* Rev. and updated ed. London: Sphere, 1987.

Ginor, Isabella, and Gideon Remez. *The Soviet-Israeli War, 1967–1973.* London: Hurst, 2017.

Glad, Betty. *An Outsider in the White House: Jimmy Carter, His Advisors, and the Making of American Foreign Policy.* Ithaca: Cornell University Press, 2009.

Gleijeses, Piero. *Visions of Freedom: Havana, Washington, Pretoria, and the Struggle for Southern Africa, 1976–1991.* Chapel Hill: University of North Carolina Press, 2013.

Golan, Galia. *Israeli Peacemaking since 1967: Factors behind the Breakthroughs and Failures.* London: Routledge, 2015.

Goldberg, J. J. *Jewish Power: Inside the American Jewish Establishment*. New York: Basic Books, 1997.

Goldstein, Amir. "Menahem Begin V'raayon Shlemut Hamoledet ad Milchemet Sheshet Hayamim" [Menachem Begin and "The Whole Land of Israel" until the Six Day War]. *Cathedra* 126 (2007): 103–28.

Gordis, Daniel. *Menachem Begin: The Battle for Israel's Soul*. New York: Nextbook, 2014.

Gordon, Neve. *Israel's Occupation*. Berkeley: University of California Press, 2008.

Gorenberg, Gershom. *The Accidental Empire: Israel and the Birth of the Settlements, 1967–1977*. New York: Times Books, 2006.

Grandin, Greg. *Empire's Workshop: Latin America, the United States, and the Rise of the New Imperialism*. New York: Henry Holt and Company, 2006.

Gresh, Alain. *The PLO: The Struggle Within: Towards an Independent Palestinian State*. Rev. and updated ed. London: Zed Books, 1988.

Gribetz, Jonathan. *Defining Neighbors: Religion, Race, and the Early Zionist-Arab Encounter*. Princeton: Princeton University Press, 2014.

———. "When *The Zionist Idea* Came to Beirut: Judaism, Christianity and the Palestine Liberation Organization's Translation of Zionism." *International Journal of Middle East Studies* 48.2 (May 2016): 243–66.

Grosbard, Ofer. *Menahem Begin: Dyokano shel Manhig—Biografiyah* [Menachem Begin: A portrait of a leader—A biography]. Tel Aviv: Resling, 2006.

Grose, Peter. *Israel in the Mind of America*. New York: Schocken, 1984.

Grossman, David. *The Yellow Wind*. New York: Farrar, Straus and Giroux, 1988.

Guha, Ranajit. *Elementary Aspects of Peasant Insurgency in Colonial India*. Durham: Duke University Press, 1999.

Haber, Eitan, Zeev Schiff, and Ehud Yaari. *The Year of the Dove*. New York: Bantam, 1979.

Hadar, Leon T. "High Noon in Washington: The Shootout over the Loan Guarantees." *Journal of Palestine Studies* 21.2 (Winter 1992): 72–87.

Hahn, Peter L. *Caught in the Middle East: U.S. Policy toward the Arab-Israeli Conflict, 1945–1961*. Chapel Hill: University of North Carolina Press, 2004.

Haig, Alexander. *Caveat: Realism, Reagan and Foreign Policy*. London: Weidenfeld and Nicolson, 1984.

Hajjar, Lisa. *Courting Conflict: The Israeli Military Court System in the West Bank and Gaza*. Berkeley: University of California Press, 2005.

Hallenbeck, Ralph A. *Military Force as an Instrument of U.S. Foreign Policy: Intervention in Lebanon, August 1982–February 1984*. New York: Praeger, 1991.

Halper, Stefan A., and Jonathan Clarke. *America Alone: The Neo-Conservatives and the Global Order*. Cambridge: Cambridge University Press, 2004.

Halperin, Liora. *Babel in Zion: Jews, Nationalism, and Language Diversity in Palestine, 1920–1948*. New Haven: Yale University Press, 2014.

Hammel, Eric M. *The Root: The Marines in Beirut, August 1982–February 1984*. San Diego: Harcourt Brace Jovanovich, 1985.

Hanhimäki, Jussi. *The Flawed Architect: Henry Kissinger and American Foreign Policy*. Oxford: Oxford University Press, 2004.

Harris, Rachel S., and Ranen Omer-Sheman, eds. *Narratives of Dissent: War in Contemporary Israeli Arts and Culture*. Detroit: Wayne State University Press, 2012.

Harrison, Olivia C. *Transcolonial Maghreb: Imagining Palestine in the Era of Decolonization*. Stanford: Stanford University Press, 2015.

Hart, Alan. *Arafat: A Political Biography*. London: Sidgwick and Jackson, 1984.

Haugbolle, Sune. *War and Memory in Lebanon*. New York: Cambridge University Press, 2010.

Heller, Daniel Kupfert. *Jabotinsky's Children: Polish Jews and the Rise of Right-Wing Zionism*. Princeton: Princeton University Press, 2017.

Herman, Tamar. *The Israeli Peace Movement: A Shattered Dream*. Cambridge: Cambridge University Press, 2009.

Hinnebusch, Raymond A. *Egyptian Politics under Sadat: The Post-Populist Development of an Authoritarian-Modernizing State*. Cambridge: Cambridge University Press, 1985.

Hirschfeld, Yair. *Track-Two Diplomacy toward an Israeli-Palestinian Solution, 1978–2014*. Washington, DC: Woodrow Wilson Center Press, 2014.

Hirschhorn, Sara Yael. *City on a Hilltop: American Jews and the Israeli Settler Movement*. Cambridge, MA: Harvard University Press, 2017.

Hiro, Dilip. *Lebanon: Fire and Embers: A History of the Lebanese Civil War*. London: Weidenfeld and Nicholson, 1993.

Hirst, David. *Beware of Small States: Lebanon, Battleground of the Middle East*. New York: Nation Books, 2010.

———. *The Gun and the Olive Branch: The Roots of Violence in the Middle East*. 3rd ed. New York: Nation Books, 2003.

Hirst, David, and Irene Beeson. *Sadat*. London: Faber and Faber, 1981.

Hochberg, Gil Z. *Visual Occupations: Violence and Visibility in a Conflict Zone*. Durham: Duke University Press, 2015.

Hogan, Michael J. "The 'Next Big Thing': The Future of Diplomatic History in a Global Age." *Diplomatic History* 28.1 (2004): 1–21.

Hudson, Michael C. *The Precarious Republic: Political Modernization in Lebanon*. Boulder, CO: Westview Press, 1985.

Hunt, Jonathan, and Simon Miles, eds. *Reagan's World: The Cold War and Beyond*. Ithaca: Cornell University Press, forthcoming.

Hutchings, Robert, and Jeremi Suri, eds. *Foreign Policy Breakthroughs: Cases in Successful Diplomacy*. New York: Oxford University Press, 2015.

Inbari, Motti. *Messianic Religious Zionism Confronts Israeli Territorial Compromises*. New York: Cambridge University Press, 2012.

Indyk, Martin. *Innocent Abroad: An Intimate Account of American Peace Diplomacy in the Middle East*. New York: Simon and Schuster, 2009.

———. *"To the Ends of the Earth": Sadat's Jerusalem Initiative*. Cambridge: Center for Middle Eastern Studies, 1984.

Isaac, Joel, and Duncan Bell, eds. *Uncertain Empire: American History and the Idea of the Cold War*. New York: Oxford University Press, 2012.

Israeli, Raphael, ed. *PLO in Lebanon: Selected Documents*. London: Weidenfeld and Nicolson, 1983.

Jacobs, Matthew F. *Imagining the Middle East: The Building of an American Foreign Policy*. Chapel Hill: University of North Carolina Press, 2011.

Jacobs, Meg. *Panic at the Pump: The Energy Crisis and the Transformation of American Politics in the 1970s*. New York: Hill and Wang, 2016.

Jacobson, Abigail, and Moshe Naor. *Oriental Neighbors: Middle Eastern Jews and Arabs in Mandatory Palestine*. Waltham, MA: Brandeis University Press, 2016.

Jansen, Jan C., and Jürgen Osterhammel. *Decolonization: A Short History*. Princeton: Princeton University Press, 2017.

Jensehaugen, Jørgen. *Arab-Israeli Diplomacy under Carter: The U.S., Israel and the Palestinians*. London: I. B. Tauris, 2018.

———. "Blueprint for Arab-Israeli Peace? President Carter and the Brookings Report." *Diplomacy & Statecraft* 25 (2014): 492–508.

Joreige, Lamia. *Objects of War*. 1999–2006. Video installation. "Here and Elsewhere." New Museum, New York, 2014.

Kalinovsky, Artemy M., and Craig Daigle, eds. *The Routledge Handbook of the Cold War*. Routledge: London, 2014.

Kamel, Mohammed Ibrahim. *The Camp David Accords: A Testimony*. London: KPI, 1986.

Kamrava, Mehran. *The Impossibility of Palestine: History, Geography and the Road Ahead*. New Haven: Yale University Press, 2016.

Kanafani, Ghassan, and Hilary Kilpatrick. *Men in the Sun & Other Palestinian Stories*. Boulder, CO: Lynne Rienner, 1999.

Kandil, Hazem. *The Power Triangle: Military, Security, and Politics in Regime Change*. Oxford: Oxford University Press, 2016.

———. *Soldiers, Spies, and Statesmen: Egypt's Road to Revolt*. London: Verso, 2012.

Kapeliouk, Amnon. *Sabra and Shatila: Inquiry into a Massacre*. Belmont, MA: Association of Arab American Graduates, 1984.

Karawan, Ibrahim A. "Sadat and the Egyptian-Israeli Peace Revisited." *International Journal of Middle East Studies* 26.2 (1994): 249–66.

Karsh, Efraim, Rory Miller, and Michael Kerr, eds. *Conflict Diplomacy and Society in Israeli-Lebanese Relations*. London: Routledge, 2010.

Kassab, Elizabeth Suzanne. *Contemporary Arab Thought: Cultural Critique in Comparative Perspective*. New York: Columbia University Press, 2009.

Kaufman, Scott. *Plans Unraveled: The Foreign Policy of the Carter Administration*. DeKalb: Northern Illinois University Press, 2008.

Kellerman, Barbara, and Jeffrey Z. Rubin, eds. *Leadership and Negotiation in the Middle East*. New York: Praeger, 1988.

Kelly, Matthew Kraig. *The Crime of Nationalism: Britain, Palestine, and Nation-Building on the Fringe of Empire*. Berkeley: University of California Press, 2017.

Kenan, Amos. *The Road to Ein Harod*. London: Al-Saqi, 1986.

Kenen, I. L. *Israel's Defense Line: Her Friends and Foes in Washington*. Buffalo: Prometheus Books, 1981.

Kepel, Gilles. *The Prophet and Pharaoh: Muslim Extremism in Egypt*. Trans. Jon Rothschild. London: Al Saqi, 1985.

Keys, Barbara J. *Reclaiming American Virtue: The Human Rights Revolution of the 1970s*. Cambridge, MA: Harvard University Press, 2014.

Khalaf, Samir. *Civil and Uncivil Violence in Lebanon: A History of the Internationalization of Communal Conflict*. New York: Columbia University Press, 2002.

Khalidi, Rashid. *Brokers of Deceit: How the U.S. Has Undermined Peace in the Middle East*. Boston: Beacon Press, 2013.

——. *The Iron Cage: The Story of the Palestinian Struggle for Statehood*. Boston: Beacon Press, 2006.

——. "1948 and After in Palestine: Universal Themes?" *Critical Inquiry* 40.4, special issue, Around 1948: Interdisciplinary Approaches to Global Transformation, edited by Leela Gandhi and Deborah L. Nelson (2014): 314–31.

——. *Palestinian Identity: The Construction of Modern National Consciousness*. New York: Columbia University Press, 1997.

——. "The Resolutions of the 19th Palestine National Council." *Journal of Palestine Studies* 19.2 (Winter 1990): 29–42.

——. *Sowing Crisis: The Cold War and American Dominance in the Middle East*. Boston: Beacon Press, 2009.

——. *Under Siege: P.L.O. Decisionmaking during the 1982 War*. 2nd ed. New York: Columbia University Press, 2014.

Khalidi, Walid. *Conflict and Violence in Lebanon: Confrontation in the Middle East*. Cambridge, MA: Center for International Affairs, Harvard University, 1983.

——. *Dayr Yasin: Al-Juma'a 9/4/1948* [Dayr Yasin: Friday 4/9/1948]. Beirut: Institute for Palestine Studies, 1999.

——. "The Half-Empty Glass of Middle East Peace." *Journal of Palestine Studies* 19.3 (1990): 14–38.

——. "Thinking the Unthinkable: A Sovereign Palestinian State." *Foreign Affairs* 56.4 (1978): 695–713.

Khalidi, Walid, ed. *All That Remains: The Palestinian Villages Occupied and Depopulated by Israel in 1948*. Washington, DC: Institute for Palestine Studies, 1992.

Khalil, Osamah. *America's Dream Palace: Middle East Expertise and the Rise of the National Security State*. Cambridge, MA: Harvard University Press, 2016.

——. "Oslo's Roots: Kissinger, the PLO and the Peace Process." *Al-Shabaka: The Palestinian Policy Network*. September 2013. https://al-shabaka.org/briefs/oslos-roots-kissinger-plo-and-peace-process/.

——. "Pax Americana: The United States, the Palestinians, and the Peace Process, 1948–2008." *New Centennial Review* 8.2 (2008): 1–41.

——. "The Radical Crescent: The United States, the Palestine Liberation Organisation, and the Lebanese Civil War, 1973–1978." *Diplomacy and Statecraft* 27.3 (2016): 496–522.

Khalili, Laleh. *Heroes and Martyrs of Palestine: The Politics of National Commemoration*. Cambridge: Cambridge University Press, 2007.

Khatib, Ghassan. *Palestinian Politics and the Middle East Peace Process: Consensus and Competition in the Palestinian Negotiating Team*. New York: Routledge, 2011.

Kieval, Gershon R. *Party Politics in Israel and the Occupied Territories*. Westport, CT: Greenwood Press, 1983.

Kimche, David. *The Last Option: After Nasser, Arafat and Saddam Hussein: The Quest for Peace in the Middle East*. New York: Scribner's, 1991.

King, Mary. *A Quiet Revolution: The First Palestinian Intifada and Nonviolent Resistance*. New York: Nation Books, 2007.

Kipnis, Yigal. *1973: The Road to War*. Charlottesville: Just World Books, 2013.

Kirkpatrick, Jeane. "Dictatorships and Double Standards." *Commentary* 68.5 (1979): 34–45.

Klagsbrun, Francine. *Lioness: Golda Meir and the Nation of Israel*. New York: Schocken Books, 2017.

Klein, Menachem. *Lives in Common: Arabs and Jews in Jerusalem, Jaffa and Hebron*. London: Hurst, 2014.

Korbani, Agnes G. *U.S. Intervention in Lebanon, 1958 and 1982: Presidential Decisionmaking*. New York: Praeger, 1991.

Koselleck, Reinhart. *The Practice of Conceptual History: Timing History, Spacing Concepts*. Trans. Todd Samuel Presner and others. Stanford: Stanford University Press, 2002.

Koskenniemi, Martti. "The Many Faces of Sovereignty: Introduction to Critical Legal Thinking." *Kutafin University Law Review* 4.2 (2017): 282–91.

Kretzmer, David. *The Occupation of Justice: The Supreme Court of Israel and the Occupied Territories*. Albany: State University of New York Press, 2002.

Kruse, Kevin. *White Flight: Atlanta and the Making of Modern Conservatism*. Princeton: Princeton University Press, 2007.

Kurtzer, Daniel C, Scott B. Lasensky, William B. Quandt, Steven L. Spiegel, and Shibley Z. Telhami. *The Peace Puzzle: America's Quest for Arab-Israeli Peace*. Ithaca: Cornell University Press, 2013.

Laham, Nicholas. *Crossing the Rubicon: Ronald Reagan and U.S. Policy in the Middle East*. Aldershot: Aldgate, 2004.

Landau, David. *Arik: The Life of Ariel Sharon*. New York: Knopf, 2013.

Laor, Dan. "The Last Chapter: Nathan Alterman and the Six-Day War." *Israel Studies* 4.2 (1999): 178–94.

Lapidoth, Ruth. "The Autonomy Negotiations." *Jerusalem Quarterly*, no. 24 (Summer 1982): 99–113.

———. "The Autonomy Negotiations: A Stocktaking." *Middle East Review* 15.3–4 (Spring/Summer 1983): 35–43.

———. "Elements of Stable Regional Autonomy Arrangements." In *The Bertelsmann Foundation*, 2001. www.cap.uni-muenchen.de/download/2001/ra/Lapidoth1.pdf.

Laqueur, Walter, and Barry M. Rubin. *The Israel-Arab Reader: A Documentary History of the Middle East Conflict*. New York: Penguin Books, 2001.

Laron, Guy. *The Six-Day War and the Breaking of the Middle East*. New Haven: Yale University Press, 2017.

Laskier, Michael M., and Hanoch Bazov. *Teror be-sherut ha-mahepekhah: Ma'arekhet ha-yehasim ben Ashaf le-ven Berit ha-Mo'atsot, 1968–1991* [Terrorism on behalf of the revolution: PLO-Soviet relations, 1968–1991]. Ramat Gan: Bar Ilan Press, 2016.

Leffler, Melvyn P. *For the Soul of Mankind: The United States, the Soviet Union, and the Cold War*. New York: Hill and Wang, 2007.

Leffler, Melvyn P., and Odd Arne Westad, eds. *The Cambridge History of the Cold War*. Vol. 3, *Endings*. New York: Cambridge University Press, 2010.

Leibowitz, Yeshayah. *Judaism, Human Values, and the Jewish State*. Cambridge, MA: Harvard University Press, 1992.

Lesch, Ann Mosely. "Israeli Settlements in the Occupied Territories, 1967–1977." *Journal of Palestine Studies* 7.1 (1977): 26–47.

Lesch, Ann Mosely, and Mark Tessler, eds. *Israel, Egypt, and the Palestinians: From Camp David to Intifada*. Bloomington: Indiana University Press, 1989.

LeVine, Mark, and Gershon Shafir, eds. *Struggle and Survival in Palestine/Israel*. Berkeley: University of California Press, 2012.

Levy, Lital. *Poetic Trespass: Writing between Hebrew and Arabic in Israel/Palestine*. Princeton: Princeton University Press, 2014.

Linowitz, Sol M. *The Making of a Public Man: A Memoir*. Boston: Little, Brown, 1985.

Litani, Yehuda. "'Village Leagues': What Kind of Carrot?" *Journal of Palestine Studies* 11.3 (April 1, 1982): 174–78.

Little, Douglas. *American Orientalism: The United States and the Middle East since 1945*. Chapel Hill: University of North Carolina Press, 2004.

Lochery, Neil. "Debunking the Myths: Margaret Thatcher, the Foreign Office and Israel, 1979–1990." *Diplomacy and Statecraft* 21 (2010): 690–706.

Lockman, Zachary. "Review: Original Sin." *Middle East Report* 152 (May–June 1988): 57–64.

Lockman, Zachary, and Joel Beinin, eds. *Intifada: The Palestinian Uprising against Israeli Occupation*. Cambridge: South End Press, 1999.

Logevall, Fredrik, and Andrew Preston, eds. *Nixon in the World: American Foreign Relations, 1969–1977*. Oxford: Oxford University Press, 2008.

Lothe, Jacob, Susan Rubin Suleiman, and James Phelan, eds. *After Testimony: The Ethics and Aesthetics of Holocaust Narrative for the Future*. Columbus: Ohio State University Press, 2012.

Louis, Wm. Roger, and Avi Shlaim, eds. *The 1967 Arab-Israeli War: Origins and Consequences*. Cambridge: Cambridge University Press, 2012.

Lukacs, Yehuda, ed. *The Israeli-Palestinian Conflict: A Documentary Record*. 2nd ed. Cambridge: Cambridge University Press, 1992.

Lustick, Ian S. *For the Land and the Lord: Jewish Fundamentalism in Israel*. New York: Council on Foreign Relations, 1988.

———. "Israel and the West Bank after Elon Moreh: The Mechanics of de facto Annexation." *Middle East Journal* 35.4 (1981): 557–77.

———. "Israeli Politics and American Foreign Policy." *Foreign Affairs* 61.2 (1982/83): 379–99.

———. "Saving Camp David: Kill the Autonomy Talks." *Foreign Policy*, no. 41 (1980–81): 21–43.

Mahmood, Zahid. "Sadat and Camp David Reappraised." *Journal of Palestine Studies* 15.1 (1985): 62–87.

Makdisi, Jean Said. *Beirut Fragments: A War Memoir.* New York: Persea Books, 1990.

Makdisi, Ussama. *Faith Misplaced: The Broken Promise of U.S.-Arab Relations, 1820–2001.* New York: PublicAffairs, 2010.

Makovsky, David. *Making Peace with the PLO: The Rabin Government's Road to the Oslo Accord.* Washington, DC: Westview Press in Cooperation with the Washington Institute for Near East Policy, 1996.

Mamdani, Mahmood. *Good Muslim, Bad Muslim: America, the Cold War, and the Roots of Terror.* New York: Pantheon Books, 2004.

Manela, Erez. *The Wilsonian Moment: Self-Determination and the International Origins of Anticolonial Nationalism.* Oxford: Oxford University Press, 2009.

Mann, James. *The Rebellion of Ronald Reagan: A History of the End of the Cold War.* New York: Viking, 2009.

——. *Rise of the Vulcans: The History of Bush's War Cabinet.* New York: Penguin Books, 2004.

Ma'oz, Moshe. *Palestinian Leadership on the West Bank: The Changing Role of the Mayors under Jordan and Israel.* London: Frank Cass, 1984.

Mart, Michelle. *Eye on Israel: How America Came to View Israel as an Ally.* Albany: State University of New York Press, 2006.

Mazzini, Giuseppe. *A Cosmopolitanism of Nations: Giuseppe Mazzini's Writings on Democracy, Nation Building, and International Relations.* Ed. Stefano Recchia and Nadia Urbinati. Princeton: Princeton University Press, 2009.

McAlister, Melani. *Epic Encounters: Culture, Media, and U.S. Interests in the Middle East since 1945.* Berkeley: University of California Press, 2005.

McDonald, Darren J. "Blessed Are the Policy Makers: Jimmy Carter's Faith-Based Approach to the Arab-Israeli Conflict." *Diplomatic History* 39.3 (2015): 452–76.

McFarlane, Robert. *Special Trust.* New York: Cadell and Davies, 1994.

McGarr, Kathryn J. *The Whole Damn Deal: Robert Strauss and the Art of Politics.* New York: Public Affairs, 2011.

Mearsheimer, John J., and Stephen Walt. *The Israel Lobby and U.S. Foreign Policy.* New York: Farrar, Straus and Giroux, 2007.

Meital, Yoram. *Egypt's Struggle for Peace: Continuity and Change, 1967–1977.* Gainesville: University Press of Florida, 1997.

Meiton, Fredrik. "Electrifying Jaffa: Boundary-Work and the Origins of the Arab-Israeli Conflict." *Past & Present* 231.1 (May 2016): 201–36.

Melman, Yossi, and Dan Raviv. *Behind the Uprising: Israelis, Jordanians, and Palestinians.* New York: Greenwood, 1989.

——. *Friends in Deed: Inside the U.S.-Israel Alliance.* New York: Hyperion, 1994.

Ménargues, Alain. *Les Secrets de la Guerre du Liban.* Paris: Albin Michel, 2004.

Merkley, Paul Charles. *American Presidents, Religion, and Israel: The Heirs of Cyrus.* Westport, CT: Praeger, 2004.

Meron, Theodor. "The West Bank and International Humanitarian Law on the Eve of the Fiftieth Anniversary of the Six-Day War." *American Society of International Law* 111.2 (2017): 357–75.

Migdal, Joel. *Shifting Sands: The United States in the Middle East*. New York: Columbia University Press, 2014.

Miller, Aaron David. *The Much Too Promised Land: America's Elusive Search for Arab-Israeli Peace*. New York: Bantam, 2008.

Milne, David. *America's Rasputin: Walt Rostow and the Vietnam War*. New York: Hill and Wang, 2008.

Milson, Menachem. "How to Make Peace with the Palestinians." *Commentary* 71.5 (1981): 25–35.

Mitchell, Nancy. *Jimmy Carter in Africa: Race and the Cold War*. Stanford: Stanford University Press, 2016.

Morgan, Iwan. *Reagan: American Icon*. London: I. B. Tauris, 2016.

Morris, Benny. *The Birth of the Palestinian Refugee Problem Revisited*. Cambridge: Cambridge University Press, 2004.

———. *Righteous Victims: A History of the Zionist-Arab Conflict, 1881–2001*. New York: Vintage, 2001.

Morris, Edmund. *Dutch: A Memoir of Ronald Reagan*. New York: Random House, 1999.

Moses, A. Dirk. "Empire, Resistance, and Security: International Law and the Transformative Occupation of Palestine." *Humanity: An International Journal of Human Rights, Humanitarianism, and Development* 8.2 (Summer 2017): 379–409.

Moyn, Samuel. *The Last Utopia: Human Rights in History*. Cambridge, MA: Harvard University Press, 2010.

Moynihan, Daniel Patrick. "Joining the Jackals: The U.S. at the U.N., 1977–1980." *Commentary* 71.2 (February 1981): 23–31.

Muslih, Muhammad. *Toward Coexistence: An Analysis of the Resolutions of the Palestine National Council*. Washington, DC: Institute for Palestine Studies, 1990.

Naor, Arye. *Begin Ba'Shilton* [Begin in power]. Jerusalem: Keter, 1984.

———. "'A Simple Historical Truth': Judea, Samaria and the Gaza Strip in Menachem Begin's Ideology." *Israel Affairs* 21.3 (2015): 462–81.

Nemchenok, Victor V. "'These People Have an Irrevocable Right to Self-Government': United States Policy and the Palestinian Question, 1977–1979." *Diplomacy & Statecraft* 20.4 (2009): 595–618.

Newman, David. "From Hitnachalut to Hitnatkut: The Impact of Gush Emunim and the Settlement Movement on Israeli Politics and Society." *Israel Studies* 10.3 (Fall 2005): 192–224.

———. *The Impact of Gush Emunim: Politics and Settlement in the West Bank*. New York: St. Martin's Press, 1985.

Newman, David, and Ghazi Falah. "Bridging the Gap: Palestinian and Israeli Discourses on Autonomy and Statehood." *Transactions of the Institute of British Geographers* 22.1 (1997): 111–29.

Njølstad, Olav, ed. *The Last Decade of the Cold War*. London: Frank Cass, 2004.

———. "Shifting Priorities: The Persian Gulf in U.S. Strategic Planning in the Carter Years." *Cold War History* 4.3 (2004): 21–55.

Norris, Jacob. *Land of Progress: Palestine in the Age of Colonial Development, 1905–1948*. Oxford: Oxford University Press, 2013.

Norton, Anne. *Leo Strauss and the Politics of American Empire*. New Haven: Yale University Press, 2004.

Norton, Augustus Richard. *Hezbollah: A Short History*. Updated ed. Princeton: Princeton University Press, 2014.

Norton, Augustus Richard, with Jillian Schwedler. "(In)Security Zones in South Lebanon." *Journal of Palestine Studies* 23.1 (1993): 61–79.

Nusseibeh, Sari. *What Is a Palestinian State Worth?* Cambridge, MA: Harvard University Press, 2011.

Nusseibeh, Sari, and Anthony David. *Once Upon a Country: A Palestinian Life*. New York: Farrar, Straus and Giroux, 2007.

O'Brien, Lee. *American Jewish Organizations and Israel*. Washington, DC: Institute for Palestine Studies, 1986.

Odom, William E. "The Cold War Origins of the U.S. Central Command." *Journal of Cold War Studies* 8.2 (2006): 52–82.

Ophir, Adi, Michal Givoni, and Sari Hanafi, eds. *The Power of Inclusive Exclusion: Anatomy of Israeli Rule in the Occupied Palestinian Territories*. New York: Zone Books, 2009.

Oz, Amos. *The Slopes of Lebanon*. San Diego: Harcourt Brace Jovanovich, 1989.

Pach, Chester. "The Reagan Doctrine: Principle, Pragmatism and Policy." *Presidential Studies Quarterly* 36.1 (March 2006): 75–88.

Pearlman, Wendy. "Spoiling Inside and Out: Internal Political Contestation and the Middle East Peace Process." *International Security* 33.3 (2008/9): 79–109.

———. *Violence, Nonviolence and the Palestinian National Movement*. Cambridge: Cambridge University Press, 2011.

Peck, Juliana S. *The Reagan Administration and the Palestinian Question: The First Thousand Days*. Washington, DC: Institute for Palestine Studies, 1984.

Pedahzur, Ami. *The Triumph of Israel's Radical Right*. Oxford: Oxford University Press, 2012.

Pedatzur, Reuven. "Coming Back Full Circle: The Palestinian Option in 1967." *Middle East Journal* 49.2 (Spring 1995): 269–91.

Pedersen, Susan. *The Guardians: The League of Nations and the Crisis of Empire*. Oxford: Oxford University Press, 2015.

Peleg, Ilan. *Begin's Foreign Policy, 1977–1983: Israel's Move to the Right*. New York: Greenwood Press, 1987.

Pennock, Pamela E. *The Rise of the Arab American Left: Activists, Allies, and Their Fight against Imperialism and Racism, 1960s–1980s*. Chapel Hill: University of North Carolina Press, 2017.

Perlstein, Rick. *Before the Storm: Barry Goldwater and the Unmaking of the American Consensus*. New York: Nation Books, 2009.

———. *The Invisible Bridge: The Fall of Nixon and the Rise of Reagan*. New York: Simon and Schuster, 2014.

———. *Nixonland: The Rise of a President and the Fracturing of America*. New York: Scribner, 2008.

Peters, Joan. *From Time Immemorial: The Origins of the Arab-Jewish Conflict over Palestine*. New York: Harper and Row, 1984.

Peterson, Christian Philip. "The Carter Administration and the Promotion of Human Rights in the Soviet Union." *Diplomatic History* 38.3 (2014): 628–56.

Phillips-Fein, Kim. *Invisible Hands: The Making of the Conservative Movement from New Deal to Reagan.* New York: W. W. Norton, 2009.

Plascov, Avi. "The 'Palestinian Gap' between Israel and Egypt." *Survival* 22 (March–April 1980): 50–57.

Podeh, Elie. *Chances for Peace: Missed Opportunities in the Arab-Israeli Conflict.* Austin: University of Texas Press, 2015.

Podhoretz, Norman. "The Future Danger." *Commentary* 71.4 (April 1981): 38.

Polakow-Suransky, Sasha. *The Unspoken Alliance: Israel's Secret Relationship with Apartheid South Africa.* New York: Pantheon Books, 2011.

Prashad, Vijay. *The Darker Nations: A People's History of the Third World.* New York: New Press, 2008.

Pressman, Jeremy. "Explaining the Carter Administration's Israeli-Palestinian Solution." *Diplomatic History* 37.5 (November 2013): 1117–47.

Quandt, William B. *Camp David: Peacemaking and Politics.* Washington, DC: Brookings Institution Press, 2016.

——. "Forty Years in Search of Arab-Israeli Peace." *Macalester International* 23.9 (2009): 24–82.

——, ed. *The Middle East: Ten Years after Camp David.* Washington, DC: Brookings Institution Press, 1988.

——. "Palestine, Apartheid, and Jimmy Carter: Reading Past the Title." *Journal of Palestine Studies* 36.3 (Spring 2007): 89–93.

——. *Peace Process: American Diplomacy and the Arab-Israeli Conflict since 1967.* Washington, DC: Brookings Institution Press, 2005.

——. "Reagan's Lebanon Policy: Trial and Error." *Middle East Journal* 38.2 (1984): 237–54.

Quandt, William B., Fuad Jabber, and Ann Mosley Lesch, eds. *The Politics of Palestinian Nationalism.* Berkeley: University of California Press, 1973.

Qurie, Ahmed. *From Oslo to Jerusalem: The Palestinian Story of the Secret Negotiations.* London: I. B. Tauris, 2006.

Raad, Walid. *The Atlas Group, 1989–2004.* "The Atlas Group Archive." http://www.theatlasgroup.org/.

Rabie, Mohamed. *U.S.-PLO Dialogue: Secret Diplomacy and Conflict Resolution.* Gainesville: University Press of Florida, 1995.

Rabin, Yitzhak. *The Rabin Memoirs.* Boston: Little, Brown, 1979.

Rabinovich, Abraham. *The Yom Kippur War: The Epic Encounter That Transformed the Middle East.* New York: Schocken, 2004.

Rabinovich, Itamar. *The Lingering Conflict: Israel, the Arabs, and the Middle East, 1948–2012.* Rev. ed. Washington, DC: Brookings Institution Press, 2013.

——. *The War for Lebanon, 1970–1985.* Rev. ed. Ithaca: Cornell University Press, 1985.

——. *Yitzhak Rabin: Soldier, Leader, Statesman.* New Haven: Yale University Press, 2017.

Rabinovitch, Simon. *Jewish Rights, National Rites: Nationalism and Autonomy in Late Imperial and Revolutionary Russia*. Stanford: Stanford University Press, 2014.

Randal, Jonathan C. *Going All the Way: Christian Warlords, Israeli Adventurers, and the War in Lebanon*. New York: Vintage, 1984.

Ravikovitch, Dahlia. *Hovering at a Low Altitude*. Trans. Chana Bloch and Chana Kronfeld. New York: W. W. Norton, 2009.

Ravitzky, Aviezer. *Messianism, Zionism, and Jewish Religious Radicalism*. Chicago: University of Chicago Press, 1996.

Raz, Avi. *The Bride and the Dowry: Israel, Jordan, and the Palestinians in the Aftermath of the June 1967 War*. New Haven: Yale University Press, 2012.

———. "The Generous Peace Offer That Was Never Offered: The Israeli Cabinet Resolution of June 19, 1967." *Diplomatic History* 37.1 (2013): 85–108.

Reagan, Ronald. *An American Life*. New York: Simon and Schuster, 1990.

Reagan, Ronald, and Douglas Brinkley. *The Reagan Diaries*. New York: HarperCollins, 2007.

Robinson, Shira. *Citizen Strangers: Palestinians and the Birth of Israel's Liberal Settler State*. Stanford: Stanford University Press, 2014.

Rodgers, Daniel T. *Age of Fracture*. Cambridge, MA: Belknap Press of Harvard University Press, 2011.

Rosenberg, John. "The Quest against Détente: Eugene Rostow, the October War, and the Origins of the Anti-Détente Movement, 1969–1976." *Diplomatic History* 39.4 (2015): 720–44.

Ross, Dennis. *The Missing Peace: The Inside Story of the Fight for Middle East Peace*. New York: Farrar, Straus and Giroux, 2005.

Rossinow, Douglas. "'The Edge of the Abyss': The Origins of the Israel Lobby, 1949–1954." *Modern American History* 1.1 (2018): 23–43.

———. *The Reagan Era: A History of the 1980s*. New York: Columbia University Press, 2015.

Rostow, Eugene V. "'Palestinian Self-Determination': Possible Futures for the Unallocated Territories of the Palestine Mandate." *International Journal of Yale Law School* 5.2 (1979): 147–72.

Rothkopf, David J. *Running the World: The Inside Story of the National Security Council and the Architects of American Power*. New York: PublicAffairs, 2005.

Rozin, Orit. *A Home for All Jews: Citizenship, Rights and National Identity in the Young Israeli State*. Waltham, MA: Brandeis University Press, 2016.

Rubenberg, Cheryl A. "The Civilian Infrastructure of the Palestine Liberation Organization." *Journal of Palestine Studies* 12.3 (1983): 54–78.

Rubin, Avshalom. *The Limits of the Land: How the Struggle for the West Bank Shaped the Arab-Israeli Conflict*. Bloomington: Indiana University Press, 2017.

Rubin, Barry. *Revolution until Victory? The Politics and History of the PLO*. Cambridge, MA: Harvard University Press, 1994.

Rubinovitz, Ziv. "Blue and White 'Black September': Israel's Role in the Jordan Crisis of 1970." *International History Review* 32.4 (2010): 687–706.

Rubinovitz, Ziv, and Gerald M. Steinberg. "Tochnit Ha'Autonomia shel Menahem Begin: Bein Rei'alizm Midini V'Ide'ologiyah" [Menachem Begin's autonomy plan: Between political realism and ideology]. *Public Sphere* 6 (2012): 75–94.

Sachar, Howard M. *Egypt and Israel*. New York: Richard Marek, 1981.

———. *A History of Israel: From the Rise of Zionism to Our Time*. 3rd ed. New York: Knopf, 2007.

Sadat, Anwar. *In Search of Identity: An Autobiography*. London: William Collins, 1978.

Sadat, Jehan. *A Woman of Egypt*. New York: Simon and Schuster, 1987.

Sa'di, Ahmad H., and Lila Abu-Lughod, eds., *Nakba: Palestine, 1948, and the Claims of Memory*. New York: Columbia University Press, 2007.

Safty, Adel. "Sadat's Negotiations with the United States and Israel: From Sinai to Camp David." *American Journal of Economics and Sociology* 50.3 (1991): 285–99.

Sahliyeh, Emile F. *The PLO after the Lebanon War*. Boulder, CO: Westview Press, 1986.

Said, Edward W. *The End of the Peace Process: Oslo and After*. New York: Vintage, 2001.

———. *The Question of Palestine*. London: Vintage, 1992.

Said, Edward W., and Christopher Hitchens, eds. *Blaming the Victims: Spurious Scholarship and the Palestinian Question*. London: Verso, 1988.

Salem, Elie. *Violence and Diplomacy in Lebanon: The Troubled Years, 1982–1988*. London: I. B. Tauris, 1995.

Salibi, Kamal S. *A House of Many Mansions: The History of Lebanon Reconsidered*. London: I. B. Tauris, 1988.

Sargent, Daniel. *A Superpower Transformed: The Remaking of American Foreign Relations in the 1970s*. New York: Oxford University Press, 2015.

Saunders, Harold. *The Other Walls: The Arab-Israeli Peace Process in a Global Perspective*. Princeton: Princeton University Press, 1991.

Savir, Uri. *The Process: 1,100 Days That Changed the Middle East*. New York: Vintage, 1998.

Sayegh, Fayez A. "The Camp David Agreement and the Palestine Problem." *Journal of Palestine Studies* 8.2 (Winter 1979): 3–40.

Sayigh, Rosemary. *Too Many Enemies: The Palestinian Experience in Lebanon*. London: Zed Books, 1993.

Sayigh, Yezid. *Armed Struggle and the Search for State: The Palestinian National Movement 1949–1993*. Oxford: Clarendon Press, 1997.

———. "Israel's Military Performance in Lebanon, June 1982." *Journal of Palestine Studies* 13.1 (1983): 24–65.

———. "Palestinian Armed Struggle: Means and Ends." *Journal of Palestine Studies* 16.1 (1986): 95–112.

———. "Palestinian Military Performance in the 1982 War." *Journal of Palestine Studies* 12.4 (1983): 3–24.

Sayigh, Yezid, and Avi Shlaim, eds. *The Cold War and the Middle East*. Oxford: Clarendon Press, 1997.

Schayegh, Cyrus. "The Many Worlds of 'Abud Yasin, or, What Narcotics Trafficking in the Interwar Middle East Can Tell Us about Territorialization." *American Historical Review* 116.2 (2011): 273–306.

———. *The Middle East and the Making of the Modern World*. Cambridge, MA: Harvard University Press, 2017.

———. "1958 Reconsidered: State Formation and the Cold War in the Early Postcolonial Middle East." *International Journal of Middle East Studies* 45.3 (2013): 421–43.

Schiff, Zeev. "The Green Light." *Foreign Policy* 50 (Spring 1983): 73–85.

Schiff, Zeev, and Ehud Yaari. *Intifada: The Palestinian Uprising—Israel's Third Front*. New York: Simon and Schuster, 1990.

———. *Israel's Lebanon War*. London: Unwin Paperbacks, 1986.

Schmidli, William Michael. "Institutionalizing Human Rights in U.S. Foreign Policy: U.S.-Argentine Relations, 1976–1980." *Diplomatic History* 35.2 (April 2011): 351–78.

Schmitz, David F., and Vanessa Walker. "Jimmy Carter and the Foreign Policy of Human Rights: The Development of a Post–Cold War Foreign Policy." *Diplomatic History* 28.1 (January 2004): 113–43.

Schneider, Suzanne. *Mandatory Separation: Religion, Education, and Mass Politics in Palestine*. Stanford: Stanford University Press, 2018.

Schrecker, Ellen, ed. *Cold War Triumphalism: The Misuse of History after the Fall of Communism*. New York: New Press, 2004.

Schulman, Bruce J., and Julian E. Zelizer, eds. *Rightward Bound: Making America Conservative in the 1970s*. Cambridge, MA: Harvard University Press, 2008.

Schulze, Kirsten E. *Israel's Covert Diplomacy in Lebanon*. New York: St. Martin's Press, 1998.

———. "Perceptions and Misperceptions: Influences on Israeli Intelligence Estimates during the 1982 Lebanon War." *Journal of Conflict Studies* 16.1 (Spring 1996): 134–52.

Seale, Patrick. *Abu Nidal: A Gun for Hire*. New York: Random House, 1992.

Segev, Tom. *1967: Israel, the War, and the Year That Transformed the Middle East*. London: Picador, 2008.

Sela, Avraham. "Civil Society, the Military and National Security: The Case of Israel's Security Zone in South Lebanon." *Israel Studies* 12.1 (Spring 2007): 53–78.

———. "The PLO at Fifty: A Historical Perspective." *Contemporary Review of the Middle East* 1.3 (2014): 269–333.

Sela, Avraham, and Moshe Maoz, eds. *The PLO and Israel: From Armed Conflict to Political Solution*. New York: Palgrave, 1997.

Sfard, Michael. *The Wall and the Gate: Israel, Palestine, and the Legal Battle for Human Rights*. New York: Metropolitan, 2018.

Shafir, Gershon. *A Half Century of Occupation: Israel, Palestine, and the World's Most Intractable Conflict*. Oakland: University of California Press, 2017.

Shahid, Leila. "The Sabra and Shatila Massacres: Eye-Witness Reports." *Journal of Palestine Studies* 32.1 (Autumn 2002): 36–58.

Shamir, Yitzhak. *Summing Up: An Autobiography*. Boston: Little, Brown, 1994.

Shapira, Anita. *Ben-Gurion, Father of Modern Israel*. New Haven: Yale University Press, 2014.

———. "Hirbet Hizah: Between Remembrance and Forgetting." *Jewish Social Studies* 7.1 (Fall 2000): 1– 62.

———. *Israel: A History*. Waltham, MA: Brandeis University Press, 2012.

———. *Land and Power: The Zionist Resort to Force, 1881–1948*. Stanford: Stanford University Press, 1999.

Shapira, Avraham, ed. *The Seventh Day: Soldiers' Talk about the Six-Day War*. New York: Charles Scribner's Sons, 1970.

Sharon, Ariel. *Warrior: The Autobiography of Ariel Sharon*. New York: Simon and Schuster, 1989.

Shehadeh, Raja. *From Occupation to Interim Accords: Israel and the Palestinian Territories*. London: Kluwer Law International, 1997.

———. *Occupier's Law: Israel and the West Bank*. Washington, DC: Institute for Palestine Studies, 1988.

———. *Palestinian Walks: Notes on a Vanishing Landscape*. New York: Scribner, 2007.

Shelef, Nadav. "From 'Both Banks of the Jordan' to the 'Whole Land of Israel': Ideological Change in Revisionist Zionism." *Israel Studies* 9.1 (Spring 2004): 125–48.

Shemesh, Moshe. "The Origins of Sadat's Strategic Volte Face." *Israel Studies* 13.2 (Summer 2008): 28–53.

Shenhav, Yehouda. *Beyond the Two-State Solution: A Jewish Political Essay*. London: Polity, 2012.

———. "The Jews of Iraq, Zionist Ideology, and the Property of the Palestinian Refugees of 1948: An Anomaly of National Accounting." *International Journal of Middle East Studies* 31.4 (November 1999): 605–30.

Shilon, Avi. *Menachem Begin: A Life*. Trans. Danielle Zilberberg and Yoram Sharett. New Haven: Yale University Press, 2012.

Shindler, Colin. *A History of Modern Israel*. Cambridge: Cambridge University Press, 2008.

———. *The Triumph of Military Zionism*. London: I. B. Tauris, 2006.

Shlaim, Avi. "The Debate about 1948." *International Journal of Middle East Studies* 27.3 (1995): 287–304.

———. "Husni Zaim and the Plan to Resettle Palestinian Refugees in Syria." *Journal of Palestine Studies* 15.4 (1986): 68–80.

———. *The Iron Wall: Israel and the Arab World*. Updated and expanded ed. New York: W. W. Norton, 2014.

———. "The Iron Wall Revisited." *Journal of Palestine Studies* 41.2 (2012): 80–98.

———. *Lion of Jordan: The Life of King Hussein in War and Peace*. London: Allen Lane, 2007.

Shultz, George. *Turmoil and Triumph: My Years as Secretary of State*. New York: Scribner's, 1993.

Shumsky, Dimitry. "Brith Shalom's Uniqueness Reconsidered: Hans Kohn and Autonomist Zionism." *Jewish History* 25.3–4 (2011): 339–53.

———. "Leon Pinsker and 'Autoemancipation!': A Reevaluation." *Jewish Social Studies* 18.1 (2011): 33–62.

Sicherman, Harvey. *Palestinian Autonomy, Self-Government and Peace*. Washington, DC: Washington Institute for Near East Policy, 1993.

Siegel, Ellen, and Lynne Barbee. "Inside and Outside the Hospital, People Were Screaming: 'Haddad, *Kataeb*, Israel—Massacre.'" *Journal of Palestine Studies* 12.2 (Winter 1983): 61–71.

Silver, M. M. *Our Exodus: Leon Uris and the Americanization of Israel's Founding Story*. Detroit: Wayne State University Press, 2010.

Simon, Reeva S., ed. *The Middle East and North Africa: Essays in Honor of J. C. Hurewitz*. New York: Middle East Institute, Columbia University, 1989.

Simpson, Bradley R. "Denying the 'First Right': The United States, Indonesia, and the Ranking of Human Rights by the Carter Administration, 1976–1980." *International History Review* 31.4 (2009): 788–826.

———. "Self-Determination, Human Rights, and the End of Empire in the 1970s." *Humanity* 4.2 (2013): 239–60.

———. "The United States and the Curious History of Self-Determination." *Diplomatic History* 36.4 (2012): 675–94.

Simpson, Christopher. *National Security Directives of the Reagan and Bush Administrations: The Declassified History of U.S. Political and Military Policy, 1981–1991*. Boulder, CO: Westview Press, 1995.

Siniora, Hanna. "An Analysis of the Current Revolt." *Journal of Palestine Studies* 17.3 (1988): 3–13.

Skinner, Kiron K., Annelise Anderson, and Martin Anderson, eds. *Reagan, in His Own Hand: The Writings of Ronald Reagan That Reveal His Revolutionary Vision for America*. New York: Simon and Schuster, 2001.

Smith, Gaddis. *Morality, Reason, and Power: American Diplomacy in the Carter Years*. New York: Hill and Wang, 1986.

Snyder, Sarah. *Human Rights Activism and the End of the Cold War: A Transnational History of the Helsinki Network*. Cambridge: Cambridge University Press, 2011.

Sparrow, Bartholomew. *The Strategist: Brent Scowcroft and the Call for National Security*. New York: Public Affairs, 2015.

Spiegel, Steven L. *The Other Arab-Israeli Conflict: Making America's Middle East Policy, from Truman to Reagan*. Chicago: University of Chicago Press, 1985.

Sprinzak, Ehud. *The Ascendance of Israel's Radical Right*. New York: Oxford University Press, 1991.

Stanislawski, Michael. *Zionism and the Fin de Siecle: Cosmopolitanism and Nationalism from Nordau to Jabotinsky*. Berkeley: University of California Press, 2001.

Staub, Michael E. *Torn at the Roots: The Crisis of Jewish Liberalism in Postwar America*. New York: Columbia University Press, 2002.

Stein, Kenneth W. *Heroic Diplomacy: Sadat, Kissinger, Carter, Begin and the Quest for Arab-Israeli Peace*. New York: Routledge, 1999.

———. "My Problem with Jimmy Carter's Book." *Middle East Quarterly* (Spring 2007): 3–15.

Stephanson, Anders. *"Simplicissimus." New Left Review* 49 (January–February 2008): 147–56.

Stocker, James. "A Historical Inevitability? Kissinger and US Contacts with the Palestinians (1973–1976)." *International History Review* 39.2 (2017): 316–37.

———. *Spheres of Intervention: US Foreign Policy and the Collapse of Lebanon, 1967–1976*. Ithaca: Cornell University Press, 2017.

Stork, Joe. "The Carter Doctrine and U.S. Bases in the Middle East." *MERIP Reports*, no. 90 (1980): 3–14, 32.

Strieff, Daniel. "Arms Wrestle: Capitol Hill Fight over Carter's 1978 Middle East 'Package' Airplane Sale." *Diplomatic History* 40.3 (June 2016): 475–99.

———. *Jimmy Carter and the Middle East: The Politics of Presidential Diplomacy.* New York: Palgrave Macmillan, 2015.

Suleiman, Michael W., ed. *U.S. Policy on Palestine from Wilson to Clinton.* Normal, IL: Association of Arab-American University Graduates, 1995.

Susser, Asher. *Israel, Jordan, and Palestine: The Two-State Imperative.* Waltham, MA: Brandeis University Press, 2012.

Svonkin, Stuart. *Jews against Prejudice: American Jews and the Fight for Civil Liberties.* New York: Columbia University Press, 1997.

Tamari, Salim. "In League with Zion: Israel's Search for a Native Pillar." *Journal of Palestine Studies* 12.4 (1983): 41–56.

Tanter, Raymond. *Who's at the Helm?: Lessons of Lebanon.* Boulder, CO: Westview Press, 1990.

Teicher, Howard, and Gayle Radley Teicher. *Twin Pillars to Desert Storm: America's Flawed Vision in the Middle East from Nixon to Bush.* New York: William Morrow, 1993.

Telhami, Shibley. *Power and Leadership in International Bargaining.* New York: Columbia University Press, 1992.

Tessler, Mark. *A History of the Israeli-Palestinian Conflict.* Bloomington: Indiana University Press, 1994.

Thrall, Nathan. *The Only Language They Understand: Forcing Compromise in Israel and Palestine.* New York: Metropolitan, 2017.

Thompson, Elizabeth. *Justice Interrupted: The Struggle for Constitutional Government in the Middle East.* Cambridge, MA: Harvard University Press, 2013.

Timmerman, Jacobo. *The Longest War.* London: Chatto and Windus, 1982.

Tivnan, Edward. *The Lobby: Jewish Political Power and American Foreign Policy.* New York: Simon and Schuster, 1987.

Toaldo, Mattia. *The Origins of the U.S. War on Terror: Lebanon, Libya and American Intervention in the Middle East.* New York: Routledge, 2013.

Touval, Saadia. *The Peace Brokers: Mediators in the Arab-Israeli Conflict, 1948–1979.* Princeton: Princeton University Press, 1982.

Troy, Gil. *Moynihan's Moment: America's Fight against Zionism as Racism.* New York: Oxford University Press, 2013.

Tucker, Robert W. "The Middle East: Carterism without Carter?" *Commentary* 72.3 (September 1981): 27–30.

Tyler, Patrick. *A World of Trouble: The White House and the Middle East, from the Cold War to the War on Terror.* New York: Farrar, Straus and Giroux, 2009.

Vaïsse, Justin. *Neoconservatism: The Biography of a Movement.* Cambridge, MA: Harvard University Press, 2010.

Vance, Cyrus R. *Hard Choices: Critical Years in America's Foreign Policy.* New York: Simon and Schuster, 1983.

Waage, Hilde Henriksen. "The 'Minnow' and the 'Whale': Norway and the United States in the Peace Process in the Middle East." *British Journal of Middle Eastern Studies* 34.2 (2007): 157–76.

———. "Norway's Role in the Middle East Peace Talks: Between a Small State and a Weak Belligerent." *Journal of Palestine Studies* 34.4 (2005): 6–24.

Waxman, Dov. *Trouble in the Tribe: The American Jewish Conflict over Israel.* Princeton: Princeton University Press, 2016.

Weinberger, Caspar W. *Fighting for Peace: Seven Critical Years in the Pentagon.* New York: Warner Books, 1990.

Weinberger, Naomi. "Peacekeeping Options in Lebanon." *Middle East Journal* 37.3 (Summer 1983): 341–69.

Weisglass, Dov. *Ariel Sharon: Rosh Memshala* [Ariel Sharon: A prime minister]. Tel Aviv: Yedioth Ahronoth, 2012.

Weitz, Yechiam. "From Peace in the South to War in the North: Menachem Begin as Prime Minister, 1977–1983." *Israel Studies* 19.1 (Spring 2014): 145–65.

Weizman, Eyal. *Hollow Land: Israel's Architecture of Occupation.* London: Verso, 2012.

Weizman, Ezer. *The Battle for Peace.* New York: Bantam, 1981.

Westad, Odd Arne. *The Cold War: A World History.* London: Allen Lane, 2017.

———. *The Global Cold War: Third World Interventions and the Making of Our Times.* Cambridge: Cambridge University Press, 2005.

Wilentz, Sean. *The Age of Reagan: A History, 1974–2008.* New York: Harper, 2008.

Wills, David C. *The First War on Terrorism: Counter-Terrorism Policy during the Reagan Administration.* Lanham, MD: Rowman and Littlefield, 2003.

Wilson, James Graham. "How Grand Was Reagan's Strategy, 1976–1984?" *Diplomacy and Statecraft* 18 (2007): 773–803.

———. *The Triumph of Improvisation: Gorbachev's Adaptability, Reagan's Engagement, and the End of the Cold War.* Ithaca: Cornell University Press, 2014.

Wright, Lawrence. *Thirteen Days in September: Carter, Begin, and Sadat at Camp David.* New York: Knopf, 2014.

Yadgar, Yaacov. *Sovereign Jews: Israel, Zionism, and Judaism.* Albany: SUNY Press, 2017.

Yaniv, Avner, and Robert J. Liber. "Personal Whim or Strategic Imperative?: The Israeli Invasion of Lebanon." *International Security* 8.2 (October 1983): 117–42.

Yaqub, Salim. *Containing Arab Nationalism: The Eisenhower Doctrine and the Middle East.* Chapel Hill: University of North Carolina Press, 2004.

———. *Imperfect Strangers: Americans, Arabs, and U.S.–Middle East Relations in the 1970s.* Ithaca: Cornell University Press, 2017.

———. "'Our Declaration of Independence': African Americans, Arab Americans, and the Arab-Israeli Conflict, 1967–1979." *Mashriq & Mahjar* 3.1 (2015): 12–29.

Yazbak, Mahmoud, and Yfaat Weiss. *Haifa Before and After 1948: Narratives of a Mixed City.* The Hague: Institute for Historical Justice and Reconciliation and Republic of Letters Publishing, 2011.

Yermiya, Dov. *My War Diary: Lebanon, June 5–July 1, 1982.* Trans. Hillel Schenker. Cambridge: South End Press, 1983.

Yizhar, S. *Khirbet Khizeh*. Trans. Nicholas de Lange and Yaacob Dweck. Jerusalem: Ibis Editions, 2008.

Yoshitani, Gail E. S. *Reagan on War: A Reappraisal of the Weinberger Doctrine, 1980–1984*. College Station: Texas A&M University Press, 2011.

Zaatari, Akram. *A Conversation with an Imagined Israeli Filmmaker Named Avi Mograbi*. Berlin: Sternberg Press, 2012.

———. *The Earth of Endless Secrets*. Frankfurt: Portikus, 2010.

———. *Letter to a Refusing Pilot*. Pavilion of Lebanon, Venice Biennale, 2013.

Zamkanei, Shayna. "Justice for Jews from Arab Countries and the Rebranding of the Jewish Refugee." *International Journal of Middle East Studies* 48.3 (2016): 511–30.

Zeiler, Thomas W. "The Diplomatic History Bandwagon: A State of the Field." *Journal of American History* 95.4 (2009): 1053–73.

Zeitz, Joshua Michael. "'If I am not for myself . . .': The American Jewish Establishment in the Aftermath of the Six Day War." *American Jewish History* 88.2 (June 2000): 253–86.

Zelizer, Julian E. "Detente and Domestic Politics." *Diplomatic History* 33.4 (2009): 653–70.

Zertal, Idith. *Israel's Holocaust and the Politics of Nationhood*. Trans. Chaya Galai. Cambridge: Cambridge University Press, 2005.

Zertal, Idith, and Akiva Eldar. *Lords of the Land: The War over Israel's Settlements in the Occupied Territories, 1967–2007*. Trans. Vivian Eden. New York: Nation Books, 2007.

A NOTE ON THE TYPE

THIS BOOK has been composed in Miller, a Scotch Roman typeface designed by Matthew Carter and first released by Font Bureau in 1997. It resembles Monticello, the typeface developed for The Papers of Thomas Jefferson in the 1940s by C. H. Griffith and P. J. Conkwright and reinterpreted in digital form by Carter in 2003.

Pleasant Jefferson ("P. J.") Conkwright (1905–1986) was Typographer at Princeton University Press from 1939 to 1970. He was an acclaimed book designer and AIGA Medalist.

The ornament used throughout this book was designed by Pierre Simon Fournier (1712–1768) and was a favorite of Conkwright's, used in his design of the *Princeton University Library Chronicle*.